The

Red Hat Society

Cookbook

The
Red Hat Society
Cookbook

INTRODUCTIONS BY
SUE ELLEN COOPER,

Founder and Exalted Queen Mother, The Red Hat Society

RECIPES BY
Members of the Red Hat Society

ILLUSTRATIONS BY
Andrea Reekstin, First Princess Daughter

RUTLEDGE HILL PRESS®
Nashville, Tennessee
A Division of Thomas Nelson Publishers
www.ThomasNelson.com

Published by Rutledge Hill Press, a Division of Thomas Nelson, Inc., P.O. Box 141000, Nashville, Tennessee 37214.

Rutledge Hill Press books may be purchased in bulk for educational, business, fund-raising, or sales promotional use.

ISBN: 978-1-4016-0246-8

Printed in the United States of America

Table of Contents

Introduction   vii

Part I – Dessert First!   1

1. Let Us Eat Cake   3
   Cakes

2. Slices of Heaven   59
   Pies

3. Bars, Bits & Bites   85
   Bars, Brownies & Cookies

4. But Wait . . . There's More!   119
   Other Desserts

Part II – Everything Else   165

5. Little Bits of Anticipation   167
   Appetizers & Beverages

6. Nurture Before Noon   199
   Breakfast, Brunch & Breads

7. Grab That Fancy Hat. We're Going for Tea!   243
   Teatime Treats & Indulgences

8. Warm and Cozy, Cool and Crisp   267
   Soups & Salads

9. Little Feasts   327
   Pizza, Sandwiches, Wraps & Burritos

10. Big Deal Meals   361
    Meats, Fish & Poultry

11. More Marvelous Mainstays   439
    Meatless Entrees, Casseroles & Main Dish Pastas

12. Embellishments and Additions   487
    Vegetables, Side Dishes, Pickles & Relishes

Part III – Table for 1   523
Recipes that Serve 1 or 2

Index of Names   555

Index of Recipes   571

∽ Introduction ∾

The Red Hat Society is, basically, one big playgroup for women of a certain age. We are all about lightening up, taking breaks, getting out, and going to recess together. We're always on the alert for new ways to play. If there's a garden show, a special exhibit at the museum, or a big sale at the mall, it's a fairly good bet that we'll be there. We still hold down the fort at home—just not as often. Probably our favorite thing to do on our outings is eat! You may have seen us in our finest purple and red regalia in tearooms and restaurants, enjoying good food and high-spirited conversation in equal measure.

Yes, we *love* to eat. Sharing meals with friends and family is one of life's premier pleasures—especially if you're a Red Hatter. We nourish more than just our bodies; we nourish our souls. Sometimes we enjoy these times in restaurants, of course. But many of us love to cook, and we know that investing our time and creativity in the personal preparation of tasty, attractive meals and serving them at home can also be immensely satisfying . . . and fun.

If you have seen Red Hatters out and about, you already know that we are zesty, active women, just full of the joy of living. We know how to have fun, and we are more than happy to share the fun with others. Red Hatters have been entertaining each other and swapping recipes since our whole movement started. No "secret ingredients" or private family recipes for us! If it's really good, it's really worth sharing with each other.

Among us, we, the hundreds of thousands of Red Hat Society members, have cooked an incalculable number of meals. Many of us are used to being asked to prepare our famous "specialties" again and again. So we decided that it would be a terrific idea to ask our members to share their absolute *best of the best* recipes. Then, we asked some highly accomplished Red Hatted cooks to serve as our testers, choosing their own top picks from among a plethora of delectables prepared with their own hands in their own kitchens. Only those recipes that truly impressed these ladies made the cut—and they are in this book you are holding!

Since Red Hatters have often been known to eat dessert first, we thought it appropriate to feature all of our scrumptious desserts in Part I. But, since we know that woman does not live by sugar alone, there are plenty of recipes for hearty, healthy fare in the chapters that follow. All of us who have contributed sincerely hope that you enjoy these little gifts of the heart. We predict that many of the recipes within will become some of *your* personal favorites!

In friendship,
Sue Ellen Cooper
Exalted Queen Mother

⊸ Part I ⊱

Dessert First!

One dictionary defines the word *dessert* as "a pastry, pudding, or ice cream served at the end of a meal." Everyone knows that it is permissible to eat a sweet treat only after finishing the meat and vegetables (yes, especially the Brussels sprouts). That is just the way that it is done, don't you know? Who among us cannot conjure up a memory or someone, somewhere, sometime, admonishing us to "Finish your (fill in the blank) or you won't get any dessert."

Apparently in reaction to this sort of thing, a humorous admonition has gained popularity in recent years: "Life is uncertain; eat dessert first!" This idea has struck a loud chord with members of the Red Hat Society. We are women who, for what seems like eons, have been fulfilling our duties and doing the things that must be done, and we are relearning how to play—with a vengeance. So, in a small act of humorous defiance of tradition, we may well choose at times to bring out the Chocolate Fudge Cake (or the pastry, pudding, or ice cream) before the Brussels sprouts.

This might be considered a little like reading the last chapter before the rest of the book. But you never know—we might do that too.

ONE

~ Let Us Eat Cake ~

CAKES

Poor Marie Antoinette! She will forever be identified with one infamous quotation she is supposed to have uttered when told that starving French peasants had no bread to eat. She is supposed to have said, "Let them eat cake," therein demonstrating both enormous ignorance and insensitivity. Scholars now agree that the poor girl got a bum rap, and almost certainly never said any such thing.

On the other hand, Red Hatters are often heard to say something quite similar: "Let US eat cake!" Eating cake is actually almost mandatory for many occasions, such as birthdays, coronations, and *Reduations*. Here are some of those most scrumptious cake recipes we could find.

Apricot Cream Cheese Pound Cake

Very moist and very rich, so cut thin slices. Testers called it attractive and easy to make.

1/2	cup chopped dried apricots
1/2	cup golden raisins
1 1/2	plus 1/4 cups sugar
2	cups water
2	cups all-purpose flour
1 1/2	teaspoons baking powder
1/2	cup chopped pecans
1	(8-ounce) package cream cheese, softened
1	cup (2 sticks) butter, softened
1 1/2	teaspoons vanilla extract
4	large eggs
	Whipped cream (optional)

In a saucepan combine the apricots, raisins, and the 1/4 cup sugar with the water, and bring the mixture to a boil. Simmer until softened, about 15 to 20 minutes. Drain the mixture, discarding the liquid, and cool.

Preheat the oven to 325°. In a bowl whisk together the flour, baking powder, and pecans. In another bowl with an electric mixer, beat together the cream cheese, butter, vanilla, and the remaining 1 1/2 cups sugar until fluffy. Beat in the eggs one at a time. Stir in the apricot mixture and fold in the flour mixture in three batches until combined. Spoon the batter evenly into a greased and floured Bundt pan, smoothing the top. Bake for 1 hour 5 minutes to 1 hour 10 minutes or until browned and a tester comes out clean. Cool the cake in the pan on a rack for 10 minutes. Turn the cake out onto the rack and cool completely. Wrap the cake in plastic wrap or foil and chill overnight. Serve at room temperature with the whipped cream if using.

Makes 16 servings

Naomi Murray, Queen Mother
Scarlet O'Hatters of the Ozarks, Springfield, Missouri

Texas White Sheet Cake

3	cups sugar
1/2	cup shortening
1	cup (2 sticks) butter, softened
5	eggs
3	cups cake flour
1	cup milk
1	teaspoon vanilla extract

Preheat the oven to 325°. In a large bowl beat together the sugar, shortening, and butter. Add the eggs one at a time, beating after each addition. Sift the flour into a bowl. Then measure out of that bowl 3 cups flour again and sift again. In a separate bowl mix the milk and vanilla together. Then alternately add some flour and milk to the butter mixture until both are used up, ending with flour. Bake in a greased and floured tube pan for 1 hour; increase the heat to 350° and bake for another 15 minutes. If your tube pan is dark inside or colored outside, turn the temperatures down by 25°.

Makes 12 to 15 servings

Gail Buss, Lady Duchess of Westminster
The Scarlette Bells, Westminster, Maryland

Blueberry Pound Cake

Very popular with testers, who noted that the texture and flavor improve after a day.

1   (8-ounce) package cream cheese, softened
3   eggs
1/2 cup (1 stick) butter, melted
3   tablespoons sugar
1   (18-ounce) box butter cake mix
2   cups fresh blueberries

Preheat the oven to 350°. In a large bowl beat the cream cheese with the eggs. Mix in the melted butter, sugar, and cake mix. Fold in the blueberries. Bake for 35 to 45 minutes in a greased and floured, 10-inch tube or Bundt pan.

Makes 16 servings

Mary Ann Bendily, Queen Mother
Red Hat Flamingal's, Denham Springs/Walker, Louisiana

Butter Cake

Instead of marmalade, you can use whipped cream and strawberries in between layers and atop this cake.

1   cup (2 sticks) butter, melted
1 1/2 cups granulated sugar
4   eggs
3   cups all-purpose flour
3   teaspoons baking powder
1   teaspoon salt
1   cup milk
1   teaspoon vanilla extract
1   (10-ounce) jar orange marmalade

FROSTING
1 1/2 cups sifted confectioners' sugar
1/2 teaspoon vanilla extract
    Orange juice

Preheat the oven to 350°. In a large bowl beat the butter with the sugar until fluffy. Add the eggs one at a time. In another bowl sift together the flour, baking powder, and salt. Add the dry mixture alternately to the batter with the milk. Add the vanilla. Bake in a greased angel food pan for 50 minutes. Let cool in the pan for 10 minutes before removing from the pan and then cool on a rack. Slice to make two layers and spread the marmalade between the layers. In a small bowl mix the confectioners' sugar with the vanilla extract and enough orange juice to make a thin frosting. Pour over the cake.

Makes 12 to 15 servings

Z. Ganaway, Queen Adazle
Radiant Redhats of Georgia, Atlanta, Georgia

Hurry-Up Pound Cake

1   (8-ounce) package cream cheese
1/2   cup warm water
2   tablespoons butter, softened
1   (18-ounce) package butter cake mix
1/2   cup vegetable oil
1/2   cup sugar
4   eggs

Preheat the oven to 350° In a large bowl beat the cream cheese, water, and butter. Add the cake mix and blend well. Beat in the oil, sugar, and eggs. Pour into a greased and floured Bundt pan. Bake for 55 to 60 minutes, or until tester comes out clean.

Makes 16 servings

Melba Holmes, Queen Melba
The Red Hatters of The Lakes
West Memphis, Arkansas

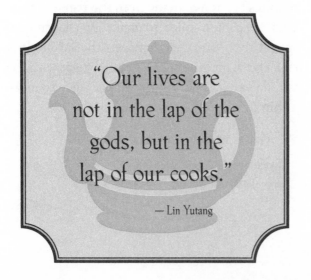

"Our lives are not in the lap of the gods, but in the lap of our cooks."

— Lin Yutang

Cream Cheese Pound Cake

1   cup (2 sticks) margarine, softened
1/2   cup (1 stick) butter, softened
1   (8-ounce) package cream cheese, softened
3   cups sugar
6   eggs
3   cups cake flour
2   teaspoons vanilla extract

Preheat the oven to 325°. Beat the margarine, butter, and cream cheese together. Add the sugar gradually and beat until fluffy. Add the eggs one at a time, beating well after each addition. Sift the flour and add it to the mixture. Stir in the vanilla. Pour into a greased 10-inch tube pan. Bake for 1 hour and 45 minutes. Cool in the pan 10 minutes then remove to a rack to cool completely.

Makes 16 servings

Phyllis Jones, Queen Mum
Carolina Belles, Charlotte, North Carolina

Chocolate Pound Cake

1   cup (2 sticks) butter, softened
1/2   cup shortening
3   cups sugar
5   eggs
3   cups all-purpose flour
1/2   cup cocoa
1/4   teaspoon salt
1/2   teaspoon baking powder
1   cup milk
1   teaspoon vanilla extract

Preheat the oven to 325°. Mix the butter, shortening, and sugar together well. Add the eggs, one at a time, and beat well. Sift together the flour, cocoa, salt, and baking powder and add alternately with the milk and vanilla extract. Bake in a greased and floured tube pan for 1 hour and 20 minutes.

Makes 1 cake

Linda Parker, Queen Mum
Carolina Jessamines, Chapin, South Carolina

Lavender Pound Cake

This cake marches to a different drum.

CAKE
2 1/2   cups all-purpose flour
1/2   teaspoon baking soda
1/2   teaspoon salt
1 1/2   plus 1/2 cups granulated sugar
1   tablespoon dried lavender
1   cup (2 sticks) unsalted butter, softened
2   teaspoons vanilla extract
4   eggs
1   cup sour cream
1/4   cup milk

FROSTING
1/4   cup water
1   tablespoon dried lavender
3/4   cup confectioners' sugar
  Few drops of purple food color

Preheat the oven to 350°. Grease and flour two 8-inch loaf pans. Mix the flour, baking soda, and salt in a medium bowl. Pulse 1/2 cup sugar with the lavender in a food processor until the lavender is ground. In a large bowl beat the butter, lavender-flavored sugar, the remaining 1 1/2 cups sugar, and the vanilla until fluffy. Beat in the eggs one at a time. In a small bowl mix the sour cream and milk on low speed. With an electric beater on low speed add the flour mixture and the sour cream mixture alternately to the egg mixture, beginning and ending with flour. Pour the batter into the pans and bake for 55 minutes, or until a tester comes out clean. Cool 10 minutes. Remove from the pans. Cool on wire racks

For the frosting, microwave the water and lavender for 30 seconds on high. Let steep 5 minutes. Drain, reserving 4 teaspoons of lavender water and discard the lavender flowers. Whisk together the reserved lavender water, the confectioners' sugar, and a few drops of the food coloring. Drizzle the frosting over the cakes.

Makes 2 cakes, 12 servings each

Maria Clapp, Redhatmaria
Hats 'R' Us, Williamstown, New Jersey

Electric Mixer Trauma

Sometime in the early 1970s, I was making our son's favorite cake, Banana Bonanza Cake. I was beating in each ingredient with my trusty electric mixer, when suddenly, it simply stopped running. I tilted it up and began wiggling the beaters to determine what had happened. Just as suddenly as it had stopped, it came on again, and the beaters went wild! Batter began spraying all over the walls, the cabinets, and the countertops. I screamed so loudly that my husband came to my rescue. When he saw the mess, he explained to me that he had been working in the garage and threw a breaker. He went to the basement to reset it and, of course, had no idea what I was doing in the kitchen. Although it wasn't very funny that day, we can laugh about it now.

Josephine Morrison
Chapterette
Purple Playground Ladies
Sand Springs, Oklahoma

Coconut Lovers Pound Cake

Transport yourself to a tropical island with this double dose of coconut—in the cake and in the frosting.

3   cups granulated sugar
1   cup shortening
1   cup (2 sticks) butter, softened
7   eggs, separated
3 1/2   cups all-purpose flour
1   cup frozen coconut, thawed
1   tablespoon coconut extract
1   cup milk
1   teaspoon baking powder

FROSTING

3   tablespoons shortening
5   tablespoons milk
2   cups confectioners' sugar
1/2   cup coconut
1   tablespoon coconut extract

In a large bowl beat the sugar, shortening, butter, and egg yolks 5 minutes. Add the flour, coconut, extract, milk, and baking powder. Beat 2 minutes. Beat the egg whites until stiff and fold into the batter. Place the mixture in a greased and floured tube pan and put into a cold oven set at 325°. Bake 1 1/2 hours or until done.

For the frosting, boil the shortening and milk in a saucepan. Add the sugar, coconut, and extract. Mix well and frost the cake while hot.

Makes 15 to 20 servings

Sally Reed, E-mail Female
Tarheel Red Hat Club of Clemmons, Clemmons, North Carolina

Jewish Apple Cake

6   cups sliced apples
2   teaspoons cinnamon
5   tablespoons sugar
3   cups all-purpose flour
2   cups sugar
3   teaspoons baking powder
4   large eggs
2 1/2 teaspoons vanilla extract
1   cup vegetable oil
1/2 cup orange juice

Preheat the oven to 350°. In a large bowl mix the apples, cinnamon, and sugar. In a separate bowl beat the flour, sugar, baking powder, eggs, vanilla, oil, and orange juice with an electric mixer on high for 5 minutes. Pour one-third of the batter into a greased and floured tube pan. Arrange one-third of the apples on the batter. Repeat, ending with apples. Bake for 1 hour 30 minutes, or until the top is golden brown.

Makes 16 servings

Agnes Mancuso, The Italian Diva
Happening Ladies of Hamilton, Lawrenceville, New Jersey

Fresh Apple Cake

This cake is even more delicious if allowed to sit a day before digging in.

1   cup vegetable oil
2   cups granulated sugar
3   eggs, beaten
3   cups all-purpose flour
1   teaspoon baking soda
2   teaspoons vanilla extract
1   cup pecans, chopped
3   cups peeled and chopped fresh apples

FROSTING
1/2 cup (1 stick) butter
1   cup light brown sugar
1/4 cup evaporated milk
1/2 teaspoon vanilla extract

Preheat the oven to 350°. In a large bowl mix the oil, sugar, and eggs. Mix in the flour and baking soda. Add the vanilla, pecans, and apples. Spread into a greased 13 x 9-inch pan. Bake for 45 to 50 minutes, or until toothpick comes out clean. Let cool in the pan.

For the frosting, boil the butter, brown sugar, milk, and vanilla in a saucepan for 2 minutes. Set the pan in cold water and beat the icing until spreading consistency. Spread the frosting over the cake before serving.

Makes 20 servings

Elaine Jimmerson, Vice Queen
The Valley Girls (of Apopka), Apopka, Florida

Stack Cake

Like most Red Hatters, this cake gets better as it ages. Let it stand overnight in a covered cake plate for maximum flavor.

CAKE
- 1/2   cup sugar
- 1/2   cup shortening
- 1/3   cup molasses
- 1/2   cup buttermilk
- 1   egg, well beaten
- 3 1/2 cups all-purpose flour
- 1 1/2 teaspoons ginger
- 2   teaspoons baking powder
- 1/2   teaspoon baking soda
- 1/2   teaspoon salt

FILLING
- 4   cups dried apples, covered in water
- 1   cup sugar
- 2   teaspoons allspice or apple pie spice

Preheat the oven to 350°. For the cake, in a large bowl beat together the sugar and shortening until fluffy. Beat in the molasses, buttermilk, and egg. In another bowl sift together the flour, ginger, baking powder, baking soda, and salt. Add to the creamed mixture. Divide the dough into four equal parts. Roll out each part and fit into an 8 or 9-inch cake pan or iron skillet that has been greased and floured. Bake at 350° for 10 to 12 minutes.

For the filling, bring the apples and water to a boil in a large saucepan then reduce the heat to medium and cook until tender, about 10 minutes. Pour off any excess water and mash or chop the apples into small pieces. Add the sugar and spice. When the cake is cool, layer it with the apple filling.

Makes 12 servings

Barbara Wachter, Queen Mother
Regal Red Hatters of Germantown, Germantown, Ohio

Rollicking Red Beet Cake

Quite an extraordinary color for a cake but just right for your Hatter gathering.

- 4   eggs, beaten
- 1 1/4 cups vegetable oil
- 1 1/2 cups puréed beets
- 1 1/2 teaspoons vanilla extract
- 2   cups sugar
- 2/3   cup cocoa
- 2   teaspoons baking soda
- 2 1/2 cups all-purpose flour
- 1   teaspoon salt

Preheat the oven to 350°. Combine the eggs, oil, beets, and vanilla. Mix and set aside. Sift together the sugar, cocoa, baking soda, flour, and salt. Add to the egg mixture, mix well, and pour into a 13 x 9-inch greased and floured pan. Bake for 40 minutes, or until a toothpick inserted comes out clean.

Makes 20 servings

Anna Marie Shaffer, Red Hatter
Red Hat Tamales of Many Towns, Sioux Falls, South Dakota

Apricot Nectar Cake

1   (18-ounce) package yellow
     cake mix
1   (3-ounce) package apricot or lemon gelatin
4   eggs
3/4 cup vegetable oil
3/4 cup apricot nectar

GLAZE
3/4 cup apricot nectar
11/2 cups confectioners' sugar
4   tablespoons butter

Preheat the oven to 300°. Combine the cake mix, gelatin, eggs, oil, and nectar in a large bowl with a wooden spoon (do not use a mixer). Pour the batter into a greased Bundt pan. Bake for 1 hour. Leave in the pan, or cool in the pan 10 minutes then turn out onto a deep platter. Poke holes all over the hot cake with an ice pick.

For the glaze, in a saucepan bring the apricot nectar, confectioners' sugar, and butter to a boil. Pour the hot mixture over the warm cake. Let stand until cool. Not all of the nectar mixture will soak in (which is why you need a deep platter).

Makes 10 servings

Joy Noll, Queen Mother
Country Girls, Paoli, Indiana

Chewy Carrot Date Cake

2   cups all-purpose flour
21/2 cups granulated sugar
2   teaspoons baking soda
1/2 teaspoon salt
2   teaspoons cinnamon
3   eggs, beaten
1   cup vegetable oil
1   teaspoon vanilla extract
1   cup chopped dates
1   cup chopped nuts
2   cups grated raw carrots
1   cup drained crushed pineapple

QUICK CARAMEL FROSTING
1/3 cup butter
1   cup firmly packed brown sugar
1/4 cup milk
21/4 cups confectioners' sugar

Preheat the oven to 350°. In a large bowl sift together the flour, sugar, baking soda, salt, and cinnamon. Make a well and add the eggs, oil, and vanilla. Mix together. Add the dates, nuts, carrots, and pineapple. Mixture will be very stiff at first, but will get thinner after carrots are added. Pour the batter into a greased 9-inch square pan and bake for about 1 hour.

For the frosting, melt the butter in a saucepan over low heat. Add the brown sugar. Cook for 2 minutes, stirring continuously. Stir in the milk and bring to a boil. Cool to luke-warm. Stir in the confectioners' sugar. Beat until smooth and creamy. Top the cake with the frosting.

Makes 10 servings

Elizabeth Fothergill, Liz the Great from Bluegrass
Bluegrass, Lexington, Kentucky

Royal Carrot Cake

FILLING
- 1   cup sugar
- 2   tablespoons all-purpose flour
- 1/4   teaspoon salt
- 1   cup whipping cream
- 1/2   cup (1 stick) butter
- 1   cup chopped pecans
- 1   teaspoon vanilla extract

CAKE
- 1 1/4 cups vegetable oil
- 2   cups sugar
- 2   cups all-purpose flour
- 2   teaspoons cinnamon
- 2   teaspoons baking powder
- 1   teaspoon baking soda
- 1   teaspoon salt
- 4   eggs
- 4   cups finely shredded carrots
- 1   cup raisins
- 1   cup chopped pecans

For the filling, in a heavy saucepan combine the sugar, flour, and salt. Stir in the cream and butter. Cook and stir over medium heat until the butter melts then bring to a boil. Reduce the heat and simmer uncovered for 30 minutes, stirring occasionally. Remove from the heat and add the pecans and vanilla. Set aside to cool.

Preheat the oven to 350°. For the cake, in a mixing bowl beat the oil and sugar with an electric mixer for 1 minute. In a separate bowl combine the flour, cinnamon, baking powder, baking soda, and salt. Add to the creamed mixture, alternating with the eggs. Mix well. Stir in the carrots, raisins, and pecans. Pour into three greased and floured 9-inch round cake pans. Bake for 35 to 40 minutes. Cool in the pans for 10 minutes then remove to a wire rack to cool completely. Spread the filling between the layers. Frost the top and sides with a cream cheese frosting (see page 31 under Swedish Pineapple Cake). Store in the refrigerator.

Makes 16 to 18 servings

Lorraine Osbahr, Lady Lorraine
Classy Dames Sisterhood, Avoca, Iowa

Blue Ribbon Banana Coconut Cake

This cake really did win a blue ribbon. Testers tinkered a bit with this recipe, adding extra bananas for flavor and moisture.

- 3/4   cup shortening
- 1 1/2 cups sugar
- 2   eggs
- 2   cups mashed bananas
- 2   cups all-purpose flour
- 1   teaspoon baking soda
- 1   teaspoon baking powder
- 1/2   teaspoon salt
- 1/2   cup buttermilk
- 1   teaspoon vanilla extract
- 1/2   cup chopped pecans
- 1/2   plus 1/2 cup flaked coconut

CREAMY NUT FILLING

1/2 cup sugar
2 tablespoons all-purpose flour
1/2 cup light cream
3 tablespoons butter
1/2 cup chopped pecans
1/4 teaspoon salt
1 teaspoon vanilla extract

Preheat the oven to 375°. In a large bowl beat the shortening and sugar until fluffy. Add the eggs and beat 2 more minutes. Beat in the bananas. In another bowl sift together the flour, baking soda, baking powder, and salt. Add the dry ingredients alternately with the buttermilk to the creamed mixture, beating well after each addition. Add the vanilla and beat 5 minutes. Stir in the pecans. Pour into two greased and floured 9-inch round cake pans. Sprinkle 1/2 cup coconut on each layer. Bake for 25 to 30 minutes, or until tester comes out clean. Cool in the pans on racks for 10 minutes then remove to a rack.

For the creamy nut filling, combine the sugar, flour, cream, and butter in a heavy saucepan. Cook, stirring constantly, until thickened. Stir in the pecans, salt, and vanilla. Cool. Use the mixture to fill the layers.

Makes 12 servings

Nancy Clemons, Exalted Queen Mother
Luscious Ladies of League City, League City, Texas

Blueberry Cake

This is the official dessert of the Sugar Plum Girls of Lebanon TN, created by our Countess of Cuisine.

CAKE

1 (14-ounce) box yellow cake mix
1 (5-ounce) box instant vanilla pudding mix
4 eggs
1 cup olive oil
1 (8-ounce) package cream cheese, at room temperature
1 (14-ounce) can blueberries, reserve the juice

FROSTING

1 cup reserved blueberry juice
2 cup confectioners' sugar

For the cake, preheat the oven to 325°. Combine the cake mix, pudding mix, eggs, olive oil, and cream cheese. With an electric mixer, beat for 2 minutes on medium speed. Fold in the drained and washed blueberries. Beat for 45 minutes. Let cool on a wire rack.

For the frosting, heat the blueberry juice in the microwave for 30 seconds. Add the confectioners' sugar and stir with fork. Adjust the sugar to desired consistency. Spread the frosting over the cake before serving.

Makes 1 cake

Vera Kirk, Countess of Cuisine
Sugar Plum Girls, Lebanon, Tennessee

Pumpkin Cake Roll

If cake cracks as you roll it, don't let it worry you. No one seems to notice.

3/4   cup all-purpose flour
1/2   teaspoon baking powder
1/2   teaspoon baking soda
1/2   teaspoon ground cinnamon
1/2   teaspoon ground cloves
1/4   teaspoon salt
3   large eggs
1   cup granulated sugar
2/3   cup canned pumpkin purée
1   cup chopped almonds
1/4   cup confectioners' sugar to sprinkle on
      towel
1   (8-ounce) package cream cheese, softened
1   cup sifted confectioners' sugar
6   tablespoons butter
1   teaspoon vanilla extract
1/4   cup confectioners' sugar (optional)

Preheat the oven to 375°. In a small bowl combine the flour, baking powder, baking soda, cinnamon, cloves, and salt. In a large bowl beat the eggs and sugar until thick. Beat in the pumpkin. Stir in the flour mixture. Spread evenly into a 15 x 10-inch jelly-roll pan that has been lined with greased and floured waxed paper. Sprinkle the almonds on top. Bake for 13 to 15 minutes, or until the top of the cake springs back when touched.

Immediately turn the cake onto a clean kitchen towel sprinkled with 1/4 cup confectioners' sugar. Carefully peel off the paper. Roll up the cake and towel together, starting with the short side. Cool on a wire rack. In a small bowl beat the cream cheese, confectioners' sugar, butter, and vanilla until smooth. Unroll the cake and remove the towel. Spread the cream cheese mixture over the cake and re-roll. Wrap the roll in plastic wrap and refrigerate at least one hour. Sprinkle with 1/4 cup confectioners' sugar before serving, if desired.

Makes about 8 servings

Patricia Foster, Queen Mother
Dusty Desert Roses, Desert Hot Springs, California

Old-Fashioned Raisin Cake

2   (1-pound) packages raisins
1   cup shortening
1 1/4 cups sugar
1   teaspoon cloves
1   teaspoon nutmeg
1   teaspoon allspice
1   teaspoon cinnamon
1   teaspoon salt
2   cups water
1/2   cup lukewarm water
1   teaspoon baking soda
2   teaspoon baking powder
5   cups all-purpose flour
1   cup chopped nuts

Preheat the oven to 250°. In a large saucepan combine the raisins, shortening, sugar, cloves, nutmeg, allspice, cinnamon, salt, and water.

Boil for 2 minutes over high heat. Cool. In a small bowl combine the lukewarm water with the baking soda. Add to the saucepan. Add the baking powder and the flour 1 cup at a time. Stir in the nuts. Pour into a greased tube pan and bake for 2 hours. Cool the cake in pan for one hour then cool completely on a rack.

Makes 12 to 16 servings

Phyllis Jenkins, Queen Momma
The Durham Dillies, Durham, North Carolina

Delicious Spice Cake

1   (4-ounce) package vanilla instant pudding mix
1   (18-ounce) package spice cake mix
2   (4-ounce) jars junior prunes with tapioca baby food
3/4   cup water or milk
1/2   cup vegetable oil
4   eggs
1   teaspoon lemon extract

BANANA GLAZE
1   small banana
1   tablespoon lemon juice
2   cups confectioners' sugar

Preheat the oven to 325°. In a large bowl combine the pudding mix, cake mix, prunes, water, oil, eggs, and lemon extract. Beat 3 minutes. Pour into a greased and floured 10-inch tube pan or Bundt pan. Bake for 50 to 55 minutes. Cool in the pan for 30 minutes. Remove the cake from the pan and let cool.

For the glaze, mash the banana with the lemon juice in a small bowl then add the sugar gradually. If too thin, add more sugar. Drizzle the glaze over the top of the cake and serve.

Makes 16 servings

Betty Monroe, Lady Betty
Scarlet Sophisticates, Fredericksburg, Virginia

Cool Coconut Do-Ahead Cake

1   (18-ounce) box yellow cake mix
1   (14-ounce) package frozen coconut, thawed
1   cup sugar
1   (16-ounce) container sour cream
1   (8-ounce) container frozen whipped topping, thawed

Prepare the cake mix in two layers according to package directions. Split the layers in half horizontally to make four layers. Mix the coconut, sugar, and sour cream, reserving 1 cup of the mixture.

Spread the remaining mixture on three of the cake layers and stack them with the fourth layer on top. Mix the reserved coconut mix with the whipped topping. Spread over the entire cake, top and sides, completely covering the cake. Wrap the cake well with plastic wrap, covering all sides and under the dish. Refrigerate at least two days before serving.

Makes 8 to 10 servings

Connie Anderson, Oldie Goldie
Bodacious Babes Of Belvedere, The Villages, Florida

Scary Cake

When my children were young, I decided to make them a special treat. I had found a recipe for a white cake that called for pouring Jell-O over after it was baked. You would first punch holes in the cake with the handle of a wooden spoon in order for the Jell-O to run down into the holes to make an interesting design.

I had made the cake and put it in the refrigerator for that night's dinner. My husband had also put a cottage cheese carton of fishing worms in the refrigerator to use later. I was at the neighbors, when my daughter Sara called screaming for me to come home. She had cut a piece of the cake to eat and a big earthworm had come crawling out of one of the holes. Apparently, one of the younger kids had earlier opened the worm carton and didn't replace the cover tightly. Needless to say, I have never made that recipe again!

Diane Denny
Queen
Berlin Center Red Hat Floozies
Saranac, Michigan

Banana–Nut Cake, aka Grammy Cake

When my grandchildren came to live with us, I would make banana-nut cake with the overripe fruit. I have a crystal footed cake plate with a crystal cover. This cake plate was always used to store the banana cake. The cake had a special place in the kitchen and the children would always look to see if there was any cake and ask for "Grammy Cake."

2   cups all-purpose flour
1/2   teaspoon baking soda
1   teaspoon baking powder
1/2   teaspoon salt
2/3   cup (10 2/3 tablespoons) butter, melted
1 1/2 cups sugar
2   eggs
1 1/2 cups mashed bananas
1/2   cup buttermilk
1   teaspoon vanilla extract
1   cup nuts (optional)

"Come along inside
. . . We'll see if tea
and buns make
the world a
better place."

—Kenneth Grahame

1   (18-ounce) package yellow
    cake mix
1/2   plus 1/2 cup (2 sticks) butter, melted
1   egg, beaten
1   (29-ounce) can pumpkin purée (with no
    added spices)
3   eggs
1/2   cup brown sugar
1/2   plus 1/2 cup granulated sugar
2/3   cup milk
1   teaspoon cinnamon
    Dash of cloves
    Dash of salt
1/2   cup chopped nuts

Preheat the oven to 350°. In a large bowl stir together the flour, baking soda, baking powder, and salt. In a separate bowl beat the butter with the sugar and eggs until fluffy. Add the bananas. Add half the dry ingredients and the buttermilk and blend well. Then add the vanilla, remaining dry ingredients, and nuts, if using. Pour the mixture into a greased and floured Bundt pan and bake for 45 minutes.

Makes 12 servings

Nancy Clemons, Exalted Queen Mother Nancy
Luscious Ladies of League City, League City, Texas

Pumpkin Pie Cake

Terrific for the autumn or holiday dessert table. Will be enjoyed by people who don't like pumpkin pie.

Preheat the oven to 350°. Reserve 1 1/4 cups cake mix. Combine the remaining cake mix with 1/2 cup melted butter and the egg. Pour the mixture into a greased and floured 13 x 9-inch pan. In a small bowl mix the pumpkin purée, eggs, brown sugar, 1/2 cup granulated sugar, milk, cinnamon, cloves, and salt. Pour over the mixture in the pan. Combine the reserved cake mix with the remaining 1/2 cup sugar and the remaining 1/2 cup melted butter. Crumble this mixture over the batter and sprinkle the nuts on top. Bake for 1 hour.

Makes 15 servings

Gayla Ashbee, Queen Babe
Fun Buddy Babes, West Chester, Pennsylvania

The Great Pumpkin Cake

No frosting is needed for this spicy cake. A dollop of whipped topping on each slice is heavenly.

1   (18-ounce) package butter brickle or spice cake mix
1   egg
1/2 cup (1 stick) butter, softened
1   (14-ounce) can sweetened condensed milk
1   (15-ounce) can pumpkin purée
2   eggs, beaten
1   cup butterscotch chips, melted
1   teaspoon ginger
1/2 teaspoon nutmeg
1   cup pecans

Preheat the oven to 350°. In a large bowl beat together the cake mix, egg, and butter. Reserve 1 1/2 cups mixture. Press the remaining cake mixture firmly into the bottom of a greased 13 x 9-inch cake pan. In a second large bowl beat the reserved mixture with the condensed milk, pumpkin, eggs, butterscotch, ginger, and nutmeg. Spread evenly into the cake pan and top with the pecans. Bake for 40 minutes, or until firm and golden brown. Cool.

Makes 12 servings

Sheryl Kneeland, Queen Mother
The Razzle Dazzlers, Elmore, Minnesota

Cheesecake Cake

Be sure your pan is at least ten inches deep to accommodate this high rising cake/cheesecake combo.

CAKE
1   (8-ounce) package cream cheese
2/3 plus 2/3 cup sugar
1/2 cup sour cream
1   plus 1 teaspoon vanilla extract
2   plus 2 eggs
1/2 cup (1 stick) butter, softened
1   tablespoon milk
1   cup all-purpose flour
1   teaspoon baking powder
1/2 teaspoon salt

TOPPING
1   cup sour cream
2   tablespoons sugar
1   teaspoon vanilla extract

Preheat the oven to 325°. For the cake, beat together the cream cheese and 2/3 cup sugar. Add the sour cream, 1 teaspoon vanilla, and 2 eggs and beat well. In a separate bowl beat together the butter, remaining 2/3 cup sugar, and remaining 2 eggs. Stir in the milk and remaining 1 teaspoon vanilla. Sift together the flour, baking powder, and salt and add to the butter mixture. Pat this mixture onto the bottom and up the sides of a 10-inch-deep springform or rectangular pan that has been greased and floured. Spoon in the cream cheese mixture. Bake for 40 minutes then remove the cake from the oven and cool slightly.

For the topping, mix the sour cream, sugar, and vanilla in a small bowl. Spread over the top of the cake and return to the oven for 5 minutes. Cool on a rack and then cover with aluminum foil and refrigerate at least 4 hours before serving.

Makes 10 to 12 servings

Alice Salvesen, Alice Blue Gown
My Fair Ladies of Lakewood, Lakewood, New Jersey

Cottage Cheese Cake

1	egg
1	teaspoon vanilla extract
1 1/2	cups all-purpose flour
1/2	cup sugar
1/2	teaspoon baking powder
1/2	cup (1 stick) butter, softened

FILLING
2	cups small curd cottage cheese
1/2	cup sugar
1	cup milk
2	tablespoons heavy whipping cream
5	egg, separated

Preheat the oven to 400°. In a large bowl beat the egg and vanilla together. Beat in the flour, sugar, baking powder, and butter to form a stiff dough. Press into the bottom of a greased 13 x 9-inch pan.

For the filling, mix the cottage cheese, sugar, milk, cream, and egg yolks in a large bowl. Fold in the beaten egg whites. Pour the filling over the dough. Bake for 15 minutes then lower the temperature to 350° for 35 additional minutes.

Makes 12 to 15 servings

Mildred Shaeffer, Lady Ma Kettle
Rural Robust Red Hatters, Ford City, Pennsylvania

Past-Perfect Fruit Cake

4	cups chopped pecans
1	pound candied pineapple
1	pound candied cherries
1	pound pitted dates
1 1/2	cups all-purpose flour
1	teaspoon baking powder
1/2	teaspoon salt
6	eggs
1 1/2	cups sugar
2	teaspoons vanilla extract

Preheat the oven to 250°. In a large bowl mix together the pecans, pineapple, cherries, and dates. In a separate bowl mix the flour, baking powder, and salt; sift the flour mixture over the fruit and nuts. Beat the eggs well but slowly. Add the sugar and vanilla and beat. Pour the egg mixture over the fruit and nut mixture. Pour into a greased, paper-lined tube pan. Bake for 2 hours, 20 minutes.

Makes 16 to 20 servings

Lucy Fuller, Lady Lucy
Elite Ladies of The Hat, Franklinton, North Carolina

Japanese Fruitcake

This elaborate cake is sure to draw raves with its unusual flavors.

CAKE

1	cup (2 sticks) butter or shortening, softened
2	cups sugar
4	eggs
3	cups all-purpose flour
1	teaspoon baking soda
1	teaspoon salt
1	cup buttermilk
1	teaspoon vanilla extract
2/3	cup chopped nuts
2/3	cup chopped raisins
3/4	teaspoon cinnamon
3/4	teaspoon allspice
3/4	teaspoon mace
1/2	teaspoon cloves

FILLING

2/3	cup sugar
1/4	teaspoon salt
1/4	cup cornstarch
1	(16-ounce) can crushed pineapple, drained (reserve 3/4 cup syrup)
1	tablespoon butter
2	tablespoons grated orange rind
1/4	cup orange juice
2	tablespoons lemon juice
1/2	cup shredded coconut
1/2	cup chopped pecans

Preheat the oven to 350°. Grease and flour three 9-inch-round pans. In a large bowl beat the butter and sugar until fluffy. Add the eggs one at a time. In a separate bowl mix the flour, baking soda, and salt. Stir into the creamed mixture alternately with the buttermilk and vanilla. Pour one-third of the batter into one of the prepared pans. Blend the nuts, raisins, cinnamon, allspice, mace, and cloves into the remaining batter. Pour the batter into the two remaining pans. Bake for 30 to 35 minutes.

For the filling, mix the sugar, salt, and cornstarch in a saucepan and slowly stir in the reserved pineapple syrup. Cook over low heat, stirring constantly until the mixture thickens and boils. Boil 1 minute. Remove from the heat. Blend in the butter, orange rind, orange juice, and lemon juice. Cool. Stir in the coconut, crushed pineapple, and pecans.

When the cake is cool, put the layers together: spread half of the filling over one of the "nut" layers of cake. Place the non-nut cake layer on top and spread the remaining filling over that. Add the final cake layer and spread a white frosting on top. (see page 37 for Red Hatters Red Cake frosting).

Makes 16 to 18 servings

Nancy Kicklighter, DuchessDotCom
Duchesses of Dorchester, Dorchester, South Carolina

Maybe the Boys Should Learn to Cook

My mother and father divorced when I was five. That left my dad, two brothers, my grandmother, and me to do the cooking. My grandmother taught me to cook when I was very young. I can remember standing on an upturned bucket so that I could reach the table to help stir.

One day when I was about six, my grandmother was out tending the garden, and I decided to make a cake. I really don't know what I put in the cake, but I can remember putting in things that I had seen my grandmother use. (She never ever used a recipe.)

When the cake was done, it looked very good—a little lopsided, but good nonetheless. I was so proud of it. When Daddy and my brothers came in from the field, my grandmother sliced the cake, and I served it with pride. Everyone ate and said it tasted pretty good.

As always, my dad and brothers drank plenty of fresh milk with their cake. I was thrilled. About two hours after dinner, my dad and brothers began complaining of stomachaches. My brothers rolled on the floor and cried.

Although we never found out exactly what I had put in the cake, my grandmother guessed I must have added a lot of baking powder, making the cake have a sponge effect. After it was eaten, the more anyone drank, the more they hurt.

To this day, forty-five years later, my brothers hesitate before eating something I bake.

Joan Burgess
Queen Jojo
Red Topped Texas Tornadoes
Branch, Texas

Spiced Eggnog Cheesecake

This special-occasion cake is full of seasonal spices and topped with festive chocolate curls.

CRUST

32	graham crackers, crushed
1	teaspoon sugar
1/4	teaspoon ground ginger
1/4	teaspoon nutmeg
1/4	teaspoon cinnamon
1/4	cup (1/2 stick) butter, melted

FILLING

4	(8-ounce) packages cream cheese, softened
3/4	cup sugar
1/4	cup all-purpose flour
1/4	teaspoon nutmeg
1/4	teaspoon cinnamon
	Pinch of cloves
1	egg
1	teaspoon vanilla extract
13/4	cups eggnog
1	(8-ounce) container sour cream

GARNISH

1	(6-ounce) package premium white chocolate baking bars
	Pinch of nutmeg

Preheat the oven to 350°. In a medium bowl mix the graham crackers, sugar, ginger, nutmeg, cinnamon, and butter. Press over the bottom of a 9-inch round springform pan. Bake for 10 minutes. Cool on a wire rack.

For the filling, beat the cream cheese in a large bowl until smooth. In a small bowl mix the sugar, flour, nutmeg, cinnamon, and cloves. Beat into the cream cheese. Beat in the egg and vanilla. Beat in the eggnog in a slow stream. Pour into the springform pan and tap the pan lightly to release air bubbles. Bake for 1 hour. Remove from the oven and spread the sour cream on top. Return to the oven and bake for 5 minutes. Cool in the pan on a rack until cool to touch. Refrigerate until ready to serve.

For the garnish, melt the chocolate in the top of a double boiler. Add the nutmeg. Line an 8 x 8 x 3-inch loaf pan with foil. Pour the chocolate into the pan, spreading it evenly. Cool until firm. Lift out of pan. Make chocolate curls, using a vegetable peeler and arrange the curls on top of the cheesecake.

Makes 16 servings

Carolyn Rogers, Queen Mum
Royal Reds, Knoxville, Tennessee

Holiday Pecan Cake

2	cups (1 pound) butter, softened
2	cups sugar
6	eggs
3	plus 1 cups all-purpose flour
1/4	teaspoon salt
1	teaspoon baking powder
1	pound pecan halves
1/2	pound red candied cherries
1/2	pound green candied cherries
1/2	pound candied pineapple, diced
2	teaspoons pure vanilla extract

Preheat the oven to 300°. In a large bowl beat the butter and sugar well. Add the eggs one at a time, beating after each addition. In a separate bowl mix 3 cups flour, the salt, and baking powder together. Add this to the butter mixture. In another bowl mix the pecan halves, cherries, and pineapple with the remaining 1 cup flour. Add this and the vanilla to the cake mixture. Bake in a greased and floured angel food or tube cake pan for 2 hours.

Makes 1 cake

Joan L. Kriner, Queen Mother
The Red Hat Society of Shippensburg,
    Shippensburg, Pennsylvania

Ruby Slipper Cake

1   (18-ounce) package yellow or lemon pudding cake mix
1   cup sour cream
1/4   cup water
2   eggs
1   (3-ounce) package raspberry gelatin*
    confectioners sugar

Preheat the oven to 350°. In a large bowl beat the cake mix, sour cream, water, and eggs. Spoon one-third of the batter into a well-greased and floured 10-inch tube pan. Sprinkle half the gelatin on top. Repeat the layers. Spread the remaining batter over the gelatin to cover. Bake for 45 to 50 minutes, or until the cake springs back when lightly pressed. Cool in the pan 5 minutes then remove to a rack to finish cooling. Sprinkle with confectioners' sugar or frost as desired.

Makes 12 to 16 servings

*Note: May reserve 1 teaspoon gelatin to tint a frosting.

Willma Zavadil, Maid of Mission
Star City Gladabouts, Lincoln, Nebraska

Pink Lady Cake

Testers rated this cake "moist and tasty."

4   eggs
1   cup vegetable oil
1/2   cup water
1   (10-ounce) package frozen strawberries, thawed and divided
1   (18-ounce) package white cake mix
1   (3-ounce) package strawberry gelatin
3   tablespoons all-purpose flour
1   (1-pound) package confectioners' sugar

Preheat the oven to 350°. Grease and flour a 13 x 9-inch pan. In a large bowl beat the eggs, oil, water, and half the strawberries. In a separate bowl blend together the cake mix, gelatin, and flour. Add this mix to the batter and beat well. Pour into the prepared pan and bake for 1 hour 15 minutes, or until a tester comes out clean. Cool the cake on a rack.

In a medium bowl mix the confectioners' sugar with the remaining strawberries. Use the mixture to frost the cake.

Makes 10 to 12 servings

Tony Horton, Queen
Crawford County Cuties, Van Buren, Arkansas

Strawberry Shortcut Cake

1   cup miniature marshmallows
2   cups frozen sliced strawberries in syrup, completely thawed
1   (3-ounce) package strawberry gelatin
2 1/4   cups all-purpose flour
1 1/2   cups sugar
1/2   cup shortening
3   teaspoons baking powder
1/2   teaspoon salt
1   cup milk
1   teaspoon vanilla extract
3   eggs

Preheat the oven to 350°. Sprinkle the marshmallows evenly over the bottom of a greased 13 x 9-inch pan. In a small bowl combine the strawberries and gelatin. In a large bowl beat the flour, sugar, shortening, baking powder, salt, milk, vanilla, and eggs. Pour this batter over the marshmallows. Spoon the strawberry-gelatin mixture evenly over the batter. Bake for 45 minutes, or until golden brown and a toothpick inserted in the center comes out clean.

Makes 12 servings

Dolly McAfee, Dutchess Snapshot
Sassy Sophistihats, Highland, New York

It's-a-Sin Cake

One bite of this rich cake, and you'll understand where the name came from.

1   (18-ounce) package butter-recipe yellow cake mix
1   cup chopped pecans
1   (15-ounce) can cream of coconut milk
1   (14-ounce) can sweetened condensed milk
1   pint strawberries, cut in half
1   (13 1/2-ounce) package strawberry glaze
1   (8-ounce) container whipped topping

Prepare the cake mix according to the directions on the package, adding the pecans. Bake in a greased 13 x 9-inch pan. In a small bowl combine the cream of coconut milk and condensed milk. When the cake is cooked and slightly cooled, poke holes on the top with the end of a wooden spoon. Pour the milk mixture over the cake. Combine the strawberries and glaze and spread on top of the cake. Refrigerate 15 minutes. Spread the whipped topping on the cool cake and refrigerate 1 hour before serving.

Makes 12 to 16 servings

Millie Lytle, Queen Bee
Red Hats On To You, Carol Stream, Illinois

Dreamsicle Cake

"Refreshing and cool," "beautiful icing," "excellent," "super cake for a formal party," chirped tasters of this pretty cake.

CAKE
1   (18-ounce) package orange cake mix
1   (3-ounce) package orange gelatin
1   (5-ounce) package vanilla instant pudding mix

4   eggs
1/2 cup vegetable oil
1 1/2 cups milk

FROSTING

1   (8-ounce) container sour cream
1   cup sugar
1   (5-ounce) package vanilla instant pudding
     mix
1   (12-ounce) can crushed pineapple, drained
1   (6-ounce) package frozen coconut, thawed
1   (8-ounce) container whipped topping

Preheat the oven to 350°. For the cake, grease and flour three 9-inch cake pans. In a large bowl combine the cake mix, gelatin, pudding mix, eggs, oil, and milk and mix with an electric mixer for 3 minutes. Pour the batter in the pans and bake for 25 to 30 minutes, or until a toothpick inserted in the cake comes out clean. Cool in the pans for 10 minutes then invert onto cooling racks and cool completely before frosting.

For the frosting, in a large bowl mix the sour cream, sugar, and pudding mix together by hand. Stir in the pineapple and coconut. Fold in the whipped topping. Spread the frosting over the cooled cake before serving. The cake must be refrigerated.

Makes 12 servings

Debbie Anderson, Lady Scarlett
The Red Hot Flashes, Advance, North Carolina

Nova Scotia Blueberry Cream Cake

1 1/2 cups all-purpose flour
1/2 plus 1/2 cup sugar
1 1/2 teaspoons baking powder
1/2 cup (1 stick) butter, softened
1   egg
1   plus 1 teaspoon vanilla extract
4   cups blueberries, fresh or frozen
2   cups sour cream
2   egg yolks

Preheat the oven to 375°. In a medium bowl stir together the flour, 1/2 cup sugar, and baking powder. Cut in the butter until the mixture resembles coarse crumbs. Stir in the egg and 1 teaspoon vanilla. Pat lightly into the bottom of a greased 9-inch springform pan. Pour the blueberries over the top. In another bowl whisk together the sour cream, the remaining sugar, egg yolks, and the remaining vanilla. Pour over the blueberries. Bake for 60 to 70 minutes, or until the top is lightly brown. Cool in the pan. Remove the outer ring of the pan and cut the cake into wedges.

Makes 8 servings

Sylvia Fallahay, Lady Sylvia
Just 14 Ladies, Elliot Lake, Ontario, Canada

Doggone Surprise

I was a nineteen-year-old bride who married a farm boy back in 1933. While my new husband was out plowing in the field, I decided I would surprise him by baking an angel food cake.

I got everything mixed, put it in the pan, and put it in the oven. When it was time to take the cake out of the oven, I discovered that something was wrong! I must have forgotten an ingredient, because the cake never rose. Embarrassed, I took the cake to the garden and buried it. I couldn't let my husband see such a mess.

A few days later, we were sitting on our porch when he noticed our English bulldog out in the garden digging. My sweet husband said, "I wonder what that dog has been digging at for so long?" The dog had found the cake and was trying to eat it, but the cake was too tough. My darling husband brought it in to me, and I had to confess that it was a cake I had made to surprise him. I guess he was pretty surprised after all.

He certainly had fun telling everyone about his surprise cake. It was a long time before I tried making another angel food cake surprise.

Anita Myers
Governess of Golf
Kiwanis Manor Ramblin' Red Hatters
Tiffin, Ohio

Lemon Cake

CAKE

- 1 (18-ounce) package lemon cake mix
- 1 (5-ounce) package instant lemon pudding
- 1/4 teaspoon lemon extract
- 3/4 cup vegetable oil
- 3/4 cup water
- 4 eggs

GLAZE

- 1 1/2 cups confectioners' sugar
- 2 tablespoons lemon juice
- 2 teaspoons butter, melted
- 2 teaspoons water

Preheat the oven to 350°. For the cake, in a large bowl beat the cake mix, pudding, lemon extract, oil, water, and eggs for 5 minutes. Pour into a greased 13 x 9-inch pan and bake for 35 to 40 minutes. Remove from the oven and prick holes in the top of the cake with a fork.

For the glaze, combine the confectioners' sugar, lemon juice, butter, and water in a bowl. Mix well and spread over the cake while it is still warm.

Makes 12 servings

Sabrena Harris, Queen Mum Too
Red Hat Jazzers, Kirkland, Washington

Sunshine Cake

We received so many recipes for this cake, many titled Pig Pickin' Cake, perhaps for its honorary status as the dessert at a pig roast, but perhaps for its effect on guests.

CAKE
1   (18-ounce) package yellow cake mix
1/2 cup vegetable oil
4   eggs
1   (11-ounce) can mandarin oranges, undrained

FROSTING
1   (8-ounce) container whipped topping
1   (8-ounce) can crushed pineapple, undrained
1   (5-ounce) package instant vanilla pudding

Preheat the oven to 350°. In a large bowl beat the cake mix, oil, eggs, and oranges with an electric mixture for 3 minutes; this will crush the oranges. Pour the batter into a greased and floured 13 x 9-inch pan and bake for 35 minutes, or until a toothpick comes out dry.

For the frosting, mix the whipped topping and pineapple in a medium bowl. Stir in the pudding mix a little at a time with a wooden spoon (not an electric mixture). Cool the cake completely before frosting with the pineapple mixture. Refrigerate.

Makes 15 servings

Diane Coombs, Queen Mother
Belles of Sun City, Sun City, California

Tangerine Cake

Like a Red Hatter, just a little out of the ordinary, but so lovable.

2   teaspoons grated tangerine peel
2   teaspoons ground cloves
1   teaspoon vanilla extract
2   cups all-purpose flour
2   cups sugar
6   eggs
1/2 cup pecans (optional)

Preheat the over to 300°. In a large bowl beat the tangerine peel, ground cloves, vanilla, flour, sugar, and eggs. Add the pecans if using. Pour the batter into a greased and floured loaf pan and bake for 1 hour, 10 minutes.

Makes 8 servings

Valerie Joye, Diva
Rouge Chapeau Divas, Richmond, Virginia

Almond Joy Cake

Because sometimes you feel like a nut. If you prefer, prepare the Texas Hot Cocoa Cake (see page 40) as the base for this rich, rich dessert.

1 (18-ounce) package chocolate or German chocolate cake mix
   Vegetable oil for preparing cake
   Eggs for preparing cake

FILLING
1 (5-ounce) can evaporated milk
1 (7 1/2-ounce) jar marshmallow creme
1 cup granulated sugar
2 (4-ounce) cans flaked coconut

FROSTING
3 tablespoons baking cocoa
1/2 cup (1 stick) butter
6 tablespoons milk
1 (1-pound) package confectioners' sugar
1 cup toasted whole almonds
1 teaspoon vanilla extract

Prepare the cake according to package directions. Pour into a greased 13 x 9-inch pan. Bake and cool the cake in the pan.

For the filling, heat the milk, marshmallow creme, and sugar until the sugar melts; stir in the coconut and pour the mixture over the cake.

For the frosting, boil the cocoa, butter, and milk; pour the mixture over the confectioners' sugar in a bowl and stir until smooth. Add the almonds and vanilla and spread over the filling. Refrigerate the cake. Serve in small pieces.

Makes about 20 servings

Virginia Hosford, Hysterian
Santa Teresa Red Hots, San Jose, California

Lemon Lime Cake

Very festive looking, and testers loved it. They noted that this cake could be baked in a 13 x 9-inch baking dish.

CAKE
1 (18-ounce) package lemon cake mix
2 (3-ounce) packages lime gelatin
5 eggs
1 1/3 cups vegetable oil
3/4 cup orange juice

FROSTING
1 (8-ounce) package cream cheese
1 (1-pound) package confectioners' sugar
1/2 cup (1 stick) butter, softened
1 teaspoon vanilla extract
1 cup nuts, chopped
2 limes for garnish (optional)
2 maraschino cherries for garnish (optional)

Preheat the oven to 350°. For the cake, in a large bowl combine the cake mix, gelatin, eggs, oil, and orange juice. Pour into three greased and floured 9-inch cake pans. Bake for 20 minutes. Cool on a rack.

For the frosting, in a medium bowl beat

together the cream cheese, confectioners' sugar, butter, and vanilla. Spread on the cake and sprinkle the nuts on top. Garnish with the sliced limes and cherries, if desired.

Makes 16 servings

Barbara Giedd, Lady Barb
Brair Patch Hattitudes, Eatonton, Georgia

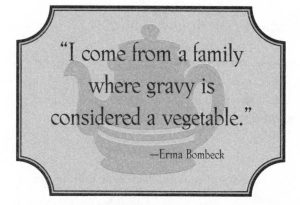

"I come from a family where gravy is considered a vegetable."

—Erma Bombeck

Lemon Nut Crunch

3/4 cup (1 1/2 sticks) butter, softened
1 1/2 cups sugar
3 eggs
3 cups all-purpose flour
3 teaspoons baking powder
1/2 teaspoon salt
1 cup milk
   Juice and grated rind of 1 lemon
1 cup chopped nuts

Preheat the oven to 375°. In a large bowl beat the butter and sugar until light and fluffy. Add the eggs and beat well. Sift the flour, baking powder, and salt together and add alternately to the creamed mixture with the milk. Stir in the lemon juice and rind. Grease a 10-inch tube pan and sprinkle the bottom of the pan with the nuts. Pour in the batter and bake for 1 hour. Turn out on a rack to cool.

Makes 12 servings

Gloria Winkes, Racing Diva
Sassy Sophistihats, Montgomery, New York

Lemon Jell-O Cake

CAKE
3/4 cup water at room temperature
3/4 cup vegetable oil
4 eggs
1 (18-ounce) package lemon supreme cake mix
1 (3-ounce) package lemon Jell-O

FROSTING
2 cups confectioners' sugar
4 1/2 tablespoons lemon juice

Preheat the oven to 350°. For the cake, in a large bowl beat the water, oil, and eggs. Mix in the cake mix and Jell-O. Pour the batter into a greased 13 x 9-inch cake pan and bake for 35 minutes.

For the frosting, in a small bowl mix the confectioners' sugar and lemon juice. Remove the cake from the oven and poke holes over the top. Spread the frosting over the cake.

Makes 24 servings

Jean Godoy Gonino, Chapterette
Sassy Scarletts of St. Augustine, St. Augustine, Florida

Lemon Meringue Cake

If you like lemon pie, you'll love this cake. An easy way to split the cake layers is to use a piece of sewing thread. Wrap it around the "equator" of each layer, cross the thread, and gently pull.

CAKE

1   (18-ounce) package lemon or yellow cake mix

3   eggs

1   cup water

1/3 cup vegetable oil

FILLING

1   cup sugar

3   tablespoons cornstarch

1/4 teaspoon salt

1/2 cup water

1/4 cup lemon juice

4   egg yolks, beaten

1   tablespoon butter

1   teaspoon grated lemon peel

MERINGUE

4   egg whites

1/4 teaspoon cream of tartar

3/4 cup sugar

Preheat the oven to 350°. For the cake, in a large bowl beat the cake mix, eggs, water, and oil for 2 minutes. Pour into two greased and floured 9-inch-round pans and bake for 25 to 30 minutes. Cool for 10 minutes then remove from the pans to finish cooling on wire racks.

For the filling, boil the sugar, cornstarch, salt, water, and lemon juice in a pan for 1 to 2 minutes, or until thickened. Remove from the heat. Stir a small amount of the hot filling into the egg yolks then add the yolks to the saucepan. Return to the heat and, stirring constantly, bring to a gentle boil and cook for 2 minutes. Remove from the heat and stir in the butter and lemon peel. Cool completely.

For the meringue, beat the egg whites and cream of tartar in a large bowl until foamy. Gradually beat in the sugar until stiff peaks form.

Split each cooled cake into two layers. Spread one-third of the filling on the bottom layer and repeat with two more layers. Spread meringue over the fourth layer and the sides of the cake. Bake for 10 to 15 minutes in a 350° oven, or until the meringue is lightly browned. Serve immediately or refrigerate.

Makes 12 to 14 servings

Janie Russell, Biker Goddess
Big D Regals, Garland, Texas

Red Hot Momma's Party Cake

Our tester held a party for tasting this cake, and everyone there agreed that it lives up to its name.

CAKE

1   (18-ounce) package lemon cake mix

1   (4-ounce) package instant vanilla pudding and pie mix

1 (16-ounce) can tropical fruit, undrained and finely chopped
1 cup coconut
4 eggs
1/4 cup canola oil
1/2 cup firmly packed brown sugar
1/2 cup chopped walnuts

GLAZE
1/2 cup (1 stick) butter
1/2 cup granulated sugar
1/2 cup evaporated milk
1 1/3 cups coconut

Preheat the oven to 325°. For the cake, in a large mixing bowl combine the cake mix, pudding mix, canned fruit with juice, coconut, eggs, and oil. Beat with a mixer for 4 minutes on medium speed. Pour into a greased and floured 13 x 9-inch pan. Sprinkle the brown sugar and nuts on top. Bake for 45 minutes. Cool in the pan for 15 minutes.

To make the glaze, combine the butter, sugar, and milk in a large saucepan over medium heat. Bring to a boil and cook for 2 minutes, stirring constantly. Stir in the coconut. Spoon the hot glaze over the warm cake.

Makes 12 to 16 servings

Lois Dill, Chapterette
River Red Hatters, DeBary, Florida

Swedish Pineapple Cake

This cake is also delicious with a mixture of almonds, pecans, and walnuts sprinkled on top of the icing.

CAKE
2 cups all-purpose flour
2 cups granulated sugar
2 eggs
1 teaspoon baking soda
1 teaspoon vanilla extract
1 (20-ounce) can crushed pineapple, undrained
1/4 cup chopped pecans

FROSTING
2 cups confectioners' sugar
1 (8-ounce) package cream cheese, softened
1/4 (1/2 stick) butter, softened
1 teaspoon vanilla extract
chopped pecans (optional)

Preheat the oven to 350°. For the cake, mix the flour, sugar, eggs, baking soda, vanilla, pineapple, and pecans. Bake in a greased 13-x-9-inch pan for 35 to 40 minutes.

For the frosting, mix the confectioners' sugar, cream cheese, butter, and vanilla. Spread over the cake while hot. Sprinkle with additional pecans, if desired.

Makes 1 cake

Illa Glandt, Queen Mother
Dakota Wild Roses, Valley City, North Dakota

Pineapple Coconut Cake

CAKE
1 (15-ounce) can crushed pineapple
1 (18-ounce) package yellow
  cake mix

FROSTING
1/2 cup (1 stick) butter
1 cup sugar
1 (5-ounce) can evaporated milk
1 cup shredded coconut
1 cup chopped pecans

For the cake, drain the pineapple and reserve the juice. Prepare the cake mix as directed on the package then fold in the pineapple. Bake the cake in a greased 13 x 9-inch pan, following directions on the package. When done, remove the cake from the oven and pierce the entire top with a fork. Pour the reserved juice over the cake.

For the frosting, cook the butter, sugar, and milk in a saucepan over low heat 3 to 4 minutes. Add the coconut and pecans. Spread the mixture on top of the cake.

Makes 12 servings

Carolyn Pitts, Lady Carolyn the Dutchess of
  Aquamarine.
Razzle Dazzle Dames of Pasadena, Azusa, California

Pineapple Angel Food Cake

It may seem like there's not enough liquid to create a batter, but the pineapple juice provides just enough. Testers declared it delicious without a frosting, but they also prepared a frosting for it by combining a 3-ounce box of vanilla instant pudding mix, an 8-ounce container of whipped topping, and a 10-ounce can crushed pineapple, drained. They called the result "excellent."

1 (16-ounce) package angel food cake mix
1 (20-ounce) can crushed pineapple,
  undrained

Preheat the oven to 350°. In a large bowl combine the cake mix with the pineapple. Pour into an ungreased 13 x 9-inch pan and bake for 30 minutes.

Makes 12 servings

Joan Judd, Queen Mom
Pool Playmates, The Villages, Florida

Watermelon Cake

This cute cake will wow your guests, who probably won't mind the chocolate chip "seeds." Testers called it "great for kids' birthday parties."

1 (18-ounce) package white
  cake mix
2 (.13-ounce) packages unsweetened
  watermelon-flavor drink mix
1/4 cup plus 2 tablespoons miniature chocolate
  chips
1 to 2 (12-ounce) containers fluffy white
  frosting
  Red and green food colors
2/3 cup green jelly beans (optional)

Preheat the oven to 350°. Grease the bottoms only of two 8 or 9-inch-round pans. Prepare the cake mix according to the directions on the package. Add the drink mix and with an electric mixer on low beat for 30 seconds, then medium for 2 minutes. Stir in the 1/4 cup chocolate chips. Pour the batter into the pans. Bake for 27 to 30 minutes. Cool 10 minutes. Remove the cakes from the pans and let cool completely. In a small bowl mix 1 cup frosting with 10 drops green food coloring. Frost the sides of the cakes with the green frosting. If using jelly beans, press them onto the sides. Add 10 drops red coloring to the remaining frosting. Frost the top of the cake. Press the remaining chocolate chips on top for seeds. Cut each cake crosswise in half and arrange to resemble four watermelon halves.

Makes 16 servings

Judy Adams, Queen Bee
B Watcha Wanna Bee Red Hatters, Shepherd, Michigan

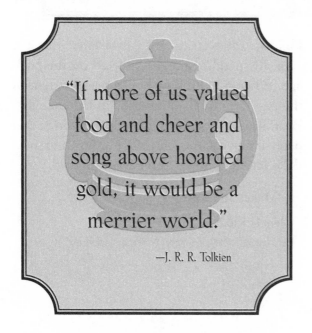

"If more of us valued food and cheer and song above hoarded gold, it would be a merrier world."

—J. R. R. Tolkien

Chocolate Upside-Down Cake

You make the topping first, so when you unmold this cake, it's topped and ready to serve. Bake the cake in an angel-food cake pan or an 8-inch-square baking pan.

3	tablespoons butter, melted
4	tablespoons brown sugar
1	cup chopped walnuts
2	tablespoons butter, softened
1	cup granulated sugar
1	egg yolk
2	squares unsweetened chocolate, melted
1	cup all-purpose flour
1	heaping teaspoon baking powder
	Pinch of salt
3/4	cup milk
1	stiffly beaten egg white

Preheat the oven to 350°. In a small bowl mix the melted butter, brown sugar, and walnuts. Sprinkle the mixture in the bottom of a greased tube pan. Beat the softened butter and granulated sugar until fluffy. Stir in the egg yolk and melted chocolate. Sift together the flour, baking powder, and salt. Add alternately to the butter mixture with the milk. Fold in the beaten egg white. Spoon the mix into the tube pan over the nut mixture. Bake for 30 minutes. Serve warm.

Makes 1 cake

Peggy Murtagh, Queen Mum
Crimson Hattitudes, Brockton, Massachusetts

The Whole Egg

When my daughter was around eleven years old, she wanted to make a cake on her own. I agreed to let her, instructing her to follow the directions in the recipe and to ask me a question if she was not sure of something. So she began making her first cake, all on her own. At one point I went over to see how things were going and looked in the bowl. There was something in the batter that looked strange. I stopped the mixer, asking what it was as I retrieved a piece of it from the batter. I realized it was an eggshell and that there were many more pieces.

I asked my daughter why there were so many pieces of the eggshell in the batter. She replied that she was following the recipe, which called for two whole eggs. And that is exactly what she put in: two whole eggs.

Of course we had to pitch the batter and start over again, but this time, without the shells.

Sandy Meller
Countess of Crafts
California Reds
Lohman, Missouri

Triple Fudge Cake

Here's an easy shot of decadence when you must have your fix of chocolate.

1　(5-ounce) package chocolate fudge pudding mix (not instant)
1　(18-ounce) package chocolate fudge cake mix
1　(6-ounce) bag chocolate chips
1　cup chopped walnuts

Preheat the oven to 350°. In a large saucepan cook the pudding mix as directed on the package. When a full rolling boil is reached, remove the pan from the heat and stir in the cake mix. Pour into a greased and floured 13 x 9-inch cake pan. Top with the chocolate chips and nuts. Bake for 30 minutes. Serve warm or cold.

Makes 16 to 20 servings

Glennis Kidder, Queen Mother
Red Hatters of the Orestimba, Newman, California

Chocolate–Chocolate Cake to Die For

CAKE

1   (18-ounce) package chocolate fudge cake mix with pudding

2   (4-ounce) packages chocolate fudge instant pudding mix

3   eggs

1   cup water

1/2   cup vegetable oil

1   cup chocolate chips

FROSTING

1   (8-ounce) container whipped topping

1   (4-ounce) package chocolate fudge instant pudding mix

1   cup half-and-half or milk

Preheat the oven to 350°. For the cake, in a large bowl combine the cake mix, pudding mix, eggs, water, oil, and chocolate chips. Pour into a greased 13 x 9-inch pan. Bake for 35 to 40 minutes. Cool the cake on a rack.

For the frosting, in a large bowl mix the whipped topping, pudding mix, and half-and-half and spread it on the cake. Refrigerate until you are ready to serve.

Makes 15 servings

Judy Howard, Chapterette
Retro Rubies, Penfield, New York

Triple Chocolate Mess Cake

Here's a ready-when-you-are chocolate dessert for your slow cooker. Testers really enjoyed working with this recipe, getting it just right. It's good with vanilla or chocolate ice cream. Dessert heaven when topped with whipped cream and a cherry. The testers wanted to rename it "Chocolate Overdose."

1   (18-ounce) package dark chocolate cake mix

1   pint sour cream

1   (6-ounce) package chocolate instant pudding mix

1   (12-ounce) bag chocolate chips

1   cup vegetable oil

4   eggs

1   cup water

Spray a slow cooker with nonstick spray. (An oval slow cooker works best.)

In a large bowl with an electric mixer, beat the cake mix, sour cream, pudding mix, chocolate chips, oil, eggs, and water until smooth. The batter will be very thick. Spoon it into the slow cooker. Cook on low for 6 to 7 hours, checking after 4 hours. (If it overcooks, it becomes bitter.) The cake is ready when the top is firm and the center is set but moist. Scoop out and serve in bowls with ice cream or whipped cream.

Makes 10 to 15 servings

Leeann Kickham, Queen Mother
Red Hat Prospects, Wentzville, Missouri

Molten Chocolate Cakes with Vanilla Ice Cream

Baked in soufflé dishes, these cakes contain a surprise liquid center. This not-too-sweet dessert is very grown-up, and definitely needs the garnish of sweet ice cream, whipped cream, or custard sauce.

1/4   cup plus 5 tablespoons sugar
 8   ounces semisweet chocolate, chopped
3/4   cup (1 1/2 sticks) butter
 3   whole eggs
 3   egg yolks
 1   tablespoon all-purpose flour
 1   quart vanilla or coffee ice cream (or whipped cream or custard sauce)

Preheat the oven to 425°. Generously butter eight 3/4-cup soufflé dishes or custard cups. Sprinkle each with 1 1/2 teaspoons sugar. In a heavy saucepan stir the chocolate and butter over low heat until smooth. Remove from the heat. In a large bowl beat the eggs, egg yolks, and the remaining 5 tablespoons sugar with an electric mixer until thick and pale yellow, about 8 minutes. Fold one-third of warm chocolate mixture into the egg mixture then fold in the remaining chocolate. Fold in the flour. Divide the batter among the soufflé dishes. (Can be made one day ahead. Cover with plastic; chill. Bring to room temperature and uncover before continuing). Place the soufflé dishes on a baking sheet and bake until the edges are puffed and slightly cracked but the center 1 inch of each moves slightly when the dishes are shaken

gently, 13 to 15 minutes. Top each cake with a scoop of vanilla ice cream and serve immediately.

Makes 8 servings

Fran Varnadore, Lady Red
Radical Fringe Red Hatters, Palos Verdes Estates, California

Mississippi Mud Cake

If you don't have a 15 x 10-inch pan, use a 13 x 9-inch pan and bake 5 minutes longer.

CAKE
 1   cup (2 sticks) butter, melted
 2   cups granulated sugar
1/2   cup unsweetened cocoa
 4   large eggs
 1   teaspoon vanilla extract
1/8   teaspoon salt
1 1/2 cups all-purpose flour
1 1/2 cups chopped pecans
 1   (10 1/2-ounce) bag miniature marshmallows

CHOCOLATE FROSTING
 1   (1-pound) package confectioners' sugar
1/2   cup milk
1/4   cup (1/2 stick) butter, softened
1/3   cup unsweetened cocoa

Preheat the oven to 350°. For the cake, in a large bowl, whisk together the butter, sugar, cocoa, eggs, vanilla, and salt. Stir in the flour and chopped pecans. Pour the batter into a greased and floured 15 x 10-inch pan. Bake for

20 to 25 minutes, or until a wooden pick inserted in the center comes out clean. Remove from the oven. Top the warm cake with marshmallows. Return it to the oven and bake 5 minutes more.

For the frosting, beat the confectioners' sugar, milk, butter, and cocoa powder together and drizzle over the warm cake. Cool completely before cutting.

Makes 36 servings

Jackie Nunes, Chapterette
Scarlet Ribbons, Elk Grove, California

Red Hatters Red Cake

The classic, but with a scrumptious buttercream frosting. The method for the frosting is unusual, but you'll enjoy the results.

CAKE
1/2	cup shortening
1/2	cup (1 stick) butter, softened
1 1/2	cups sugar
2	eggs
2	(1-ounce) bottles red food coloring
2 1/4	cups cake flour
2	teaspoons unsweetened cocoa
1	teaspoon salt
1	cup buttermilk
1	teaspoon baking soda
1	tablespoon vinegar
1	teaspoon almond extract

FROSTING
1	cup milk
5	tablespoons all-purpose flour
1/4	teaspoon salt
1/2	cup (1 stick) butter, softened
1/2	cup shortening
1	cup sugar
2	teaspoons almond extract

Preheat the oven to 350°. For the cake, in a large bowl beat the shortening, butter, sugar, eggs, and red food coloring. Sift together the flour, cocoa, and salt. Add the flour mixture and buttermilk alternately to the creamed shortening mixture, beating after each addition. Mix the baking soda and vinegar and add to the cake batter. Add the almond extract. Pour into two 8-inch well-greased and floured round cake pans. Bake for 25 minutes or until a tester comes out clean. Cool. Cut each layer in half crosswise.

For the frosting, cook the milk, flour, and salt in a saucepan over low heat until thick. Cool completely and strain. Beat together the butter, shortening, and sugar. Add the cooled flour mixture to the butter mixture and beat until creamy and white. Add the almond extract. Frost the top of each layer, stack the layers, and frost the sides of the cake. Store in the refrigerator.

Makes 12 servings

Gerry Benassi, Clean Gerry
Red Hatted League of Duluth, Duluth, Minnesota

Chocolate Mayonnaise Cake

CAKE
2 cups all-purpose flour
1 teaspoon baking soda
1 cup granulated sugar
4 heaping teaspoons cocoa
1 cup mayonnaise
1 cup milk
1 teaspoon vanilla extract

FROSTING
2 tablespoons butter, softened
2 cups confectioners' sugar
2 heaping teaspoons cocoa
1 teaspoon vanilla extract
1/4 cup coffee or milk

Preheat the oven to 350°. For the cake, sift the flour with the baking soda. In a large bowl combine the sugar, cocoa, mayonnaise, milk, vanilla, and flour mixture. Pour the batter into two 8-inch greased round cake pans. Bake for 25 minutes. Cool.

For the frosting, beat the butter with the sugar, cocoa, and vanilla. Gradually add the coffee or milk to moisten and make the frosting spreadable. Spread on top and sides of cake.

Makes 10 servings

Linda Denton, Queen
Chapeau Rouge, Richmond, Virginia

All-American Chocolate Cake

While wonderful straight out of the refrigerator, the flavor of this cake improves by allowing it to come to room temperature before serving.

CAKE
1 2/3 cups all-purpose flour
1 1/2 cups superfine sugar
3/4 cup (1 1/2 sticks) butter, softened
3/4 cup milk
1/3 cup unsweetened cocoa
1 teaspoon vanilla extract
3/4 teaspoon baking powder
1/2 teaspoon salt
1/4 teaspoon baking soda
3 large eggs

FROSTING
1 1/4 cups heavy cream
3/4 cup granulated sugar
6 ounces unsweetened chocolate, coarsely chopped
2/3 cup (10 2/3 tablespoons) butter
1 teaspoon vanilla extract

Preheat the oven to 325°. For the cake, in a large bowl with the mixer at low speed, beat the flour, sugar, butter, milk, cocoa, vanilla, baking powder, salt, baking soda, and eggs for 2 minutes. Spoon the batter into two greased 9-inch round cake pans that have been dusted with cocoa. Bake for 30 to 35 minutes, or until a toothpick inserted in the center of the cake comes out clean. Cool in pans on racks 10 minutes then remove from the pans.

For the frosting, in a large saucepan over medium heat, boil the cream and sugar for 1 minute. Remove from the heat and stir in the chocolate, butter, and vanilla. Refrigerate the mixture until it thickens. With a mixer at high speed, beat until smooth and high peaks are formed. Use 3/4 to 1 cup frosting between the layers. Refrigerate the cake until ready to serve.

Makes 12 servings

Joann Kelly, Queen Julep Magnolia Blossom
Hobart Scarlett O'Hatters, West Hobart,
    Tasmania, Australia

Last-Minute Chocolate Cake

A real help for the harried cook since ingredients are those usually found in the pantry. Our tester was very fond of this cake, and recommended a quick cream cheese frosting. You can also use the batter to make twelve cupcakes.

1 1/2   cups all-purpose flour
1   cup sugar
3   tablespoons cocoa
1   teaspoon baking soda
1/2   cup (1 stick) butter, melted
1/2   cup milk
1/2   cup warm water
1   teaspoon vanilla extract

Preheat the oven to 350°. In a large bowl mix the flour, sugar, cocoa, and baking soda together with a wooden spoon until well blended. Beat in the melted butter, milk, water, and vanilla. Pour into a greased 8-inch square cake pan. Bake for

25 to 30 minutes, or until toothpick comes out clean. Let cool completely and frost with your favorite buttercream frosting.

Makes 9 servings

Cynthia West, Queen Cookie
Traveling Cooks with Hattitude, Marshalltown, Indiana

Old-Fashioned Devil's Food Cake

This moist cake is best served warm with ice cream or whipped topping, but is also delicious with a white buttercream frosting.

2   cups all-purpose flour
1 3/4   cups sugar
1/2   cup cocoa
1/2   teaspoon salt
1   tablespoon baking soda
1   egg
1   cup buttermilk
2/3   cup vegetable oil
1   cup strong coffee, hot

Preheat the oven to 350°. In a large bowl stir together the flour, sugar, cocoa, salt, and baking soda. Add the egg, buttermilk, and oil. Stir well. Blend in the hot coffee. No need to beat. Pour the batter into a greased and floured 13 x 9-inch pan and bake for 40 minutes.

Makes 9 to 12 servings

Linda Glenn, Queen Linda
Rowdy Red Hat Mamas of N.W. Wisconsin, Luck,
    Wisconsin

Chocolate Chip Rum Cake

1   (18-ounce) yellow cake mix
1   (3-ounce) package chocolate instant
     pudding mix
1   cup sour cream
4   eggs
1/2 cup vegetable oil
1   teaspoon vanilla extract
2   tablespoons rum
1   cup chopped walnuts or almonds
1   cup chocolate chips

Preheat the oven to 350°. In a large bowl beat the cake mix, pudding mix, sour cream, eggs, oil, vanilla, rum, nuts, and chocolate chips for 7 to 10 minutes. Pour into a greased and floured Bundt pan and bake for 58 minutes. Let stand 7 minutes then turn onto a rack or plate. Timing is crucial.

Makes 16 to 20 servings

Sharon Sheaver, Crafty Contessa
Red Hats of the Purple Stage, Hereford, Arizona

Black Forest Cake

1   (18-ounce) package devil's food cake mix
1   (21-ounce) can cherry pie filling
1   teaspoon almond flavoring
1   (5-ounce) package vanilla instant
     pudding mix
2   tablespoons vanilla extract
1   (8-ounce) container whipped topping,
     thawed

2   tablespoons chocolate sprinkles or
     chocolate chips
     Maraschino cherries

Bake the cake according to manufacturer's directions in a 13 x 9-inch pan. Mix the pie filling and almond flavoring. While the cake is still warm, poke the top with a fork and spread the cherry pie filling over the top of the cake. While the cake cools, prepare the pudding mix as directed on the package, adding the vanilla extract. Fold the pudding into the whipped topping. Spread the pudding mixture over the cake, carefully covering the cherry pie filling. Decorate with chocolate sprinkles and maraschino cherries. Cover and refrigerate.

Makes 12 servings

Judith Ausmus, Lady of Resourcefulness
Purple Plumes, Santa Ana, California

Texas Hot Cocoa Cake

This cake's success depends on good old-fashioned hand stirring, so skip the mixer when making this cake.

CAKE
2   cups all-purpose flour
2   cups granulated sugar
1/2 cup (1 stick) butter
6   rounded tablespoons cocoa
1/2 cup shortening
1   cup water
1   cup buttermilk
2   eggs
1   teaspoon salt

1 teaspoon baking soda
1 teaspoon vanilla extract
1/4 teaspoon cinnamon

FROSTING
1/2 cup (1 stick) butter
6 tablespoons evaporated milk
6 rounded tablespoons cocoa
1 teaspoon vanilla extract
1 (1-pound) package confectioners' sugar
Pecans (optional)

Preheat the oven to 375°. For the cake, in a medium bowl stir the flour and sugar together. In a saucepan combine the butter, cocoa, shortening, and water and bring to a boil. Pour this mixture over the flour and sugar and mix well. Add the buttermilk, eggs, salt, baking soda, vanilla, and cinnamon and mix well. Pour into a greased and floured 13 x 9-inch pan. Bake for 30 to 35 minutes.

For the frosting, in a saucepan heat to a boil the butter, milk, cocoa, vanilla, and confectioners' sugar. Add the pecans if using. Spread over the hot cake and serve warm.

Makes 16 to 20 servings
Lady Barbara Noakes Aldrich, Queen Mother
Tootee Flutee Red Hats, Omaha, Nebraska

Graham Cracker Cake with Mocha Frosting

This meringue-like cake is filled and topped with a fluffy mocha frosting.

CAKE
2 sleeves plus 3 more graham crackers
12 eggs, separated
2 cups granulated sugar
1/2 pound walnuts, chopped

MOCHA FROSTING
1 tablespoon instant coffee
1/2 cup cocoa
1/4 cup water
1/2 cup (1 stick) butter, softened
1 teaspoon vanilla extract
2 cups confectioners' sugar, or more

Preheat the oven to 325°. For the cake, grease two 9-inch cake pans and line the bottoms with greased waxed paper. Crush the graham crackers (not too finely). Beat the egg yolks and sugar until thick and lemony in color with an electric mixer, about 2 minutes. In a separate bowl beat the egg whites until stiff but not dry. Stir the graham crackers and walnuts into the egg yolk mixture. Gently fold in the egg whites. Place in the prepared cake pans and bake for about 25 minutes. Do not overbake. Cool in the pans then transfer to a serving plate.

For the mocha frosting, mix the coffee, cocoa, and water together in a medium bowl to make a paste. Add the softened butter, vanilla, and confectioners' sugar to make a spreadable consistency. Spread the frosting over the cake.

Makes 12 servings
Margaret LeRoy, Queen Mother
Red Flamingos of Grandezza, Estero, Florida

Polka-Dot Cake

My mother started teaching me how to cook when I was nine. I could only cook a few things, but I was pretty sure I could follow a recipe well enough to bake my dad a birthday cake. I waited until they had gone grocery shopping and started getting everything together.

Did I forget to tell you that we were poor? Yeah, I know everyone says that, but in our case it was true. While we did have running water and electricity, we didn't have hot water, and our stove was an old, cast-iron cookstove fueled by coal instead of wood, since we lived in a coal-mining town. There was no electric mixer either.

I decided on a devil's food cake, since it was Dad's favorite. I followed the recipe to the letter, except for the sifting part because I didn't know what sifting was. When my parents returned, they were quite surprised to see what a good job I had done. They were even more surprised when Mom cut the cake and revealed little white polka dots of unsifted flour throughout the cake!

Dad said it was the best cake he ever had, and he was sure no other father had ever received a polka-dot cake!

Joyce Bacon
Queen of Tarts
The Elderberry Tarts
Baltimore, Maryland

Rum Cake

This moist cake is delicious served with whipped cream.

CAKE

- 1/2 cup chopped walnuts
- 1 (18-ounce) package yellow cake mix
- 1/2 cup vegetable or corn oil
- 4 eggs
- 1 cup water
- 1/2 cup dark rum

SAUCE

- 1/2 cup (1 stick) butter
- 1 cup sugar
- 1/2 cup dark rum
- 1/4 cup water

Preheat the oven to 350°. For the cake, grease a Bundt cake pan and sprinkle chopped walnuts on the bottom. In a large bowl mix together the cake mix, oil, eggs, water, and rum. Pour into the cake pan and bake for 1 hour.

For the sauce, bring the butter, sugar, rum, and water to a boil in a saucepan. Boil and stir for 5 minutes. Cool the cake and punch holes in the top with a fork. Pour the sauce over the cake.

Makes 12 servings

Marsha Hendrickson, Dessert Queen
Red Roses of Brampton, Brampton, Ontario, Canada

Crazy Cake

This one is known by other names, such as Wacky Cake or Funny Cake, due to the fill-in-the-holes method of mixing.

- 3   cups all-purpose flour
- 2   cups sugar
- 1/3 cup cocoa
- 2   teaspoons baking soda
- 1/2 teaspoon salt
- 1   teaspoon vanilla extract
- 2   tablespoons vinegar
- 3/4 cup vegetable oil
- 2   cups cold water

Preheat the oven to 350°. Sift together the flour, sugar, cocoa, baking soda, and salt into a greased 13 x 9-inch cake pan. Make three holes in the mixture. Put the vanilla in the first hole, vinegar in the second and oil in the third hole. Add the water and blend with a fork until smooth. Bake for 30 to 35 minutes.

Makes 15 servings

Peg Warriner, Queen Diva
Red Hat Divas, Villa Grove, Illinois

Earthquake Cake

This cake gets its name from the cracks that appear on the surface as it bakes.

- 1 1/2 cups chopped pecans
- 2   cups coconut flakes
- 1   (18-ounce) package pudding-in the-mix German chocolate cake mix
- 1   (8-ounce) package cream cheese
- 1/2   cup (1 stick) butter
- 4   cups confectioners' sugar

Preheat the oven to 350°. Spread the pecans on the bottom of a greased 13 x 9-inch pan. Sprinkle the coconut on top. Prepare the cake according to the package directions and pour into the pan. Beat together cream cheese, butter, and confectioners' sugar and spread on top of the batter. Bake for 1 hour.

Makes 12 to 15 servings

Carole Hayes, Baroness Butterfly
Jewels of the Prairie, Jamestown, North Dakota

Sugar Storm

Have you ever tried to mix up a recipe while sitting in a chair? It's like being a child, because you can't see into the bowl. And you would think that stirring up a recipe for frosting would be easy enough, whether you were sitting or standing.

I use a wheelchair due to a mobility challenge, and that's exactly what I thought as I got out the ingredients and utensils for:

Decorator Buttercream Frosting

1 cup butter

1 cup shortening

2 pounds confectioners' sugar

5 tablespoons milk

1 1/2 tablespoons vanilla

With mixer at medium speed, beat the butter and shortening. With mixer off or set at low speed, add the confectioners' sugar in several parts, beating after each addition. (Having mixer on low or off will prevent a cloud of sugar going everywhere.) Add milk slowly, a tablespoon at a time after each addition of sugar. Add vanilla and mix well.

I beat the butter and shortening, peeking over the bowl's edge and down into the mixture to make sure it was creamy before adding the first cup of sugar. The phone was in my lap, and it began to ring. I didn't turn off the mixer but instead answered the phone while stretching to see if the frosting ingredients in the mixer were getting creamy.

As I held the cordless phone to my ear with my shoulder, without thinking, I picked up another portion of sugar and poured it into the mixer, forgetting to turn the mixer down or off. It took just seconds for the sugar to hit the air current made by the speed of the mixer and blow up into a sugar storm! A confectioners' sugar cloud went everywhere, covering me and the kitchen counter. I had sugar in my lap, sugar in my hair. It covered me like snow.

I didn't tell my sister-in-law (who was still on the other end of the phone, remember) what a mess I had made. Instead, I told her I needed to call her back. That was an understatement! I wanted to clean up the mess quickly, before my husband got home. Just as I hung up the phone, I heard the front door open and my husband walked in. What was I to do, covered in sugar from head to toe?

As he walked into the room to see his wife covered with sugar, I asked him, "Do you want some sugar?"

He replied by singing, "Sugar in the morning, sugar in the evening, sugar at suppertime." We laughed and shook off the sugar while giving each other a bit of the best kind of "sugar."

Shirley Williams
Queen
The Red Hat Mermaids
Knoxville, Tennessee

Popcorn Candy Cake

Use whatever candies you want in this fun, no-bake cake, including seasonal choices such as candy corn, red and green M&M's, etc. Don't use a springform pan.

1   (10½-ounce) package miniature marshmallows
3/4 cup vegetable oil
1/2 cup (1 stick) butter or margarine
3   quarts popped popcorn, not popped kernels removed
1   (16-ounce) package spiced gumdrops
1   (16-ounce) package (2 cups) M&M's
1   cup salted peanuts or mixed nuts

In a large saucepan melt the marshmallows, oil, and butter until smooth. In a large bowl combine the popcorn, candies, and nuts. Add the marshmallow mixture and mix well. Press into a well greased 10-inch tube pan. Cover and refrigerate for 5 hours or overnight. Dip the pan in hot water for no more than 5 to 10 seconds to remove the cake from the pan. Slice with an electric or serrated knife.

Makes 10 to 12 servings

Mary Goodell, Queen Mother
Razzle Dazzle Darlins', Sun City West, Arizona

Solid Walnut Cake

Black walnuts can be difficult to find at your grocery, but if you have a walnut tree, or a neighbor with one, you know how wonderful their distinctive taste is.

1/2   cup (1 stick) butter, softened
2   cups sugar
4   eggs, separated
3   cups sifted all-purpose flour
1/4   teaspoon salt
2   teaspoons baking powder
1   cup milk
1   teaspoon vanilla extract
1   cup chopped black walnuts

Preheat the oven to 350°. In a large bowl beat the butter and sugar until fluffy. Beat in the egg yolks. In a medium bowl combine the flour, salt, and baking powder. Add the dry ingredients to the creamed mixture alternately with the milk and vanilla, beating well after each addition. Beat the egg whites until stiff peaks form. Fold in the walnuts and egg whites. Pour into a greased tube pan. Bake for 1 hour, or until a cake tester comes out clean.

Makes 12 to 15 servings

Joan Plitt, Queen Mother
The Cats in the Hats, York, Pennsylvania

Black Walnut Cake

For walnut lovers, a cake that's good with tea.

1/3   cup (5 1/3 tablespoons) butter, softened
1 3/4   cups sugar
2   eggs
2 3/4   cups all-purpose flour
4 1/2   teaspoons baking powder
1/4   teaspoon salt
1   cup milk
2   teaspoons vanilla extract
1 1/2   cups chopped black walnuts

Preheat the oven to 375°. In a large bowl beat the butter and sugar until fluffy. Beat in the eggs, flour, baking powder, salt, milk, and vanilla. Add the nuts. Bake in a greased and floured angel food cake pan for 1 hour.

Makes 10 to 12 servings

Mitzi Wilson, QueenMumFunDames
Fun and Fantastic Dames, Charlotte, North Carolina

Pistachio Cake

1   (18-ounce) box white or yellow cake mix
1   (14-ounce) can cream of coconut
1   (8-ounce) container whipped topping
1   cup chopped pistachios

Bake the cake according to package directions in a 13 x 9-inch pan. Remove from the oven and poke holes in the cake with a fork. Pour the cream of coconut over the cake. When cool, spread the whipped topping over the cake and sprinkle the pistachios on top.

Makes 20 servings

Elizabeth Kirk, Queen Elizabeth III
Rocking Red Hatters, Lumberton, North Carolina

Pistachio Marble Cake

"Perfect," "removed easily from pan," "nice and moist," "delicious," "would be great with coffee" were among comments from the tester. Try a drizzling of melted chocolate chips and butter for the top.

1 (18-ounce) package yellow cake mix
1 (3-ounce) package pistachio pudding mix
4 eggs
1 cup water
1/2 cup vegetable oil
1/2 teaspoon almond extract
1/4 cup chocolate syrup
  Confectioners' sugar (optional)

Preheat the oven to 350°. In a large bowl beat together the cake mix, pudding mix, eggs, water, oil, and almond extract for 2 minutes. Remove 1 1/2 cups batter and place it in a small bowl. Mix in the chocolate syrup. Spoon the yellow and chocolate batter alternately into a greased and floured 10-inch tube or Bundt pan. Marble the batters with a knife. Bake for 50 minutes. Cool in the pan for 15 minutes. Remove from the pan and finish cooling on a rack. Sprinkle confectioners' sugar on top, if desired.

Makes 12 servings

Judy Fabian, Duchess of DoLittle
Rural Robust Red Hatters, Ford City, Pennsylvania

Chocolate Chip Kahlua Cake

1 (18-ounce) package German chocolate cake mix
1 (4-ounce) package chocolate instant pudding mix
2 cups sour cream
4 eggs
3/4 cup vegetable oil
1/3 cup Kahlua
1 (6-ounce) package chocolate chips

Preheat the oven to 350°. In a large bowl mix together the cake mix, pudding mix, sour cream, eggs, oil, Kahlua, and chocolate chips. Pour into a greased Bundt pan and bake for 1 hour. Cool in the pan for 15 minutes then transfer the cake to a cooling rack. Serve with whipped cream or vanilla ice cream.

Makes 12 to 15 servings

Rose Marie Fischer, FQM RoseBud
Red Hot Roses, South St. Paul, Minnesota

Black Russian Cake

The glaze is not necessary for this tasty cake, but it adds a special touch.

CAKE

1   (18-ounce) package yellow cake mix
4   eggs
1/4   cup vegetable oil
1/4   cup Kahlua
1   (5-ounce) package chocolate instant pudding mix
3/4   cup strong brewed coffee (decaffeinated is fine)
1/4   cup vodka

GLAZE

1   cup sugar
2   tablespoons butter
1/4   cup water
1/4   cup rum

Preheat the oven to 350°. For the cake, grease a tube or Bundt pan. Mix together the cake mix, eggs, oil, Kahlua, pudding mix, coffee, and vodka until smooth. Pour into the pan and bake for 50 minutes; cool.

For the glaze, mix the sugar, butter, water, and rum in a saucepan over medium heat. Bring to a boil then cool slightly. Pour the glaze over the cake.

Makes 16 servings

Lynn Borg, Duchess of Information
The Grateful Red Hatters, Encinitas, California

Almond Lovers' Cake

2   cups all-purpose flour
1   teaspoon baking soda
1   teaspoon baking powder
1/4   teaspoon salt
1   cup granulated sugar
1/2   cup (1 stick) plus 1 tablespoon butter
2   eggs, beaten
1   teaspoon vanilla extract
1   cup sour cream
1   plus 1/2 cups sliced almonds
1/2   cup half-and-half
1/4   cup brandy (or 1 teaspoon brandy flavoring)
1   (8-ounce) can almond paste
4   tablespoons milk
4   tablespoons confectioners' sugar
    Sliced almonds for garnish

Sift together the flour, baking soda, baking powder, and salt. In a separate bowl, beat the sugar and 1/2 cup butter until fluffy. Mix in the eggs and vanilla. Add the dry ingredients alternately with the sour cream. The batter will be stiff. Stir in 1 cup almonds. In a small bowl combine the half-and-half, brandy, and the remaining 1/2 cup almonds. Knead the almond paste until soft and add it to the brandy mixture a little at a time until well blended.

Preheat the oven to 350°. Spread half the cake batter in a greased and floured 9 or 10-inch tube pan. Spread half the almond paste mixture over the batter then spread the remaining cake batter on top. To the remaining almond paste mixture, add the milk and confectioners' sugar. Pour over the cake. Bake for 30 minutes. Remove from the oven and garnish with sliced almonds. Bake 30 minutes longer, or until a toothpick inserted in the center comes out clean. Cool on a wire rack for 30 minutes. Carefully remove the cake from the pan and cool completely. Melt the remaining tablespoon butter and brush the top of the cake.

Makes 10 to 12 servings

Marie Haney, Her-Marie-ness
The Cats in the Hats, Ogden, Utah

Oatmeal Chocolate Chip Cake

This is one handy cake—it makes its own frosting. The chocolate chips melt as the cake bakes.

13/4   cups boiling water
1   cup quick-cooking oatmeal
1   cup firmly packed brown sugar
1   cup granulated sugar
1/2   cup (1 stick) butter, softened
2   eggs
13/4   cups all-purpose flour
1/2   teaspoon salt
1   teaspoon baking soda
1   tablespoon cocoa
1   (12-ounce) package chocolate chips
3/4   cup walnuts

Preheat the oven to 350°. In a large bowl pour the water over the oatmeal and let it stand for 10 minutes. Add the brown and granulated sugars

and butter, stirring until the butter melts. Add the eggs, flour, salt, baking soda, and cocoa. Add half the chocolate chips and mix well. Pour into a greased 13 x 9-inch pan. Sprinkle the remaining chocolate chips and walnuts over the top of the cake. Bake for 40 minutes.

Makes 12 servings

Beverly Schmedel, Queen Mum
Purple Posies, Indianapolis, Indiana

Shoofly Cake

Here are the sweet tastes of the famous shoofly pie in cake form.

4   cups all-purpose flour
1   cup (2 sticks) butter, softened
2   cups sugar
1   cup molasses
2   cups warm water
1   teaspoon baking soda

Preheat the oven to 350°. In a large bowl mix the flour, butter, and sugar. Reserve 11/3 cups for the topping. To the main bowl, add the molasses, water, and baking soda. Mix well and pour into a 13 x 9-inch greased and floured pan. Top with the reserved crumb mixture. Bake for 45 to 50 minutes, or until the top springs back when pressed with a finger.

Makes 15 servings

Joan L. Kriner, Queen Mother
The Red Hat Society of Shippensburg,
Shippensburg, Pennsylvania

Birth of the Red Hat Society

While visiting a friend in Tucson several years ago, Sue Ellen Cooper impulsively bought a bright red fedora at a thrift shop, for no other reason than that it was cheap and, she thought, quite dashing. A year or two later she read the poem "Warning" by Jenny Joseph, which describes an older woman who has decided to become a bit eccentric, wearing purple clothing with a red hat. Sue Ellen gave a red hat and a copy of the poem to her dear friend, Linda Murphy, as a whimsical birthday gift. Intrigued, other friends requested the same gift for their birthdays.

*One day it occurred to these friends that they were becoming a sort of "Red Hat Society" and that perhaps they should go out to tea . . . in full regalia. They decided they would find **purple dresses** which didn't go with their red hats to complete the poem's image. The tea was a smashing success.*

Soon, each of them thought of another woman or two she wanted to include, and they bought more red hats. One of their members passed along the idea to a friend of hers in Florida, and their first sister chapter was born. When the group began getting publicity, they began to encourage other interested women to start their own chapters, which many, many thousands of them have done.

*Sue Ellen's fondest hope is that these societies will proliferate far and wide. We have now held three successful Red Hat Society conventions—entire hotels filled with women of a certain age wearing red hats and **purple outfits**! Could world domination be far behind?*

Kentucky Jam Cake

This century-old recipe was developed in Tennessee and Kentucky as a way to substitute bountiful preserves and to preserve scarce sugar. It's a great way to use up all those little jars of jam that accumulate. You may wish to start with just 3/4 cup sugar, since the jams provide lots of sweetening power.

CAKE

 1 cup (2 sticks) butter, softened
1 1/2 cups granulated sugar
 3 eggs
1 1/2 teaspoons baking soda
 1 cup buttermilk
 3 cups all-purpose flour
 1 teaspoon cinnamon
 1 teaspoon cloves
 1 teaspoon nutmeg
 1 cup strawberry preserves
 1 cup blackberry jam
 1 cup chopped pecans

FROSTING

1/2 cup (1 stick) butter, softened
 1 cup packed brown sugar
1/4 cup milk
 2 cups confectioners' sugar
 1 teaspoon vanilla extract

Preheat the oven to 325°. For the cake, in a large bowl beat the butter and sugar until fluffy. Mix in the eggs. Add the baking soda and buttermilk. Sift the flour, cinnamon, cloves, and nutmeg and add to the mixture. Stir in the preserves, jam, and pecans. Pour into a lightly greased, 9-inch-round cake pan and bake for 1 hour. Remove from the pan and cool on a rack.

For the frosting, boil the butter, brown sugar, and milk in a saucepan. Cool to lukewarm. Add the confectioners' sugar and vanilla, beating until thick and creamy and until the mixture loses its gloss. Spread over the cooled cake.

Makes 12 servings

Lena Caswell, Madam Cracker
Traveling Cooks with Hattitude, Greenfield, Indiana

Upside-Down Rhubarb Cake

Adjust the amount of sugar you use, depending on the tartness of your rhubarb.

 5 cups rhubarb, chopped
 1 cup sugar
 1 (3-ounce) package strawberry gelatin mix
 3 cups miniature marshmallows
 1 (18-ounce) package yellow cake mix

Preheat the oven to 350°. In a large bowl mix together the rhubarb, sugar, gelatin, and marshmallows. Pour into the bottom of a 13 x 9-inch greased and floured pan. Prepare the cake mix as directed on the package and pour over the rhubarb mixture. Bake for 1 hour. Let the cake cool for 10 minutes before turning out onto a cake dish. When cool, store in the refrigerator.

Makes 16 servings

Deb Schmoll, Duchess of Doing
The Purple Apron Gals, Champlin, Minnesota

Little Baker

When my oldest daughter was five years old, she already had a one-and-a-half-year-old sister and another sibling on the way. I was so tired during the pregnancy that I would often put the two girls down for naps so that I could take one myself. Of course, Julie, the five-year-old, wasn't taking naps anymore, but I'd put her down anyway and give her books to read or quiet games to play.

One afternoon when I woke up, imagine my surprise when she told me she had "baked a cake" while I was sleeping! Rushing to the kitchen, I pulled a "cake" from the oven that was about as heavy as a brick. Naturally, we had to taste it. After a sampling, I asked her what recipe she used. She said she didn't use a recipe. So I asked what she put in it. She said proudly, "Flour, sugar, eggs, milk, and peanut butter." When I asked her why the peanut butter, she said brightly, "Because I like it!"

For her next birthday, I made coupons for twelve at-home "cooking lessons" to be given once a month over the following year, to be sure that if she decided to "cook," it would at least be something we'd be able to eat!

It must have worked, because many years later, she went to culinary school to become a pastry chef!

Polly Tomlinson
Queen Tacobelle
Red Hat Chili Peppers
Randallstown, Maryland

Milky Way Cake

This is a very light, moist cake with very mild chocolate taste. Choose a caramel or orange glaze or sauce for a light finish. For a more intense chocolate experience, go with a fudge frosting. Good for a potluck because you know it's a conversation starter.

6   regular size Milky Way candy bars

1/2 plus 1/2 cup (2 sticks) butter, softened

2   cups sugar

4   eggs

21/2 cups all-purpose flour

1/2 teaspoon baking soda

11/4 cup buttermilk

1   teaspoon vanilla extract

1   cup chopped nuts

Preheat the oven to 350°. In a medium saucepan melt the candy bars and 1/2 cup butter over low heat. In a large bowl beat the remaining 1/2 cup butter with the sugar until fluffy. Beat in the eggs one at a time. Sift the flour with the baking soda and add alternately to the batter with the buttermilk. Mix in the melted candy. Stir in the vanilla and nuts. Pour the batter into a greased and floured tube pan. Bake for 1 hour to 1 hour, 10 minutes.

Makes 15 servings

Jo Ann Fain, Hysterian

Red Hats and Ready Hearts, Hendersonville, North Carolina

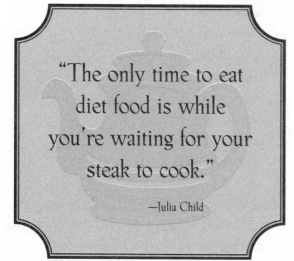

"The only time to eat diet food is while you're waiting for your steak to cook."

—Julia Child

Poppy Seed Bundt Cake

1/4	cup poppy seeds
1	cup buttermilk
1	cup (2 sticks) butter, softened
1 1/2 plus 1/2	cups sugar
4	eggs
1	teaspoon vanilla extract
2 1/2	cups all-purpose flour
1/2	teaspoon salt
1	teaspoon baking soda
1 1/2	tablespoons cinnamon

Soak the poppy seeds in the buttermilk for 6 to 8 hours.

Preheat the oven to 350°. In a large bowl beat the butter with 1 1/2 cups sugar until fluffy. Beat in eggs one at a time. Add the vanilla. Sift the flour, salt, and baking soda; add to the batter alternately with the buttermilk mixture. Blend well. In a small bowl combine the remaining 1/2 cup sugar with the cinnamon. Grease a Bundt pan, and sprinkle part of the cinnamon mixture over the bottom and sides of the pan. Spoon the batter into the pan in two or three layers, sprinkling the cinnamon sugar between each layer. Bake for 50 minutes or until a toothpick comes out clean. Cool the cake in the pan for 1 hour then remove the cake to a rack.

Makes 16 servings

Barbara Yost, Queen Floozie

Bodacious Floozies, Jacksonville, North Carolina

Pink Champagne Cake

A great way to use up leftover champagne—if there is such a thing.

CAKE

1	(18-ounce) box white cake mix
1 1/4	cups pink champagne
1/3	cup vegetable oil
3	eggs
1	cup milk
1/2	teaspoon salt
3	tablespoons all-purpose flour
1	cup (2 sticks) butter, softened
1	cup sugar
1	teaspoon vanilla extract
2	to 3 drops red food coloring

FROSTING

1	cup milk
1/2	teaspoon salt
3	tablespoons all-purpose flour
1	cup (2 sticks) butter, softened
1	cup sugar
1	teaspoon vanilla extract

Preheat the oven to 350°. For the cake, in a large bowl beat the cake mix, champagne, oil, eggs, milk, salt, flour, butter, sugar, vanilla, and food coloring at low speed for 2 to 3 minutes. Pour into a greased and floured, 13 x 9-inch pan, or two, 8-inch-round pans. Bake for 30 to 35 minutes, or until a toothpick inserted in the center comes out clean. Let cool.

For the frosting, cook the milk, salt, and flour in a small saucepan over medium heat until thick. Remove from the heat and cool. In a large bowl beat the butter, sugar, and vanilla. Beat in the cooled flour mixture until the icing resembles whipped cream. Spread on top of the cake.

Makes 12 servings

Cindi Carter, Antiparlimentarian
Monroe Hotsy Totsys, Monroe, Iowa

Peanut Butter Sheet Cake

1	cup water
1	cup (2 sticks) butter
1/2	teaspoon salt
1/4	cup peanut butter
2	cups all-purpose flour
2	cups sugar
2	eggs
1/2	cup buttermilk
1	teaspoon baking soda
1	teaspoon vanilla extract

Preheat the oven to 350°. In a large saucepan mix the water, butter, salt, and peanut butter over medium heat. Mix in the flour, sugar, eggs, buttermilk, baking soda, and vanilla. Pour into a greased 13 x 9-inch pan. Bake for 20 minutes. Be careful not to overbake.

Makes 12 to 15 servings

Marge McGovney, Queen
The Red Hattitudes, DeWitt, Michigan

French Cream Frosting

In some older cookbooks this mixture is also known as Mystery Icing.

5   tablespoons all-purpose flour
1   cup milk
1   cup (2 sticks) butter, softened
1   cup sugar
1   teaspoon vanilla extract

In a saucepan over medium-low heat cook the flour and milk, stirring until thick. Cool completely. In a large bowl beat the butter and sugar until fluffy. Add the flour mixture a small amount at a time. Mix in the vanilla until smooth.

Makes enough to frost a two-layer cake

J. Sue Ziltener, Diva of Script
Sassy Society Sisters, Janesville, Wisconsin

Strawberry YaYa Cake

CAKE
1   (18-ounce) package strawberry cake mix
1   (3-ounce) box vanilla instant pudding mix
1   (3-ounce) box strawberry gelatin mix
1/4 cup vegetable oil
4   large eggs
1 1/4 cups cold water

FROSTING
1   (8-ounce) package cream cheese
1/2 cup granulated sugar
1/2 cup confectioners' sugar
1   (16-ounce) container whipped topping
1   (15-ounce) can strawberry pie filling
1   pint fresh strawberries, sliced for garnish

Preheat the oven to 350°. For the cake, pour the cake mix, pudding mix, and gelatin mix directly into an ungreased 13 x 9-inch baking pan. Add the oil, eggs, and water and mix until smooth. Bake for 45 minutes. Let cool.

For the frosting, with a mixer on low setting, beat the cream cheese with the granulated and confectioners' sugars. Fold in the whipped topping and blend well. Spread half the frosting on the cooled cake. Now spread all the strawberry pie filling on top of the frosting. Spread the remaining frosting on top of the strawberry pie filling. Garnish the top of the cake with freshly sliced strawberries. Then refrigerate for 2 to 3 hours prior to serving. Cut the cake into squares to serve.

Makes 20 servings

Mary Davis, YaYaGranny
Red Hat Vintage Belles, West Columbia, South Carolina

Chocolate Ganache

Pour over cake for a quick topping that's glossy and smooth-looking (and deliciously chocolaty).

3/4   cup heavy cream
8   ounces bittersweet or semisweet chocolate morsels
1   tablespoon liqueur of choice (optional)

In a medium saucepan heat the cream to hot, not boiling. Pour over the chocolate morsels and stir to melt the chocolate. Add the liqueur. When melted and smooth, let stand for 10 minutes. Pour over cooled cakes or cookies.

Makes enough for a double-layer cake

Janet Gilbert, Royal Spinner
Red Hat Hotties, Newark, Delaware

Peanut Butter Squares

4   large eggs
2   cups sugar
2   cups all-purpose flour
2   teaspoons baking powder
       Pinch of salt
1   cup milk
1   (18-ounce) jar creamy peanut butter
1   (12-ounce) package milk chocolate chips

Preheat the oven to 350°. Grease and flour a jelly-roll pan Beat the eggs and sugar with a mixer in a large bowl. Stir the flour, baking powder, and salt together in a separate bowl.

Add the milk and dry ingredients alternately to the creamed mixture. Pour the batter into the prepared pan. Bake for 20 minutes. Spread the peanut butter on top of the hot cake immediately. Place in the freezer for 30 minutes (until the peanut butter is not tacky). Melt the chocolate chips in a saucepan or microwave. Spread on top of the cooled cake and cut into squares.

Makes 24 servings

Dolores Fiori, Queen of Tea-light
Tea-lightful Red Hatters, Hammonton, New Jersey

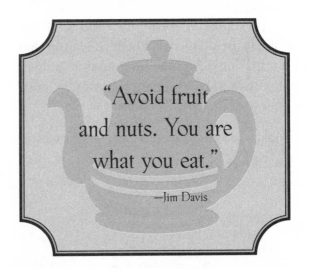

"Avoid fruit and nuts. You are what you eat."

—Jim Davis

White Wine Cake

To vary the flavor, use sherry in place of white wine.

CAKE
1/2   cup finely chopped pecans
1   (18-ounce) package yellow cake mix
1   (5-ounce) package French vanilla instant pudding mix

1/2 cup white wine
1/2 cup water
1/2 cup vegetable oil
4 eggs

TOPPING
1/2 cup (1 stick) butter or margarine
1 cup sugar
1/4 cup white wine
1/4 cup water

Preheat the oven to 350°. For the cake, spray the bottom of a tube pan with nonstick cooking spray then sprinkle the pan with pecans. In a large bowl beat together the cake mix, pudding mix, wine, water, oil, and eggs. Pour into the pan. Bake for 45 to 50 minutes, or until a toothpick comes out clean.

For the topping, boil the butter, sugar, wine, and water in a saucepan for 2 1/2 minutes. Poke holes in the top of the cake, and spoon the topping over the cake while it is still hot. Let sit for 5 minutes then remove from the mold onto a serving plate.

Makes 16 servings

Wendy Works Gibson, Queen Wendybird
Red Hat Readers Society, Moneta, Virginia

Tres Leches Cake

Tres leches *is Spanish for "three milks." Those three milks plus sour cream give the cake a rich, mild flavor and intensely moist body.*

2 cups buttermilk pancake mix
1 teaspoon baking powder
1 cup sugar
1 cup milk
1 teaspoon vanilla extract
4 eggs
3/4 cup vegetable oil
1 (12-ounce) can evaporated milk
1 (10-ounce) can sweetened condensed milk
2 tablespoons sour cream
1 (8-ounce) container whipped topping
Chopped nuts or cinnamon (optional)

Preheat the oven to 350°. In a large bowl beat together the pancake mix, baking powder, sugar, milk, vanilla, eggs, and oil. Pour into a greased and floured 13 x 9-inch pan. Bake for 30 minutes. Meanwhile, in a blender mix the evaporated milk, condensed milk, and sour cream. Take the cake out of the oven and immediately poke holes all over the cake with a wooden spoon handle. Pour the milk mixture into the holes. Pour a little more on the edges. Let cool, and frost with the whipped topping. Refrigerate several hours or overnight before serving. Sprinkle with chopped pecans or cinnamon if desired.

Makes 15 to 20 servings

Jo Anne Silva, Founding Queen Mother
El Paso Red Hat Border Babes, El Paso, Texas

Chocolate Zucchini Cake

1   cup firmly packed brown sugar
1/2   cup granulated sugar
1/2   cup (1 stick) butter, softened
1/2   cup canola oil
3   eggs
1   teaspoon vanilla extract
1/2   cup buttermilk
2 1/2 cups all-purpose flour
1/2   teaspoon allspice
1/2   teaspoon cinnamon
1/2   teaspoon salt
2   teaspoons baking soda
4   tablespoons unsweetened cocoa
3   zucchini, about 6 inches long
1   cup chocolate chips

Preheat the oven to 350°. In a large bowl beat the sugars, butter, and oil. Add the eggs, vanilla, and buttermilk. In a separate bowl mix the flour, allspice, cinnamon, salt, baking soda, and cocoa. Add to the batter. Grate the zucchini into the batter and stir. Pour into a greased and floured 13 x 9-inch pan. Sprinkle with the chocolate chips. Bake for 45 minutes, or until a tester inserted in the center comes out clean.

Makes 15 servings

Nancy Parkhurst, Vice Queen
Feathers and Flowers, Bedford, Virginia

ꙥ Slices of Heaven ꙥ

PIES

"Pie in the sky, by and by." Many of us think that sounds pretty good. But the future is still out there—in the future. Since we can't change that (and why should we want to anyway?), we Red Hatters are perfectly content to take life as it comes, one day at a time. We look for the bright spots in life—and we find them too. So while we're content to wait to see whatever the future may bring, we Red Hatters choose to look for the sweeter things in life . . . and enjoy them right now, too!

Some of the "slices of Heaven" available to us here and now are: Lemon Meringue, Chocolate Cream, Apple Crumble, Boysenberry, Fresh Peach, Cherry, Custard, Apricot, Banana Cream, Coconut Cream, Black Bottom, Strawberry, Blackberry, Raspberry, Butterscotch, Key Lime, Pumpkin, Sweet Potato, Sour Cream Raisin, Mince, Rhubarb, etc.

Need I say more?

Brown Bag Apple Pie

A fun recipe—make sure everyone is watching when you pull the pie out of the oven. Veteran bakers say new grocery bags are thinner than old-style bags, so double-bag the pie.

CRUST
1 1/2 cups all-purpose flour
1/2 cup vegetable oil
1/4 cup milk
Dash of salt

FILLING
4 large Granny Smith apples
1/2 cup sugar
3 tablespoons all-purpose flour
1/2 teaspoon cinnamon

TOPPING
1/2 cup sugar
1/2 cup all-purpose flour
1/2 teaspoon cinnamon
1/2 cup (1 stick) butter or margarine, slightly softened

Preheat the oven to 375°. For the crust, combine the flour, oil, milk, and salt in a bowl and mix until the dough holds together. Roll dough to 1/8-inch thick, large enough to fit in an 8 or 9-inch pie pan. Bake for 10 minutes.

For the filling, peel, core, and slice the apples. In a large bowl toss the apples with the sugar, flour, and cinnamon. Arrange them in the piecrust.

For the topping, combine the sugar, flour, and cinnamon. Cut in the butter with a pastry blender, two knives, or a food processor. Spread over the apple mixture, pressing down slightly. Slide the pie into a brown paper grocery bag. Fold the top of the bag to close then fasten with paper clips. Bake for 1 hour.

Makes 8 servings

Peggy Krickbaum, Princess Knit Wit
Flashy Sassies, Montrose, Colorado

Grandma's Apple Pot Pie

Is it a dumpling? A lasagna? Or a pie?

2 cups all-purpose flour
4 tablespoons sugar
1/2 teaspoon salt
2 teaspoons baking powder
5 tablespoons shortening
2/3 cup milk
3 to 4 apples, peeled, cored, and sliced
Sugar for sprinkling

Preheat the oven to 375°. Sift the flour, sugar, salt, and baking powder together. Cut in the shortening with a pastry cutter or in a food processor until crumbly. Add the milk and stir with a fork until the dough comes together. Roll out on a board until about 1/4-inch thick. Cut into squares or rectangles. Grease a loaf pan. Cover the bottom with a layer of dough, then a layer of apples. Sprinkle sugar on top of the apples. Add another layer of dough and apples.

Sprinkle with sugar again. Put a scant layer of dough on top. Add enough boiling water to come half way up the side of the pan. Bake for about 1 hour, or until golden brown. Serve warm. Pour milk over individual servings if desired.

Makes 4 servings

Cassandra DeAngelis, Queen
Charming Ladies with Hattitude, Mill Run, Pennsylvania

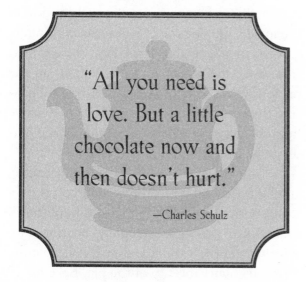

"All you need is love. But a little chocolate now and then doesn't hurt."

—Charles Schulz

Three Sisters Pie

A trio of berries yields an intriguing flavor.

2   cups all-purpose flour
1   teaspoon salt
2/3 cup vegetable shortening or lard
6   to 7 tablespoons ice water
1 1/2 cups fresh or thawed unsweetened sliced strawberries

1 1/2 cups fresh or frozen blueberries
1 1/2 cups fresh or frozen raspberries
3   tablespoons cornstarch
1/4 cup apple juice
1   cup sugar
1/2 teaspoon cinnamon
2   tablespoons unsalted butter, cut into bits

Combine the flour and salt in a bowl. Cut in the shortening until the mixture is crumbly. Add the water 1 teaspoon at a time, tossing with a fork until the pastry holds together. Shape into two balls, one slightly larger than the other; flatten into disks. Gently toss the strawberries, blueberries, and raspberries, with mixture of cornstarch, and apple juice in a bowl. Let stand 15 minutes. Gently mix in the sugar and cinnamon.

Preheat the oven to 450°. On a lightly floured surface, roll the larger pastry disk into a 12-inch circle. Fit it into a 9-inch pie pan, leaving a 1-inch overhang. Spoon in the filling and dot with the butter. Roll the remaining disk into an 11-inch circle. Cut into 1/2-inch strips. Twist each strip. Arrange the strips in a lattice pattern on top of the filling. Trim the ends and flute the edge. Place on a cookie sheet and bake 15 minutes. Reduce the temperature to 350° and bake 55 more minutes, or until the filling is bubbly and the crust is golden brown. Serve warm with ice cream.

Makes 8 to 10 servings

Ronda Tucker, Royal Pain In The Ass
Red Hot Readers of Decatur, Ten Mile, Tennessee

Unbaked Fresh Blueberry Pie

The unusual method here yields a flavor that testers found intense and surprising. Be sure your berries are ripe.

3   tablespoons cornstarch
1   cup cold water
3/4 cup sugar
1   plus 5 cups fresh blueberries
2   teaspoons fresh lemon juice
1   unbaked (8- or 9-inch) graham cracker crust

Combine the cornstarch and water in a saucepan and bring to a boil. Add the sugar, 1 cup blueberries, and lemon juice. Cook until thickened. Pour the remaining 5 cups blueberries into the piecrust. Pour the thickened blueberry mixture over the fresh blueberries. Chill until set, and serve with ice cream or whipped cream.

Makes 8 servings

Dolores R. Buckley, Queen Mom
#1 Low-Fat Red Hatters, Worcester, Massachusetts

Butterscotch Pie

FILLING
3   eggs, separated
2 3/4 cups milk
1 1/4 cups firmly packed brown sugar
1/4 cup cornstarch
1/2 teaspoon salt
1/2 teaspoon vanilla extract

1   teaspoon butter, melted
1   (9-inch) prebaked pie shell

MERINGUE
1/2 teaspoon salt
1   teaspoon cornstarch
6   tablespoons granulated sugar
1   teaspoon vanilla extract

For the filling, beat the egg yolks slightly. Beat in the milk. Combine the brown sugar, cornstarch, and salt in a large glass bowl. Beat the egg mixture into the sugar mixture. Cook in the microwave on high for 10 minutes, or until mixture thickens and boils, stirring twice. Remove from the microwave; stir in the vanilla and butter. Immediately pour into the baked shell.

Preheat the oven to 400°. For the meringue, combine the egg whites, salt, and cornstarch. Beat constantly until the mixture holds up in peaks. Add the sugar gradually, beating constantly. Add the vanilla and mix well. Pile the meringue lightly on top of the pie. Bake for 10 minutes until the meringue is light brown.

Makes 6 to 8 servings

Sharon Buchanan, Gourmet Par Excellence
Celtic Bells Red Hatters, Baddeck, Nova Scotia,
   Canada

Chocolate Angel Pie

Meringue stands in for crust in this heavenly creation. The tester thought a decorative drizzle of chocolate syrup would be a nice finish.

Special Homemade Pie

A friend went berry picking and left a bag of her efforts on my doorstep. Upon returning home from work, I was delighted with the plump berries that awaited me and decided to bake a homemade blueberry pie for my family. After dinner, I served my husband and children each a generous slice of pie, and we all dove in to enjoy a special treat. Then there was a loud crunch, crunch. *It seems that my luscious blueberries were actually grapes, seeds and all. It was not my best pie ever, but then, not many gals can lay claim to baking a grape pie.*

Carol Kiernan
Sergeant–in–Gloves
Scarlett O'Hatters of Trinity (SoHot)
Trinity, Florida

1/2 cup sugar
1/8 teaspoon cream of tartar
2 egg whites
1/4 plus 1/4 cup chopped walnuts
3/4 cup chocolate chips
3 tablespoons hot water
1 teaspoon vanilla extract
1 cup heavy whipping cream, whipped
1 (9-inch) prebaked pie shell

Preheat the oven to 275°. Stir together the sugar and cream of tartar. Beat the egg whites until stiff but not dry; add the sugar mixture gradually, beating until the meringue is smooth and glossy. Line a well-buttered 9-inch pie plate with the meringue, keeping the bottom just 1/4 inch thick. Sprinkle 1/4 cup walnuts on top and bake for about 1 hour, or until delicately browned. Let cool.

Melt the chocolate chips in the top of a double boiler set over simmering water; stir in the hot water, and cook until thickened. Cool the mixture slightly, add the vanilla, and fold in the whipped cream. Pour into the pie shell. Sprinkle with the remaining walnuts. Chill 2 to 3 hours, or until the filling is set.

Makes 6 to 8 servings

Connie McGrath, Queen of Cabernet
Last of the Red Hat Mommas, Riverside, California

Blender Cheese Pie

Easier than cheesecake, but equally flavorful. Top with any topping that suits you—pie filling is nice and easy.

2 eggs
1 teaspoon vanilla extract
3/4 cup milk
3/4 cup sugar
2 (8-ounce) packages cream cheese
1 (9-inch) graham cracker piecrust
1 (20-ounce) can fruit pie filling (optional)

Preheat the oven to 350°. Blend the eggs, vanilla, milk, and sugar in a blender. Add the cream cheese and blend until smooth. Pour the mixture into the piecrust. Bake for 30 to 35 minutes (may vary). Test with a toothpick in center. Let cool and then refrigerate until firm. Top with pie filing before serving

Makes 8 to 10 servings

Ann Szczerbicki, Secretary
Nine to Fivers, Jupiter, Florida

Chocolate Chess Pie

Tender and rich, but simple enough that you'll find yourself making it often. We've offered a variation to keep it interesting time after time. Southern cooks are usually taught for best texture to mix chess pie with a spoon or whisk, but not an electric mixer.

4 eggs, beaten
2 1/2 cups sugar
2 tablespoons all-purpose flour
1/2 cup (1 stick) butter, melted
6 tablespoons cocoa
1 (12-ounce) can evaporated milk
2 teaspoons vanilla extract
2 (9-inch) pie shells, unbaked
   Whipped cream (optional)

Preheat the oven to 350°. Whisk the eggs and sugar in a large bowl. Whisk in the flour and butter. Add the cocoa, milk, and vanilla and mix well. Pour into the pie shells. Bake for 30 minutes, or until firm when tested. Serve with whipped cream, if desired.

Makes 12 servings

Variation: For a heartier pie, add 2 cups coconut and 2 cups chopped nuts to the batter.

Leah Wright, Lady Winnie
Elite Ladies of the Hat, Franklinton, North Carolina

Cranberry Walnut Pie

A winter delight, and in the perfect color for a Red Hat gathering. Testers called it very good and ideal for the winter holidays.

1 refrigerated pie pastry
1 1/2 cups fresh cranberries
1/2 cup chopped walnuts
1/2 cup firmly packed brown sugar
1 egg
3/4 cup granulated sugar
1/2 cup all-purpose flour
1/3 cup butter, melted

Preheat the oven to 325°. Fit the pastry into a 9-inch pie pan. Spread the cranberries and walnuts evenly over the crust then sprinkle with the brown sugar. In a bowl beat the egg, sugar, flour, and butter. Spoon evenly over the pie to form a crust. Bake for 40 to 45 minutes. Serve warm with a topping or sauce if you like.

Makes 8 servings

Diana Grosz, Queen Mum
Platinum Valley Plum Tarts, Sioux Falls, South Dakota

Crustless Coconut Pies

The tester called this a quick way to make two pies, and added a teaspoon of vanilla for extra flavor.

4   eggs
2   cups milk
1   teaspoon vanilla extract
2   cups sugar
1/2 cup (1 stick) butter, melted
1/2 cup self-rising flour
2   cups coconut

Preheat the oven to 350°. In a bowl beat the eggs, milk, vanilla, sugar, butter, and flour until well blended. Pour the mixture into two greased pie pans. Sprinkle the coconut over the pies. Bake for 45 minutes.

Makes 12 servings

Frances Piper, Lady Godiver
Elite Ladies of the Hat, Franklinton, North Carolina

Cantaloupe Chiffon Pie

"An unusual and refreshing summer dessert," testers wrote.

1   medium cantaloupe, peeled and seeded
1   envelope unflavored gelatin
3   eggs, separated
1/2 plus 1/4 cup sugar
1/2 teaspoon salt
1/4 cup lemon juice
1   cup heavy cream, whipped
1   (9-inch) baked graham cracker crust

Finely shred or purée half the cantaloupe, or enough to make 1 cup. Pour into the top part of a small double boiler. Add the gelatin and let soften for 5 minutes. Slightly beat the egg yolks and add them to the cantaloupe along with 1/4 cup sugar and the salt. Cook over boiling water, stirring, until thickened. Add the lemon juice and cool.

Cut the remaining cantaloupe into small cubes and add to the cooled mixture. Beat the egg whites until foamy. Gradually add the remaining 1/2 cup sugar and beat until stiff but not dry. Fold the meringue and half the whipped cream into the cantaloupe mixture. Pour into the crust. Spread the remaining whipped cream over the pie, and chill until firm.

Makes 6 to 8 servings

Darlene Schlemmer, Princess Dar
Red Rovers, Kent, Ohio

Microwave Choc Pie

All the rich, old-fashioned goodness of a chocolate pie, but without the fuss of the double boiler.

3/4   cup plus 6 tablespoons sugar
3   tablespoons cocoa
6   tablespoons all-purpose flour
    Dash of salt
2   cups milk
3   eggs, separated
1/4   cup (1/2 stick) butter or margarine
1   plus 1 teaspoons vanilla extract
1   (9-inch) baked piecrust

Mix 3/4 cup sugar, the cocoa, flour, and salt in a microwaveable bowl. Stir in the milk and egg yolks. Microwave on high for 8 minutes, stirring every 2 minutes. When the mixture is thick, stir in the butter and 1 teaspoon vanilla. Pour into the baked and cooled piecrust.

Preheat the oven to 350°. Beat the egg whites until soft peaks form. Gradually add the remaining 6 tablespoons sugar and the remaining 1 teaspoon vanilla, beating until stiff but not dry. Spread over the filling. Bake for 15 to 20 minutes, or until browned.

Makes 6 to 8 servings

Nancy Burnett, Lady Luv
Red Hat Chicks of Murfreesboro, Smyrna, Tennessee

Hospitality Pies

Fluffy and crunchy at the same time. All of the testers on the panel gave this pie a "5," the highest score.

1   (14-ounce) can sweetened condensed milk
1   (8-ounce) package cream cheese, softened
1   (16-ounce) container whipped topping
1 1/2   to 2 cups chopped pecans
2   cups coconut
1/2   cup (1 stick) butter, cut into pieces
1   (12-ounce) jar caramel ice cream topping
2   (8-inch) graham cracker crusts

Preheat the oven to 350°. In a bowl beat the condensed milk and cream cheese until smooth. Fold in the whipped topping. Mix the pecans, coconut, and butter and toast them, stirring every 5 minutes, for 15 minutes, or until golden. Cool. Spoon a layer of the cream cheese mixture into each crust. Top with the coconut mixture and drizzle with the caramel topping. Repeat to make a second layer. Freeze. Let stand at room temperature for 10 to 15 minutes before ready to serve.

Makes 2 pies

Nancy Kicklighter, DuchessDotCom
Duchesses of Dorchester, Dorchester, South Carolina

A+ for Ingenuity

"Quantitative Cooking" was a required course when I studied Home Economics at Salem College in Winston-Salem, North Carolina. I chose Lemon Meringue Pie as my lab research project. One assignment involved developing a recipe and then changing the ingredients for one pie to the correct proportions for preparing ten.

The course culminating activity was preparing a complete meal that we would serve to the faculty. Dessert was my responsibility. After weeks of experimenting with the right proportions of eggs, sugar, and lemon juice, my final product was ready for the big party. The afternoon of the faculty banquet, my pies came out of the oven with perfectly browned peaks of meringue over a thick, lemon filling in a crusty shell. The desserts were left on a counter, lightly covered with waxed paper, while I finished afternoon classes and dressed for the evening. I had learned that refrigeration would make the meringue "weep" and I wanted a perfect presentation.

Tables had to be set up, so I returned to the Home Ec building early and peeked in on my pies. To my surprise, they were decorated with what appeared to be chocolate chips. Upon closer examination, I saw that the chips were moving! An army of black ants had arrived and taken over the meringues!

With guests arriving in less than an hour, I closed the door and set about retrieving the struggling ants, one by one, from the pies. To cover their tracks, I used a fork to "mess up" the pretty egg-white peaks and cut the slices, ready to serve them just so. The dinner received high marks, and although the dessert would not rate an A+ for appearance, the chef deserved one for ingenuity in saving it from the ants. . . . And the faculty never knew.

Lucinda Denton
Founding Queen Mother (FQM)
Nonpareils
Knoxville, Tennessee

Macaroon Pie

Corn syrup gives the pie a delectably, chewy texture. The tester called it "awesome."

3   eggs
1   cup light corn syrup
1/2   cup sugar
2   tablespoons butter, melted
1/4   teaspoon almond extract
1/8   teaspoon salt
1   (3 1/2-ounce) can flaked coconut
1   cup sliced almonds or chopped pecans
1   (9-inch) unbaked piecrust

Preheat the oven to 350°. In a medium bowl, beat the eggs slightly. Beat in the corn syrup, sugar, butter, almond extract, and salt. Stir in the coconut and nuts. Pour into a piecrust. Bake for 50 minutes, or until a knife inserted halfway between the center and edge comes out clean. Cool before serving.

Makes 8 servings

Linda Dobbs, Princess Yazzie
Red Hat Ya-Yas, Beaumont, Texas

Coconut Buttermilk Pies

Sure to get raves from family and friends. The contributor practically guarantees it.

1/2   cup (1 stick) butter, melted
2   cups sugar
4   eggs, separated

1   cup buttermilk
1   teaspoon all-purpose flour
1   teaspoon vanilla extract
1   cup flaked coconut
2   unbaked piecrusts

Preheat the oven to 300°. Mix the butter, sugar, and egg yolks. Add the buttermilk, flour, and vanilla. In a separate bowl beat the egg whites until stiff and add to the egg mixture. Add the coconut. Pour into the piecrusts. Bake for 1 hour.

Makes 12 servings

Joan Wall, Queen Mother
Randleman Red Hat Darlin's, Randleman, North Carolina

Lemon Cake Pie

A lemon pudding cake naturally separates into a cake layer and a pudding layer. This one is baked in a piecrust, for a lemon pudding cake pie. Sort of. Very lemony and said by the tester to be a nice alternative to lemon meringue pie. It was also noted that bottled lemon juice makes an acceptable substitute for the fresh lemon juice.

3/4   cup sugar
1/4   cup all-purpose flour
1/4   cup (1/2 stick) butter, melted
     Dash of salt
2   eggs, separated
     Grated rind and juice of 2 lemons
1   cup milk
1   (8-inch) unbaked piecrust

In a bowl combine the sugar, flour, butter, and salt. Add the egg yolks and beat until smooth. Beat in the lemon rind and juice, and then beat in the milk. In a separate bowl beat the egg whites until stiff peaks form and fold them into the lemon mixture.

Preheat the oven to 350°. With a fork prick holes on the bottom and around the side of the piecrust. Prebake the piecrust for 6 minutes. Remove the piecrust from the oven and pour in the batter. Return the pie to the oven and bake for 30 to 40 minutes, or until the pie is set and a cake has formed on the top. Cool or serve slightly warm with either whipped cream or vanilla ice cream. Good with a cup of coffee or a glass of milk because of the pie's sweetness.

Makes 8 servings

Jeanne Fritsche, Queen Mum
Classie Lassies, Elkhorn, Wisconsin

Self-Frosting Lemon Pie

Use the lesser amount of sugar if you like it puckery, like our tester, or the greater amount for a mellower sweetness.

- 3   eggs, separated
- 1/2 to 3/4 cup sugar
       Grated rind and juice of 1 lemon
- 1   tablespoon all-purpose flour
- 2   tablespoons butter
- 1   cup milk
- 1/8 teaspoon salt
- 1   (9-inch) unbaked piecrust

Preheat the oven to 350°. Mix the egg yolks, sugar, lemon rind and juice, flour, butter, milk, and salt in a large bowl. Beat the egg whites until stiff. Fold into the lemon mixture. Pour the mixture into the piecrust. Bake for 30 to 40 minutes, or until cooked through and set.

Makes 6 to 8 servings

Mary Dobens, Queen
Red Hat Tomatoes, Poland, Maine

Lemonade Stand Pie

A frozen ice cream pie—very refreshing on a hot evening.

- 1/3 cup sweetened lemonade powdered drink mix
- 1/2 cup water
- 2   cups vanilla ice cream, softened
- 1   (8-ounce) container whipped topping (thawed if frozen)
- 1   (9-inch) piecrust

Stir the drink mix into the water. Beat the lemonade mixture and ice cream in a large bowl on low until blended. Stir in the whipped topping and mix well. Spoon the filling into the piecrust and freeze for at least 4 hours until firm. Let stand at room temperature for 15 minutes before serving. Store leftovers in the freezer.

Makes 6 to 8 servings

Jeanette Camp, Queen
Red Hot Hens, Hemet, California

Pie in the Sky

A secret pal gift was brought to a Red Hat meeting for a recipient who was away on vacation. As was my custom, I brought the gift home to be delivered later. I noticed a delicious looking piece of pie sitting on the top, some kind of fruit with meringue on top, and a cherry, as I recollect, so I put it in the refrigerator for safekeeping.

A couple of days later I was hungering for something sweet and kept looking at that piece of pie. I finally rationalized that it wasn't going to keep, and I could always replace it. Temptation overwhelmed me, and I tore open the plastic container. Just before plunging my fork into the pie, I noticed the candlewick! All this time, I had lovingly nurtured and been tempted by a candle!

Barbara Diemler
Queen
Classy Red Hatters
Jefferson City, Missouri

Glazed Fruit Tarts

GLAZE

1/4 cup sugar

1 tablespoon cornstarch

Dash of salt

1/3 cup orange juice (or apple juice or pineapple juice)

3 tablespoons water

PASTRY CREAM

1 (4-serving size) vanilla instant pudding mix

1 cup milk

1/2 cup heavy cream

14 to 15 (3-inch) tart shells, baked and cooled
Sliced fresh fruit

For the glaze, combine the sugar, cornstarch, and salt in a saucepan. Stir in the juice and water. Cook over medium heat, stirring constantly, until the mixture thickens and boils. Boil for 1 minute, stirring constantly; cool.

For the pastry cream, combine the pudding mix and milk in a bowl and beat until thickened. In another bowl whip the cream until stiff. Fold into the pudding. Spoon into the baked and cooled tart shells.

To assemble, dip the fresh fruit slices into the glaze to coat completely, and then tuck an edge into the pastry cream so the fruit sits at an angle on the tarts. Slices of banana, strawberry, kiwi, mandarin oranges, pineapple, and grapes are a great color combination on each tart.

Makes 14 or 15 tarts

Joy Bryson, Royal Page
Red–Red Robins, Winnipeg, Manitoba

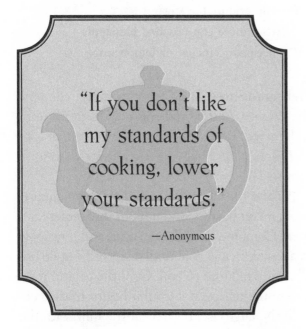

"If you don't like my standards of cooking, lower your standards."

—Anonymous

Margarita Pie

A 3.3-ounce package of Bartender's brand instant margarita mix contains eight individual packets. You'll have six of them left over, so plan for a margarita party with friends.

1   (8-ounce) package cream cheese, softened
1/2   cup sugar
2   (3.3-ounce) packets instant margarita mix

1   (8-ounce) container whipped topping
1   (9-inch) prepared graham cracker or vanilla wafer piecrust

In a bowl beat the cream cheese and sugar until fluffy and smooth. Add the dry margarita mix and beat until thoroughly combined. Add the whipped topping and mix well. Pour into the prepared piecrust. Freeze until firm, and then cut into slices.

Makes 6 to 8 servings

Grace McCollum, Sister Superior
Red Hat Twisted Sisters Of Brotherly Love, Philadelphia, Pennsylvania

Pink Lemonade Pie

Another lemonade pie even simpler to mix up.

1   (12-ounce) can frozen pink lemonade concentrate, thawed
1   (8-ounce) container whipped topping
1   (14-ounce) can sweetened condensed milk
1   (8-inch) graham cracker piecrust

In a bowl combine the lemonade, whipped topping, and sweetened condensed milk until thoroughly blended. Spoon into the piecrust. Chill in the refrigerator until firm.

Makes 8 servings

Judy Ramer, Dazzling Judy
Dazzling Diamond Divas, North Little Rock, Arkansaas

Peaches-and-Cream Pie

2 (9-inch) piecrusts, fresh or refrigerated
7 or 8 peaches, peeled and sliced
1 cup sugar
1/2 cup sour cream
5 tablespoons all-purpose flour
1/8 teaspoon salt
1/4 teaspoon cinnamon mixed with 1 teaspoon sugar

Preheat the oven to 400°. Fit one piecrust in a pie pan. Fill with the peach slices. In a bowl combine the sugar, sour cream, flour, and salt and mix well. Pour over the peaches, spreading to cover. Fit a top crust over the peach filling. Press the edges to seal. Cut steam vents in the top. Sprinkle with the cinnamon sugar. Bake for 40 minutes. Check the pie while cooking, covering the edges of the pastry with aluminum foil if necessary to prevent burning.

Makes 8 servings

Jo Anne Schultz, Queen of Moonbeams and Magic
The Red Hat Hoydens, Delmar, Delaware

Frosty Fruit Pie

You make your own buttery, delicious graham cracker crust for this pie. Any graham cracker crust, homemade or store-bought, will hold together better and have a wonderfully crisp texture if baked and cooled before filling.

CRUST
2 cups graham cracker crumbs
1/2 cup (1 stick) butter, melted
1/4 cup brown sugar or granulated sugar

FILLING
1 (12-ounce) can evaporated milk
1 (3-ounce) package cherry gelatin
3/4 cup granulated sugar
1 (8-ounce) can crushed pineapple
1/2 teaspoon vinegar or lemon juice

Preheat the oven to 400°. For the crust, combine the crumbs, butter, and sugar with a fork until well mixed. Press firmly into the bottom of a 13 x 9-inch pan. Bake for 15 minutes, or until browned.

For the filling, chill a very large glass mixing bowl, mixer beaters, and milk in the freezer for 1 hour. Combine the gelatin, sugar, and pineapple in a saucepan and heat until dissolved, but do not allow the mixture to boil. Cool the gelatin mixture in the refrigerator until it begins to thicken.

In the large cold bowl, beat the milk with the vinegar until the mixture forms peaks. Fold the gelatin mixture into the whipped milk and gently mix until the color is an even pink. Pour into the prepared, cooled crust. Chill for 12 hours.

Makes 16 servings

Linda Young, Queen Bee
HmmmDingers, Cedar Mountain, North Carolina

Citrus Meringue Pie

1 1/2 plus 1/2 cups sugar
6 tablespoons cornstarch
1/4 teaspoon salt
1 1/2 teaspoons grated orange rind
3 cups orange juice
6 tablespoons lemon juice
4 eggs, separated
1 tablespoon butter or margarine
1 (9-inch) piecrust, baked and cooled
1/4 teaspoon cream of tartar

Combine 1 1/2 cups sugar, the cornstarch, salt, and orange rind in a heavy saucepan. Gradually add the orange juice, lemon juice, and egg yolks. Bring the mixture to a boil, stirring constantly. Stir in the butter. Cook over medium heat for 10 to 12 minutes, or until mixture is smooth and thick. Pour the filling into the baked piecrust.

Preheat the oven to 350°. In a bowl beat the egg whites. (They will beat more quickly and fluffier if the whites are at room temperature.) Add the cream of tartar and beat until foamy. Gradually add the remaining 1/2 cup sugar, 1 spoonful at a time. Beat until stiff peaks form. Spread the meringue over the pie filling. Bake until the meringue is golden brown. Chill well before serving.

Makes 8 servings

Dokie Bledsoe, Queen Ritzy Red Lady
Coleman County Texans, Valera, Texas

Peach & Cranberry Pie

2 (9-inch) piecrusts, fresh or refrigerated
3/4 cup sugar plus more for sprinkling
1/4 cup all-purpose flour
1 teaspoon cinnamon
1/4 teaspoon nutmeg
4 cups peeled and sliced McIntosh or other cooking apples
2 cups sliced canned peaches, drained
1 cup whole fresh cranberries
1 tablespoon lemon juice
2 tablespoons butter or margarine

Preheat the oven to 425°. Fit one piecrust into a pie pan. In a bowl combine the sugar, flour, cinnamon, and nutmeg . Add the apples, peaches, cranberries, and lemon juice. Mix well. Spoon the fruit mixture into the crust. Dot with the butter. Arrange the remaining piecrust over the filling. Seal and flute the edge. Cut steam vents in the top crust. Sprinkle a few drops of water over the top, along with a sprinkling of sugar. Place the pie dish on a baking sheet. Bake on the lower rack of the oven for 15 minutes. Reduce the temperature to 350° and bake 35 to 40 minutes longer, or until the fruit is tender and the piecrust is golden.

Makes 8 servings

Yolande Hollis, Queen of Fiddledom
The Fiddle-Reds, Shelburne, Ontario, Canada

Fresh Peach Custard Pie

1   (9-inch) piecrust
1/2 cup (1 stick) butter, softened
1/2 cup shortening
2   eggs
3/4 cup sugar
3   tablespoons all-purpose flour
6   fresh peaches, peeled and sliced

Preheat the oven to 350°. Line a pie pan with the piecrust. Beat the butter, shortening, eggs, and sugar. Add the flour gradually. Place the peaches into the piecrust. Pour the batter over the peaches. Bake for 50 minutes, or until barely set in the center. Let stand to firm up before slicing.

Makes 6 to 8 servings

Joan McClelland, Ms. Reddie
Niagara Hatties, St. Catharines, Ontario, Canada

Fresh Peach Pie with No-Roll Crust

Easier to work with since a crumb mixture replaces traditional pastry. Delicious with ice cream.

CRUST
1/2 cup sugar
1 1/2 cups sifted all-purpose flour
    Pinch of salt
1/2 cup (1 stick) butter, softened

FILLING
4   cups sliced fresh peaches
2   tablespoons cornstarch
1/2 cup sugar
1   tablespoon lemon juice

Preheat the oven to 425°. For the crust, combine the sugar, flour, and salt. Cut in the butter and mix with a pastry blender or fork until crumbly. Reserve 3/4 cup of the "crumbs" for the topping. Press the remaining crumbs into the bottom and up the side of a 9-inch pie pan.

For the filling, combine the peaches, cornstarch, sugar, and lemon juice. Mix well. Pour the peach mixture into the crumb shell. Bake for 20 minutes. Remove from the oven and sprinkle the top with the reserved crumbs. Return the pie to the oven and continue to bake for 20 to 30 minutes, or until the top is lightly brown and the peaches have softened. Serve warm. Ice cream makes an excellent topping.

Makes 6 to 8 servings

Shirley Wright, Queen Sweetie
Super Sun Sweeties, Apache Junction, Arizona

Pear Custard Pie

Testers loved this pie, calling it "fancy and elegant" and "picture perfect," but easy to make. They termed it the best of the desserts they tested.

1   (9-inch) piecrust
8   to 9 pears (not too hard or soft)
    Juice of 1/2 lemon

1/4 cup (1/2 stick) butter or margarine, softened
1   cup sugar
1/4 cup all-purpose flour
3   eggs
1   teaspoon vanilla extract
1/8 teaspoon salt
1/8 teaspoon ground mace

Preheat the oven to 350°. Fit the piecrust into a pie pan. Peel and core the pears and cut into slices. Sprinkle with the lemon juice. Fill the pastry crust with the pears.

In a bowl beat the butter with the sugar. Beat in the flour, eggs, vanilla, and salt. Pour the butter mixture evenly over the pears. (The mixture will settle by itself over and through the pears.) Sprinkle lightly with the ground mace, which is important because it gives the pie its flavor. Bake for 45 minutes, or until the filling is set and lightly brown. Cool. Serve with whipped cream.

Makes 8 servings

Catie McIntyre Walker, Queen Cabernet Catie
Les Merlot Chapeaux, Walla Walla, Washington

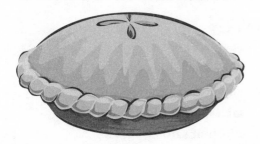

Bourbon Pecan Pie

Two great Southerners meet in one great pie.

1 1/4 cups pecan halves
1/3   cup bourbon
1   cup brown sugar, firmly packed
2   tablespoons all-purpose flour
1   teaspoon butter, softened
1   cup dark corn syrup
3   eggs, beaten
1/4   teaspoon salt
1   (8 or 9-inch) piecrust

Toss the pecans and bourbon until the pecans are coated. Let stand at least 1 hour or up to 12 hours until most of the bourbon is absorbed.

Preheat the oven to 325°. Mix the brown sugar and flour. Beat in the butter until creamy. Beat in the corn syrup, eggs, and salt. Stir in the pecans and bourbon. Pour into the piecrust. Cover the edges with a 1/2-inch aluminum foil strip to prevent excessive browning. Bake for 40 to 45 minutes, or until the pie is firm. Remove the foil during the last 15 minutes of baking.

Makes 6 to 8 servings

Jewel Simmons, Oldie But Goodie
High Hatters, Santee, California

An Apple Pie to Remember

Many years ago, when I was a young housewife and mother of three young children, I had occasion to entertain some old family friends from my hometown. Between my three children and their four children, we had to do some makeshift seating arrangements to accommodate all of us around the kitchen table.

I had made apple pie for dessert and had lined the oven with aluminum foil to catch any drips. For some reason, a cloud of gray film lifted off the foil and settled on top of the pies. Not having the money or the time to come up with an alternative dessert, I scraped off what I could and explained to my guests what had happened, hoping the pie would taste good enough that they would overlook the color.

The father suggested that his young son try the pie first, and jokingly suggested that if nothing happened to him, it would be safe for the rest of us to eat the pie. At the exact moment the child took a bite of the pie, he fell off his chair!

Of course, each time we have seen these friends over the years, this story has been retold, providing us with many years of laughter!

Kathleen Smith
Queen Kate au Contraire
Steel Magnolias
Ancaster, Ontario
Canada

Pecan Tarts

If you haven't discovered how easy and foolproof cream cheese pastry is, now is the time.

CRUST

3   ounces cream cheese, softened

1/2 cup (1 stick) butter, softened

1   cup all-purpose flour

FILLING

1   egg

1   teaspoon vanilla extract

3/4 cup brown sugar, packed

1   tablespoon melted butter

Pinch of salt

Pecan pieces

For the crust, combine the cream cheese, butter, and flour in a bowl and mix well. Chill until firm enough to handle. Pinch off bits of dough and press into 24 tart pans, pressing on the bottom and up the side.

Preheat the oven to 325°. For the filling, beat the egg, vanilla, brown sugar, butter, and salt in a bowl until well combined. Arrange some pecans in each shell. Spoon the filling over the pecans. Bake for 25 minutes.

Makes 24 tarts

Agnes Mancuso, The Italian Diva
Happening Ladies of Hamilton, Lawrenceville, New Jersey

Rhubarb Cream Pie

1   tablespoon butter
3/4 plus 1/4 cup plus 2 tablespoons sugar
2   cups finely chopped rhubarb
1/4 cup whipping cream
2   eggs, separated
     Pinch of salt
1   (9-inch) baked piecrust

Combine the butter, 3/4 cup sugar, and rhubarb in a saucepan and cook until the rhubarb is just tender but not puréed. Mix together in a small bowl the whipping cream, the egg yolks, salt, and the 1/4 cup sugar. Add some of the rhubarb sauce to the egg mixture to warm it slightly, and then add the egg mix to the rhubarb. Mix well and cook for 2 to 3 minutes to thicken. (If the rhubarb is very juicy, stir in about 2 teaspoons cornstarch mixed with just a little water.) Remove from the heat and pour the mixture into the baked piecrust.

Preheat the oven to 350°. Beat the egg whites with the remaining 2 tablespoons sugar until stiff. Arrange the meringue on top of the rhubarb mixture, making sure the meringue touches the pastry on all sides. Bake until the meringue has browned to an attractive golden color.

Makes 6 servings

Millie Sandahl, Queen
Red Baronettes, Sechelt, British Columbia, Canada

Sugar-Free Pineapple Pie

A little something sweet for the sugarless ladies and gentlemen. The new sucralose sweeteners are so close to the flavor of sugar that you can hardly tell the difference in a traditional pie and a sugar-free pie. (Don't forget, though, that the crust has sugar in it.)

1   (20-ounce) can crushed pineapple
1   cup low-fat sour cream
2   (1-ounce) packages sugar-free instant
     vanilla pudding mix
1   (8-inch) graham cracker crust
1   (8-ounce) container whipped topping

In a medium bowl combine the pineapple, sour cream, and pudding mix and blend well. Spoon the mixture into the crust. Top with the whipped topping and refrigerate for an hour or more. (This pie firms up quickly.)

Makes 6 to 8 servings

Dolores Allen, Queen Mother
Awesome Sisters McAlester Red Hatters, McAlester, Oklahoma

Pecan-Topped Pumpkin Pie Squares

Imagine a pumpkin pie in a crumbly oat crust with a buttery pecan topping—a real crowd pleaser and a nice change for the holiday buffet.

CRUST

1	cup sifted all-purpose flour
1/2	cup quick rolled oats
1/2	cup firmly packed brown sugar
1/2	cup (1 stick) butter, softened

FILLING

2	cups solid-pack pumpkin
1	(12-ounce) can evaporated milk
2	eggs
3/4	cup granulated sugar
1/4	teaspoon salt
1	teaspoon cinnamon
1/2	teaspoon ginger
1/4	teaspoon cloves

TOPPING

1/2	cup chopped pecans
1/2	cup firmly packed brown sugar
2	tablespoons butter, softened

Preheat the oven to 350°. For the crust, combine the flour, oats, brown sugar, and butter with a pastry blender or fork until the mixture is the consistency of crumbs. Press in the bottom and slightly up the side of an ungreased 13 x 9-inch pan. Bake 15 minutes.

For the filling, combine the pumpkin, milk, eggs, sugar, salt, cinnamon, ginger, and cloves in a medium bowl. Mix well and pour over the crust. Bake for 20 minutes. (Filling will not be set.)

For the topping, combine the pecans, brown sugar, and butter in a bowl until well blended. Sprinkle over the pumpkin filling. Return to the oven and bake for 15 to 20 minutes, or until the filling is set. Cool in the pan. Cut into 2-inch squares. Serve with whipped cream or whipped topping.

Makes about 24 servings

Brenda Holtz, Queen Brenda
Vintage Vines of Kingsley, Iowa, Kingsley, Iowa

"My cooking is so bad my kids thought Thanksgiving was to commemorate Pearl Harbor."

—Phyllis Diller

Red and Purple Berry Pie

What a treat black raspberries are! Share them with friends in this sweet-tart pie.

1   cup sugar
1   (3-ounce) package strawberry gelatin, divided
3   tablespoons cornstarch
1   to 2 tablespoons Minute brand tapioca (depending on juiciness of fruits)
2 1/2   cups chopped or sliced rhubarb in 1/4 to 1/2-inch pieces
1 1/2   cups black raspberries
2   (9-inch) piecrusts

Preheat the oven to 425°. Blend the sugar, gelatin, cornstarch, and tapioca in a large bowl. Add the rhubarb and raspberries and stir gently to mix well. Let stand, stirring occasionally, while lining the pie plate with 1 piecrust. Pour the rhubarb mixture into the crust and add a lattice top using the remaining piecrust. (If preferred, a solid top crust may be used; cut several slits in the top to vent.)

Shield the edge of the crust with strips of aluminum foil to prevent over browning. Bake for 15 minutes. Reduce the oven temperature to 375° and bake for 30 minutes. Remove the protective foil strips for the last 10 minutes of baking time.

Makes 6 to 8 servings

Joanne Harter, Lady Hi-Jinks, Court Jester
Hot Tamales of Watertown, Harrisville, New York

Red Hat Berry Cream Pie

Everyone loves this old favorite for its rich, smooth sweetness. This version replaces some of the lemon juice with lime juice.

1   (8-ounce) package cream cheese, softened
1   (14-ounce) can sweetened condensed milk
1/4   cup lemon juice
2   tablespoons lime juice
1   teaspoon vanilla extract
1/2   cup chopped pecans
1   (8-inch) graham cracker crust
1/2   cup whipped topping
    Blueberries and strawberries

In a bowl stir or beat the cream cheese and condensed milk until smooth. Add the lemon juice, lime juice, and vanilla and mix well. Arrange the chopped pecans on the graham cracker crust, and then pour in the cream cheese mixture. Chill until firm. Top the pie with the whipped topping. Decorate with blueberries and strawberries. Use your imagination and decorate it like a Red Hat.

Makes 6 to 8 servings

Rita Christian, Queen Mother Assistant
Yesterday's Teens, Wake Village, Texas

Playing Dress-Up

Every little girl, at one time or another, pretends to be a princess. There may or may not be a prince involved. Perhaps there won't even be an imaginary kingdom (queendom?). The attraction of playing royalty more than likely revolves around the frills and glitter of fancy dress-up clothes. That, more than anything, is what being a princess, a queen, a duchess or a baroness in the Red Hat Society is all about!

Modern life rarely finds us grown-ups receiving invitations to occasions calling for sumptuous, satin-skirted ball gowns or "diamond" tiaras. Nor do we get the chance to wield bejeweled scepters and make pronouncements (at least not to anyone who is really listening).

Therefore, if a "girl" of whatever age wants to play at being royalty, she must manufacture her own appropriate occasions. That is what we Red Hat Society members do—for ourselves and for our friends. A chapter's first outing, and the outfits the women wear, are usually a bit low key. But, given time, every group discovers there is nerve in numbers. The costumes get grander and fancier. The red hats get taller, wider and more ostentatiously ornamented. The resultant attention paid by onlookers serves only to encourage RHS royalty, and egg them on to new levels of showmanship. Thus, one of our slogans has evolved: "Gaudy is good!" Being gaudy royalty is even better!

Raspberry White Chocolate Pie

1   cup heavy whipping cream
1   tablespoon superfine sugar (or Splenda)
1/2 teaspoon vanilla extract
2   tablespoons raspberry liqueur or syrup
4   ounces white chocolate, melted
2   cups fresh raspberries
1   (8-inch) chocolate piecrust

Beat the cream, sugar, vanilla, and raspberry liqueur until the mixture forms soft peaks. Fold in the melted chocolate then the raspberries. Pour the mixture into the chocolate crust. Chill for 2 hours until firm before serving.

Makes 8 servings

Judy Ziegler, Royal Varmint
Farragut Classy Red Hots, Knoxville, Tennessee

Fresh Strawberry Pie with Pecan Crust

If you wish, decorate the pie with an abundance of whipped cream and eight chocolate- dipped strawberries.

PECAN CRUST
1/2 cup (1 stick) butter, softened
1/4 cup firmly packed brown sugar
1   cup plus 1 tablespoon all-purpose flour
3/4 cup chopped pecans

STRAWBERRY GLAZE
1   cup granulated sugar
1   cup water
2   tablespoons cornstarch
1   (3-ounce) package strawberry gelatin
1   quart fresh whole strawberries, cleaned, stemmed, and dried

For the pecan crust, preheat the oven to 350°. Mix the butter, brown sugar, flour, and pecans with a pastry blender or in a food processor until well combined. Pat into a 9-inch pie plate. Bake for 10 to 12 minutes. Cool.

For the strawberry glaze, combine the sugar, water, and cornstarch in a saucepan. Cook, stirring, until the mixture becomes translucent and slightly thickened. Remove from the heat and add the gelatin. Cool 5 minutes. Fill the pecan crust with the whole strawberries. Pour the glaze over the strawberries and chill for 4 hours. Serve with whipping cream.

Makes 8 servings

Gerry Benassi, Clean Gerry
Red Hatted League of Duluth, Duluth, Minnesota

Fresh Strawberry Tart

Sweet, buttery pastry; chocolate and strawberry filling—all the elements for a great dessert.

CRUST

1/2　cup (1 stick) butter, very cold
1 1/2　cups all-purpose flour
1/4　teaspoon salt
2　tablespoons sugar
1　egg

FILLING

2　quarts fresh strawberries
2/3　cup semisweet chocolate chips
1/2　cup strawberry jam
　　Freshly whipped cream (optional)

Preheat the oven to 375°. For the crust, cut the butter into pieces. In a food processor fitted with the metal blade, combine the flour, salt, sugar, and butter. Pulse until it forms crumbs. Beat the egg and add it to the food processor. Mix until the ingredients form a ball. Press the ball of dough into an 11-inch pie or tart pan. Chill 20 minutes or more. With a fork, prick the bottom and sides of the crust. Press a double thickness of foil into the pan over the dough. Bake for 15 minutes. Remove the foil and bake for 10 to 15 minutes longer until golden. Let the crust cool.

For the filling, wash and stem the strawberries. Melt the chocolate chips in a saucepan over low heat or in the microwave. Spread over the cooled crust with the back of a spoon.

Arrange the whole strawberries on top of the warm chocolate, points up, beginning in the center and working toward the outside of the crust. Melt the jam in the microwave briefly and brush it over the top of the strawberries. Let the pie stand to firm up the jam before serving. Top with the whipped cream if desired.

Makes 8 servings

Vicki Beidelman, Contessa of Chocolate
Foxy Roxys, Fullerton, California

Toffee Bar Crunch Pie

1 1/2　cups cold half-and-half
1　(5.2-ounce) package vanilla instant pudding mix
1　(8-ounce) container whipped topping
1　cup chopped chocolate-covered English toffee bars
1　(8-inch) graham cracker crust

Pour the half-and-half into a large bowl. Add the pudding mix. Beat with a wire whisk until well blended, about 1 minute. Let stand 5 minutes. Fold in the whipped topping and toffee. Spoon into the crust. Freeze until firm, about 6 hours or overnight. Remove from the freezer and let stand 10 minutes to soften before serving. Store any leftover pie in the freezer.

Makes 6 to 8 servings

Kali Sitton, Princess Need 4 Speed
Rhat Pacque, Canyon Country, California

Low-Fat Lemon Icebox Pie

Another delectable treat for those watching their sugar. Sugar-free lemonade crystals are packed into little plastic tubs. Typically there are four of these in a canister.

1   package light lemonade mix
2   (1-ounce) packages sugar-free vanilla instant pudding mix
3 3/4 cups skim milk
2   tablespoons light sour cream
Juice of 1 lemon
1   (12-ounce) container light whipped topping, divided
1   (9-inch) graham cracker piecrust

Mix the lemonade crystals with the vanilla pudding mix. Add the milk and mix well. Let stand for 5 minutes. Add the sour cream, lemon juice, and about 1/4 cup whipped topping and mix well. Pour the mixture into the piecrust. Refrigerate for 1 hour. Spread with the remaining whipped topping to serve.

Makes 6 to 8 servings

Debbie Divine, Main Dame
Divine Dames, Wagoner, Oklahoma

THREE

Bars, Bits & Bites

BARS, BROWNIES & COOKIES

Pies are served in slices. Cakes are served in pieces. Bars and other desserts are baked in rectangular or square pans, then cut into small pieces . . . aren't they? Sometimes this kind of dessert poses a challenge for the person cutting them up. If she cuts them into tiny pieces, will she look stingy? If she cuts them in slabs, will it appear that she is encouraging gluttony?

Most women, when confronted with this, will say they want "just a little." After all, no one wants to be perceived as a hog. But an awful lot of us will indiscreetly return to the serving table for one or two more "just a littles." After all, it tastes so good!

No, it's not a good idea to do this all the time. But, when something tastes that good, sometimes it's OK to have "just a little" . . . more.

Surprise Brownies

For a shortcut, use a package of brownie mix instead of making the brownies from scratch. One tester said her brownies fell in the middle but were still delicious.

CREAM CHEESE FILLING

1   (8-ounce) package soft cream cheese

1/3   cup sugar

1   egg

1/2   teaspoon vanilla extract

BROWNIE BATTER

2   (1-ounce) squares unsweetened chocolate

1/2   cup (1 stick) butter or margarine

2   eggs

1   cup sugar

1   teaspoon vanilla extract

3/4   cup sifted all-purpose flour

1/2   teaspoon baking powder

1/2   teaspoon salt
    Sliced almonds (optional)

For the filling, beat together the cream cheese, sugar, egg, and vanilla until fluffy.

For the batter, melt the chocolate and butter in a saucepan over low heat; cool. Beat the eggs in a medium bowl. Add the sugar, vanilla, and chocolate mixture and mix well. In separate bowl combine the flour, baking powder, and salt; add to the chocolate mixture, blending well.

Preheat the oven to 350°. Spread half of chocolate batter into a greased 8-inch-square pan; spread the cream cheese filling on top. Top with the remaining batter. Sprinkle the sliced almonds on top if desired. Bake for 45 minutes, or until a toothpick inserted 1 inch from the edge comes out clean.

Makes 6 to 8 servings

Susan Wilson, Princess with the Pea
Iron Butterflies, Mont Alto, Pennsylvania

Apple Brownies

"A cake-like result with good texture and flavor," said testers.

1   cup (2 sticks) butter, melted

2   cups granulated sugar

2   eggs

1   cup chopped nuts

6   medium apples, peeled and thinly sliced

2   cups all-purpose flour

1   teaspoon baking powder

1   teaspoon baking soda

1/2   teaspoon salt

2   teaspoons cinnamon
    Confectioners' sugar

Preheat the oven to 350°. In a bowl combine the butter, sugar, and eggs and mix well. Stir in the nuts and apples. Combine the flour, baking powder, baking soda, salt, and cinnamon in a large bowl. Add to the butter mixture in three parts, mixing well after each addition. Pour into a 13 x 9-inch greased and floured pan. Bake for 40 to

45 minutes. Cool and cut into squares. Sprinkle with the confectioners' sugar and serve alone or with ice cream or whipped cream.

Makes 20 to 24 servings

Laura Lee Wierzbinski, Lady Laura Lee of Grendale
Raspberry Preserves, New Berlin, Wisconsin

Brown Sugar Brownies

Baby Boomers get positively misty-eyed about chewy, rich Brown Sugar Brownies.

1   cup (2 sticks) butter, melted
2   cups brown sugar
2   eggs
1   cup all-purpose flour
1   teaspoon baking powder
1   teaspoon vanilla extract
1   cup chopped walnuts
    Confectioners' sugar (optional)

Preheat the oven to 350°. In a large bowl combine the butter and brown sugar. Mix well. Add the eggs and mix well. Add the flour, baking powder, and vanilla. Stir in the nuts. Spoon into a greased and floured 8-inch square pan. Bake for 30 to 40 minutes (Brownies will not seem completely firm.) Let cool for 15 minutes and then cut into squares. Cool completely, remove from the pan, and shake the brownies in a bag with the confectioners' sugar, if desired.

Makes 16 to 20 brownies

Mary Grisaffi, Lady Merry Mary
Spicy Red Hats of Santa Clarita Valley, Valencia, California

German Chocolate Luscious Bars

Double the chocolate, plus extra caramel.

14   ounces caramels, unwrapped
1/3   plus 1/3 cup evaporated milk
1   (18-ounce) box German Chocolate Cake Mix
3/4   cup butter, melted
1   cup chopped English walnuts or pecans
6   ounces semisweet chocolate chips

Preheat the oven to 350°. Microwave in a glass bowl the caramels and 1/3 cup evaporated milk. Mix together the cake mix, butter, the remaining 1/3 cup evaporated milk, and the nuts. Spoon half the mixture into a greased and floured 13 x 9-inch pan. Bake for 8 minutes. Sprinkle the chocolate chips and caramel mixture over the baked crust. Carefully spoon the remaining batter over that and bake for 15 minutes more. Cool, then refrigerate until the caramels are firm. Cut into roughly 2-inch square pieces.

Makes 24 pieces

Marlene Fleeman, Contessa Marl
Simply Red, Kingsville, Missouri

Kahlúa Brownies

What's better with after-dinner coffee than a coffee brownie?

10 tablespoons butter (no substitutes), softened
2   cups sugar
3   eggs
3   (1-ounce) squares unsweetened chocolate
1/2 teaspoon salt
1/2 teaspoon baking powder
1 1/2 cups all-purpose flour
1/3 cup Kahlúa plus 3 tablespoon for brushing

Preheat the oven to 350°. In a bowl beat the butter and sugar until fluffy. Add the eggs one at a time and blend well. Melt the chocolate in the top of a double boiler. Cool and add to the butter mixture. Add the salt, baking powder, and flour and blend well. Slowly add the Kahlúa. Spoon into a greased 9-inch-square pan and bake for 30 minutes. Remove from the oven and brush with additional Kahlúa.

Makes 16 to 18 servings

Nancy Clemons, Exalted Queen Mother Nancy
Luscious Ladies of League City, League City, Texas

Almond-Sesame Bars

Graham crackers
3/4 cup (1 1/2 sticks) butter
3/4 cup firmly packed brown sugar
1 1/2 to 2 tablespoons sesame seeds
1 1/2 cups sliced almonds

Preheat the oven to 375°. Line a 13 x 9-inch baking sheet with foil, shiny side down. Arrange enough graham crackers to cover the foil. In a skillet melt the butter. Add the brown sugar, sesame seeds, and almonds. Bring to a simmer and cook for 4 minutes, stirring continuously. Pour the mixture over the graham squares, spreading it evenly. Bake for 7 minutes. Shift the baking pan to the top rack (or into the broiler) and broil for 1 minute or less, just until golden brown. Watch closely since it burns quickly. Cool on a rack on foil. Cut into bars at the perforations. Store in a foil-lined cookie tin.

Makes 30 cookies

Christine Austin, Princess Sunshine
Sassy Squaws of Seminole Lakes, Punta Gorda, Florida

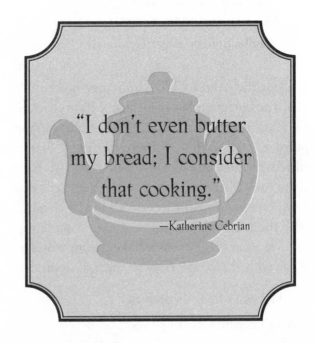

"I don't even butter my bread; I consider that cooking."

—Katherine Cebrian

Oatmeal Brownies

Two layers of oaty goodness surrounding a traditional fudge brownie layer got a top score from testers.

2   cups uncooked quick-cooking oats
1   cup all-purpose flour
1   cup firmly packed brown sugar
1   cup chopped walnuts
1   teaspoon baking soda
1   cup (2 sticks) butter, melted
1³/4 cups semisweet mini chocolate chips
1   (19- to 21-ounce) package fudge brownie mix, prepared according to package directions

Preheat the oven to 350°. In a large bowl combine the oats, flour, brown sugar, walnuts, and baking soda. Beat in the butter until the mixture forms coarse crumbs. Stir in the chocolate chips and mix well. Reserve 3 cups of the mixture. Pat the remaining mixture onto the bottom of a 15 x 10-inch jelly-roll pan to form the crust. Pour the prepared brownie mix over the crust, spreading it into a thin layer. Sprinkle the reserved crumb mixture over the top of the brownie mixture; pat down lightly. Bake 25 to 30 minutes, or until a toothpick inserted in center comes out with moist crumbs. Cool completely. Cut into bars.

Makes 48 bars

Linda Kirbach, Lady Lou
Fiesty Femmes, Jacksonville, Illinois

Turtle Brownies

Gooey, gorgeous, and good, good, good. Fantastic frozen too. Testers noted that the cake mix, milk, and butter should be mixed like a piecrust, using a fork or pastry blender. They said they preferred the result made with Betty Crocker brand cake mix.

1   (14-ounce) package caramels
1/3 plus 1/3 cup evaporated milk
1   (18-ounce) package German chocolate cake mix
3/4 cup (1 1/2 sticks) butter, softened
1   cup walnuts or pecans, toasted
12   ounces semisweet chocolate chips

Combine the caramels with 1/3 cup milk in the top of a double boiler. Cook, stirring, until the caramels are melted and the mixture is well blended.

Preheat the oven to 350°. In a bowl combine the cake mix, the remaining 1/3 cup milk, and butter. Blend until the mixture holds together. Stir in the nuts. Press half the cake mixture into a thin layer in a greased 13 x 9-inch pan. Bake for 6 minutes. Remove from the oven and sprinkle the top of the cake with the chocolate chips. Pour the melted caramels evenly over the top. Crumble the remaining cake mixture over the caramel. Bake for 15 to 20 minutes longer. Cool slightly and cut into bars.

Makes 8 to 12 servings

Lois Garfield, Queen Mum
Jen Jo's Crown Jewels, San Diego, California

Just Plain Great Brownies

A dusting of sugar in the pan adds a little something to these treats.

1   tablespoon shortening
1   cup plus 1 tablespoon sugar
1/2 cup (1 stick) lightly salted butter
2   (1-ounce) squares unsweetened chocolate
2   large eggs
1   teaspoon vanilla extract
1/2 cup all-purpose flour
1   cup semisweet chocolate chips
1   cup chopped walnuts (optional)

Preheat the oven to 350°. Grease an 8 or 9-inch square pan with shortening and coat with 1 tablespoon sugar. Melt the butter and unsweetened chocolate in a small saucepan over low heat. Allow it to cool for 5 minutes.

In a large mixing bowl lightly beat together the eggs and the remaining 1 cup sugar with a whisk. Add the vanilla. Gradually whisk the chocolate mixture into the egg mixture. Add the flour and stir until just blended. Add the chocolate chips and nuts (if desired). Pour the batter into the prepared pan. Bake for 25 to 30 minutes. Cool and cut into 12 squares.

Makes 12 brownies

Barbara Weinberg, Princess of Past and Present
Dusty Desert Roses, Cathedral City, California

Choco-Cherry Bars

Quick and popular, so a good choice for a take-along dessert. Bake in a disposable pan so it's totally portable.

CAKE
1   (18-ounce) package chocolate fudge cake mix
1   (21-ounce) can cherry pie filling
2   eggs
1   teaspoon almond extract

FROSTING
1/3 cup milk
1   cup sugar
5   tablespoon butter
1   (6-ounce) package chocolate chips

Preheat the oven to 350°. For the cake, in a large bowl with a wooden spoon, combine the cake mix, cherry pie filling, eggs, and almond extract. Pour into a greased 15 x 10-inch jelly-roll pan. Bake 25 to 30 minutes.

For the frosting, bring the milk, sugar, and butter to a boil in a saucepan over medium-high heat. Boil for 1 minute. Add the chocolate chips. Reduce the heat to low, and cook until smooth, stirring constantly. Spread over the cooled cake. Cut into bars.

Makes 12 servings

Sally Reed, E-mail Female
Tarheel Red Hat Club of Clemmons, Clemmons, North Carolina

Bake Shop Brownies

Corn syrup and dark brown sugar give these brownies some extra chew and a deep, delicious flavor.

1   cup (2 sticks) butter, at room temperature
2   cups granulated sugar
1   cup firmly packed light brown sugar
2/3 cup dark corn syrup
6   large eggs
6   (1-ounce) squares unsweetened chocolate
2   cups all-purpose flour
2   cups pecan halves or coarsely broken walnuts

Line the bottom and sides of a 15 x 10-inch jelly-roll pan with a sheet of foil. In a large mixing bowl using a wooden spoon, combine the butter, granulated sugar, brown sugar, and syrup. Stir in the eggs, one at a time, until blended. Preheat the oven to 350°. In a small saucepan over very low heat (or over hot water), melt the chocolate; stir into the sugar mixture until blended. Add the flour and stir until smooth. Add the pecans and mix well. Spoon into the prepared pan; spread the batter evenly. Bake for 40 minutes, or until a wooden pick inserted in the center comes out clean. Cool on a wire rack. Refrigerate, uncovered, until chilled. Invert the pan and remove the foil from the brownies. Cut into 30 brownies. Store brownies in the refrigerator.

Makes 30 brownies

Lorraine Tollefson, Queen
Chapeau Rouge of Crystal River, Crystal River, Florida

Viennese Apricot Jam Macaroons

1 1/2 cups ground walnuts
2/3   cup sugar
2   egg whites, slightly beaten
2/3   cup apricot jam

Preheat the oven to 350°. Grease and flour a baking sheet. Combine the nuts and sugar and mix well. Add the egg whites and mix. Drop by the teaspoonful onto a baking sheet. Bake for approximately 20 minutes, or until lightly browned. Allow to cool a few minutes and transfer from the pan to a wire rack. In a small saucepan melt the jam. Pour approximately 1/2 teaspoon onto each cookie.

Makes 18 to 24 cookies

Violet Lancer, Princess
Fuschia Fillies, Dublin, California

Monday Night Baking

When my kids were growing up, we would bake every Monday night for the week. We baked cookies for school snacks, whoopie pies, pies, and cakes. It was a night that the neighborhood kids looked forward to as well. The kids would gather around the table and we would bake and talk and eat. (I believe this is where my son learned his love for cooking.)

I have a much younger brother who is about the age of my children. He was home for Christmas during his freshman year at college and visiting my house. About eleven o'clock one night he asked if we could make some Christmas cookies.

I looked at him as if he had two heads. I asked if he knew what time it was and if he remembered how long it took to mix, roll, cut, bake, and decorate the cookies. He realized all of that, but really wanted to make Christmas cookies, so we did, late into the night.

It was probably one of the longest cooking sessions I've ever experienced. But it is one of my fondest cooking memories too. You see, I think he really wanted to talk, and the cooking was a way for him to do that comfortably. I still remember those cookies, and I just love the memories!

Sally Davidson
Queen Bee
Purple Pips
Northfield, Vermont

Amaretto Cookies

COOKIES
1 1/2 cups (3 sticks) butter, softened
1   cup sugar
1/4 cup almond-flavored liqueur
3   cups old-fashioned or quick (but not instant) oats
2   cups all-purpose flour

FROSTING
12   ounces chocolate chips
2   tablespoons shortening

Preheat the oven to 350°. For the cookies, mix the butter and sugar until light and fluffy. Blend in the liqueur. Add the oats and flour and mix well. Refrigerate 10 minutes. Shape the dough into balls and arrange on an ungreased baking sheet. Press into circles with the bottom of a glass (it helps to flour the bottom of the glass each time you press). Bake for 10 to 12 minutes. Cool.

For the frosting, combine the chocolate chips and shortening in a microwaveable bowl. Microwave, stirring occasionally, until the chips are melted and the mixture is smooth. Spread the chocolate on the back side of one cookie and top with another.

Makes 36 cookies

Rogene Lis, Rougie Rogene
Sassy Classy Ladies, Roselle, Illinois

Apricot Fold-Ups

Each rich square holds a tender apricot half.

DOUGH
- 2   cups all-purpose flour
- 1   teaspoon salt
- 1   (8-ounce) package soft cream cheese
- 1   tablespoon vegetable oil
- 1/2 to 2/3 cup milk, as needed
- 1   tablespoon white vinegar

FILLING
- 2   (6-ounce) packages dried apricots
- 2   cups water
- 1 1/2 cups granulated sugar

GLAZE
- 3/4 cup confectioners' sugar
- 1   tablespoon water

For the dough, combine the flour and salt in a medium bowl. With a pastry blender, cut in the cream cheese and oil until mixture resembles coarse crumbs. Add the milk and vinegar and work till dough holds together. Divide the dough into four portions and roll into a ball. Wrap each in waxed paper and chill 2 hours.

For the filling, combine the apricots, water, and sugar in a saucepan. Bring to a boil and cook until the apricots soften. Cool and drain.

Preheat the oven to 400°. On a lightly floured surface, roll each ball to 1/8-inch thickness. Cut into 2 1/2-inch squares. Place an apricot half in the center of each square. Fold each corner into the center and pinch tightly together to seal. Arrange on a baking sheet and bake for 15 minutes, or until golden. Place on wire racks to cool.

For the glaze, combine the confectioners' sugar and water till smooth. Drizzle on the cookies when slightly cooled.

Makes 4 servings

Sandy Meller, Lady Rocking Grammy
California Reds, Lohman, Missouri

Melt-In-Your-Mouth Butter Cookies

This delectable cookie has a touch of almond flavor.

COOKIES
1   cup (2 sticks) butter, softened
3/4   cup granulated sugar
1   teaspoon almond extract
2   cups all-purpose flour
1/2   teaspoon baking powder

GLAZE
1 1/2   cups confectioners' sugar
1   teaspoon almond extract
4   to 5 teaspoons water
   Red food coloring
   Purple food coloring
   Sliced almonds

Preheat the oven to 400°. For the cookies, combine the butter, sugar, almond extract, flour, and baking powder in a large bowl of an electric mixer. Beat at medium speed, scraping the bowl often, until creamy. Drop the dough by round teaspoonfuls 2 inches apart onto an ungreased baking sheet. Flatten the balls to 1/4-inch thickness with the bottom of a buttered glass dipped into sugar. Bake for 7 to 9 minutes, or until the edges are very lightly browned. Cool for 1 minute on the baking sheet. Remove and cool completely.

For the glaze, combine the confectioners' sugar, almond extract, and water and whisk together. Divide the icing into two small bowls, adding one food color to each bowl. Ice each cookie with both colors. Sprinkle the cookies with sliced almonds.

Makes about 80 cookies

Barb Witges, Cookie Princess
LuLu's Scarlet Ladies, Wentzville, Missouri

Forget-Me-Nots

A meringue cookie dotted with mini chocolate chips, these are very sweet, almost like candy. Remember to take them out of the oven before turning it on the next day.

2   egg whites, at room temperature
3/4   cup sugar
3/4   teaspoon mint extract
8   to 12 ounces mini chocolate chips

Preheat the oven to 375°. In a bowl with an electric mixer beat the egg whites until stiff, adding the sugar gradually. Add the mint extract and chocolate chips. Drop the mixture by the spoonful onto a baking sheet and place it in the oven. Turn the oven off and leave the sheet for 6 to 8 hours or overnight. Do not open the door.

Makes 24 cookies

Kathleen Fiocca, Vice Queen
Red Hat Philly Beach Babes, Langhorne, Pennsylvania

Homemade Crème Sandwiches

You'll need an empty potato chip can, such as a Pringles can, for storing the sandwiches.

1   (1-ounce) package sugar-free instant chocolate pudding mix
     Milk for preparing pudding
1   (8-ounce) container whipped topping
1   (12-ounce) box vanilla wafers
     Nonstick cooking spray

In a bowl prepare the pudding according to the package directions. Fold in the whipped topping. Spoon a generous amount of the mixture onto a vanilla wafer and top with another wafer. Place each crème sandwich in a paper-lined muffin cup. Repeat until all ingredients are used. Freeze the sandwiches. Serve frozen. For compact, secure storage, spray the inside of a potato chip canister with nonstick spray and fill the can with frozen sandwiches.

Makes 12 to 15 servings

Dana Burns, Queen Mystic
Mystical Dixie Pixies, Oxford, Alabama

Chewy Double Chocolate Cookies

These cookies will keep for one week, if they last that long.

1   (18-ounce) package pudding-in-the-mix devil's food cake mix
2   large eggs
1/2 cup (1 stick) butter or margarine, softened
1   cup semisweet chocolate chips
1/2 cup coarsely chopped walnuts

Preheat the oven to 375°. Combine the cake mix, eggs, and butter in a large mixing bowl, stirring until no streaks of cake mix remain. Dough will be very thick. Add the chocolate chips and walnuts. Drop by the tablespoonful onto lightly greased baking sheets. Press the cookies down with wet fingers. Bake for 12 to 14 minutes. Store in an airtight plastic container.

Makes 48 large cookies

Rosa West, Queen Bee
Red Hat Seagalls, Hudson, Florida

Chocolate Turtles

Great when you don't want to fire up the oven. One tester who made these said that when batter stuck to her waffle iron, she baked the rest in mini muffin cups, which worked well.

1/2 cup (1 stick) butter, melted
3/4 cup sugar
2   eggs
1/2 cup unsweetened cocoa
1   cup all-purpose flour
1/2 teaspoon baking powder
1   teaspoon vanilla extract
1/2 cup chopped pecans

Combine the butter and sugar in a large bowl. Beat the eggs in a separate bowl and add to the sugar mixture. Mix in the cocoa, flour, baking powder, vanilla, and pecans. Drop by the spoonfuls onto a hot waffle iron. Cook for about 50 seconds. (If using a Belgium waffle iron, cook for 3 minutes and remove with a pancake turner.) Cool and frost with your favorite chocolate icing.

Makes 24 turtles

Marge Byford, Queen Ladybug
Titian Queens & Ladies-in-Waiting, Helena, Montana

Sour Cream Chocolate Drops

1/2   cup shortening
1 1/2 cups sugar
2   eggs
1   cup sour cream
1   teaspoon vanilla extract
2 3/4 cups sifted all-purpose flour
1/2   teaspoon baking soda
1/2   teaspoon baking powder
1/2   teaspoon salt
2   (1-ounce) squares baking chocolate, melted
1   (15-ounce) can chocolate frosting

Preheat the oven to 350°. In a bowl beat the shortening, sugar, eggs, sour cream, and vanilla. Add the flour, baking soda, baking powder, and salt and blend well. Stir in the melted chocolate. Drop by tablespoonfuls 1 inch apart onto an ungreased baking sheet. Bake for 12 to 15 minutes. Transfer drops to a wire rack to cool. When cool, frost with the chocolate frosting.

Makes 48 cookies

Letitia Schonebaum, Queen Mum
Red Hot To Trots, Honey Brook, Pennsylvania

Cookie Dough Cream Cheese Cups

These are like little individual cheesecakes.

1   (8-ounce) tube refrigerated chocolate chip cookie dough

Peanut Brittle Block

I've always made peanut brittle for Christmas. It's a pretty easy recipe to follow, and, if I must say so myself, it turns out well.

We had just bought a new house in July with a nice big kitchen. In my kitchen is an island with a butcher block top. As Christmas drew near, it was time to make the brittle. I brought out the recipe and prepared it. But instead of pouring the brittle into greased pans like I have always done, I thought, Why not butter up the ole butcher block and pour the brittle onto it? Well, guess what? It stuck like cement.

It took three days to get that mess off the butcher block. First, I hammered at the mess to loosen what I could. Then, I kept wet towels over it while it kind of melted away. Finally, I could get a knife under the mass to loosen it.

The moral of that experiment: peanut brittle and butcher block tops do not mix.

Claudia Beene
Queen Mother
Scarlett O'Hatters
Bossier City, Louisiana

---

1   (8-ounce) package cream cheese, softened
1/4   cup (1/2 stick) butter, softened
1   teaspoon vanilla extract
2 1/2   cups confectioners' sugar

Preheat the oven to 350°. With floured hands, press about 1 tablespoon of the cookie dough onto the bottom and up the sides of each of 24, ungreased, miniature, muffin cups. Bake for 8 minutes or until lightly browned.

Using the end of a wooden spoon handle, reshape the puffed cookie cups. Cool for 5 minutes before removing from the pan to a wire rack to cool completely. In a small mixing bowl beat the cream cheese, butter, and vanilla until blended. Gradually beat in the confectioners' sugar. Spoon the mixture into the cookie cups. Store in the refrigerator.

Makes 24 cups

Lynn Lengel, Queen Mother
Red Hat Cardinals, Nazareth, Pennsylvania

Coconut Mounds Bars

1/2   cup (1 stick) butter or margarine
24   saltine crackers, finely crushed
1/4   cup sugar
1   (14-ounce) can sweetened condensed milk
1   (7-ounce) package shredded coconut
1   cup semisweet chocolate chips

Preheat the oven to 350°. Melt the butter and add the cracker crumbs and sugar. Mix well. Press into the bottom of a 9-inch baking pan. Bake for 10 to 12 minutes until the edges are golden and then remove. In a separate bowl mix the sweetened condensed milk and coconut. Spread over the baked crust. Return to the oven and bake for 15 minutes. Remove from the oven and sprinkle the chocolate chips on top. Return to the oven and bake for 1 minute longer, just long enough to melt the chocolate. Remove from the oven. Use a knife to spread the chocolate to cover the coconut. Cool. Cut into 16 squares.

Makes 16 servings

Mary Beth Palmer, Lady McBeth, Vice Queen
Columbine Cuties, Colorado Springs, Colorado

Swedish Courtyard Coconut Cookies

This deliciously melting cookie was truly enjoyed by testers, who noted that the recipe "makes lots of cookies." Look to this recipe when you need a super big batch.

2   cups shortening
2   cups (4 sticks) butter, softened
4   cups sugar
6   cups all-purpose flour
2   teaspoons baking soda
2   teaspoons baking powder
2   teaspoons vanilla extract
2   cups flaked coconut

Preheat the oven to 350°. In a large bowl beat the shortening, butter, and sugar. Sift the flour, baking soda, and baking powder. Add to the shortening mixture and mix well. Add the vanilla and coconut and mix well. Drop by rounded teaspoonfuls onto ungreased baking sheets. Dip the bottom of a glass in sugar and flatten each cookie. Bake for 10 minutes until lightly browned.

Makes about 140 cookies

Verla Shaw, E-Mail Female
Breezy Belles in Bonnets, Pequot Lakes, Minnesota

Coconut Kiss Cookies

1/2   cup (1 stick) butter, softened
1   (3-ounce) package cream cheese
3/4   cup sugar
1   egg yolk
2   teaspoons almond extract
2   teaspoons orange juice
1 1/4 cups all-purpose flour
2   teaspoons baking powder
1/4   teaspoon salt

3 plus 2 cups flaked coconut
54 Hershey Kisses with wrappers removed

In a large bowl beat the butter, cream cheese, and sugar until light and fluffy. Add the egg yolk, almond extract, and orange juice and mix well. In another bowl combine the flour, baking powder, and salt. Add to the butter mixture. Stir in 3 cups coconut. Refrigerate for 1 hour.

Preheat the oven to 350°. Shape the mixture into 1-inch balls and roll in the remaining 2 cups coconut. Arrange on an ungreased baking sheet and bake for 10 to 12 minutes. Press a Kiss into the middle of each cookie. Cool for 2 minutes on the baking sheet. Remove and cool completely.

Makes 54 cookies

Gail Buss, The Lady Duchess of Westminster
The Scarlette Belles, Westminster, Maryland

Coconut Macaroons with Red Tops

A macaroon with a light chewy texture.

3 egg whites
1 cup sugar
3 cups flaked coconut
2 tablespoons cornstarch
1 teaspoon almond extract
  Candied red cherries

Preheat the oven to 300°. Beat the egg whites until stiff but not dry. Gradually beat in the sugar. Combine the coconut and cornstarch in a small bowl. Stir into the egg whites. Transfer the mixture to a double boiler. Cook over simmering water for about 15 minutes, stirring often. Remove from the heat and stir in the almond extract. Drop by teaspoonfuls 1½ inches apart onto greased baking sheets. Top each with a candied red cherry. Bake for 20 to 25 minutes, or until the macaroons are a delicate brown. Store between sheets of waxed paper in a cookie tin.

Makes 30 cookies

Mary Ann Saint, The Cookie Lady
The Happy Hatters, Plymouth, Michigan

"I do not like broccoli. And I haven't liked it since I was a little kid and my mother made me eat it. And I'm President of the United States and I'm not going to eat any more broccoli."

—George Bush

Date Swirl Cookies

A great looking cookie that makes a nice addition to a cookie platter. If you have whole dates, use a food processor to chop them, sprinkling them with a tiny bit of flour. A large, sharp knife dipped into hot water occasionally also works nicely.

COOKIE DOUGH

- 1/2 cup shortening
- 1/2 cup firmly packed brown sugar
- 1/2 cup sugar
- 1 egg, slightly beaten
- 2 cups sifted all-purpose flour
- 1/2 teaspoon baking soda
- 1/4 cup salt

FILLING

- 1/3 cup water
- 1/2 cup granulated sugar
- 8 ounces chopped dates
- 1/8 teaspoon salt
- 8 ounces chopped nuts

For the cookie dough, cream the shortening and sugars and add the egg. In a bowl sift the flour, baking soda, and salt. Add to the sugar mixture and mix well. Chill this dough in the refrigerator while you prepare the filling.

For the filling, combine the water, sugar, and dates in a saucepan over medium heat. Cook for 5 minutes. Add the salt. Cool. Roll the dough into a rectangle 1/8 inch thick. Spread the filling on the dough and sprinkle it with nuts. Roll up the dough to enclose the filling, jelly-roll style, and refrigerate for at least 6 hours. Preheat the oven to 350°. Cut the roll into 1/8-inch slices and arrange them on a greased baking sheet. Bake for 10 to 12 minutes.

Makes 60 cookies

Martha Kiker, Her Royal Hatness Queen Martha
The Heavenly Hatters of Cedar Hill, De Soto, Texas

Corn Flake No-Bakes

This recipe arrived with the charming (but fortunately not descriptive) name June Bug Cookies;—every family seems to have given this beloved cookie its own special name.

- 1 cup white corn syrup
- 1 cup sugar
- 2 cups peanut butter
- 4 cups fresh corn flakes (fresh is key)

Bring the corn syrup and sugar to a boil in a large saucepan. Boil for 1 minute, stirring constantly so not to scorch. Remove from the heat. Stir in the peanut butter then the corn flakes. Drop by teaspoons (or tablespoons) onto a cool surface. Hide the cookies before the family comes.

Makes 36 to 48 cookies

Mayme Easton, Royal Granny Nanny
Red Hats of Oz, Olathe, Kansas

Chocolate Chip Crisps

Adding a bit of crunch to chocolate chippers results in a whole new dimension to love. Testers said the corn flakes make the cookies taste as if they had nuts. They used the corn flakes as they came from the package, not crushing them any farther.

2   cups all-purpose flour
1   teaspoon baking soda
1/2   teaspoon salt
1   cup (2 sticks) butter, softened
1 1/2   cup sugar
2   eggs
1   teaspoon vanilla extract
4   cups corn flakes
1   cup semisweet chocolate chips

Preheat the oven to 375°. Combine the flour, baking soda, and salt and mix well. In a seperate bowl beat the butter and sugar until light and fluffy; add the eggs and vanilla and beat well. Stir in the corn flakes and chocolate chips. Add the flour mixture and mix well. Drop the dough by teaspoonfuls on ungreased baking sheets. Bake for about 12 minutes. Cool 2 minutes on the baking sheet. Remove and cool completely.

Makes about 90 cookies

Sheila Hannan, Queen

The Merry Madams of Merritt Island, Merritt Island, Florida

Cranberry–Pistachio Biscotti

1/4   cup light olive oil
3/4   cup sugar
2   teaspoons vanilla extract
1/2   teaspoon almond extract
2   eggs (or egg beaters)
1 3/4   cups all-purpose flour
1/4   teaspoon salt
1   teaspoon baking powder
1/2   cup dried cranberries
1 1/2   cups pistachio nuts

Preheat the oven to 300°. Line a baking sheet with parchment paper. In a large bowl mix the oil and sugar until well blended. Mix in the vanilla and almond extracts and then beat in the eggs. Combine the flour, salt, and baking powder in a seperate bowl; gradually stir into the egg mixture. Fold in the cranberries and nuts by hand. Divide the dough in half. Form two logs on a 13 x 9 x 2-inch baking sheet. If the dough is too sticky, wet your hands with cool water to handle. Bake for 35 minutes until the logs are light brown. Remove from the oven and let cool 10 minutes. Reduce the heat to 275°. Cut the logs on the diagonal into 3/4-inch-thick slices. Lay the slices on their sides onto a parchment-covered baking sheet. Bake 8 to 10 minutes or until dry.

Makes 28 to 30 cookies

Joanne Saulsbery, Duchess of Dance
Violettas, Colonie, New York

World's Greatest Corn Flake Cookie

Meltingly delicious, with a chewy inside and crisp exterior. The tester recommended buying sugar in a shaker for quicker sugar sprinkling.

1	cup (2 sticks) butter, softened
1	cup firmly packed light brown sugar
1	egg
1	cup vegetable oil
1	teaspoon vanilla extract
3 1/2	cups all-purpose flour
1	teaspoon baking soda
1	teaspoon salt
1	cup rolled oats
1	cup crushed corn flakes
1	cup shredded coconut
1/2	cup chopped pecans
1	cup granulated sugar

Preheat the oven to 325°. Cream the butter and brown sugar in an electric mixer. Add the egg, oil, and vanilla extract. In a separate bowl, mix the flour with the baking soda and salt and add to the cream mixture with the oats, corn flakes, coconut, and pecans. Mix well at medium speed. Roll the dough into walnut-size balls or use a small scoop, and put the balls on an ungreased baking sheet 1 1/2 inches apart. Push the balls down with a fork. Bake for 12 minutes (cookies will still be light in color). Remove from the oven. Sprinkle the tops with granulated sugar. Let cool on the baking sheet for 5 minutes, and then remove the cookies to a wire rack.

Makes about 60 cookies

Robin Yancey, Lady of Stroll
Ruby Red Hats of Joy, San Ramon, California

Josephines

A no-bake cookie that doesn't taste no-bake.

1	pound graham crackers
1	cup (2 sticks) butter
1	cup granulated sugar
1	egg, beaten
1/2	cup milk
1	cup angel flake coconut
1	cup chopped nuts (walnuts or pecans)
1	cup graham cracker crumbs

FROSTING

4	to 6 tablespoons butter
2	cups confectioners' sugar
1	teaspoon vanilla extract
1	tablespoon milk

Cover the entire bottom of a 13 x 9-inch baking pan with whole graham crackers. In a saucepan melt the butter and add the sugar, beaten egg, and milk. Cook over medium heat until thick, about 10 minutes. Add the coconut, nuts and graham cracker crumbs to the mixture. Spread over the graham cracker layer. Cover with a second layer of whole graham crackers. Or you may wish to crumble the top layer of crackers.

For the frosting, combine the butter, sugar, vanilla, and milk and beat until fluffy and well blended. Spread the frosting over the top layer of graham crackers. Refrigerate until chilled. Cut into squares and serve.

Make 12 to 16 servings

Dell Goodwin, Queen of Arts
Crabtown Ladies, Hampton, Virginia

Dunking Platter Cookies

Corn flakes make these crunchy, and dates make them chewy. Testers noted that chilling the dough helped control their spread on the baking sheet. If you want a lot of cookies, use only one tablespoon dough per cookie and—you'll get eight dozen.

2	cups (4 sticks) butter, melted
2	cups granulated sugar
2	cups packed dark brown sugar
4	large eggs, slightly beaten
2	teaspoons vanilla extract
2	cups oatmeal
2	cups corn flakes
2	teaspoons baking soda
2	teaspoons baking powder
4	cups all-purpose flour
2	teaspoons cinnamon (optional)
1 1/2	cups chopped dates (or chocolate chips or raisins)
1	cup chopped nuts

Preheat the oven to 350°. In a large bowl beat the butter and sugars. Stir in the eggs and vanilla. Mix in the oatmeal and corn flakes.

Sift together the baking soda, baking powder, flour, and cinnamon, if using, and add this to the cornflake mixture. Add the dates and nuts. Drop tablespoonfuls at least 2 inches apart onto an ungreased baking sheet. (They spread a lot.) Bake for 12 to 15 minutes. Cool 2 minutes on the sheet. Remove and cool completely.

Makes 48 to 60 cookies

Joanne Thill, Princess of Thin
London Bridge Red Hots, Lake Havasu City, Arizona

Nut Balls

A rich, plain, and straightforward cookie that's just right with coffee and tea.

1 1/2	cups (3 sticks) butter, softened
3	tablespoons granulated sugar
3	teaspoons vanilla extract
3	cup chopped walnuts
3	cups all-purpose flour
2	cups confectioners' sugar

Preheat the oven to 300°. In a large mixing bowl beat the butter, sugar, and vanilla. Add the walnuts and then mix in the flour. Form the dough into small balls. Arrange on a greased baking sheet. Bake for 35 minutes. Roll the hot cookies in the confectioners' sugar. Let cool and then roll in the sugar again.

Makes about 84 cookies

Sylvia Fiedler, Historian
Bowdle WOWS, Bowdle, South Dekota

Cookie Decorating

When our own children were younger, my Christmas gift to our siblings was to take everyone's children for the whole day one Saturday near Christmas so that the parents could go shopping in peace. Since I am one of six children and my husband is one of three, that meant there would be a lot of children at our house—between ten and nineteen each year.

I would set up low tables covered with vinyl tablecloths. The kids and I would make and decorate sugar cookies. We would learn how to follow a recipe, how to measure ingredients, how to roll out the dough, and how to cut out the shapes. We would then have lunch and maybe a little nap or movie while sheet after sheet of cookies baked and cooled. All afternoon we would frost and decorate their masterpieces.

At the end of the day, we would fill a take-home bag for each child with his or her best works so they could share the edible art with their families. It was messy, it was mayhem, and it was marvelous!

Sandy Wright
Scarlet Scribe
Simply Red
Pleasant Hill, Missouri

Frosted Cranberry–Orange Cookies

Great holiday flavors and a touch of frosting.

COOKIES
1 1/2 cups firmly packed brown sugar
1　cup (2 sticks) butter, softened
1　teaspoon vanilla extract
2　eggs
2 1/4 cups all-purpose flour
2　teaspoons baking powder
1　teaspoon baking soda
1/2　teaspoon salt
2　cups quick-cooking oats
1　cup sweetened dried cranberries
1　cup chopped orange slice candies

GLAZE
1 1/2 cups confectioners' sugar
4　to 6 teaspoons orange juice

Preheat the oven to 350°. For the cookies, in a large bowl combine the brown sugar and butter; beat until light and fluffy. Add the vanilla and eggs; blend well. Add the flour, baking powder, baking soda, and salt; mix well. Stir in the oats, cranberries, and chopped candies. Drop the dough by rounded teaspoonfuls 2 inches apart onto ungreased baking sheets. Bake for 9 to 11 minutes or until golden brown. Cool for 1 minute; remove from the baking sheets. Cool completely, about 15 minutes.

For the glaze, combine the confectioners' sugar and orange juice in a small bowl for the desired drizzling consistency. Drizzle the glaze over the cooled cookies.

Makes about 60 cookies

Phyllis Sturgill, Queen
Red Hatted Faithful Few, Omaha, Nebraska

Fruitcake Cookies

The great taste of Christmas in a cookie. One batch makes enough to share, plus lots to spare.

8   ounces candied green cherries, chopped
8   ounces candied red cherries, chopped
8   ounces candied pineapple, chopped
1   pound golden raisins or dates, chopped
1   cup sherry
3   eggs
10 tablespoons butter, melted
1   cup brown sugar
3   cups all-purpose flour
1   teaspoon ground cloves
    Pinch of allspice
2   teaspoons cinnamon
    Pinch of nutmeg
1   teaspoon baking soda
1   tablespoon buttermilk
1   teaspoon vanilla extract
8   ounces almonds, chopped
8   ounces pecans, chopped

In a large bowl soak the fruits in the sherry for 6 or more hours. In a separate bowl beat the eggs, butter, and sugar. Sift the flour with the spices and add to the brown sugar mixture. Dissolve the baking soda in the buttermilk. Add to the batter along with the vanilla, nuts, and soaked fruit. Chill for 15 minutes. Preheat the oven to 325°. Drop the batter by rounded teaspoonfuls onto a baking sheet. Bake for 15 to 20 minutes. Store in an airtight container or tin. Cookies will stay fresh at least 3 weeks.

Makes 120 to 140 cookies

Pam Burke, Queen Mum
Ruby Mermaids, Sanibel, Florida

Christmas Cake Cookies

The ingredients are indulgent, but what the heck—Christmas comes but once a year. The tester substituted hazelnuts for Brazil nuts and pronounced them very nice.

2¹/2 cups all-purpose flour
1   teaspoon baking soda
1   teaspoon salt
1   teaspoon cinnamon
1   cup (2 sticks) butter, softened
1¹/2 cups sugar
2   eggs
1   pound dates, cut into chunks
¹/2 pound candied red and green cherries, quartered
¹/2 pound candied pineapples, thinly sliced
¹/2 pound blanched toasted almonds, coarsely chopped
¹/2 pound Brazil nuts or hazel nuts

Preheat the oven to 350°. Sift the flour, baking soda, salt, and cinnamon together. In a separate bowl, beat the butter until soft and creamy. Add the sugar gradually and continue to work until the mixture is smooth. Beat in the eggs, mixing thoroughly. Stir in the sifted ingredients, mixing well. Stir in the fruits and nuts. Drop balls about the size of a small walnut onto the cookie sheets. Bake for 10 to 13 minutes. Do not overbake. Remove from the sheets to cool. The cookies store well. Keep in airtight containers or freeze.

Makes about 120 cookies

Elizabeth Ann Deeter, Countess Chatterbug
Gettys Garnets, Thurmont, Maryland

Macadamia Snowballs

¹/2 cup confectioners' sugar plus additional for sprinkling
1   cup (2 sticks) butter (no substitutes), softened
3   tablespoons vanilla extract
2¹/2 cups all-purpose flour
1   cup finely chopped macadamia nuts (about 5 ounces)

Preheat the oven to 350°. Beat ¹/2 cup confectioners' sugar, the butter, and vanilla in a medium bowl till blended. Stir in the flour and nuts until well blended. Gather the dough into a ball. If the mixture is too dry, add another tablespoon of vanilla. Roll the dough into 1-inch balls. Arrange 1 inch apart on an ungreased baking sheet. Bake for 12 to 15 minutes, or until somewhat browned on the bottoms. Cool the cookies for 1 minute on the baking sheet and then coat with additional sifted confectioners' sugar. Cool on wire racks. Sprinkle the cookies with additional confectioners' sugar to store. Before serving, roll in additional sugar if desired.

Makes 48 cookies

Carol Kennedy, Queen Red Beauty
Under–Aged Beauties, Van Alstyne, Texas

Snappy Gingersnaps

If the bite of ginger is your favorite, make these with a piece of crystallized ginger inside each cookie.

3   cups all-purpose flour.
1   tablespoon baking soda
1/2   teaspoon salt
1 1/2   teaspoons cinnamon
1 1/2   teaspoons cloves
1 1/2   teaspoons ginger
8   ounces shortening
1 1/2   cups firmly packed dark brown sugar
2   eggs
1/2   cup molasses
1/4   cup crystallized ginger, chopped (optional)
   Turbinado (raw) sugar or regular sugar for
   rolling

Preheat the oven to 375°. Mix together the flour, baking soda, salt, cinnamon, cloves, and ginger. In a mixing bowl beat the shortening with a mixer for 5 minutes. Gradually add the brown sugar and beat 5 more minutes until light and fluffy. In a separate bowl beat the eggs with a fork. Add the eggs and molasses to the shortening. Add the flour and spice mixture fairly quickly on low speed. Beat only until the flour disappears. Do not overmix. Form tablespoons of dough into balls (handle as little as possible). Press a piece of ginger into the middle of each ball and roll it in raw sugar. Arrange on a parchment-lined baking sheet and bake for about 10 minutes.

Makes about 72 cookies

Karen Ridout, Duchess of Dessert
Red Hat Dollies of Calgary, Calgary, Alberta, Canada

Spiced Oatmeal Cookies

1   cup raisins
1   cup sugar
3   beaten eggs
1   cup (2 sticks) butter or shortening, softened
2   cups all-purpose flour
1/2   teaspoon salt
1/2   teaspoon baking soda
1   teaspoon ground cinnamon
1/2   teaspoon ground allspice
1/2   teaspoon ground cloves
2   cups quick-cooking oatmeal

Preheat the oven to 375°. In a small pan combine the raisins with enough water almost to cover. Bring to a boil. Remove from the heat and cover. Let the raisins plump for 15 minutes. Pour off the liquid and reserve 6 tablespoons. Beat the sugar, eggs, and butter together in a large bowl. Sift together the flour, salt, baking soda, cinnamon, allspice, cloves, and oatmeal. Gradually pour them into the creamed butter mixture. Add the raisins and reserved raisin liquid. Grease a cookie sheet and drop the cookie dough 1 tablespoon at a time onto the sheet. Bake the cookies for about 8 minutes. They should be slightly brown. If the batter is too warm, place it in the refrigerator for about half an hour. The cookies should be slightly rounded on top, not flat. You can add coconut or nuts to the cookies before baking.

Makes 48 cookies

Shirley Keas, Queen Mum
South Bay Babes, Torrance, California

Ginger-Lavender Sugar Cookies

Unusual and glamorous and perfect for tea. The cookies keep well (if there are any left over).

1 1/3 cups all-purpose flour
2/3   cup corn flour (or regular cornmeal)
1/2   teaspoon baking powder
1/4   teaspoon salt
1   cup (2 sticks) unsalted butter, softened
1   cup granulated sugar
1   tablespoon brown sugar
1   tablespoon finely grated fresh gingerroot
1   tablespoon dried culinary lavender blossoms (found in bulk/health food stores)
1   large egg, beaten
1 1/2 teaspoons vanilla extract
     Chopped crystallized ginger

Preheat the oven to 375°. Line two baking sheets with parchment. Sift together the flours, baking powder, and salt. In a large bowl beat the butter, sugars, gingerroot, and lavender until light and fluffy. Add the egg and vanilla. Add the dry ingredients, incorporating them well after each addition. Let the dough rest in the fridge for 20 minutes. Roll the dough into 1-inch balls or use a small ice cream scoop to shape the dough. Roll each ball in the ginger and arrange on a baking sheet (12 to 15 cookies per sheet). Bake 15 to 18 minutes until golden brown and just set. Cool on baking sheets for 5 minutes. Remove and cool completely.

Makes 24 cookies

LuLu (Linda-Rose) Thomsett, Divalicious LuLu Ruby Royal Majes-"Teas," Port Townsend, Washington

Honey Bars

Let this chewy bar—with its secret-ingredient frosting—be the topic of conversation at your next gathering.

BARS
3/4   cup vegetable oil
1/4   cup honey
1   egg
1   cup granulated sugar
2   cups all-purpose flour
1   teaspoon baking soda
1/2   teaspoon salt
1 1/4 teaspoons cinnamon
1   cup chopped pecans

GLAZE
1   cup confectioners' sugar
2   tablespoons mayonnaise
2   tablespoons water
1   teaspoon vanilla extract

Preheat the oven to 350°. For the bars, in a bowl beat the oil, honey, and egg. In a separate bowl combine the sugar, flour, baking soda, salt, and cinnamon and add to the egg mixture. Mix well and then stir in the pecans. The batter will be stiff. Press into a greased baking sheet with a lip. Bake for 15 to 20 minutes.

For the glaze, combine the confectioners' sugar, mayonnaise, water, and vanilla in a saucepan. Cook over medium heat just to heat through. Pour over the cookies. Let stand until the glaze has firmed a little and then cut into bars.

Makes 24 bars

Dokie Bledsoe, Queen Ritzy Red Lady
Coleman County Texans, Valera, Texas

Peanut Butter Kisses

1   (18-ounce) package yellow cake mix
1   cup peanut butter
1/3 cup water
1   egg
1   (22-ounce) package chocolate kisses, unwrapped

Preheat the oven to 350°. In a large bowl combine the cake mix, peanut butter, water, and egg and mix well. Shape the mixture into 1-inch balls. Arrange them 2 inches apart on an ungreased baking sheet. Bake for 9 to 11 minutes. Remove from the oven and immediately press a chocolate kiss into the center of each hot cookie. Remove from the baking sheet and cool completely.

Makes 60 cookies

Nancy Mans, Purple Participant
Sassy Classy Ladies, Roselle, Illinois

Potato Chip Cookies

A clever cook can turn just about anything into a delicious cookie. Surprise young children with this long-time family favorite.

1   cup granulated sugar
1   cup firmly packed light brown sugar
1   cup (2 sticks) butter, softened
2   eggs, well beaten
2   cups all-purpose flour
1   teaspoon baking soda
2   teaspoons vanilla extract
1   cup finely crushed potato chips
1/2 cup chopped nuts (any kind) (optional)
    Confectioners' sugar

Preheat the oven to 350°. In a large bowl beat the sugars and butter until fluffy. Beat in the eggs. In a separate bowl sift the flour with the baking soda; add to the creamed butter mixture. Stir in the vanilla, potato chips, and nuts. Drop by teaspoonfuls 3 inches apart on ungreased baking sheets. Bake for 10 to 12 minutes. When cool, sprinkle with the confectioners' sugar for a nice touch.

Makes 60 cookies

Sue Scott, Queen of My Kitchen
Over The Seven Hills of Marlborough Red Hat Society, Marlborough, Massachusetts

Ricotta Cookies

Soft and cake-like. Add a pinch of ground nutmeg to the frosting if you are a fan of nutmeg. Turn these into a holiday treat by tinting the frosting.

COOKIES

2   cups granulated sugar

1   cup (2 sticks) butter, softened

1   (15-ounce) container ricotta cheese

2   teaspoons vanilla extract

2   large eggs

4   cups all-purpose flour

2   tablespoons baking powder

1   teaspoon salt

FROSTING

1 1/2 cups confectioners' sugar

3   tablespoons milk

Sprinkles for decorating

Preheat the oven to 350°. For the cookies, in a large bowl with a mixer at low speed, beat the sugar and butter until light and fluffy. At medium speed, beat in the ricotta, vanilla, and eggs until well combined. Reduce the speed to low. Add the flour, baking powder, and salt; beat until soft dough forms. Drop the dough by level tablespoonfuls about 2 inches apart onto ungreased baking sheets. Bake 15 minutes, or until the cookies are lightly golden. (Cookies will be soft.) With a spatula, remove the cookies to a wire rack to cool.

For the frosting, stir the confectioners' sugar and milk in a small bowl until smooth. Spread the icing on the cookies; decorate with the sprinkles. Set the cookies aside for the icing to firm.

Makes about 70 cookies

Mary Finley, Queen Mother
Violettas, Albany, New York

Pumpkin & Chocolate Chip Cookies

A surprising combination that's surprisingly well-matched.

1   cup shortening

1   cup sugar

1   egg

1   cup canned solid-pack pumpkin

2   cups all-purpose flour

1   teaspoon baking soda

1   teaspoon baking powder

1/2 teaspoon salt

1   teaspoon cinnamon
    (or pumpkin pie spice)

1   teaspoon vanilla extract

1   cup chocolate chips

1/2 cup chopped pecans (optional)

Preheat the oven to 350°. Beat the shortening and sugar at medium speed with an electric mixer until fluffy. Add the egg and pumpkin, mixing well. Combine the flour, baking soda, baking powder, salt, and cinnamon and add to the pumpkin mixture. Stir in the vanilla, chocolate chips, and pecans, if using. Drop the dough by tablespoonfuls onto lightly greased baking sheets. Bake for 13 minutes. Let cool 2 minutes on the baking sheets. Remove and cool completely.

Makes about 60 cookies

Catie McIntyre Walker, Queen Cabernet Catie
Les Merlot Chapeaux, Walla Walla, Washington

Peanut Butter Miracles

No flour? Can they possibly work? They do, and that is where the name originated. Add 1 teaspoon vanilla extract if you like. Our tester took them to a children's party, and the little ones ate every last cookie.

- 1   cup peanut butter (creamy or crunchy)
- 1   cup sugar
- 1   egg, beaten

Preheat the oven to 375°. In a medium bowl combine the peanut butter, sugar, and egg until well mixed and stir until the dough forms a ball. Shape the dough by the teaspoonful into small balls. Arrange the balls on ungreased baking sheets. Use a fork to press a crisscross pattern on the top. Bake for about 7 minutes.

Makes 24 cookies

Sara Menke, Princess of Threads
Rosie Red Hats, Wellington, New York

Piña Colada Squares

Scrumptious squares flavored with pineapple, coconut, and rum flavoring.

- 1   cup all-purpose flour
- 1   tablespoon baking powder
- 1/4   cup cold butter, cut into small cubes
- 3   large eggs, divided
- 2   tablespoons half-and-half or light cream
- 1   (19-ounce) can unsweetened crushed pineapple, drained
- 1   cup unsweetened coconut flakes
- 1   cup sugar
- 2   tablespoons melted butter
- 1   teaspoon rum extract

Preheat the oven to 350°. Combine the flour and baking powder in a bowl. Cut in the cold butter until the mixture is crumbly. Beat 1 egg with the half-and-half and stir into the flour mixture. Spread the mixture in an 8-inch square nonstick or greased baking pan. Spread the pineapple over the batter. Mix the coconut, sugar, remaining 2 eggs, melted butter, and rum extract together and spread over the pineapple, gently pressing it down. Bake for 35 to 40 minutes. Cool on a rack. Cool and then chill thoroughly. Cut into 16 squares.

Makes 16 servings

Maureen McDermott, Princess Maureen
Delta Gals, Delta, British Columbia, Canada

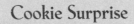

Cookie Surprise

My mother made wonderful cookies called Sour Cream Chocolate Drops. Once they were baked, she stored them in an old Dutch oven on the counter.

One Sunday morning, I came downstairs and saw the Dutch oven. Cookies for breakfast! Sleepily, I walked to the Dutch oven, lifted the lid, and reached my hand in for a treat. To my surprise, there was salt mackerel soaking in there for my father's special Sunday breakfast. I learned at an early age to "Look before you leap."

Letitia Schonebaum
Queen Mum
Red Hot to Trots
Honey Brook, Pennsylvania

Raspberry Meringue Kisses

3   egg whites
1/8   teaspoon salt
3 1/2   tablespoons raspberry gelatin (half a small box)
3/4   cup sugar
1   teaspoon vinegar
1   cup miniature chocolate bits

Preheat the oven to 250°. Line at least two baking sheets with parchment paper. Use a mixer to beat the egg whites with the salt until foamy. Add the raspberry gelatin and sugar gradually. Beat until stiff peaks form and the sugar is dissolved. Gently stir in the vinegar. Fold in the chocolate bits. Drop the dough by teaspoonfuls onto the baking sheets. Bake for 25 minutes. Turn the oven off but leave the cookies in the oven for 20 minutes longer. Remove from the oven and loosen from the parchment paper.

Makes about 60 cookies

Maryanne Niesen, Queen
Chapter Name: Red Hot Cheesy Chicks, Whitefish Bay, Wisconsin

Root Beer Cookies

Definitely not a garden variety cookie. The McCormick spice company makes a root beer concentrate. Testers found the icing too sweet and recommended a cream cheese frosting instead. Better yet, they said, make ice cream sandwiches from them for a portable float.

COOKIES

- 1   cup firmly packed dark brown sugar
- 1/2   cup (1/4 stick) margarine
- 1/4   cup unsalted butter, softened
- 1   egg
- 1   teaspoon vanilla extract
- 1/2   teaspoon baking soda
- 1/2   teaspoon salt
- 1 3/4   cups all-purpose flour
- 2   teaspoons root beer concentrate

ICING

- 2   cups confectioners' sugar
- 1/3   cup unsalted butter, softened
- 1   to 2 tablespoons water
- 1   teaspoon root beer concentrate

For the cookies, beat the brown sugar, margarine, butter, and egg until well blended and fluffy. Stir in the vanilla, baking soda, salt, flour, and root beer concentrate. The batter will be stiff. Cover and refrigerate for 1 hour. Preheat the oven to 375°. Cover a baking sheet with parchment paper. Drop the dough by teaspoonfuls onto the prepared sheet. Bake for 6 to 8 minutes.

For the icing, combine the confectioners' sugar with the butter in a bowl and beat well. Combine the water and root beer concentrate and add to the sugar mixture. Mix well. Spread on the cooled cookies.

Makes 24 cookies

Beverly Hofecker, Lady Crimson
Red Hat Hotties, Johnstown, Pennsylvania

Spice Cookies

Think Mexican wedding cookies with a dash of spice. One easy way to coat the cookies with confectioners' sugar is to pour the sugar into a large paper grocery sack, and then add six to eight cookies and shake.

- 3/4   cup shortening
- 1   cup granulated sugar
- 1   egg
- 1/4   cup molasses
- 2   cups all-purpose flour
- 2   teaspoons baking soda
- 1   teaspoon cinnamon
- 3/4   teaspoon cloves
- 3/4   teaspoon ginger
-    Dash of salt
-    Confectioners' sugar for coating

Preheat the oven to 350°. In a large bowl beat the shortening and sugar until light and fluffy. Beat in the egg and then the molasses. Combine the flour, baking soda, cinnamon, cloves, ginger, and salt and mix well. Add the flour mixture to the shortening mixture and mix well. Drop by rounded tablespoonfuls onto baking sheets. Bake for 10 minutes. While still warm, roll or shake the cookies with confectioners' sugar to coat. Cool slightly and then roll or shake again.

Makes about 50 cookies

Patricia Wick, Queen Mum
Wecandogals, Gowanda, New York

Snicker Cookies

A peanut butter cookie with a candy bar inside. Testers called these "much better than peanut butter kiss cookies."

1   cup granulated sugar
1   cup firmly packed brown sugar
1   cup (2 sticks) butter, softened
1   cup peanut butter
2   teaspoons vanilla extract
2   eggs, beaten
3   cups all-purpose flour
1   teaspoon baking powder
1   teaspoon baking soda
1   (16-ounce) package small
     Snickers candy bars

Preheat the oven to 350°. Combine the sugars and butter in a bowl and beat until fluffy. Beat in the peanut butter, then the vanilla and eggs. In a seperate bowl, combine the flour, baking powder, and baking soda. Add to the batter and mix well. Cut the candy bars into thirds. Wrap the dough around each piece. Arrange on a greased baking sheet. Bake for 12 to 18 minutes. These freeze well if kept covered, if they last that long.

Makes 30 cookies

Audrey Ouhl, Queen Knit Wit
Prairie Dames of Elgin, Elgin, North Dakota

Zucchini Cookies

Another zucchini recipe to the rescue. If you know any super-picky children, you might even consider these for their breakfast.

1   cup shredded zucchini
     (with or without peel)
1   teaspoon baking soda
1   cup sugar
1/2 cup (1 stick) butter, melted
1   egg
2 1/2 cups all-purpose flour
1   teaspoon cinnamon
1/2 teaspoon allspice
1/2 teaspoon salt
1   cup chopped walnuts
1   cup golden raisins

Preheat the oven to 375°. In a bowl combine the zucchini, baking soda, sugar, butter, and egg. Sift together the flour, cinnamon, allspice, and salt and stir into the zucchini mixture. Stir in the walnuts and raisins. Drop by tablespoonfuls onto greased baking sheets. Bake 12 to 15 minutes.

Makes about 48 cookies

Sally Clowers, Lady Mustang Sally
Tennessee Tootsies (TNTs), Tullahoma, Tennessee

Website

WWW.REDHATSOCIETY.COM

The website address above is the key to connection for many women of high spirits. The modern miracle of the Internet has enabled us to share many aspects of our lives with our red-hatted sisters. No matter how far away they may be from us geographically, they are only a few key taps from hearing our latest news and sharing our latest trial or joy.

Our website contains tools to help our members communicate with each other in a myriad of ways. There is our Queen Mother Board, our chat room, and our Events Calendar, just for starters. Once compatible women have found each other and begun sharing, it is very common for meaningful friendships to take root and develop. At our conventions it is not unusual for women who have known each other only in cyberspace to run into each other's arms with cries, such as "How wonderful to meet you in person!"

This is just one more way that the Red Hat Society is changing the lives of many women for the better. The conventional wisdom has always been that one's circle of friends almost always shrinks as one gets older. We women of the Red Hat Society are here to say, "It ain't necessarily so!"

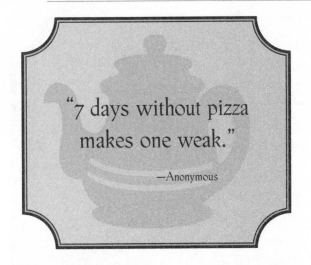

"7 days without pizza makes one weak."

—Anonymous

No-Bake Bars

3   cups Oatie Os cereal
2   cups crisp rice cereal
2   cups dry roasted peanuts
2   cups M & Ms
1   cup light corn syrup
1   cup sugar
1 1/2 cups creamy peanut butter
1   teaspoon vanilla extract

In a large bowl combine the cereals, peanuts, and M & M's. In a saucepan bring the corn syrup and sugar to a boil, stirring frequently. Remove from the heat and stir in the peanut butter and vanilla. Pour over the cereal mixture and toss to coat evenly. Spread in a greased 15 x 10-inch jelly-roll pan. Cool. Cut into 3-inch squares.

Makes 15 bars

Bonita Shaw, Queen Mother
Cardinal Hattitudes, Roseland, Nebraska

Sweet Marie Bars

Another great unbaked cookie, but with a chocolate layer. The recipe is easily doubled; use a 14 x 9-pan. At Christmas, make the bars in a large mold or several small holiday molds.

2   cups crisp rice cereal
1   cup peanuts
1/2 cup firmly packed brown sugar
1/2 cup light corn syrup
1   tablespoon butter or margarine
1/2 cup peanut butter
1   (6 to 8-ounce) package chocolate chips (semisweet or milk chocolate)

Mix the cereal and peanuts in large bowl. Mix the brown sugar, corn syrup, and butter in a 2-quart pot. Bring to a boil. Remove from the heat and add the peanut butter. Mix well. Pour the warm mixture over the cereal mixture and mix well. Press into a greased 8-inch square pan. Melt the chocolate chips and spread evenly on top. Refrigerate for several hours. Cut into bars or squares.

Makes 12 or 16 pieces

Sue Haizelden, Queen Mother
Preemie Donnas of Jacksonville, Jacksonville, Florida

Refrigerator Fruit Cake

It's called a cake, but it's really somewhere between a bar and a candy. This no-bake sweet features the fine flavors of Christmas past. Nearly every tester recommended using a jelly-roll pan or a 13 x 9-inch pan, which makes for easy cutting and serving.

1   cup milk
1   (16-ounce) bag marshmallows
1   (16-ounce) box graham crackers, crushed
2   cups chopped mixed candied fruits
4   cups chopped mixed nuts
1   (16-ounce) bag or box raisins
1   (8-ounce) package dates
1   (8-ounce) bag coconut

In a large saucepan scald the milk and add the marshmallows. Stir until melted. Combine the graham crackers, candied fruits, nuts, raisins, dates, and coconut. Add to the marshmallow mixture. Pack into a greased tube pan or spread in a jelly-roll pan for easy cutting. Chill in the refrigerator at least 4 hours.

Makes 20 servings

Bonnie Adams, Queen Bee
Red Bonnet Sisters, Lakeland, Florida

FOUR

But Wait . . . There's More!

OTHER DESSERTS

One of the most enjoyable (and sometimes the most vexing) aspect of life is the infinite variety of choices life sets before us. Even some of the inconsequential choices can seem weighty at times. Have you ever been confronted with an array of fabulous-looking concoctions displayed on a dessert table? It can be wrenching to try to choose between the 11-layer chocolate torte and the luscious custard-laden bread pudding. Oh, such agony. Perhaps you made a selection and, after a few bites, regretted that you hadn't chosen something else. Maybe that Apricot Souffle à la Mode was even more delicious.

Human nature being what it is, we always want the thing that we don't have, don't we? May we make a suggestion? Take samples of every item that you don't think you can live without and savor each bite. That's the only way I know to eat your cake and have it too. A little bit of a lot of things can be terrific.

Paradise Pudding

*This almond-lemon-cherry dessert recipe makes a large
bowl full, so be sure to have lots of Red Hatters on hand.*

2   (3-ounce) packages lemon gelatin
2   cups boiling water
1/2 cup chopped blanched almonds
12   large marshmallows, cut into 8 pieces each
12   maraschino cherries, quartered
6   macaroons, crushed
1/4 cup sugar
1/4 teaspoon salt
1   cup heavy whipping cream, whipped

In a large bowl combine the lemon gelatin and
boiling water. Refrigerate until thickened, but
not solid. Stir in the almonds, marshmallows,
cherries, macaroons, sugar, and salt. Fold in the
whipped cream. Refrigerate until ready to serve.

Makes 8 to 12 servings

Paula Whitledge, Queen Mum
Ruby and Amethyst Jewels, Bartonville, Illinois

Easy Amaretto Flan

CARAMEL
2   cups sugar
1/4 cup water
1/4 cup sliced almonds, lightly toasted

FILLING
4   ounces softened cream cheese
1/4 cup sugar
2   tablespoons almond liqueur
1 1/2 teaspoons vanilla extract
3   large eggs
1   (12-ounce) can evaporated milk
3/4 cup sweetened condensed milk
1   cup whole milk

For the caramel, combine the sugar and water in
a heavy saucepan. Bring to a boil and cook, stirring, until the sugar is dissolved. Reduce the heat
and boil without stirring until the mixture turns
a rich caramel color. (Watch carefully because
the mixture continues to darken after it is
removed from the heat.) Carefully pour the syrup
into a 9-inch non-metal round flan dish or pie
pan with sides at least 2 inches high. Tilt the pan
to coat with caramel up the sides, and sprinkle
the almonds over the caramel, lightly pressing
them in if necessary.

For the filling, preheat the oven to 300°. With
a food processor or electric mixer, beat together
the cream cheese, sugar, almond liqueur, vanilla,
eggs, and the milks until completely smooth.
Pour into the prepared dish. Place a metal rack
in a large pan big enough to hold the dish, put
the flan dish on the rack, and pour enough hot
water into the pan to reach halfway up the side
of the flan dish.

Bake in the middle of the oven for about 40
minutes and remove when the flan is just set

in the center. Cool on a rack and chill at least 4 hours. To serve, run a thin knife around the sides of the flan dish. Dip the bottom in a pan of very warm water for 10 seconds and then invert the dish onto a serving platter. Garnish with additional toasted sliced almonds if desired.

Makes 8 to 10 servings

Elsie Wollaston, Regina of Recipes
Red Snappers, Vancouver, British Columbia, Canada

Apple Dumplings

A taste of comfort and love, and easy enough that testers say they'd make it again.

1   large Granny Smith apple, peeled, cored, and cut into 8 slices
1   (8-ounce) package refrigerated crescent dinner roll dough
1   plus 3/4 cup sugar
1   tablespoon cinnamon
1/2 cup (1 stick) butter
1 1/4 cups sparkling lemon-lime soda
1   teaspoon vanilla extract
1/2 cup chopped pecans

Preheat the oven to 350°. Place each apple slice on a crescent roll. Combine 3/4 cup sugar with the cinnamon. Sprinkle each apple slice with 1 to 2 tablespoons of the cinnamon sugar. Roll to enclose the apple slice. In a greased baking dish

arrange the rolls fairly close together. Heat the remaining 1 cup sugar, the butter, and lemon-lime soda in the microwave until the butter is melted. Pour over the crescent rolls. Sprinkle with any remaining cinnamon sugar. Sprinkle with the pecans. Bake uncovered for 35 to 45 minutes. Remove from the oven and immediately baste the top of each apple dumpling with the liquid in the baking dish.

Makes 8 dumplings

Edith Keith, Royal Baker
Betty's Bonnets, Fort Worth, Texas

Toasted Almond Dessert

A spirited milkshake. Use a fun glass—parfait glasses, sherbet glasses, or martini glasses—for serving to set the mood.

2   ounces (1/4 cup) Kahlúa
2   ounces (1/4 cup) Amaretto
2/3 to 3/4 of a half gallon vanilla ice cream, softened

Mix the Kahlúa, Amaretto, and ice cream in a blender until the ice cream is smooth. Serve in fancy glasses.

Makes 4 servings

Elaine Jimmerson, Vice Queen
The Valley Girls (of Apopka), Apopka, Florida

Sally's Apple and Nut Bread Pudding

Country-style bread has a coarser, more open texture than refined white bread. It soaks up the custard mixture beautifully and then puffs as it bakes.

1   (1-pound) loaf country white bread, cut into cubes
2   cups sugar
4   eggs
3   cups whole milk
2   teaspoons ground cinnamon
1/2   teaspoon vanilla extract
1   (21-ounce) can premium apple pie filling
1   cup coarsely chopped pecans
1   cup golden raisins
4   tablespoons butter, softened

In a very large bowl gently combine the bread and sugar. In a large bowl beat together the eggs, milk, cinnamon, and vanilla until foamy. Pour the mixture over the bread and toss gently. Cover and refrigerate for 2 hours. Preheat the oven to 350°. Add the pie filling, pecans, raisins, and butter to the bread mixture. Pour into a greased 13 x 9-inch baking dish. Bake for 40 minutes, or until firm. Cool and cut into squares. Serve warm or cold with ice cream or whipped cream.

Makes 6 servings

Sally Carbone, Lady-In-Waiting
Razzle Dazzle Red Hats of Colchester, Colchester, Connecticut

Banana Split Dessert

CRUST
2   cups crumbs from cream-filled chocolate sandwich cookies
1   tablespoon granulated sugar
6   tablespoons butter, melted

FILLING
1   cup (2 sticks) butter, softened
3   cups confectioners' sugar
1   teaspoon vanilla extract
4   large bananas, sliced
1   (20-ounce) can crushed pineapple, drained
1   pint strawberries, washed, sliced
1   (12-ounce) container whipped topping
1   (10-ounce) jar maraschino cherries, stems removed, cherries halved
1   (4-ounce) bag pecan pieces
    Chocolate syrup

For the crust, in a bowl blend the cookie crumbs, sugar, and butter. Press into the bottom of a 13 x 9-inch pan.

For the filling, with a mixer, blend the butter, confectioners' sugar, and vanilla until very fluffy. Spread over the crust. Top the filling with the bananas, following with the pineapple. Then add the strawberries. Cover the fruit with the whipped topping. Top with the cherries and sprinkle with the pecans. Drizzle with the chocolate syrup. Refrigerate until ready to serve.

Makes about 16 servings

Lady Barbara Noakes Aldrich, Queen Mother
Tootee Flutee Red Hats, Omaha, Nebraska

Blueberry Bread Pudding with Caramel Sauce

PUDDING

2 cups milk
1 (8-ounce) container pasteurized egg substitute (such as Egg Beaters)
2/3 cup sugar
1 teaspoon vanilla extract
1/4 teaspoon ground cinnamon
8 slices bread, cubed (about 4 cups)
1 cup fresh or frozen blueberries

CARAMEL SAUCE

1/4 cup milk
14 vanilla caramels

For the pudding, in large bowl blend together the milk, egg substitute, sugar, vanilla, and cinnamon.

Preheat the oven to 350°. Arrange the bread cubes in the bottom of a lightly greased 8-inch-square baking dish. Sprinkle with the blueberries. Pour the egg mixture evenly over the bread mixture. Set the dish in a pan filled with 1 inch of hot water. Bake for 1 hour or until set.

For the caramel sauce, warm the milk and caramels in a small saucepan over low heat until the caramels are melted, stirring frequently. Pour the caramel sauce over the pudding to serve.

Makes 9 servings

Camilla Damiens, Mississippi Lady
Swinging Mississippi Belles, Carriere, Mississippi

Simplified Fruit Cobbler

Forget making pastry—this smart recipe makes its own yummy dough.

1/2 cup all-purpose flour
1/2 cup sugar
1 teaspoon baking powder
   Pinch of salt
1/2 cup milk
4 tablespoons butter or margarine
2 cups sweetened fruit (fresh, defrosted, or canned)
   Whipped cream, custard sauce, or ice cream for serving

Preheat the oven to 350°. In a bowl mix well the flour, sugar, baking powder, and salt. Add the milk. Melt the butter in an 8 or 9-inch-square baking dish. Pour in the batter but do not stir. Top with the fruit but do not stir. Bake for 45 to 50 minutes until light brown. The batter will come to the top to cover the fruit. Serve warm with whipped cream, custard sauce, or ice cream.

Makes 6 to 8 servings

Lola Heldenbrand, Queen
Red Bud Belles, Bethany, Oklahoma

Blueberry Nut Crunch

Something like Dump Cake, but uses fresh blueberries and a little sugar. A little cinnamon is nice added to the sugar and mixed with the berries. Don't worry if it seems a bit liquid when the cooking time is over; the juices thicken as it stands.

1   (20-ounce) can crushed pineapple with juice
4   cups blueberries (fresh or frozen)
1/2   plus 1/4 cup sugar
1   (18-ounce) box yellow cake mix
1/2   cup (1 stick) butter or margarine, melted
1/2   to 1 cup chopped pecans

Preheat the oven to 350°. Mix the pineapple, blueberries and 1/2 cup sugar in a greased 13 x 9-inch pan. (If you like a juicy cobbler, add 1/2 cup water.) Sprinkle the dry cake mix evenly over the fruit. Drizzle the butter over cake mix. Sprinkle the pecans over the butter and the remaining 1/4 cup sugar over the pecans. Bake for 50 to 60 minutes.

Makes 12 servings

Louise Bragg, Duchess Sylvia
Elite Ladies of The Hat, Franklinton, North Carolina

Blueberries and Cream Dessert

Another wonderfully creamy and light dessert that's just irresistible.

CRUST
1   cup all-purpose flour
1/2   cup (1 stick) butter
1   cup chopped pecans

CREAM CHEESE
1   (8-ounce) package cream cheese
1   (8-ounce) container whipped topping
1   cup sugar

BERRY LAYER
3   cups blueberries
1   cup sugar
1/4   plus 1/4 cup water
1/4   cup cornstarch

For the crust, preheat the oven to 350°. Combine the flour, butter, and pecans with a pastry blender or mixer. Mix well and press into a greased 13 x 9-inch baking dish. Bake for about 15 to 20 minutes, or until light brown. Set aside to cool.

For the cream cheese layer, combine the cream cheese, whipped topping, and sugar in a bowl. Stir until well blended. Spread over the cooled first layer.

For the berry layer, cook the blueberries, sugar, and 1/4 cup water over medium heat until soft, about 15 minutes. Combine the cornstarch with the remaining 1/4 cup water and add to the blueberries. Cook until translucent and thickened. Allow the blueberries to cool, and then spread them over the cream cheese layer. Chill until firm.

Makes 10 to 12 servings

Tammy Strickland, Queen Mum Tammy of Osyka
Osyka Red Hat Society, Osyka, Mississippi

Eggnog Flan

Just one word for this big, beautiful dessert: Wow!

CARAMEL
1 1/2 cups sugar
1/2 cup water

CUSTARD
1 quart sweetened condensed milk
1 teaspoon instant coffee granules
2 tablespoons brown sugar
1/4 teaspoon cinnamon
8 large eggs
4 large egg yolks
1 cup plus 2 tablespoons sugar
Violets, nasturtiums, or edible flowers, or selected fresh berries for garnish
Fresh whipped cream

Preheat the oven to 325°.

For the caramel, combine the sugar and water in a medium saucepan. Cook over moderate heat, swirling the pan occasionally, for 12 to 15 minutes, or until the mixture is golden brown and smells like caramel. As it cooks, be sure all the sugar granules are stirred down from the sides of the pan (use a wet pastry brush). Pour the caramel into a 9-inch cake pan or pan large enough to hold the flan ingredients and, holding the pan with an oven glove, swirl it around to generously coat the bottom and sides.

For the custard, combine the sweetened condensed milk, coffee granules, brown sugar, and cinnamon in a large bowl and mix well. In a large mixing bowl gently whisk together the eggs, egg yolks, sugar, and 2 cups of the eggnog mixture to blend, but not until foamy. In a small saucepan, bring the remaining eggnog mixture to a simmer. Whisk this into the egg mixture a little at a time, whisking constantly until it is all incorporated. Pour through a strainer into the prepared cake pan. Place the cake pan inside a large roasting pan and pour very hot tap water into the pan so that it comes halfway up the sides of the cake pan. Bake for about 1 to 1 1/4 hours, or until the center is slightly jiggly but not wavy. Cool to room temperature and then cover with plastic wrap with the plastic gently touching the top of the flan. Refrigerate for at least 3 hours and up to 4 days.

To unmold the custard, run a small sharp knife around the inside edge of the dish several times to loosen it. Invert a round platter over the dish and turn them both over together, shaking the two a little to help release the custard. The caramel sauce will run out around the edges of the platter. Garnish the top of the flan with edible flowers or fresh raspberries, blueberries, and blackberries and freshly whipped cream.

Makes 8 to 12 servings

Eileen Cannon, Princess of Pomp and Circumstance
Crimson Chapeau Club, Tulsa, Oklahoma

Doughnut Bread Pudding with Butter Rum Sauce

For the very, very sweet tooth—testers found it too sweet for the average person, but your crowd may find it just right. If you don't have a Krispy Kreme nearby, use any yeast-raised glazed doughnut. Or do as testers recommend and make it with ordinary bread.

PUDDING
2   dozen Krispy Kreme plain doughnuts
1   (14-ounce) can sweetened condensed milk
2   (14.5-ounce) cans fruit cocktail, drained
2   eggs, beaten
1   (9-ounce) box raisins
     Pinch of salt
1   to 2 teaspoons ground cinnamon

BUTTER RUM SAUCE
1/2   cup (1 stick) butter
1   (1-pound) package confectioners' sugar
     Rum to taste

Preheat the oven to 350°. For the pudding, cut the doughnuts into cubes and combine in a large bowl with the condensed milk, fruit cocktail, eggs, raisins, salt, and cinnamon. Let stand several minutes for doughnuts to absorb the liquid. Pour into a greased 13 x 9-inch baking dish. Bake for 1 hour, or until the center is set, covering with foil if the top seems to be browning before the interior is set.

For the sauce, melt the butter and stir in the confectioners' sugar. Add a little rum for flavor-ing and heat until bubbly. Serve on top of the bread pudding.

Makes 12 servings

Edith Ralls, Vice Queen Mother
Sassy Angels, Houston, Texas

Lamingtons

These little cakes look impressive and are the ideal size for tea.

1   (18-ounce) package yellow cake mix
1   (16-ounce) box confectioners' sugar
1/3   cup unsweetened cocoa powder
1/4   cup (1/2 stick) butter, melted
1/2   cup milk
1   cup coconut
     Whipped cream or ice cream for serving

Bake the cake according to the package directions in an 11 x 7-inch pan. Let cool completely. (Making it a day ahead is best.) Mix together the confectioners' sugar and cocoa. Slowly add the butter and milk and stir until well mixed. Cut the cake into twelve squares and dip each square into the chocolate mixture and then into the coconut until well covered. Serve with whipped cream or ice cream.

Makes 12 servings

Karen Burgess, Queen Mum
Sydney RHS, Gladesville, New South Wales
    Australia

Chocolate Cream Torte Delight

Names for this popular dessert abound—3-Layer Dessert, Better-Than You-Know-What Dessert, Sin Pie, Better Than Robert Redford. A pecan crust is topped with a cream cheese layer then a chocolate layer—simplicity itself. And you want to know a secret? It's delicious frozen, too.

CRUST

1 cup all-purpose flour
1/2 cup (1 stick) butter
1/2 cup chopped nuts

CREAM CHEESE LAYER

1 cup confectioners' sugar
1 (8-ounce) package cream cheese
1 (12-ounce) container whipped topping, divided

CHOCOLATE LAYER

2 1/2 cups milk
1 (5-ounce) package chocolate instant pudding mix
1/2 cup chopped nuts

For the crust, preheat the oven to 350°. In a bowl combine the flour, butter, and nuts with a pastry blender or food processor. Pat into a 13 x 9-inch baking dish. Bake for 10 minutes. Let cool completely.

For the cream cheese layer, beat together in a bowl the confectioners' sugar, cream cheese, and half the whipped topping. Spread over the crust. Chill until slightly firm.

For the chocolate layer, combine the milk and chocolate pudding mix according to the package directions. Spread over the cream cheese layer. Top with remaining whipped topping and chopped nuts.

Makes 10 to 12 servings

Loretta Shank, Queen Mum
Santa Teresa Red Hots, San Jose, California

Cherries in the Snow

Yet another creamy berry dessert. Hatters can't seem to get enough of them.

1 (8-ounce) package cream cheese, softened
1 cup confectioners' sugar
1 (12-ounce) container whipped topping
1 (8-ounce) angel food cake
1 (21-ounce) can cherry pie filling

In a bowl beat the cream cheese and sugar until smooth. Fold in the whipped topping. In a large clear serving bowl layer the cake, cream cheese mixture, and cherry pie filling; then repeat the layers. Chill at least 4 hours.

Makes 10 to 15 servings

Gloria Fletcher, Queennan
First of The Red Hat Mammas, Charlottesville, Virginia

Red Hat Gelatin Trifle

A trifle with a cool gelatin layer. Use frozen berries for this and the gelatin will set faster.

2   (3-ounce) packages strawberry or grape gelatin
1   (16-ounce) package frozen strawberries or mixed berries, thawed and well drained
2   (3³/4-ounce) packages cook-and-serve vanilla pudding
1/2   cup sherry
1   package ladyfingers or pound cake
     Whipped cream, fresh strawberries or raspberries, maraschino cherries for garnish

Prepare the gelatin according to the package directions. Pour into a 4-cup glass serving bowl. Add the drained berries and refrigerate until set. Prepare the vanilla pudding according to the package directions, substituting 1/2 cup sherry for the milk. Cool the pudding until it thickens. Arrange the ladyfingers on top of the gelatin in a spiral pattern. Top with the pudding. Return the bowl to the refrigerator for about 3 hours, or until the pudding is completely set. Before serving, garnish with whipped cream, fresh berries, and/or maraschino cherries.

Makes 10 servings

Caroline Gerstley, Chapterette
Radical Fringe Red Hatters, Santa Monica, California

Dirt Dessert

Versions of this recipe abound. Add gummy worms and any other inspired "garden" choices.

1   (8-ounce) package cream cheese
1/2   cup (1 stick) butter, melted
1   cup confectioners' sugar
3   to 3¹/2 cups milk
2   (5-ounce) packages instant French vanilla pudding mix
1   (12-ounce) container whipped topping
2   (18-ounce) packages chocolate cream sandwich cookies, crumbled
10   to 12 clean, new flowerpots
     Small silk flowers

In a bowl beat the cream cheese, butter, and confectioners' sugar until well mixed. In another bowl combine the milk and pudding mix and mix well. Fold the whipped topping into cream cheese mixture. Combine the pudding mixture and cream cheese mixture.

Set aside 1 cup of the crushed cookies. Line the bottom of each flowerpot with waxed paper, plastic wrap, or aluminum foil. Spoon a layer of cookie crumbs into each pot. Top with a layer of the pudding mixture, then a layer of cookies. Repeat until there are three layers of each or until all ingredients are used. Top with the reserved crushed cookies. Push 3 to 4 small silk flowers into each pot. Refrigerate.

Makes 10 to 12 servings

Pamela Bibbee, Head Rebel
Springfield Globetrotters, Springfield, Ohio

Charlotte Royale Mousse Trifle

2   (7-ounce) packages ladyfingers
1   (16-ounce) package mini marshmallows
1   (6-ounce) package chopped pecans
1/2 (16-ounce) jar maraschino cherries, drained
2   (8-ounce) containers chocolate-flavored whipped topping
2   (10-ounce) packages frozen strawberries, thawed and drained
1   (20-ounce) can pineapple chunks, drained and cut into pieces
1   (11-ounce) can mandarin oranges, drained and cut into pieces
2   envelopes unflavored gelatin

Line a glass trifle bowl with the ladyfingers. Press them down. Reserve a few marshmallows, pecans, and cherries for garnish. In a large bowl combine the remaining marshmallows, pecans, and cherries, the whipped topping, strawberries, pineapple, mandarin oranges, and unflavored gelatin. Spoon half the mixture over the ladyfingers. Top with another row of ladyfingers. Scoop a second row of marshmallow whipped topping mixture onto this. Add the reserved chopped pecans, marshmallows, and cherries to decorate.

Makes 10 to 12 servings

Charlotte Beasley, Queen CharlotteB
Southern Belles of Boca Raton, Boca Raton, Florida

Chocolate Pudding Cake

Pudding cakes seem so magical. Somehow they separate into a soft, sauce-like layer and a chewy cake layer.

CAKE LAYER
3/4 cup granulated sugar
1   cup all-purpose flour
2   tablespoons unsweetened baking cocoa
2   teaspoons baking powder
1/4 teaspoon salt
1/2 cup milk
3   tablespoons butter or margarine, melted
1   teaspoon vanilla extract

SAUCE LAYER
1/2 cup granulated sugar
1/2 cup firmly packed brown sugar
1/4 cup unsweetened baking cocoa
1 1/2 cups water
     Whipped cream or ice cream for serving

For the cake layer, preheat the oven to 350°. Sift the sugar, flour, cocoa, baking powder, and salt into a 9-inch square pan. Stir in the milk, butter, and vanilla. Spread the batter evenly in the pan.

For the sauce layer, combine the sugars with the cocoa in a small bowl. Sprinkle the mixture over the batter. Pour the water over the top. Bake for 40 minutes. Serve with whipped cream or ice cream if desired.

Makes 6 servings

Leah Wright, Lady Winnie
Elite Ladies of The Hat, Franklinton, North Carolina

Funnel Cakes

Country cooks know this goodie from back when, and they know it's best to get 'em while they're hot. A fun group activity and a delight for children.

2²/3   cups all-purpose flour
1/4   cup granulated sugar
2   teaspoons baking powder
1/2   teaspoon salt
2   eggs
2   cups milk
1/2   teaspoon vanilla extract
      Vegetable oil for frying
      Confectioners' sugar for sprinkling

In a large bowl combine the flour, sugar, baking powder, and salt. In another bowl beat the eggs, milk, and vanilla. Add to the dry ingredients and stir just until blended.

Heat 1 inch of oil in a frying pan. Hold your finger over the bottom of a funnel and pour in 1/2 cup of the batter. Holding the funnel over the hot oil, drizzle the batter into the oil. Cook until golden brown, turn and cook the other side. Drain on paper towels and sprinkle with confectioners' sugar.

Makes 5 to 6 servings

Nancy Sharkey, Queen Mum Nanette
The Budding Red Roses of Arizona, Glendale, Arizona

Toffee-Topped Brownie Trifle Delight

What becomes a Hatter most? Her hat, of course, and a big chocolate dessert to share. Declared "quite rich" by testers.

1   (19-ounce) package fudge brownie mix
1/2   cup Kahlua (optional)
3   (4-ounce) packages chocolate instant pudding mix
4   cups milk for pudding
1   (12-ounce) container whipped topping, thawed
6   (1.4-ounce) Heath Bars, crushed

Prepare the brownies according to package directions, using a 13 x 9-inch pan. Poke holes in the top of the baked brownies and pour the Kahlua over them. If not using Kahlua, cool, then crumble the brownies. While the brownies are cooling make the pudding with the milk. (No need to chill the pudding.)

In an attractive clear serving bowl or trifle bowl, lay one-third of the crumbled brownies in the bottom. Top with one-third of the pudding, then one-third of the whipped topping, and then one-third of the crushed Heath Bars. Repeat the layers two more times, ending with Heath Bars. Cover and chill for at least 8 hours.

Makes 15 to 20 servings

Gloria Gauthier, Princess G
Growing Up Gawdy, The Gawdy Girls, Conway, Arkansas

The Cheesecake Dog

At my daughter's house I made two of my mother-in-law's most wonderful pineapple cheesecakes. Yummy, yummy! When transporting them home, I put them on a large cookie tray with a towel over them. My husband put them on the back set of the car, as I came out to the car carrying bags with my puppy on a leash. The puppy jumped into the car to her favorite spot between the two front seats on the floor. I was distracted, looking through my bags for something, and then I remembered the puppy. She wasn't between the seats! Oh, my! Could she?!

Yes, there she was on the back seat, prancing all over my cheesecakes and licking her lips. Yummy, yummy! So you can imagine what happened to those beautiful pineapple cheesecakes. They turned to mush, but the puppy thought they were delicious. We laughed and laughed. It was a funny scene.

Doris Shaw
Visa Queen
The Red Fedora Flora Doras of Gilbert,
Arizona
Mesa, Arizona

Italian Cheesecake

1   (two-crust) piecrust
1 1/2 pounds ricotta cheese
2 1/2 tablespoons all-purpose flour
4   ounces semisweet chocolate chips
3   eggs
3/4   cup sugar
1 1/2 teaspoons orange rind
4   tablespoons citron (optional)

Preheat the oven to 400°. Line a pie plate with 1 piecrust. In a large bowl mix the ricotta, flour, chocolate chips, eggs, sugar, orange rind, and citron (if using). Pour into the piecrust. Cover with the remaining piecrust. Cut steam vents in the top crust. Bake for 15 minutes, and then reduce the heat to 300°. Bake for another 55 minutes.

Makes 8 servings

Mary Chiocchi, Queen Mother
Red Hat Rebels, Port Charlotte, Florida

Cassis & White Chocolate Cheesecake

A soft, soft cheesecake with the bewitching fragrance of cassis.

CRUST
2   cups vanilla wafer crumbs (1 box)

2   tablespoons sugar

1/2 cup (1 stick) unsalted butter, melted

FILLING
2   (16-ounce) packages cream cheese, at room temperature

1   cup sugar

4   ounces (3/4 cup) grated white chocolate

3   tablespoons crème de cassis

4   large eggs

TOPPING
2   cups (1 pint) sour cream

1/4 cup sugar

1   teaspoon pure vanilla extract

For the crust, combine the crumbs and sugar in a mixing bowl. Add the melted butter, mixing with a fork to distribute well. Press onto the bottom of and halfway up the sides of an ungreased 9-inch springform pan (the top edge need not be even).

For the filling, preheat the oven to 350°, and set the rack one-third up from the bottom. In a large bowl of an electric mixer cream the softened cream cheese until it is very smooth. Gradually beat in the sugar, then the grated white chocolate and cassis, beating just until well blended. Beat in the eggs, one at a time, and continue beating until smooth. Pour the filling into the crust. Tap the pan lightly on the counter two to three times to eliminate any large air bubbles. Bake 40 to 45 minutes. (The edge may have a few cracks, and the center of the filling will not appear set). Remove from the oven, and place the pan on a wire rack away from drafts to cool for 10 minutes. Do not turn off the oven.

For the topping, combine the sour cream, sugar, and vanilla in a small mixing bowl. Stir with a spoon until blended. Pour over the slightly cooled filling, and spread evenly to the edges. Return the cheesecake to the oven and bake 10 minutes longer. The topping will quiver but should appear set. Return the baked cheesecake to the wire rack and allow to cool completely. Cover the pan loosely with foil; refrigerate for at least 12 hours before serving.

To serve, carefully remove the sides of the pan, cut the cake into wedges, and serve immediately. The cheesecake is creamy-soft in its chilled state.

Makes 12 servings

Ann Hofer, Queen
Kootenay Red Belles, Castlegar, British Columbia, Canada

Peanut Butter Cheesecake

CRUST
2   tablespoons melted peanut butter

1/4 cup (1/2 stick) butter or margarine, melted

1/4 cup granulated sugar

3   cups graham cracker crumbs

FILLING

3   (8-ounce) packages cream cheese, softened

1   cup creamy peanut butter

1/2 cup firmly packed dark brown sugar

2   teaspoons vanilla extract

1/3 cup lemon juice

1   (14-ounce) can sweetened condensed milk

1   (12-ounce) container whipped topping

2   tablespoons peanuts for garnish (if desired)

For the crust, combine the melted peanut butter, butter, sugar, and graham cracker crumbs. Mix well to make sure all the crumbs are moistened, and then line two 8-inch pie pans with the mixture. Refrigerate while you prepare the other ingredients.

For the filling, in a large mixing bowl beat the cream cheese. Blend in the peanut butter, brown sugar, vanilla, and lemon juice and mix very well. Beat in the sweetened condensed milk and mix for several minutes, scraping the sides of the bowl. Then carefully fold in the whipped topping. Pour the mixture into the crusts and smooth the top. If desired, you may garnish with some graham cracker crumbs or chopped peanuts. Chill for at least 3 hours before serving.

Makes 8 servings

Patricia Macomber, Queen Trish
Tickled Pink, Hertford, North Carolina

No-Need-to-Share Individual Cheesecakes

Everyone gets her own. Use foil bake cups for a festive presentation.

12   chocolate-filled vanilla sandwich cookies

2   (8-ounce) packages cream cheese

1/2   cup sugar

1 1/4 teaspoons vanilla extract

2   eggs

      Red sugar sprinkles

Preheat the oven to 325°. Split the cookies, keeping the filling on one half. Line a muffin pan with foil baking cups. Arrange the filling-covered cookie halves in the baking cups, filling side up.

In a medium mixing bowl beat the cream cheese, sugar, and vanilla until smooth and fluffy. Beat in the eggs just until well mixed. Spoon about 1/4 cup of the cream cheese mixture into each baking cup. Sprinkle red sugar sprinkles on top or crush the remaining cookies and sprinkle them over the cream cheese mixture.

Place the muffin pan in a larger pan and add about 1 inch water. Bake, uncovered, for about 25 minutes, or until set.

Makes 12 single cheesecakes

Paula Rae Espy, Red Hat Accountess
Red Hot River Babes, Burlington, Iowa

Fudge Rum Cheesecake

Six ounces of chocolate makes this definitely a sweet for those who like rich and chocolaty desserts.

CRUST
1 1/4 cups graham cracker crumbs
2   tablespoons sugar
1/4   cup (1/2 stick) butter, melted

FILLING
6   ounces bittersweet baking chocolate
1/4   cup dark rum
2   (8-ounce) packages cream cheese
3/4   cup sugar
1/2   cup sour cream
1   tablespoon vanilla extract
4   large eggs

For the crust, mix the graham cracker crumbs, sugar, and butter. Pat into the bottom of a 10-inch springform pan. Chill.

For the filling, melt the chocolate with the rum over low heat. Beat the cream cheese until fluffy. Gradually beat in the sugar, sour cream, and vanilla. Add the eggs, one at a time. Mix until smooth.

Preheat the oven to 350°. Pour a generous cup of the batter into another bowl and set aside. Mix the remaining batter with the chocolate mixture until smooth. Fill the prepared springform pan with the chocolate batter. Gently pour the plain batter over the top and swirl with a fork for a marble effect. Bake for 50 minutes.

Cool to room temperature and remove the rim of the pan. Chill overnight for flavors to blend.

Makes 12 servings

JoEllen Smith, Queen Mum
Scarlett Darlings, Clearwater, Florida

Classic Cheesecake

As every Red Hatter knows, it's tough to do better than a time-tested classic.

CRUST
1 1/2   cups crushed graham crackers
1/2   cup (1 stick) butter, melted
1/2   cup sugar

FILLING
1   pound cream cheese
1/2   cup sugar
3   eggs
1   teaspoon vanilla extract

TOPPING
1   pint sour cream
1/4   cup sugar
1   teaspoon vanilla extract

Preheat the oven to 350°. For the crust, mix the graham crackers, butter, and sugar in a small bowl. Press the mixture into the bottom of a 13 x 9-inch pan.

For the filling, beat the cream cheese, sugar, eggs, and vanilla in a large bowl until smooth.

Pour the filling into the crust. Bake for 20 minutes. Remove from the oven and cool for 10 minutes.

For the topping, mix the sour cream, sugar, and vanilla and pour over the filling. Bake another 10 minutes. Cool and serve.

Makes 15 servings

Marland Cannella, Chapter Instigator
Falls–Overfield Scarlet Sages Injoying Lotsa Silliness
(FOSSILS), Falls, Pennsylvania

Dessert Cheese Ball

Great for holiday parties, and a real conversation piece. French vanilla pudding gives it a golden glow, but vanilla will do.

2   (8-ounce) packages cream cheese
1   (3.4-ounce) package French vanilla instant pudding mix
1   (14-ounce) can fruit cocktail, drained
    Chopped nuts for garnish
    Maraschino cherries for garnish
    Cinnamon Crisps, sugar cookies, graham crackers for dipping

In a bowl combine the cream cheese and pudding mix and mix well. Stir in the drained fruit cocktail. Form the mixture into 1 large ball or 2 small balls. Roll or press nuts or cherries on the ball(s), if desired. Serve with Cinnamon Crisps, sugar cookies, or graham crackers. (My personal favorite is Cinnamon Crisps.)

Makes 8 to 12 servings

Joyce Killett, Queen Mother
Spiffy with Hattitude, Sykesville, Maryland

Fruit and Cream Cooler

Light, creamy, and slightly tangy, this is nice after a heavy meal. (And, of course, it has a touch of chocolate.)

1   (12-ounce) container whipped topping, thawed
1   cup buttermilk
1   (5-ounce) package instant vanilla pudding mix
1   (11-ounce) can mandarin orange segments, drained
1   (16-ounce) can crushed pineapple, drained
1/2 (11-ounce) package fudge-stripe cookies

In a bowl combine the whipped topping, buttermilk, and pudding mix and mix well. Add the oranges and pineapple and mix well. Refrigerate until thoroughly chilled. (May be prepared the day before serving.) Just before serving, break up the fudge-stripe cookies and stir them in. Serve and sit back and listen to the raves.

Makes 8 servings

Nancy Ellis, Queen Mother
Desert Flowers, Palm Desert, California

French Cream

Something like Coeur à la Crème, a lightly sweet French dessert course served with light sugar cookies, butter cookies, or with a topping of sweetened fruit. It's traditionally made in a heart-shaped ("coeur") mold. Serve as a dip or as a pudding.

CREAM

1 (8-ounce) carton sour cream
1 cup whipping cream
3/4 cup sugar
1 envelope unflavored gelatin
1/4 cup boiling water
1 (8-ounce) package cream cheese, softened
1/2 teaspoon vanilla extract

FROSTED GRAPES

Small bunches clean dry grapes on stems
1 egg white, beaten
Sugar

For the cream, combine the sour cream and whipping cream in a medium saucepan, and beat at medium speed until blended. Gradually add the sugar, beat well, and then cook over low heat until warm. Dissolve the gelatin in boiling water. Add to the sour cream mixture and remove from the heat. Beat the cream cheese with an electric mixer until light and fluffy. Add the sour cream mixture and vanilla, beating until smooth. Pour lightly into an oiled 4-cup mold. Chill until firm. Unmold onto a platter.

For the grapes, dip them into the beaten egg white. Coat with sugar. Set on a rack to dry at room temperature. Use for garnishing the French Cream.

Makes 8 servings

Note: Grapes are for decorative purposes only!

Dale Bullock, Mini Paws
The Hummingbirds, Glen Allen, Virginia

Creamy Cream Puffs

For a quick filling, prepare instant pudding using whipped topping for a portion of the milk.

CREAM PUFFS

1/2 cup (1 stick) butter
1 cup boiling water
1 cup self-rising flour
4 eggs
Prepared pudding
Whipped topping

CHOCOLATE GLAZE

2 tablespoons butter
2 tablespoons unsweetened cocoa powder
1/4 cup heavy whipping cream
1 cup confectioners' sugar
1 teaspoon vanilla extract

Preheat the oven to 375°. For the cream puffs, melt the butter in a saucepan over medium heat by pouring the boiling water over it. Bring back to a boil, remove from the heat, and stir in the flour all at once, mixing quickly. The mixture will form a ball. Let stand a couple of minutes to cool. Add the eggs, one at a time, mixing well after each addition (a whisk or a fork works best). Drop by large heaping tablespoonfuls onto a greased baking sheet, forming 12 mounds. Bake for 45 minutes. Cool. Cut off the top one-fourth of each puff and fill the puff with prepared pudding, whipped topping, or other cream filling.

For the chocolate glaze, melt the butter in a saucepan. Stir in the cocoa and cream and heat but do not boil. Remove from the heat and stir in confectioners' sugar and vanilla. Drizzle over the cream puffs.

Makes 12 servings

Brenda Donovan, Princess Brenda
Northern Maine Classie Lassies, Presque Isle, Maine

Red Hat Cranberry Pudding Cake with Butter Sauce

Testers gave this "thumbs up," calling it "a winner." Surprise! You can also make this cake with dried cranberries.

CAKE
- 3 cups all-purpose flour
- 3 3/4 teaspoons baking powder
- 1 1/2 cups granulated sugar
- 2 large eggs
- 1 cup whole milk (or half-and-half)
- 4 1/2 tablespoons butter, melted
- 3 cups fresh cranberries

BUTTER SAUCE
- 1 cup firmly packed brown sugar
- 1 tablespoon cornstarch
- 3/4 cup (1 1/2 sticks) butter
- 3/4 cup heavy cream
- Whipped cream for garnish

Preheat the oven to 350°. Grease and flour a 13 x 9-inch pan.

For the cake, combine the flour, baking powder, and sugar in a large bowl. Add the eggs, milk, and butter and mix well. Fold in the cranberries. Batter will be heavy and thick. Spoon into the prepared pan. Bake for 40 to 45 minutes, or until the top appears lightly browned.

For the butter sauce, combine the brown sugar, cornstarch, butter, and cream in a 2-quart saucepan while the cake is baking. Bring to a boil over medium heat, stirring occasionally. Boil for 2 minutes and remove from the heat.

Cut the cake into 20 pieces. Serve the cake in a small bowl topped with warm butter sauce (1 to 2 tablespoons) over each piece. Top with whipped cream or whipped topping.

Makes 20 servings

Linda Glenn, FQM, Queen Linda Glenn, Mistress of Mischief and Merriment
Rowdy Red Hat Mamas of N.W. Wisconsin, Luck, Wisconsin

Cranberry Apple Crisp

A sweet apple crisp, "tarted up" with (what else?) cranberries.

2	cups fresh or thawed cranberries
2	cups chopped, peeled apples
1/2	cup granulated sugar
1	cup all-purpose flour
3/4	cup firmly packed brown sugar
1/2	cup quick-cooking oats
1/2	cup (1 stick) butter, melted

Preheat the oven to 350°. In a bowl toss the cranberries, apples, and sugar. Spoon into a greased 8-inch square baking pan. Combine the flour, brown sugar, oats, and butter. Sprinkle over the cranberry mixture. Bake for 35 minutes or until the topping has browned and the fruit is tender. Serve with whipped cream or ice cream.

Makes 4 to 6 servings

Linda Beer, Queen 'Amma
Red Hot Super Chicks, Bethany, Ontario, Canada

Baked Custard with Caramel Sauce

Homey and comforting. On a cold night, indulge yourself with a dinner of just custard.

3/4	cup firmly packed brown sugar
4	cups milk
2	tablespoons rum or flavored liqueur (optional)
6	slightly beaten eggs
1/4	teaspoon salt
1	teaspoon vanilla extract

Sprinkle the brown sugar in the bottom of a 2-quart glass casserole. In a saucepan bring the milk and rum, if using, nearly to a boil, stirring. Cool slightly. Preheat the oven to 350°. Beat the eggs in a large bowl. Gradually stir the hot milk into the eggs, beating constantly. Stir in the salt and vanilla. Pour the mix over the brown sugar. Do not stir. Place the casserole in a larger pan and pour in enough water to rise about 1 to 2 inches up the side of the glass dish. Bake for about 1 hour, or until a knife inserted in the custard comes out clean.

Makes 6 to 8 servings

Mary Woolsey, Marquisa De Martini
RHS Red Queens, Canoga Park, California

"A balanced diet
is a cookie
in each hand."

—Anonymous

Foundation Ice Cream

Homemade ice cream is the classic summer project, either with friends in the evening or with kids to while away a hot afternoon.

2/3 cup sugar
1 tablespoon all-purpose flour
   Dash of salt
2 cups milk, scalded
1 egg or 2 egg yolks
1 teaspoon vanilla extract
1 pint heavy whipping cream, whipped

Combine the sugar, flour, and salt in a saucepan. Add the milk and stir. Cook over medium-low heat, stirring, for 15 minutes, or until thickened. Beat the egg or yolks and add to the milk mixture, stirring constantly until cooked. Remove the pan from the heat and add the vanilla. Pour into a bowl and cool. Place the mix in a freezer and when half frozen, add the whipped cream and any of the variations described below. Freeze until firm.

Makes 6 servings

VARIATIONS:

Fruit Ice Cream: Add 1 cup puréed or crushed fruit when the ice cream mixture is partly frozen.

Chocolate Ice Cream: Increase the sugar to 1 cup. Add 2 squares chipped bittersweet or sweet chocolate to the scalded milk. Mix well.

Nut Ice Cream: Add 3/4 cup chopped pecans when the ice cream mixture is half frozen.

Caramel Ice Cream: Increase the sugar to 1 cup and caramelize the sugar in a saucepan. Pour into the scalded milk, and cook until melted.

Peanut Brittle Ice Cream: Reduce the sugar to 1/4 cup. Add 1 cup chopped peanut brittle when the ice cream mixture is partially frozen.

Vickie Robb, FQM Socialitist
Friends of The Red Hatters, Springville, Indiana

Heavenly Ice Cream Dessert

Very fast and looks like a lot more effort than it actually requires.

2 (24-ounce) boxes ice cream sandwiches
2 (12-ounce) jars caramel, butterscotch, or fudge ice cream topping
1 (16-ounce) container whipped topping
   Crushed toffee bits

In a 13 x 9-inch pan arrange 1 layer of ice cream sandwiches followed by 1 jar of ice cream topping. Top with the remaining ice cream sandwiches followed by the remaining jar of ice cream topping. Spread the whipped topping on the top, and then sprinkle with crushed toffee bits. Freeze until ready to serve.

Makes 20 servings

Marcia Taddey, Queen
Damsels in Dis–Order, West Allis, Wisconsin

Ice Cream Crunch Torte

If the idea of a sweet, salty, creamy dessert appeals to you, try Ice Cream Crunch Torte.

- 68 round buttery crackers
- 1/2 cup (1 stick) butter, melted
- 4 tablespoons sugar
- 2 (5-ounce) packages instant vanilla pudding mix
- 2 cups milk
- 1 quart vanilla ice cream, melted
- 1 (8-ounce) container whipped topping

With a rolling pin, crush the crackers to fine crumbs. In a bowl mix the crackers with the butter and sugar. Put half the mixture into a 13 x 9-inch pan, pressing it down firmly. Beat the pudding mix and milk until thick. Add the ice cream and beat until thick. Pour into the crust. Cover with the whipped topping. Finally, cover with the remaining half of the cracker mixture. Store in the refrigerator. May be prepared a day in advance.

Makes 15 to 20 servings

Linda Wheeler, Scrapbooker
Tazwell Scarlett Ladies, Creve Coeur, Illinois

Kiwi-Banana Kuchen

Serve this desert on a pretty pedestal cake stand.

- 1/2 cup (1 stick) butter, softened
- 1/4 cup sugar
- 1 teaspoon vanilla extract
- 1 egg
- 1 cup sifted all-purpose flour
- 1/2 teaspoon baking powder
- 2 kiwifruit, peeled and sliced
- 1 banana, peeled and sliced
- 2 tablespoons sugar
- 1 teaspoon cinnamon

Preheat the oven to 350°. Grease a 9-inch springform pan and sprinkle with a little flour. In a bowl beat the butter, sugar, vanilla, and egg until smooth. Add the sifted flour and baking powder and mix well. Spread the dough over the bottom of the prepared pan. Arrange the slices of kiwifruit and banana over the dough. Sprinkle with the sugar and cinnamon.

Bake for 35 minutes. Cool for 5 minutes. Remove the side of the pan.

Makes 10 servings

Roxie Freitas, Sequin Butterfly
Big Island Beauties, Kailua-Kona, Hawaii

Lemon Lush

Lemon pairs with a cream layer and a pastry layer.

CRUST
- 1 cup all-purpose flour
- 5 tablespoons butter, softened
- 1/2 cup finely chopped walnuts or pecans

Mistaken Identity

As the hostess of one of our monthly Red Hat luncheons, I had wrapped squares of strawberry scented soap (made by my son) in red tissue paper with purple ribbon so that they looked like little wrapped presents. I gave one to each of the ladies at the luncheon as a party favor. Before I got around to explaining that they were homemade soap squares, one lady unwrapped hers and took a bite of what looked to her like a creamy, white chocolate square. Talk about washing your mouth out with soap. It reminded me of my grandmother telling me what she'd do to me if I wasn't a "good" little girl. The gal is a really good friend with a wonderful sense of humor, and we all had a good laugh about it.

Carol Hendon,
Queen
Red Toppers
Katy, Texas

CREAM LAYER
1   (8-ounce) package cream cheese, softened
1   cup confectioners' sugar
1   (16-ounce) container whipped topping, divided

LEMON LAYER
2   (3-ounce) packages lemon instant pudding mix
3   cups cold milk

Preheat the oven to 350°. For the crust, combine the flour, butter, and nuts and stir until the mixture is crumbly. Pat into the bottom of an 11 x 9-inch pan. Bake for 10 minutes. Cool.

For the cream layer, combine the cream cheese, confectioners' sugar, and 1 cup of the whipped topping. (The remaining topping is for the top of the Lemon Lush.) Spread on top of the cooled crust and chill for 5 minutes.

For the lemon layer, combine the pudding mix with the cold milk. Let it begin to thicken. Pour the pudding on top of the cream cheese mixture. Chill for another 5 minutes.

Spread the remaining whipped topping on top of the pudding. Chill for at least 1 hour. Serve in small pieces because it is rich.

Makes 12 to 16 servings

Gayle Rudd, Recipe Diva
Red Chicks, Springville, Alabama

Frosty Fruit Pops

Make this kid-pleaser in paper drinking cups with wooden sticks.

3   cups grape juice or orange juice
1   (14-ounce) can sweetened condensed milk
1/4 cup lemon juice

In a large bowl stir together the juice, condensed milk, and lemon juice. Pour into paper cups. Cover each cup with foil. Make a small hole in the center of the foil with a knife. Insert a wooden stick or plastic spoon into each cup through the hole. Freeze until firm. To serve, remove the foil and tear off the paper.

Makes 10 servings

Nancy Mans, Purple Participant
Sassy Classy Ladies, Roselle, Illinois

Quick Lemon Mousse

For theme gatherings, make the mousse in tea cups.

1   envelope unflavored gelatin
1   (12-ounce) can frozen lemonade or limeade concentrate, divided
1   cup boiling water
    Zest of 1 lemon or lime
1   cup heavy whipping cream, divided

In a large bowl sprinkle the gelatin over 1/2 cup of the concentrate. Let stand 5 minutes. Pour the boiling water over the gelatin and stir to dissolve. Add the lemon zest and the remaining concentrate. Refrigerate, stirring every 20 minutes, for 40 to 60 minutes until the mixture has thickened to the consistency of raw egg whites. Whip the cream to soft peaks. Add one-third of the whipped cream to the mixture and whisk in thoroughly to lighten. Fold in the remaining

whipped cream until no white streaks remain. Pour into serving dishes or a serving bowl. Refrigerate for at least 6 hours.

Makes 6 servings

Karen Ridout, Duchess of Dessert
Red Hat Dollies of Calgary, Calgary, Alberta, Canada

Fluffy Lime Cantaloupe

1   medium cantaloupe
3/4 cup boiling water
1   (3-ounce) package lime gelatin
1/2 cup cold orange juice
1/2 cup thawed whipped topping
    Whipped topping and lime zest for garnish

Cut the cantaloupe into halves, removing the seeds. Scoop out the melon, leaving 1-inch melon inside the shell. Dice the scooped-out melon; drain well. Cut a thin slice from the bottom of each melon half to allow it to stand upright. In a bowl stir the water into the gelatin until it dissolves. Stir in the orange juice. Refrigerate until slightly thickened. Gently stir in the whipped topping. Stir in the reserved diced melon. Pour this mixture into the melon halves. Refrigerate until firm. Cut into wedges. Lay a slice of melon on a plate of lettuce, and top with a spoonful of whipped topping and lime zest.

Makes 8 servings

Lorraine Sayas, Queen Mother Gem
Tidewaters Gems, Virginia Beach, Virginia

Fruit Pizza

Not for dinner, naturally, but we won't tell if you don't. Berries are a nice addition to the fruit.

1   (18-ounce) tube refrigerated sugar cookie dough
1   (8-ounce) package cream cheese, softened
1/3 cup sugar
1   tablespoon vanilla extract
2   medium firm bananas, sliced
2   teaspoons lemon juice
1   (20-ounce) can pineapple chunks, drained
1   pint fresh strawberries, halved
1   (11-ounce) can mandarin oranges, drained
1/3 cup orange marmalade
1   tablespoon water

Preheat the oven to 375°. Grease a 14-inch pizza pan and press the cookie dough onto it in a 12-inch circle. Bake for 10 to 12 minutes or until lightly browned. Cool completely on a wire rack.

In a mixing bowl beat the cream cheese, sugar, and vanilla until smooth. Spread over the cooled cookie crust. Toss the bananas with the lemon juice. Arrange the bananas, pineapple, strawberries, and oranges over the cream cheese mixture. Refrigerate for 1 hour. Combine the marmalade and water and drizzle over the fruit.

Makes 12 to 14 servings

Bonnie Tinch, Red Hatter
Cathie's Cuties, Cookeville, Tennessee

Grapes and Cream

Some ladies call this a salad, but it's creamy, sweet, and loaded with goodies; so we put it here with the desserts.

GRAPES

1	(8-ounce) package cream cheese, softened
1	(8-ounce) carton sour cream
1/2	cup granulated sugar
1	teaspoon vanilla extract
2	pounds white seedless grapes
2	pounds red seedless grapes

TOPPING

1/2	cup firmly packed brown sugar
1/2	cup pecans
3	large Butterfinger bars, crushed

For the grapes, beat together with an electric mixer the cream cheese, sour cream, sugar, and vanilla. Lightly fold in the grapes and pour into a deep 2-quart bowl.

For the topping, combine the brown sugar, pecans, and Butterfingers in a medium bowl. Sprinkle the mixture thickly over the top of the grape mixture. Refrigerate until completely chilled.

Makes 12 servings

Sheila Childress, Anna Belle
Bonnett Belles of Blountville, Blountville, Tennessee

Nutty Baklava

An ancient treat that's absolutely delicious with coffee and tea.

4 1/2	cups finely chopped walnuts
1/2	cup sugar
1 1/2	teaspoons cinnamon
1	pound phyllo pastry dough
1	cup (2 sticks) butter or margarine, melted
1	cup unseasoned breadcrumbs
1	cup honey

Preheat the oven to 300°. Grease a 13 x 9-inch pan.

In a large bowl mix the nuts, sugar, and cinnamon. Fit 1 sheet of pastry into the prepared pan, extending up the sides of the pan. Brush with butter and sprinkle with breadcrumbs. Repeat for five layers. Then sprinkle with 1 cup of the nut mixture.

Cut the rest of the phyllo into 13 x 9-inch rectangles. Repeat the layering process four more times. It is fine to overlap the narrow pieces of phyllo. Arrange the remaining phyllo on top of the final nut layer. With a sharp knife, trim any pastry extending over the top or edge. With the knife, cut a diamond pattern halfway down through all layers. Bake for 1 hour 15 minutes, or until the top layer is golden brown.

Heat the honey until hot but not boiling.

Spoon over the hot baklava. Cool at least 1 hour. Finish cutting through the layers before serving.

Makes 12 servings

Mary McGee, Queenie
Scarlet Women of Portsmouth, Portsmouth, New Hampshire

Mini Hamburger Dessert

1/4   cup flaked coconut
      A few drops of green food coloring
1   tube red decorator frosting
48   vanilla wafers
24   miniature peppermint patties (be sure to use chocolate-covered peppermint patties)
1   tube yellow decorator frosting

Put the coconut into a zip-top bag and add just about three drops of the green food coloring. Close the bag and shake until the coconut is a nice lettuce-green color. Place a dab of red frosting on the flat side of 1 vanilla wafer. Arrange a peppermint patty on top of the red frosting. Place a dab of yellow frosting on the flat side of another vanilla wafer. Add a small pinch of green coconut on the yellow frosting. Sandwich the yellow half onto the peppermint patty. If it does not stick well, add a drop or two more yellow frosting. Repeat the process until you have assembled all 24 "hamburgers."

Makes 24 "hamburgers"

Dee Kozlowski, Duchess of Hat
Scarlett Harlotts, Edgewood, Maryland

"Help me keep the kitchen clean —eat out."

—Anonymous

Baked Peaches

6   canned peach halves with juice
2   teaspoons granulated sugar
2   teaspoons brown sugar
1   teaspoon lemon juice
1/2   cup coconut (1/4 cup nuts may be substituted)

Preheat the oven to 350°. Drain the juice from the peaches into a saucepan. Add the sugars and lemon juice to the peach juice; boil 3 minutes. Arrange the peach halves in a 6-inch baking dish. Pour the peach juice mixture over them. Bake for 15 minutes. Sprinkle the coconut (or nuts) on the peaches during the last 3 minutes of baking.

Makes 6 servings

Mary Yarbrough, Lady Lucille
Elite Ladies of The Hat, Franklinton, North Carolina

Lazy Peach Party Dessert

CRUST
1 1/2 cups all-purpose flour
1/4 cup sugar
3/4 cup (1 1/2 sticks) butter

GLAZE
2 cups sugar
1/4 cup cornstarch
2 cups water
2 (3-ounce) boxes peach gelatin

FILLING
16 to 20 peaches

Preheat the oven to 350°. For the crust, mix the flour and sugar together. Cut in the butter and mix until pea size. Pat into a 13 x 9-inch pan. Bake 10 to 15 minutes at 350°. Cool.

For the glaze, combine the sugar, cornstarch, and water in a saucepan over medium heat and cook until thickened. Add the peach gelatin. Stir until dissolved and let cool.

For the filling, blanch the peaches. Peel and slice 2 peaches into the glaze and the remaining peaches onto the cooled crust. Pour the cooled glaze over the peaches on the crust and refrigerate. If possible, don't put a lid on until completely cooled or condensation forms on the lid and makes it runny and the crust soggy.

Makes 12 to 18 servings

Pat Kiebach, Princess
Sweet T.A.R.T.S., Harrisburg, South Dakota

Christmas Plum Duff

2 cups self-rising flour
1 cup all-purpose flour
Pinch of salt
1 1/2 cups sugar
1 cup sultanas
1 cup currants
1/2 teaspoon baking soda
1 teaspoon butter melted in 1 cup boiling water
2 tablespoons plum jam
1 egg, beaten

Sift the flours and salt into a bowl. Add the sugar and fruits and mix well. Add the baking soda, butter/water, and jam and mix. Add the egg (and a little milk if necessary) and beat to make a fairly stiff consistency. Carefully spoon into a floured pudding cloth or oiled pudding basin and place into a large pot of boiling water. Simmer for 2 to 2 1/2 hours. Don't allow to boil dry.

Makes 10 generous servings

Colleen Atkinson, Countess
Red Hat Dames Down Under, Adelaide, Australia

Praline Pumpkin Torte

GLAZE
3/4 cup packed brown sugar
5 tablespoons butter (no substitute)
3 tablespoons whipping cream
3/4 cup chopped pecans

CAKE

4	eggs
1 2/3	cups granulated sugar
1	cup canola oil
2	cups cooked or canned pumpkin (not the pumpkin pie mix)
1/4	teaspoon vanilla extract
2	cups all-purpose flour
2	teaspoons baking powder
2	teaspoons pumpkin pie spice
1	teaspoon baking soda
1	teaspoon salt

TOPPING

1 3/4	cups whipping cream
1/4	teaspoon vanilla extract
1/4	cup confectioners' sugar
	Additional pecans

Preheat the oven to 350°. For the glaze, combine the brown sugar, butter, and cream in a heavy saucepan. Cook and stir over low heat until the sugar is dissolved. Pour into two well-greased 9-inch round baking pans. Sprinkle with the pecans; cool.

For the cake, beat the eggs, sugar, and oil in a mixing bowl. Add the pumpkin and vanilla. Combine the flour, baking powder, pie spice, baking soda, and salt and add to the pumpkin mixture. Beat just until blended. Carefully spoon the cake mixture over the brown sugar mixture in the pans. Bake for 30 to 35 minutes, or until a toothpick inserted near the center comes out clean. Cool for 5 minutes; remove from the pans to wire racks to cool completely. Arrange one cake layer, praline side up, on a serving plate.

For the topping, beat the cream in a mixing bowl until soft peaks form. Beat in the vanilla and confectioners' sugar. Spread two-thirds of the topping over the cake layer. Top with the second cake layer and remaining whipped cream. Sprinkle with additional pecans if desired. Store in the refrigerator.

Makes 12 to 14 servings

Judy Aremka, Queen Mum of Cooking
Purple & Proud, Kenosha, Wisconsin

Pineapple Upside-Down Biscuits

1/2	cup firmly packed brown sugar
1	(10-ounce) can crushed pineapple, drain and reserve liquid
1/4	cup (1/2 stick) butter
10	red cherries
1	(10-count) can biscuits

Preheat the oven to 350°. Thoroughly mix together the sugar, pineapple, and butter. Pour the pineapple mixture into a 12-cup muffin pan that has been sprayed with nonstick cooking spray, filling 10 of the cups. Put one red cherry in the center of each muffin cup and push it all the way to the bottom. Put one biscuit on top of each muffin cup. Pour a small amount of reserved pineapple juice on top of each biscuit. Bake for 10 to 12 minutes.

Makes 10 biscuits

Barbara Simpson, Assistant Queen Mother
Highbanks Hatters, DeBary, Florida

Pistachio Delight Torte

1 1/2 cups all-purpose flour
3/4 cup (1 1/2 sticks) butter, melted
3/4 cup chopped walnuts
1 (8-ounce) package cream cheese, softened
1 cup confectioners' sugar
2 (8-ounce) containers whipped topping
3 cups milk
2 (3.4-ounce) boxes pistachio instant pudding mix

Preheat the oven to 350°. Mix the flour, butter, and walnuts together and pat into a 13 x 9-inch cake pan. Bake for 15 to 20 minutes, or until golden brown. Blend the cream cheese, confectioners' sugar, and 1 container whipped topping and mix well. Pour the cream cheese mixture over the cool crust. Combine the milk and pudding mix and stir until thick. Pour the pudding mixture over the cream cheese mixture. Top with the remaining 1 container whipped topping. Sprinkle additional chopped nuts on top if desired.

Makes 18 servings

Mary Androff, Chapterette
Razzle Dazzle of Clinton Twp. Maine, Clinton Township, Maine

Pumpkin Crunch

1 (16-ounce) can solid pack pumpkin
1 (12-ounce) can evaporated milk
3 eggs
1 1/2 cups sugar
4 teaspoons pumpkin pie spice
1/2 teaspoon salt
1 (18-ounce) package yellow cake mix
1 cup chopped pecans
1 cup (2 sticks) butter, melted
 Whipped topping

Preheat the oven to 350°. Grease the bottom of a 13 x 9-inch pan. Combine the pumpkin, milk, eggs, sugar, spice, and salt in a large bowl. Pour into the prepared pan. Sprinkle the dry cake mix evenly over the pumpkin mixture. Top with the chopped pecans. Drizzle the melted butter over the top. Bake for 50 to 55 minutes, or until golden brown. Cool completely. Serve with whipped topping. Refrigerate leftovers.

Makes 12 to 15 servings

Barbara Ostrander, Baroness of Birthdays
Crimson Croonies, Lexington Park, Maryland

Rhubarb Dessert

2 plus 1/4 cups all-purpose flour
1 cup (2 sticks) butter
5 cups rhubarb (frozen or fresh), thaw if frozen
1 cup whipping cream
2 plus 1/2 cups sugar
5 eggs, separated
1/4 teaspoon salt

Preheat the oven to 325°. Blend 2 cups flour and butter and press into a 13 x 9-inch pan.

Mix the rhubarb, cream, the remaining 1/4 cup flour, 2 cups sugar, egg yolks, and salt. Pour over the unbaked crust. Bake for 45 minutes, or until the rhubarb custard mixture has set. Beat the egg whites with the remaining 1/2 cup sugar until stiff. Spread them onto the baked rhubarb mixture and brown in the oven. Cool.

Makes 15 servings

Candice Lawson, Queen of Hearts
Cinnamon Hearts, Winnipeg, Manitoba, Canada

Rice Pudding

Use whole milk and traditional cook-and-serve pudding for this recipe. Add raisins, if you like, when adding the vanilla extract.

1/2 gallon whole milk
1 rounded cup uncooked long-grain rice
1 (5-ounce) package cook-and-serve vanilla pudding
1 cup sugar
3 eggs
1 teaspoon vanilla extract
Cinnamon or nutmeg

Place the milk and uncooked rice in a saucepan. Stir so the rice does not stick to the bottom of the pan. Cover and cook on medium heat. Keep watch over the pot and stir frequently so the mixture does not boil over. Cook until the rice is tender, about 40 minutes (taste for doneness). In a small bowl combine the vanilla pudding mix and sugar; stir to mix. Add the eggs and stir well. When the rice is tender,

spoon some hot milk mixture into the bowl containing the egg and pudding mixture and stir to warm the egg mixture. This step is important. (The egg mixture must be warmed before adding to the milk mixture or you will have scrambled eggs.) Add the egg mixture to the milk mixture and cook for about 5 minutes while stirring. The mixture will thicken. Add the vanilla and stir. Pour into a 13 x 9-inch glass casserole. Sprinkle with cinnamon or nutmeg. Refrigerate.

Makes 10 servings

Mildred Tucci, Vice Queen
Dazzling Damzels, Lodi, New Jersey

Creamy Strawberry Freeze

Try a topping of shaved white and dark chocolate. The tester liked this just as well refrigerated as frozen.

1 (8-ounce) container whipped topping
1 (16-ounce) can strawberry pie filling
1 (14-ounce) can sweetened condensed milk
1 (20-ounce) can crushed pineapple, drained
1/4 cup lemon juice

Mix together the whipped topping, pie filling, condensed milk, pineapple, and lemon juice. Pour into a 13 x 9-inch pan and freeze. Serve frozen.

Makes 10 to 12 servings

Joyce Christian, Red Hatter
Chester County's Classy Chassis, Downingtown, Pennsylvania

Strawberry and Caramel–Banana Trifle

1   large package vanilla pudding mix

CARAMEL SYRUP
1   cup sugar
1/3   cup plus 3 plus 2 tablespoons water

TRIFLE
2   pound cakes, sliced into 1/3-inch slices
1/3   plus 1/3 cup raspberry jam
1 1/2 plus 1 1/2 tablespoons dark rum
3   pints strawberries, hulled and sliced
3   medium bananas, peeled and sliced
1   container whipped topping

Prepare the pudding according to the package directions.

For the caramel syrup, stir the sugar and 1/3 cup water in a small, heavy saucepan over low heat until the sugar dissolves. Increase the heat to boiling without stirring until the syrup turns a deep amber color, brushing down the sides of the pan with a wet pastry brush and swirling the pan occasionally. Remove from the heat. Add 3 tablespoons water (over the sink, since the mixture will bubble vigorously). Stir until the caramel is smooth. Pour into a medium bowl and mix in the remaining 2 tablespoons water. Set aside to cool.

To assemble the trifle, arrange one-fourth of the cake slices in a trifle bowl or punch bowl to cover the bottom of the bowl. Spread with 1/3 cup jam and top with another layer of cake slices. Brush the cake layer with 1 1/2 tablespoons rum. Top with a layer of half the strawberries. Add the banana slices to the caramel syrup; gently stir to coat. Using a slotted spoon, remove the banana slices a few at a time, draining the excess caramel back into the bowl. Layer half the banana slices atop the strawberries. Spoon half the pudding over the bananas, spreading to the sides of the dish with the back of the spoon to press the pudding to the edge of the bowl in a clearly defined layer. Repeat the layering with cake, jam, cake, rum, berries, banana slices, and pudding; press gently to compact. Top with the whipped cream, cover and chill at least 4 hours.

Makes 16 servings

Fran Hemenway, Queen
Creole Red Hat Divas, River Ridge, Louisiana

Simple Strawberry Trifle

Not quite the complex blend of subtle tastes you'd find in a real trifle, but less work and more familiar ingredients.

1   (5-ounce) box vanilla pudding mix (regular or instant)
1   (12-ounce) box vanilla wafers
1/2   cup brandy
1   (8-ounce) container whipped topping
    Fresh strawberries, sliced

Make the pudding according to the package instructions. (You can use a few drops of red food coloring to make it pink or red. But the strawberries are red enough.) In a glass trifle bowl arrange the vanilla wafers on the bottom and around the bottom edge (standing up against the glass). Pour the brandy over them and add one more layer of wafers. Spread half the pudding on top of the wafer layer. Top with half the sliced strawberries. Add another layer of pudding, using half the remaining pudding, then a layer of whipped topping. Repeat the layers, reserving a few strawberries to garnish the top.

Makes 6 servings

Stephanie Layer, Queen Cosmo
The Red Cosmopolitans, Maplewood, Minnesota

Crescent Cream Squares

All the testers on the panel gave a score of 5 to this light but rich dessert.

2   (8-ounce) packages cream cheese
1   plus 1/2 cup sugar
1   tablespoon vanilla extract
2   (8-ounce) cans crescent rolls
4   tablespoons butter
1   tablespoon cinnamon plus for topping
1/2   cup chopped pecans

Preheat the oven to 350°. Combine the cream cheese, 1 cup sugar, and vanilla in a bowl and mix well. Arrange 1 can of crescent rolls in a greased 13 x 9-inch pan. Spread the cream cheese mixture on top of the rolls. Arrange the remaining can of crescent rolls over the cream cheese. Combine the remaining 1/2 cup sugar, butter, and cinnamon. Sprinkle over the second layer of crescent rolls. Top with the pecans and additional cinnamon. Bake for 35 to 40 minutes. Cool and then cut into small squares.

Makes 15 to 20 servings

Valerie Joye, Diva
Rouge Chapeau Divas, Richmond, Virginia

Tiramisu

1　plus 1/2 cup cold water
1　(14-ounce) can sweetened condensed milk
1　(3-ounce) package vanilla instant pudding mix
1　(8-ounce) package soft cream cheese
1　(12-ounce) container frozen whipped topping, thawed
1　tablespoon instant espresso coffee powder
1/2　cup Kahlúa
1/2　cup hot water
24　soft ladyfingers
1　plus 1 plus 1 tablespoons unsweetened cocoa

Combine 1 cup cold water, condensed milk, and vanilla pudding mix in a large bowl. Whisk until thoroughly combined. Cover with plastic wrap, and chill for 30 minutes. Beat in the cream cheese with a mixer on medium speed until well blended. Gently fold in the whipped topping. Combine the instant coffee, Kahlúa, hot water, and 1/2 cup cold water. Split the ladyfingers into halves. Arrange 16 halves flat side down in a trifle bowl or large glass bowl. Drizzle with 1/2 cup of the Kahlúa mixture. Spread one-third of the pudding mixture evenly over the ladyfingers and sprinkle with 1 tablespoon cocoa. Repeat the layers, ending with cocoa. Cover and chill at least 8 hours before serving.

Makes 12 servings

Patricia Johnson, Lady Secretary
Cugini Bei, Aurora, Colorado

Blitz Torten

Blitz means "lightning" and torte is a German word for a rich, short dessert.

TORTE
1/2　cup (1 stick) butter, softened
1/2　cup sugar
4　egg yolks
1　teaspoon baking powder
1/2　cup all purpose flour
4　tablespoons milk
1　teaspoon vanilla extract

TOPPING
4　egg whites
1　cup sugar

FILLING
1　(8-ounce) container whipped topping
1/2　(10-ounce) package frozen strawberries

Preheat the oven to 325°. For the torte, beat the butter and sugar. Add the egg yolks one at a time. Mix thoroughly. Mix the baking powder with the flour. Add the flour mixture alternately with the milk to the batter, stirring after each addition. Add the vanilla. Pour the batter into two greased 8 or 9-inch layer pans that have rim cutters (or use springform pans).

For the topping, beat the egg whites until stiff and fairly dry. Fold in the sugar. Divide evenly over both layers of the batter and spread out to the edges of the pan. Bake for 30 minutes. Cool the cakes in the pans.

For the filling, combine the whipped topping and frozen strawberries.

Using rim cutters, remove each layer from the pan. (Or remove the side of the springform pans.) Place the first layer upside down (meringue on the bottom) on a serving dish, taking care to not damage the top. Spread the filling over the first layer. Then place the second layer right side up (meringue on the top) on top. Refrigerate and serve. Cut in slices with a sharp knife.

Makes 8 to 12 servings

Marjorie Inman, Secretary
Jazzy Belles, Chocowinity, North Carolina

Twinkie Casserole

2   dozen Twinkies
1   (11 3/4-ounce) jar caramel topping
1   (10 1/2-ounce) bag miniature marshmallows
1   (11 3/4-ounce) jar hot fudge topping
1   teaspoon cinnamon
1   (1 pound 2-ounce) bag cream-filled chocolate sandwich cookies

Line the bottom of a large casserole with the Twinkies. Pour the caramel topping over evenly and smooth with knife. Spread the marshmallows over the caramel, covering the caramel completely. Pour the hot fudge sauce over the marshmallows. Sprinkle the cinnamon over the hot fudge. Layer the cookies on top. Serve immediately.

Makes 20 to 30 servings

Variations: Break the cookies into small pieces before layering. Microwave the casserole for 20 seconds or until the marshmallows are gooey. Better for mixing. This is wonderful with vanilla ice cream.

Diana Baker, Lady Di
ParTeaGals, Burke, Virginia

Vanilla Snowbank

This delicate, white gelatin with a vanilla flavor is a novelty for dinner or a pretty base for berries and grapes on a buffet.

1   (1/4-ounce) envelope unflavored gelatin
1/4   cup cold water
1   cup boiling water
2/3   cup sugar
1   teaspoon vanilla extract
2   cups sour cream
8   ounces whipped topping
     Strawberries or blueberries

In a medium bowl dissolve the gelatin in the cold water. Add the boiling water and stir to dissolve. Add the sugar and vanilla and stir until the sugar is dissolved. Whisk in the sour cream until smooth. Whisk in the whipped topping. Pour the mixture into a large (6 cup) ring mold. Refrigerate until set. Pile strawberries or blueberries into the center of the mold when serving.

Makes 8 to 10 servings

Mary Vander Ploeg, Royal Red Hatter
Rivertown Belles, Wyoming, Michigan

Vanilla Pecan Delight

Biscuit mix makes a quicker-than-usual crust. The contributor says she doubles the crust mixture for a substantial layer.

1 1/4 cups biscuit mix

1 tablespoon brown sugar

3 tablespoons butter, melted

1/2 cup chopped pecans plus extra for garnish

1 cup plus 1 tablespoon confectioners' sugar

1 (8-ounce) package cream cheese

2 cups heavy whipping cream

2 (3-ounce) packages instant vanilla pudding mix

2 1/2 cups milk

Preheat the oven to 375°. Combine the biscuit mix, brown sugar, and butter; mix until crumbly. Mix in the chopped pecans. Press into a lightly greased 13 x 9-inch glass pan. Bake for 10 minutes; cool. In a bowl beat 1 cup confectioners' sugar with the cream cheese until smooth. Beat the whipping cream until stiff. Fold 1 cup whipped cream into the cream cheese mixture. Spread over the cooled baked layer.

Prepare the pudding with the 2 1/2 cups milk. Pour over the cream cheese mixture. Cover and refrigerate until firm. Fold the remaining 1 tablespoon confectioners' sugar into the remaining whipped cream and spread over the dessert. Sprinkle a few chopped pecans on top.

Makes 15 servings

Sandy Van Der Linden, Queen Mum
Vintage Valley Girls, Hemet, California

Zeppole

A light, yeasty, fried pastry similar to a doughnut.

1 teaspoon active dry yeast

3/4 cup warm water

1 teaspoon granulated sugar (to activate the yeast)

1 egg

2 cups all-purpose flour

1/2 teaspoon salt
Shortening or vegetable oil
Confectioners' sugar

Sprinkle the yeast over the warm water and add the sugar; lightly mix. Let stand until the yeast is dissolved.

Beat in the egg; add the flour and salt and blend until smooth. Place in a warm spot (cover with a towel to add heat to the yeast). When the dough has doubled in size, about 30 minutes, punch down and repeat to double again.

Pour the shortening or vegetable oil into a Dutch oven or other pot to a depth of several inches. Heat the shortening over medium-high heat until hot. Drop the dough by the teaspoonful into the oil. Cook until brown; they turn over by themselves. Drain on paper towels and shake in a bag with confectioners' sugar to coat.

Makes about 20.

Eletta Werlock, The Royal E-mail Female
Crafty Cats in Crimson Hats, Tom's River, New Jersey

Microwave Hot Fudge Sauce

1/2 cup sugar
3 tablespoons cocoa
1 1/2 tablespoons cornstarch
1/2 cup cold water
2 tablespoons butter
1 teaspoon vanilla extract

In 1 quart glass microwavable bowl, combine the sugar, cocoa, and cornstarch and mix until combined. Stir in the water. Mix briefly with a spoon. Cook on full power in a microwave for 1 minute, 30 seconds, stirring halfway through cooking time; the mixture will be thick. Blend in the butter and microwave on full power for 15 seconds; stir. Add the vanilla and stir until smooth. Serve over ice cream, pound cake, or strawberries.

Makes 1 cup

Tip: Leftover sauce may be stored in a covered container in the refrigerator and briefly reheated in the microwave.

Cynthia West, Queen Cookie
Traveling Cooks with Hattitude, Marshalltown, Iowa

Lemon Fluff Sauce

2 tablespoons butter
1/4 cup plus 2 tablespoons sugar
1 tablespoon cornstarch
Dash of salt
3/4 cup water
2 eggs, separated
1/3 cup frozen lemonade concentrate, defrosted

In a 1 1/2-quart saucepan melt the butter, and blend in 1/4 cup sugar and the cornstarch. Add the salt and water. Cook over medium heat, stirring constantly until thickened. Beat the egg yolks and combine them with the lemonade concentrate. Whisk the lemonade mixture into the hot cornstarch mixture and continue to stir; heat just to boiling. Remove from the heat. Beat the egg whites until foamy and gradually add the remaining 2 tablespoons sugar. Beat until stiff. Bring the sauce back to a boil and fold in the egg whites just until blended. Remove from the heat. Serve warm over cake or persimmon pudding or chilled in small stemmed glasses for a light and elegant desert.

Makes 3 cups

Diana Fuller, Dame Diana
Modoc Red Hot Hatters, Alturas, California

The Eggnog Debacle

My husband and I were married in June of 1968, and the following December we threw our first Christmas party. Like most new brides, I was anxious to impress our guests with my prowess at homemaking and hostessing. The food was prepared, the apartment shiny clean, and the last-minute touches were complete. The doorbell rang, our guests arrived, and many made straight for the homemade eggnog. Within seconds, several guests ran for the kitchen sink to spit out their libations. Horrified, I raised my voice, over the sound of retching, to ask what was wrong with the eggnog.

I pulled out the recipe card and began to read the ingredients aloud, beginning with "Beat one dozen egg yolks. . . ." Uh-oh!

I had carefully separated the yolks from the whites, but had thrown out the yolks and beaten the whites. My "eggnog" consisted of egg whites, spices, and a fifth of straight rum! No wonder the punch bowl was billowing with mounds of white froth! The party went on, but the guests have never forgotten my first attempt at providing Christmas cheer!

Sue Ellen Cooper
Founder & Exalted Queen Mother
The Fabulous Founders
Fullerton, California

Hot Fudge Sauce

1/2   cup (1 stick) butter
4   heaping tablespoons cocoa
1   (14-ounce) can sweetened condensed milk
1/2   cup light corn syrup
1   teaspoon vanilla extract

Melt the butter and add the cocoa. Stir to mix well. Add the sweetened condensed milk and cook until small bubbles begin to form. Add the corn syrup and heat until almost boiling. Stir in the vanilla and remove from the heat.

Makes about 3 cups

Gail Davis, Red Snapper, Princess of Photos and Hysterian
Sassy Survivors (A Group for Breast Cancer Survivors), Fort Smith, Arkansas

Bourbon Balls

2 cups fine vanilla wafer crumbs
1/4 cup unsweetened cocoa
Dash of salt
1 cup sifted confectioners' sugar
1 cup chopped walnuts
3 tablespoons dark corn syrup
6 tablespoons bourbon or rum

In a large bowl combine the wafer crumbs, cocoa, salt, sugar, walnuts, corn syrup, and bourbon and mix thoroughly. Roll into small balls. Store in the refrigerator in an airtight container.

Makes about 24 pieces

Oleta Reinhart, Princess of Poultry
Kiwanis Manor Ramblin' Red Hatters, Tiffin, Ohio

Butter Mints

Use any flavoring you like; these don't have to taste like mint.

3 ounces soft cream cheese
2 teaspoons butter flavoring
1/8 teaspoon mint extract (or alternate flavoring)
16 ounces confectioners' sugar
Food coloring (very small amount)

Beat the cream cheese, butter flavoring, extract, sugar, and food coloring together in a bowl with a mixer at low speed. Roll into balls or ropes and slice. Flatten with a fork or what-ever shape the occasion calls for. Set on waxed paper and let dry for about 8 hours. Store in an airtight, plastic container.

Makes about 80 mints

Diane Morey, Queen Mother Nature
Secret Society of Southern Scarlet Sisters, Hardeeville, South Carolina

Velveeta Fudge

An unusual recipe from Southern Hatters—definitely fun to make. Let your chapter judge whether it's fun to eat.

1 cup (2 sticks) butter, softened
8 ounces Velveeta cheese, cubed
1 1/2 pounds confectioners' sugar
1/2 cup unsweetened cocoa
1/2 cup nonfat dry milk
2 teaspoons vanilla extract
2 cups coarsely chopped pecans or walnuts

In a large saucepan over medium heat melt the butter and cheese cubes, stirring frequently. Remove from the heat. Sift together the confectioners' sugar and cocoa and add to the cheese, mixing well. Stir in the dry milk, vanilla, and nuts. Pour into a lightly greased 9-inch square pan and chill until firm. Cut into squares.

Makes 4 dozen servings

Melonee Jackson, Her Royal Pink Highness Princess Sister Von Webmistress
Donelson Red Hat Honeys, Nashville, Tennessee

Almond Butter Crunch

Tastes like a chocolate-covered toffee bar.

1   cup (2 sticks) butter
1 1/3 cups sugar
3   tablespoons water
1   tablespoon light corn syrup
1   cup coarsely chopped blanched almonds, toasted
1   cup melted semisweet chocolate chips
1   cup finely chopped blanched almonds, toasted

In a large saucepan, melt the butter. Add the sugar, water, and corn syrup. Cook over medium heat, stirring occasionally, to the hard-crack stage (300°). Quickly stir in the coarsely chopped almonds and spread in a large, well-greased baking pan. Cool thoroughly. Turn out onto waxed paper. Spread with half the melted chocolate and sprinkle with half the nuts. Cover with waxed paper and invert. Spread again with the remainig chocolate and sprinkle with the remaining nuts. If necessary, chill to firm the chocolate.

Makes about 1 1/2 pounds

Marlene O'Malley, Vice Queen
Ruby Revellers, Dartmouth, Nova Scotia, Canada

Butterscotch Haystacks

Shoestring potato sticks stand in for chow mein noodles in this sweet-and-salty snack.

1   (11-ounce) package butterscotch morsels
2   cups unsalted dry-roasted peanuts
2   cups shoestring potato sticks

In a large saucepan melt the butterscotch morsels over low heat, stirring occasionally. When melted and smooth, remove from the heat. Stir in the peanuts. Stir in the potato sticks, breaking some up as you stir. Drop onto waxed paper with a large spoon. Push any stray peanuts back into the "stack" so they will adhere. Cool completely.

Makes 20 pieces

Marsha Gerber, Queen Mother
Marsha, Marsha, Marsha and her Marvelous Mates, Parkland, Florida

Micro Fudge

The fudge gets a little soft if left at room temperature for a long period, so store it in the refrigerator.

3   cups sugar
3/4 cup (1 1/2 sticks) butter
1   (5-ounce) can evaporated milk
1   cup chopped nuts
1   (10-ounce) jar marshmallow creme
1   (12-ounce) bag chocolate chips
1   teaspoon vanilla extract

Combine the sugar, butter, and milk in a large glass bowl and cover with plastic wrap. Microwave 10 minutes on medium power. Remove, uncover, and stir. Be careful, because the steam will be very hot. Return the mixture to the microwave and continue to cook for 5 more minutes. Remove the bowl from the microwave. Stir in the nuts, marshmallow creame, chocolate chips, and vanilla. Pour into a buttered 13 x 9-inch pan. Chill until firm.

Makes 74 pieces

Brenda Hansen, Vice Queen
Happy Red Hatters, Youngtown, Arizona

Quick Foolproof Fudge

1   (12-ounce) bag semisweet chocolate chips
1   cup milk chocolate chips
1   (14-ounce) can sweetened condensed milk
2   cups miniature marshmallows
    Dash of salt (optional)
1/2 to 1 cup chopped pecans or walnuts
1 1/2 teaspoons vanilla extract

In a 1 1/2-quart microwavable bowl combine the chocolate chips, condensed milk, marshmallows, and salt. Cover and microwave for 3 minutes on high power. Remove from the microwave and stir until all the chips and marshmallows are melted and the mixture is smooth. Add the nuts and vanilla extract and mix well. Line an 8 or 9-inch square pan with waxed paper. Spread the fudge into the pan. Chill for 2 hours, or until firm. Turn the fudge onto a cutting board. Peel off the waxed paper and cut into squares. Store loosely covered in the refrigerator.

Makes 2 pounds

Dolores Rose, Grand Dame Diva Do–Little
Isle de Grand Red Hat Divas, Grand Island, Nebraska

Peanut Butter Cups

1/2 cup granulated sugar
1/2 cup packed brown sugar
1/2 cup (1 stick) butter, softened
1/2 cup creamy peanut butter
1   egg
1/2 teaspoon vanilla extract
1 1/4 cups all-purpose flour
3/4 teaspoon baking soda
1/2 teaspoon salt
1   (13-ounce) package miniature peanut butter cups, unwrapped

Preheat the oven to 350°. Spray a miniature muffin pan with nonstick cooking spray. Combine the sugars, butter, and peanut butter in a large mixing bowl. Beat at medium speed until creamy. Add the egg and vanilla and mix well. Reduce the speed to low and add the flour, baking soda, and salt. Beat, scraping the bowl often. Shape the dough into 1-inch balls. Place each ball into the prepared muffin pan. Bake for 11 to 13 minutes, or until lightly browned. Remove from the oven and press a peanut butter cup in the center of each cookie. Let cool 30 minutes. Remove from the pan. Cool completely.

Makes 4 dozen.

Colleen Helgerson, Contessa of Courtesies
Red Hatters and That's What Matters, Aurora, Colorado

Stained Glass Windows

Each slice of this confection is pretty to look at and offers that great combination of chocolate and marshmallow.

1/2 cup (1 stick) butter or margarine
1 (12-ounce) package chocolate chips
1 (12-ounce) package colored miniature marshmallows

Heat the butter and chocolate chips in a double boiler or in a microwave until melted. Cool. Stir in the marshmallows. Roll the mixture on waxed paper to form two 6 to 8-inch logs. Place in the refrigerator until hardened. Cut into thin slices.

Makes 24 slices

Mary Flynn, Princess
Scarlet Splashers, Torrington, Connecticut

Crunch Candy

Be prepared to share the recipe for this easy candy.

　　Saltine crackers, salted or not
1 1/4 cups (2 1/2 sticks) butter
1 1/2 cups firmly packed brown sugar
2 cups chocolate chips
　　Sliced almonds or chopped pecans (optional)

Grease a jelly-roll pan well. Cover the bottom completely with saltine crackers. Preheat the oven to 350°. In a saucepan bring the butter and brown sugar to a boil. Boil for 4 minutes. Pour over the crackers, spreading well. Bake for just 6 minutes. Turn off the oven and remove the pan. Sprinkle the chocolate chips evenly over the crackers and return to the oven for 10 minutes to soften. Spread the melted chocolate all over the surface. Sprinkle with the nuts if desired. Refrigerate for 2 hours and then break into pieces.

Makes 12 servings

Tove Cravens, Queen of Quite-a-Lot
Red Hatters, Fun and Chatters, Orion, Illinois

English Toffee

1 cup sugar
1 cup (2 sticks) butter (no substitutes)
3 tablespoons water
1 teaspoon vanilla extract
4 (1-ounce) milk chocolate bars, broken in pieces
1 to 2 cups finely chopped walnuts (or almonds)

In a large saucepan combine the sugar, butter, and water over high heat. Using a candy thermometer bring to a boil at 300°. Stir often over medium heat to keep from burning. Stir in the vanilla and then quickly pour onto a large buttered pan or baking sheet. Spread the mixture out evenly and then cover with the broken chocolate bars. Once melted, evenly spread out the chocolate until the mixture is covered. Spread the nuts over the chocolate and press firmly into the candy. Cover the candy with waxed paper and then press the nuts into the chocolate. Cool completely, and then break into pieces.

Makes about 1 pound

Cyntra Giboney, Purple Haze Royale
Ruby Red Girls of Martinez, Pleasant Hill, California

Pecan Caramel Candies

63 miniature pretzels
1   (13-ounce) package Rolo candies (or use eight 1.7-ounce rolls)
63 pecan or walnut halves

Preheat the oven to 250°. Line baking sheets with foil. Arrange the pretzels on the foil and top each pretzel with a candy. Bake for 4 minutes, or until the candies are softened. (The chocolate will retain its shape.) Remove from the oven and immediately place a pecan or walnut half on each Rolo. Press down so the candy fills the pretzel. Cool slightly. Refrigerate for 10 minutes, or until set.

Makes 63 pieces

Carol Bobo, Countess of Creativity
Heavenly Hatters, Santa Cruz, California

Macadamia Nut Truffles

1/4 cup heavy whipping cream
2   pounds milk or semisweet chocolate, divided (Guttiard or Ghiradelli work well)
1/4 cup macadamia nut liqueur
1/2 cup finely chopped macadamia nuts

Heat the cream in the top of a double boiler set over simmering water. Add 1 pound of the chocolate, let heat for a few minutes, and then mix well. Add the liqueur and mix well. Pour the hot mixture into an air-tight container with a tight-fitting lid. Refrigerate for 24 hours. When ready to mold the truffles, remove and let stand at room temperature for at least 4 hours.

Using a teaspoon, scrape across the chocolate mixture about 2 or 3 times. Lightly powder your hands with confectioners' sugar, and then roll the chocolate mixture into a ball. Set the truffle onto waxed paper. Repeat with the remaining chocolate mixture.

Melt the remaining 1 pound chocolate and dip the truffles into the chocolate. You can use a dipping tool found at a craft store or a fork. Let the excess chocolate drip back into the pan. Roll the truffles in the nuts and arrange them on a baking sheet covered with waxed paper. Allow the truffles to firm up, and then store in an airtight container.

Makes 30 truffles

Joann Heisch, Truffle Queen
Home & Heartstrings Red Hatters, Auburn, California

Orange-Coconut Balls

Serving size: as many as you'd like.

1   (12-ounce) box vanilla wafers, crushed
1   (6-ounce) can orange juice concentrate, thawed
1/2 cup (1 stick) butter, melted
3/4 cup chopped nuts (optional)
     Shredded coconut (optional)

Mix together the wafers, juice, butter, and nuts, if using. Roll into balls, then roll the balls in coconut, if using. Tastes best when chilled.

Makes 12 to 14 servings

Lyn Rogers, The Queen of Everything
The Victorian Roses, San Jose, California

Peanut Butter Snowballs

This little candy is like a buckeye, but made with a white coating. A coating of sugar makes them pretty. Look for sparkling sugar—it's extra special.

1 1/2 cups peanut butter
1/2   cup (1 stick) butter or margarine, softened
1   box (16 ounces) confectioners' sugar
1   package (12 ounces) white chocolate chips
1   tablespoon vegetable shortening
      Confectioners' sugar or edible glitter for dusting

In a large bowl, combine peanut butter and butter and beat until blended. Beat in the confectioners' sugar 1/2 cup at a time. Line a baking sheet with foil. Shape the peanut butter mixture into 1-inch balls. Arrange the balls on the prepared baking sheet and chill for about 1 hour until firm. Place the white chocolate and shortening in a large microwave-safe bowl. Microwave on medium, stirring every 30 seconds, until the chocolate is melted and smooth, about 2 minutes. Line a baking sheet with waxed paper. Using a spoon, dip each peanut butter ball into the melted chocolate, spooning chocolate over the ball to coat, if necessary. Transfer the snowballs to the waxed paper–lined baking sheet. Sprinkle the tops with confectioners' sugar or edible glitter. Chill the snowballs until set, about 30 minutes.

Makes about 24 cookies

Carol Hendon, Queen
Red Toppers, Katy, Texas

Buckeyes

They say buckeyes bring good luck, but you won't need it to succeed with this easy candy.

2 1/2 cups confectioners' sugar
1/2   cup (1 stick) butter or margarine, softened
1/2   cup plus 2 tablespoons creamy peanut butter
1/2   teaspoon vanilla extract
1/8   cake paraffin
6   ounces semisweet chocolate chips

In a large bowl, combine the confectioners' sugar, butter, peanut butter, and vanilla and mix well. Roll into small balls and freeze on waxed paper. Melt the paraffin in the top of a double boiler over boiling water. Add chocolate chips and heat, stirring, until melted. Insert a toothpick into each frozen ball. Dip each ball two-thirds deep into the warm chocolate, leaving a portion of the peanut butter center showing. Set on waxed paper to cool until firm. (Doing this in the refrigerator is quicker).

Makes about 48

Susan Duncan, Queen Susie Q
Derby City Ladybugs of Louisville, Kentucky, Louisville, Kentucky

Microwave Peanut Brittle

The microwave oven is brilliant for candy-making. Try this one and discover how easy it is.

1 1/2 cups unsalted dry-roasted peanuts
1 cup sugar
1/2 cup light corn syrup
1/8 teaspoon salt
1 tablespoon butter or margarine
1 teaspoon vanilla extract
1 teaspoon baking soda

In a microwaveable bowl combine the peanuts, sugar, corn syrup, and salt. Microwave on high power for 7 to 9 minutes, or until the mixture is bubbling and the peanuts are brown. Quickly stir in the butter and vanilla; cook on high 2 to

3 minutes longer. Add the baking soda and stir quickly, just until the mixture is foamy. Pour immediately onto a greased baking sheet. Let cool about 15 minutes until firm. Break the peanut brittle into pieces; store in an airtight container.

Makes 20 ounces

Lorraine Tollefson, Queen
Chapeau Rouge of Crystal River, Crystal River, Florida

Crunchy Peanut Bark

Look for confectionery coating in the baking section of the supermarket. It's often labeled "candy coating."

1 pound white confectionery coating
1/2 cup peanut butter
1 1/2 cups crisp rice cereal
1 cup dry roasted peanuts
1 cup miniature marshmallows

Place the confectionery coating in a large microwave-safe bowl. Microwave at 50 percent power until melted, about 5 minutes, stirring every minute or so. Add the peanut butter, rice cereal, peanuts, and marshmallows. Stir to mix well. Drop by heaping teaspoonfuls onto waxed paper. Let set until firm.

Makes about 60 pieces

Dee Boyes, Diva Dee
Lusty Ladies in Red of Loveland, Loveland, Colorado

Creamy Pralines

1 1/2 cups packed brown sugar
1 1/2 cups granulated sugar
1/2 cup milk
1/2 cup whipping cream
1/4 teaspoon cream of tartar
1/4 cup (1/2 stick) unsalted butter
1 1/2 teaspoons vanilla extract
2 cups pecan halves

Combine the sugars, milk, cream, and cream of tartar in a heavy saucepan. Heat, stirring to dissolve the sugars. Bring to a boil and cook until the mixture reaches the softball stage, about 235° to 240° on a candy thermometer. Remove from the heat and cool for 5 minutes. Stir in the butter, vanilla, and pecans. Stir until the mixture starts to look creamy. Drop by teaspoonfuls onto waxed paper. Let cool thoroughly before storing in an airtight container.

Makes 8 to 10 servings

Claudia Beene, Queen Mother
Scarlett O'Hatters, Bossier City, Louisiana

Sherry Pralines

1 cup granulated sugar
1 cup packed brown sugar
1 cup evaporated milk
1 to 2 cups pecan pieces (not small)
1 tablespoon sherry

Combine the sugars and milk in a heavy saucepan. Bring to a boil over low heat and cook to the soft ball stage, about 236° on a candy thermometer, stirring frequently. When the syrup begins to thicken, stir constantly and remove from the heat. Add the pecans and sherry and mix thoroughly. Let cool slightly and then beat until the mixture starts to thicken. Drop by teaspoonfuls onto waxed paper or a greased baking pan. Let cool.

Makes 20 pieces

Beverly Trahan, Lady B
Swinging Mississippi Belles, Carriere, Mississippi

Toffee Bar Squares

1 package round buttery crackers
1 package chocolate covered toffee chips, such as Skor or Heath
1 (12-ounce) can sweetened condensed milk

Preheat the oven to 350°. Crush the crackers. In a large bowl combine the crackers, toffee chips, and milk and mix well. Press the mixture into a greased, 8-inch pan. Bake for 12 minutes. Cool completely and then cut into squares.

Makes 36 squares

Lorna McDowell, Queen Charles
Scarlett O'Haras, Garson, Ontario, Canada

~ Part II ~

Everything Else

Sweets all the time?
Nah! We want it all.

We Red Hatters may be playful, but we actually are grown-ups, and we even behave like adults when we have to. We know that women do not live by sugar alone. And the truth is, we love the great food that precedes the sweets just as much as we love our desserts. Sometimes nothing will do but a big slice of roast beef or a crunchy medley of vegetables. We also know that our bodies need the nutritional benefits of hearty, healthy food just as much as our taste buds need satisfying.

Preparing a whole meal, using foods that complement each other in terms of flavor, texture, and color is an art, one that a lot of Red Hatters have spent many years perfecting. They find pleasure in cooking beautiful, nourishing meals, and they still find fulfillment in nurturing loved ones, including their chapterettes, by preparing enjoyable meals for them and exchanging treasured recipes.

As we collected these recipes from our members, it quickly became apparent that, collectively, we members of the Red Hat Society have managed to gather the crème de la crème of them. Our chapter editors winnowed the number of these down even further, resulting in the real gems that follow.

FIVE

~ Little Bits of Anticipation ~

APPETIZERS & BEVERAGES

The funny thing about appetizers is that they are those things we eat *before* we eat. In some ways this may not seem to make sense, but there is no denying that appetizers are among the most intriguing foods. They are meant to be sampled in small amounts and savored, not heaped up on plates and devoured. They are the little jewels of cuisine, often juxtaposing flavors and textures to intrigue the palate.

If a gathering is held in a private home, appetizers are often served, with drinks of various kinds as guests arrive and begin to socialize. They help break the ice and get the party going. Much like a rousing overture played by the orchestra right before a musical play begins, they whet the appetite for what is to follow, creating an air of anticipation and promote a relaxed atmosphere for enjoyable conversation. Sounds good, doesn't it? Here are some winning recipes.

BLT Dip

What a great idea—all the flavors you love in a BLT, but in a party-ful format.

1	pound bacon
1	cup sour cream
1	cup mayonnaise
1	tomato, chopped

In a skillet sauté the bacon until crisp. Drain and crumble. In a small bowl the mix sour cream, mayonnaise, tomato, and cooked bacon. Serve with favorite crackers or vegetables.

Makes 16 servings

Kathi Asigner, Pink Hatter
Red Hot Flashes, St. Ann, Missouri

Colby Bean Dip

Take that old bean dip to a new level.

1	(8-ounce) package cream cheese, softened
1	(8-ounce) container sour cream
1	(10 1/2-ounce) can bean dip
2	tablespoons taco seasoning
10	drops Tabasco sauce
2	cups grated Colby cheese

Preheat the oven to 350°. In a large bowl mix together the cream cheese, sour cream, bean dip, seasoning, and Tabasco. Spread half the mixture in a lightly greased casserole dish, top with half the grated cheese, and then spread with the remaining bean mixture. Bake at 300° for 25 minutes. Top with the remaining grated cheese and return to the oven for 5 minutes. Serve with tortilla chips.

Makes 20 servings

Susie Van Foeken, Queen
Hilmar Red Hat Readers, Hilmar, California

Corned Beef Pâté

Satisfyingly savory—good for a group of hearty eaters.

2	tablespoons finely minced onion
2	tablespoons water
1	(12-ounce) can corned beef
8	ounces braunschweiger (liverwurst)
1/2	cup mayonnaise
1	tablespoon apple cider vinegar
2	teaspoons mustard

In a small bowl mix the onion and water. In another bowl flake the corned beef with a fork. Add the braunschweiger, mayonnaise, vinegar, mustard, and onion mixture. Mix well.

Spoon 1/2 cup of the mixture into a blender or food processor and blend until smooth. Remove and blend the remaining mixture. Spoon into a 3 1/2-cup mold or bowl. Refrigerate until chilled. At this point, the pâté may be shaped or decorated and is ready to serve with rye crackers or rye bread. Can be frozen for up to a month.

Makes 20 servings

Diane Jackson, Kountess Kazooest-in-Charge
Glitz & Glamour, Albuquerque, New Mexico

Beefy Picadillo Dip

This handy recipe is good for an entrée too.

1	pound ground beef
1	small onion, chopped
3/4	cup chopped pimientos
4	ounces black olives, chopped
1	cup golden raisins
1	(14 1/2-ounce) can tomatoes with green chiles
1	pound Velveeta cheese, cut into chunks
2	to 3 garlic cloves, minced
3/4	teaspoon dried oregano
3/4	cup slivered almonds, toasted

In a large skillet brown the beef; drain. Add the onion, pimientos, olives, raisins, tomatoes, cheese, garlic, oregano, and almonds. Simmer for 30 minutes, stirring frequently. Serve hot in a chafing dish with tortilla chips.

Makes 12 servings

Linda Pennington, Queen Mum
Sassy Hattitudes, Loganville, Georgia

Chocolate Chip Cheese Ball

Testers found low-fat cream cheese worked just as well as regular cream cheese in this unusual cheese ball. Especially good for serving to little children.

1	(8-ounce) package cream cheese, softened
1/2	cup (1 stick) butter, softened
1/4	teaspoon vanilla extract
3/4	cup granulated sugar
2	tablespoons brown sugar
3/4	cup mini chocolate chips

In a large bowl mix the cream cheese, butter, vanilla, and sugars. Add the chocolate chips and form a ball. Refrigerate and serve with cinnamon or honey graham sticks.

Makes 10 servings

Donna McElroy, Founding Queen Mother
Rosebud Hues, Venice, Florida

Cheese Bombay

Curry powder, sherry, and chutney make this cheese ball a standout.

1	(8-ounce) package cream cheese, softened
6	ounces sharp cheddar cheese, grated
1	tablespoon curry powder
2	tablespoons sherry
3	large garlic cloves, minced
1/2	cup mango chutney (or other chutney)
2	tablespoons minced scallions (optional)

In a large bowl mix the cream cheese, cheddar cheese, curry powder, sherry, and garlic. Shape into a ball and chill for several hours. Top with the chutney and sprinkle the scallions on top. Serve with crackers.

Makes 12 servings

Peggy Krickbaum, Princess Knit Wit
Flashy Sassies, Montrose, Colorado

Hot Corn Cheese Dip

That easy favorite, Ro-Tel Dip, gets a remake here with corn and cream cheese.

1   (15-ounce) can white corn, drained
1   (15-ounce) can yellow corn, drained
1   (10-ounce) can diced tomatoes with green chiles (the hot variety is best)
2   (4-ounce) cans green chiles, drained
1   (8-ounce) package cream cheese
12   slices American cheese

Combine the corn, tomatoes, green chiles, cream cheese, and cheese slices in large pot over medium-low heat. Cook, stirring frequently, until the cheese melts. Serve warm with chips, crackers, or bread pieces.

Makes 8 to 12 servings

Betty Yates, Queen Mother
Willowing Mad Hatters, Steens, Mississippi

"Do chickens think rubber humans are funny?"

—Anonymous

Warm Chicken Dip

1   (8-ounce) package cream cheese
1   (10¾-ounce) can cream of chicken soup
1   to 2 poached chicken breasts, shredded
1   (4-ounce) can green chiles, drained
     Toasted bread triangles, assorted crackers

In small slow cooker combine the cream cheese and soup. Add the chicken and chiles and stir. Heat on low. When warm, serve with crackers or toast.

Makes 20 servings

Millie Lytle, Queen Bee
Red Hats On To You, Carol Stream, Illinois

Chili Cheese Dip

1   (8-ounce) package cream cheese
1   (15-ounce) can chili without beans
1   cup shredded sharp cheddar cheese
1   tomato, chopped
     Chopped green onions (optional)

Preheat the oven to 350°. Line the bottom of a quiche or pie dish with the cream cheese. Pour the chili over the top and sprinkle with the cheddar cheese. Bake for 20 minutes. Remove from the oven and sprinkle with the chopped tomato and green onions, if using. Serve with corn chips or tortilla chips.

Makes 8 servings

Maggie Smith, Purple Playmate
The Hart Throb and Socialites of Hartwell, Buford, Georgia

Mexicorn Dip

2   (7-ounce) cans Mexican corn, drained
8   ounces sharp cheddar cheese, grated
8   ounces sour cream
1   cup mayonnaise
1   (4-ounce) can chopped green chiles
1/2 medium-size white onion, chopped
    Jalapeño peppers to taste

In a large bowl mix together the corn, cheese, sour cream, mayonnaise, chiles, onion, and jalapeños. Serve immediately or chill until ready to serve. Stir before serving. Serve with tortilla chips.

Makes 16 servings

Sandy Meller, Lady Rocking Grammy
California Reds, Lohman, Missouri

Joyce Moore's Crab Crunch

Testers loved this. And it's ideal for gals who entertain often—it's already in the freezer, ready to bake and serve.

6   tablespoons butter
2   tablespoons mayonnaise
2 1/2 teaspoons onion powder
1 1/2 teaspoons garlic salt
1 1/2 teaspoons garlic powder
1/2 teaspoon seasoned pepper
1   (6-ounce) can crabmeat, drained
1   (5-ounce) jar Kraft Old English cheese
    spread
6   English muffins, halved

Mix well the butter, mayonnaise, onion powder, garlic salt, garlic powder, seasoned pepper, crabmeat, and cheese spread. Spread with the mixture over the English muffin halves and freeze until firm. Remove from the freezer and cut into fourths. Return to the freezer until ready to bake. Preheat the oven to 375° and bake for 15 minutes on an ungreased jelly roll pan.

Makes 24 servings

Delora Jo Koscielski, Queen
Red Hot Hatters, Quincy, Illinois

Hot Crab Dip

This dish is best when made a day in advance and heated thoroughly before serving.

1   (8-ounce) package cream cheese
1/2 cup (1 stick) butter
1   pound fresh crabmeat, shells picked out
6   green onions, finely chopped
1   tablespoon Worcestershire sauce
1/4 cup dry sherry
    Garlic powder to taste
    White pepper to taste
    Salt to taste

In a large dish melt the cream cheese and butter in the microwave. Add the crabmeat, onions, Worcestershire, sherry, garlic powder, white pepper, and salt. Mix well. Return to the microwave and heat until hot and bubbly.

Makes 12 servings

Sonja Sheffield, Queen Mother
Red Hatted Stepchild, Gulfport, Mississippi

Texas Crab Grass

Selected by testers as worthy of a tip of the hat.

1   (10-ounce) package frozen chopped
    spinach, thawed
1/2   cup (1 stick) butter
1/2   medium onion, chopped
1   (6-ounce) can lump crabmeat
3/4   cup grated Parmesan cheese

Preheat the oven to 300°. Squeeze the water from the spinach. In a skillet melt the butter over medium heat and sauté the spinach and onion. Add the crabmeat and cheese and blend well. Transfer to a 1-quart casserole. Bake for 15 to 20 minutes. Spread on crackers or celery sticks.

Makes 4 to 6 servings

Wilma Day, Queen Yakety–Yak
Daring Audacious Yakety–Yaks, Oak Ridge North, Texas

High Society Dip

You can use hot or mild sausage in this recipe, depending on your spice quotient.

1   pound bulk pork sausage, hot or mild
1   (8-ounce) package cream cheese
1   (16-ounce) jar salsa
3   or 4 fresh jalapeño peppers
1   bag white corn tortilla chips

Cook the sausage in a medium-size saucepan over medium heat until thoroughly brown. Drain off the grease. Add the cream cheese and stir until melted. Add the salsa and mix well. Thinly slice the peppers and add them to the mixture or serve separately, depending on the tastes of your guests. Serve with tortilla chips.

Makes 10 servings

Evelyn Tidy, Princess Evelyn
Siler City Royal Belles, Siler City, North Carolina

Layered Nacho Dip

1   (16-ounce) can refried beans
2   tablespoons taco seasoning mix
1   (8-ounce) container sour cream
1   (4 1/2-ounce) can chopped black olives,
    drained
2   large tomatoes, diced
1   small onion, finely chopped
1   (4-ounce) can green chiles, drained
3/4   cup shredded Monterey Jack cheese
3/4   cup medium sharp cheddar cheese

In a bowl combine the beans with the taco seasoning mix. Spread the mixture in a 12 x 8 x 2-inch dish. Layer the sour cream, olives, tomatoes, onion, chiles, Jack cheese, and Cheddar cheese in that order. Serve with tortilla chips or corn chips.

Makes 15 servings

Tonia Finger, Princess
His Glorious Gals, Rustburg, Virginia

Pineapple Cheese Ball

2 (8-ounce) packages cream cheese, softened
1 (15-ounce) can crushed pineapple, drained
1 to 2 cups chopped pecans, divided
1/4 cup chopped green bell pepper
2 teaspoons chopped onion
1 teaspoon seasoned salt

In a large bowl mix the cream cheese, pineapple, two-thirds of the pecans, green pepper, onion, and salt. Shape into a ball. Roll the ball in the remaining pecans, pressing them onto the outside of the cheese ball. Chill and serve with crackers.

Makes 12 servings

Louise Bragg, Duchess Sylvia
Elite Ladies of The Hat, Franklinton, North Carolina

Hot Onion Dip

2 (8-ounce) packages cream cheese
1 cup mayonnaise
1 1/2 cups grated Parmesan cheese
1 1/2 cups chopped onions
1 teaspoon garlic salt
1 tablespoon white wine (optional)
1 tablespoon chopped chives or green onions

Preheat the oven to 350°. In a large bowl mix the cream cheese, mayonnaise, Parmesan cheese, onions, garlic salt, and wine, if using. Transfer to a 2-quart dish and sprinkle with the chives or onions. Bake for 50 minutes, or until the mixture looks firm. Serve warm with crackers and chips.

Makes 16 servings

Maryellen Grimes, Queen Meg
Glamorous Gallavanting Gals, Fort Worth, Texas

A Cup, A Cup, A Cup Dip

Another hot onion dip, but in an easy-to-remember recipe, because there's one cup of everything. The contributor said she thought this was crab dip the first time she tried it.

1 cup mayonnaise
1 cup shredded sharp cheddar cheese
1 cup finely chopped Vidalia onion

Preheat the oven to 350°. In a large bowl mix the mayonnaise, cheese, and onion. Pour into a lightly greased ovenproof serving dish. Bake for 30 minutes. Serve with crackers or corn chips.

Makes 24 servings

Fran Maurer, Queen Mother
Chesapeake Bay Red Hatters of Baltimore, Baltimore, Maryland

Reuben Spread

8   ounces Swiss cheese, diced
1½   cups mayonnaise
½   cup chopped onions
2   (12-ounce) packages chopped corned beef
1   cup sauerkraut, drained

Preheat the oven to 350°. Mix together the cheese, mayonnaise, onions, corned beef, and sauerkraut; bake in a lightly greased 1-quart dish for 25 minutes. Serve with chips, scoopers, or rye bread.

Makes 20 to 24 servings

Sherry McCoy, Gracious Lady of Golf
Star City Scarlett O'Hatters, Roanoke, Virginia

Fresh Vegetable Dip

Serve with a clever array of vegetables and include some unusual choices: steamed sugar snap peas, zucchini sticks, tiny boiled potatoes, and slices of fresh fennel.

2   cups mayonnaise
2   cups sour cream
2   tablespoons chopped chives
2   tablespoons chopped fresh parsley
2   teaspoons chopped fresh dill weed
1   teaspoon seasoned salt
1   teaspoon celery salt
1   teaspoon chopped onion
1   teaspoon Worcestershire sauce
5   drops Tabasco sauce

In a medium bowl combine the mayonnaise, sour cream, chives, parsley, dill weed, seasoned and celery salts, onion, Worcestershire, and Tabasco and mix well. Refrigerate for a day before serving so the flavors will blend.

Makes 4 cups, about 30 servings

Linda Dzwonkiewicz, Queen Mother
Bloom Violets, Mundelein, Illinois

Taco Dip

Crisp, fresh vegetables are a good contrast to the seasoned meat.

1   to 1½ pounds ground beef
1   (1¼-ounce) package taco seasoning
½   head lettuce, shredded
4   to 5 tomatoes, diced
2   cups shredded taco cheese
8   ounces Ranch salad dressing
1   bag nacho tortilla cheese chips

In a skillet brown the beef. Drain and add the taco seasoning. Let cool. When ready to serve, layer the lettuce, tomatoes, cheese, and dressing in a serving dish. Serve with the chips.

Makes 20 servings

Dawn Lovas, Ruby Tuesday
Red Tarts of SBC CSS, Cudahy, Wisconsin

Mississippi Sin Dip

So rich, so delicious, you could be forgiven for overindulging.

1   (16-ounce) container sour cream
1   (8-ounce) package cream cheese, softened
1   package bacon, cooked, drained, and crumbled
1   cup shredded mild cheddar cheese
1   (16-ounce) package cubed ham
1   bunch green onions, chopped
1   (4-ounce) can green chiles, drained

Preheat the oven to 350°. Mix together well the sour cream, cream cheese, bacon, cheddar cheese, ham, onions, and chiles, and pour into a lightly greased 10 x 8-inch baking dish. Bake for 30 to 45 minutes. Serve warm with Ritz crackers or corn chips.

Makes 8 servings

Rhonda Graves, Princess of Nonsense
Red Hot Hatters of Mid–Mississippi, Ridgeland, Mississippi

Annie's Sassy Salsa

Summer gardens and produce stands will yield the best tomatoes and peppers for this salsa.

8   large tomatoes, chopped
     Juice of 4 limes
5   tablespoons lime zest
1   to 2 hot peppers, chopped
1   medium onion, chopped
1   to 2 garlic cloves, chopped
1   bunch cilantro, chopped
1/2 cup vinegar, white or apple cider

Mix together the tomatoes, lime juice, lime zest, peppers, onion, garlic, cilantro, and vinegar. Marinate at room temperature for 1 hour. Refrigerate.

Makes 4 servings

Anne Snowden Crosman, Queen of Young at Heart Curvaceous Cuties, Sedona, Arizona

Shoe Peg Salsa

2   (16-ounce) cans black-eyed peas, drained
2   (10-ounce) cans white shoe peg corn, drained
2   (15-ounce) cans diced tomatoes with green chiles, drained
2   large sweet bell peppers, chopped
12   small green onions, chopped
6   Italian or 3 medium-size tomatoes, seeded and chopped
1   teaspoon garlic powder
1   teaspoon dried parsley
1   (16-ounce) bottle Italian dressing

Combine the peas, corn, tomatoes, bell peppers, onions, fresh tomatoes, garlic powder, parsley, and dressing in a large salad bowl, tossing well. Refrigerate overnight. Serve with tortilla chips as a dip or as a salad.

Makes 40 servings

Marylin Wallace, Queen Mom
Sophisticated Ladies, Centre, Alabama

Little Hat on the Prairie

Every July, western Washington's Sequim-Dungeness Prairie bursts into glorious purple blooms of fragrant lavender, and we enjoy the popular "Celebrate Lavender" Festival. The balmy microclimate makes everyone thirsty for quenching beverages like my Lavender-Hibiscus Cooler! Hibiscus-blossom infusions add a crimson hue to any drink— and anything else it lands on.

Business was brisk at the big lavender farm that afternoon—patrons clamored for the festive refresher they had enjoyed in previous years. I usually wear a big red hat, but on this breezy day, I wore a lovely, white, straw tea hat replete with veil and dainty ecru and lavender flowers. What was I thinking? Nevertheless, I was ready with three icy tumblers full of the Cooler for enthusiastic Red Hatters. Just as I was handing them the drinks, confessing that I was "in disguise" without my red hat, several sharp gusts of wind threatened to blow my pretty hat away. Still with all three tumblers firmly grasped in my hands, I quickly reached up to keep that hat from flying away and—oh no!—I was drenched in Lavender Hibiscus Cooler . . . and my hat was red! That'll teach me about leaving home without my colors.

LuLu Thomsett
Divalicious LuLu
Ruby Royal Majes–"Teas" . . . Regal
Dalliances for Queens
Port Townsend, Washington

Gawdy Girls Party Salsa

A salsa for mid-winter, when fresh, vine ripe tomatoes are scarce.

1/4 cup diced onion

1 tablespoon plus 1 teaspoon chopped jalapeño peppers

1 (14 1/2-ounce) can tomatoes with green chiles

1 (14 1/2-ounce) can whole peeled tomatoes, not drained

3/4 teaspoon minced garlic

1/2 teaspoon cumin

1/4 teaspoon sugar

Salt to taste

Blend the onion and jalapeños in a food processor or blender. Add the tomatoes, garlic, cumin, sugar, and salt and blend.

Makes 24 servings

Cathi Murphy, Queen Mother
Growin' Up Gawdy, Conway, Arkansas

Cowboy Caviar

1   (15-ounce) can black-eyed peas, drained
1/4 cup chopped green onions
1/4 cup chopped red bell pepper
2   cloves minced garlic
2   tablespoons olive oil
2   tablespoons cider vinegar
1   to 2 fresh jalapeños, chopped and seeded
1/4 teaspoon salt
1/4 teaspoon pepper

In a medium bowl combine the peas, onions, pepper, garlic, olive oil, vinegar, jalapeños, salt, and pepper. Refrigerate for at least 4 hours before serving. Serve with corn chips or tortilla chips.

Makes 6 servings

Ann Burns, Lady Astor
Red Hot Hatters of Euless, Euless, Texas

Mango Salsa

Delicious with chips and also great with grilled fish and flank steak.

2   mangos, peeled and chopped
2   large tomatoes, seeded and chopped

1   medium red onion, finely chopped
1   to 2 jalapeño peppers, finely chopped
    Juice of 1 lime
1   to 2 tablespoons chopped cilantro

Combine the mangos, tomatoes, onion, peppers, lime juice, and cilantro together and refrigerate. Allow to come to room temperature to enjoy the fullest flavor. Serve with your favorite chips.

Makes 8 servings

Tina Gayer, Founding Queen Mother
The Water Lilies, Strongsville, Ohio

Zesty Brussels Sprouts

Serve as a first course or offer cocktail picks.

2   (10-ounce) bags frozen Brussels sprouts
1 1/2 cups sugar
1   cup cider vinegar
5   tablespoons horseradish
    Salt to taste
2   teaspoons dry mustard

Cook the Brussels sprouts according to the package directions; drain. In a large bowl mix the sugar, vinegar, horseradish, salt, and mustard. Add the Brussels sprouts and toss lightly. Refrigerate at least 6 hours or overnight.

Makes 6 servings

Phyllis Carver, Anti-Parliamentarian
Red Bonnet Sisters, Lakeland, Florida

Caviar Pie

Impress guests with this attractively presented dip. Be sure to drain the caviar well.

4   to 6 chopped hard-boiled eggs
1   to 2 finely chopped green onions
2   sprigs celery, finely chopped
2   to 3 tablespoons mayonnaise
1/2 pint sour cream
1   small jar caviar, drained
    Chopped chives for garnish

In a small bowl mix the eggs, onions, celery, and mayonnaise. Spread on the bottom of a 9-inch glass pie plate. Spread the sour cream on top and refrigerate overnight. Carefully spread the caviar over the center of the sour cream. Place the chopped chives around the rim to meet the caviar. Refrigerate until ready to serve with crackers.

Makes 8 servings

Carol Marks, Lady Lapis
Silver Star Jewels, Vernon, British Columbia,
    Canada

Cheese and Pesto Spread

Deliciously creamy with the tantalizing flavor of pesto.

1   cup firmly packed fresh basil leaves
1/2 cup firmly packed fresh parsley sprigs
1/2 cup grated fresh Parmesan cheese
1/4 cup pine nuts, chopped walnuts, or
    slivered almonds

2   cloves garlic, quartered
2   plus 2 tablespoons olive oil or cooking oil
1   (8-ounce) package cream cheese, softened
4 1/2 ounces brie
1/2 cup whipping cream
    Wheat thin crackers or sliced French bread

In a blender combine the basil, parsley, Parmesan cheese, nuts, garlic, and 2 tablespoons oil and process until a paste forms. Gradually blend in the remaining 2 tablespoons oil. In a separate bowl beat the cream cheese and brie with a mixer until smooth.

In another bowl beat the whipping cream at medium speed until soft peaks form. Fold the whipped cream into the cheese mixture.

Line a 3 1/2 or 4-cup mold with plastic wrap. Spread one-quarter of the cream cheese mixture into mold. Top with one-third of the pesto. Repeat the layers twice. Top with the cheese mixture. Chill 6 to 24 hours. Unmold onto a serving plate and remove the plastic wrap. Garnish with fresh basil leaves and serve with crackers.

Makes 24 servings

Susanna Shirlock, Queen of Money
Scarlet Splashers, Goshen, Connecticut

Flat and Uglies

    Softened butter
6   (8-inch) flour tortillas
1 1/2 cups (12 ounces) sour cream
1   to 2 pounds Monterey Jack cheese,
    shredded
2   (4 1/2-ounce) cans chopped green chiles

Preheat the oven to 350°. Butter the tortillas and lay one in an 8 to 9-inch cake pan. Follow with layers of sour cream, cheese, and chiles. Continue layering at least six tortillas high. Bake until heated through and the cheese is melted, about 10 minutes. Cut into wedges and serve warm.

Makes 12 servings

Roxie Becker, Queen
Foxy Roxy's, Fullerton, California

Roasted Red Pepper Cheesecake

Impressive and delicious, this makes abundant servings.

1   cup butter cracker crumbs
1/4 cup (1/2 stick) butter, softened
2   (8-ounce) packages cream cheese, softened
1   cup ricotta cheese
3   eggs
1/2 cup grated Parmesan cheese
1/2 cup pesto sauce
1/2 cup roasted red peppers, puréed and drained

Preheat the oven to 325°. Mix the cracker crumbs and butter. Press onto the bottom of a 9-inch springform pan. Bake for 10 minutes. Mix the cream cheese and ricotta cheese with an electric mixer on medium speed until well blended. Add the eggs one at a time, mixing well after each addition. Blend in the Parmesan, pesto sauce, and red peppers. Pour over the crust. Bake for 55 minutes to 1 hour, or until a knife inserted

into the center comes out dry. Run a knife or metal spatula around the rim of the pan to loosen the cake. Cool before removing from the pan. Refrigerate 4 hours or overnight. Let stand 15 minutes at room temperature before serving. Garnish if desired. Serve with crackers.

Makes 20 servings

Judy Sausto, Dame Judy
Dames with a Par-Tea Hat-titude, Egg Harbor Township, New Jersey

Tuna Spread

Testers described this dip as "much better than your average tuna spread."

1   (7-ounce) can white chunk tuna, drained
2   tablespoons lemon juice
1   (8-ounce) package cream cheese
1   (5-ounce) can black olives, drained and chopped
1/2 cup mayonnaise-style salad dressing
1   cup finely chopped pecans
1   large loaf sliced bread

In a large bowl combine the tuna, lemon juice, cream cheese, olives, salad dressing, and pecans and mix well. Trim the crusts from the bread slices. Spread the tuna mixture evenly on one slice of bread and cover with a second slice. Cut into desired shapes or serve on crackers.

Makes 16 servings

Mary Francinn Parker, Queen Mom of Grandyville
The Happy Hatters, Georgetown, Texas

Fresh Tomato Tart

An easy appetizer that scored well with testers.

1   unbaked piecrust
1   cup shredded Swiss, mozzarella, or
    Gruyère cheese
1   teaspoon Italian or pizza seasoning
1/2 teaspoon dried rosemary leaves
3   medium plum tomatoes, thinly sliced
1/4 teaspoon pepper
1/8 teaspoon garlic powder

Preheat the oven to 400°. Let the piecrust stand at room temperature for 15 minutes. Line a 12-inch pizza pan or baking sheet with foil. Unroll the crust onto the prepared pan. Sprinkle the cheese, seasoning, and rosemary onto the crust. Arrange the tomato slices on top of the cheese. Mix the pepper and garlic powder together and sprinkle over the tomatoes. Bake for 20 to 22 minutes, or until golden brown. Let stand for 5 minutes. Use foil to transfer the tart to a serving platter. Cut into wedges to serve.

Makes 12 servings

Nancy Herbers, Queen Mum
Ruby Fashionettes, Holmen, Wisconsin

Taco Tartlets

Leftovers are good reheated the next day. Testers noted that tartlets made in an ordinary size muffin cup were easier to make and to remove from the pans, and the right size for one person.

1   pound lean ground beef, uncooked
1   (1 1/4-ounce) package taco seasoning mix
2   tablespoons cold water
1 1/2 cups sour cream
2   tablespoons taco sauce
1/2 cup (2 1/4 ounces) black olives, chopped
    (or more to taste)
1   cup shredded sharp cheddar cheese
3/4 cup tortilla chips, coarsely crushed

Preheat the oven to 425°. In a medium bowl mix the beef, taco seasoning, and water with your hands. Press into the bottom and up the sides of mini muffin cups. In a small bowl mix the sour cream, taco sauce, and olives. Place a spoonful of filling into each shell, mounding slightly. Sprinkle each tartlet with the cheese and crushed chips. Bake for 7 to 8 minutes. Remove the tartlets from the pan with the tip of a knife. Serve immediately or cool and freeze.

Makes 30 servings

Carol Boshaw, Queen Mother
Fun Hatters of Holiday Acres, McHenry, Illinois

Cheesy Artichoke Hearts Appetizer

2   (8-ounce) cans refrigerated crescent dinner
    rolls
3/4 cup (3 ounces) shredded mozzarella cheese
1   (3-ounce) can grated Parmesan cheese
    (3/4 cup)
1/2 cup mayonnaise or whipped salad dressing

1   (4-ounce) can artichoke hearts, drained
     and finely chopped
1   (4 1/2-ounce) can chopped green chiles,
     drained
1   (2-ounce) jar chopped pimientos, drained

Preheat the oven to 375°. Unroll the dough into rectangles. Press into the bottom and sides of a 15 x 10 x 1-inch jelly-roll pan to form a crust. Bake for 10 minutes. Combine the cheeses, mayonnaise, artichoke hearts, chiles, and pimientos; mix well. Spread over the crust. Bake an additional 15 minutes, or until the cheese is melted. Let stand for 5 minutes before cutting into squares to serve.

Makes about 12 servings

Shirley Klinner, Queen Mother
Crimson C'Hatters, Medford, Wisconsin

Bitty Beef Calzones

1   pound ground beef, uncooked
1/2 cup chopped celery
1/2 cup chopped onion
1   (4-ounce) can mushroom stems and pieces,
     drained
2   tablespoons soy sauce
     Salt and pepper to taste
2   (10-count) cans refrigerated biscuits

Preheat the oven to 325°. Combine the beef, celery, and onion in a large bowl. Mix in the mushrooms, soy sauce, salt and pepper. Flatten each biscuit into a circle. Spoon a little of the beef mixture onto each biscuit. Fold over and seal the edges. Bake for about 20 minutes.

Makes about 10 servings

Tillie Van Sickle, The Imperial Empress of Images
Western Wayne County Red Hat Society, Westland, Michigan

Gougères

This French recipe is somewhere between a popover and cheese bread. Serve them hot and watch them disappear!

1/2 cup (1 stick) butter
1   cup water
1   cup all-purpose flour
1/2 teaspoon garlic or onion salt
4   eggs
1   to 2 cups Gruyère or cheddar cheese

Preheat the oven to 375°. In a large saucepan bring the butter and water to a boil. Remove from the heat and add the flour and salt. By hand or with an electric mixer, beat in the eggs one at a time. Stir in the cheese. Drop heaping tablespoons into a circle on a greased cookie sheet. Bake 35 to 45 minutes.

Makes 10 servings

Rubye Erickson, Queen Mother
Red Hat Adventurers, Edina, Minnesota

Baked Cheese Bundles

These are tasty served hot or cold.

1   (8-ounce) package cream cheese, softened
1   tablespoon minced onion
1/4   cup grated Parmesan cheese
8   slices bacon, cooked and crumbled
2   (8-ounce) cans refrigerated crescent rolls
1   tablespoon water
1   egg white

The day before baking, mix the cream cheese, onion, Parmesan cheese, and bacon. Store covered in the refrigerator overnight. Remove the cheese mixture and form 32 balls. Preheat the oven to 350°. Unfold the crescent rolls. Cut each triangle in half. Place 1 cream cheese ball on each of the 32 triangles. Fold the dough over and crimp the edges to seal. Combine the water and egg white and beat well. Brush the egg white mixture over each triangle and bake for 15 to 17 minutes, or until golden.

Makes 15 servings

Bobbee Wilcox, Chapterette
Foxy Red Hatters, Canton, Pennslyvania

Sausage Balls

The classic, easy-to-make, everyone-loves-them snack. You can bake them, cool, and freeze in zip-top plastic bags for a ready-to-heat appetizer.

1   pound Italian sausage, removed from casing
1   pound cheddar cheese, grated
3   cups biscuit baking mix

In a skillet cook the sausage until browned and crumbly; drain. Combine the sausage and cheese. Add the biscuit mix and enough water to moisten.

Preheat the oven to 450°. Roll the mixture into walnut-size balls and arrange on an ungreased baking sheet. Bake for 8 to 10 minutes. Serve hot with mustard for dipping.

Makes about 40 pieces

Sheila Cassella, Marchioness of Mirth
Purple Passion Majesties, Chicago, Illinois

Oh-So-Easy Sweet Kielbasa

4   (1-pound) packages beef kielbasa
2   pounds brown sugar

Slice the kielbasa into 1-inch pieces. Put into a 5-quart slow cooker. Pour the brown sugar on top. Cook for 3 hours on high or 6 hours on low. Stir occasionally. The sugar will melt and glaze the meat.

Makes 32 servings

Debbie Gilio, Chapterette
Coastal Rose Buds, Pismo Beach, California

Pepperoni Loaf

Cut into small pieces for a snack or appetizer, or serve as a casual entrée.

1 (1-pound) loaf frozen white bread dough, thawed and at room temperature
1 (8-ounce) package sliced provolone cheese
1 (8-ounce) package sliced pepperoni
1 (8-ounce) package shredded cheddar cheese
1 egg white
   Garlic salt and pepper to taste

Preheat the oven to 350°. Roll out the dough on a 13 x 11-inch baking sheet and let rise for about 20 minutes. Arrange the provolone cheese over the entire dough. Lay the pepperoni slices in rows. Cover with the cheddar cheese. Roll up jelly-roll style and pinch the ends to seal. Brush the egg white over the entire loaf and then sprinkle the garlic salt and pepper and any other spices you enjoy on top. Cut slits in the loaf before baking to let out the steam. Bake for 30 minutes. Let cool and then slice. Serve with spaghetti sauce as a dip.

Makes 6 to 8 servings

Erika Eidam, Sparkles
Naples Knoties, Long Beach, California

BLT Bites

You may need to cut a thin slice from the bottom of each tomato so it will stand up on a serving plate.

16 to 20 cherry tomatoes
1 pound bacon, cooked and crumbled
1/2 cup mayonnaise
1/3 cup chopped green onions
3 tablespoons grated Parmesan cheese
2 tablespoons chopped fresh parsley

Cut a thin slice off each tomato top, and scoop out the insides with a small spoon. Discard the insides. In a small bowl combine the bacon, mayonnaise, onions, cheese, and parsley. Spoon into the tomatoes. Refrigerate for several hours.

Makes 16 to 20 servings

Winnie Corbett, Queen Mother
Les Grande Dames of Cecil County, North East, Maryland

Drunken Hot Dogs

1 cup firmly packed brown sugar
1 cup ketchup
1 cup bourbon
1 pound mini party franks

In a saucepan simmer the brown sugar, ketchup, and bourbon for 20 minutes, or until the sugar is melted and the alcohol smell has evaporated. Add the franks and simmer 15 more minutes, or until they are plump. Serve with toothpicks in a fondue pot or chafing dish to keep them warm.

Makes 16 servings

Linda LoPresti, Vice Queen
Bergen Beauties, Paramus, New Jersey

Stuffed Mushrooms

1   pound sweet Italian sausage, casing
     removed
1/4 cup grated Parmesan cheese, plus more for
     sprinkling
1/2 cup Italian breadcrumbs
1/4 cup (1/2 stick) salted butter
1   pound large mushrooms

In a large skillet fry the sausage over medium heat, breaking the meat up into small pieces. Add 1/4 cup Parmesan cheese, breadcrumbs, and butter, heating and stirring until the butter melts. Remove from the heat.

Preheat the oven to 350°. Clean the mushrooms and remove the stems. Chop the stems finely, add them to the sausage mixture and mix well. Arrange the mushroom caps in a baking dish. Stuff each mushroom cap with about 1 tablespoon sausage mixture. Sprinkle each mushroom with a little cheese. Bake for about 15 minutes, or until the mushrooms have slightly softened and the tops are brown. Drain on paper towels.

Makes 12 to 18 servings

Barbara Weinberg, Princess of Past and Present
Dusty Desert Roses, Cathedral City, California

Garlic Mushrooms Morgan Hill

4   garlic cloves, minced
1/3 cup olive oil
2/3 cup white wine vinegar
1/3 cup dry red or white wine
2   tablespoons soy sauce
2   tablespoons honey
2   tablespoons chopped fresh parsley
1   teaspoon salt
2   pounds fresh mushrooms

In a skillet over medium heat, sauté the garlic in the oil. Add the vinegar, wine, soy sauce, honey, parsley, and salt. Stir until the mixture is well blended and hot. Place the mushrooms in a heat-proof container with a tight fitting lid. Pour the hot mixture over the mushrooms; allow to marinate for 1 to 3 hours or more, stirring several times. Save the marinade for later use on more mushrooms or use it as a salad dressing.

Makes 5 to 8 servings

Linda Tarvin, Court Jester
The Stinkin' Red Roses, Morgan Hill, California

Bacon Roll-Ups

If you're a kitchen experimenter, try using chive-flavored cream cheese. Once cooked, these can be frozen for later reheating.

13   to 16 slices white bread, crusts removed
1   (8-ounce) package cream cheese, softened
1   pound bacon, each slice halved
     horizontally

Preheat the oven to 400°. Spread each bread slice thinly with cream cheese. Cut each slice of bread

Her Queenship Joan of the Red Hat Gang of Purple Persuasion,
Mistress of Mayhem Carole O'Brien, and Queen Judy of the Red Hat
Mommas celebrating high tea at the Plaza in New York

The Villages First Red Hatters Hope De Armond
and Barb Quail hamming it up at a Christmas tea

Hannah Belle's Hottenannies
in Knoxville, Tennessee

Photo courtesy of Mary Finley, Queen Mother of the Violettas

Violettas of Albany, New York, enjoying a buffet lunch
at the Saratoga Race Track

Photo courtesy of Carol R. Ritter of the Beaded Babes

The Beaded Babes of Fullerton, California

The Rowdy Red Hat Mommas after a day of recipe testing

The Goodwill Ambassadors from Dazzling Darlings presenting
Exalted Queen Mother Sue Ellen Cooper (second from left)
with a blueberry cake (page 13)

The Dallas Red Hat Flashes of Dallas, Texas, enjoying lunch at Jorg's in historic Plano, Texas

The Villages First Red Hatter Penny gives a big smile as she rides in the golf cart for the Red Hat Parade in The Villages, Florida

Wild Roses of Peoria, Illinois, at Pumpkin Patch of Second Baptist Church

"How many pies can we make with this one, girls?" Lady Arleen Hempel, Lady Kelley Hemple, Royal Equestrian Brittany Mabusth, and Queen Mum Nadia Giordana of the Merry Mad Hatters or Dayton, Minnesota

The Missouri Livewires at Café Italia in Kansas City, Missouri

Red Hat Seagulls celebrating life

Pinehurst Crimson Camellias
decorating cookies, and their tongues,
in Pinehurst, North Carolina

Red Hat Honey Queen Mum Toni
Garmaneating dessert first on her birthday

Photo courtesy of Lucinda Denton

Hannah Belles's Hootenannies in Knoxville, Tennessee

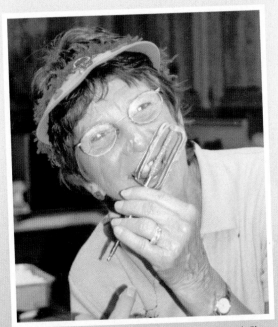

Photo courtesy of Queen Mother Linda Glenn

Rowdy Red Hat Momma Hilda Trudeau
tasting the beater in Luck, Wisconsin

Photo by Kevin Farrington

Modoc Red Hot Hatter Diana Fuller
wears a purple hat during
her birthday month

Queen Marge of the Titian Queens
and Ladies-in-Waiting holding her
birthday cake in Virginia City, Montana

Patricia Stiles of the Aloha Girls of Apple Valley making
her mom's homemade baked beans

into thirds. Roll up and wrap with half a slice of bacon. Spear with a toothpick. Bake for 30 minutes, or until the bacon is completely cooked.

Makes about 40 pieces

Marilyn Barr, Queen
Red Hot Royals of Roxbury, Ledgewood, New Jersey

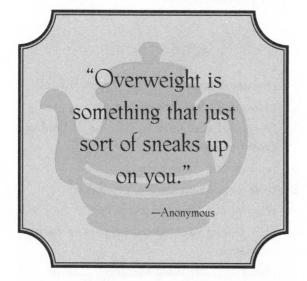

"Overweight is something that just sort of sneaks up on you."

—Anonymous

Pickled Shrimp

4   pounds small unpeeled shrimp (26 to 30 size)
2   onions, thinly sliced
1   cup olive oil
1/4   cup tarragon vinegar
2   tablespoons pickling spice
2   teaspoons salt
1/2   teaspoon dry mustard
6   bay leaves
   Dash of cayenne pepper
   Lettuce
   Cherry tomatoes for garnish

In a large pot cook the shrimp in boiling water for 3 to 5 minutes. Drain, rinse in cold water, and peel. In a large zip-top bag or covered bowl, combine the shrimp with the onions, oil, vinegar, pickling spice, salt, mustard, bay leaves, and cayenne pepper. Refrigerate overnight. When ready to serve, line a serving dish with lettuce. Use a dark variety for contrast. Remove the shrimp from the marinade and place them on the lettuce. Garnish with cherry tomatoes.

Makes 12 servings

Kathleen Rivest, Duchess of Dough
Sassy Red Hatters, Winston-Salem, North Carolina

Shrimp Puff Oriental

1/4   cup vegetable oil
1   (8-ounce) package cream cheese, softened
2   (41/4-ounce) cans shrimp, drained
3   teaspoons soft breadcrumbs
3   drops sesame oil
3   tablespoons pineapple juice
1   package wonton wrappers

In a skillet heat the vegetable oil to 370°. In a large bowl mix the cream cheese, shrimp, breadcrumbs, sesame oil, and pineapple juice. Place 1 tablespoon filling in each wonton wrapper. Fold over and seal. Deep fry in the hot vegetable oil for about 3 minutes, or until lightly browned. Drain on paper towels and serve with sweet and sour sauce or mustard.

Makes 6 to 8 servings

Hisako Hampshire, Queen Mother
Sassy Silly Sisters, Lawton, Oklahoma

Tortilla Rollups

1 1/2 (8-ounce) containers cream cheese
1/2 cup chopped onions
1 (2 1/2-ounce) can chopped olives, drained
1 green pepper, chopped
Picante sauce to taste
6 (6-inch) flour tortillas

In a large bowl mix the cream cheese, onions, olives, green pepper, and picante sauce. Spread the mixture on each tortilla and roll up. Refrigerate at least one hour. Cut each into bite-size pieces and serve.

Makes 24 servings

Doreen Bohrer, Queen Mother
The Red Razzle Dazzles, Wimberley, Texas

Hot Sweet Little Sausages

1 1/2 pounds medium link sausage
1 (20-ounce) can pineapple chunks
1/2 cup firmly packed light brown sugar
2 tablespoons cornstarch
1 tablespoon soy sauce
1/4 cup lemon juice
1/3 cup maraschino cherries
1 green bell pepper, chopped

In a skillet over medium heat, cook the sausage until done. Cut into small pieces. Drain the pineapple, reserving the juice. Add enough water to the pineapple juice to make 1 cup. In a small saucepan mix the pineapple juice with the brown sugar, cornstarch, soy sauce, and lemon juice. Cook over medium heat for about 10 minutes, or until thick. Add the sausage, pineapple, cherries, and green pepper. Serve warm in a chafing dish.

Makes 12 to 15 servings

Sally Battle, Queen Fun
Shamrock Red Hatters, Dublin, Georgia

Spinach Florentine Antipasto

3 (8-ounce) cans refrigerated crescent rolls
1 (16-ounce) bag frozen spinach
1 (8-ounce) container light chive and onion cream cheese
6 tablespoons cottage cheese
2 tablespoons feta cheese, crumbled
1/4 plus 1/4 cup sliced black olives
1/4 plus 1/4 cup sautéed red peppers or roasted red peppers
1 plus 1 cup shredded Monterey Jack or mozzarella cheese
7 eggs
1/4 plus 1/4 cup grated fresh Parmesan cheese

Preheat the oven to 375°. Spray a 13 x 9-inch deep-dish pan with cooking spray. Roll out 1 can crescent rolls into a rectangle and place it in the pan, pressing until the bottom of pan is entirely covered.

Cook the spinach according to the package directions. Drain and press out all the liquid. In a large bowl mix the cream cheese, cottage cheese, and feta cheese until smooth and spread half the mixture over the rectangle. Sprinkle half the spinach, 1/4 cup olives, 1/4 cup red peppers, and 1 cup Jack cheese on top. Beat together 3 of the eggs with 1/4 cup of the Parmesan cheese and pour evenly on top.

Repeat the layering with the second can of crescent rolls, the remaining half of the cream cheese mixture and the spinach, the remaining 1/4 cup olives, 1/4 cup red peppers, and 1 cup Jack cheese. Beat 3 more eggs with the remaining 1/4 cup Parmesan cheese and pour on top. Roll out the remaining can of crescent rolls and place it on top. Beat the remaining egg and brush it on top. Freely prick the crust with a fork.

Cover with a loose tent of aluminum foil and bake for 30 minutes. Uncover and bake an additional 10 to 20 minutes, or until brown on top and bubbly on the bottom.

After baking, let sit for 1 hour before serving; serve at room temperature. Refrigerate leftovers.

Makes 12 to 15 servings

Carol A. Kinelski, Husband's Royal Pain
Cats in the Red Hat, Richmond, Kentucky

Smashed Green Olives

1   (16-ounce) jar large green Spanish olives with pits, drained
1   celery stalk, finely chopped
1   teaspoon dried oregano
2   garlic cloves, minced
1   teaspoon cider vinegar
    Few drops of olive oil

Soak the olives in cold water 1 hour. Drain. Smash the olives with meat tenderizer. Soak another 30 minutes in clean cold water. Drain and combine with the celery, oregano, garlic, vinegar, and olive oil in a container with a lid. Shake the container to mix evenly. Store the olives in the refrigerator, shaking the container occasionally until serving time. Use within two weeks.

Makes 10 servings

Theresa Cassidy, Queen Mum
REDucators R Us, Forestburgh, New York

Hot Peanuts

Hot pepper flakes and chili powder give peanuts some dash.

3   tablespoons olive oil
1   to 2 tablespoons dried crushed red pepper
4   garlic cloves, pressed
1   (12-ounce) can cocktail peanuts
1   (12-ounce) can Spanish peanuts
1   teaspoon salt
1/2 teaspoon chili powder

In a large skillet heat the oil over medium heat. Add the crushed red pepper and cook for 1 minute. Stir in the garlic and peanuts and cook for 5 minutes, stirring constantly. Remove from the heat and sprinkle with the salt and chili powder. Drain on paper towels and cool completely. Store in an airtight container.

Makes 24 servings

Sue Stein, Hysterian
Hen–der–Hatters, Hendersonville, Tennessee

Spiced Pecan Halves

A little something sweet for the snack table. If you like a heavy glaze, use 2 cups pecans. For a lighter coating, add the other cup of nuts.

1   cup sugar
1/3 cup evaporated milk
1/2 teaspoon cinnamon
2   to 3 cups pecan halves
1/2 teaspoon vanilla extract

In a large saucepan boil the sugar, milk, and cinnamon until it starts to thicken. Add the pecan halves and vanilla. With a slotted spoon, remove the pecans individually onto waxed paper.

Makes 16 to 24 servings

Gena Walls, Queen Mamabear
The BEARables, Richmond, Texas

Bonna's Tipsy Tomatoes

Think of these as a one-bite Bloody Mary.

3   or 4 cartons cherry tomatoes
     Vodka
     Seasoned Salt
     Lemon Pepper

Pierce the bottom of each tomato several times with a toothpick. Place the tomatoes, pierced side down, in a wide, shallow bowl or glass baking dish. Pour vodka into the dish halfway up the sides of the tomatoes. Refrigerate overnight.

Skewer each tomato with a decorative toothpick to serve. Mix equal portions of seasoned salt and lemon pepper (start with 2 tablespoons of each) and add to the vodka. Dip the tomatoes into the mixture to eat.

Makes 20 servings

Beth Wheeler, Queen Mother
Scarlett's Starlets, Jonesboro, Georgia

Shrimp Salsa

1   (2-pound) package frozen cooked salad shrimp, thawed
     Juice of 3 to 4 lemons
1   onion, chopped
4   pickled chile peppers, sliced very thin
1   tomato, peeled and diced
4   tablespoons canola or olive oil
1   tablespoon white vinegar
     Salt and pepper to taste
     Cilantro
     Celery (optional)
     Red or orange peppers (optional)

Place the shrimp and enough lemon juice to cover them in a glass bowl. Refrigerate for 1 to 2 hours, stirring occasionally. Add the onion, chile peppers, tomato, oil, vinegar, salt and pepper, cilantro, celery, and peppers. Serve with corn chips.

Makes 20 servings

Gaylene Miller, Vice Queen GiGi
The Red Hattitudes of Galveston, Ticki Island, Texas

Baptist Punch

We were having our yearly Christmas Drop-In, and the guests included many people in the senior group of which I was program director. Knowing that many in this group were teetotalers, I decided to have two punches: one with alcohol, the other without.

The plan was for me to label each bowl so guests would know which punch was which, but as luck would have it, we had a rush of drop-ins before I could get the labels in place. By the time I got a look at the punch bowls, it was clear that everyone preferred the punch with alcohol. I was so embarrassed for making the error. I came out to my guests from the kitchen, saw the punch bowl almost finished, and said, "Oh my, I am so sorry, but I did not get time to label the punch, and I believe some of you drank the punch with alcohol in it." In reply, one of my most admired seniors said, "Shhhh child, what we don't know won't hurt us, and the good Lord knows we were ignorant." At that, I giggled and made more punch this time with the correct labeling.

Dana Burns
Queen Mystic
Mystical Dixie Pixies
Oxford, Alabama

Hot Mulled Apple Cider

1   quart apple cider
1   liter raspberry ginger ale
4   cinnamon sticks
1/2 teaspoon freshly grated nutmeg
1   apple, cored and quartered

In a slow cooker combine the cider, ginger ale, 3 cinnamon sticks, and nutmeg. Heat on low for 30 minutes to 1 hour. Before serving, grate the remaining cinnamon stick on the apple slices and float them on top.

Makes 20 servings

Vonnie Clark, Mother Superior
Dames with a Par-tea Hat-titude, Absecon, New Jersey

Coffee Punch

1   cup boiling water
1   (2-ounce) jar instant coffee
3   cups sugar
1   gallon milk
1/2   gallon chocolate ice cream
1/2   gallon vanilla ice cream

In a large saucepan boil the water and stir in the coffee and sugar. Cool and refrigerate. When ready to serve, transfer the coffee mixture to a punch bowl. Stir in the milk and ice creams.

Makes 60 servings

Katie Griffin, Dynamite
Women in Time, Houston, Texas

Spinach Things

Easy to make and fun to pop into your mouth. Testers thought lemon juice or lemon pepper would add more zing and a dipping sauce would be fun. Recipe can be halved.

2   cups herb-seasoned stuffing mix
1   large onion, chopped fine
4   eggs, beaten
3/4   cup (1 1/2 sticks) butter, melted
1/2   cup grated Parmesan cheese
1/2   teaspoon garlic salt or powder
1/4   teaspoon pepper or lemon pepper
1   teaspoon Accent (optional)

1/4   teaspoon dried thyme
2   (10-ounce) boxes frozen chopped spinach, thawed and squeezed dry

In a large bowl mix the stuffing, onion, eggs, butter, cheese, garlic powder, pepper, Accent, thyme, and spinach. Roll into small balls and freeze. (For ease in freezing, place the balls on a cookie sheet until frozen and then transfer them to a plastic bag). When ready to serve, preheat the oven to 350°. Place the balls on a cookie sheet and bake for 20 minutes.

Makes 20 to 24 servings

Dianne Buehrer, Sister
Ramblin' Red Rose, Canton, Ohio

Eggnog

If properly mixed, this eggnog results in a fluffy delight that has to be dipped into cups and eaten with a spoon. A far cry from store-bought. Beware, this recipe contains raw eggs, which can pose a health risk.

6   eggs, separated
6   tablespoons sugar
1   pint heavy whipping cream
1   cup bourbon
     Nutmeg for sprinkling

In a large bowl beat the egg yolks until lemon colored. Fold in the sugar and refrigerate. Using clean beaters, whip the egg whites until very stiff. Refrigerate. In another bowl beat the whipping cream until stiff and refrigerate. Fold the bourbon into the egg yolk mixture and pour into the punch bowl. Using a slotted spoon, fold the egg whites into the punch bowl. Slowly fold the whipped cream into punch bowl. Sprinkle nutmeg on top of each serving.

Makes 20 servings

Cil Mace, Vice QM
Vintage Roses, Warner Robins, Georgia

Orange Eggnog

Take a shortcut by doctoring up store-bought eggnog with a few select ingredients.

1   quart eggnog
1 1/2   cups milk
1   (16-ounce) can frozen orange juice concentrate, thawed
1/2   cup (or less) light rum
1/4   cup (or less) orange-flavored liqueur
    Ground nutmeg
    Orange zest

In a large pitcher mix the eggnog, milk, orange juice, rum, and orange liqueur. Refrigerate several hours or overnight to blend the flavors. To serve, pour into small glasses and sprinkle with the nutmeg and fresh orange zest.

Makes 16 servings

Susan Roe, Queen Mother Sue
Heavenly Hatters, Seal Beach, California

Red Hat Diva Holiday Tea

This spicy drink is good hot or cold.

1   quart plus 6 cups water
3   cups sugar
    Cinnamon sticks to taste
    Whole cloves to taste
    Whole allspice to taste
8   tea bags
1/2   cup lemon juice
23   ounces grapefruit juice
1   (64-ounce) bottle apple juice
2   (46-ounce) cans pineapple-orange juice
1/2   teaspoon salt
1/2   pint apricot brandy (optional)

In a large saucepan combine 1 quart water, sugar, cinnamon sticks, cloves, and allspice. Boil rapidly for at least 10 minutes. Bring the remaining 6 cups of water to a boil over the tea bags. Steep for 20 minutes until very strong. Strain the syrup into a large bowl. Add 1 or 2 cinnamon sticks to the bowl. Pour the lemon juice, grapefruit juice, apple juice, and pineapple-orange juice into the bowl and stir to mix. Add the tea and salt. If desired, add the apricot brandy. Stir to mix.

Makes 50 servings

Mary Waters, Queen Mum
Red Hat Divas, Moseley, Virginia

Rhubarb Slush

If you grow rhubarb, you'll welcome this recipe. It's super-refreshing in the summer.

16   pounds rhubarb
2   gallons (32 cups) water
4   cups sugar
1   cup lemon juice
1   (3-ounce) package strawberry gelatin
4   cups vodka, gin, or rum
     Lemon-lime soda

Wash the rhubarb and remove all the leaves. Chop the stalks and place them in a large saucepan with the water and sugar. Bring to a boil over medium-high heat. Cook the rhubarb until tender. Add the lemon juice and gelatin. Cool and add your preferred liquor. Purée the rhubarb mixture in a blender in batches. Pour into a 13 x 9-inch pan, cover and freeze 6 hours or overnight. To serve, scoop a little of the mixture into a glass and top it off with lemon-lime soda.

Makes 26 servings

Pat Kiebach, Princess
Sweet T.A.R.T.S., Harrisburg, South Dakota

Snowman Soup

If your gathering includes children, bring them joy with Snowman Soup.

1   cup hot water
1   envelope cocoa mix

1   Hershey kiss candy
1   candy cane
     Mini marshmallows

Fill a cup with steaming water. Add the cocoa mix. Add a Hershey kiss. Stir with a magic stick (candy cane). Top with snowman dumplings (mini marshmallows). Enjoy while warm and yummy.

Makes 1 serving.

Bonnie Jameson, Lady Bonnie
Bloomin' Tea Roses, San Dimas, California

Peach Iced Tea

3   (11 1/2-ounce) cans peach nectar
2 1/4   quarts brewed tea
1   cup sugar
1/4 cup fresh lemon juice

Stir together the peach nectar, tea, sugar and lemon juice and chill until ready to serve.

Makes 10 servings

Leah Wright, Lady Winnie
Elite Ladies of The Hat, Franklinton, North Carolina

Pink Hatter Lemonade

2   (12-ounce) containers frozen pink lemonade concentrate
1   (750-milliliter) bottle vodka (or to taste)
2   liters lemon-lime soda

Thaw the lemonade concentrate and pour it into a gallon container. Add the vodka to suit your taste. Add the lemon-lime soda. Secure a top on the container and do the "Pink Hat Twist." Hold the container tightly and twist your hips from side to side while listening to your favorite upbeat song. Repeat until all the ingredients are mixed together or anytime you add more ingredients to the mixture.

Makes 10 to 12 servings

Tiffany Cunningham, Princess SuperStar
Sugar Plum Girls, Lebanon, Tennessee

Scandinavian Almond Tea

5	tea bags
2	cups hot water
1 1/2	cups sugar
2 1/2	cups cool water
	Juice of 3 lemons
1	teaspoon almond extract
1	teaspoon vanilla extract

Steep the tea bags in the hot water. Add the sugar and cool water. Stir in the lemon juice and extracts. Refrigerate 6 hours or more. Serve over ice.

Makes 3 quarts, about 12 servings

Diana Grosz, Queen Mum
Platinum Valley Plum Tarts, Sioux Falls, South Dakota

Brandy Slush

Make the base up to a week or more in advance and keep in the freezer. Also good made with bourbon instead of brandy.

7	plus 2 cups water
2	cups sugar
4	tea bags
1	(12-ounce) can frozen lemonade concentrate, thawed
1	(12-ounce) can frozen orange juice concentrate, thawed
2	cups brandy
	Lemon-lime soda

Boil 7 cups water with the sugar for 10 minutes. In a separate saucepan, boil the remaining 2 cups water and steep the tea bags for 20 minutes. Mix the tea with the sugar water and add the lemon and orange concentrates and brandy. Put in the freezer. To serve, scoop a tablespoon or so of slush into a glass and fill with soda.

Makes about 80 servings

Sharon Smith, Queen of Hearts
Ruby Rebels with Purple Passion, Palmyra, Nebraska

Bay Leaves or Bailey's

One evening, a group of friends met for dinner. At the end of our meal, our waiter asked if we wished to order an after dinner drink, and I ordered coffee with a shot of Bailey's Irish Cream, but I shortened it to "Bailey's."

With my coffee, the young, inexperienced server brought me a saucer of bay leaves! The group of friends thought this was hilarious, and we laughed until tears streamed down our cheeks.

Despite the hilarity, I didn't want to embarrass the employee, so I put the leaves in my coat pocket. He returned to our table, and, seeing the plate empty of bay leaves, asked if I needed more!

Jo Anne Silva
Chapterette
El Paso Red Hat Border Babes
El Paso, Texas

Homemade Kahlúa

10   teaspoons instant coffee
2 1/2   cups sugar
4   cups water
3   cups vodka
5   teaspoons vanilla extract

In a large saucepan boil the coffee, sugar, and water for 1 hour. Cool and add the vodka and vanilla. Can be served right away.

Makes 12 servings

Shirley Ramby, *Princess*
Red Hat Divas Too, Spring Hill, Florida

Red Head's Irish Cream

Decorate the decanter with ribbon and you have a lovely gift. If raw eggs are a problem in your area, substitute an equal amount of pasteurized egg substitute.

1 1/4   cups light rum
1   (14-ounce) can sweetened condensed milk
1/2   pint whipping cream
4   eggs
2   tablespoons dark chocolate syrup
2   teaspoons instant coffee granules
1   teaspoon vanilla extract
1/2   teaspoon almond extract
2   (16-ounce) glass decanters

Pour the rum, condensed milk, cream, eggs, syrup, coffee granules, and extracts into a blender. Purée until well blended. Pour the mixture into two decanters. Cover and refrigerate 3 to 4 hours. To serve, remove from the refrigerator, shake the bottle gently to redistribute the chocolate, and pour into small glasses. If by some chance there are leftovers, recap the bottle and return it to the refrigerator. This will keep up to two weeks.

Makes 10 servings

Sami Botelho, Sun Queen
Sleepless in Seattle Sassy Scarlet Sisterhood, Seattle, Washington

Cosmotini

Just leave out the vodka for a "virgin" version of this tasty drink.

2   cups vanilla ice cream
1   cup cranberry juice
1/2 cup vodka
4   strawberries or any red fruit

Combine the ice cream, cranberry juice, and vodka in a blender. Purée until smooth. Pour into martini glasses and garnish with a strawberry or fruit of your choice.

Makes 4 servings

Stephanie Layer, Queen Cosmo
The Red Cosmopolitans, Maplewood, Minnesota

Gin Julep

This julep is so party-ready that it's made in a portable cooler.

2   (10-pound) bags crushed ice
3   (6-ounce) cans frozen limeade concentrate, thawed
3   (6-ounce) cans frozen orange juice concentrate, thawed
6   (12-ounce) cans lemon-lime soda
25   fresh mint leaves
1   (750-milliter) bottle gin
     Additional mint leaves for garnishing drinks

In a medium-size portable cooler that has been washed, spread 1 bag of the ice. Pour 1 can of limeade concentrate, 1 can of orange juice concentrate, 2 cans of soda, and 8 to 10 mint leaves evenly over the ice. Layer twice more, dividing the remaining 1 bag of ice and ending with some of the ice on top. Pour the gin evenly over top. Let sit for 30 minutes or longer. Ladle into plastic beverage cups and garnish with fresh mint.

Makes 25 servings

Jane Ross, Baroness
High Steppin' Red Hatters, Carrollton, Missouri

Strawberry Champagne Fancy Schmancy Drink

For those times you really have something to celebrate.

1   quart pineapple sherbet
1 1/2   cups sliced fresh strawberries, divided
3/4   cup champagne or sparkling white grape juice

Spoon the sherbet evenly into six stemmed glasses. Top each with 1/4 cup strawberries. Pour champagne over each serving. Serve immediately.

Makes 6 servings

Susan Duncan, Queen Susie Q
Derby City Ladybugs of Louisville, Kentucky, Louisville, Kentucky

Strawberry and Cream Cooler

Treat yourself like the queen you are.

1/2   cup sugar
1   envelope unsweetened strawberry drink mix (Kool-Aid)
1   cup milk
1   small scoop vanilla ice cream
2   strawberries, cleaned and hulled, plus 1 whole

Stir together the sugar and drink mix. Store in a tightly covered container until ready to use. In a blender combine the milk, ice cream, 2 strawberries, and 1 to 2 tablespoons of the drink mix mixture until smooth. Pour into a tall glass and garnish with the remaining strawberry on the rim of the glass.

Makes 1 serving.

Mary Sanders, Queen Mom Mary
Royal Tea Red Hatters, Peoria, Arizona

Bloomer Droppers

Both the virgin and "spirited" versions of this party drink drew rave reviews from testers.

2   cups crushed ice
1   (6-ounce) can frozen pink lemonade concentrate, thawed
6   ounces (3/4 cup) vodka (optional)
2   to 3 peaches pitted with skins
1   tablespoon confectioners' sugar

In a blender combine the ice, lemonade, vodka, peaches, and sugar. Process until well blended. Serve at once.

Makes 4 servings

Elaine Spader, Queen
Red Hat Honeys, Randolph, Nebraska

Pink Hatters

Some people are surprised to learn that not every member of the Red Hat Society actually wears a red hat! The red hat and purple regalia are reserved for those members of our "disorganization" who have celebrated (!) their fiftieth birthdays—and beyond. Did we pick this birthday arbitrarily? Well . . . yes! We think that one's fiftieth birthday is quite a milestone in life. After all, surviving fifty years of living (with one's sense of humor intact) is something to be proud of! Donning a glamorous purple ensemble and a bright red hat (with, perhaps, a mysterious veil or a sweep of plumes) is a Red Hatter's way of showing the world that she has arrived!

But what about those younger women who want to join our party early? When some of these "youngsters" clamored to join us, we were, at first, surprised. Then we were pleased and flattered. We decided to welcome them in with open arms. But we did agree that purple and red must still be earned. A woman under 50 (no matter how many years under) is asked to wear lavender clothing and a pink hat. These are just paler versions of the bolder purple and red. She'll grow up (and into) the colors. And, when she does, her chapter will throw a "Reduation" for her. She will turn her pink and lavender in for her purple and red. Because now she is a "big girl"!

Fresh Strawberry Daiquiri

1   pint fresh strawberries, sliced
1   (6-ounce) can lemonade frozen
    concentrate, thawed
2   tablespoons confectioners' sugar
1   cup light rum

In a blender combine the strawberries, lemonade, sugar, and rum. Purée to mix well. Add ice to the 5-cup level, cover, and blend until smooth. Pour into glasses. Garnish the glasses with a whole fresh strawberry.

Makes 6 servings

Esther Taylor, Queen Bee
Frolicking Fuchsias, Lakeville, Minnesota

Holiday Wine Coolers

A light, sparkling drink with just a hint of wine flavor.

1   bottle white Zinfandel wine
1   (2-liter) bottle ginger ale
1   gallon lemonade
1/4 cup grenadine syrup
    Fresh mint

In several large pitchers or a punch bowl, combine the wine, ginger ale, lemonade, and syrup. Refrigerate to chill thoroughly. Serve garnished with the mint leaves.

Makes 50 servings

Joan L. Kriner, Queen Mother Lady Joan
The Red Hat Society of Shippensburg,
    Shippensburg, Pennsylvania

Holiday Wassail Punch

1   (48-ounce) can unsweetened pineapple
    juice
1   (48-ounce) can cranberry juice
1   cup brown sugar
1/2 teaspoon salt
1   teaspoon whole cloves
2   sticks cinnamon
2 2/3 cups water

In the carafe of a 20-cup coffeemaker, combine the pineapple and cranberry juices, brown sugar, and salt. Put the cloves and cinnamon in the basket. Pour the water into the reservoir and run the coffeemaker through its brew cycle.

Makes 20 servings

Lani Zimmerman, Lady of the Lake
Colonie Red Hatters, Nassau, New York

SIX

⸙ Nurture Before Noon ⸙

BREAKFAST, BRUNCH & BREADS

It is said that breakfast is the most important meal of the day. Since most Red Hat Society gatherings include food of some type, it may be said that we consider every meal to be the most important meal of the day (at least at the time we're eating it).

It wasn't long after the Red Hat Society began to spread that we began to be entertained by stories of imaginative chapter events. What fun to hear that many chapters decided to resurrect that old standby from our earlier years, the slumber party. These get-togethers often begin in the early evening and continue well into the next morning—and even beyond. After watching movies, exchanging stories, and giggling into the night, chapterettes find that nothing is more fun than sharing breakfast the next morning, still in their pajamas.

And who knows, after refueling lavishly, the ladies may just decide to put on their "regular" regalia and hit the mall together. It's hard to let the really good events end too soon.

Elephant Ears

2   cups milk
5   tablespoons butter-flavored or regular
    shortening
5   tablespoons sugar
2   teaspoons salt
2   packages active dry yeast
1/2 cup warm water
4   plus 2 cups all-purpose flour
    Vegetable oil for frying

In a saucepan bring the milk nearly to a boil, stirring often to prevent sticking. It should be steaming and have small bubbles around the edge. Cool to lukewarm. Add the shortening, sugar, and salt. In a large bowl sprinkle the yeast into the warm water to soften. Let stand 5 minutes. Add the warm milk mixture and mix well. Beat in 2 cups of the flour until smooth. Stir in enough of the remaining flour to make a stiff dough. Knead the dough 10 minutes until smooth and elastic. Transfer the dough into a greased bowl and allow to rise until doubled in size. Pinch off egg-size pieces of the dough and stretch into elephant ear shapes. Deep fry in 375° vegetable oil.

Makes 12 to 18 pastries

Judy Hudson, Subject
Red Mint Hatters, Sturgis, Michigan

Danish Puff

Although this Danish is best prepared on serving day, it can be prepared one day ahead of time and refrigerated. Bring to room temperature before serving.

CRUST
1   cup all-purpose flour
1/2 cup (1 stick) butter
2   tablespoons cold water

DANISH
1/2 cup (1 stick) butter
1   cup water
1   cup all-purpose flour
3   large eggs
1   teaspoon vanilla extract
1   teaspoon almond extract

FROSTING
2   tablespoons butter, softened
1   (3-ounce) package cream cheese, softened
8   ounces confectioners' sugar
2   teaspoons vanilla extract
    Milk to thin
    Chopped nuts
    Sliced maraschino cherries

Preheat the oven to 350°. For the crust, blend the flour and butter with a fork. Add the water. Mix like piecrust dough. Divide the dough into two portions. Pat each portion into an 8 to 9-inch strip about 7 inches wide on ungreased cookie sheets. (Use 2 sheets.)

For the Danish, place the butter and water in a small saucepan and bring to a boil. Reduce the heat to low and add the flour, stirring vigorously until the mixture leaves the sides of the pan in a smooth ball. Remove from the heat and quickly beat in the eggs one at a time until the mixture is smooth and shiny. Beat in the vanilla and almond extracts. Spread this mixture over the dough strips. Bake for 1 hour. Cool slightly on a rack and frost while warm.

For the frosting, combine the butter, cream cheese, sugar, and vanilla. Mix well. Thin with a little milk. Spread on the warm Danishes. Decorate with the chopped nuts and cherries.

Makes 20 to 25 servings

Irene Findorff, Queen Irene
Red Hat Divas of Metairie, Metairie, Louisiana

"My next house will have no kitchen—just vending machines."

—Anonymous

Danish Kringle

A brunch or breakfast treat for pastry lovers that's also nice for tea.

DOUGH
2 1/2 cups all-purpose flour
2 tablespoons granulated sugar
1/2 teaspoon salt

1/2 cup (1 stick) butter, softened
1 egg, separated
1/2 cup milk
1/4 cup warm water
1 package active dry yeast

FILLING
4 tablespoons butter, softened
1/2 cup firmly packed brown sugar
Chopped nuts (optional)

For the dough, blend the flour, sugar, salt, and butter in a bowl. In a separate bowl combine the egg yolk and milk and mix well. Add to the flour mixture and mix well. Combine the warm water and yeast in a small bowl. Let stand for 5 minutes until foamy. Add to the dough mixture and beat until well combined; the dough will be very soft. Cover the dough and chill in the refrigerator. (The dough can be used after 2 hours or chilled up to 48 hours.) Divide the dough in half. Roll each half into a 6 x 9-inch rectangle. Beat the egg white and spread over the halves.

For the filling, beat or stir together the butter, sugar, and nuts, if using, in a small bowl. Spread half the mixture over the dough. Roll to enclose the filling. Place the kringle on a greased baking sheet. Repeat with the other half of the dough. Cut slits about 1 inch apart in the top of the dough. Let rise about 45 minutes. Preheat the oven to 350°. Bake the kringle for 20 to 25 minutes.

Makes 10 servings

Betty Keiper, Chapterette
Red Hat Angels, Atkins, Iowa

Monkey Bread

3   (12-ounce) cans old-fashioned buttermilk biscuits
1/2 cup granulated sugar
1/2 cup firmly packed brown sugar
3/4 cup (1 1/2 sticks) butter
2   teaspoons cinnamon

Preheat the oven to 350°. Cut the biscuits into quarters and arrange in a greased and floured Bundt pan. Fill the pan about half full. In a small saucepan or microwaveable bowl, heat the sugars, butter, and cinnamon until the butter is melted. Pour over the biscuits quarters. Bake for 34 to 40 minutes, or until lightly brown.

Makes 6 to 8 servings

Sherry Pell, Queen
West Coast Sisterhood of The Red Hat Society, Huntington Beach, California

Red Raspberry Cheese Danish

Start this pastry the night before you plan to serve it.

2   (8-ounce) cans crescent rolls
2   (8-ounce) packages cream cheese, softened
1   cup granulated sugar
1   egg, separated
1   teaspoon vanilla extract
1   (12-ounce) jar red raspberry jam
1   cup confectioners' sugar
2   tablespoons milk

Preheat the oven to 350°. Press 1 can crescent rolls out flat in a lightly greased 13 x 9-inch glass baking dish. Mix the cream cheese, granulated sugar, egg yolk, and vanilla in a bowl. Spread the mixture over the rolls. Spread the jam very gently over the cheese mixture so that the jam and cheese do not get swirled together. (You may wish to soften the jam first and drop it by the spoonful instead.) Roll out the remaining can of crescent rolls to fit on top of the jam. Brush the top of the rolls with the egg white. Bake for 30 to 35 minutes. Cool.

Mix the confectioners' sugar and milk. Spread over the pastry. Refrigerate 6 to 8 hours or overnight.

Makes 12 servings

Patricia Mickley, Queen Mother
Redbuds of Bedford, Thaxton, Virginia

Overnight Pancakes with Fruit Sauce

Testers adored this "excellent" dish that looks and tastes great. They also liked the idea of preparing the batter the night before serving. One big bonus of this recipe—the fruit sauce is great with ham, too.

PANCAKES

1   package active dry yeast
1/4 cup warm water
4   cups all-purpose flour
2   tablespoons baking powder
2   teaspoons baking soda
2   teaspoons sugar
1   teaspoon salt

6   large eggs
1   quart buttermilk
1/4 cup vegetable oil

Fruit Sauce
1   (20-ounce) can cherry pie filling
1   (15-ounce) can jellied or whole cranberry sauce
1/4 cup maple syrup
1/4 cup orange juice
3   tablespoons butter

In a small bowl dissolve the yeast in warm water and let stand for 5 minutes. Meanwhile in a large bowl combine the flour, baking powder, baking soda, sugar, and salt. In a medium bowl beat the eggs, buttermilk, and oil together. Stir the wet ingredients into the bowl of dry ingredients until the batter is moist. Stir in the yeast mixture. Cover the bowl with plastic wrap and refrigerate 6 to 8 hours or overnight.

Stir when ready to use. Pour 1/4 cup batter for each pancake onto a hot, lightly greased griddle. When bubbles form on the pancake, turn it over and continue cooking until golden brown. Cool any leftover pancakes and freeze for later use.

For the fruit sauce, combine the pie filling, cranberry sauce, syrup, orange juice, and butter in a pan and heat until the butter has melted and the sauce is hot, stirring occasionally. Serve the sauce warm.

Makes 2½ dozen pancakes, about 8 servings

Ann Sample, Vice Mother
Jewels of the Desert, Albuquerque, New Mexico

Raised Czech Dumplings

An adventurous breakfast for cooks who like a little something different.

1   package active dry yeast
1/4 cup warm water
1   teaspoon sugar
3/4 cup warm milk
1   egg
1   teaspoon salt
2   slices white bread, cubed
3   cups all-purpose flour

Dissolve the yeast in the warm water. Combine the sugar and warm milk in a medium bowl. Beat in the egg and salt; add the bread cubes and flour and mix to make a stiff dough. On a floured flat service divide the dough into four small football shapes. Cover with a clean kitchen towel and let rise 30 to 45 minutes.

Fill a large pot more than half full of water and bring to boil. Place the dumplings into the water. Cover and boil for 20 minutes. To slice, use a string or thread—a knife may shred the delicate dumplings. Serve with a thick brown gravy.

Makes 6 dumplings

Diana Blazek, Queen Mum
The Red Hot Grand Hatters, Surprise, Arizona

Foreseeing the Future

As the Red Hat Society has grown—to many thousands of chapters, in many countries—I have had occasion to answer the questions of countless reporters. One of their first questions, in almost every case, goes something like this: "Did you ever, in your wildest dreams, envision something this huge coming out of one simple idea?"

The answer, of course, is always "No!" When the first five women met for tea, wearing purple clothing and red hats, we were quite aware that we were being silly. We thought that we would probably do this once; then we would move on to something else. No one could have been more surprised than we were when we found ourselves having more fun than we had enjoyed in a long time! Before those tea pots were even empty, we found ourselves making plans to continue going out together in our red and purple. We dubbed ourselves "The Red Hat Society." And I proclaimed myself Queen! The entire concept seemed to appear, full-blown, in one afternoon. So . . . do we Red Hatters believe in magic?

What do you think?

Great Granola

Visit a Whole Foods store for some of the ingredients, including rolled wheat flakes and bulk sesame seeds.

2	cups old-fashioned rolled oats
2	cups rolled wheat flakes
1	cup shredded coconut
2/3	cup roasted peanuts
2/3	cup sunflower seeds
1/2	cup coconut oil
1/2	cup honey
1	teaspoon vanilla extract
1/3	cup sesame seeds
1/3	cup wheat germ
1	cup or more raisins

Preheat the oven to 350°. Mix the oats, wheat flakes, coconut, peanuts, and sunflower seeds in a large bowl. Do not mix too long or mixture will become sticky. In a small saucepan heat the oil, honey, and vanilla slightly. Pour over the dry ingredients. Spread the mixture thinly on a cookie sheet. Bake, stirring often, for 25 to 30 minutes, or until desired brownness. Cool. Add desired amount of raisins. Store in an airtight container.

Makes 8 cups

Fay Warta, Queen
Pearls & Red Hat Society, Delano, Minnesota

Wheat Germ–Cashew Granola

Serve with fresh fruit, strawberries, yogurt, or milk.

6	cups old-fashioned rolled oats
1	cup shredded coconut
1	cup wheat germ
1/2	cup sunflower seeds
3/4	cup cashews halves
1/2	cup vegetable oil
1/2	cup honey
1/3	cup water
1 1/2	teaspoons salt
1 1/2	teaspoons vanilla extract
1	cup raisins or craisins

Preheat the oven to 350°. In a large bowl, combine the oats, coconut, wheat germ, sunflower seeds, and cashews. In a small bowl mix together the oil, honey, water, salt, and vanilla. Pour the honey mix over the oatmeal mixture. Stir to coat well. Spread the mixture onto greased baking sheets. Bake, stirring often, for about 30 minutes. Cool thoroughly. Add the raisins. Store in an airtight container until ready to serve.

Makes 12 servings

Roxie Becker, Queen
Foxy Roxy's, Fullerton, California

Fresh Fruit Salad Pita

Got a big bunch? This makes twenty-four servings and is portable, so it's good for serving breakfast out of the back of the car, at a golf tournament, at the beach, or other "away" location.

1/2   cup orange juice (about 1 orange)
2   large oranges, peeled, sectioned, and coarsely chopped
2   large apples, coarsely chopped
2   cups green grapes
1   cantaloupe, cut into 1-inch cubes
1   pint fresh strawberries, sliced
1   pint fresh blueberries
12   pita breads, halved
1   (8-ounce) container nonfat vanilla yogurt
3   tablespoons brown sugar

Combine the orange juice, oranges, apples, grapes, cantaloupe, strawberries, and blueberries in a bowl and toss to distribute. Spoon 1/2 cup of the fruit mixture into each pita half with a slotted spoon. Top each with a spoonful of yogurt and then sprinkle with the brown sugar. Serve immediately.

Makes 24 servings

Cara Rodgers, Queen Cara
Coral Springs Sweethearts, Coral Springs, Florida

Cinnamon–Raisin French Toast Soufflé

Rich, unusual, flavorful, and "perfect for brunch," raved testers.

1   loaf cinnamon-raisin bread (cut into small cubes)
12   ounces cream cheese, softened
3/4   cup (1 1/2 sticks) butter, softened
1/4   plus 1/2 cup maple syrup
10   eggs
3   cups half-and-half
     Cinnamon sugar
     Confectioners' sugar

Place the chopped bread in a well-buttered 13 x 9-inch glass pan. Mix the cream cheese, butter, and 1/4 cup maple syrup until smooth. Spread on top of the bread, leaving some openings through which to pour an egg mixture. (This is a thick mixture; you'll spread it out with a knife.) Beat the eggs and half-and-half with the remaining 1/2 cup maple syrup. Pour over the bread and sprinkle with cinnamon sugar. Cover and refrigerate 6 to 8 hours or overnight. When ready to bake, uncover and bake for 50 to 55 minutes at 350°. Cut into squares and sprinkle with confectioners' sugar.

Makes 8 to 12 servings

Arlene Reid, Princess of Fun
Dakota Wild Roses, Valley City, North Dakota

Rise of the Yeast Monster

One day the kitchen was a little more drafty than usual, and my bread dough stubbornly refused to rise as quickly as I thought it should. But it was a beautiful spring day, and I certainly didn't want to close up the doors and windows.

Inspiration struck, and I decided to place the large bowl in the microwave—not to cook it, but just to get it out of the draft. An emergency came up, and the dough was promptly forgotten as the kids and I raced out of the house.

When we returned home hours later, we were dumbfounded to find that the dough had finally risen. And risen. And risen! It had actually pushed the door open and had blobbed out all around! We had a hearty laugh over it, punched it down, shaped, and baked it anyway. It tasted great!

JoEllen Smith
Queen Mum
Scarlet Darlings
Clearwater, Florida

Bread Pudding

Pretend it's a soufflé and you could be eating dessert for breakfast.

3   eggs, beaten
1   (14-ounce) can sweetened condensed milk
2   tablespoon butter, melted
6   cups cubed bread or rolls
    Blueberries, raspberries, cherries, nuts, etc.

Preheat the oven to 350°. Mix together the eggs, milk, and butter. Place the bread cubes in a buttered 13 x 9-inch casserole. Place desired fruit and nuts on top. Add 2 1/2 cups hot water to the milk and egg mixture. Pour the mixture evenly over the bread and fruit. Bake for 40 minutes, or until a knife comes out clean.

Makes 6 to 9 servings

Billie Sperry, Lady Billie
Desert Darlins, Mesa, Arizona

Double Berry Multi-Grain Pancakes

Flax seed, oats, wheat germ, and olive oil—a breakfast treat that's great for glowing good health.

1/2 cup rolled oats
1/2 cup whole wheat flour
1/4 cup ground flax seed
1/4 cup toasted wheat germ
2 tablespoons sugar
1 tablespoon baking powder
1/4 teaspoon salt
1 1/3 cups low-fat milk
2 eggs, beaten
2 tablespoons olive oil
1/2 cup dried cranberries
1/2 to 1 cup blueberries

In a large bowl combine the oats, flour, flax seed, wheat germ, sugar, baking powder, and salt and mix well In a medium bowl combine the milk, eggs, and oil and mix until well combined. Add to the dry ingredients and mix just until moistened. Stir in the cranberries and blueberries. Heat a greased griddle over medium-high heat. For each pancake, pour 1/4 cup batter onto the hot griddle. Cook until bubbles form and break on the surface and the top seems dry. Turn and brown the other side.

Makes about 12 (4-pancake) servings

Saima Davis, Queen Saima
Gateway Red Hatters, St. Louis, Missouri

Sourdough Pancakes

A yeast pancake batter that's prepared the night before—ideal for quick breakfasts and morning entertaining.

2 cups all-purpose flour
1 package active dry yeast
2 cups warm milk
1 or 2 eggs
1 teaspoon baking soda
1/2 teaspoon salt
1 tablespoon sugar
2 tablespoons melted butter or bacon grease

Mix the flour, yeast, and warm milk in a large bowl. Cover and let stand at room temperature for at least 8 hours. When ready to cook, beat the eggs, baking soda, salt, sugar, and butter in a bowl. Add to the yeast mixture and mix well. Spoon about 1/4 cup batter onto a hot griddle. Cook until bubbles form and burst and pancakes appear dry. Turn and brown the other side.

Makes 6 servings

Sally Widby, Lady Night in Gale
Sassy Lassies, Pekin, Illinois

Apple-Stuffed French Toast with Praline Topping

Start with the lesser quantity of apples, adding more the next time you make it, if you like. The dish is also good without the sauce.

FRENCH TOAST

1/4 cup (1/2 stick) butter

6 to 8 apples, peeled and sliced

1 plus 1/4 teaspoons ground cinnamon

1/2 plus 1/4 teaspoons ground nutmeg

1/2 cup firmly packed light brown sugar

1 loaf cinnamon-raisin bread

8 large eggs

3 cups milk

2 tablespoons granulated sugar

TOPPING

1 cup (2 sticks) butter, softened

1 cup firmly packed brown sugar

1 cup chopped pecans

2 tablespoons light corn syrup

1/2 teaspoon cinnamon

1/2 teaspoon nutmeg

For the French toast, melt the butter in a saucepan over medium heat. Add the apples, 1 teaspoon cinnamon, 1/2 teaspoon nutmeg, and brown sugar. Cook until blended. Arrange a row of buttered raisin bread in a greased 13 x 9-inch pan. Layer the apples on top and add another row of bread. Combine the eggs, milk, granulated sugar, the remaining 1/4 teaspoon cinnamon, and the remaining 1/4 teaspoon nutmeg until blended. Pour over the bread slices, making sure all are covered evenly with the egg mixture. Spoon some mixture in between the slices. Cover with foil and refrigerate overnight.

Preheat the oven to 350°. For the praline topping, combine the butter, brown sugar, pecans, corn syrup, cinnamon, and nutmeg in a medium bowl and beat well. Spread over the French toast before baking. Bake for 40 to 50 minutes until puffed and lightly brown. Serve with maple syrup.

Makes 6 to 8 servings

Roma Scriven, Madame of Music
Star City Scarlett O'Hatters, Roanoke, Virginia

Pajama Party Breakfast Bake

Good served with sliced spiced apples.

7 slices bread

8 ounces grated cheese (low-fat works well)

5 tablespoons butter, melted

3 eggs, beaten

1/2 cup ham cubes or bacon bits (optional)

2 cups milk

In a greased 13 x 9-inch baking dish layer the bread and cheese. Combine the butter, eggs, and ham. Pour over the bread and cheese mixture. Pour the milk over all, cover, and refrigerate for at least 6 hours. When ready, bake at 300° for 1 hour.

Makes 12 to 15 servings

Connie Cummings, Queen Connie
Red Hatter Chatters, Silver Springs, Florida

Crème Brulée French Toast

You'll need to dress up especially sparkly for this rich, wonderful brunch meal.

Make it in advance and then heat up the slices with a drizzling of butter.

1	quart heavy whipping cream
2	to 3 tablespoons vanilla extract
3/4	cup sugar
8	egg yolks
1	to 2 loaves challah or other egg bread, cut into 1/2-inch slices
1/2	cup (1 stick) butter, melted
	Fresh berries and maple syrup for serving

In a large saucepan over low heat warm the whipping cream, vanilla, and sugar until the sugar dissolves. Gradually whisk in the egg yolks. Set the cream mixture aside to cool. Grease a 10 1/2-inch springform pan and line it with foil. Layer the bottom of the pan with the slices of bread. Pour one-fourth of the cream mixture over the bread. Layer the bread and cream mixture three more times. Press a layer of aluminum foil directly on the top layer of bread. Top with a plate, a can of beans, or other weight and refrigerate for 1 hour.

Preheat the oven to 325°. Place the springform pan in a larger pan and pour in 1 inch of water. Bake for 1 1/2 hours. Let cool and then refrigerate until ready to use.

When ready to serve, heat the oven to 350°. Turn the bread mixture out of the pan and cut into slices. Arrange the slices on a baking sheet. Brush each slice with the melted butter. Heat for 15 to 20 minutes. Serve with fresh berries and pure maple syrup.

Makes 14 to 16 servings

Janie Bee, Queen
Scarlett O'Hatters of Howard County, Ellicott City, Maryland

Crab Quiche Deluxe

If you can find frozen crabmeat, treat your chapterettes to that; the flavor is superior to canned.

8	ounces crabmeat
1	(4-ounce) jar sliced mushrooms, drained, or 4 ounces sliced fresh mushrooms
1/2	cup shredded mozzarella cheese
1/2	cup shredded provolone cheese
4	eggs
1	cup sour cream
1	cup cottage cheese
1/2	grated Parmesan cheese
1/4	cup buttermilk biscuit mix
1	teaspoon Old Bay Seasoning

Preheat the oven to 350°. Lightly grease a 10-inch pie or quiche dish. Layer the crabmeat, mushrooms, and cheeses in the dish. In a blender or food processor combine the eggs, sour cream, cottage cheese, Parmesan, biscuit mix, and Old Bay. Blend until smooth. Pour into the dish. Bake for 45 minutes, or until set. Cool 5 minutes before serving.

Makes 4 to 6 servings

Pat Frederick, Lady-on-the-Go
Spiffy with Hattitude, Clarksville, Maryland

Hattitude Breakfast–Brunch Egg Bake

6 to 7 slices white bread, crusts removed
1 pound pork sausage, browned, casing removed
6 eggs
4 cups shredded cheddar cheese
2 cups half-and-half or heavy whipping cream
1 teaspoon salt
1 teaspoon dry mustard

Preheat the oven to 350°. Grease a 13 x 9-inch baking dish. Spread butter on both sides of each slice of bread and layer the bread in the bottom of the prepared baking dish. Brown the sausage in a skillet over medium heat, breaking into pieces; drain. Layer the sausage over the bread, then sprinkle the cheese over the sausage. In a bowl beat the eggs, half-and-half, salt, and mustard. Pour the egg mixture over cheese. Bake, uncovered, for 45 minutes.

Makes 6 to 8 servings

Patty Kobus, Chapterette
Brookfield Scarlet Hattitudes, Brookfield, Wisconsin

Crab Soufflé

Special occasions call for a special touch—crabmeat is suitably indulgent.

6 slices bread, crusts removed, cubed
1 pound fresh crabmeat
2 tablespoons minced onion
2 tablespoons chopped green bell pepper or pimiento
1/2 cup diced celery
1/2 teaspoon salt
1/4 teaspoon dry mustard
1 tablespoon lemon juice
1/2 cup mayonnaise
2 eggs, beaten
1 1/2 cups milk or 1 cup half-and-half plus 1/2 cup milk
1/2 cup sour cream (or enough to cover top of casserole)
3 tablespoons grated Parmesan cheese

Place half the bread in a large bowl. In another bowl combine the crabmeat, onion, bell pepper, celery, salt, mustard, lemon juice, and mayonnaise. Mix well. Pour over the cubed bread in the large bowl. Then add the remaining bread. Mix the eggs and milk and pour over the crab mixture. Let stand 1 hour or overnight, or until the milk is absorbed. Preheat the oven to 325°. Put in an ungreased soufflé dish. Spoon the sour cream over the top of the crab mixture. Sprinkle with the Parmesan cheese. Bake for 45 minutes, or until set and light golden brown. Serve immediately.

Makes 6 servings

Dee Wunderlich, Queen Dee
PARFF—Purple And Red For Fun, Napa, California

Sausage Stars

"Looks good, taste good, and lots of fun," wrote one tester. Wonderful for brunch and also a terrific appetizer for a finger-food buffet.

1   pound (2 cups) bulk pork sausage, cooked
1 1/2 cups grated sharp cheddar cheese
1 1/2 cups grated Monterey Jack cheese
1   cup Ranch salad dressing
1   (2-ounce) can sliced ripe olives, drained
1/2   cup chopped red bell pepper
     Vegetable oil or nonstick cooking spray
1   package fresh or frozen wonton wrappers

Preheat the oven to 350°. Drain the cooked sausage with paper towels. Combine the sausage, cheeses, salad dressing, olives, and bell pepper in a large bowl. Lightly grease (or spray) a mini (or regular) size muffin tin. Press 1 wonton wrapper into each cup. Brush the top (or spray) with oil. Bake for 5 minutes or until golden brown. Removed the baked wonton wrappers from the muffin tin and place on a baking sheet. Repeat this process until you have 4 to 5 dozen shells. Fill the wonton shells with the sausage mixture. Arrange on a baking sheet and bake until bubbly.

Makes 4 to 5 dozen.

Betty Spencer, Queen
Scarlet Divas, Atoka, Tennessee

Ham-N-Cheddar Broccoli Quiche

Great for dinner too, and packs well for take-along lunches.

1   (9-inch) refrigerated piecrust
1   cup milk
4   eggs, slightly beaten
1/2   teaspoon dry mustard
1/4   teaspoon pepper
1   cup cubed cooked ham
1 1/2 cups shredded cheddar cheese
1   cup frozen broccoli flowerets, thawed
1   tablespoon chopped onion

Press the piecrust into a 9-inch pie dish. Preheat the oven to 350°. In a bowl combine the milk, eggs, mustard, and pepper. Layer the ham, cheese, broccoli, and onion in the piecrust. Pour the egg mixture over the ham mixture. Bake for 40 to 50 minutes, or unitl a knife inserted in the center comes out clean. Cool for 5 minutes; cut into wedges. Refrigerate any remaining quiche.

Makes 6 servings

Elsie Stacy, Just Me . . . El See
Red Hot Red Hat Readers of Decatur, Decatur, Tennessee

Sausage-Rice Brunch Casserole

Unusual and delicious for a change of pace in the morning.

2 pounds bulk pork sausage

1 small onion, chopped

2 plus 2 cups crisp rice cereal

3 cups cooked white rice

4 cups shredded mild cheddar cheese

6 eggs slightly beaten

2 (10³/4-ounce) cans cream of celery soup

1/2 cup milk

Preheat the oven to 325°. Brown the sausage and onion; drain. Grease the bottom of a 13 x 9-inch pan. Cover the bottom of the pan with 2 cups rice cereal. Sprinkle half the sausage mixture over the cereal. Layer half the rice and half the cheese over the sausage. Mix the eggs, soup, and milk together and pour half the mixture over the cheese. Repeat the layers with the remaining 2 cups rice cereal, sausage mixture, rice, cheese, and egg mixture. Bake 30 to 35 minutes. You can prepare the casserole the night before and refrigerate but increase the baking time to 45 minutes.

Makes 12 to 15 servings

Louise Hauck, Queen
Red Hat Rockers, Humboldt, Iowa

English Toad in the Hole

In England little sausage links are the "toad." The "hole" is a small Yorkshire pudding, which is shaped like a puff pastry shell. This version is simpler.

1¹/2 cups all-purpose flour

2 teaspoons baking powder

1/2 teaspoon salt

3 tablespoons vegetable oil

2 eggs

1 to 1¹/4 cups milk

12 small link sausages

Preheat the oven to 350°. Combine the flour, baking powder, salt, oil, eggs, and milk in a bowl and stir until well blended. Place the sausages in a greased 13 x 9-inch pan. Pour the mixture over the sausages. Bake for 40 to 45 minutes until golden brown. Serve hot with maple syrup or apple butter.

Makes 6 to 8 servings

Patt Kudron, Lady IMAGINE!
Raspberry Tarts, Lincoln, Nebraska

Baked Cheese

Baked Cheese is one useful dish—you can serve it for breakfast, lunch, or dinner.

2 cups grated Colby cheese

2 cups grated cheddar cheese

1 (15-ounce) carton egg substitute
Chopped ham, cooked sausage, chopped onions, cooked bacon (optional)

Preheat the oven to 350°. Mix the cheeses and egg substitute together until well blended. Add any of the optional ingredients. Bake for 25 to 30 minutes, or until the center is set. Cut into wedges to serve.

Makes 6 servings

Debbie Divine, Main Dame
Divine Dames, Wagoner, Oklahoma

Creamy Sausage Brunch Soufflé

Use ordinary bread for this rather than light or diet bread.

8   slices bread, crusts removed and cubed
1 1/2 pounds pork sausage, browned and drained
12   ounces cheddar cheese, grated
2 1/2 cups plus 1/2 cup milk
4   eggs
2   tablespoons self-rising or all-purpose flour
1   (10 3/4-ounce) can cream of mushroom
     soup
1   cup sliced fresh mushrooms

Spread the bread cubes over the bottom of a greased 13 x 9-inch casserole dish. Top with the sausage. Sprinkle the cheese over the top. Combine 2 1/2 cups milk, eggs, and flour and beat until smooth. Pour over the cheese. Cover and refrigerate at least 8 hours.

To bake, preheat the oven to 300°. Blend the remaining 1/2 cup milk, soup, and mushrooms. Pour over the casserole. Bake for 1 1/2 hours.

Makes 8 to 10 servings

Alice Duvall, Queen Alice
Red Hat Valley Chicks, Minden, Nevada

Baked Eggs Dijon

Quietly elegant and suitable for dinner as well as breakfast or brunch.

1   garlic clove, cut in half lengthwise
6   to 8 eggs
1   cup sour cream
1/4 cup grated cheddar cheese
1   tablespoon white wine
1   to 2 tablespoons Dijon mustard
1   teaspoon salt
1/3 cup buttered breadcrumbs

Preheat the oven to 350°. Rub the inside of a 1 1/2 to 2-quart baking dish with the garlic. Grease the dish and break the eggs into the dish. Combine the sour cream, cheese, wine, mustard, and salt in a bowl and mix well. Pour the mixture over the eggs, spreading as needed to cover evenly. Sprinkle with the breadcrumbs. Place the baking dish in a larger dish or pan and pour in 2 inches hot water. Bake for 15 minutes, or until the eggs are set.

Makes 3 to 4 servings

Sheila Cassella, Marchioness of Mirth
Purple Passion Majesties, Chicago, Illinois

Breakfast Burrito Bar

All of the elements except the scrambled eggs are easily prepared the night before. Then just scramble the eggs (and heat the tortillas, if you like), bring out the dishes, and line up the royal subjects for breakfast.

1   pound hot bulk pork sausage
1   bunch green onions
1   cup grated hot pepper cheese
2   cups grated cheddar cheese
12   eggs
1   (16-ounce) can refried beans

MOM!

Ten years after I was married, I finally had to admit to my mother that I could not fix pork that tasted like that wonderful pork she had served every morning with pancakes and hash browns when I was a child, back in the central Minnesota logging country. We had lived off the land mostly, catching, growing, and gathering what we ate, including blueberries, fish, wild game and two gardens. Now, we didn't raise pigs, just turkeys and sheep. However, from hunting and fishing, we ate all sorts of meat that other people might not have ventured to try, including turtle, fish, venison, bear, and moose.

My little mother laughed and confessed to me that "that great pork" I had been eating was yet another wild food: raccoon. I would never knowingly agree to eat a "masked bandit," but she knew me well, and knew how much I liked to eat pork when visiting my grandparents' farm in North Dakota. The power of suggestion is strong!

Jackie Tarpinian
Queen Mother
Jewels of the Prairie
Jamestown, North Dakota

1   (16-ounce) carton sour cream
1   jar salsa
1   package 8-inch flour tortillas

The night before serving, brown and drain the sausage, slice the green onions, and combine the cheeses in a bowl. Refrigerate.

When ready to serve, scramble the eggs and mound in a serving bowl. Heat the refried beans and place them in a bowl. Spoon the sour cream and salsa into bowls. Heat the tortillas if desired.

Arrange the bowls, placing the tortillas and eggs first, and let the guests build their own burritos.

Makes 10 to 12 servings

Elaine Busby, Exalted Queen Mother
Flaming Fedoras, Rancho Palos Verdes, California

Ham and Egg Strata

There's a lot of great morning eating going on in Red Hat homes judging from the number of great strata recipes we received.

4   eggs
3   cups milk
3   tablespoons all-purpose flour
1   tablespoon dry mustard
3   cups cubed ham
3   cups cubed French bread
1/2 pound shredded cheddar cheese
3   tablespoons melted butter

Beat the eggs and milk until frothy. In a small bowl combine the flour and dry mustard. Layer the ham, bread, and cheese in a greased 13 x 9-inch casserole dish. Sprinkle the flour mixture on top and drizzle the melted butter over all. Pour the eggs and milk over all. Cover and refrigerate 6 to 8 hours or overnight. To serve, bake at 350° for 45 minutes.

Makes 8 servings

Joan Kania, Princess
Hat'Attudes of Safety Harbor, Clearwater, Florida

Sausage Fondue

8   slices bread, cubed
2   cups grated sharp cheddar cheese
1   pound sausage links
4   eggs
2 1/2 cups plus 1/2 cup milk

1/2 teaspoon salt
3/4 teaspoon dry mustard
1   (10 3/4-ounce) can cream of mushroom soup
1/2 cup milk

Arrange the cubed bread in a greased 13 x 9-inch baking dish. Top with the cheese. Brown the sausage, drain, and cut each link into three pieces. Arrange the pieces over the cheese. Beat the eggs with 2 1/2 cups milk, salt, and mustard and pour over the sausage. Cover and refrigerate for at least 6 hours.

When ready to serve, preheat the oven to 300°. Dilute the soup with the remaining 1/2 cup milk and pour over the casserole. Bake for 1 1/2 hours, or until set.

Makes 8 to 10 servings

Jacqueline Pickering, Chapterette
Queen City Crimson Belles, Cincinnati, Ohio

Potato Crust Ham and Cheese Quiche

Clever idea. Hash browns form the crust of the quiche.

3   cups frozen prepared hash browns, thawed
5   tablespoons butter, melted
1   cup diced, cooked ham
1   cup shredded cheddar cheese
1/4 cup green chiles, diced
2   eggs
1/2 cup milk

1/2 teaspoon salt
1/4 teaspoon pepper

Preheat the oven to 425°. Press the hash browns between paper towels to remove any excess moisture. Press into the bottom and sides of an ungreased 8-inch pie pan. Drizzle with the butter and bake for 25 minutes, or until browned.

In a bowl combine the ham, cheese, and green chiles. Spoon over the crust. In a small bowl beat the eggs, milk, salt, and pepper. Pour the mixture over all. Reduce the heat to 350° and bake for 25 to 30 minutes, or until the center is set.

Makes 8 servings

Kali Sitton, Princess Need 4 Speed
Rhat Pacque, Canyon Country, California

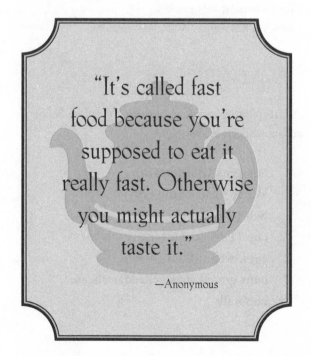

"It's called fast food because you're supposed to eat it really fast. Otherwise you might actually taste it."

—Anonymous

Sausage Quiche

It's just as easy to make two quiches as one. Once baked, they keep nicely in the refrigerator for a couple of days.

1 pound bulk pork sausage
1 pound button mushrooms, coarsely chopped
1/4 red bell pepper, finely chopped
3 green onions, finely chopped
1 (10-ounce) package chopped spinach, thawed and well drained
2 cups shredded Cheddar or Jack cheese
2 (8-inch) piecrusts
6 eggs
1 1/2 cups heavy cream or half-and-half
1/4 teaspoon ground nutmeg

Preheat the oven to 350°. In a skillet, brown the sausage and drain slightly. Sauté the mushrooms, bell pepper, and onions over medium-high heat for about 5 minutes, or until tender. Add the spinach and heat through. Remove from the heat and stir in the cheese and cooked sausage. Bake the piecrusts for 7 to 8 minutes. Let cool slightly to firm up, and then spoon the sausage mixture into the crusts, dividing equally. In a bowl beat the eggs, cream, and nutmeg. Pour over the sausage mixture in the piecrusts. Bake for 35 minutes, or until the center is set and a knife inserted in the quiche comes out clean.

Makes 2 quiches, 4 to 6 servings each

Evelyn Wolf, Queen Mother
Crimson Bonnets, Sublimity, Oregon

Sausage and Rye Brunch Bake

Bake up a change-of-pace with hearty sausage and flavorful rye bread.

4   slices seeded rye bread
1   pound sausage links
1   cup grated cheddar cheese
7   eggs
2   cups milk
1   teaspoon dry mustard
     Dash of pepper

Preheat the oven to 350°. Tear up the bread. Arrange the bread in a well greased 13 x 9-inch casserole. Brown and cook the sausage. Drain well. Cut into thin slices and cover the bread. Sprinkle with the cheese. Beat the eggs, milk, mustard, and pepper. Pour over the cheese. Bake for 30 or 40 minutes. Test with a knife. Serve hot with fruit.

Makes 6 servings

Maureen Warner, Queen Mom Pat
The Belles of Bridgewater, Bridgewater, Connecticut

Spanish Sauce

If you love Huevos Rancheros or salsa with your sunny-side-ups, you know the great taste of peppers and tomatoes with eggs. Spicy food lovers can add a little heat with fresh jalapeños.

3   tablespoons vegetable oil
1/3   cup chopped onion

1/4   cup chopped green bell pepper
3/4   cup sliced mushrooms
1   (14-ounce) can diced tomatoes
1   tablespoon cornstarch
1   teaspoon salt
     Dash of pepper
2   teaspoons sugar

Heat the oil in a skillet over medium heat. Sauté the onion, bell pepper, and mushrooms. Drain the tomatoes, reserving 2 tablespoons juice. Blend the cornstarch with the reserved juice. Add the tomatoes, cornstarch mixture, salt, pepper, and sugar to the skillet. Cook over low heat, stirring, for 15 minutes, or until thickened. Offer this sauce for scrambled eggs with sausage on the side.

Makes 1 quart.

Rita Rennels, Reluctant Rita
Ravishing Red Hatters, Westfield Center, Ohio

Grits Soufflé

A little paprika sprinkled over the top before baking adds a reddish, golden glow.

1   cup grits (not instant)
     Water for cooking grits
     Salt to taste
1/2   cup (1 stick) butter
2   eggs, well beaten
2   cups grated sharp cheddar cheese
1/4   cup milk

Preheat the oven to 350°. Cook the grits in water with salt according to package directions. Stir the butter into the hot cooked grits. Stir in the beaten eggs, cheese, and milk. Spoon the mixture into a greased, 1 1/2-quart baking dish or round casserole. Bake for 20 minutes, or until set. Serve at once.

Makes 5 to 6 servings

Sandra Calhoun, Duchess of Bargains
Delightful Anderson Hattitude Sisterhood, Anderson, South Carolina

Frozen Fruit Cups

Margarita mix has just the right puckery sweet and sour quality to wake up your appetite. When you want to create an attractive serving table, spoon the mixture into freezer-safe parfait or sherbet dishes.

1   (6-ounce) can frozen orange juice concentrate, thawed
2   large bananas, sliced
1   (6-ounce) can mandarin oranges, drained
1   cup red grapes, sliced
1   (8.5-ounce) can pineapple tidbits, drained
1   (10-ounce) package frozen strawberries in syrup, thawed
2   cups lime margarita drink mix

Combine the orange juice concentrate, bananas, oranges, grapes, pineapple, strawberries, and margarita mix in a large bowl. Spoon into twelve 6-ounce clear, plastic cups or ramekins. Cover with clear plastic wrap. Freeze for at least 6 hours. Let stand at room temperature 30 to 40 minutes before serving.

Makes 12 (4-ounce) servings

Virginia Houdyshell, Vice Queenie
Serendipity Reds, Pratt, Kansas

Hot Fruit Casserole

1   (20-ounce) can peach halves
1   (20-ounce) can pear halves
1   (20-ounce) can apricot halves
1   (20-ounce) can pineapple chunks
1   (10 to 16-ounce) bottle red maraschino cherries
4   tablespoons butter
1/2 cup firmly packed brown sugar
1   dozen macaroon cookies, crushed
1/4 cup (2 ounces) slivered almonds

Preheat the oven to 350°. Drain the peaches, pears, apricots, pineapple, and cherries, reserving 1/2 cup of each of the juices. In a clear glass baking dish, layer the fruit. In a saucepan combine the reserved juice, butter, and brown sugar and bring to a boil. Pour over the fruit. Top with the macaroons and almonds. Cover with foil and bake for 20 minutes. Uncover and bake 10 minutes longer.

Make 10 to 15 servings

Linda Sauer, Princess of Pennies
Crimson Cruisers/Wells Belles, Wells, Minnesota

Artichoke Bake

Testers loved the "gourmet flavor." Sophisticated enough for a special occasion, Artichoke Bake is also great when you need a brunch vegetable.

2   (6-ounce) jars marinated artichoke hearts, drained and chopped
8   ounces grated sharp cheddar cheese
3   large green onions, finely chopped
4   eggs
5   soda crackers, crushed
     Dash of Tabasco
     Salt and pepper to taste

Preheat the oven to 325°. Combine the artichoke hearts, cheese, onions, eggs, crackers, Tabasco, and salt and pepper in a bowl. Pour the mixture into a greased 9-inch baking pan. Bake for 45 minutes. Serve warm or cold.

Makes 6 to 8 servings

Jo Ann Caldwell, Sergeant of Gloves
Red Hat Jezebels, Brentwood, Tennessee

Rice Croquettes

Put your rice cooker to use with this unusual recipe.

3/4   cup uncooked rice
1 1/2   cups boiling water
3   tablespoons butter
1   teaspoon salt
1 1/2   cups hot milk
3   tablespoons sugar

4   egg yolks, beaten
     Vegetable oil
2   eggs, beaten
     Fine cracker crumbs, graham cracker crumbs, or bread crumbs

Cook the rice, water, butter, and salt in a rice cooker until the rice is dry. Stir in the hot milk. Cook until the milk is absorbed. Add the sugar and egg yolks and mix well. Turn into a shallow dish and chill in the refrigerator. Form the mixture into 1 1/2-inch-round balls and make a small indention in each with your thumb. Chill again. Heat two inches of oil in a skillet over high heat to 370°. Dip the rice balls in the 2 beaten eggs then in the cracker crumbs. Deep-fry in hot oil until golden brown.

Makes 6 servings

Pat Cooper, Queen of Texas
Red Hatter Sweethearts, Shreveport, Louisiana

Country-Style Sausage Gravy

One classic country topping for hot biscuits.

1   pound sage-seasoned sausage
2   tablespoons finely chopped onion
6   tablespoons all-purpose flour
1   quart 2% milk
1/2   teaspoon poultry seasoning
1/2   teaspoon ground nutmeg
1/4   teaspoon salt
     Dash of Worcestershire sauce
     Dash of hot pepper sauce

All Puffed Up

When I was six years old, I lived with my aunt in Texas. She is the best cook in the world (or I think so, anyway)! She had a great recipe for biscuits, which called for 1/2 teaspoon of baking powder. One day, pretending I was working in an office, I typed out the recipe on her old, black Royal typewriter. I didn't know about the forward slash, the one that separates the numerals in a fraction, so I left it out. I wasn't really focused on preserving the recipe accurately—I just loved playing with my aunt's typewriter.

When I got out the recipe to make the biscuits some months later, I put in 12 teaspoons of baking powder. That's what the paper said, right? Those biscuits rose and rose and rose, until the whole baking sheet looked like one big biscuit. They were easily twice as big as ordinary biscuits. They didn't really fall exactly, but more or less rippled, high and low. They looked very odd. My mother told me when I was grown that they tasted very bad, but, being dear parents, my mother and father ate them anyway.

My younger sisters ate them too. But they didn't know whether they tasted good. They were so little that they ate dirt, so what did they know?

Over the years, I eventually learned how to both type and cook.

Glenda Mitchell
Queen Mum
Red Hat Wine Mamas
Darrington, Washington

Cook the sausage in a skillet over medium heat, breaking up the pieces. Add the onion and cook until the onion is tender and the sausage is cooked through. Drain, discarding all but 2 tablespoons drippings. Stir in the flour and cook over medium-low heat for about 6 minutes, or until the mixture bubbles and turns golden. Stir in the milk and add the poultry seasoning, nutmeg, salt, Worcestershire, and pepper sauce. Cook, stirring, until thickened. Spoon over fresh, warm biscuits while hot.

Makes 4 to 6 servings

Betty Gideon, Email Female
Classi Lassies, Lamar, Missouri

Morning Potatoes

1/4 cup olive oil
5   white potatoes, peeled, diced
1   red onion, sliced
1/2 green bell pepper, sliced
1/2 teaspoon salt
     Black pepper to taste
1   teaspoon garlic powder
1/2 cup water

Heat the olive oil in a skillet over medium-high heat and sauté the potatoes, onion, and bell pepper until the onion is slightly wilted. Add the salt and the black pepper, then add the garlic powder. Pour in the water. Cover the skillet and let simmer until the potatoes are tender.

Makes 4 servings

Pam Jones, Queen Mother Pam
Rose–Mary Virtuous Divas, Birmingham, Alabama

Omelets in a Bag

This fun meal is brunch and entertainment all in one. Serve this "wow" brunch entrée with coffee cake, hash browns, and sliced fresh fruit. We combined two contributors' recipes for one fantastic recipe.

     Water for boiling
1   large zip-top freezer bag per person
1   permanent black marking pen
2   large or extra large eggs per person
     Shredded cheese of your choice

Sautéed onions or sliced green onions
Sautéed green bell peppers
Chopped ham
Crumbled cooked bacon
Diced tomatoes
Salsa
Hot red pepper sauce

For each 6 to 8 people, have a large pot of water boiling. Have each person write his or her name on a zip-top bag in permanent marker. Let each guest crack 2 eggs into the labeled bag. Zip shut and then squeeze the bag to scramble the eggs.

Let the guests add any of the other ingredients to their bag. Squeeze and shake to blend. Press all the air out of the bag and seal securely. Drop the bags into the boiling water. Boil for exactly 13 minutes. Omelets will slide out onto an eagerly awaiting plate.

Makes 6 to 8 omelets per pot

Lynda Herzog–Pope, Queen Mother
Herzog's Hilarious Hellyun Hairdressers and Healthcare
Heifers of Haughton, Haughton, Louisiana

Cheddar–Apple Breakfast Lasagna

Testers hailed this as "something really different for brunch." Some liked the "lasagna" just as well without the sour cream and granola topping. Use prepared frozen French toast from the supermarket or make your own.

1   cup sour cream
1/2   cup firmly packed brown sugar
6   plus 6 slices French toast
1   (8-ounce) package sliced ham
1   plus 1 cup shredded sharp cheddar cheese
1   (20-ounce) can apple pie filling
1   cup granola

1   teaspoon vanilla extract
1   teaspoon ground cinnamon
1/2   teaspoon ground nutmeg
1/2   cup chopped pecans
1/3   cup firmly packed brown sugar
    Confectioners' sugar, strawberries, bananas for garnish

Blend the sour cream and brown sugar and refrigerate until chilled. Preheat the oven to 350°. Layer 6 slices of the French toast in a buttered 13 x 9-inch baking pan. Layer the ham and 1 cup cheese over the toast. Place the remaining 6 toast slices on top. Spread the apple pie filling over the toast and sprinkle with the remaining 1 cup cheese and the granola. Bake for 25 to 35 minutes, or until warmed through. Serve with a dollop of sour cream topping or warm maple syrup.

Makes 8 to 10 servings

Donna Deaton, Hat Scrapbooker
Happy Hatters, McMinnville, Tennessee

Banana Cream Coffeecake

Fresh bananas give packaged cake mix a homemade taste.

2   bananas, mashed
1   (18-ounce) package yellow cake mix
1   (3-ounce) package vanilla instant pudding mix
1/2   cup vegetable oil
4   eggs

Preheat the oven to 300°. In a large bowl combine the mashed bananas, cake mix, pudding mix, oil, eggs, and vanilla. Beat for 8 minutes with mixer at medium speed, scraping the bowl occasionally. In a separate bowl combine the cinnamon, nutmeg, pecans, and brown sugar. Pour half the cake mix batter into a well greased and floured Bundt cake pan. Sprinkle the brown sugar mixture over the batter. Cover with the remaining batter. Insert a knife in the batter and swirl the layers in a figure-eight pattern. Bake for 1 hour. Cool in the pan for 10 minutes on a wire rack. Invert the pan and cool completely. Dust with the confectioners' sugar and garnish with fresh strawberries and bananas if desired.

Makes 12 to 14 servings

Cindi Carter, Antiparlimentarian
Monroe Hotsy Totsys, Monroe, Iowa

Omelet Biscuit Cups

1   (12-ounce) can refrigerated buttermilk biscuits (not Grands)
4   eggs
1/4 cup milk
1/8 teaspoon salt
1/8 teaspoon pepper
1   cup diced, fully cooked ham
1/4 plus 1/2 cup shredded cheddar cheese
1/3 cup chopped canned mushrooms, drained
1   tablespoon butter

Preheat the oven to 375°. Press the biscuits onto the bottom and up the sides of greased muffin cups. In a large bowl beat the eggs, milk, salt, and pepper. Add the ham, 1/4 cup cheese, and the mushrooms; mix well. In a skillet melt the butter and add the egg mixture. Cook and stir until the eggs are nearly set. Spoon the eggs into the biscuit cups. Bake for 10 to 15 minutes, or until the biscuits are golden brown. Sprinkle with the remaining 1/2 cup cheese. Bake 2 minutes longer, or until the cheese is melted.

Makes 5 servings

Sylvia Wagner, Queen Mumm
Red Bonnet LB Chapter, Cincinnati, Ohio

Cranberry Coffeecake

A Big Red Brunch calls for a Big Red Taste in coffeecake.

1/2 cup firmly packed brown sugar
1   cup chopped walnuts
1/2 teaspoon cinnamon
1/4 teaspoon apple pie spice
4   cups baking mix
4   tablespoons granulated sugar
2   eggs
1 1/3 cups milk
1 1/3 cups (16 ounces) cranberry sauce
2   cups confectioners' sugar
2   tablespoons water
1   teaspoon vanilla extract

Preheat the oven to 400°. In a small bowl mix the brown sugar, nuts, cinnamon, and pie spice. In a large bowl combine the baking mix, sugar, eggs, and milk and mix well. Spread the batter in a greased 13 x 9-inch pan. Sprinkle the batter with the nut mixture. Spoon the cranberry sauce over the nut mixture. Bake for 20 to 25 minutes. Combine the confectioners' sugar, water, and vanilla in a medium bowl. Spread or drizzle over the warm cake.

Makes 6 to 8 servings

Rose Marie Snow, Ravishing Rose
Blushing Bells, Campbell, California

The Best Darn Coffeecake Ever

A bold claim, but every tester agreed it was delicious.

2 1/2 cups sifted all-purpose flour
2 cups firmly packed brown sugar
1/2 teaspoon salt
2/3 cup shortening
1/2 teaspoon baking soda
2 teaspoons baking powder
1/2 teaspoon cinnamon
1/2 teaspoon nutmeg
1 cup buttermilk or sour milk (made by mixing 1 cup milk with 1 teaspoon vinegar)
2 eggs, beaten

Preheat the oven to 375°. Mix the flour, brown sugar, salt, and shortening until crumbly. Measure out 1/2 cup and reserve for the topping.

To the remaining flour mixture, add the baking soda, baking powder, cinnamon, and nutmeg; mix well. Add the buttermilk and eggs and mix well. Pour into a greased and floured 8 or 9-inch round cake pan. Cover with the reserved 1/2 cup crumbs. Bake for 25 to 30 minutes.

Makes 8 servings

Suzanne Russo, The Lady Firenze
Sizzlin' Sisters, Melbourne, Florida

Shortcut Cinnamon Rolls

Prepared bread dough gets a royal treatment that turns it into a royal treat.

Chopped nuts (optional)
2 loaves frozen bread dough, thawed
1 (3-ounce) package cook-and-serve vanilla pudding mix
1/2 cup (1 stick) butter, melted
1 cup firmly packed brown sugar
1 teaspoon cinnamon
2 tablespoons milk

Grease a 13 x 9-inch pan. Spread the nuts over the bottom of the pan, if desired. Cut or break the bread into 24 pieces and arrange in the pan. Mix together the pudding mix, butter, brown sugar, cinnamon, and milk. Dribble this mixture over the bread pieces. Refrigerate 6 to 8 hours or overnight. Bake at 375° for 30 minutes.

Makes 12 servings

Deanna Riley, Queen
Razzler–Dazzlers, Chatfield, Minnesota

Sour Cream Coffeecake

This simple, not-too-sweet cake scored well with testers.

COFFEE CAKE

1/2 cup (1 stick) butter, softened

1 cup granulated sugar

2 eggs

1 teaspoon vanilla extract

1 (8-ounce) container sour cream

1 teaspoon baking soda

1 1/2 cups all-purpose flour

1 1/2 teaspoons baking powder

NUT TOPPING

1/4 cup firmly packed brown sugar

1/4 cup chopped nuts

1 teaspoon cinnamon

Preheat the oven to 350°. For the coffee cake, beat the butter and sugar in a bowl until fluffy. Beat in the eggs and vanilla. Combine the sour cream and baking soda in a small bowl and let stand for about 2 minutes. Add to the butter mixture. Combine the flour and baking powder and add to the mixture. Grease a springform or tube pan.

For the topping, combine the brown sugar, nuts, and cinnamon in a small bowl. Spread over the bottom of the pan. Spoon the batter over the topping. Bake for 45 to 50 minutes. Let cool. Invert on a plate to serve.

Makes 8 to 10 servings

Mary Jane MacVicar, Queen Scarlettness
Scarlett Shady Ladies, Leamington, Ontario, Canada

Land-Of-Nod Cinnamon Buns

Bring them back from the Land of Nod with these dressed up cinnamon rolls.

20 frozen uncooked dinner rolls, thawed

1 cup firmly packed brown sugar

1 to 2 tablespoons cinnamon

3/4 cup raisins (optional)

1/2 cup (1 stick) butter, melted

Before you put the cat out and turn out the lights, grease a 10-inch Bundt pan and arrange the frozen rolls in it. Sprinkle the brown sugar, cinnamon, and raisins, if using, over the rolls. You can also add cherries and pecans if you wish. Pour the melted butter over all and cover with a clean, damp cloth. Leave out at room temperature 6 to 8 hours or overnight. When ready to bake, preheat the oven to 350° and bake for 25 minutes. Let stand for 5 minutes and then turn out on a serving plate.

Makes 8 servings

Betty Nowlan, Lady Rose Bud
Chocolate River Cuties, Moncton, New Brunswick, Canada

Crescent Caramel Swirl

Great-looking results with just five ingredients.

1/2 cup (1 stick) butter, melted

1/2 cup chopped nuts

1 cup firmly packed brown sugar

2 tablespoons water

2 (8-ounce) cans refrigerated crescent rolls

Preheat the oven to 375°. Coat the bottom and sides of a 12-cup fluted tube pan or angel food cake pan with 2 tablespoons melted butter. Sprinkle the pan with about 3 tablespoons of the nuts. Combine the remaining nuts, the brown sugar, and water with the remaining butter in a saucepan and heat to boiling. Boil for approximately 5 minutes. Remove the crescent rolls from the cans in rolled sections; do not unroll. Cut each roll into quarters. Separate each quarter of dough and layer 8 of the quarters in the bottom of the tube pan. Spoon half the caramel sauce over the dough. Add a second layer of dough quarters to the pan. Pour the remaining sauce over the second layer of dough. Bake for 25 to 30 minutes, or until golden brown. Cool for 3 minutes. Invert onto a serving platter.

Makes 10 to 12 servings

Gladys Brown, Queen
Red Hat Gems, San Diego, California

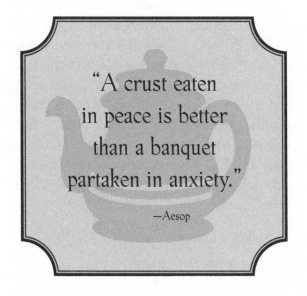

"A crust eaten in peace is better than a banquet partaken in anxiety."

—Aesop

Avocado Quick Bread

Not your everyday bread and great for all kinds of theme parties.

1 1/3 cups sugar
1/2 cup (1 stick) butter, softened
2 large eggs
1 teaspoon vanilla extract
1 cup mashed avocado
1 1/2 cups all-purpose flour
1/2 teaspoon cinnamon
1/2 teaspoon allspice
1/2 teaspoon salt
1 1/2 teaspoons baking soda
1/3 cup buttermilk
1 cup raisins
1/2 cup chopped walnuts

Preheat the oven to 350°. In a bowl beat the sugar, butter, eggs, vanilla, and avocado until light and fluffy. In another bowl stir together the flour, cinnamon, allspice, salt, and baking soda. Add the flour mixture to the creamed mixture alternately with the buttermilk and mix well. Stir in the raisins and nuts; the batter will be stiff. Spoon into a greased and floured loaf pan. Bake for 1 hour 15 minutes.

Makes 1 loaf

Joanne Thill, Princess of Thin
London Bridge Red Hots, Lake Havasu City, Arizona

Honey-Sweet Banana-Nut Bread

A slice of this honey sweetened bread is extra good when spread with a little cream cheese.

2   eggs, beaten
4   ripe bananas, mashed
1   cup honey
2   tablespoons wheat germ
2   tablespoons orange juice
1 1/2   teaspoons baking powder
1   teaspoon baking soda
1   teaspoon salt
3   cups all-purpose flour
    Raisins and chopped walnuts (optional)

Preheat the oven to 375°. In a medium bowl combine the eggs, bananas, and honey and stir to mix. Add the wheat germ and orange juice and mix well. In a large bowl combine the baking powder, baking soda, salt, and flour. Add the wet ingredients to the dry ingredients and mix until blended. Stir in the raisins and walnuts, if desired.

Pour into two greased loaf pans. Bake for 40 to 45 minutes, or until a tester inserted in the center comes out clean.

Makes 2 loaves

Karen White, Santo's Red Hats Queen Mum
Santo's Red Hats, The Villages, Florida

Banana Blueberry Bread

Fruit-filled and sour cream enriched loaves for breakfast, snacking, tea, or gift-giving. For a completely different loaf, use an equal amount of nuts in place of the berries.

1   cup (2 sticks) butter, softened
1 2/3   cups sugar
4   eggs
5   medium ripe bananas, mashed
2   teaspoons vanilla extract
1   cup sour cream
3   cups all-purpose flour
2   teaspoons baking soda
1   teaspoon salt
1   cup blueberries, dried

Preheat the oven to 350°. Grease the bottoms of two 8 or 9-inch loaf pans. Beat the butter and sugar in a large bowl with an electric mixer on medium speed until fluffy. Add the eggs and mix until well blended. Add the bananas, vanilla, and sour cream and mix well. Add the flour, baking soda, and salt and mix until moistened. Add the blueberries and mix. Pour the batter into the prepared pans. Bake for about 1 hour, or until a tester inserted in the center comes out clean. Cool 10 minutes. Remove from the pans and cool completely. Wrap tightly and store in the refrigerator up to 1 week.

Makes 2 loaves

Jowanna James, Lady Anna Doll
Sweeny Hatters, Sweeny, Texas

Carrot-Date-Nut Bread

All those goodies in every slice of this scrumptious bread. These loaves can be frozen for several weeks.

1 (18-ounce) package carrot cake mix
1 (3-ounce) package instant coconut
 pudding mix
4 eggs
1/2 cup vegetable oil
1 cup hot water
1 (8-ounce) package chopped dates
1/2 to 1 cup chopped pecans or walnuts

Preheat the oven to 350°. Combine the cake mix, pudding mix, eggs, oil, and water in a large bowl. Beat with an electric mixer until well combined. Stir in the chopped dates and nuts; the mixture will be thick. Pour into two greased loaf pans or 5 mini loaf pans. Bake for 40 to 45 minutes for regular-size pans or 34 to 38 minutes for mini pans. Cool on a wire rack.

Makes 2 large or 5 small loaves

Sylvia M. Schoen, Queen Mum
Perky Purple Pixies of Minnesota, Minneapolis, Minnesota

Baking Mix Muffins

Won't the family be surprised to see you pop open a beer in the morning? Hoist it proudly and announce, "I'm making the breakfast of champions."

4 cups baking mix
5 tablespoons sugar
1 (12-ounce) can or bottle cold beer

Preheat the oven to 350°. Combine the baking mix and sugar. Add the beer and mix well. Spoon into twelve well-greased muffin cups. Bake for 40 minutes, or until golden.

Makes 12 servings

Betty Gabel, Chapterette
La Vida Real Red Hats, El Cajon, California

Cherry Bread

2 eggs
3/4 cup sugar
1 1/2 cups all-purpose flour
1 1/2 teaspoons baking powder
1/4 teaspoon salt
1 (6-ounce) bottle chopped maraschino
 cherries, not drained
3/4 cup chopped pecans

Preheat the oven to 350°. Beat the eggs and sugar in a bowl until light and fluffy. Combine the flour, baking powder, and salt. Drain the cherries, reserving 1/3 cup juice. Add the flour mixture to the egg mixture alternately with the cherry juice. Mix in the chopped cherries and nuts. Line the bottom of an 8 to 9-inch loaf pan with waxed paper and grease the sides. Spoon the batter into the pan. Bake for 45 to 50 minutes.

Makes 8 servings

Mary Ann Swip, Queen Mum
Heartland Red Hat Doll Society, Collinsville, Illinois

Red Jewel Bread

Love those cranberries when they're combined with a touch of orange peel.

2 cups all-purpose flour
1 cup sugar
1 1/2 tablespoons baking powder
1/2 teaspoon baking soda
2 tablespoons butter or margarine, melted
3/4 cup milk
1 egg, beaten
2 teaspoons grated orange peel
1 cup halved fresh cranberries
1/2 cup chopped nuts

Preheat the oven to 350°. Grease an 8 to 9-inch loaf pan. Combine the flour, sugar, baking powder, and baking soda in a large bowl. Add the butter, milk, egg, and orange peel and mix well. Fold in the cranberries and nuts. Batter will be thick. Pour or spoon into the prepared pan. Bake for 60 minutes. Cool on a rack 15 minutes and then remove the bread from the pan and cool completely.

Makes 8 to 10 servings

Mary Page, Queen Mary
Lovely Ladies of Pevely, Pevely, Missouri

Gridiron Blueberry Muffins

Make these muffins with sugar or sugar substitute; they're beautiful, blue, and scrumptious either way.

1/2 (15-ounce) can blueberries
1/2 cup (1 stick) butter, softened
1/2 cup vegetable oil
1 3/4 cups sugar or sucralose (Splenda)
2 eggs or equivalent egg substitute
1 tablespoon vanilla, butter, or almond extract
3 cups all-purpose flour
1 tablespoon baking powder
1 teaspoon baking soda
1/2 teaspoon salt
1 cup buttermilk

Preheat the oven to 400°. Drain the blueberries, reserving 1/2 cup juice. In a large bowl beat the butter and oil until well blended. Add the sugar and eggs, and then beat in the flavoring. In a medium bowl sift together the flour, baking powder, baking soda, and salt. Slowly add to the sugar mixture. Add the buttermilk and the reserved blueberry juice. Gently stir in the blueberries. Fill well-greased muffin cups one-half full. Bake for 15 minutes for miniature cups or 20 minutes for regular-size muffins.

Makes 12 regular-size muffins or 36 miniature muffins

Marilyn Dudley, Lavender Librarian
La Feria Femmes in Red Hats, Harlingen, Texas

Aloha Loaf

Add a handful of chopped nuts to the loaf if that strikes your fancy.

1/2 cup (1 stick) butter
1   cup sugar
2   eggs
2   cups all-purpose flour
1   teaspoon baking powder
1/2 teaspoon baking soda
1/4 teaspoon salt
1   ripe banana, mashed
1   (7-ounce) can crushed pineapple
1/2 cup shredded coconut

Preheat the oven to 350°. Grease and flour a 9-inch loaf pan. Beat the butter, sugar, and eggs until fluffy. Sift together the flour, baking powder, baking soda, and salt. Add to the butter mixture. Fold in the undrained pineapple and coconut. Pour into the prepared loaf pan. Bake for 1 hour 15 minutes.

Makes 8 to 10 servings

Wanda Suminski, Chapterette
Classy Clarettes, Lake, Michigan

Nutty Rhubarb Muffins

"Fabulous" flavor and excellent moist texture, testers rated.

MUFFINS
3/4 cup firmly packed brown sugar
1/3 cup buttermilk
1/3 cup vegetable oil
1   egg
1   teaspoon vanilla extract
2   cups all-purpose flour
1/2 teaspoon salt
3/4 teaspoon baking soda
1   cup diced rhubarb
1/2 cup chopped nuts

TOPPING
1/4 cup firmly packed brown sugar
1/4 cup chopped nuts
1/2 teaspoon ground cinnamon

Preheat the oven to 375°. For the muffins, in a small bowl mix the brown sugar, buttermilk, oil, egg, and vanilla. In a medium bowl mix the flour, salt, and baking soda. Stir the buttermilk mixture into the flour mixture and blend until evenly moistened. Stir in the rhubarb and nuts. Spoon into a well-greased 12-cup muffin tin.

For the topping, stir together the brown sugar, nuts, and cinnamon, and sprinkle evenly over each muffin. Bake about 20 minutes, or until the center springs up when touched.

Makes 12 muffins

Joann Dickerson, Lady Classy Clarette
Classy Clarettes, Clare, Michigan

Go, Dough, Go!

Many years ago, in the days before air-conditioning and widespread car ownership, I worked in a wholesale bakery. Very often I would bring home a loaf of bread dough, packed by the bakers in a brown paper bag, to make pizza or fried dough.

I didn't have a car, so I took two buses to get to work and home again. This particular July day was hot and steamy, and the buses were not air-conditioned. The dough loved the conditions, and by the time I transferred to the second bus, my bag of dough was beginning to expand and expand. My bread and I captured the attention of the passengers; everyone watched the bread rising through the top of the bag and pushing out the sides. People giggled as they watched me struggle to keep the dough in the bag to prevent it from taking over the bus. I had no idea a loaf of bread could take on a life of its own like that. I was scarlet with embarrassment. Believe me, I never tried that again on a hot day. And now I have a deep understanding of what "let rise in a warm place" really involves.

Ruth Harding
Queen
Classy Lady Red Hats of Worcester
Worcester, Massachusetts

Date-Nut Bread

The contributor figures she's prepared about three hundred loaves of this bread over the years, and she can attest that they freeze very well. You can double the recipe, but make it in two separate pots.

1   cup chopped pitted dates (39 to 40 pieces) or 1 (10-ounce) package

1 1/2   teaspoons baking soda

1   cup chopped walnuts or pecans

1   cup (2 sticks) butter, at room temperature

3/4   cup boiling water

2   eggs, beaten

1   teaspoon vanilla extract

1   cup sugar

1 1/2   cups sifted all-purpose flour

1/2   teaspoon salt

Combine the dates, baking soda, nuts, butter, and boiling water in a large pot. Set aside for 20 minutes, stirring occasionally with a spatula to break up the butter. Preheat the oven to 350°. Grease a large loaf pan. Add the eggs, vanilla, sugar, flour, and salt to the date mixture and mix well. Spoon the batter into the loaf pan. Bake for 1 hour 15 minutes.

Makes 9 servings

Elsie Hinkson, Queen Mother
The Red Hatters of Bay Ridge, Brooklyn, New York

Sunday Yeast Rolls

Make them on the weekend; bake them all week.

1   envelope active dry yeast
1   cup water, lukewarm
1/2 cup vegetable oil
4   cups all-purpose flour
1   teaspoon salt
1/2 cup sugar
2   eggs, beaten

Dissolve the yeast in the water in large mixing bowl. Add the oil, flour, salt, sugar, and eggs and mix thoroughly. Cover and let stand 8 to 12 hours or overnight on the kitchen counter.

When ready to bake, turn the dough out onto a floured board and knead lightly. Roll out to 1/2-inch thickness. Cut with a biscuit cutter dipped into flour. Arrange the rolls on one or two greased 13 x 9-inch pans. Lightly cover with plastic wrap. Let rise 4 to 6 hours. Bake at 400° for 10 to 12 minutes.

Makes 8 to 12 servings

Lynda Barker, Lady in Waiting
Texas Red Bonnets, Mansfield, Texas

Pound Cake Muffins

Testers loved the flavor but found the texture a little dry, so experiment with the amount of sour cream, and serve the muffins with a smear of cream cheese and a generous dollop of jam.

13/4 cups all-purpose flour
1/2 teaspoon salt
1/4 teaspoon baking powder
1   cup sugar
1/2 cup (1 stick) butter or margarine, softened
1/2 to 1 cup sour cream
1   teaspoon vanilla extract
1/2 teaspoon lemon extract
2   eggs

Preheat the oven to 400°. In a large bowl combine the flour, salt, baking powder, and sugar. In a smaller bowl mix the butter, sour cream, vanilla extract, lemon extract, and eggs. Add the butter mixture to the flour mixture and mix until the flour is moistened. Batter will be lumpy. Spoon into greased muffin tins. Bake for 22 minutes.

Makes 12 muffins

Jackie Tarpinian, Queen Mother
Jewels of the Prairie, Jamestown, North Dakota

Cloverleaf Dinner Rolls

A make-ahead dough for turning into clover leaf or any shape rolls.

2	cups milk
1/2	cup sugar
1/2	cup canola oil
2	teaspoons salt
2	eggs, slightly beaten
2	envelopes active dry yeast
1/2	cup lukewarm water
6 1/2	to 7 cups all-purpose flour

Bring the milk nearly to a boil in a saucepan over low heat. Stir in the sugar, oil, salt, and beaten eggs. Dissolve the yeast in the lukewarm water in large bowl. Stir in the milk mixture. Sift the flour into a large bowl. Add the milk mixture. Stir till a soft dough forms. Turn out on a lightly floured surface and knead till soft and elastic. Place in a clean, greased bowl, turning to grease the entire surface. Let the dough rise, covered, until doubled in size. Preheat the oven to 375°. Shape into small balls. Place 2 to 3 balls into each cup of a greased 24-cup muffin tin. Bake for 15 to 20 minutes or until golden brown.

Makes 24 rolls

Shirley Bennett, Queen Mother
Red Hot Ladies, Franklin, Massachusetts

Pumpkin Spice Bread

This recipe makes three loaves of delicious pumpkin bread. They freeze well.

1	(30-ounce) can pumpkin or 4 cups mashed cooked pumpkin
4	cups sugar
1	egg, beaten
1	cup canola oil
2	teaspoons salt
1	teaspoon nutmeg
1	teaspoon cinnamon
1/4	teaspoon ginger
1/2	teaspoon ground cloves
5	cups all-purpose flour
4	teaspoons baking soda
1	cup chopped dates
1	cup raisins
1	cup chopped nuts (optional)

Preheat the oven to 350°. In an extra large mixing bowl combine the pumpkin, sugar, egg, oil, salt, nutmeg, cinnamon, ginger, and cloves and mix well. Stir in the flour, baking soda, dates, raisins, and nuts, if using. Bake in three greased 7-inch loaf pans for 1 to 1 1/2 hours. Test for doneness with a toothpick. Cool for 10 minutes in the pans; then remove and cool completely.

Makes 3 loaves

Cherie Dutton, Queen of Mizchef
Red Hot Tea Bags of Shoreline, Shoreline, Washington

Quick and Easy Rolls

For something more special, add half a cup shredded cheese and one pound sausage, browned and drained, to the mixture.

3/4   cup (1 1/2 sticks) butter
2   cups self-rising flour
8   ounces sour cream

Preheat the oven to 375°. In a medium bowl mix the butter, flour, and sour cream together until well blended. Spoon into ungreased muffin tins. Bake for 15 to18 minutes.

Makes 3 dozen mini rolls or 2 dozen large rolls

Brenda Moxley, Vice Queen
Bold 'N Classy, Macon, Georgia

Oatmeal Bread

"Nice and soft" noted the tester.

1   cup quick oats
1/2   cup whole wheat flour
1/2   cup firmly packed brown sugar
1   tablespoon salt
2   tablespoons butter
2   cups boiling water
1/2   cup water
1   package active dry yeast
1/2   cup lukewarm water (110°)
1   teaspoon granulated sugar
4   plus 1 cups all-purpose flour

In a large bowl combine the oats, whole wheat flour, brown sugar, salt, and butter. Pour the boiling water over all. Mix well and let cool to about 110°. Meanwhile heat the 1/2 cup water to 110°, add the yeast and 1 teaspoon sugar. Stir and let the yeast sit to begin to work. When the batter has cooled to 110°, stir in the yeast mixture and then add 4 cups of flour, one cup at a time. Mix until it forms a dough.

Pour the remaining 1 cup flour on a work surface and place the dough on the floured surface. Knead in the flour until the dough is smooth and elastic. Place in a greased bowl, cover with a towel, and let rise until double in size, about 60 minutes.

Divide the dough into two parts and shape into loaves. Place in two greased loaf pans and let rise until double in size, about 60 minutes. Heat the oven to 350°. Bake the bread 30 to 40 minutes. Cool 2 minutes in the pans. Remove from the pans, butter the tops of the loaves, and cool completely.

Makes 2 loaves

Sherry Schweinhagen, Queen Sherry
Tri-County Reds, Archbold, Ohio

Cottage Dill Bread for Bread Machine

3/4 cup small curd cottage cheese
11/2 tablespoons butter
3/4 cup warm water
3   cups bread flour
11/2 tablespoons nonfat dry milk
2   tablespoons sugar
11/2 teaspoons salt
1   tablespoon dry minced onion
1   tablespoon dill seed
1   tablespoon dill weed
2   envelopes active dry yeast
1   teaspoon lemon juice
3   tablespoons wheat flour
1   tablespoon gluten

Set your bread machine to its white bread setting, light crust. Heat the cottage cheese and butter together to warm. Load the ingredients into the bread machine in the order listed and turn on the machine.

If you don't have a machine, preheat the oven to 350°. Heat the butter and cottage cheese together, and then add the remaining ingredients together in a large bowl. Stir to form a dough. Put the dough in greased loaf pans and bake until golden brown on top and a toothpick inserted into the center comes out clean.

Makes one 2-pound loaf

Carol Verkennis, Royal Songbird
Ruby Red Hat's Ramblers, Westland, Michigan

Sheepherder's Bread

An impressive bread and bountiful enough to serve a crowd, or cut into halves and freeze part for later.

3   cups hot water
1/2 cup (1 stick) butter or margarine
1/2 cup sugar
21/2 teaspoons salt
2   packages active dry yeast
91/2 cups all-purpose flour

Grease the inside of an 8 to 10-inch Dutch oven and lid. In a bowl combine the hot water, butter, sugar, and salt. Stir until the butter melts; then cool to 110°. Stir in the yeast, cover, and set in a warm place for about 12 minutes. Add 5 cups flour and beat with a wooden spoon. (I use a Kitchen Aid mixer with dough hooks.) Add another 31/2 cups flour and stir into a stiff dough. Knead on a floured surface or with mixer for 10 minutes, or until smooth, adding the remaining 1 cup flour as needed. Place in a greased bowl. Cover and let rise until doubled in size, about 60 minutes. Punch the dough down and knead to form a smooth ball. Place the ball in the Dutch oven and put the lid on top. Let rise until the dough just touches the lid. Bake in a 375° oven with the lid on for 12 minutes. Remove the lid and bake 30 to 35 minutes longer.

Makes 1 loaf

Jan Eason, Rodeo City Jan
Windy Hat Snatchers, Ellensburg, Washington

French Baguettes

1   cup lukewarm water
1 1/2   teaspoons sugar
1 1/2   teaspoons salt
3   cups bread flour
2   teaspoons (about 1 envelope) active dry yeast
    Cornmeal

If you have a bread machine set it on the dough cycle. Add the ingredients according to your bread machine's instructions and turn it on to mix the ingredients. Otherwise, in a large bowl combine the water, sugar, salt, flour, and yeast. Mix until it forms a dough. Place the dough in a greased bowl. Cover and let rise for 60 minutes. Divide it into two or three pieces, depending upon how long you would like your baguettes to be. Preheat the oven to 400°. Roll the dough into long loaves and arrange (diagonally if necessary) on a baking sheet sprinkled generously with cornmeal. With a very sharp knife, slash the tops of the baguettes with three diagonal cuts. Bake for 30 minutes, or until the loaves sound hollow when thumped.

Makes 2 or 3 loaves

Joan Lemmuler, Dancing Queen
Swinging Mississippi Belles, Picayune, Mississippi

Texican Corn Bread

Any extra corn bread freezes well. Drizzle with butter when reheating.

2   cups cornmeal (white or yellow)
1   cup all-purpose flour
3   eggs
1/2   teaspoon baking soda
2   teaspoons baking powder
1   teaspoon salt
2   tablespoons sugar
1/2   to 3/4 cup buttermilk
1   (16-ounce) can cream-style corn
1/2   cup vegetable oil
2   tablespoons minced onion
1   cup grated sharp cheddar cheese
1   jalapeño pepper or 1 (4-ounce) can chopped green chiles
1   garlic clove, minced

Preheat the oven to 375°. Generously grease a 13 x 9-inch pan or iron skillet and put it in the oven to heat. In a large bowl mix the cornmeal, flour, eggs, baking soda, baking powder, salt, and sugar. In a smaller bowl combine the buttermilk, corn, and oil. Mix well. Add the onion, cheese, pepper, and garlic. Add the wet ingredients to the dry ingredients and mix just until no streaks of flour remain. Pour the mixture into the hot pan. Bake for 35 to 45 minutes.

Makes 10 to 12 servings

Sue Hobson, Queen Mother
Classi Lassies, Lamar, Missouri

Hot Hot Jalapeño Corn Bread

Use fresh jalapeños or the ones packed in cans or jars.
Vary the number of them to suit your taste.

1	tablespoon shortening or bacon drippings
1	cup corn bread mix
1	(8-ounce) can cream-style corn
1	cup grated cheddar cheese
1/3	cup vegetable oil
1/2	cup buttermilk
2	eggs
3	jalapeño peppers, chopped

Preheat the oven to 400°. Spoon the shortening or bacon drippings into a 9-inch cast-iron skillet and place in the oven. In a large bowl combine the corn bread mix, corn, cheese, oil, buttermilk, eggs, and peppers. Pour the mixture into the skillet. Bake for 35 to 40 minutes, or until brown.

Makes 8 servings

Maida Burns, Queen Mum
Houston Heights Red Hat Honeys, Houston, Texas

Cake Corn Bread

This corn bread has a smooth texture and a taste like a
moist pound cake.

3	large eggs
3/4	to 1 cup sugar
	Pinch of salt
1	cup water
1	cup fine stone-ground enriched white cornmeal (Alabama King brand)
1	cup milk
1/2	teaspoon vanilla extract
1	biscuit or bread slice, crumbled
1	tablespoon shortening

Preheat the oven to 400°. In a bowl beat the eggs, sugar, and salt. Boil the water in a 2-quart saucepan. When it reaches a rapid boil, remove from the heat and mix in the cornmeal, using an electric mixer. Beat in the milk. Add the egg mixture and mix well. Add the vanilla and biscuit. Mix well. Spoon the shortening into an 8-inch square pan and place it in the oven to melt. When the shortening is melted, take out the pan and tilt to cover the bottom. Pour the batter into the hot pan. Bake for about 30 minutes, or until set and slightly brown on top. Refrigerate leftovers and warm in the microwave.

Makes 6 to 8 servings

Delilah Horsfield, Queen Mum
The Villages 1st Red Hatters, The Villages, Florida

"Grandpa, What's for Breakfast?"

My dad and grandpa had an ice delivery business, and the business office was in our home. Their day started at five o'clock, so every morning my grandpa was at our house working well before we children were awake. He would occasionally cook something wonderful for our breakfast.

One morning, when I was still half asleep, I saw a pot simmering away on the stove. The vision of something warm and filling, like Grandpa's oatmeal, was suddenly sparking energy through my body. My steps came faster as I got closer to the stove and my mouth was watering. . . . Oh, yummy! I looked in and "Yummy!" turned to "Yuck!" He was boiling a horned toad's head to make a tie slider for my little brother's Boy Scout scarf.

Beverly Johnson
Vice Queen
Tahoe REDS (Rowdy, Energetic,
    Diva Sisters)
South Lake Tahoe, California

Cheese Biscuits

Be sure to use sharp cheese for the best flavor. Using an ice cream scoop to drop the biscuits gives them a nice shape.

2	cups self-rising flour
1	teaspoon baking powder
1	teaspoon sugar
1/3	cup shortening
3/4	cup grated cheddar cheese
1	cup buttermilk

Preheat the oven to 350°. In a bowl mix the flour, baking powder, and sugar with a fork. Cut in the shortening until the mixture resembles coarse crumbs. Stir in the cheese and then stir in the buttermilk all at once. Mix just until blended; do not overmix. Drop by tablespoon-fuls onto a well-greased baking sheet. Bake for 12 to 15 minutes.

Makes 10 to 12 biscuits

Helen Burns, Red Hatter
Sassy Angels, Houston, Texas

Queen Mom Angel Biscuits

These foolproof biscuits get a roll-like texture from the yeast, but they don't need to rise. The dough may be kept in the refrigerator for up to several weeks; then give it a brief stirring and shape and bake as needed.

1/2 cup warm water
1 teaspoon sugar
2 1/4 teaspoons (one envelope) active dry yeast
4 1/2 cups all-purpose flour
4 teaspoons baking powder
1/4 to 1/2 teaspoon baking soda
1 teaspoon salt
1/2 cup sugar
2 cups buttermilk
1/2 cup canola oil

Mix the water, sugar, and yeast together and set aside for 5 minutes. In a very large bowl sift together the flour, baking powder, baking soda, salt, and sugar. Make a well in the dry ingredients and add the buttermilk, oil, and the yeast mixture. Mix well. Cover the bowl, refrigerate, and use as needed.

When ready to bake, preheat the oven to 375°. Flour a cutting board and pat out the amount of dough you want to bake. Roll out the dough and cut with a biscuit cutter. Arrange the biscuits 1 1/2 inches apart on a greased baking sheet. Bake for 20 to 25 minutes, or until lightly brown.

Makes about 30 biscuits

Mary Francinn Parker, Queen Mom of Grandyville
The Happy Hatters, Georgetown, Texas

Green Tomato Bread

If you've ever grown tomatoes, you know how useful this recipe will be, especially at the end of the season. Tester comments ranged from "fabulous" to "excellent" to "very good," and everyone noted the bread's moist crumb.

3 eggs
1 cup vegetable oil
2 cups sugar
2 teaspoons vanilla extract
2 cups finely chopped green tomatoes
1 cup well-drained, crushed pineapple
3 cups all-purpose flour
2 teaspoons baking soda
1 teaspoon salt
1/2 teaspoon baking powder
1 teaspoon cinnamon
1/2 teaspoon mace
1 cup chopped nuts
1/2 cup golden raisins
2 tablespoons sesame seeds

Preheat the oven to 350°. In a large bowl beat the eggs with the oil, sugar, and vanilla until light and fluffy. Stir in the tomatoes and pineapple. Sift the flour, baking soda, salt, baking powder, cinnamon, and mace and add to the mixture. Blend well. Stir in the nuts, raisins, and sesame seeds. Pour into two greased and floured loaf pans. Bake for 1 hour 15 minutes. Test before removing from oven.

Makes 2 loaves

Sharon Beadle, Countess Crafty
Sassy Sophistihats, Wallkill, New York

Onion Bread

A yeast-batter bread needs no kneading, just a good beating with an electric mixer. Testers called it "wonderful with ham."

1 1/2   cups warm water (105° to 115°)
1   envelope active dry yeast
1   tablespoon dried onion flakes
1   tablespoon sugar
2   teaspoons seasoned salt
2   tablespoons shortening
1/2   teaspoon dried oregano
2   plus 1 1/2 cups all-purpose flour
1   medium onion, sliced into rings
      Melted butter

Put the warm water into a bowl. Sprinkle in the yeast and stir to dissolve. Add the onion flakes, sugar, seasoned salt, shortening, oregano, and 2 cups flour. Beat with an electric mixer for 2 minutes at medium speed. Stir in the remaining 1 1/2 cups flour. Let rise in a warm place (85°) free from draft for about 1 hour, or until doubled in size. Punch or beat down.

Spread into a greased 9-inch loaf pan. Pat the top into shape with lightly floured hands. Cover with a clean kitchen towel, and let rise in a warm place about 40 minutes, or until the batter is about 1/2 inch from the top of the pan.

Preheat the oven to 375°. Dip the onion rings into the melted butter, and place on top of the loaf. Bake 35 to 40 minutes. Remove from the pan and cool on a rack.

Makes 1 loaf

Jackie Bauder, Lady-Quilt-a-Lot
A Gathering of Hats, West Hills, California

SEVEN

❧ Grab That Fancy Hat, ❧ We're Going for Tea!

TEATIME TREATS & INDULGENCES

The first gathering ever of what later became the Red Hat Society was held in a tea room with five women gathered around the table, each wearing a red hat and some sort of purple clothing. Since we were being such ladies, wearing such hoity-toity get-ups (some of us even wore red gloves), a tea room just seemed like the best place to go. (Lunch in a coffee shop just wouldn't have done.) As we lingered over our ginger peach tea, scones, clotted cream, and other delicacies, the concept of the Red Hat Society began to take shape.

The atmosphere in the lace-curtained tea room contributed much to the tone we set for our "disorganizaton." As we held our pinkies aloft, gently spoofing gentility, adorned in our silly clothes, we established the values that have held true from that day in April 1998 up to today: Fun, sisterhood, dress-up, and good humor—and, of course, good food.

Coronation Citrus Tea Punch

For those summer ceremonies when a cool tea drink is the very thing a wilting Hatter needs.

6 cups water
6 tea bags
1 1/2 cups sugar (or to taste)
3 cups chilled club soda
2 cups orange juice
1 cup lemon juice
    Mint sprigs and raspberries for garnish

Bring the water to a boil and steep the tea bags for 15 minutes. Discard the bags and add the sugar. Mix well. Add the club soda, orange juice, and lemon juice. Chill 2 to 3 hours. Serve over crushed ice with mint sprigs and raspberries for garnish.

Makes 24 servings

Diane White, Summer Vice Perpetrator of Tomfoolery, Royal Raspberry Tarts, Levittown, Pennsylvania

Chocolate Hazelnut Torte

2 tablespoons unsalted butter, softened
1 plus 1 cups chopped hazelnuts
5 eggs
3 (4-ounce) packages chocolate fudge pudding mix
1/2 cup (1 stick) butter, melted
    Cocoa powder
    Confectioners' sugar

Preheat the oven to 350°. Grease a 10-inch springform pan with the unsalted butter. Sprinkle 1 cup chopped hazelnuts over the bottom. Grind the remaining 1 cup nuts in a blender or food processor. Combine the ground nuts, eggs, pudding mix, and melted butter; mix well. Pour into the pan. Bake for 20 minutes. Edges should be set but the center should jiggle when shaken. Cool slightly and dust with the cocoa powder and confectioners' sugar.

Makes 12 servings

Mahel Da Petrillo, Chapterette
Newton Redglows, Newton, New Jersey

Sour Cream Muffins

1 egg
2 tablespoons sugar
1 tablespoon shortening
1 cup sour cream
1 1/3 cups all-purpose flour
1 teaspoon baking powder
1/2 teaspoon baking soda
1/2 teaspoon salt

Preheat the oven to 400°. In a large bowl beat the egg until light in color. Add the sugar and shortening and mix well. Beat in the sour cream. Combine the flour, baking powder, baking soda, and salt and add to the shortening mixture. Fill greased muffin cups two-thirds full. Bake for 20 to 25 minutes.

Makes 12 servings

Barbara Hodnett , Queen Mother
Clinton Fairlaydes, Clinton, Maine

Apple Slices

2 cups plus 2 tablespoons sifted
  all-purpose flour
1/2 teaspoon salt
2/3 cup shortening or lard
2 egg yolks
1 tablespoon lemon juice
1/4 cup cold water
4 to 6 tart cooking apples, peeled and sliced
1 cup granulated sugar
1/2 teaspoon cinnamon
1 cup confectioners' sugar
2 tablespoons butter
1/2 teaspoon vanilla extract
2 tablespoons milk

In a large bowl sift 2 cups flour with the salt. Cut in the shortening. Lightly blend in the egg yolks, lemon juice, and water. Divide the dough in half. Roll one half to fit the bottom and sides of a 13 x 9-inch pan. Arrange the apple slices in the crust. In a small bowl mix the sugar, the remaining 2 tablespoons flour, and cinnamon. Sprinkle over the apples. Roll out the remaining half of the dough to fit over the filling and seal the edges. Cut steam vents in the crust. Bake for 30 to 40 minutes. To frost, combine the confectioners' sugar, butter, vanilla, and milk in a small bowl. Frost while still warm.

Makes 12 servings

Marie Rubietta, Chapterette
Red Hat Sweethearts for Atkinson, Jefferson, Wisconsin

Flowerpot Apple Muffins

Testers enjoyed this recipe, but found a 4-inch pot made a very large serving. If you can, find miniature pots, about 3 inches across, and use those and decrease baking time to 35 minutes.

1/2 cup sugar
1/4 cup apple cider or apple juice
1 teaspoon vanilla extract
1 teaspoon cinnamon
1 egg
1 cup all-purpose flour
1 teaspoon baking soda
1 teaspoon baking powder
2 Granny Smith medium apples, diced
  (peeling optional)

Grease the inside of five clean, unused 4-inch clay flowerpots. Place a 10-inch square sheet of foil over each flowerpot and with a small jar or juice glass gently push the foil into the flowerpot, guiding with your other hand. Gently fold the foil around the flowerpot. Grease the foil.

Preheat the oven to 350°. Combine the sugar, cider, vanilla, cinnamon, and egg in a bowl and mix well. Add the flour, baking soda, and baking powder. Mix well, but don't overmix. Stir in the apples. Mix and evenly divide into the five foil-lined flowerpots. Bake for 45 minutes. Serve with a faux flower, tucking the stem of flower between the clay pot and foil liner.

Makes 5 pots, about 10 servings

Roxie Freitas, Sequin Butterfly
Big Island Beauties, Kailua-Kona, Hawaii

Dream Bars

CRUST

1/2   cup (1 stick) butter
1/2   cup firmly packed brown sugar
1   cup all-purpose flour

TOPPING

2   eggs, beaten
1   cup brown sugar
1   teaspoon vanilla extract
2   tablespoons all-purpose flour
1   teaspoon baking powder
1/2   teaspoon salt
1   cup shredded coconut
1   cup slivered almonds

Preheat the oven to 350°. For the crust, beat the butter and brown sugar until fluffy. Stir in the flour. Press the mixture into a lightly greased 13 x 9-inch pan. Bake for 10 minutes.

For the topping, in a large bowl beat the eggs, brown sugar, and vanilla. In a small bowl mix the flour, baking powder, and salt. Add the flour mixture to the egg mixture. Stir in the coconut and nuts. Pour over the base and bake 25 minutes longer, or until golden. Cool and cut into bars.

Makes 36 bars

Marge Pritchard, Chapterette
Scarlet Dames at Tea, Hudson, Florida

Orange Sour Cream Fruit Dip

1   (6-ounce) can frozen orange juice
      concentrate, thawed
1 1/4 cups milk
1   (3-ounce) package vanilla instant pudding
      mix
1/4   cup sour cream

In a large bowl combine the orange juice concentrate, milk, and pudding mix. Beat until smooth. Stir in the sour cream. Chill for 2 hours. Serve with fresh fruit.

Makes 8 to 12 servings

Rose Marie Dawes, Chapterette
Camarillo Red Hatters, Camarillo, California

Marshmallow Fruit Dip

1   (1/2-ounce) jar marshmallow creme
1   (8-ounce) package cream cheese
1/2   teaspoon vanilla extract

In a bowl combine the marshmallow creme, cream cheese, and vanilla. Chill for up to 1 day. Serve with fresh fruit.

Makes 8 to 12 servings

Dottie Koehler, Chapterette
Sassy Angels, Houston, Texas

Port Wine Cheese Spread

1 (8-ounce) package shredded sharp cheddar cheese
1 (8-ounce) package cream cheese
1/4 cup port wine
1/2 cup chopped walnuts

In a microwaveable bowl combine the Cheddar and cream cheese. Microwave on high for 45 seconds to soften. Add the port and mix vigorously to blend. Fold in the walnuts and spoon into a serving bowl. Serve with apples, pears, grapes, celery sticks, and crackers.

Makes 12 servings

Bessie Moseley, Chapterette
Sassy Angels, Houston, Texas

Banana Butter

Cloves bring out the best in bananas. See for yourself.

4 large bananas
2 tablespoons lemon juice
1 1/2 cups sugar
1/2 teaspoon cinnamon
1/8 teaspoon ground cloves

Peel the bananas and cut into chunks. Put the bananas into a blender and sprinkle with the lemon juice; blend thoroughly. In a large saucepan combine the bananas with the sugar, cinnamon, and cloves. Bring to a boil and sim-

mer for 15 minutes. Put in a jar and store in the refrigerator for a quick treat. Use within 2 weeks.

Makes 1 pint.

Diane Morey, Queen Mother Nature
Secret Society of Southern Scarlet Sisters, Hardeeville, South Carolina

Microwave Lemon Curd

Testers declared this much better than commercial lemon curd.

2 to 3 lemons
1/4 cup (1/2 stick) butter (no substitutes)
3/4 cup sugar
2 large eggs, beaten

Finely grate the outer rind of the lemons. Squeeze the lemons and measure 1/2 cup lemon juice into a 4-cup glass measuring bowl. Stir in the rind, butter, and sugar. Microwave, uncovered, on high (100%) for 2 minutes, or until the butter is melted and the mixture is hot. Gradually add the hot lemon mixture to the eggs, stirring constantly. Return the mixture to the glass measuring bowl and microwave, uncovered, on medium (50%) for 2 minutes, stirring every 30 seconds. Do not allow the mixture to boil; the mixture will thicken as it cools. Pour the cooled curd into a tightly sealed container. Refrigerate up to 2 weeks or freeze for longer storage.

Makes 1 2/3 cups

Phyllis Sturgill, Queen
Red Hatted Faithful Few, Omaha, Nebraska

Devonshire Cream

It's difficult to find real, super-rich Devon cream in the United States. This dreamy approximation helps make tea a little more authentic.

1   teaspoon unflavored gelatin powder
1/2   cup cold water
1   cup chilled sour cream
1   cup chilled whipping cream
1/4   cup sugar
2   teaspoons vanilla extract

Sprinkle the gelatin over the water in a small saucepan. Let stand 10 minutes, or until the gelatin softens. Heat the mixture over low heat until the gelatin dissolves. Remove from the heat and cool for about 10 minutes (but not much longer or the gelatin will begin to set). Combine the sour cream and gelatin mixture in a medium bowl. Beat the whipping cream, sugar, and vanilla in another bowl until soft peaks form. Fold into the sour cream mixture in two additions. Cover and chill for at least 1 hour. (Or make up to 1 day ahead and refrigerate.)

Makes 3 cups

Ina Lee, Duchess Ina
Scarlett Sugars, Mesa, Arizona

Cornflake Macaroons

This soft, sweet cookie scored high with testers. This cookie really sticks to the pan, so be sure to use parchment paper (or one of those terrific Silpat mats). Testers recommend that to get the measurement of cornflakes right, crush them first and then measure 1 1/2 cups.

3/4   cup sugar
1/3   cup evaporated milk
1 1/2 cups crushed cornflakes
1   cup shredded coconut
1/2   tablespoon vanilla extract
2   tablespoons butter

Preheat the oven to 350°. Mix the sugar and evaporated milk in a saucepan. Bring to a boil. Add the cornflakes, coconut, vanilla, and butter. Drop by the teaspoonful onto a parchment-lined cookie sheet. Bake for 10 to 12 minutes, or until light brown.

Makes 12 to 20 servings

Sylvia Joseph, Queen Mother Troubles
Kool Katz's, Warren, Michigan

Fancy Rich Butter Cookies

Forget those store-bought ones; make a batch of these to remind yourself how good a real butter cookie can be.

1   cup (2 sticks) butter
1 1/2 cups confectioners' sugar
2   eggs, separated

2 cups all-purpose flour
1 teaspoon vanilla extract
1 cup chopped candied cherries or nuts

Preheat the oven to 350°. Beat the butter and sugar until fluffy. Beat in the egg yolks. Fold in the flour and vanilla. Shape the dough into small balls. Place on a baking sheet and flatten with a fork. Beat the egg whites and brush the dough with the egg whites. Top with the cherries or nuts. Bake for 10 minutes.

Makes 4 to 5 dozen

Carol Ranieri, Chapterette
Belles of the Hooch, Columbus, Georgia

Pecan–Cinnamon Tea Ring

TEA RING
1 package active dry yeast
1 tablespoon granulated sugar
1/4 cup warm water
2/3 cup warm milk (about 105°)
1 egg
2 to 3 cups baking mix

FILLING
3/4 cup (1 1/2 sticks) butter, melted
1 1/2 cups granulated sugar
1 1/2 cups firmly packed brown sugar
Cinnamon to taste
1 cup finely chopped pecans

FROSTING
1 (1-pound) box confectioners' sugar
1/2 cup (1 stick) butter, melted
1 teaspoon vanilla extract
1/8 teaspoon salt
1/4 to 1/2 cup milk

For the tea ring, in a large bowl combine the yeast with the sugar and warm water; let stand for 5 minutes until foamy. Add the milk and stir in the egg and baking mix. Knead on a floured surface for 5 minutes. Roll out in a large circle about 1/4-inch thick.

For the filling, pour the butter over the dough. Spread the granulated sugar, brown sugar, cinnamon, and pecans on top. Roll up in a spiral and put on a round baking pan. Press ends together to seal. Cut into pie wedges about 2 inches wide, but leave the dough intact at the center so you still have a ring. Flip the wedge on its side to show the swirled interior. Cover and let rise in a warm place until double in size. Bake in a preheated 400° oven for 15 to 20 minutes, or until brown. Remove from the oven.

For the frosting, mix together the confectioners' sugar, melted butter, vanilla, salt, and milk. Pour the frosting on top of the ring while it is still warm. Cool and serve.

Makes 16 servings

Sydney Snedegar, Vice Queen Mother
Real Extraordinary Dames, Rushville, Indiana

Coal Camp Survivor Cooking

Some cook for pleasure, some for the love of eating, and others for survival. For my dear Granny and her fifteen children, it was survival.

The coal camp where they lived—Granny, seven daughters, and eight sons trying to earn a dollar—was a melting pot of nationalities. All were poor, all grew gardens, all cooked, and all shared what they had.

Granny made marble cake every Sunday, and at the end of the evening, not a crumb was left. When the taffy was pulled, never a bit was wasted. Homemade bread was made—ten loaves every day. Cut the crust off? Never! It was the best part, crisp and golden. Fruit season meant bushels, bushels, and more bushels of fruit from their own trees to "put up" as jams and preserves. There was always plenty of jam for that warm and aromatic fresh-baked bread! Granny was known in the coal camp for her wonderful chili, which she served to the town children before the Thursday free movie! Those good ole beans were the staple of the community.

She did it for necessity, not pleasure. But she left a legacy of good food, and now cooking for pleasure is part of the lives of the 15 children, 45 grandchildren, 123 great-grandchildren, and 109 great-great-grandchildren. This granddaughter gives thanks to those who suffered rough times in order to make my life easier!

Vickie Robb
FQM Socialitist
Friends of the Red Hatters
Springville, Indiana

Applesauce Cake

Old-fashioned, easy to make, and not too sweet. A wonderful winter tea treat.

1/2	cup shortening
1	cup sugar
1	teaspoon cinnamon
1/2	teaspoon cloves

1/2   teaspoon nutmeg

1   teaspoon baking soda

1 1/2   cups applesauce

1   egg

4   tablespoons hot water

2 1/2   cups all-purpose flour

1   cup raisins

Preheat the oven to 350°. Beat the shortening with the sugar, cinnamon, cloves, and nutmeg. Dissolve the baking soda in the applesauce. Add to the shortening mixture. Beat in the egg. Slowly add the hot water and flour. Add the raisins. Spoon the mixture into a greased loaf pan. Bake for 45 minutes. Cool the cake in the pan and serve in slices.

Makes 12 servings

Helene Mills, Chapterette
Birmingham Red Hat Belles, Birmingham, Michigan

Pecan Pound Cake

Serve in slices, or better yet, cut into "fingers" as a tempting morsel for the tea tray.

1   (18-ounce) box butter pecan cake mix

1   (8-ounce) can coconut-pecan frosting

3/4   cup vegetable oil

4   eggs

1   cup water

1/4   cup confectioners' sugar

Preheat the oven to 350°. In a large bowl beat the cake mix, frosting, oil, eggs, and water with a mixer. Grease a tube pan and dust it with the confectioner's sugar. Pour the batter into the pan and bake for 1 hour. Cool in the pan for about 10 minutes; then remove to a rack to finish cooling. When the cake is completely cooled, frost with a cream cheese frosting or an additional can of coconut-pecan frosting.

Makes 15 to 20 servings

Maggie Smith, Purple Playmate
The Hart Throb and Socialites of Hartwell, Buford, Georgia

Figgy Date Bars

Fruit and nuts make a wholesome snack with tea.

1   cup figs

1   cup pitted dates

2   cups chopped walnuts
   Confectioners' sugar

Chop the figs, dates, and walnuts in a food processor. Press the mixture firmly into a buttered 9-inch square pan. Sprinkle with the confectioners' sugar and cut into squares, or shape into balls and roll in confectioners' sugar.

Makes 12 servings

Judy Emily Huitt, Queen Mother
Norby's Red Rowdies, Anaheim, California

Apple Loaves

A moist, flavorful cake that keeps well for days, if it lasts that long.

2½ cups sugar
1 cup vegetable oil
4 eggs
1 teaspoon vanilla extract
3 cups all-purpose flour
1½ teaspoons salt
1½ teaspoons baking soda
½ teaspoon baking powder
1 teaspoon ground cloves
2 teaspoons cinnamon
3 cups chopped, peeled apples
2/3 cup raisins
½ cup chopped nuts

Preheat the oven to 325°. In a bowl beat the sugar, oil, eggs, and vanilla until light. Sift together the flour, salt, baking soda, baking powder, cloves, and cinnamon and stir into the batter. Stir in the apples, raisins, and nuts. Pour into two greased loaf pans. Bake for 1 hour.

Dee Tuisku, Chapterette
Hat'attudes of Safety Harbor, Safety Harbor, Florida

Cherry Coconut Tea Dainties

PASTRY
3 tablespoons confectioners' sugar
1 cup all-purpose flour
½ cup (1 stick) butter, softened

FILLING
1/4 cup all-purpose flour
1/2 teaspoon baking powder
1/4 teaspoon salt
2 eggs
1 cup granulated sugar
1 teaspoon vanilla extract
3/4 cup chopped walnuts
1/2 cup shredded coconut
1/2 cup maraschino cherries, cut into quarters

Preheat the oven to 350°. For the pastry, combine in a medium bowl the confectioners' sugar and flour. Add the butter and mix thoroughly. Spread the mixture into a lightly greased 8-inch square cake pan.

For the filling, in a small bowl combine the flour, baking powder, and salt. In a large bowl whisk the eggs just until frothy; add the sugar and vanilla and whisk again until thoroughly mixed. Fold in the flour mixture. Slowly stir in the walnuts, coconut, and cherries. Pour the filling over the top of the pastry and spread evenly to cover. Bake 25 to 30 minutes. Remove from the oven and let cool. Cut into squares and serve on small lace doilies.

Makes 16 squares

Carmella Chris, Queen Mamma
Divine Desert Divas of Las Vegas, Las Vegas, Nevada

Chocolate Zucchini Bread

Zucchini makes a moist bread, especially in this cake-like version tailor-made for tea.

3	eggs
1 1/2	cups sugar
1	cup vegetable oil
1	tablespoon vanilla extract
2	cups grated zucchini
3	cups all-purpose flour
1	teaspoon salt
1	teaspoon baking soda
1/2	teaspoon baking powder
1	tablespoon cinnamon
1	(3-ounce) box instant chocolate pudding mix
1/2	cup shredded coconut
1/2	cup chopped nuts
1/2	cup chocolate chips

Preheat the oven to 350°. In a large mixing bowl beat the eggs, sugar, oil, and vanilla until light in color. Fold in the zucchini. Combine the flour, salt, baking soda, baking powder, cinnamon, and pudding mix. Add to the egg mixture and mix well. Fold in the coconut, nuts, and chocolate chips. Pour into two greased loaf pans. Bake for 1 hour, or until a wooden pick inserted in the center comes out clean. Cool on a rack for 10 minutes; remove from the pans and cool completely.

Makes 2 loaves

Sue Tisdale, Chapterette
Red Hat Society Crones and Cronies, Pekin, Illinois

Amaretto Apricot Chews

CHEWS

1	cup butter, softened
1/2	cup granulated sugar
3/4	cup firmly packed brown sugar
1	egg
1	cup all-purpose flour
1	teaspoon baking soda
1	teaspoon almond extract
2 1/2	cups quick-cooking oats
1	cup chopped dried apricots
1/2	cup sliced almonds

GLAZE

2	cups confectioners' sugar
2/3	teaspoons water

Preheat the oven to 375°. For the "chews," beat the butter and sugars with an electric mixer on low speed until fluffy. Add the egg, flour, baking soda, and almond extract and continue beating on low until mixed. Add the oats, apricots, and almonds and stir with a spatula. Drop tablespoonfuls of batter onto a greased baking sheet. Bake for 8 to 10 minutes. Transfer to a wire rack to cool.

For the glaze, combine the confectioners' sugar and water and stir until smooth. Spread the glaze over the cooled chews before serving.

Makes about 36 cookies

Betty Graf, Drive-In Queen
O'Really Reds, Nixa, Missouri

Real Scottish Shortbread

Cornstarch gives shortbread a wonderfully crisp texture. Rice flour works too.

2   cups (4 sticks) butter (no substitutes), softened
1   cup sugar
4   cups all-purpose flour
1   cup cornstarch

Preheat the oven to 250°. Beat the butter and sugar until fluffy, about 10 minutes. Combine the flour and cornstarch and gradually add to the butter mixture 1/2 cup at a time. The mixture will become stiff after about 3 cups. Finish mixing in the flour and cornstarch by hand. Dough will be crumbly. Turn out on a pastry board and knead 10 to 12 times. Press the entire mixture into a 13 x 9-inch pan and prick all over with a fork. Bake for 11/2 to 2 hours, or until the shortbread starts to brown around the edges. Remove from the oven and let cool 15 minutes. Cut into very thin slices and let cool completely before serving. Store covered in a cookie tin or equivalent.

Makes 30 servings

Barbara Gowans, Queen Mother
Birmingham Red Hat Belles, Waterford, Michigan

Rich Nut and Jam Squares

Also called Czechoslovakian Cookies, this is a time-tested recipe using the best ingredients and makes fine cookies; you'll agree.

1   cup (2 sticks) butter, softened
1   cup granulated sugar
2   large egg yolks
2   cups all-purpose flour
1   cup chopped walnuts
1   (10-ounce) jar apricot preserves
    Confectioners' sugar (optional)

Preheat the oven to 325°. Combine the butter and sugar and beat until light and fluffy. Add the egg yolks and blend well. Gradually add the flour and mix thoroughly. Fold in the walnuts. The mixture will be thick. Spoon half the batter into a greased and floured 8-inch square pan. Top with the preserves, then the remaining batter. Bake for one hour until brown. Sprinkle lightly with confectioners' sugar, if desired, while still warm.

Makes 16 squares

Irvaleen Ogletree, Queen
Alpine Red Hat Society, Alpine, Texas

Orange Cream Scones

Yogurt gives the scones a light texture and is wonderful with the citrus flavors.

2   cups all-purpose flour
1/3 cup sugar
2   teaspoons baking powder
1/2 teaspoon baking soda
1/4 teaspoon salt
3   tablespoons chilled butter
1   (8-ounce) carton lemon yogurt
1/4 plus 1/4 cup orange juice

2 teaspoons grated orange peel

1/2 cup toasted, chopped pecans

12 sugar cubes

Preheat the oven to 400°. Combine the flour, sugar, baking powder, baking soda, and salt. Cut in the butter until crumbly. Add the yogurt, 1/4 cup orange juice, and orange peel and mix until just moistened (dough will be sticky). Add the pecans. Using an ice cream scoop that has been dipped in warm water, scoop the batter onto a parchment-lined cookie sheet. Dip the cubes of sugar in the remaining 1/4 cup orange juice and place one cube in the center of each scone. Bake for 16 minutes, or until nicely browned.

Makes 12 servings

Phyllis Souza, Queen Bee of Disorganization
Red Hot Hatter's of San Jose, San Jose, California

Red Hat Venetians for Teatime

Beautiful, fancy cookies for a gal who loves a project, or for the perfectionist baker.

1 (8-ounce) can almond paste

1 1/2 cups (3 sticks) butter, softened

1 cup sugar

4 egg yolks

1 teaspoon almond extract

2 cups all-purpose flour

1/4 teaspoon salt

4 egg whites

Red and purple paste food colors

6 ounces seedless raspberry preserves

2/3 cup semisweet chocolate chips

2 tablespoons butter

Preheat the oven to 350°. Prepare two or three 13 x 9-inch pans by lightly buttering the bottoms and sides, then lining them with waxed paper and buttering again. Beat the almond paste, butter, and sugar together. Add the egg yolks and almond extract and beat until light and fluffy. Add the flour and salt and mix until blended. Beat the egg whites until stiff peaks form and then fold into the mixture. Divide into two equal amounts in separate bowls. Add a small amount of red food coloring to one bowl and purple food coloring to the other. Spread each color batter into a different pan. Bake for 15 minutes. Cool.

Heat the preserves to soften, and then spread on one layer. Turn the plain layer out onto a wire rack and remove the waxed paper. Place this layer on top of the preserves. Cover the top with a layer of waxed paper and set a clean pan on top. Weight the pan down with a phone book or something heavy. Allow to cool to room temperature, and then remove the weighted pan. Melt the chocolate and butter together, spread over the top, and cool. Slice into small squares and store in a cool place or freeze.

With icing, create red and/or purple swirls or hats on the top of each square, or dye marzipan red and purple and make miniature hats and flowers for the top of each square.

Makes 30 servings

Jackie Seppy, Hysterian
Scarlet O'Hatters, Gaithersburg, Maryland

Raisin Scones

Raisin scones are delicious with a raisin spread: Combine cream cheese, a little sugar, raisins, and vanilla extract.

2   cups all-purpose flour
2   tablespoons granulated sugar
2   teaspoons baking powder
1/2 teaspoon salt
1/2 teaspoon baking soda
1/2 teaspoon ground nutmeg
1/2 cup (1 stick) cold butter or margarine
1   cup raisins
3/4 cup buttermilk
1   egg white
     Cinnamon sugar

Preheat the oven to 425°. Combine the flour, sugar, baking powder, salt, baking soda, and nutmeg in a bowl. Cut in the butter until crumbly. Stir in the raisins and buttermilk. Turn onto a floured surface and knead gently six to eight times. Pat into an 8-inch circle and cut into 12 wedges. Place 1 inch apart on a greased baking sheet. Beat the egg white until foamy and brush over the scones. Sprinkle with the cinnamon sugar. Bake for 12 to 15 minutes, or until golden.

Makes 12 servings

Mary Flynn, Princess
Scarlet Splashers, Torrington, Connecticut

Ginger–Orange Scones

Sassy and spicy.

2   cups all-purpose flour
2   tablespoons granulated sugar
2   teaspoons baking powder
2   teaspoons ground ginger
1/4 teaspoon baking soda
1/2 cup (1 stick) cold butter
1   cup raisins or dried currants
1   egg
3/4 cup sour cream
1 1/2 teaspoons grated orange peel
1/2 cup confectioners' sugar
1   tablespoon orange juice

Preheat the oven to 400°. Combine the flour, sugar, baking powder, ginger, and baking soda in a bowl. Cut in the butter until the mixture resembles coarse crumbs. Stir in the raisins. In a separate bowl combine the egg, sour cream, and orange peel; add to the crumb mixture and stir to form a soft dough. Turn onto a floured surface and knead a few times. Divide the dough in half. Pat each portion into a 7-inch circle; cut each circle into six wedges. Place the wedges 1 inch apart on an ungreased baking sheet. Bake for 10 to 12 minutes. Stir together the confectioners' sugar and orange juice. Drizzle over the scones while slightly warm.

Makes 12 scones

Dawn Praino, Duchess des Fleurs
Red Hot Colonial Sister, Dumfries, Virginia

Swedish Scones

For bakers who love trying something new, a yeast-raised scone is an intriguing change.

1   (0.6-ounce) cake of yeast (1/4-ounce envelope active dry yeast)
1/4   plus 3/4 cup milk
1/2   cup plus 1 teaspoon sugar
5   tablespoons butter plus for brushing
1   teaspoon salt
3   eggs, beaten
2   plus 2 cups all-purpose flour

Dissolve the yeast in 1/4 cup warm milk with 1 teaspoon sugar. Scald the remaining 3/4 cup milk and pour over the remaining 1/2 cup sugar, butter, and salt. Add the beaten eggs. Beat in 2 cups flour. Add the remaining 2 cups flour slowly. Add the yeast mixture and stir. Cover and put in the refrigerator for 6 to 8 hours or overnight. Remove from the refrigerator for 4 hours before baking. Divide the dough into four balls, rolling each out 1/4 inch thick. Brush with melted butter. Cut into pie-shaped wedges. Roll each wedge, beginning with the large end. Let rise for 4 hours. Bake at 350° for 20 minutes.

Makes 24 servings

Evelyn Garrett, Milkmaid
Happy Red Hatters of Somerset, Somerset, Kentucky

Weathervane Inn Irish Soda Bread

Soda bread slices are nice warm with butter and jam, and the bread makes a great base for little ham sandwiches.

4   cups all-purpose flour
1   teaspoon baking soda
2   teaspoons baking powder
1   teaspoon salt
1/2   cup (1 stick) butter, softened
1   cup plus 2 teaspoons sugar
2   eggs
1 1/4   cups buttermilk
1   tablespoon caraway seeds
1   cup raisins

Preheat the oven to 350°. Combine the flour, baking soda, baking powder, salt, butter, 1 cup sugar, the eggs, buttermilk, caraway seeds, and raisins and mix until blended (batter will be stiff). Turn into a well-greased and floured 4-quart round cast-iron Dutch oven. With a knife, cut a cross on the top of the batter about 1/4 inch deep by 4 inches long. Sprinkle the remaining 2 teaspoons sugar over the top. Bake for 1 hour. Cool 15 minutes in the pan. Remove and cool completely.

Makes 16 servings

Patricia D. Barlow, Queen Mum Pat
The Belles of Bridgewater, Bridgewater, Connecticut

Pumpkin Tea Bread

1   cup vegetable oil
1   cup granulated sugar
1   cup brown sugar
4   beaten eggs
1   (1-pound) can solid-pack pumpkin
3   cups sifted all-purpose flour
1 1/2 teaspoons salt
1   teaspoon cinnamon
1   teaspoon nutmeg or pumpkin pie spice
2   teaspoons baking soda
2/3 cup walnuts
2/3 cup chopped dates
     Whipped cream for topping (optional)

Blend the oil with the sugars in a bowl. Stir in the eggs and pumpkin. Sift together in a bowl the flour, salt, cinnamon, nutmeg, and baking soda. Stir in the nuts and dates. Add to the pumpkin mixture. Pour the batter into a greased and floured 3-pound coffee can. Put the can in a slow cooker. Cover the slow cooker and cook for 4 1/2 hours on low setting. No peeking. Remove the bread from the can. Slice and serve with a little bit of whipped cream on top.

Makes 6 to 8 servings

Diana Forrest, Queen of Forgetfullness
Fab 50s, Athens, Tennessee

Strawberry Bread

Unusual and delicious. The baked loaves freeze well. Testers called this "good and very moist."

3   cups all-purpose flour
1   teaspoon baking soda
1   teaspoon salt
1   tablespoon cinnamon
1 1/4 cups vegetable oil
2   cups sugar
4   eggs, beaten
2   cups sliced strawberries
1 1/4 cups chopped pecans or walnuts

Preheat the oven to 350° In a medium bowl sift the flour, baking soda, salt, and cinnamon together. Beat the oil with the sugar. Beat in the eggs and strawberries. Add the wet ingredients to the dry ingredients and mix until blended. Stir in the nuts. Pour into two greased loaf pans. Bake for 1 hour.

Makes 24 servings

Natalie Youngstead, Princess
The Nonpareils, Loudon, Tennessee

Asparagus Lovelies

For a full tea offer some savory tidbits, such as the next few goodies, along with the cakes and cookies.

16   fresh asparagus spears
16   slices sandwich bread, crusts removed
1   (8-ounce) package cream cheese, softened
8   bacon strips, cooked and crumbled
2   tablespoons minced fresh chives
     (or scallions)
1/4 cup (1/2 stick) butter or margarine, melted
3   tablespoons grated Parmesan cheese

Preheat the oven to 400°. In a skillet combine the asparagus with a small amount of water and cook over medium heat until crisp-tender, about 6 minutes. Drain. Flatten the bread with a rolling pin. Combine the cream cheese, bacon, and chives. Spread 1 tablespoon on each slice of bread. Top with an asparagus spear and roll up tightly. Place seam side down on a greased baking sheet. Brush with the melted butter and sprinkle with Parmesan cheese. Cut the rolls in half and bake for 10 to12 minutes, or until lightly browned.

Makes 15 servings

Linda Siatt, Chapterette
Rio Red Hots, Sun City West, Arizona

Asparagus Rolls

Any really good deli meat, such as smoked turkey, will substitute for the prosciutto. Any cheese spread will substitute for the Boursin. Or make your own spread with cream cheese and dip mix or fresh or dried herbs and spices.

20 asparagus spears
10 slices prosciutto, sliced about 1/8-inch thick
1   (5-ounce) container Boursin cheese, softened

Break off the tough ends of the asparagus. Steam or microwave 2 to 3 minutes, just until tender-crisp. Immediately rinse in cold water and dry on paper towels. Stack the prosciutto and cut in half. Spread a slice of prosciutto with a small bit of Boursin and place an asparagus spear on the long edge. Roll up and place on a plate.

Makes 8 to 10 servings

Susan Raymond, Madame Sew 'n' Sew
Brewster Wild Flowers, Pawling, New York

Apple-Almond Chicken Sandwiches

Dainty but filling.

3/4 cup mayonnaise
1/4 cup chopped celery
1/4 cup dried cranberries
1/4 cup chopped toasted almonds
     Dash of dried mustard or curry powder
1   cooked chicken breast, chopped
1   medium tart apple, finely chopped
4   plus 4 slices bread (12-grain and sourdough are good choices)
     Lettuce leaves

In a bowl combine the mayonnaise, celery, cranberries, almonds, and mustard. Add the chicken and mix well. Stir in apple and mix. Spread the mixture on 4 slices bread. Top with lettuce and the remaining 4 slices of bread. Cut into "fingers," triangles, or squares.

Makes 12 pieces

Eleanor Fossati, Queen Mother
Scarlet Splashers, Torrington, Connecticut

Making a Treasure

I enjoy cooking and love cookbooks, so one of my goals after retiring was to create a family cookbook. It took about a year, but with the help of my two sisters, we created a big family cookbook. Our book has more than three hundred recipes, plus stories and family favorites.

My daughters say it's so nice having the recipes at hand in the cookbook rather than hunting for papers. My seven grandchildren and four nephews contributed recipes and love seeing their names in print. Our book even includes a recipe for popcorn and another for scrambled eggs that Dad taught his son to make. It's such an accomplishment and a way to preserve your family history.

I recommend that anyone who loves cooking and sharing recipes to do a cookbook, because old family recipes have a way of getting lost.

Faith Eaton
Queen Mother Faith
Jamaica Bay YaYas
Fort Myers, Florida

Big Batch Tea Sandwich

You'll get four different fillings with this one recipe.

2 (8-ounce) packages cream cheese
1/2 cup mayonnaise
1/2 cup crushed pineapple, drained, patted dry
1/2 cup finely minced green olives
1/2 cup finely chopped cucumber
1/2 cup finely chopped pecans
1 loaf soft white bread, crusts removed
1 loaf soft wheat bread, crusts removed

Chopped parsley, crumbled bacon, poppy seeds, and pecans for garnish (optional)

In a medium bowl beat the cream cheese and mayonnaise. Divide the mixture evenly among four bowls. Add the pineapple to one bowl and mix well. Add the green olives to another bowl and mix well. Add the cucumbers to a third bowl and mix well. Add the pecans to the fourth bowl and mix well. Spread the fillings on the white bread and cover with the wheat bread. Cut each sandwich into triangles or other shapes. Arrange on a large platter, grouping by fillings. Garnish with the parsley, bacon, poppy seeds, or pecans. Label the sandwiches.

Makes about 32 full-size sandwiches

Paula Holdren, Vice Queen Paul DeLovely
Scarlett Ladies of Littleton, Littleton, Colorado

Bonnet Tea Chicken Cranberry Sandwiches

Savory, with a bit of scarlet sparkle. Try the Harry and David's Web site for the cranberry relish.

1	medium yellow onion
6	whole black peppercorns
1	bay leaf
2	sprigs fresh thyme
1 1/2	pounds boneless chicken breasts
	Cold water
2	(8-ounce) packages cream cheese
1	(12 1/4-ounce) jar cranberry relish
1	cup chopped pecans (optional)
1	pound (4 sticks) unsalted butter, softened
4	large loaves firm deli sandwich bread

A day or two before serving, combine the onion, peppercorns, bay leaf, thyme, and chicken in a pot; add cold water to cover. Bring to a boil and simmer about 1 hour, or until tender. Remove the chicken from the broth and reserve the broth for another use. Shred and chop the chicken. Chill. Beat the cream cheese in a large bowl until fluffy. Add the cranberry relish and mix well. Fold in the chicken. (You may refrigerate at this point until ready to make sandwiches. Let the filling stand at room temperature to soften before making sandwiches.) Fold in the pecans. Spread the softened butter on the bread. Spread the chicken mixture on the bread slices to make sandwiches. Cut the crusts from bread and cut the sandwiches into serving pieces. Cover with dampened dish towels and plastic wrap and refrigerate until ready to serve.

Makes about 40 whole sandwiches

Judith C. (Judy) Kockx, Queen Mother Hen
Red Chalice Chicks, Medford, Oregon

Cucumber Tea Sandwiches

The classic tea-time tidbit.

1	(8-ounce) package cream cheese
1	(.7-ounce) package dry Italian dressing mix
1	loaf cocktail rye bread
3	medium cucumbers, cut into 1/4-inch slices
	Dill weed

Mix the cream cheese with the Italian dressing with an electric mixer. Spread each slice of bread with the cheese mixture. Top with 1 slice cucumber and sprinkle with dill weed. Store in an airtight container until serving time. These sandwiches may be stacked with waxed paper between layers.

Makes 4 dozen tea sandwiches

Dorothy Jensen, Hattitude Hattie
Red Hat Honeys, Randolph, Nebraska

Chicken Salad Delight

Serve in hollowed out tomatoes, or spoon into cucumber halves and cut into bite-size pieces.

4   cups diced cooked chicken, chilled
1   (4-ounce) can sliced water chestnuts, drained, chopped
2   green onions, sliced
1/2 cup chopped pecans (optional)
1   (4-ounce) jar pimientos, drained and chopped
1   tablespoon sweet relish
1   teaspoon chopped parsley
2   tablespoons mayonnaise
     Salt and pepper to taste

In a large bowl combine the chicken, water chestnuts, green onions, pecans, pimientos, relish, parsley, mayonnaise, and salt and pepper. Mix well and chill. Serve with crackers or use as a sandwich filling.

Makes 6 to 8 servings

Yvonne Spencer Robinson, Foxy Nana
2 Many Foxy Red Hat Divas with Hattitude, Rockingham, North Carolina

Strawberry Tea Sandwiches

Irresistibly dainty and pretty.

1   (8-ounce) package strawberry cream cheese, softened
32   slices buttered white bread or nut bread
1/2 cup finely chopped toasted walnuts or almonds
8   ripe strawberries, cut in half

Spread the cream cheese on one side of each of the slices of bread. Sprinkle the walnuts over the cheese on one slice. Assemble the sandwiches. Trim the crusts and cut into desired shapes. (Little hats are cute.) Just before serving, insert a toothpick into half a strawberry and put it into the top of the sandwich.

Makes 16 servings

Marilyn Preston, Queen Mom
Red Ladyslippers, Maplewood, Minnesota

Melt-In-Your-Mouth Cheese Tarts

You can practically taste these when you read the ingredients.

CRUST

6   tablespoons butter
1   (3-ounce) package low-fat cream cheese, softened
1   cup all-purpose flour

FILLING

1	cup grated Muenster cheese
1/4	cup mayonnaise
1/4	cup sour cream
	Paprika
	Chopped nuts (optional)

For the crust, beat the butter and cream cheese and then stir in the flour. Chill about 1 hour. Roll into 24 balls and press each ball into a small muffin tin.

Preheat the oven to 350°. For the filling, mix the cheese, mayonnaise, and sour cream together. Spoon into the tarts and sprinkle with the paprika and chopped nuts. Bake for 30 minutes.

Makes 2 dozen tarts

Shirley Jackson, Queen
Totally Eccentric Adventurous Red Hatters of Vienna
Vienna, Virginia

Pear Tea Sandwiches

1	(8-ounce) package cream cheese, softened
4	ounces blue cheese, crumbled
1/4	plus 1/4 cup chopped walnuts
6	plus 6 slices cinnamon raisin bread
2	(16-ounce) cans pears, drained and sliced
8	ounces thinly sliced honey-baked ham

In a small bowl combine the cream cheese, blue cheese, and 1/4 cup walnuts. Spread the cheese mixture on 6 slices of the bread and then add a layer of pears and ham. Top the sandwiches with the 6 remaining slices of bread. Cut the crust from the bread with a sharp knife and then cut into quarters. Place on a pretty plate and garnish with the remaining 1/4 cup walnuts.

Makes 24 tea sandwiches

Sandy Guilbeaux, Princess of Royal Teas
Shrewd Hatters of Shrewsbury, Stewartstown, Pennsylvania

Nut Tea Sandwiches

You don't have to keep a well-stocked pantry to make these.

1	(8-ounce) package cream cheese, softened
3	to 4 tablespoons mayonnaise
1/4	teaspoon salt
1/4	teaspoon paprika
1 1/2	cups chopped pecans or walnuts
1	loaf wheat bread

Beat the cream cheese with a whisk until smooth. Add the mayonnaise and stir until blended. Add the salt, paprika, and chopped nuts. Trim the crusts from the bread; spread the mixture on one slice and top with another slice. Slice the sandwiches diagonally into quarters.

Makes 2 dozen tea sandwiches

Sandra Morales, The Traveling Contessa
New Braunfels Colleens, Wimberley, Texas

Pecan-Tuna Crunch Spread

You can spread the mixture onto fancy crackers instead of bread if you prefer.

1   (7-ounce) can white chunk tuna in water, drained
2   tablespoons lemon juice
1   (8-ounce) package cream cheese, softened
1   small can black olives, drained and chopped
1/2 cup mayonnaise-type salad dressing
1   cup finely chopped pecans
1   large loaf sliced bread, crusts trimmed

Mix the tuna, lemon juice, cream cheese, olives, salad dressing, and pecans in a bowl. Spread the tuna mixture evenly on one slice of bread and cover with the second slice. Cut into desired shapes. Store between layers of waxed paper. Can also serve on fancy little crackers as hors d'oeuvre.

Makes about 12 sandwiches

Note: For a special presentation, cut the crusts from the sandwiches. Moisten the edges with a little salad dressing and press into chopped nuts to create a crunchy border.

Mary Francinn Parker, Queen Mom of Grandyville
The Happy Hatters, Georgetown, Texas

Peppernut Sandwich Spread or Dip

2   (8-ounce) packages cream cheese, softened
1   medium green bell pepper, finely chopped
1/4 cup finely chopped onion
1/2 cup sour cream
1/4 cup mayonnaise
1   cup finely chopped pecans
    Bread or crackers

Blend together the cream cheese, bell pepper, onion, sour cream, mayonnaise, and pecans. Spread on bread or crackers. Or use as a dip with chips. This can be made the day before and refrigerated.

Makes 1 dozen sandwiches

Carolyn Wetherby, Lady Carolyn
Regal Foxie Fillies, Cumby, Texas

Slumguneon

Slumguneon is one of those recipes that is better the day after it is made. Serve with little crackers or make tea sandwiches from the mixture.

1   (8-ounce) package cream cheese
2   hard-boiled eggs
1   (8-ounce) bottle salad olives, drained
1   small onion, finely chopped
1   tablespoon butter, softened

Soften the cream cheese. Dice the eggs finely. Chop the salad olives. In a bowl combine the cream cheese, eggs, olives, onion, and butter. Mix well. Add some of the liquid from the olives, if needed to thin the mixture. Spoon into a little serving bowl.

Makes 20 servings

Barbara Cowan, Vice Queen Mum
Hacienda Red Hatters, Seven Springs, Florida

Stovetop Raisin Cakes

Part tea cake, part English muffin, these are served warm with jam and Devonshire cream (see page 248) or butter. They are cooked on a griddle, like a crumpet.

1/2   cup sugar
2   cups all-purpose flour
2   teaspoons baking powder
1/2   teaspoon salt
1/2   cup (1 stick) butter, softened
1/2   cup milk
1   egg
1   cup currants or raisins

Combine the sugar, flour, baking powder, and salt in a bowl and mix well. Cut in the butter until the mixture resembles coarse crumbs. Add the milk, egg, and raisins. Mix until well moistened. Roll out the dough on a floured surface and cut into large circles. Cook on a griddle or nonstick skillet until golden brown, turning just once.

Makes 8 to 10 cakes

Vano Gust, Lady Shutterley
The Sassy R.E.D.s, Alberta, Canada

Dill Egg Spread

1   cup mayonnaise
1 1/2 tablespoons fresh lemon juice
2   teaspoons Dijon mustard
1   tablespoon finely chopped onion
1/2   teaspoon fresh lemon zest
1/2   teaspoon hot pepper sauce (or to taste)
6   hard-boiled eggs
1   (3-ounce) package low-fat cream cheese, softened
1/2   teaspoon seasoned salt
       Pinch of pepper
2   teaspoons chopped fresh dill, plus sprigs for garnish
       Rye bread
1   (6-ounce) can sliced stuffed olives

Combine the mayonnaise, lemon juice, mustard, onion, lemon zest, and hot pepper sauce in a blender and process until well blended. Add the eggs, one at a time, adding some cream cheese after each egg. Add the salt and pepper; blend until smooth. Fold in the dill. Let rest at least 1 hour. Spread on rye bread. Top with the sliced olives and a sprig of dill.

Makes 2 cups

Dorothy Bono, Lady Shelby
Silly Sassy Shelby Sisters, Washington Twp., Michigan

Oat Cakes

Serve with clotted cream and jam or honey butter or cream cheese spread. Also great with slivers of blue cheese or a blue cheese spread.

3   cups rolled oats

2   cups all-purpose flour

1/2 cup sugar (white or brown)

1   teaspoon baking powder

1   teaspoon baking soda

1/4 teaspoon salt

1   cup shortening

2   tablespoons butter, softened

1/4 cup cold water

Preheat the oven to 375°. In a large bowl mix the oats, flour, sugar, baking powder, baking soda, and salt. Mix in the shortening and butter until coarse. Add the cold water and mix until the dough forms a ball. Roll out to 1/4 inch thickness. Cut into 3-inch squares and put on a greased cookie sheet. Bake for 10 to 12 minutes. Cool 2 minutes and then remove to a rack.

Makes 4 dozen

Judy Ross, Chapterette

Celtic Bells Red Hatters, Baddeck, Nova Scotia, Canada

EIGHT

⸜ Warm and Cozy, ⸝ Cool and Crisp

SOUPS & SALADS

When the weather turns cold, just about every woman who has meals to cook finds herself rummaging for her best soup recipes. Blustery weather inevitably conjures up images of rain on the windowpanes and a fire in the fireplace. A thick, hearty soup may be the most nurturing food in existence. Salads seem almost to have been invented solely to accompany soup. The warm, creamy soup cries out for a crunchy salad, most often filled with vegetables.

The children's book entitled *Stone Soup* is often used as an analogy for the Red Hat Society itself. In the story, a village full of starving people manages to make a huge kettle of hearty soup, enough for all, by pooling the little bits of food that each has. Every woman who joins our "disorganization" contributes something unique, and helps to make the Red Hat Society what it has become.

Artichoke Chicken Pasta Salad

3   bone-in chicken breast halves
1   pound thin spaghetti
1   cup good-quality Italian salad dressing
3   celery stalks
3   green onions
1   (14-ounce) can water-packed artichoke
    hearts, drained
1   (2-ounce) can sliced black olives
1   cup good-quality mayonnaise
    Salt and pepper to taste

Steam the chicken until cooked through. Cool, remove the meat from the bones, and cut into bite-size pieces. Cook the spaghetti according to package instructions, breaking it into 2-inch pieces when adding to the boiling water. Drain the cooked spaghetti in a colander and rinse with cold water. Combine the spaghetti with the salad dressing and chicken in a bowl.

Chill the chicken mixture in the refrigerator while you finely chop the celery, green onions, and artichoke hearts. Add to the spaghetti along with the sliced black olives, mayonnaise, salt, and pepper. Chill for at least 1 hour.

Makes 6 generous servings

Nancy Ellis, Queen Mother
Desert Flowers, Palm Desert, California

Caramel Apple Salad

1   cup milk
1   (5.1-ounce) package vanilla instant
    pudding mix
1   (12-ounce) container whipped topping
6   Snickers bars, cut into bite-size pieces
4   Granny Smith apples, cut into bite-size
    pieces

Mix together the milk and pudding mix in a large bowl and beat or whisk until thickened. Stir in the whipped topping, Snickers, and apples. Refrigerate until serving time.

Makes 6 to 8 servings

Karen Pickett, Madam Pompidou, Queen of Hearts
Young @ Hearts, Racy Reds & Perky Pinks, Evansville, Indiana

Marinated Asparagus Salad

DRESSING
1 1/3 cups olive oil
2/3   cup tarragon vinegar
2   tablespoons lemon juice
2   garlic cloves, minced
2   teaspoons salt
1   tablespoon sugar
1   teaspoon dill weed
1   teaspoon dry mustard
1/4   cup Durkee's famous sauce

SALAD

2 pounds asparagus
1 large red onion, peeled and sliced
1 cucumber, peeled and sliced
   Bibb or Boston lettuce

To make the dressing, combine the oil, vinegar, lemon juice, garlic, salt, sugar, dill, mustard, and Durkee's in a bottle or cruet with a tight-fitting lid. Shake to combine.

For the salad, wash and trim the asparagus spears. Cook until just tender. Marinate the asparagus, onion slices, and cucumber slices in the dressing for several hours or overnight. The longer they marinate the better they taste. To serve, place the vegetables on lettuce leaves and pour the dressing over all.

Makes 8 servings

Sheila Bougher, Queenie
Holy Rollers, Owasso, Oklahoma

Asparagus Raspberry Salad

The essence of California bounty and a wonderful salad for a Red Hat gathering.

3 pounds fresh asparagus
1 carton fresh raspberries
   Prepared raspberry vinaigrette dressing

Prepare the asparagus by snapping off the ends. Lightly steam in the microwave on high for about 2 minutes, or until tender. Cool. Arrange on plates and top with the raspberries. Drizzle with the dressing and serve.

Makes 8 servings

Barbara Boxold, Contessa Bee in My Bonnet
Notorious Tacky Hatters of Norco
Riverside, California

Avocado Cocktail

1   tablespoon mayonnaise
1   tablespoon ketchup
1/2 teaspoon Worcestershire sauce
1/4 teaspoon onion juice
1/8 teaspoon chili powder
1   large ripe avocado
2   slices chopped bacon, cooked and drained

Combine the mayonnaise, ketchup, Worcestershire sauce, onion juice, and chili powder in a bowl. Cut the avocado into cubes. Arrange in custard cups or cocktail glasses. Top each serving with the mayonnaise mixture. Garnish with the bacon.

Makes 2 servings

Kali Sitton, Princess Need 4 Speed
Rhat Pacque, Canyon Country, California

Broccoli Bacon Salad

SALAD

2 heads fresh broccoli, florets only
12 slices bacon, crisply cooked and crumbled
1 cup chopped celery
1/2 cup chopped green onions
1 cup seedless green grapes
1 cup seedless red grapes
1/2 cup blanched slivered almonds
2 cups shredded cheddar cheese

DRESSING

1 cup mayonnaise
1 tablespoon white or red wine vinegar
1/4 cup sugar

In a large salad bowl toss together the broccoli, bacon, celery, green onions, grapes, and almonds. Sprinkle the cheese on top.

For the dressing, whisk together the mayonnaise, vinegar, and sugar. Pour the dressing over the salad and toss to combine.

Makes 6 to 8 servings

Della Waynick, Queenette
The Hot Foxy Ladies, Warren, Michigan

Black-Eyed-Pea Salad

Black-eyed peas on New Year's Day mean good luck—try this salad for a rollicking great year.

SALAD

3 cans plain black-eyed peas, drained
1 (4-ounce) jar chopped pimientos, drained
6 green onions with tender tops, sliced
4 celery stalks, chopped
1 large green bell pepper, diced
1 large red bell pepper, diced
1 fresh jalapeño, seeds removed, diced
1 large ripe tomato, cubed
1 bunch cilantro, leaves chopped

DRESSING

3 large cloves garlic, minced
1/3 cup olive oil
1/3 cup balsamic vinegar
2 teaspoons seasoned salt
Leaf lettuce or parsley (optional)
4 strips crisp-cooked bacon, crumbled (optional)

For the salad, combine the peas, pimientos, green onions, celery, bell peppers, jalapeño, tomato, and cilantro in a large serving bowl and toss to distribute evenly.

For the dressing, whisk together the garlic, olive oil, vinegar, and seasoned salt.

The salad does not have to be refrigerated. Flavor develops if it is made several hours prior to serving. Leftovers should be refrigerated. Garnish with leafy lettuce or parsley. Crisp bacon can be sprinkled on top just before serving.

Makes 15 to 20 servings

Lucinda Denton, Founding Queen Mother (FQM)
Nonpareils, Knoxville, Tennessee

Fresh Green Bean and Squash Salad

1/2 cup fresh green beans, broken into 1-inch pieces

1/2 cup sliced fresh yellow squash

3 fresh plum tomatoes, diced

4 ounces mozzarella cheese, cut into 1/2-inch cubes

1/4 cup roasted garlic & Parmesan salad dressing

Pinch of black pepper

1 1/2 ounces chopped fresh basil (about 3 tablespoons)

Combine the green beans, squash, plum tomatoes, and mozzarella in a medium bowl. Add the dressing, pepper, and basil and toss to combine. Cover and refrigerate for about an hour.

Makes 2 large servings

Peggy Giddens, Queen Mum Peg
Red Hot Red Hat Readers of Decatur, Ten Mile, Tennessee

Brussels Sprout Salad

A new role for an underused ingredient.

3 pounds Brussels sprouts

2 tablespoons chopped green onions

2 tablespoons chopped green bell pepper

2 tablespoons chopped fresh parsley

1 (2-ounce) jar chopped pimientos

2 cups Italian salad dressing

2 tablespoons capers, drained

2 tablespoon lemon juice

1/2 teaspoon hot pepper sauce

1/4 teaspoon ground black pepper

Clean the Brussels sprouts by peeling off the outer layer of leaves and cutting off the ends. Place the Brussels sprouts in a large pot and cover with water. Cover and bring to a boil, lower the temperature, and cook for about 20 minutes, or until tender and easily pierced with a knife. Drain and immediately immerse in cold water to retain their green color. Drain and transfer to a large bowl. Add the green onions, bell pepper, parsley, and pimientos. Add Italian salad dressing, capers, lemon juice, hot sauce, and ground black pepper. Toss to combine. Chill for at least 8 hours. Serve cold.

Makes 12 servings

Mara Willick, Queen of SASCI
SASCI (Sexy Adventurous Sun City Instigators), Henderson, Nevada

"Life is a banquet and most poor suckers are starving."

—Rosalind Russell

Cauliflower Salad

Full of fiber, flavor, and antioxidants.

1   (12-ounce) bag romaine lettuce
1   large or 2 small heads cauliflower, cut into bite-size pieces
5   to 7 ounces (about 2 cups) roasted cashew pieces
2   cups shredded mozzarella cheese or other mild white cheese
     Sweet and sour salad dressing

Empty the lettuce into a large bowl or onto a serving platter. Top with the cauliflower, cashews, and cheese. Just before serving, drizzle with the dressing.

Makes 5 to 6 servings

Della Waynick, Queenette
The Hot Foxy Ladies, Warren, Michigan

Layered Spinach Salad

1   (9-ounce) package refrigerated uncooked cheese tortellini
2   cups shredded red cabbage
6   cups torn spinach leaves
1   cup halved cherry tomatoes
1/2 cup sliced green onions
1   (8-ounce) bottle ranch dressing
8   slices bacon, cooked and crumbled

Cook the tortellini according to the package directions. Drain and rinse with cold water. Layer the cabbage, spinach, tortellini, tomatoes and green onions in a 13 x 9-inch glass baking dish. Pour dressing evenly over the top. Sprinkle with bacon. Cover and refrigerate until serving time.

Makes 8 servings

Gail K. Sykora, Queen Mother
Magenta Madames, Meno. Falls, Wisconsin

Curried Beet Salad

Some of us get flushed just thinking about those gorgeous red beets.

CURRY VINAIGRETTE
1   garlic clove, minced
1/2 teaspoon salt
2   teaspoons curry powder
1/2 teaspoon ground ginger
1 1/2 tablespoons lemon juice
6   tablespoons olive oil

SALAD
1   (15-ounce) can sliced beets
6   green onions, sliced
1/2 cup currants
2   sweet apples, cut into chunks
2   celery stalks, cut into chunks
3/4 cup walnut pieces
     Lettuce for serving

For the curry vinaigrette, combine the garlic, salt, curry powder, ginger, lemon juice, and olive oil in a bowl or jar with a tight-fitting lid. Whisk or shake to blend

For the salad, combine the beets, green onions, currants, apples, celery, and walnuts in a bowl. Pour the dressing over the beet mixture. Chill and serve on a bed of lettuce.

Makes 6 to 8 servings

Barbara Sendall, Mama Sunshine
Red Hot Dollies, Port Charlotte, Florida

Cantaloupe Surprise

The surprise is that each slice of cantaloupe is filled with berries in gelatin. Serve this tableside so everyone can see the "surprise" when you cut open the cantaloupe. Not a dish for eating on your lap, as it requires a knife and some balance. Testers used blueberries and sugar-free gelatin and pronounced them good.

1   (3-ounce) package raspberry gelatin
1   (10 to 12-ounce) package frozen raspberries (or other berries), thawed
2   cantaloupes

Prepare the gelatin using package directions. Add the berries after the mixture has thickened slightly. Cut a small opening in each cantaloupe and scoop out the seeds. Pour the gelatin mixture into the cantaloupes through the opening. Refrigerate the cantaloupes until the gelatin is set. Cut each cantaloupe into six sections.

Makes 12 servings

Judy Emily Huitt, Queen Mother
Norby's Red Rowdies, Anaheim, California

Cucumber Cream Salad

When this salad chills in the refrigerator overnight, the cucumbers absorb the flavors of the gelatin and sour cream and don't taste like cucumbers anymore.

1   (3-ounce) package lime gelatin
1   cup hot water
1   teaspoon salt
2   teaspoons white vinegar
1   teaspoon onion juice
1/2 cup mayonnaise
1   cup sour cream
2   cups chopped cucumbers

Dissolve the gelatin in the hot water in a medium bowl. Add the salt, vinegar, and onion juice. Chill until slightly thickened. Fold in the mayonnaise. Whip the sour cream until fluffy. Fold into the gelatin mixture. Add the cucumbers and mix well. Chill until firm.

Makes 4 to 6 servings

Roseanna Newberry, Royal Red Hatter
The Fort Scott Ladies of Oz, Fort Scott, Kansas

Taste of Hawaii Chicken Salad

Save yourself some clean-up time by mixing the dressing right in the bowl you use for making the salad.

DRESSING
- 8 ounces Italian dressing
- 4 tablespoons soy sauce
- 4 tablespoons brown sugar

SALAD
- 6 chicken breast halves, cooked and shredded
- 1 (20-ounce) can unsweetened pineapple chunks, drained
- 6 green onions, thinly sliced on the diagonal
- 1 head romaine or iceberg lettuce
- 1 cup chopped fresh parsley
- 1 cup shredded coconut
- 1 cup chopped macadamia nuts

For the dressing, combine the Italian dressing, soy sauce, and brown sugar in a jar with a tight-fitting lid. Shake to mix well.

For the salad, combine the chicken, pineapple, and green onions in a large bowl. Top with the dressing and toss to combine. Refrigerate, covered, for at least 6 hours. To serve, shred or chop the lettuce and layer it in a large, chilled serving bowl. Drain the chicken mixture and layer it over the lettuce. Sprinkle with the chopped parsley, coconut, and nuts.

Makes 4 to 6 servings

Judy Pettersen, Dutchess of Disarray
Big Island Beauties, Kailua-Kona, Hawaii

Baby Blue Salad

A stand-out salad requires stand-out components. Fortunately, the pecans and dressing can be made well ahead and kept handy, so you can have gourmet any day. The pecans keep for a week or more in an air-tight container, and the dressing keeps for more than two weeks.

PECANS
- 1/4 cup plus 2 tablespoons sugar
- 1 cup warm water
- 1 cup pecan halves
- 1 tablespoon chili powder
- 1/8 teaspoon ground red pepper

VINAIGRETTE
- 1/2 cup balsamic vinegar
- 3 tablespoons Dijon mustard
- 3 tablespoons honey
- 2 large garlic cloves, minced
- 2 small shallots, minced
- 1/4 teaspoon salt
- 1/4 teaspoon pepper
- 1 cup olive oil

SALAD
- 3/4 pound gourmet-mix salad greens
- 1 (4-ounce) package crumbled blue cheese
- 2 oranges, peeled and cut into squares
- 1 pint fresh strawberries, quartered

For the pecans, stir together 1/4 cup sugar and warm water in a bowl until the sugar dissolves. Add the pecans and soak for 10 minutes. Drain, discarding the syrup. Preheat the oven to 350°. Combine the remaining 2 tablespoons sugar, chili powder, and red pepper. Add the pecans, tossing to coat. Arrange the pecans on a lightly greased baking sheet. Bake for 10 minutes, or until golden brown, stirring once.

For the vinaigrette, whisk together the vinegar, mustard, honey, garlic, shallots, salt, and pepper until blended. Gradually whisk in the olive oil, blending well.

For the salad, toss together the greens, cheese, oranges, and strawberries in a large bowl. Drizzle with the balsamic vinaigrette. Top with the pecans to serve.

Makes 6 servings

Sue Southerland, Queen Mum
Sassy Bodacious Ladies, Greeneville, Tennessee

Corn Bread Salad

Homemade corn bread is the best option—the pieces are larger and more attractive and they absorb just the right amount of dressing. A summer version of this salad substitutes tomatoes, basil, and bacon for the vegetables.

Some cooks mix up the salad and refrigerate it for several hours before serving, while others wait until just before serving to stir in the corn bread pieces.

CORN BREAD
1 1/4 cups cornmeal
3/4 cup all-purpose flour
3 tablespoons sugar
1/2 teaspoon salt
1 1/2 tablespoons baking powder

1 cup milk
1/4 cup (1/2 stick) butter, melted
1 egg, beaten

SALAD
3/4 cup chopped cauliflower
3/4 cup chopped broccoli
3/4 cup chopped red or green bell peppers
3/4 cup chopped carrots
3/4 cup chopped red or green onions
3/4 cup chopped celery
1/2 cup chopped radishes
1/2 to 3/4 cup sweet pickle juice
1 cup good-quality mayonnaise

For the corn bread, preheat the oven to 400°. Grease an 8-inch square pan. In a large bowl combine the cornmeal, flour, sugar, salt, and baking powder. Add the milk, butter, and egg all at once and stir to combine. Pour the batter into the prepared pan and bake for about 20 minutes. Cool completely and crumble.

For the salad, combine the vegetables in a large bowl. Mix the pickle juice and mayonnaise in a small bowl and toss with the vegetables. Add the corn bread and mix well to ensure the corn bread is coated. Seal and chill overnight. Toss to serve the next day.

Makes 6 to 8 servings

Anna Belle Fulford, Queen Mum
West Orange Red Hat Society, Winter Garden, Florida

Pink Stuff

We received hundreds of recipes like this one, some classified as salad (though they contain no fresh fruit or vegetables) and others as dessert. At our age, who cares what it's called, so long as it's delicious.

1   can sweetened condensed milk
1   (12-ounce) container whipped topping, thawed
1   (20-ounce) can cherry pie filling
1   (15-ounce) can crushed pineapple, well drained
1   (15-ounce) can mandarin oranges, drained

Stir together the condensed milk and whipped topping. Fold in the cherry pie filling. Fold in the pineapple and oranges. If you want a deeper pink color, add few drops of red food coloring. Refrigerate at least 4 hours prior to serving.

Makes 12 servings

Doris Hoyt, Queen Mom
Red Hatted Ya Yas, Houston, Texas

Banana Cream Salad

We received dozens of versions of this salad, which is as much of a dessert as a salad. Red Hatters can't seem to get enough of it.

2   (3-ounce) packages vanilla instant pudding mix
2   cups buttermilk

1   (16-ounce) container whipped topping, thawed
2   (30-ounce) cans fruit cocktail, drained
2   (15-ounce) cans mandarin oranges, drained
2   (16-ounce) jars maraschino cherries, drained
1   (20-ounce) can crushed pineapple, drained
2   bananas, sliced

Combine the pudding mix and buttermilk and beat for 1 minute with an electric mixer. Add the whipped topping and mix well. Add the fruit cocktail, oranges, cherries, pineapple, and bananas, and stir to combine. Chill.

Makes 20 servings

Patti Ingli, Queen Patti
Ellsworth Red Hatters, Ellsworth, Wisconsin

Grapefruit Salad

1   teaspoon salt
1   teaspoon dry mustard
1   teaspoon celery salt
1   teaspoon paprika
1/2 cup sugar or honey
1   teaspoon grated onion
1/4 cup vinegar
1   cup vegetable oil
4   cups grapefruit sections
     Lettuce leaves

Combine the salt, mustard, celery salt, paprika, and sugar in a bowl or jar with a tight-fitting lid. Add the onion and vinegar and mix well. Whisk in the oil or shake to combine. (Store in the refrigerator but let stand at room temperature before serving.) Arrange the grapefruit sections on the lettuce leaves. Serve with the fruit dressing.

Makes 6 servings

Pat Callicutt, Anti-Parlimentarian
Little Red Hens, Seagrove, North Carolina

Italian Macaroni Salad

1   (1-pound) package whole wheat elbow macaroni
1   cup freshly grated Parmesan cheese
3/4 cup Italian dressing
3/4 cup sliced pimiento-stuffed olives
1   cup julienned pepperoni
1   cup shredded mild cheddar cheese
    Salt and pepper to taste

Cook the pasta according to package directions. Drain, rinse with cold water (this stops the cooking process), and drain again. Combine the Parmesan cheese, dressing, olives, pepperoni, cheese, and salt and pepper in a large bowl. Add the pasta and mix well. You may need to adjust the dressing to taste.

Makes 6 to 8 servings

Nancy Clemons, Exalted Queen Mother Nancy
Luscious Ladies of League City, League City, Texas

Macaroni and Cheese Salad

Fun pasta shape, simple ingredients, and great taste ensure this one is a keeper—oh, and it makes an abundant batch, too.

SALAD
1   pound dry ruffle macaroni
2   cups diced celery
2   cups diced or grated green bell pepper
2   cups grated Vidalia onion
2   cups shredded carrots
2   cups sharp cheddar cheese cubes

DRESSING
1 1/2 cups cider vinegar
2   cups sugar
3   tablespoons vegetable oil

Cook the macaroni according to the package directions. Drain and transfer to a large serving bowl. Add the celery, bell pepper, onion, and carrots to the pasta. Add the cheese and toss to combine.

For the dressing, combine the vinegar, sugar, and oil in a bowl with a whisk (or a blender, or a jar with a tight-fitting lid). Mix or shake to blend. Pour the dressing over the salad and mix well. Refrigerate for at least 8 hours.

Makes 20 to 25 servings

Irene Andrews, Chapterette
The Ruby Red Hats, Lakewood, New York

Czarina's Cranberry Borscht Salad with Horseradish Dressing

Bold flavors for ladies looking for something different.

SALAD
1 (16-ounce) jar pickled beets, not drained
3/4 cup cold water
2 cups cranberry juice
1/4 teaspoon salt
1/8 teaspoon pepper
1 bay leaf
2 (3-ounce) packages lemon gelatin
2 tablespoons fresh lemon juice
3 tablespoons red wine vinegar
3 tablespoons finely minced beets
3 tablespoons finely minced celery
2 tablespoons finely minced onion
1/2 cup sliced radishes for garnish

DRESSING
1 cup sour cream
3 tablespoons skim milk
1 tablespoon prepared horseradish
1/4 teaspoon salt
1 teaspoon sugar

For the salad, drain the beet liquid into a 2-quart saucepan. And the water, cranberry juice, salt, pepper, and bay leaf. Heat to boiling, remove from the heat, and remove the bay leaf. Add the gelatin and lemon juice. Stir until the gelatin is dissolved, 3 to 5 minutes. Add the red wine vinegar. Chill to the consistency of egg whites, about 30 to 45 minutes. Add the beets, celery and onion. Pour into an oiled gelatin mold with a 5-cup or larger capacity. Refrigerate until firm, 4 to 6 hours. Unmold onto a plate of lettuce leaves, garnish with radishes, and serve with the horseradish dressing.

For the dressing, combine the sour cream, skim milk, horseradish, salt, and sugar in a small bowl that will fit in the center of the gelatin mold.

Makes 6 to 8 servings

Sharon Brown, Queen
The Saintly Red Germain–iums, St. Germain, Wisconsin

Marinated Fresh Mushrooms

A really versatile recipe to keep around since it can be served as a salad, side dish, or appetizer. The recipe doubles well.

1/2 pound fresh button mushrooms
3 tablespoons lemon juice
1/2 cup olive oil
1/2 teaspoon salt
    Freshly ground pepper to taste
1/2 teaspoon dried oregano

Clean the mushrooms. Mix the lemon juice, oil, salt, pepper, and oregano. Toss the mushrooms in the dressing and let stand overnight at room temperature. Serve with toothpicks. If desired, slice the mushrooms for antipasto at the table.

Makes 2 to 3 salad servings

Janet MacVicar, Queen Mother
Jubilee Jewels, Montreal, Quebec,
    Canada

Red Hat Magic!

As we have often explained, there was, initially, no conscious plan to spread the Red Hat Society concept. But spread (like wildfire) it did! In retrospect, over six years later, it is not difficult to analyze some of the reasons for its popularity. The elements, casually put in place from the beginning—without conscious planning—proved to have universal appeal to other women "of a certain age." Some of them are:

Playing dress-up! What grown-up little girl doesn't love to wear pretty clothes and devise costumes?

Taking time for ourselves! Women are natural-born nurturers, and we are proud of it. But, as we get older, we may realize that we have forgotten how to nurture ourselves.

Fun! Red Hat Society activities are required to be fun! We are collectively rediscovering our ability to play, and going out to recess together!

Friends! Almost anything worth doing is even more worth doing with your girlfriends. And, in the Red Hat Society, you can reconnect with old friends and make new ones as well!

No rules! The Red Hat Society is a "disorganization," which encourages its chapters to do things their own way!

Big-Hearted Salad

1   (14-ounce) can hearts of palm, drained and cut into 1/2-inch slices
1   (14-ounce) can artichoke hearts, drained and cut into eighths
1   sweet purple onion, sliced very thinly
1   bottle good-quality vinaigrette dressing
8   to 12 cups romaine lettuce or spinach, or a combination

Combine the hearts of palm, artichoke hearts, onion, and salad dressing in a zip-top bag. (May be prepared ahead of time and refrigerated until serving time.) Arrange the lettuce and/or spinach in a large bowl. At serving time, pour the vegetable mixture over the greens.

Makes 8 to 10 servings

Roxy Rock, Queen
Spring Elite Red Hatters, Tomball, Texas

Sun-Dried Tomato Pasta Salad

Start this salad the day before you plan to serve it for the deepest flavor and best texture.

SALAD
8   ounces penne pasta
1   cup finely chopped, oil-packed, sun-dried tomatoes
2   tablespoons finely chopped red onion
1/2   cup chopped fresh parsley
2   tablespoons grated Parmesan cheese

BALSAMIC ORANGE DRESSING
1/4   cup balsamic vinegar
1/4   cup orange juice
1/4   olive oil
1   garlic clove, minced
2   teaspoons Dijon mustard
1   teaspoon finely chopped fresh basil for garnish

The day before you plan to serve the salad, prepare the penne pasta according to the package directions. Rinse and drain. Combine with the tomatoes, red onion, parsley, and Parmesan cheese in a large bowl.

For the dressing, mix the vinegar, orange juice, olive oil, garlic, and mustard in a jar with a tight-fitting lid. Pour half the dressing over the salad the day before serving. Several hours before serving, toss with the remaining dressing. Garnish with the chopped basil.

Makes 4 to 6 servings

Virginia Caldwell, Princess Virginia
Delta Gals, Delta, British Columbia, Canada

Vidalia Onion Salad

A composed salad is so nice, and so rare these days. Be brave and try this bold combination at your next luncheon.

SALAD
1   fresh pineapple
2   large tomatoes
1   large Vidalia or other sweet onion

BALSAMIC VINAIGRETTE

3/4 cup water
1/4 cup balsamic vinegar
2 teaspoons Dijon mustard
1 1/2 teaspoons dried basil
1 tablespoon parsley, chopped

For the salad, peel the pineapple and cut out the eyes. Cut into quarters and trim out the core. Cut the "spears" into six slices each. Slice the tomatoes into 12 slices. Slice the onion into 12 slices. To assemble the salad, place 2 pineapple slices on a plate, stagger-stack a slice of tomato and then an onion slice; repeat once to complete one serving. Assemble five more salads. Drizzle with the balsamic vinaigrette.

For the vinaigrette, combine the water, vinegar, mustard, basil, and parsley. Adjust the vinegar to taste. Drizzle over the salads. Store any leftover vinaigrette in the refrigerator.

Makes 6 servings

Brenda Parker, Queen Mum
Sun City Grand Dames, Surprise, Arizona

Orzo & Pine Nut Salad

Don't let the list of ingredients intimidate you. This dressing gets its fantastic flavor from a little of this and a little of that.

SOY ORANGE GINGER DRESSING

1 teaspoon salt
1/2 cup vegetable oil
2 tablespoons sesame oil
1/2 cup rice vinegar
1/2 teaspoon grated orange peel
1 teaspoon soy sauce
2 tablespoons thinly sliced green onion
1 teaspoon minced fresh ginger
1/2 teaspoon minced garlic
1/4 teaspoon crushed red pepper flakes
1 teaspoon ground black pepper
1 tablespoon sugar
2 tablespoons chopped fresh parsley

SALAD

1 (16-ounce) package orzo pasta
1 tablespoon sesame oil
3 cups shredded carrots
2 cups raisins
3/4 cup pine nuts

For the dressing, combine the salt, vegetable oil, sesame oil, vinegar, orange peel, soy sauce, green onion, ginger, garlic, pepper flakes, black pepper, sugar, and parsley in a bowl or a jar with a tight-fitting lid. Whisk or shake to combine.

For the salad, prepare the orzo according to package directions. Drain, rinse with cold water, and drain again. Combine the orzo with the sesame oil. Let cool completely. Add the carrots, raisins, pine nuts, and dressing mixture. Gently toss all together and refrigerate, covered, until serving time.

Makes 6 to 8 servings

Louise Carlotto, Contessa Cannoli
The Ladybugs RHS, Orwell, Vermont

Green Pearls Salad

Halve the recipe for a nice small portion to feed one person for two meals.

SALAD

2   cups dry, small-shell macaroni

1 1/2 cups frozen petite green peas

6   (8-ounce) cans salad shrimp (or freshly cooked tiny shrimp)

1/2 cup chopped celery

1 1/2 tablespoons minced fresh onion

1   tablespoon minced fresh parsley

DRESSING

1/2 cup mayonnaise-type salad dressing

1/2 cup mayonnaise

1   to 2 tablespoons Dijon mustard

For the salad, cook the macaroni in large amount of salted boiling water until almost done. Add the frozen peas and bring back to a boil. Immediately drain in a colander and immerse in cold water until cooled. Drain well and transfer to a large bowl. Add the shrimp, celery, onion, and parsley. Toss gently to mix.

For the dressing, whisk together the salad dressing, mayonnaise, and mustard. Add to the salad and toss gently to mix thoroughly. Chill.

Makes 8 servings

Diana Fuller, Dame Diana
Modoc Red Hot Hatters, Alturas, California

Peas and Peanuts Salad

Hooray for legumes—good, and good for you. Serve right away for the best texture.

1   (10-ounce) package frozen peas, thawed

3   green onions, chopped

2   celery stalks, finely chopped

1/2 cup plain yogurt or good-quality mayonnaise

2   tablespoons lemon juice

1/2 cup chopped cooked bacon

1 1/2 cups salted peanuts

In a large bowl combine the peas, onions, celery, yogurt, and lemon juice. Just before serving, add the bacon and peanuts and stir well. If you want it creamier, add a little more mayonnaise. Serve immediately.

Makes 12 servings

Gena Walls, Queen Mamabear
The BEARables, Richmond, Texas

Pineapple Boat Salad

A showstopper for company or special occasions.

SALAD

1   fresh pineapple

1   pint fresh strawberries, sliced

2   bananas, sliced

1   (11-ounce) can mandarin oranges, juice reserved

Celebration Dinner in Red and Purple

After the rigors of being a committee of only six to do our first successful annual National Red Hat Day here in Gainesville, Florida, a friend and I decided to have a Thank-God-It's-Over-Dinner for our husbands who had patiently seen us through the recent weeks of hair-pulling and nerve-wracking duties. We made them leave the room, and we changed into our outfits, complete with boas. The table was set with all purple and red, from stem to stern, including red candles and red roses. The food was red tomato juice served tacky from a red can into a fancy red stemmed glass, red cabbage, red Spanish rice, red-leaf salad, baked pork chops covered in red catsup, purple sparkling grape juice, and blueberry pie for dessert. It was a most interesting combination of flavors! Our husbands were privately discussing whether or not the next day they would go potty and it would be red and purple! We did not ask any questions the next day!

Judy Bloss
Queen Judy B
Vintage Gals
Alachua, Florida

DRESSING
1/4 cup honey
Juice of 1 lime
Coconut flakes
Fresh mint leaves for garnish

For the salad cut the pineapple in half lengthwise. Cut out and discard the hard core that runs through the center. Cut the fruit from the shell, leaving the shell intact. Dice the pineapple, and combine with the strawberries, bananas, and mandarin oranges together in a large bowl.

For the dressing, combine the reserved mandarin orange juice (about 1/2 cup), the honey, and lime juice together and mix well. Pour over the fruit and toss. Spoon into the pineapple shells. Sprinkle with the coconut and garnish with the mint leaves.

Makes 8 to 10 servings

Janet Gurdgiel, Queen Mom
Ladies of Grace, Merritt Island, Florida

Popcorn Salad

Surprising and different, this fun salad can be served when you want to amuse guests as well as feed them. A red onion in place of the green onions is a nice addition, as is a little chopped green or red bell pepper.

1   cup chopped celery
1   cup sliced water chestnuts
1   cup grated sharp or medium cheddar
     cheese
1/2 cup chopped green onions
1   cup mayonnaise or salad dressing
1   pound bacon, crisply cooked and crumbled
6   cups popped popcorn, any unpopped
     kernels removed

Combine the celery, water chestnuts, cheese, onions, and mayonnaise. Can be refrigerated overnight. Before serving, add the bacon and popcorn. Mix well.

Makes 6 servings

Sylvia M. Schoen, Queen Mum
Perky Purple Pixies of Minnesota, Minneapolis, Minnesota

Never-Fail Secret Potato Salad

When you're asked for the recipe, smile and proclaim loudly that this is a secret family recipe.

2   pounds deli potato salad
3   hard-boiled eggs, chopped
6   green onions and tops, sliced thinly
2   carrots, sliced very thin

1 1/2 cups sliced celery
3   hard-boiled eggs
1/2   teaspoon celery salt
       Paprika for garnish
       Sliced black olives (optional)
       Cheddar cheese (optional)

Put the potato salad into a large bowl. Add the chopped eggs, the onions, carrots, and celery. Slice and garnish with the whole eggs, and sprinkle with the celery salt and paprika. Add olives and cheese if desired.

Makes 10 servings

Gayle Brune, Lady Sparkles, Grand Duchess of Chocolate Bodacious Biddies, La Quinta, California

Pomegranate Salad

Here's a trick for getting pomegranate seeds out easily. Cut the pomegranate in half around the "equator." Hold a half cut side down over a bowl. With a wooden spoon, tap firmly over and over. Seeds will loosen and fall into the bowl.

3   red apples, peeled and chopped
3   bananas, sliced
2   pomegranates
1   (16-ounce) package walnuts
1   pint (2 cups) heavy cream
2   tablespoons sugar

Combine the apples and bananas in a large bowl. Get the pomegranate seeds out as described above. (Or, if you prefer, soak the pomegranates in a bowl of water for a few minutes to make them easier to peel. Peel and spoon out the seeds into the bowl.) Dice and add to fruit mixture.

Top the fruit with the walnuts. Beat the cream with the sugar until stiff peaks form. Spoon the sweetened whipped cream over the fruit. Serve right away.

Makes 6 to 8 servings

Pam Dolge, Queen
Sophisticated Sisters, St. George, Utah

Chilled Rice Salad

3 1/2 cups cooked white rice
1/3 cup finely chopped tomatoes
1/3 cup sliced green onions
1/3 cup diced cucumber
1 tablespoon vegetable oil
1 tablespoon red wine vinegar
  Salt and pepper to taste

Combine the rice, tomatoes, green onions, and cucumber in a medium serving bowl. Blend the oil, vinegar, and salt and pepper in a small bowl or jar with a tight-fitting lid. Shake well and pour the dressing over the rice mixture. Cover and refrigerate at least 2 hours. Stir before serving.

Makes 4 to 6 servings

Marilyn Steines, Princess
Bodacious Bastrop Belles, Bastrop, Texas

Old-Fashioned German-Style Potato Salad

6 cups cooked white potatoes, peeled and sliced
4 strips pork bacon
1/3 cup all-purpose flour
3/4 cup sugar
3/4 cup good-quality white vinegar
3/4 cup water
1 teaspoon salt
1/2 teaspoon ground black pepper
1/4 teaspoon celery seed (optional)
1 medium white onion, diced finely

Pile the potatoes into a large serving bowl. Fry the bacon until crisp, remove from the skillet, and crumble into small pieces. Leave the bacon drippings in the skillet and turn the heat to low. Stir the flour and sugar into the drippings. Stirring slowly, add the vinegar and water. Bring this mixture to a low boil and cook for 2 to 3 minutes, stirring, until smooth and thickened. Pour this sauce over the cooked potatoes. Add the bacon pieces, salt, pepper, celery seed, and onion. Toss lightly. Can be served immediately or refrigerated and kept up to 24 hours. Can be reheated by adding more water and vinegar in equal parts to keep the salad moist. Adjust the salt and pepper to taste.

Makes 6 servings

Judith Lewis, Empress of Events/Vice-Queen Mother
Les Chapeaux Rouges of Bristol Village, Waverly, Ohio

Something-In-Red Potato Salad

A refined potato salad of uncommon good taste.

1 1/2   pounds baby red potatoes, cooked and chopped

3   hard-boiled eggs, chopped

1/2   cup diced sweet red onion

6   slices smoked bacon, cooked and crumbled

5   oil-packed sun-dried tomatoes, drained and finely chopped

1/2   cup sour cream

1/2   cup mayonnaise

1   tablespoon cider vinegar

3   tablespoons premium sweet pickle relish

2   tablespoons sweet and tangy honey mustard

1/4   teaspoon dry mustard

1   teaspoon salt (or to taste)

1   teaspoon white pepper

In a large bowl combine the potatoes, eggs, onion, bacon, and tomatoes. In a separate bowl combine the sour cream, mayonnaise, vinegar, relish, honey mustard, dry mustard, salt, and white pepper. Mix well. Add to the potato mixture and gently toss until well combined. Refrigerate several hours before serving to allow flavors to blend.

Makes 6 servings

Lana Davenport, Queen Mum

California Central Coast Femme Fatales, Vandenberg AFB, California

Real Italian Salad Dressing

1/2   cup olive oil

1/4   cup rice vinegar

1/2   cup cold water

1   teaspoon dried basil

1/2   teaspoon dried oregano

1/2   teaspoon dried marjoram

2   tablespoons garlic powder

1   teaspoon onion powder

1   teaspoon sugar or artificial sweetener

1/8   teaspoon pepper

Mix together in a jar with a tight-fitting lid the oil, vinegar, water, basil, oregano, marjoram, garlic powder, onion powder, sugar, and pepper. Shake to blend. Use right away or store in the refrigerator up to 1 week.

Makes enough for 8 dinner salads

Jeani Flannery, Countess Jeani

Devine Divas of Algood, Algood, Tennessee

Presto Change-O Chicken and Rice Salad

The chicken is optional if you prefer this as a side dish. To transform the salad into a casserole, add a topping of about 1 cup of crushed cornflakes sautéed in a little butter, then a 15-minute turn in the oven to heat the ingredients and crisp the topping.

1   (7-ounce) package chicken-flavored
    rice mix

1   cup chopped celery

3/4 cup chopped green onions

1   (2-ounce) jar chopped pimientos, drained

1   (6-ounce) jar marinated artichoke hearts,
    undrained, chopped

3/4 cup mayonnaise

1   to 2 cups chopped cooked chicken (optional)

Prepare the rice mix as directed on the package. Fluff with a fork and cool. Add the celery, green onions, pimientos, artichoke hearts with marinade, and mayonnaise. Stop here for a side salad. Add the chicken if desired and either serve at room temperature or heat in a 350° oven for about 15 minutes.

Makes 6 to 8 servings

Carolyn Pitts, Lady Carolyn the Duchess of
    Aquamarine
Razzle Dazzle Dames of Pasadena, Azusa, California

German Rice Salad

Excellent served hot or cold, and hearty enough to be a one-dish meal, with a fruit side dish.

DRESSING

2   cups cider vinegar

1   cup sugar

1   teaspoon celery seeds

1/2 teaspoon black pepper

SALAD

3   cups uncooked white rice

6   eggs

10 slices bacon

1   medium onion, chopped

1   green bell pepper, chopped

1   cup chopped celery

1   (16-ounce) package little smoked sausage
    links

1   (4-ounce) jar diced pimientos, drained

Prepare the dressing by combining the vinegar, sugar, celery seeds, and pepper in a bowl or jar with a tight-fitting lid.

For the salad, cook the rice in water in a very large saucepan according to package directions. When it is almost done, crack and drop the eggs on top of the rice, but don't stir. Cover and continue cooking. Fry the bacon until crisp. Drain, reserving 3 to 4 tablespoons drippings and crumble the bacon. Cook the onion, bell pepper, and celery in the reserved bacon drippings over medium heat until tender. Add the sausages and heat through. When the rice is done, chop the eggs. Add the dressing to the rice and eggs and toss lightly. Add the vegetables and sausages to the rice mixture and cook a little longer to mix the flavors. Stir in the diced pimientos.

Makes 8 to 10 servings

Marlene Fleeman, Contessa Marl
Simply Red, Kingsville, Missouri

Southwest-Style Potato Salad

If the thought appeals to your taste, use sour cream and full-fat mayonnaise instead for a classic potato salad texture.

1/2 cup plain nonfat yogurt

1/2 cup low-fat mayonnaise

2   tablespoons lemon juice

1   teaspoon coriander

1   teaspoon cumin

     Salt and pepper to taste

6   large red potatoes, cooked, cooled, and cubed

1   small red onion, finely diced

3   celery stalks, finely diced

1   poblano pepper, minced

2   pickled jalapeño peppers, minced

10   green Spanish olives with pimientos, thinly sliced

2   tablespoons finely chopped cilantro

Combine the yogurt, mayonnaise, lemon juice, coriander, and cumin in a large bowl. Add salt and pepper; add the potatoes, onion, celery, poblano and jalapeño peppers, olives, and cilantro. Mix well. Refrigerate until ready to serve.

Makes 12 servings

Joyce Pillitteri, Princess Joy
Reddy Set Goes, Jacksonville, Florida

Sunflower Pasta Salad

Dressy for the table, with some unexpected flavors and a nice crunch, according to testers.

1/2 pound vegetable rotini pasta, cooked

3/4 cup dried fruit

1/4 cup real bacon bits

3/4 cup frozen petite peas, rinsed in hot tap water

1/2 cup sunflower seeds (or to taste)

1   bunch finely chopped green onions

1   (16-ounce jar) lite or low-fat slaw dressing

In a large bowl combine the pasta, dried fruit, bacon bits, peas, sunflower seeds, and green onions and gently mix together. Add about two-thirds of the slaw dressing or enough to moisten. Refrigerate until serving time. Salad can be prepared the day before and chilled so the flavors can mingle.

Makes 8 servings

Marilyn Martin, Queen
The Royal Court of Live a Lot, Avon, Indiana

Roquefort Dressing

3   plus 2 ounces Roquefort or other blue cheese

1   tablespoon white wine vinegar

2   teaspoons lemon juice

1   garlic clove, minced
5   drops hot pepper sauce
2   tablespoons sour cream
1   cup heavy cream
    Salt and pepper to taste

Beat 3 ounces of the cheese with the vinegar, lemon juice, garlic, pepper sauce, sour cream, heavy cream, and salt and pepper with an electric mixer, blender, or food processor. Crumble in the remaining 2 ounces cheese. Refrigerate several hours before using to allow flavors to "marry."

Makes about 2 cups

Joann Rouston, Madam Nomad
Hats Amore, Northville, Michigan

Tancook Island Sauerkraut Salad

Surprising, different and declared by testers "very colorful and easy to prepare."

4   cups sauerkraut
1   cup chopped celery
1   green bell pepper, chopped
1   red bell pepper, chopped
     (or a 4-ounce jar of pimientos, drained and chopped)
1   cup sweet pickles, chopped
1   cup crushed pineapple with juice
1   cup sugar
1/2 cup canola or vegetable oil
1/2 cup white vinegar

Pour the sauerkraut into a colander or sieve and rinse under cold water for a few moments. Drain well. In a large bowl combine the sauerkraut, celery, green bell pepper, red bell pepper, sweet pickles, and pineapple with juice. In a separate bowl combine the sugar, oil, and vinegar. Mix well and pour over the sauerkraut mixture. Chill for at least 6 hours. (Leftover mixture keeps well in the refrigerator for a week.)

Makes 12 to 14 servings

Ruth Nevills, Line Dancing Chick
Red Hat'll Do Ya, Halifax, Nova Scotia, Canada

Scarlet Sparkle Spinach Salad

10   to 14 ounces baby spinach
1   (11-ounce) can mandarin oranges, drained
1   cup dried sweetened cranberries
8   ounces fresh strawberries, chopped
2   ounces crumbled blue cheese
1/2 cup chopped walnuts
     Raspberry or raspberry-walnut vinaigrette dressing

Combine the spinach, oranges, cranberries, strawberries, and blue cheese in a large bowl and toss lightly to combine. Top with the walnuts. If serving right away, toss with the dressing. Otherwise, serve the dressing on the side.

Makes 8 to 10 servings

Linda Enrico, Lady Sewsalot
Red Hot Taters, Boise, Idaho

Wilted Spinach Salad

8 cups fresh spinach

1 cup fresh bean sprouts

1/2 cup sliced radishes

4 slices bacon, cut into small pieces

1/4 cup finely chopped onion

3 tablespoons white vinegar

3 tablespoons ketchup

1 tablespoon sugar or sugar substitute

1 hard-boiled egg, sliced (optional)

Tear the spinach leaves into bite-size pieces or use baby spinach). Combine in a large bowl with the bean sprouts and radishes. Fry the bacon until crisp; do not drain. Add the onion, vinegar, ketchup, and sugar to the skillet. Cook and stir until the mixture is bubbly; remove from the heat. Add the spinach mixture to the skillet. Cook, tossing constantly, until the greens are slightly wilted and well-coated with the dressing mixture. Spoon into a serving bowl. Serve at once. Garnish with the egg slices if desired.

Makes 8 servings

Linda Shiflett, DARling RedHatter
San Carlos She Shells, Liberty Lake, Washington

Red Hat Summer Salad

Sometimes the simplest things are just about perfect.

1 seedless watermelon

1 large bunch seedless purple grapes

4 tablespoons poppy seeds

1/2 cup slivered almonds

Cut the watermelon into bite-size pieces. Combine with the grapes, poppy seeds, and almonds in an attractive bowl. Serve right away so the nuts stay crisp.

Makes 12 to 20 servings

Linda Tarvin, Court Jester
The Stinkin' Red Roses, Morgan Hill, California

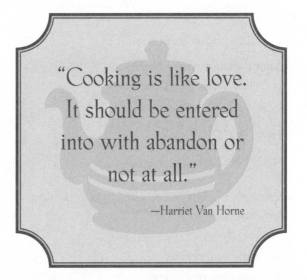

"Cooking is like love. It should be entered into with abandon or not at all."

—Harriet Van Horne

Tofu Ginger Salad

If you're trying to eat more tofu (for those hot flashes), here's an addition to your options. You may wish to add a tablespoon of vegetable oil (and perhaps a pinch of sugar) to the soy and vinegar mixture.

1 pound tofu, medium firm

1 teaspoon chopped fresh ginger

1 teaspoon chopped fresh garlic

5   tablespoons chopped fresh cilantro
5   tablespoons soy sauce
5   tablespoons vinegar, white or apple cider
     Romaine lettuce or endive leaves, for serving

Combine the tofu, ginger, garlic, and cilantro in a bowl. Mix the soy sauce and vinegar and pour over the tofu mixture. Spoon onto the Romaine or endive leaves.

Makes 2 servings

Anne Snowden Crosman, Queen of Young at Heart
Curvaceous Cuties, Sedona, Arizona

Redelicious Red Hat Salad

Stunning and yummy.

5   ripe plum or Roma tomatoes
3   large beefsteak tomatoes
1   red onion
1   head iceberg lettuce
     Real bacon bits
     Walnuts
     Seedless purple grapes
     Raspberry vinaigrette

Cut each plum tomato down the middle and put the 10 domes (tops of hat) aside. Slice the beefsteak tomatoes into 1/4-inch slices (these are the brims). Cut the onion into thin rings. Stack them up and cut into quarters. Separate the pieces.

Arrange a layer of lettuce leaves on ten salad plates. Place sliced tomatoes on the lettuce. Top each "brim" with the hat dome. Poke a small hole in the top and insert two pieces of onion ring into hole (for the plume). Top with the bacon bits, walnuts, and grapes, and any other desired garnishes. Drizzle with the vinaigrette or serve it alongside.

Makes 10 servings

Judy Sheppard, Loquacious Quipster
Hunnies with Hattitude, Hornell, New York

Summer Tomato and Basil Salad

Also known as Caprese Salad, for the Italian island of Capri. It's a gorgeous red, white, and green combination that looks as lovely as it tastes.

1   pound tomatoes, cut into slices
1/2   Vidalia or any sweet onion, thinly sliced
        Fresh mozzarella cheese, thinly sliced
1/2   teaspoon garlic salt
1 1/4   teaspoon cracked black pepper or freshly ground black pepper
2   tablespoons olive oil
2   tablespoons balsamic vinegar
1/4   to 1/2 cup chopped or torn fresh basil

Layer the tomatoes, onion slices, and mozzarella slices on a serving plate. (Make sure the plate has a lip; this salad can be juicy.) Sprinkle the garlic salt and black pepper over all. Drizzle the olive oil and balsamic vinegar over all. Sprinkle with the fresh basil.

Makes 6 servings

Dorothy Romanczuk, Queen Mum
Red Hot Zingers, Hamburg, New york

Gracious Goodness Tossed Green Salad

Almonds, Swiss cheese, and a lemon-garlic dressing make this a shortcut, sophisticated salad hearty enough to be a light main dish.

DRESSING

1/4 cup vegetable oil
1/4 cup fresh lemon juice
2   garlic cloves, minced (or more to liking)
1/2 teaspoon salt
1/2 teaspoon pepper

SALAD

2   (1-pound) heads romaine lettuce, torn
2   cups chopped tomatoes
1   cup (4 ounces) shredded Swiss cheese
2/3 cup slivered almonds, toasted
1/2 cup grated Parmesan cheese
8   bacon strips, cooked and crumbled
1   cup Caesar salad croutons

For the dressing, in a jar with a tight fitting lid combine the oil, lemon juice, garlic, salt, and pepper. Cover and shake well. Chill.

For the salad, toss the lettuce, tomatoes, Swiss cheese, almonds, Parmesan cheese, and bacon in a bowl. Shake the dressing again and pour over the salad. Toss to coat the vegetables. Add the croutons and serve immediately.

Makes 14 servings

Kathy Kauno, Kathryn the Great (Scribe of Birthdays)
Lynnwood Red Hat Flashes, Mountlake Terrace, Washington

Festive Layered Salad

1 1/2 cups small macaroni shells, uncooked
4   cups shredded romaine lettuce
4   carrots, peeled, cut into 2-inch strips
1   (10-ounce) package frozen green peas, thawed
1   small red onion, sliced into rings
2   cups cubed cooked ham
2   cups (8 ounces) shredded Swiss cheese
2 1/2 cups light mayonnaise
1   tablespoon dill weed (or to taste)
4   hard-boiled eggs, cut into slices

Cook the macaroni according to directions and drain. Cool to room temperature.

Arrange the lettuce in an even layer in the bottom of a 3 to 4-quart glass bowl. Arrange the carrot sticks in an even layer over the lettuce. Cover with a layer of macaroni, then the peas, onion, and ham. Sprinkle the top with the Swiss cheese.

Combine the mayonnaise and dill weed in a small bowl. Spread the dressing over the top of the salad and top with the egg slices. Chill for several hours. Just before serving, toss well to coat.

Makes 8 servings

Phyllis Sturgill, Queen
Red Hatted Faithful Few, Omaha, Nebraska

Autumn Treasure Green Salad

Fresh fruit, dried cranberries, and classic poppy seed dressing transform greens into a crunchy and irresistible salad.

DRESSING
2/3 cup vegetable oil
1/3 cup lemon juice
1/4 cup sugar
2 teaspoons chopped green onions
3/4 teaspoon salt
1 teaspoon poppy seeds

SALAD
8 cups torn mixed salad greens (I buy the bags)
2 medium red apples, chopped
2 pears, chopped
1 cup chopped pecans
1 cup (4 ounces) shredded Swiss cheese
1 cup dried cranberries

For the dressing, combine the oil, lemon juice, sugar, green onions, salt, and poppy seeds in a jar with a tight lid. Shake to combine. Refrigerate.

For the salad, combine the salad greens, apples, pears, pecans, cheese, and cranberries in a large bowl and toss lightly to combine. Just before serving, drizzle the dressing over the salad and toss gently. Serve immediately.

Makes 16 servings

Sheryl Kneeland, Queen Mother
The Razzle Dazzlers, Elmore, Minnesota

Caraway Cabbage Toss

A quick supper side dish made with items you probably keep on hand.

1 medium head cabbage
2/3 cup canola oil
1/3 cup white or cider vinegar
1 tablespoon caraway seeds
1 teaspoon sugar
1/2 teaspoon salt
    Dash of pepper
3 medium apples
    Large romaine leaves (optional), for serving

Shred the cabbage finely (approximately 9 cups). Place it in a large bowl. Combine the canola oil, vinegar, caraway seeds, sugar, salt, and pepper in a container with a tight-fitting lid. Shake well to mix. Pour over the cabbage and toss lightly. Cover and chill for several hours. When ready to serve, quarter the apples, core, and slice thinly crosswise. Set aside a few slices for garnish. If you prefer, you may dice the apples. Toss the remaining apples with the cabbage mixture. Spoon into a romaine-lined salad bowl. Overlap the remaining apple slices on top.

Makes 8 to 10 servings

Connie Ferlita, Chapterette
Late Bloomers W/Red Hattitude, Cocoa, Florida

Cranberry–Walnut Cabbage Slaw

1/4   cup mayonnaise or salad dressing
1   tablespoon sweet pickle relish
1   tablespoon honey mustard
1   tablespoon honey
1/4   teaspoon white or black pepper
1/8   teaspoon salt
1/4   teaspoon celery seeds
5   cups shredded green cabbage
1/3   cup chopped walnuts
1/4   cup finely chopped onion
1/4   cup finely chopped celery
1/4   cup finely chopped red sweet pepper
1/4   cup dried cranberries

Stir together the mayonnaise, relish, honey mustard, honey, pepper, salt, and celery seeds in a small bowl. In a large bowl combine the cabbage, walnuts, onion, celery, red bell pepper, and cranberries. Add the mayonnaise mixture to the cabbage mixture; toss to coat. Cover and chill at least 1 hour or up to 4 hours before serving.

Makes 8 to 10 servings

Shirley Klinner, Queen Mother
Crimson C'Hatters, Medford, Wisconsin

Picnic German Coleslaw

1   large cabbage, shredded
2   large onions, finely chopped
1   large green bell pepper, chopped
1   cup sugar

MARINADE
2   teaspoons sugar
1   tablespoon celery seed
2   teaspoons dry mustard
1   cup white vinegar
1   tablespoon salt
3/4   cup corn oil

Layer one-third of the cabbage, then one-third of the onions, one-third of the green bell pepper, and one-third of the sugar in a large bowl. Repeat twice more.

For the marinade, combine the sugar, celery seeds, dry mustard, vinegar, salt, and oil in a saucepan and bring to a rolling boil. Pour over the slaw, cover, and let stand at room temperature for 4 hours. Mix together and then chill.

Makes 12 servings

Emma King, Duchess of Url
Roses on the Go, Jamul, California

WARM AND COZY, COOL AND CRISP

Acorn Squash Soup

2   acorn squash
1   tablespoon butter or margarine
1   large yellow onion, chopped
2   tablespoons light brown sugar
1   cup chicken broth
1   teaspoon salt
1   teaspoon cinnamon
1   teaspoon coriander
1/4 teaspoon pepper
1   cup heavy cream

Preheat the oven to 400°. Cut the squash in half crosswise and remove the seeds. Place the squash cut side down in a greased, shallow, baking dish. Bake for 45 minutes, or until tender. Cool completely. Scoop out the pulp, discarding the shells.

Melt the butter in a Dutch oven over medium-high heat and sauté the onion for 7 to 8 minutes, or until lightly browned. Add the brown sugar; cook 2 minutes, stirring often. Add the squash pulp; cook 5 minutes, stirring often. Add the broth, salt, cinnamon, coriander, pepper, and cream. Cover, reduce the heat to medium low, and simmer 5 minutes. Remove from the heat and cool slightly. Process the soup in batches in a food processor or blender until smooth. Return the soup to a Dutch oven and simmer 5 minutes over low heat. Drizzle each serving with a little heavy cream.

Makes 8 cups

Elaine Crum, Royal PITA
Red Hatters of Anthem, Anthem, Arizona

Lemon Asparagus Soup

Springtime flavors come together in a special soup.

4   tablespoons butter
1   medium onion, chopped
1/2 cup chopped celery
2   teaspoons cornstarch
1   cup water
2   chicken bouillon cubes
12 ounces fresh asparagus, trimmed and cut into 1-inch pieces
2   cups milk
1/2 teaspoon grated lemon peel
1/8 teaspoon nutmeg
    Dash of seasoned salt

In a 2-quart saucepan melt the butter over medium-high heat. Sauté the onion and celery until tender. Dissolve the cornstarch in the water. Add to the saucepan along with the bouillon cubes. Bring to a boil over medium heat. Cook and stir for 2 minutes. Add the asparagus. Reduce the heat, cover, and simmer for 3 to 4 minutes, or until the asparagus is tender-crisp. Stir in the milk, lemon peel, nutmeg, and seasoned salt. Cover and simmer for 25 minutes, stirring occasionally.

Makes 4 to 6 servings

Carol Park-Coen, Lady Carol-Countess of Conveance
Rowdy Red Hat Mamas of NW Wisconsin, Luck, Wisconsin

Italian Pasta Fazool

Fazool is an Italian dialect for "beans." There are lots of different recipes for this homey dish, but all feature a chunky combination of meat, beans, and pasta.

1	pound ground beef
3	ounces pancetta (Italian bacon)
1	cup diced onions
1	cup chopped celery
1	cup sliced carrots
2	garlic cloves, minced
1	(16-ounce) can diced tomatoes, drained
1	(16-ounce) can tomato sauce
1	(16-ounce) can red kidney beans, not drained
2	cups water
2	(14-ounce) cans beef broth
1	teaspoon fresh or 1/2 teaspoon dried parsley flakes
1	teaspoon salt
1/2	teaspoon oregano
1/2	teaspoon basil
1/2	teaspoon pepper
2	cups shredded cabbage
1	(14-ounce) can green beans, cut into bite-size pieces
1/2	cup elbow macaroni
	Parmesan cheese for serving

Brown the ground beef and drain off the fat. Add the pancetta, onions, celery, carrots, garlic, tomatoes, tomato sauce, beans, water, broth, parsley, salt, oregano, basil, and pepper. Bring to a boil, cover, and simmer for 20 minutes. Add the cabbage, green beans, and macaroni. Simmer until tender, approximately 10 minutes. After serving in bowls, sprinkle with fresh Parmesan cheese. Serve with warm crusty bread for a great warm-up on cool nights.

Makes 8 to 10 servings

Nancy Keefner, Princess Smiley
Red Hatted Ya Yas, Richmond, Texas

Mexican Kitchen Black Bean and Sausage Posole

Posole is a Christmas holiday tradition in the Mexican state of Jalisco. Serve with bowls of shredded lettuce, chopped tomato, diced onion, and shredded cheese for garnishing.

1	(12-ounce) package light ground turkey and pork sausage
2	(14 1/2-ounce) cans reduced-sodium chicken broth
1	(15-ounce) can black beans, rinsed and drained
1	(14 1/2-ounce) can golden hominy, rinsed and drained
1	(14 1/2-ounce) can Mexican-style stewed tomatoes
1	cup frozen, loosely packed, diced hash-brown potatoes
1/2	cup chopped green bell pepper
1/3	cup chopped onion
1	garlic clove, minced
1/2	teaspoon chili powder
1	teaspoon dried oregano, crushed

In a large saucepan brown the sausage and drain. Stir in the broth, black beans, hominy, tomatoes, potatoes, bell pepper, onion, garlic, chili powder, and oregano. Bring to a boil. Reduce the heat to low. Cover and simmer for 30 minutes.

Makes 6 servings

Alice Duvall, Queen Alice
Red Hat Valley Chicks, Minden, Nevada

Chick Pea Soup

1   cup dried chick peas or garbanzo beans
6   garlic cloves, peeled
1   tablespoon olive oil
3/4 cup fettuccini broken into 2-inch pieces
     Dash of salt

Place the chick peas in a medium-size saucepan and cover with water to 1/2-inch above the chick peas. Bring to a boil, turn off the heat, and let sit for 1 hour. Add enough water to cover the chick peas by 1 inch; add the garlic cloves and simmer for 1 1/2 hours. Check occasionally and add water as needed. (If using a slow cooker for this stage, the water won't evaporate.)

Bring the liquid to a boil again. Add the olive oil and pasta and cook according to the package instructions.

Makes 4 servings

Deborah Eckart, Co-Queen
Bronx Bombshells, Bronx, New York

Cream of Fresh Broccoli Soup

4   cups (about 1 pound) broccoli stems, cut very fine
1   quart chicken broth
1/2   cup finely chopped onion
4   to 6 chicken bouillon cubes
1/4   cup (1/2 stick) butter
1/4   cup all-purpose flour
1   cup half-and-half
1 1/2 cups finely cut broccoli florets
1/4   teaspoon white pepper

Combine the broccoli stems, chicken broth, and onion in a saucepan. Bring to a boil and cook for 10 minutes. Add the bouillon cubes and cook 3 minutes longer. Strain, reserving the broth. Process the cooked broccoli stems and onion in a food processor. Return to the broth. In a separate saucepan melt the butter and add the flour. Cook and stir for 5 minutes over low heat, being careful not to brown. Add the half-and-half and broth mixture. Stir until the mixture boils and is thickened. Add the broccoli florets and white pepper. Let simmer over low heat for 20 minutes, stirring constantly. This soup is also good served cold.

Makes 4 to 8 servings

Kathy T. Wilson, M.D., Hey Doc
Fondrem Femme Fatales, Jackson, Mississippi

Pantry Soup

Bring out the food processor to make short work of chopping the vegetables. Like many soups, this one gets better after a day in the refrigerator.

1   pound lean ground beef
1   onion, chopped
1   celery stalk, chopped
1   small zucchini, sliced
2   carrots, sliced
2   garlic cloves, minced
1   (15-ounce) can chopped tomatoes
1   (15-ounce) can white kidney beans
    (cannelloni)
3/4 cup barley or 1 cup elbow macaroni
2   (beef or chicken) bouillon cubes
1   bay leaf
    Pinch of thyme
2   dashes Maggi or Worcestershire sauce
    Salt and pepper to taste
    Sour cream and Parmesan cheese for
    serving

In a big pot or Dutch oven brown the ground beef with the onion and then drain. Add the celery, zucchini, carrots, garlic, tomatoes, and beans, and cover with water. Cover and cook at a low, steady boil for 10 minutes. Add 1 more cup water and the macaroni, bouillon cubes, bay leaf, thyme, Worcestershire, and salt and pepper to taste. Cook for 10 to 15 minutes until the noodles and veggies are done. (Barley takes a little longer.) Top each serving with a teaspoon of sour cream and a sprinkle of Parmesan.

Serve with bread. You can stretch this soup with more water and bouillon to share with a large group of friends.

Makes 6 to 8 servings

Rosemarie Goos, Purple Rose
Nine to Five Divas, Kingwood, Texas

Steak Lovers' Soup

Serve this with herb bread and you've got a great, hearty meal.

2   tablespoons olive oil
2   garlic cloves, minced
1 1/2 pounds good-quality, 1-inch-thick steak
     (strip steak, T-bone, rib-eye, etc.), cut into
     1-inch cubes
3/4   cup diced white or yellow onion
1/2   cup A-1 sauce
1/2   cup Worcestershire sauce
2   (10 to 14-ounce) cans beef broth
1   quart regular or spicy tomato-based
     vegetable juice such as V-8, divided
1   (20-ounce) can tomatoes, chopped, not
     drained
3   cups diced potatoes
     Freshly ground black pepper to taste
2   pounds frozen mixed vegetables

Heat the olive oil in a large Dutch oven or soup pot over medium-high heat and sauté the garlic until tender. Add the meat and sear on all sides. Add the onion and the A-1 and Worcestershire sauces. Cook until the onion is translucent. Add the beef broth, 2 to 3 cups V-8, tomatoes with juice, potatoes, and black pepper. Cook over medium heat for 15 minutes, or until the potatoes are tender. Add the frozen vegetables, cover the pot, and simmer for 1½ to 2 hours. Add the remaining V-8 as liquid is needed.

Makes 10 to 12 servings

Karen Miller, Vixen of Vice
Diamond Lil's Red Hot Hatters, Kansas City, Missouri

Slow Cooker Broccoli Soup

You can never have too many recipes for hot soup, ready and waiting at suppertime.

1 (10-ounce) package chopped frozen broccoli
3 cups milk
2 (10¾-ounce) cans condensed cheddar cheese soup
1 cup frozen, loosely packed hash-brown potatoes
1 small onion, chopped

Break up the broccoli a little. Combine with the milk, soup, potatoes, and onion in a slow cooker. Stir to mix. Cover and cook on low 7 to 9 hours.

Makes 4 to 6 servings

Marsha Konken, Lady Raspberry
Red Raspberry Tarts, Sterling, Colorado

Special Red Bean Recipe

1 pound red beans, soaked overnight
1 pound smoked beef sausage
2 bay leaves

5 slices bacon, cut into 1-inch pieces
1 onion, chopped
1 cup chopped green or red bell pepper
2 celery stalks, chopped
4 garlic cloves, minced
¼ teaspoon thyme leaves
½ teaspoon basil leaves
1 teaspoon oregano
½ cup parsley
1 tablespoon Worcestershire sauce
1 teaspoon chili powder
½ tablespoon sugar
4 ounces tomato sauce
1 pound bulk pork sausage
  Salt and pepper to taste

The night before cooking, sort the beans, wash, and drain. Soak overnight, covered in water about 2 inches above the beans. Drain the water and rinse the beans. To cook, cover with water three inches above the beans, add the sausage and bay leaves, and bring to a boil. Turn the heat to low and simmer. Meanwhile, sauté the bacon with the onion, bell pepper, celery, garlic, thyme, basil, and oregano. Add to the beans with the parsley, Worcestershire sauce, chili powder, sugar, and tomato sauce. Cook the sausage in a skillet until done, drain, and add to the beans after they have been cooking at least 45 minutes. Continue to cook until the beans are done. Just before turning them off add the salt and pepper.

Makes 12 cups

Jeanette Chedotal, Queen Mom
Classy Sassy Ladies, Gulfport, Mississippi

Summer Corn Gazpacho

When the living is easy, but the weather is hot, serve this cool, refreshing soup to perk up appetites.

3   tablespoons plus 2 teaspoons olive oil
3   to 4 ears white corn, kernels shaved from the cob
1/2   cup chopped onion
2   cups diced red tomatoes
1/2   cup peeled, seeded, and diced cucumbers
1/3   cup finely diced red or green bell pepper
1/3   cup finely diced celery
4   cups V-8 juice
1   tablespoon red wine vinegar
1/8   teaspoon celery seeds
1/4   teaspoon fresh ground black pepper
1/8   teaspoon salt
1/8   teaspoon basil
2   garlic cloves, chopped finely
1   teaspoon Worcestershire sauce
1/8   teaspoon hot pepper sauce (or to taste)
1   teaspoon sugar (or to taste)
4   tablespoons finely diced fresh parsley
     Reduced-fat sour cream for garnish
     Snipped chives for garnish

Heat 2 teaspoons oil in a skillet over medium heat and sauté the corn kernels for 2 minutes. In a blender combine half of each of the following: the onion, tomatoes, cucumbers, peppers, celery, and V-8. Blend. Add to the blender the vinegar, celery seeds, pepper, salt, basil, garlic, Worcestershire sauce, hot sauce, sugar, parsley, and the remaining 3 tablespoons olive oil. Blend thoroughly.

Pour the contents into a glass bowl or non-metal bowl. Add the corn and the remaining half of the vegetables. Cover and refrigerate for at least 6 hours or overnight.

Before serving, top with sour cream and sprinkle with snipped chives.

Makes 12 servings

Lynne Wixom, Gray Fox
Red Hat TeasHers, Silver Spring, Maryland

Creamy Roasted Cauliflower Soup

A marvelous change occurs when cauliflower is roasted— the natural sugars caramelize into a roasted sweetness. Half-and-half and fresh thyme are the ideal complements.

1   large head cauliflower (3 pounds), cut into florets (10 cups)
1   large onion, sliced
2   garlic cloves, halved
2   tablespoons olive oil
2   (14-ounce) cans chicken broth
1   cup water
1   bay leaf
1   teaspoon chopped fresh thyme
1   cup half-and-half
1   teaspoon salt
1/8   teaspoon black pepper

Preheat the oven to 400°. In a large roasting pan toss the cauliflower, onion, and garlic with the olive oil. Roast for 30 minutes, stirring after 15 minutes. In a large saucepan combine the roasted cauliflower mixture with the chicken broth, water, bay leaf, and thyme. Cover and bring to a boil. Reduce the heat. Simmer, covered, 20 minutes.

Discard the bay leaf. In a blender or food processor, purée the soup in batches. Return the soup to the saucepan. Stir in the half-and-half, salt, and pepper. Heat through.

Makes 8 servings

Rita Cunningham, Co-Queen
Red Hat Mommas of Western Maine, Dixfield, Maine

In-a-Snap Crab Bisque

Not in the mood to cook a big meal? Condensed soup gets the job done, and crabmeat adds its special flair.

1   (10-ounce) can condensed tomato soup
1   (10-ounce) can condensed green pea soup
1   quart half-and-half
7   ounces lump crabmeat (canned is fine)
1   tablespoon sherry or cooking sherry (or to taste)

Combine the tomato and green pea soups in a saucepan set over low heat, stirring to blend well. Gradually add the half-and-half. Add the crabmeat. Cook until thick. Add the sherry just before serving.

Makes 5 servings

Rosanne Bridges, Vice Mother
Ruby Hatters, Bethlehem, Pennsylvania

Clam Chowder

Testers enjoyed tinkering with this soup. They recommended sautéing a rib, or stalk, of celery with the onion.

4   slices bacon
1   leek or onion, chopped
1 1/4 cups diced potatoes
1 1/2 cups clam juice and/or water
2   cups half-and-half
18   to 20 ounces canned clams
1   teaspoon salt
     Pepper to taste
     Pinch of dried thyme
2   tablespoons butter
1   tablespoon chopped fresh parsley

Cook the bacon in a soup pot until crisp. Remove the bacon from the pot, leaving the drippings. Cook the leek in the drippings until golden brown. Add the potatoes, clam juice, and half-and-half. Cook until the potatoes are tender. Drain the clams, pouring the liquid into the soup pot. Chop the clams and add to the pot. Add the salt, pepper to taste, and the thyme. Simmer until thoroughly heated, but do not boil. Float several pats of butter in the soup. Serve in bowls, garnished with the parsley and crumbled bacon.

Makes 6 servings

Laurette Godard, Digital Photographer
Tuesday Linedancers, Winnipeg, Manitoba, Canada

Hamburger Noodle Soup

A hard-working, everyday soup you'll serve again and again.

1   pound ground beef
1   medium onion, chopped
1/2   cup chopped celery
1/2   cup chopped carrots
1   teaspoon minced garlic
3   (14-ounce) cans beef broth
1 1/2   tablespoons soy sauce
1   (4.5-ounce) jar sliced mushrooms, drained
2   cups frozen peas, thawed
3   cups cooked noodles
     Salt and pepper to taste

Brown the ground beef in a skillet over medium heat. Drain if desired. Add the onion, celery, carrots, and garlic to the skillet. Cook until the vegetables are tender-crisp. Add the broth, soy sauce, and mushrooms. Simmer for about 20 minutes, or until the vegetables are tender. Add the peas and noodles. Cook until heated through. Season with salt and pepper.

Makes 8 servings

Kathleen Rivest, Duchess of Dough
Sassy Red Hatters, Winston-Salem, North Carolina

Deluxe Crab Soup

Special friends coming over? Want to indulge your loved ones? Rich cream, a sparkling drop of sherry, and rare crabmeat are suitably glorious.

1/2   cup (1 stick) unsalted butter
1   cup chopped onion
1 1/2   cups chopped celery
3   to 4 tablespoons all-purpose flour
2   (14-ounce) cans chicken broth
1   to 2 cubes chicken bouillon
1   quart half-and-half
1   pint whipping cream
1/3   to 1/2 cup cream sherry
1   pound lump back fin crabmeat
     Dash of ground nutmeg
     Old Bay Seasoning to taste
     Freshly ground pepper to taste
     Chopped fresh parsley

In a large soup pot over medium heat, melt the butter and sauté the onion and celery until tender. For a thick textured soup, stir in the flour at this time. Stir until no dry flour is visible. Stir in the chicken broth and 1 bouillon cube. Add the half-and-half, whipping cream, and cream sherry. Simmer briefly to heat through. Blend with an immersion just enough to chop up the celery and onion into smaller pieces. Add the crabmeat to the soup. Add another bouillon cube if necessary. Season with the nutmeg and several heavy-handed dashes of Old Bay Seasoning and freshly ground pepper. Simmer a few minutes before serving. Garnish with parsley.

Makes 4 to 6 servings

Judy Bloss, Queen Judy B
Vintage Gals, Alachua, Florida

Carrot Soup with Ginger

Racy fresh ginger is delicious with carrots and great for those with sensitive stomachs.

2	tablespoons butter or margarine
1	onion, chopped
1	celery stalk, chopped
1	medium potato, chopped
5 1/2	cups chopped carrots
2	tablespoons minced fresh gingerroot
1 1/2	quarts chicken or vegetable stock
7	tablespoons whipping cream (optional)
	A good pinch of freshly grated nutmeg
	Salt and freshly ground black pepper to taste

Heat the butter in a soup pot over medium heat and sauté the onion and celery for about 5 minutes, or until soft. Stir in the potato, carrots, ginger, and stock. Bring to a boil. Reduce the heat to low, cover, and simmer for about 20 minutes. Process the soup in a food processor or blender until smooth. (Alternately, use a vegetable mill to purée the soup.) Return the soup to the pan. Stir in the cream and nutmeg. Add the salt and pepper to taste. Reheat slowly to serve, or serve cold.

Makes 6 servings

Winnie Ching, Wiki Wiki Winnie
Papa O Ka Papale Ulaula Ahahui, Kaneohe, Hawaii

Carrot and Leek soup

The contributor says, "Some times my boys would not wait for the purée process. That's ok too."

4	carrots
4	leeks
2	large potatoes
4	tablespoon butter
4	cups chicken stock
	Salt and pepper (white pepper is best)

Wash the vegetables. Peel and slice the carrots. Slice or chop the leeks, and be sure to use the green part as well as the white part. Peel and slice the potatoes. Melt the butter in a large, heavy pot over low heat. Add the vegetables. Stir to cover with the butter. Cover to "sweat" the vegetables, stirring as needed. Add a little water if needed, and do not let the vegetables brown. Cook for 5 to 8 minutes until the veggies start to become tender. Add the chicken stock. Simmer for about 25 minutes, or until the vegetables are cooked. Add the salt and pepper to taste. Purée in a food processor, blender, or food mill. Reheat on low if the soup cools too much. It should be served warm.

Makes 5 to 6 servings

Dot Evans, Vice Queen Mother & Princess of Purple Passion
Not Young and Not Restless, Piedmont, South Carolina

Crawfish and Corn Chowder

Testers called this "a hearty flavorful soup that is easy to prepare."

1/2   cup (1 stick) butter or margarine
1/2   bunch green onions, chopped
1   cup chopped celery
1   cup chopped onion
1   cup chopped green bell pepper
2   tablespoons all-purpose flour
1   (10-ounce) can cream of potato soup
1   (14 3/4-ounce) can whole kernel corn, drained
1   pound cooked crawfish
3   cups milk
1   to 2 teaspoons Accent
1   teaspoons Worcestershire sauce
1   teaspoon Cajun seasoning

In a Dutch oven or large saucepan melt the butter over medium heat. Sauté the green onions, celery, onion, and bell pepper in the butter until tender. Sprinkle the flour over the vegetables and mix well. Add the soup, corn, crawfish, milk, Accent, Worcestershire sauce, and Cajun seasoning. Simmer for 45 minutes, stirring often.

Makes 6 servings

Jeanette Chedotal, Queen Mom
Classy Sassy Ladies, Gulfport, Mississippi

Meatball Soup

If you prefer fresh carrots to canned, use baby carrots, cut into halves, and partially cook them in the microwave while you work on the rest of the soup.

1   large onion, chopped
1   cup chopped celery
1   tablespoon olive oil
1   (16-ounce) can chopped tomatoes, not drained
1   (15-ounce) can kidney beans, not drained
1   (10 1/2-ounce) package chopped frozen spinach
8   beef bouillon cubes
1   (15-ounce) can sliced carrots
1/2   teaspoon basil
1/2   teaspoon oregano
8   cups water
      Frozen cooked meatballs, thawed
1   cup spiral pasta

Brown the onion and celery in the olive oil in a Dutch oven over medium heat. Add the tomatoes with juice, beans with juice, spinach, bouillon cubes, carrots, basil, oregano, and water. Bring to a boil over medium heat. Add the meatballs and return to a boil. Add the pasta and cook until tender.

Makes 6 servings

Kay Huston, Royal Rostarian
Santa Teresa Red Hots, San Jose, California

Beef Barley Soup

When I was first married, I wanted to impress my new husband with some beef barley soup. I didn't think it would be too difficult; after all, I had made vegetable soup before. But I had never cooked with barley. When it was time to serve the soup, I ladled it into bowls and called him to the dinner table. After he looked at it for a few minutes, he picked up his knife and fork to proceed to eat it. The soup was very tasty but extremely thick. Barley only looks small in the bag, I learned. And my husband has never forgotten this little mishap.

Patti Waszak
Queen
Red Tarts of SBC CSS
Cudahy, Wisconsin

Slap-It-Together Beer Cheese Soup

Smart shortcut. Use packaged soup mix rather than make a broth from scratch. The contributor warns not to reheat in the microwave or the beer will foam up and make the soup overflow.

1   envelope dry packaged leek soup mix
1   envelope dry packaged French onion
    soup mix
6   cups plus 1/2 cup water
1   (10 3/4-ounce) can cream of chicken soup
1   (10 3/4-ounce) can cream of celery soup
1   pound Velveeta cheese, cut into cubes
1   cup beer

Combine the two dry soup mixes in 6 cups water in a large pot. Bring to a boil and reduce to simmer for 15 minutes. Strain, reserving the broth. In a blender process the chicken and celery soups and the remaining 1/2 cup water. Add to the broth. Add the cheese and beer. Cook over low heat until the cheese is melted.

Makes 10 servings

Joy T. Jones, Queen
Le Rouge Chapeaux of Rockdale, Conyers, Georgia

Chicken Barley Soup

Don't be tempted to use more barley; it expands and expands.

2 1/2   quarts (10 cups) chicken broth
1/3   cup medium barley
2   large celery stalks, diced
2   large carrots, peeled and chopped
1   large onion, minced
    Salt and pepper to taste

Bring the chicken broth and barley to a bowl over high heat. Reduce the heat to medium, cover, and simmer for 45 minutes. Add the celery and boil 15 more minutes. Add the carrots and onion and boil 15 more minutes. Season with salt and pepper.

Makes 6 to 8 servings

Kay Riley, Queen Mum Kay
Chapter Name: Hunt for the Red Hats, Gainesville, Virginia

Chicken-Cheese Tortellini Soup with Spinach

Convenience products make a quick soup with a gourmet taste.

2   tablespoons olive oil
1 1/2   cups sliced fresh mushrooms
2   large garlic cloves, chopped
4   (14-ounce) cans fat-free chicken broth
1   (9-ounce) package fresh cheese tortellini

Whole rotisserie chicken, skinned, meat removed from bones, or 4 boneless, skinless chicken breast halves, cooked and coarsely chopped.
1   (5-ounce) bag spinach leaves, thinly sliced
2   tablespoons freshly grated Parmesan cheese
    Additional Parmesan cheese for serving

Heat the oil in a 6-quart Dutch oven over medium-high heat. Add the mushrooms and garlic and sauté, stirring constantly, for about 5 minutes, or until tender. Add the broth and bring to a boil. Add the tortellini and cover. Reduce the heat to medium. Cook the pasta until al dente according to package directions. Add the chicken and spinach, and cook until the spinach wilts and the chicken is heated through, about 3 minutes. Add the Parmesan cheese and remove from the heat. Serve with additional cheese and place salt and pepper on the table for seasoning.

Makes about 12 servings

Charlene Chambers, Diva in the Kitchen
Scarlet O'Bearas, Ormond Beach, Florida

Rowdy Red Chili

Spices and chocolate are easy additions that make all the difference. Tastes even better the next day, and freezes well too.

1   pound bacon
2 1/2   to 3 cups chopped onions
8   to 12 large garlic cloves, chopped
4   pounds lean ground chuck

8 to 9 tablespoons good-quality chili powder

2 tablespoons ground cumin

1/2 teaspoon ground coriander

1 teaspoon cinnamon

2 ounces semisweet chocolate, grated or melted

2 (28-ounce) cans plus 1 (15-ounce) can crushed tomatoes, not drained

2 (12-ounce) bottles beer

2 (6-ounce) cans tomato paste

1 or 2 (15 to 16-ounce) cans chicken broth

2 (15 to 16-ounce) cans kidney beans

1 (15 to 16-ounce) can pinto beans

1 (15 to 16-ounce) can black beans, rinsed and drained

Cook the bacon over medium heat in a heavy, large Dutch oven. Remove the bacon and crumble. Increase heat to medium high and sauté the onions and garlic in the bacon drippings for 8 minutes, or until the onions are translucent. Add the ground chuck and sauté until brown, breaking up the meat with the back of the spoon. Stir in the chili powder, cumin, coriander, and cinnamon. Cook, stirring, for 2 minutes. Add the chocolate, crushed tomatoes with juice, beer, and tomato paste. Add the bacon and mix well. Stir in the chicken broth, and simmer until thickened to desired consistency, stirring occasionally to prevent sticking, about 1 hour 15 minutes. Mix in the kidney, pinto, and black beans. Simmer 10 to 15 minutes, to heat beans through.

Makes 18 to 20 servings

Mikayla DeRosier, Queen Mum of Sonoma
Le Chapeau Rouge D'Elegance, Sonoma, California

White Chili

1 pound ground turkey

2 garlic cloves, finely chopped

2 (15-ounce) cans white kidney beans, drained

2 (4-ounce) cans chopped green chiles

2/3 plus 2/3 cups French-fried onions

1 cup frozen whole kernel corn, thawed

1/4 cup chopped fresh cilantro

3 tablespoon lime juice

1 tablespoon ground cumin

1/4 teaspoon ground white pepper

1 large tomato, chopped

1/4 cup sour cream

Cook the ground turkey and garlic in a large nonstick skillet or Dutch oven over medium heat for about 5 minutes, or until the turkey is no longer pink. Stir in the beans, green chiles, 2/3 cup French-fried onions, corn, cilantro, lime juice, cumin, and white pepper. Bring to a boil over high heat. Reduce the heat to low and simmer 5 minutes, stirring often. Add the tomato and sour cream; cook, stirring, until hot and bubbly. Sprinkle with the remaining 2/3 cup french-fried onions.

Makes 4 to 6 servings

Marie Preston, Vice Queen Mother
Vintage Roses, Perry, Georgia

Fast and Easy Chicken Chili

A slow-cooker recipe for a day that you're away from the kitchen. Add a salad and corn bread for a complete meal.

1   tablespoon vegetable oil
1/2 cup finely chopped onion
1   pound ground turkey or chicken
1   (15-ounce) can pinto beans
1   (15-ounce) can kidney beans
1   (15-ounce) can whole kernel corn
1   (15-ounce) can stewed tomatoes
2   envelopes chili seasoning
     Sour cream for garnish
     Shredded cheese for garnish
     Chopped onions for garnish
     Cilantro for garnish

Heat the oil in a skillet over medium heat. Brown the onion in the oil. Add the ground turkey or chicken. Cook until brown and crumbly. Transfer to a slow cooker. Add the beans, corn, tomatoes, and chili seasoning and mix well. Cook on high for 3 to 4 hours or low for 6 to 8 hours. Ladle into bowls. Serve garnishes in bowls alongside.

Makes 10 servings

Monica Maylasang, E-mail Princess
Der Tahs of Orange County, Tustin, California

Cool Cucumber Soup

English cucumbers are long and slightly ridged. They are often shrink-wrapped to keep them fresh longer. They have a sweet, pure cucumber flavor, tiny seeds, and a delicate, tender texture.

2   English cucumbers
1   plus 3 cups buttermilk
1/4 cup chopped parsley
2   green onions, chopped
1   pint (2 cups) sour cream
1   teaspoon salt
2   tablespoons lemon juice
     Sprigs of fresh dill for garnish

Save a few thin slices of cucumber for garnish. Peel and chop the remaining cucumbers. Place half the cucumbers and 1 cup buttermilk in a blender. In a separate bowl, mix the parsley and green onions. Add half the parsley mixture to the blender and blend. Repeat with the remaining half of the cucumbers and the remaining half of the parsley mixture. Pour into a large bowl and with a wire whisk beat in the remaining 3 cups buttermilk, the sour cream, salt, and lemon juice. Cover and refrigerate. To serve, float a cucumber slice and a sprig of dill on top of each bowl.

Makes 4 to 6 servings

Kathleen Smith, Queen Kate au Contraire
Steel Magnolias, Ancaster, Ontario, Canada

Escarole and Bean Soup

In some parts of the country, escarole is labeled "curly endive." Its slightly bitter flavor pairs well with rich beans and cheese in this traditional Italian soup.

- 2 tablespoons olive oil
- 2 garlic cloves, chopped
- 1 pound escarole, chopped
  Pinch of salt
- 4 cups low-salt chicken broth
- 1 (15-ounce) can cannellini beans, drained and rinsed
- 1 (1-ounce) piece Parmesan cheese
  Salt and freshly ground black pepper to taste
- 6 teaspoons extra-virgin olive oil

Heat the olive oil in a heavy large pot over medium heat. Add the garlic and sauté until fragrant, about 15 seconds. Add the escarole and sauté until wilted, about 2 minutes. Add the pinch of salt. Add the chicken broth, beans, and Parmesan cheese. Cover and simmer until the beans are heated through, about 5 minutes. Season with salt and pepper to taste. Drizzle each serving with a teaspoon of good-quality, extra-virgin olive oil.

Makes 6 servings

Edel Kerr, Lady Edelweiss
Sensuous Hens, Lilburn, Georgia

Mulligatawny Soup

Get out of a rut with this Anglo-Indian classic, which pairs familiar flavors in unusual ways.

- 1 tablespoon vegetable oil
- 1/4 cup finely chopped onion
- 1 1/2 teaspoons curry powder
- 1 tart apple, peeled, cored, and chopped
- 1/4 cup chopped carrot
- 1/4 cup chopped celery
- 1 tablespoon chopped green bell pepper
- 3 tablespoons all-purpose flour
- 4 cups chicken broth
- 1 (16-ounce) can diced tomatoes with juice
- 1 tablespoon chopped fresh parsley
- 2 teaspoons lemon juice
- 1 teaspoon sugar
- 1/4 teaspoon salt
  Dash of pepper
- 1 1/2 cups diced cooked chicken

Heat the oil in a large saucepan over medium-high heat. Cook the onion and curry powder in the oil until the onion is tender. Stir in the apple, carrot, celery, and bell pepper. Cook, stirring occasionally, for 5 minutes, or until the vegetables are tender. Sprinkle the flour over the vegetables and mix well. Add the broth, tomatoes, parsley, lemon juice, sugar, salt, and pepper. Bring to a boil, add the chicken, and simmer, stirring occasionally, for about 30 minutes.

Makes 6 servings

Cynthia Glansdorp, Queen Cynthia
Carolina Crimson Camellias, Pinehurst, Nebraska

Red Hot Taco Soup

We received dozens of taco soup recipes. Testers tried several versions of this soup and declared it easy to make and deliciously similar to chili. Makes a big pot full, and it's a bit spicy, so be sure to have a tall glass of iced tea at hand. To serve more people (or for planned leftovers), add a can of black beans and a can of pinto beans and serve over rice.

2   pounds ground beef
1   medium onion
1   (15-ounce) can kidney beans
1   (15-ounce) can chili hot beans
1   (4-ounce) can green chiles
1   (11-ounce) can Mexican style corn
1   (15-ounce) can shoe peg corn
3   (14-ounce) cans Mexican-style stewed
     tomatoes
1   (1 1/4-ounce) package taco seasoning
1   (.7-ounce) package dry ranch dressing mix
     Grated cheese and corn chips for serving

Cook the ground beef and onion in a skillet over medium heat until the beef is browned and crumbly. Combine the beef, onion, undrained beans, green chiles, corns, tomatoes, taco seasoning, and ranch dressing mix in a slow cooker. Cook 8 hours on low or 4 hours on high. (The soup can be prepared on the stovetop, cooking for about 2 hours.) Serve with grated cheese on top and corn chips on the side.

Makes about 1 gallon, 10 to 12 servings

Paula Smith, Queen Mother of Naptime
Red Hot Hatters of Mid-Mississippi, Ridgeland, Mississippi

Mint Melon Soup

2   cantaloupes
1/2 pint strawberries, halved
1/2 pint raspberries
1/2 pint blueberries
1/2 pint blackberries
1   (16-ounce) container cottage cheese
     Fresh mint leaves

Peel, seed, and cut the cantaloupes into quarters. Purée in a blender or food processor. Divide the berries equally into 6 large soup plates. Pour the cantaloupe purée over the berries. Top with a dollop of cottage cheese and a sprig of mint.

Makes 6 servings

Donna Boyd, Duchess of the Desert
Crazy Daiseys, Palm Desert, California

Onion and Wine Soup

Unusual and economical. Serve with hot, crusty, French bread. One tester noted that the mixture could be prepared in advance up to the point of adding the cream and then refrigerated. When ready to serve, reheat, adding cream, salt, and pepper.

1/4 cup (1/2 stick) butter
5   large onions, chopped
5   cups beef broth
1/2 cup celery leaves
1   large potato, sliced
1   cup dry white wine
1   tablespoon vinegar
2   teaspoon sugar

1   cup light cream

1   tablespoon minced fresh parsley

    Salt and pepper to taste

Melt the butter in a large saucepan over medium heat. Add the onions and mix well. Add the beef broth, celery leaves, and potato. Bring to a boil. Cover and simmer for 30 minutes. Purée the mixture in a blender. Return to the saucepan and stir in the wine, vinegar, and sugar. Bring to a boil and simmer for 5 minutes. Stir in the cream, parsley, and salt and pepper. Heat thoroughly, but do not boil.

Makes 6 to 8 servings

Shirley Branthoover, Lady Green Thumb
Fayette–Greene Mama Mias, Alverton, Pennsylvania

Oyster Stew

A taste of seaside vacations and fishing villages.

24   fresh oysters or 1 (12-ounce) package frozen oysters with liquid, thawed

2   cups milk or 1 cup half-and-half and 1 cup milk

2   tablespoons butter or margarine

1/4   teaspoon black pepper

1/4   teaspoon salt

1/4   teaspoon paprika

    Dash of celery salt

    Chowder crackers or oyster crackers (optional)

In a medium saucepan heat the oysters in their own liquid on low heat just until the edges curl.

Add the milk, butter, pepper, salt, paprika, and celery salt. Heat gently just until the mixture is hot. Do not boil or overcook. This recipe may easily be doubled.

Makes 4 servings, 1 1/2 quarts

Reyes Smith, Queen
Carefree Crimson Court of Coventry, Royal Oak, Michigan

Dill Pickle Soup

Fun for a chapter gathering—award a prize to the guest who can guess what kind of soup it is. Tasters called it "the most surprising soup" of their tasting, and most gave it a score of 4 out of a possible 5.

1   (14-ounce) can chicken broth

1   (14-ounce) can water

1   medium carrot, peeled and julienned

1   small onion, minced

1/2   cup minced celery

3   to 4 medium dill pickles, coarsely chopped

2   (18-ounce) cans creamy potato with roasted garlic soup

1   cup milk

1/2   cup instant potato flakes

In a medium saucepan combine the broth, water, carrot, onion, celery, and pickles. Cook over medium heat until the vegetables are nearly tender, 5 to 8 minutes. Stir in the soup, milk, and potato flakes (to thicken). Simmer 5 minutes longer.

Makes 6 to 8 servings

MJ Lawrence, Duchess of Many Hats
Scarlett Strutters, Carlsbad, New Mexico

Nearly Instantaneous Swiss Onion Soup

Customize canned soup for a quick supper.

1   (10³/4-ounce) can cream of mushroom soup
1   (10³/4-ounce) can onion soup
1   (10³/4-ounce) can water
6   tablespoons all-purpose flour
1   (15-ounce) can chicken broth
1   soup can milk
    Shredded Swiss cheese

Mix the mushroom soup, onion soup, water, and flour in a blender. Process until the flour is thoroughly blended. Add the chicken broth to the mixture and process again. Pour into a soup pot and cook over medium-high heat, stirring constantly. When the mixture begins to thicken, add the milk. Cook, stirring, until the soup is thick and hot. Pour over shredded Swiss cheese in a soup bowl and stir to string the cheese.

Makes 6 servings

Cathy Smith, No Count Dutchess
Crawford County Cuties, Charleston, Arkansas

The Best French Onion Soup Ever

Traditionally served in thick, white, ovenproof bowls.

2   tablespoons vegetable oil
3   tablespoons butter

5   cups thinly sliced onions
1   teaspoon sugar
2   cups (or cans) beef broth
2   (10-ounce) cans beef consommé
3   tablespoons all-purpose flour
    Salt and pepper to taste
1/2 cup white wine
    Toasted white bread, 1 slice for each bowl (May substitute croutons)
2   cups grated Gruyere or Swiss cheese

Heat the oil in a Dutch oven or soup pot over medium heat. Add the butter and sauté the onions, stirring often, for 5 minutes, or until they are translucent. Stir in the sugar and continue cooking, stirring often, until the onions are golden brown, 15 to 20 minutes. While the onions are cooking, heat the broth and consommé in a separate pan. Preheat the oven to 350°.

Stir the flour into the onions and cook about 2 minutes, stirring constantly. Stir in the hot broth. Add the salt and pepper. Add the wine and bring to a boil. Remove from the heat. Trim the edges from the toast and fit one slice of toast (or croutons) in each ovenproof serving bowl. Pour the soup into the serving bowls. Sprinkle with the cheese. Bake for 20 minutes (or broil for 5 to 7), or until the cheese is slightly bubbly.

Makes 6 to 8 servings

Dot Evans, Vice Queen Mother & Princess of Purple Passion
Not Young and Not Restless, Piedmont, South Carolina

Potato and Sausage Soup

Brimming with flavors, some of them out of the ordinary.

6 to 8 Yukon gold potatoes, peeled and diced
4 cups chicken stock
2 pounds hot pork sausage
1 1/2 cups diced onion
1 3/4 cups finely diced celery
1/2 cup (1 stick) butter
1 quart heavy cream
3 to 4 tablespoons balsamic vinegar
1 tablespoon vanilla extract
1/4 cup finely chopped flat-leaf parsley
   Salt and pepper to taste

In a soup pot cook the potatoes in the chicken stock. Simmer for 20 minutes until tender. In a large skillet sauté the sausage and onions until tender. Drain, add the celery and sauté a few minutes longer. Add the sausage mixture to the soup pot. Add the butter and cream and more broth if needed. Add the vinegar, vanilla, and parsley at the end of cooking. Season with the salt and pepper.

Makes 4 to 6 servings

Paula Thomas, The I-Can-Help Gal
Red Hat Honeys, Spokane, Washington

Scrumptious Green Pea Soup

4 to 5 tablespoons unsalted butter
1 medium onion, chopped
2 tablespoons all-purpose flour

1/4 teaspoon white pepper
1 teaspoon salt
   Pinch of grated nutmeg
1 bay leaf
1/8 to 1/4 teaspoon curry powder (optional)
5 cups chicken or vegetable broth
3 3/4 cups frozen peas, thawed
1/2 cup frozen chopped spinach, thawed
1 1/2 teaspoons sugar
2 cups half-and-half or mixture of milk and half-and-half
1/2 teaspoon grated lemon rind for garnish
   Ground pepper for garnish
   Chopped parsley, tarragon, or basil for garnish
   Sour cream or plain yogurt for garnish

Heat the butter in a saucepan or soup pot over medium heat. Sauté the onion for 5 minutes. Add the flour and cook 3 minutes, stirring. Add the white pepper, salt, nutmeg, bay leaf, curry, and broth. Bring to a boil and stir thoroughly from the bottom. Simmer for 5 to 6 minutes and then add the peas, spinach, and sugar. Simmer for 10 more minutes. Purée in batches in a blender or food processor and then strain through a sieve into the soup pot, stirring with a wooden spoon. Add the half-and-half and very slowly reheat the soup over very low heat. Do not boil. Ladle into bowls. Garnish with the lemon rind, pepper, parsley, and sour cream.

Makes 6 to 8 first course servings, 4 to 6 entrée servings

LuLu (Linda-Rose) Thomsett, Divalicious LuLu
Ruby Royal Majes-"Teas," Port Townsend, Washington

Green Chili Stew

Two meats and plenty of seasonings in a slow cooker mean good food, ready when you are, for company or family.

3   tablespoons vegetable oil
2   garlic cloves, minced
1   large onion, chopped
1   pound ground sirloin
1/2 pound ground pork
3   cups chicken broth
2   cups water
2   (4-ounce) cans diced green chiles
4   large potatoes, diced
1   (10-ounce) package frozen corn, thawed
1   teaspoon black pepper
1   teaspoon crushed dried oregano
1/2 teaspoon ground cumin
1   teaspoon salt

Heat the oil in a skillet over medium-high heat. Add the garlic, onion, sirloin, and pork. Cook until the meat is no longer pink. Transfer to a slow cooker and add the chicken broth, water, green chiles, potatoes, corn, black pepper, oregano, cumin, and salt. Cover and cook on high 6 hours or longer, at least until the potatoes are soft. Serve with warm flour tortillas.

Makes 8 to 12 servings

Judy Stacey, Jovial Judy
Vim, Vigor and Vitality Gals, Surprise, Arizona

Strawberry Soup

Testers worked with several strawberry soups and selected this one, which they declared "simple and refreshing."

16   ounces frozen strawberries
1/2 cup freshly squeezed orange juice
1/2 cup cold water
1/4 cup sugar
2   (6-ounce) cartons nonfat or low-fat strawberry yogurt
     Fresh mint or lime slice for garnish

Partially thaw the strawberries (about an hour at room temperature). Combine the strawberries, orange juice, water, and sugar in a blender or food processor. Blend until smooth. Add the yogurt and process until well blended. Refrigerate until serving time. Serve in small glass bowls. Garnish with fresh mint or a lime slice.

Makes 6 one-cup servings

Judy Davison, Jazzy Judy Duchess of Dixieland
Ladybugs, Dana Point, California

Baked Potato Soup

A creamy and cheesy soup that features all the appealing flavors of a loaded baked potato.

8   slices bacon
1   cup diced yellow onions
2/3 cup all-purpose flour
6   cups (48 ounces) hot chicken broth

The Accountant Chef

For our first Valentine's Day dinner, I surprised my new husband with my "cooking" skills—steak, baked potatoes, biscuits, and roasted vegetables, all of which had to be cooked in the oven at different times and different temperatures. As a career accountant, I did what I would have done in a professional situation and averaged the cooking times and temperatures so that everything would be ready at the same time. As experienced cooks would know, that didn't work very well, and dinner was a disaster. My husband was so wonderful about the dinner; he said he married me for my money, not my domestic abilities. Boy, did he get shortchanged!

Aleene Kann
Queen Mother
Princesses of the Pines
Summerville, South Carolina

4   cups diced, peeled, baked potatoes
2   cups (1 pint) heavy cream
1/4   cup chopped fresh parsley
1 1/2   teaspoons granulated garlic
1 1/2   teaspoons dried basil
1 1/2   teaspoons salt
1 1/2   teaspoons red pepper sauce
1 1/2   teaspoons coarse black pepper
1   cup grated cheddar cheese
1/4   cup diced green onions (white part only)
    Additional chopped bacon, grated cheese, and parsley for garnish

Fry the bacon in a soup pot until crisp. Remove the bacon and crumble. Cook the onions in the bacon drippings over medium-high heat for 3 minutes, or until transparent. Sprinkle with the flour and stir until no white streaks of flour remain. Add the chicken broth gradually, whisking to prevent lumps. Cook until the liquid thickens. Add the potatoes, cream, bacon, parsley, garlic, basil, salt, pepper sauce, and black pepper. Reduce the heat to low and simmer for 10 minutes. Do not allow to boil. Add the grated cheese and green onions. Heat until the cheese melts smoothly. Garnish each serving as desired.

Makes 2 quarts

Stella Lewis, Queen Mother
Antique Rose Hatters, Farmers Branch, Texas

Queen's Cream of Reuben Soup

Our testers loved the idea of this soup, so they massaged the recipe until everyone gave it a thumbs-up. If you're a big Reuben fan, serve the soup with rye croutons or in rye bread bowls.

1/4   cup (1/2 stick) butter
3   celery stalks, chopped
1   large onion, chopped
1/4   cup coarsely chopped green bell pepper
2   garlic cloves, minced
1   (14-ounce) can sauerkraut, rinsed and drained
2   cups coarsely chopped canned corned beef
2   cups beef broth
1/3   cup chili sauce
1   tablespoon Worcestershire sauce
1   tablespoon caraway seeds
2   tablespoons cornstarch dissolved in 3 tablespoons water
1   cup shredded Swiss cheese
1   quart half-and-half
      Chopped fresh chives for garnish

In a large soup pot over medium heat, melt the butter and sauté the celery, onion, bell pepper, and garlic until tender. Add the sauerkraut and corned beef and sauté 3 minutes longer. Heat the broth to almost boiling. Add to the pot and bring to a boil. Lower the heat and add the chili sauce, Worcestershire sauce, and caraway seeds. Simmer for 20 minutes. Add the cornstarch mixture and simmer, stirring constantly, until the mixture thickens. Reduce the heat to low and add the cheese and half-and-half. Cook, stirring occasionally, until the cheese is melted (but do not boil). Garnish with the chives.

Makes 3 quarts

Kristen McWilliams, Quite Queenly Kris
Red Hot Raspberries, Richfield, Minnesota

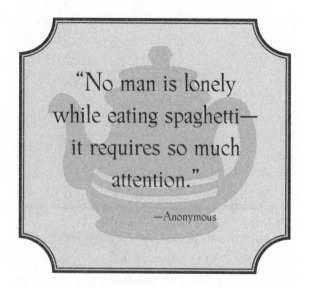

"No man is lonely while eating spaghetti—it requires so much attention."

—Anonymous

Icy Cold Vichyssoise

Our tester loved working with this soup.

2   tablespoons butter
1   bay leaf
2   cups diced leeks, white parts only, thoroughly washed
2   cups peeled and diced potatoes (about 1 pound russet or baking potatoes)
2   cups reduced-sodium chicken broth
2   plus 1 cups half-and-half
1/4   teaspoon hot pepper sauce

Kosher salt to taste

Ground white pepper to taste

2 tablespoons chopped chives for garnish

In a medium saucepan over medium heat, melt the butter. Add the bay leaf and leeks. Cover and cook for 6 to 8 minutes, stirring occasionally, or until the leeks are tender but not browned. Add the potatoes and broth; increase the heat to medium-high and bring to a boil. Cook for 12 to 15 minutes, or until the potatoes are fork tender. Remove and discard the bay leaf.

Cool to room temperature. Combine the potato mixture and 2 cups half-and-half in a blender and purée until smooth. Add the remaining 1 cup half-and-half and the hot sauce and process until blended. Pour through a strainer (this step is optional). Season with the salt and pepper to taste. (This will take more salt than you think, so keep tasting). Chill the soup thoroughly. Serve the soup in cups, garnishing each with a teaspoon of chopped chives.

Makes 6 servings

Sally Cecil, The Countess of Cuisine
Rose's Rosebuds, Pittsburgh, Pennsylvania

Sausage Soup

Add any other vegetable you like to this soup for variety. Be sure to taste the broth before adding the salt, pepper, or hot pepper flakes, because your sausage can vary in its spices and some people might not like it as spicy as others. The soup freezes well.

1 1/2 to 2 pounds Polish, sweet or hot, Italian sausage (not smoked)

10 to 12 cups water

1 1/2 cups chopped sweet onions

1 1/2 cups chopped celery

1 cup chopped green bell pepper

1 cup chopped red bell pepper

1 chopped jalapeño pepper

8 to 10 ounces baby carrots, chopped

4 to 6 cups chopped zucchini

1 (28-ounce) can diced tomatoes

3 garlic cloves, minced

6 fresh sweet basil leaves (or 1 tablespoon dried)

2 teaspoons oregano

Red pepper flakes (optional)

2 tablespoons beef stock

1 pound small pasta

In a large pot boil the sausage in water over medium-high heat. Drain, reserving the water and skimming off the grease. Let the sausage cool; then slice. Combine the reserved water with the onions, celery, bell peppers, jalapeño, carrots, zucchini, and tomatoes with juice. Add the garlic, basil, oregano, pepper flakes, and stock. Bring to a boil over medium-high heat; reduce the heat to medium-low and simmer until the vegetables are tender. Add the cooked, sliced sausage and simmer 10 minutes longer.

Cook the pasta in salted water, drain, and add to the soup bowl when ready to serve.

Makes 6 to 8 servings

Barbara Skibinski, Queen Mother Barbie
The Lake Side Red Hatters, Erie, Pennsylvania

Seafood Soup

So rich it can also be used as a sauce over pasta, rice, split rolls, or biscuits.

1/2   cup (1 stick) butter
2/3   cup green onions, chopped
2/3   cup sliced mushrooms
      (fresh or canned)
1   (8-ounce) package cream cheese
2   (10-ounce) cans cream of potato soup
2   (10-ounce) cans cream of mushroom soup
2   (8-ounce) cans corn, drained
1   quart half-and-half
2   pounds crawfish tails, peeled shrimp,
      crabmeat, or a combination
1   to 2 tablespoons Creole seasoning (start
      with the lesser amount—this stuff is spicy)

Melt the butter in a soup pot over medium-high heat. Sauté the onions and mushrooms in the butter until tender. Add the cream cheese and heat until smooth. Add the soups, corn, half-and-half, seafood, and Creole seasoning and cook over medium-low heat until warm, stirring constantly. (It can easily stick and scorch. Don't leave it. Trust me on this.)

Makes 12 to 15 servings

Charla Jordan, Queen of Quite a Lot
Brandon's Bodacious Babes, Brandon, Mississippi

Turkey Soup (My Way)

BROTH
1   (18-plus pound) turkey carcass
2   to 3 carrots, chopped
2   to 3 celery stalks, chopped
1   medium onion, sliced
2   parsley bunches, chopped
      Salt and pepper to taste

SOUP
4   to 5 medium carrots, sliced
2   large celery stalks, sliced
1   medium onion, chopped
1   (14-ounce) can diced tomatoes
1/2   to 3/4 cup barley
2   cups chopped spinach or kale
2   zucchini, diced or sliced
1   russet potato, diced
1   to 2 tablespoons beef base (optional)
      Salt and pepper to taste

Make the broth from the turkey carcass. In a large pot over high heat, cover the carcass with water and add the carrots, celery, onion, parsley, and salt and pepper. Bring to a boil, reduce the heat to medium-low, and simmer for 2 to 3 hours. Strain the broth; it will make about 12 cups. Remove the meat from the carcass and set it aside for the soup.

For the soup, in a large soup pot over high heat combine the broth with the carrots, celery, onion, tomatoes with juice, barley, spinach, zucchini, potato, beef base, if using, salt and pepper, and the pieces of turkey. Bring to a boil, reduce the heat to medium-low, and simmer till the vegetables are cooked.

Makes about 12 servings

Mary Woolsey, Member
RHS Red Queens, Canoga Park, California

Quick Creamy Tomato-Basil Soup

Choose good-quality, canned, crushed tomatoes for best flavor.

4   cups canned, crushed, whole tomatoes and juice
14   washed fresh whole basil leaves
1   cup heavy cream
1/2 cup (1 stick), unsalted butter
1/4 teaspoon freshly cracked black pepper
     Salt to taste

Put the tomatoes with juice in a saucepan. Simmer 30 minutes over medium heat. In a blender or food processor purée the cooked tomatoes and juice mixture in batches along with the basil leaves. Return the mixture to the saucepan. Add the heavy cream, butter, black pepper, and salt. Cook, stirring, over low heat until the butter is melted and the soup is warm. Garnish with additional basil leaves and serve with your favorite bread.

Serves 4 as a main dish or 8 as an appetizer

Sandy Guilbeaux, Princess of Royal Teas,
Shrewd Hatters of Shrewsburg, Stewartstown, Pennsylvania

Tuscan Soup

1   teaspoon olive oil or vegetable oil
1   small onion, chopped
1   small carrot, sliced
2   (14-ounce) cans chicken broth
1   cup water
3/4 teaspoon salt
1/4 teaspoon pepper
1   (15 to 16-ounce) can white kidney or great northern beans, rinsed and drained
2/3 cup uncooked small spiral pasta
3   cups fresh spinach, thinly sliced

In a two-quart saucepan heat the oil over medium-high heat. Sauté the onion and carrot until tender. Add the broth, water, salt, and pepper; bring to a boil. Stir in the beans and pasta; return to a boil. Reduce the heat to low, cover, and simmer for 15 minutes, or until the pasta is cooked, stirring occasionally. Add the spinach and heat through.

Makes 4 servings

Dottie Phelps, Queen Mother
Les Dames aux Chapeaux Rouges, Malden, Missouri

Are We There Yet?

The Red Hat Society has been called "the second women's movement"! A heady thought! So, where is this "movement" moving to?

That is a good question. Since it came into being without conscious planning, those of us at Hatquarters (the Red Hat Society hub) were initially tempted to sit back and watch it develop in the same way. In fact, for the first few years, we did that. We coined the term, "disorganization" to define ourselves, and we did a pretty good job of living up to that description.

However, reality eventually made itself felt, and we realized that positive leadership was required to keep this movement on the right track and to bring its potential to fruition. Although we continue to eschew "rules," we have constructed a few guidelines, formed policies, and exerted leadership. If we had not done this, we would have found ourselves (and our chapters) galloping off in all sorts of different directions at once.

Through our website and our staff, Hatquarters facilitates connection among its members and encourages multiple forms of interaction. We engage in give and take with our chapters, learning from each other and sharing ideas. We organize and present large events—and larger events!

So, the question again arises, where are we moving to? We're still not overly interested in naming a particular destination. What we are interested in is making the journey valuable, interesting (and fun)—and in making the journey together!

One Tomato, Two Tomato Soup

Canned crushed tomatoes and fresh tomatoes are mellowed by sour cream and a smidge of honey.

1   tablespoon olive oil
1   tablespoon butter
1 1/2 cups chopped onions
3   to 4 garlic cloves, minced
1/2 teaspoon salt
1   teaspoon dill
3   to 4 teaspoons ground black pepper
1   (28-ounce) can crushed concentrated tomatoes (or puréed canned tomatoes)
2   cups water
1   tablespoon honey
1   tablespoon sour cream
2   medium fresh tomatoes, diced
    Plain yogurt, parsley and/or basil, snipped chives for garnish

Heat the olive oil and butter in a kettle over medium heat. Sauté the onions, garlic, salt, dill, and black pepper for 5 to 10 minutes, or until the onion is translucent. Add the crushed tomatoes with juice, water, and honey. Cover, reduce the heat to low, and simmer for 20 to 30 minutes. About 5 minutes before serving, whisk in the sour cream and stir in the diced fresh tomatoes. Serve hot. Top with the yogurt and freshly minced herbs.

Makes 4 to 6 servings

Marian Ferris, Vice Mum
The Rural Red Hats, Attica, New York

Fresh Mushroom Soup

Fun if you like the stringiness of mozzarella cheese. Testers noted that it's not a good choice for a formal ladies' luncheon. If you want a less "interactive" soup, add croutons to "grab" the cheese, or choose freshly grated Parmesan, aged gouda, or gruyere.

4   slices bacon
2   tablespoons butter
1   large onion, chopped
1   or 2 garlic cloves, minced
1   pound sliced mushrooms
1   (7-ounce) can tomato paste
4   tablespoons sweet vermouth or wine
6   cups chicken stock
    Salt and pepper to taste
    Grated mozzarella cheese
    Parsley for garnish

In a soup pot cook the bacon until crisp. Set aside to cool. Drain the fat from the pan if desired. Melt the butter over medium heat in the soup pot and cook the onion and garlic until soft. Add the sliced mushrooms. Cook for 10 minutes, stirring occasionally. Stir in the tomato paste, vermouth, and chicken stock. Crumble the bacon and add to the pot. Simmer for 10 to 15 minutes. Add the salt and pepper.

Add a handful of mozzarella cheese to each soup bowl, and ladle the hot soup over the cheese. Top with fresh parsley.

Makes 4 to 6 servings

Laurette Godard, Chapterette
Tuesday Linedancers, Winnipeg, Manitoba, Canada

Turkey Tortilla Soup

1 teaspoon olive oil
1 1/4 pounds lean ground turkey
2 (14-ounce) cans chicken broth
1 (16-ounce) jar salsa
1 (11-ounce) can Mexican-style corn, drained
1 tablespoon lime juice
2 tablespoons chopped cilantro
Salt and pepper to taste
Lime wedges for garnish

Heat the oil in a large saucepan over medium heat and cook the turkey 6 to 8 minutes, or until brown and crumbled. Add the chicken broth, salsa, corn, and lime juice and mix well. Reduce the heat to low. Cover and simmer for 10 minutes. Add the cilantro and salt and pepper. Spoon into soup bowls and garnish with wedges of lime. Serve with tortilla chips.

Makes 8 servings

Mary Van Atta, Vice Queen Mother
Vintage Roses, Warner Robins, Georgia

Sauerkraut Soup

Serve hot with a hearty, crusty bread, such as pumpernickel or rye. Use the sauerkraut packed in plastic bags for the freshest taste.

4 medium potatoes, washed and diced in 1/2-inch cubes
1/2 cup frozen diced onion, thawed and drained
2 (14-ounce) cans chicken broth, plus water

to make 4 1/2 cups liquid
1 (16-ounce) package sauerkraut
2 teaspoons dill weed
1 pound kielbasa, sliced and quartered
Salt and pepper to taste
1 cup sour cream
1 tablespoon all-purpose flour

In a saucepan over high heat combine the potatoes and onion with the broth and water and boil until the vegetables are tender. Rinse and drain the sauerkraut in a colander. Add the sauerkraut, dill weed, kielbasa, and salt and pepper to the potatoes. Mix well. Simmer for 5 minutes. Combine the sour cream and flour with 1/2 cup liquid from the soup, and then stir the mixture into the soup. Simmer until thickened, but do not boil.

Make 4 to 6 servings

Joanne Harter, Lady Hi-Jinks, Court Jester
Hot Tamales of Watertown, Harrisville, New York

Wild Rice Soup

Testers liked the flavor of the soup, but felt that the butter could be reduced by half.

3 boneless chicken breasts, cut into chunks
3 plus 3 cups water
4 tablespoons chicken soup base
1 to 2 tablespoons seasoned salt
1/2 plus 1/4 cup butter (1 1/2 sticks)
1 medium onion, chopped
3 celery stalks, chopped

4 tablespoons all-purpose flour

4 cups milk

1 1/4 cups cooked wild rice

1 head cauliflower, chopped

3 carrots, grated or finely chopped

1/2 pound American cheese, shredded

In a large soup pot combine the chicken breasts, 3 cups of the water, chicken soup base, and seasoned salt. Bring to a boil over high heat; reduce the heat to medium-low and simmer for about 15 minutes, or until the juice is clear.

In a separate pot, melt 1/2 cup of the butter over medium-high heat. Sauté the onion and celery until the onion is translucent. Add the flour and cook until thick. Slowly add the remaining 3 cups water and cook, stirring, until thickened. Stir in the milk and cook until thickened. Add to the chicken. Add the wild rice, cauliflower, and carrots. Simmer gently for about 2 hours uncovered. Do not allow to boil. Shortly before serving, add the American cheese. Cook until it melts.

Makes 6 servings

Lynette Huovinen, Queen Mother
Babbitt Just-for-Fun Red Hatters, Babbitt, Minnesota

Fresh Shrimp Chowder

Boiling shrimp shells gives the soup extra depth of flavor.

2 pounds large fresh shrimp, shells on

1/4 cup (1/2 stick) butter

1 bunch green onions, thinly sliced

1 large onion, finely chopped

1 large potato, diced

1 tablespoon hot paprika

2 (15-ounce) cans whole kernal corn, drained

1 (8-ounce) package cream cheese

Salt and pepper to taste

Peel and devein the shrimp. Combine the shells, tails, and 3 to 4 cups of water in a saucepan and simmer for 15 to 20 minutes. Drain and reserve the stock.

In a large pot melt the butter over medium-high heat and sauté the green onions, onion, potato, and paprika for 10 minutes. Add the shrimp stock and mix well. Cover and simmer until the potatoes are tender. Add the corn and mix well. When hot, add the cream cheese and cook until melted. Add the shrimp and cook 3 to 4 minutes longer until cooked thoroughly. Season with the salt and pepper. Serve with a crusty bread.

Makes 6 to 8 servings

Paula Thomas, The I-Can-Help Gal
Red Hat Honeys, Spokane, Washington

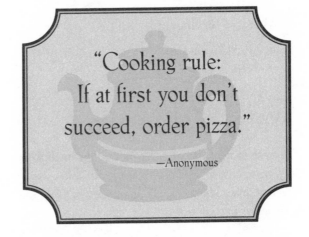

"Cooking rule:
If at first you don't
succeed, order pizza."

—Anonymous

Salmon Cheese Chowder

2   tablespoons butter

1/2   cup chopped celery

1/2   cup chopped carrots

1/4   cup all-purpose flour

1/4   teaspoon paprika

1/8   teaspoon pepper

2   cups chicken broth

2   cups milk

1   (15-ounce) can salmon, drained, bones removed

1/2   cup shredded cheese

2   teaspoons chopped fresh parsley

In a 3-quart saucepan melt the butter over medium-high heat. Cook the celery and carrots for 4 to 5 minutes, or until tender but not brown, stirring often. Stir in the flour, paprika, and pepper. Add the chicken broth and milk all at once. Reduce the heat to medium and cook, stirring, until the mixture is thickened and bubbly. Stir in the salmon, cheese, and parsley. Cook, stirring, until the cheese melts. Ladle into soup bowls.

Makes 4 servings

Nancy Rosi, Queen Mother
Jolly Red Hatters, Denver, Colorado

Manhattan Fish Chowder

The fresh taste of this soup depends on the quality of the fish, so choose good quality fish. Our tester used frozen, skinless, boneless, cod loins. Better still if you have access to fresh fish.

4   bacon slices, cut into bite-sized pieces

1/2   cup chopped onion

2   cups boiling water

1   (16-ounce) can chopped tomatoes

1   cup diced potatoes

1/2   cup diced carrots

1/2   cup chopped celery

1/4   cup ketchup

1   tablespoon Worcestershire sauce

1/2   teaspoon salt

1/4   teaspoon pepper

1/4   teaspoon thyme

1   pound fresh fish fillet, cut into 1-inch pieces

Chopped fresh parsley for garnish

In a large saucepan over medium heat, fry the bacon until crisp. Add the onion and cook until tender. Add the water, tomatoes, potatoes, carrots, celery, ketchup, Worcestershire sauce, salt, pepper, and thyme. Cover, reduce the heat to medium-low and simmer for 40 to 45 minutes, or until the vegetables are tender. Add the fish, cover, and simmer about 10 minutes longer, or until the fish flakes easily. Garnish with the parsley.

Makes 4 servings

Christine Austin, Princess Sunshine
Sassy Squaws of Seminole Lakes, Punta Gorda, Florida

Lentil Spinach Soup

A powerhouse of a soup, bursting with color, flavor, and nutrition.

1   tablespoon olive oil
2   onions, chopped
2   carrots, chopped
1/2   teaspoon minced garlic
4   cups water
1 1/4   cups (8 ounces) dried lentils
1   (14-ounce) can stewed tomatoes
1   (10-ounce) package frozen spinach, thawed
1   tablespoon lemon juice
1   teaspoon grated lemon peel or 2 teaspoons red wine vinegar (optional)

Heat the olive oil in a soup pot over medium-high heat. Sauté the onions, carrots, and garlic in the oil for 2 minutes. Add the water, lentils, and tomatoes. Cover and bring to a boil. Reduce the heat to low and simmer for 45 minutes. Add the spinach, lemon juice, and lemon peel. Simmer 5 minutes longer.

Makes 6 servings

Jill Davis, Crimson Queen Jill
Crimson Crones, Beaverton, Oregon

Microwave Cream of Zucchini Soup

This summer's garden a bit too abundant in zucchini? Serve a hearty soup that uses that abundance but keeps the kitchen cool. Tasters were impressed, and the soup was popular even with those who didn't like zucchini.

6   cups sliced zucchini (4 medium to large)
1/2   tablespoon dried minced onion
3   chicken bouillon cubes (or 3 teaspoons bouillon granules)
1/4   cup (1/2 stick) butter
1/3   cup all-purpose flour
1   teaspoon seasoned salt
3   cups milk

Combine the zucchini, onion, and crumbled bouillon cubes in a 2 1/2-quart glass casserole. Heat in the microwave for 11 minutes at full power, or until the zucchini is tender. Process in a blender or food processor until puréed. In the same glass dish, heat the butter for 1 minute in the microwave. Stir in the flour and seasoned salt. Whisk in the milk until the mixture is smooth. Cook in the microwave for 8 minutes, stirring often. Sauce should be thick and bubbling. Combine the sauce and zucchini. Heat 2 minutes more. If the soup is too thick, add milk to achieve desired consistency, then heat through.

Makes 8 servings

Dee Boyes, Diva Dee
Lusty Ladies in Red of Loveland, Loveland, Colorado

NINE

❧ Little Feasts ❧

PIZZA, SANDWICHES, WRAPS & BURRITOS

Who says that cooking has to be complicated? Some of the most enjoyable foods can be put together in a hurry, either as easy entrées or as snacks. The Earl of Sandwich is credited with inventing the concoction that bears his name. He probably just slapped a few things together and put them between two pieces of bread to make the whole thing easier to eat. But it was a stroke of genius that has been a life-saver for everyone from school lunch packers to picnickers.

Pizza (originally developed in China) is every bit as beloved as the lowly sandwich, though a little more labor-intensive to prepare. It doesn't matter though; when you're in the mood for your favorite dish, a little effort won't usually stop you.

These foods are perfect for Red Hat Society get-togethers. They are "fun" foods that can often be prepared spontaneously. Fun and spontaneity? Perfect.

Bruschetta Sauce

3   to 4 tablespons olive oil
4   large fresh garlic cloves, finely chopped
1   teaspoon ground oregano
1/2   teaspoon oregano leaves
1 1/4   teaspoons basil
1   teaspoon parsley leaves
1/3   teaspoon salt
1/3   teaspoon pepper (white or black)
3   tablespoons dijon mustard

Mix the olive oil, garlic, oregano, basil, parsley, salt, pepper, and mustard in a blender. Refrigerate 6 to 8 hours or longer.

Serving size: 6 to 8

Lucy Barwick, E-mail Female
Ladies of the Lake, Vicksburg, Mississippi

Gourmet Gingerburgers

Like them spicy? You can increase the amounts of ginger and Worcestershire and add minced fresh garlic.

2   pounds ground chuck
    Garlic salt to taste
4   teaspoons ground ginger
4   tablespoons butter
4   teaspoons Worcestershire sauce
4   hamburger buns, buttered
    Lettuce and tomato

Form the meat into four patties. Sprinkle each patty with garlic salt and rub with 1 teaspoon ground ginger. Grilled, broil, or pan-fry the patties to desired doneness. Top each patty with a tablespoon of butter and 1 teaspoon Worcestershire sauce. Cover and let the butter melt. Sprinkle a little garlic salt on the buns and lightly toast. Top the toasted buns with the hamburgers. Add the lettuce and tomato before serving.

Makes 4 servings

Janet Shannon, Crafty Queen
Crafty Cats In Crimson Hats, Tom's River, New Jersey

Shrimp Burger

Testers called this "Yummy." It can also be served over lettuce as a salad.

1   celery stalk with tops, coarsely chopped
1/2   small yellow onion, coarsely chopped
1/2   green bell pepper, seeded and coarsely chopped
1   garlic clove
1/2   cup chopped fresh parsley
1   pound fresh small shrimp, peeled and deveined
1   tablespoon Old Bay seasoning
1/2   teaspoon cayenne pepper
1   lime, zested
    Salt and pepper to taste
2   tablespoons extra-virgin olive oil
1/4   cup mayonnaise or horseradish mayonnaise
1/4   cup chili sauce
    Juice of 1 lime
    Mixed lettuce leaves

Put the celery, onion, bell pepper, garlic, and parsley in a food processor and process until finely chopped. Spoon into a mixing bowl. Divide the shrimp in half. Put half the shrimp into a food processor and process. Add to the chopped vegetables. Add the whole shrimp to the bowl. (If you are using medium shrimp, cut them in half before adding.) Add the Old Bay, cayenne pepper, lime zest, and salt and pepper. Mix well. Heat the olive oil in a large nonstick skillet over medium to medium-high heat. Form four patties with the shrimp mixture and fry for 3 to 5 minutes on each side, or until they firm up and the shrimp turn pink. Combine the mayonnaise and chili sauce and mix well. Drizzle the lime juice over the lettuce. Serve the shrimp burgers on toasted English muffins with the mayonnaise sauce and lettuce.

Makes 4 servings

Judy Sensi, Lady Babalot
Ladies with HATtitude, Reston, Springfield, Virginia

Dynamites

Another great way to serve a group with the kick of bell pepper.

3	tablespoons olive oil
2	large onions, sliced
5	celery stalks, diced
1 1/2	pounds ground chuck
5	green bell peppers, sliced into 1/2-inch strips
1	(28-ounce) can tomato purée
	Salt and red pepper flakes to taste
12	individual French or Italian rolls

Heat the olive oil in a large sauce pan over medium-high heat. Sauté the onions and celery in the oil for 10 minutes, or until tender. Remove from the pan. Brown the ground chuck in the same pan, breaking it into small pieces. Return the onions and celery to the pan; add the green peppers and tomato purée. Mix well and a bring to a boil. Reduce the heat to low and add the salt and red pepper flakes. Cover and simmer for about 2 hours, stirring every 30 minutes. Slice the rolls lengthwise and fill with the beef mixture.

Makes 12 servings

Thelma Montecalvo, Queen Supreme
Little Rhody Red Hens, Woonsocket, Rhode Island

"What my mother believed about cooking is that if you worked hard and prospered, someone else would do it for you."

—Nora Ephron

Meal in a Bun

If you're in charge of feeding the troops, this one can't be beat for economy.

2   cups shredded sharp cheddar cheese
1/2 cup chopped green bell pepper
1   small onion, chopped
3   hard boiled eggs, peeled and chopped
1/4 cup sliced pimiento-stuffed olives
2   cups ground cooked bologna or ham
1   teaspoon Worcestershire sauce
1   tablespoon ketchup
24   medium hamburger buns

Preheat the oven to 350°. Mix together the cheese, bell pepper, onion, eggs, olives, bologna or ham, Worcestershire sauce, and ketchup. Remove some of the inside of the buns to make a space for the filling. Fill with the mixture and wrap each bun in aluminum foil. Place the wrapped buns on a cookie sheet and heat in the oven for 20 minutes, or until the filling is heated and the cheese is slightly melted.

Makes 24 sandwiches

Barbara Telkamp, Queen Mother
Le Chapeau Rouge, Brookings, South Dakota

Memories of Philly Burgers

1   pound ground beef
1   plus 1 tablespoons Worcestershire sauce
3   plus 1 teaspoons Dijon mustard
1   (2.8-ounce) can french-fried onions, divided

1   (3-ounce) package cream cheese, softened
1   (2.5-ounce) jar sliced mushrooms, drained
1   teaspoon dried parsley flakes
4   kaiser rolls

Combine the ground beef with 1 tablespoon Worcestershire sauce, 3 teaspoons mustard, and half the onions. Form into four patties and broil or grill to desired doneness. In a small bowl, combine the cream cheese, the remaining 1 tablespoon Worcestershire sauce, the remaining 1 teaspoon mustard, the mushrooms, and parsley; mix well. Spread the cheese mixture on the cooked patties; top with the remaining reserved onions and broil or grill 30 seconds more, or until the onions are golden. Serve on the kaiser rolls.

Makes 4 servings

Nancy Parkhurst, Vice Queen
Feathers and Flowers, Bedford, Virginia

Beef and Chile Cheese Rolls

Expecting a crowd? Make this in advance and serve it to a grateful group.

3 1/2 pounds ground round
1   onion, chopped
1   (4-ounce) can green chiles
2   (8-ounce) cans tomato sauce
       Salt and pepper to taste
       Chili powder to taste
1 1/2 pounds cheddar cheese, sliced or shredded
24   French rolls

Preheat the oven to 225°. Brown the ground round and onion in a skillet over medium heat. Add the chiles, tomato sauce, salt, pepper, and chili powder. Stir in the cheese. Scoop out the center of the rolls and fill with the beef mixture. Wrap the rolls in waxed paper or aluminum foil. Bake for 20 to 30 minutes, or until the filling is hot.

Makes 24 servings

Sue Hemphill, Queen Sue
Sassy Classy Red Hatters, San Leandro, California

Pizza Burgers

English muffins stand in for pizza crust, and cheese holds the beef mixture together for neater eating.

1	pound ground beef
1	package sliced pepperoni, chopped
1	small onion, chopped
1/2	teaspoon garlic powder
1/2	teaspoon oregano
	Salt and pepper to taste
1	(6-ounce) can tomato paste
1	(14 1/2-ounce) can tomato sauce
	Water if needed
1	(6-count) package English muffins
2	(8 ounces) cups shredded mozzarella cheese
1	(2-ounce) can sliced olives (optional)

Preheat broiler. Brown the ground beef with the pepperoni and onion in a large skillet over medium heat. Add the garlic powder, oregano, salt, pepper, tomato paste, and tomato sauce and mix well. Mixture should be thick. Add a little water if needed to thin and blend the tomato paste. Slice the English muffins in half. Spread some mixture on each muffin. Top with the cheese and sliced olives. Broil until the cheese is melted.

Makes 12 servings

Beth Grahl, Queen Bee
Red Hat Belles of Fenton, Fenton, Michigan

Tunaburgers

This old standby has served many a cook well for decades.

1	(7-ounce) can tuna, drained
1	cup chopped celery
1	cup shredded mozzarella cheese
1	cup shredded mild cheddar cheese
1	small onion, minced
1/4	cup mayonnaise
4	tablespoons butter, softened
4	hamburger buns

Preheat the oven to 350°. In a bowl combine the tuna, celery, cheeses, onion, and mayonnaise. Butter the buns. Spread with the tuna mixture. Wrap in aluminum foil and place on a baking sheet. Bake for 15 minutes. Serve hot.

Makes 4 servings

Celia Cloud Walker, La Chef de Hattitude
Pink & Purple Pampered Prissies, Dothan, Alabama

Tuna Cheese Broil

You know your friend is your really dear friend when you can serve this tasty but humble meal to her.

1   (7-ounce) can tuna, drained
3   hard-boiled eggs, finely chopped
1/2   cup Cheez Whiz
1/2   cup mayonnaise-type salad dressing
1/4   cup sweet green pickle relish
1   small onion, diced finely
   Chopped chives (optional)
4   hamburger buns

Preheat the broiler. Mix together the tuna, eggs, Cheez Whiz, salad dressing, relish, onion, and chives. Spread on the hamburger buns and put under the broiler until the tops start to bubble and turn lightly browned. Serve hot.

Makes 4 servings

Mary Jane MacVicar, Queen Scarlettness
Chapter Name: Scarlett Shady Ladies, Leamington, Ontario, Canada

Beef-Stuffed French Loaf

Ground or cooked cubed chicken is a good option, too.

1   pound ground beef
1   package (1/3 cup) dry onion soup mix
1   (10-ounce) can cream of mushroom soup
1   (10-ounce) can cream of celery soup
1 1/2   cups shredded cheese
1   cup cooked rice
1   loaf French bread

In a large skillet brown the ground beef over medium heat. Stir in the onion soup mix. Add both cans of soup, the cheese, and rice and mix well.

Preheat the oven to 350°. Cut the French bread in half lengthwise with one-third for the top and two-thirds for the bottom. Hollow out the bottom half of the bread, leaving at least a 1/2-inch shell. Add the removed bread to the hamburger mixture and mix well. Pack the meat mixture into the hollowed bread. Cover with the top half. Wrap in foil and bake for 30 minutes.

Makes 4 to 6 servings

Judy Roth, Queen MUM
Rockin Red Hatters, Warner, South Dakota

Veggie Burgers

Testers were enthusiastic about Veggie Burgers, saying, "Taste, texture, and convenience are all there. This was a big surprise to our ladies. We thought it would need seasonings, but it didn't. We loved it."

1   celery stalk, chopped
1   carrot, peeled and chopped
1/2   onion, chopped
1/2   cup chopped broccoli
1/2   cup chopped zucchini
3/4   to 1 cup bread crumbs plus more for coating patties
1   egg, beaten
   Vegetable oil for frying

In a medium bowl combine the vegetables, bread crumbs, and egg and mix well. The mixture will be soft. Carefully form into patties and coat the patties in the bread crumbs. Heat the oil in a skillet over medium-high heat. Fry the patties until browned on both sides.

Makes 6 servings

Yvonne Gonzalez, Lady I. Lavender
The Sunshine Girls, Massapequa Park, New York

The Ol' Ball Game Hot Dog Chili

Testers called this a "very easy" recipe "with good flavor and texture." A build-your-own hot dog bar is a great way to feed a mixed group of children and adults.

1	pound ground London broil (flank) steak
1/2	cup chopped onion
1 1/2	cups water
3	tablespoons ketchup
2	tablespoons yellow mustard
2	tablespoons Worcestershire sauce
2	tablespoons chili powder
1/2	teaspoon salt
1/4	teaspoon pepper

Combine the ground steak, onion, and water in a medium-size saucepan and cook over high heat, stirring, for 3 to 5 minutes, or until the meat is brown. (Since this meat is very lean, there is no fat to drain.) Add the ketchup, mustard, Worcestershire sauce, chili powder, salt, and pepper and mix well. Reduce the heat to low and simmer, uncovered, for 30 minutes. Add a little water if the mixture becomes dry. Use to top eight hot dogs.

Makes 8 servings

Barbara Mitchell, Queen Mother
Royal, Regal, Red Hat Rounders, Mechanicsville, Virginia

Red Hot Topper

More fun-in-a-bun eats for entertaining or just serving up a casual meal.

1	tablespoon vegetable oil
1/2	pound ground beef
1	small onion, finely chopped
1	(10 3/4-ounce) can tomato soup
1/4	cup water
1/2	teaspoon paprika
1/2	teaspoon dry mustard
1/2	teaspoon sugar
1	tablespoon Worcestershire sauce
1	tablespoon chili powder
2	bay leaves
	Dash of ground cloves
	Salt and black pepper to taste
	Cayenne to taste

Heat the oil in a saucepan over medium-high heat and sauté the beef and onion until browned and crumbly; drain. Add the soup, water, paprika, mustard, sugar, Worcestershire sauce, chili powder, bay leaves, cloves, and salt, pepper, and cayenne. Reduce the heat to low and cook, stirring regularly, for about 20 minutes. Remove bay leaves before serving.

Makes enough to top 6 to 8 hot dogs

Sally Claydon, Vice Queen (NOT Queen of Vice)
Glad Abouts, Gasport, New York

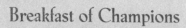

Breakfast of Champions

Very early one morning, I was beginning to prepare Italian Beef Sandwiches in the slow cooker. It was six o'clock in the morning, and I was adding the secret ingredient. My daughter, who was home from college, walked into the kitchen just at that moment. You can just imagine the shock on her face when she saw me opening that can of beer at six in the morning, and the situation definitely called for some impromptu humor on my part.

Sandy Kangas
Lady Laughable
Red Hatters of the North
Menominee, Michigan

Sirloin French Dip

Indulge your loved ones with this top-shelf French dip. Be sure to use chicken bouillon—the combination of beef and chicken is the secret to the complex flavors here.

1   (2-pound) sirloin tip roast (round roast) trimmed very lean
4   to 6 tablespoons butter or margarine
2   large onions, sliced
4   chicken bouillon cubes
2   cups boiling water
3/4   cup Burgundy wine
    Salt and pepper to taste
    Italian rolls

Cut the beef into thin slices. Heat the butter in a large saucepan over medium-high heat. Sauté the meat and onions in the hot butter until the onions are tender. Dissolve the bouillon cubes in the water. Add to the skillet. Add the Burgundy. Bring to a boil, reduce the heat to low, and simmer for 30 minutes. Add the salt and pepper. Cut the rolls in half. Spoon the beef mixture over the rolls and serve.

Makes 6 servings

Kathy Corrado, Queen Mother
Red Hat Chicks, Pittsburgh, Pensylvania

A Big Sandwich, Red-Hat Style

This one takes a little planning ahead. You'll have to order the bread, but the looks on people's faces are worth the effort.

1 (6-foot) loaf colored bread
4 pounds assorted cold cuts
2 pounds sliced cheeses
1 (4-ounce) can sliced or chopped black olives
1 red onion, cut into thin rings
2 cucumbers, thinly sliced
1 green bell pepper, cut into rings or slices
1 red bell pepper, cut into rings or slices
1 yellow bell pepper, cut into rings or slices
1 head lettuce, shredded
   Mayonnaise, mustard, and/or vinaigrette
   to taste

Slice the bread in half lengthwise and layer on the meats, cheeses, black olives, onion rings, cucumber slices, and bell peppers. Mix the lettuce with the mayonnaise, mustard, and/or vinaigrette. Top the sub with the lettuce. Replace the top and secure with toothpicks. Place on a six foot platter (or cutting board) wrapped in colorful paper to serve.

Makes 25 to 30 servings

Note: You can order a 6-foot loaf of colored, specialty bread (red, of course, but purple is nice too) from your favorite bakery or grocery.

Karen Fitzsimmons, Lady Still Nameless
Red Hot Taters, Meridian, Idaho

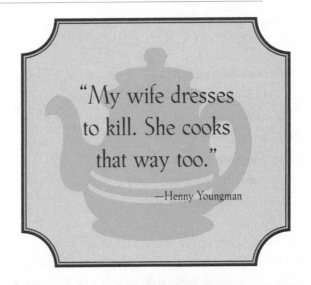

"My wife dresses to kill. She cooks that way too."

—Henny Youngman

Slow Cooker Italian Sandwich Beef

Super easy and so good.

1 (3 to 4-pound) rolled and tied beef rump roast
1 (10-ounce) jar pepperoncini peppers
1 (12-ounce) can beer
1 (14-ounce) can beef broth
16 hoagie rolls

Put the beef roast in a slow cooker. Add the pepperoncini peppers with liquid, beer, and beef broth to the slow cooker. Cook on low for 6 to 8 hours. Serve the meat piled onto hoagie rolls. Spoon the juice into small cups for dipping. Cut the sandwiches in half to serve.

Makes 16 servings

Margaret Metz, Countess of Barter and Bride
The Hottie Red Hatters of Coralville, Coralville, Iowa

Beef Barbecue for a Bunch

4   pounds chuck roast
1   (15-ounce) bottle barbecue sauce
1/2   cup mayonnaise
1/2   teaspoon salt
1/4   teaspoon pepper
4   cups shredded cabbage
8   to 10 hamburger buns

In a large pot, cover the chuck roast with water and bring to a boil. Reduce the heat to low and simmer, making sure that water always covers the roast, for about 3 hours, or until you can shred the meat with a fork. Shred the meat and combine with the barbecue sauce. Mix well.

In large mixing bowl combine the mayonnaise, salt, and pepper. Add the cabbage and mix well. Spoon the barbecue over the bottom halves of the buns; top with the cabbage mix and the tops of the buns.

Makes 8 to 10 sandwiches

Gwendolyn Crawford, Queen
Ladie Gone Purple, Victorville, California

Pizza-wiches

A quick mixture to stuff into rolls, then broil.

1   pound ground beef, cooked and drained
    Salt and pepper to taste
2   (8-ounce) packages shredded mozzarella cheese
2   medium onions, ground or finely chopped
1 1/2   tablespoons ripe olives, chopped
1   (10 3/4-ounce) can tomato soup
1   teaspoon garlic salt
1/2   teaspoon oregano
    Italian rolls, buttered

Combine the beef, salt and pepper, cheese, onions, olives, tomato soup, garlic salt, and oregano. Mix well and refrigerate for a few hours before serving. (Will keep one week in the refrigerator or can be frozen up to six months.) Spread the beef mixture on the Italian rolls and broil for 5 to 10 minutes, or until the cheese bubbles.

Makes 15 servings

Joann Walters, Arts and Travel Coordinator
Husker Honeys, Omaha, Nebraska

Bologna Sandwich Spread

1   pound bologna
6   hard-boiled eggs
1   large onion
1   (10-ounce) jar dill pickle relish
1   teaspoon garlic powder
    Salt and pepper to taste
1   cup mayonnaise

Grind the bologna, eggs, and onion in a meat grinder or food processor. Add the relish, garlic powder, and salt and pepper. Stir in the mayonnaise. Spread on bread slices to serve. Refrigerate any leftover spread.

Makes enough for 18 to 24 sandwiches

Evelyn Sinast, Queen Mom
Taft Red Hat Ladies, Taft, Texas

Baked Chicken Sandwiches

2   cups cubed cooked chicken
1   (8-ounce) package cream cheese, softened
2   tablespoons butter, softened
2   tablespoons milk
1   tablespoon grated onion
    Salt and pepper to taste
1   (8-ounce) can crescent roll dough
2   tablespoons butter, softened
    Herb-seasoned bread crumbs
1   (10¾-ounce) can cream of mushroom soup
1   tablespoon chopped pimiento

Preheat the oven to 375°. In a large bowl combine the chicken, cream cheese, butter, milk, onion, and salt and pepper. Mix well. Unroll the crescent roll dough, leaving two sections attached in a rectangular shape. Press the seams together. Spoon 1/2 cup of the chicken mixture into each rectangle. Roll tightly to enclose the chicken filling. Brush with the butter and roll in the bread crumbs. Arrange on a baking sheet and bake for 20 to 30 minutes. Heat the soup, undiluted, and add the pimiento. Pour over the baked sandwiches and serve.

Makes 4 servings

Barbara Giedd, Lady Barb
Brair Patch Hattitudes, Eatonton, Georgia

Honey-Pecan Chicken Salad

This chunky salad is a natural on bread and also good on salad garnished with grapes. The tester also made it with sweet relish, which was another good choice; but the tasters slightly preferred dill relish.

1   cup mayonnaise
1/2   cup dill pickle relish
2   tablespoons minced onion
1   tablespoon honey
1½   tablespoons sugar
1   teaspoon salt
1/4   teaspoon white pepper
3/4   cup chopped celery
3/4   cup coarsely chopped toasted pecans
1½   pounds chopped cooked chicken
      (about 4 cups)

Combine the mayonnaise, relish, onion, honey, sugar, salt, and white pepper in a bowl and mix well. Stir in the celery and pecans. Fold in the chicken. Adjust the seasonings to taste. Chill, covered, in the refrigerator. Serve on crusty French bread rolls with potato chips and carrot sticks.

Makes 6 to 8 servings

Alice Russell, Vice Mum
Sassy Bodacious Ladies, Greeneville, Tennessee

Maryland Crab Cake Sandwich

2   pounds lump crabmeat

2   jumbo eggs, slightly beaten

2   tablespoons butter

1/4 cup minced onion

1   teaspoon Old Bay seasoning
     (or shrimp seasoning, if not available)

16   saltine crackers, crushed finely
     (a rolling pin helps)

1   teaspoon Dijon mustard

2   to 3 heaping tablespoons mayonnaise

1   tablespoon parsley flakes
     Peanut or canola oil for frying

10   hamburger buns
     Mayonnaise
     Shredded lettuce
     Sliced tomato

In a large bowl combine the crabmeat and eggs, tossing gently. In a small skillet heat the butter over medium-high heat and sauté the onion for 5 minutes, or until tender. Stir into the crabmeat mixture. Add the Old Bay, cracker crumbs, mustard, mayonnaise, and parsley flakes. Mix gently but thoroughly. Refrigerate for 1 to 2 hours. When ready to cook, shape the crabmeat mixture into 10 patties. Heat a small amount of the oil in a large frying pan over medium-high heat. Fry the crab cakes, several at a time, for a few minutes on each side until golden. Serve on buns with mayonnaise, lettuce, and tomato.

Makes 10 large crabcakes

Cecile Jantz, Quilting Diva
Queen Anne Red Hat Swingers, Queenstown, Maryland

Crab Salad Rounds

For Crab Hots, spread on English muffins, top with a slice of cheese, and broil until the cheese melts.

1   (12-ounce) package imitation crabmeat,
     flaked

4   bacon strips, cooked and crumbled

2   hard-boiled eggs, chopped

1/3 cup chopped celery

1/3 cup chopped onion

1/4 cup chopped green pepper
     Salt and pepper to taste

1/2 cup shredded cheddar cheese
     Mayonnaise to bind

Combine the crabmeat, bacon, eggs, celery, onion, green pepper, and salt and pepper in a large mixing bowl. Add the shredded cheese last. Add enough mayonnaise to hold the mixture together. Spread on toasted bread or buns, or fill pita pockets.

Makes 2 servings

Elsie Stacy, Just Me . . . El See
Red Hot Red Hat Readers of Decatur, Decatur, Tennessee

Baked Crab Rolls

3   tablespoons butter, softened

4   French rolls, split

1   pound fresh or frozen imitation crabmeat,
     chopped

1   cup shredded cheddar cheese or Monterey
     Jack cheese (I use half of each)

1/3 cup sliced green onions

1/8 teaspoon nutmeg or 1/2 teaspoon dill weed

1/2 cup mayonnaise

3 tablespoons sour cream

1 tablespoon lemon juice

Preheat the oven to 400°. Spread the butter on the rolls. Arrange on a cookie sheet buttered side up and bake for 5 to 7 minutes, or until lightly toasted.

In a bowl combine the crabmeat, cheese, onions, and nutmeg or dill weed. Add the mayonnaise, sour cream, and lemon juice and mix until well blended. Spoon the crabmeat onto the rolls. Top with extra cheese if desired and bake for 5 to 10 minutes, or until the cheese is melted.

Makes 4 servings

Fran Pritchert, Empress of Ebay
Scarlet Sophisticates, Woodbridge, Virginia

Hot Crab Sandwiches

Testers loved this rich, luxurious sandwich, only recommending that the English muffins be toasted first. Keep the whole thing for yourself, or cut into dainty, bite-size pieces for tea or with drinks.

1 (7 1/2-ounce) can crabmeat, drained, picked over, flaked

1/4 cup mayonnaise

1 (3-ounce) package cream cheese, softened

1 egg yolk

1 teaspoon chopped onion

1/4 teaspoon prepared mustard
    Dash of salt

2 tablespoons butter, softened

3 English muffins, halved

In a small bowl combine the crabmeat and mayonnaise. In another bowl beat the cream cheese, egg yolk, onion, mustard, and salt until creamy. Butter the muffin halves. Divide the crab mixture evenly among them. Top with the cheese mixture. Broil for 2 to 3 minutes, or until hot and bubbly.

Makes 3 to 6 servings

Reyes Smith, Queen
Carefree Crimson Court of Coventry, Royal Oak, Michigan

Big Bunch Barbecued Chopped Ham

2 cups chopped celery

1 cup white or cider vinegar

2 cups diced onions

2 teaspoons Worcestershire sauce

1 teaspoon salt

4 cups ketchup

1 cup water

2 teaspoons chili powder

5 pounds chopped ham

Combine the celery, vinegar, onions, Worcestershire sauce, salt, ketchup, water, and chili powder in a large pot. Bring to a simmer over medium heat. Reduce the heat and simmer for 45 minutes. Add the ham and mix well. Simmer another 15 minutes.

Makes enough for 50 sandwiches

Linda Gibb, Founding Queen Mum
Red Hat Roadrunners, Marlinton, West Virginia

Egg Spread

More flavorful and smoother in texture than your average egg spread.

1/2 cup mayonnaise
1 1/2 tablespoons fresh lemon juice
2 teaspoons Dijon mustard
1 tablespoon finely chopped onion
1/2 teaspoon fresh lemon zest
1/2 teaspoon hot pepper sauce
(or to taste)
6 hard-boiled eggs
1 (3-ounce) package low-fat cream cheese, softened
1/2 teaspoon seasoned salt
Pinch of pepper
2 teaspoons chopped fresh dill
1 small can sliced stuffed olives
Dill sprigs

In a blender combine the mayonnaise, lemon juice, mustard, onion, lemon zest, and hot pepper sauce. Add the eggs one at a time. After each egg add some of the cream cheese. Add the salt and pepper. Blend until smooth. Fold in the dill. Chill for at least an hour. Spread on rye bread. Top with the sliced olives and a sprig of dill.

Makes 2 cups

Dorothy Bono, Lady Shelby
Silly Sassy Shelby Sisters, Washington Twp., Michigan

Muffulettas

Bring back memories of New Orleans with this muffuletta. For the most dramatic presentation, choose a big round loaf and slice it into wedges at the table. Gorgeous.

OLIVE SALAD
4 cups pimiento-stuffed olives, drained and chopped
1 cup sliced black olives
1 (14-ounce) can artichoke hearts, drained and chopped
3 celery stalks, finely chopped
2 teaspoons minced garlic
2 carrots, peeled and grated
1/2 cup olive oil
1/4 cup red wine vinegar
1 1/2 teaspoons dried oregano
Dash of pepper

SANDWICH
Sesame seed sandwich buns or round loaf sourdough bread, cut in half horizontally
4 ounces thinly sliced honey ham
4 ounces sliced Genoa salami
4 ounces sliced provolone cheese
4 ounces sliced Swiss cheese
1 1/2 cups olive salad (recipe above)

For the olive salad, combine the olives, artichoke hearts, celery, garlic, carrots, oil, vinegar, oregano, and pepper in a large bowl and

Greaseless Potatoes

After a long day of shopping, my grandmother and I were in a rush to cook supper for Grandpa, and for his part, he was patiently waiting for his meat and fried potatoes. We carefully cut up the potatoes and threw them in the pan to fry. Grandma kept her large bottle of cooking oil under the sink because it was close to the stove. She reached down and grabbed a bottle and poured in the oil. After a few minutes of cooking, I noticed that the potatoes were not browning. I was only twelve years old and didn't know much about cooking, but I knew something was wrong, so I asked "Gram" to come look at them.

"I poured enough oil in there. They should be browning by now," she said and grabbed the bottle again. As she started to pour, I noticed it wasn't oil; it was concentrated degreaser!

"Quick! Wash them off!" she said.

I asked, "Are you sure?"

"Yes," she said, "rinse them off!"

It was a total disaster: there were soapsuds everywhere, even after five minutes of rinsing. At that point, we decided to start over.

That night, Grandpa got his supper just a little later than we had promised. And now Gram keeps her cooking oil in the pantry, instead of under the kitchen sink.

Karen Kersey
Queen Culture Vulture
Diamond Valley Divas
Cushing, Oklahoma

mix well. Cover and chill at least 8 hours. Mixture will keep in the refrigerator for up to one week.

For the sandwich, preheat the oven to 350°. Place the bread on a baking sheet. Layer the ham, salami, and cheeses; then top with the olive salad. Wrap in foil and bake for 20 minutes.

Makes 4 servings

Claudia Huye, Maiden of Memories
GRITS (Girls Raised in the South), Montgomery, Texas

Shrimp Pocket Sandwich

Finally, creative use for frozen fried shrimp. If you like, add fried catfish nuggets, sliced avocado, chopped cilantro—make it your own.

1   (6-ounce) box frozen small fried shrimp
4   pita bread rounds
1   (8-ounce) bottle Thousand Island dressing
1/4   head lettuce, chopped
1   small tomato, diced

Cook the shrimp according to package directions. Cut the pita bread into halves across the middle. Split the pitas to make a pocket. Divide the shrimp among the pita halves and then drizzle with a little dressing. Top with the lettuce and tomato and add a little more dressing.

Makes 8 servings

Trish Brooke, Queen
Sassy But Classy Carolina Girls, Sumter, South Carolina

Sourdough Turkey Sandwich

Like an abbreviated version of a muffuletta.

1   large, round loaf sourdough bread
1   (7.5-ounce) jar marinated artichoke hearts
1/4   cup mayonnaise
1 1/2   pounds thinly sliced smoked turkey breast
6   slices onion jack cheese
    Lettuce, tomatoes, sliced red onion, pepperoncini, pickles

Cut a 4-inch circle out of the top of the loaf of bread. Tear the inside out of the loaf, leaving a 1-inch shell. Place half the artichoke liquid in a small bowl with the mayonnaise and mix well; brush over the inside of the bread bowl. Chop the artichoke hearts and spread on the bottom of the bread bowl. Layer alternate slices of the turkey, cheese, and any of the other sandwich fixings desired: lettuce, tomatoes, onion, pepperoncini, pickles, etc. Replace the top of the bread and press down firmly on top of the sandwich to press ingredients together. Cut into large wedges to serve.

Makes 6 servings

Donna Boyd, Duchess of the Desert
Crazy Daiseys, Palm Desert, California

Hot Brown Sandwich

Named for the Brown Hotel in Louisville, this hot turkey sandwich in a rich sauce is fantastic after Thanksgiving.

5   plus 1 tablespoons butter
1   medium small onion, chopped
1/3   cup all-purpose flour
3   cups milk
1   teaspoon salt
1/8   teaspoon red pepper
4   ounces Velveeta cheese, grated
2   eggs, well beaten
8   slices white bread, toasted
8   1/4-inch thick slices cooked chicken or turkey

Sliced fresh tomatoes

Sliced mushrooms

8   strips bacon, fried

Parmesan cheese

Paprika

Melt 5 tablespoons of the butter in a heavy saucepan over medium heat. Sauté the onion until tender but not brown. Add the flour and stir to make a smooth paste. Add the milk, salt, and red pepper. Stir and cook until thick and smooth. Add the cheese and cook, stirring, until melted. Pour some of the cheese mixture into the beaten eggs, mix well, and pour back into the saucepan. Heat through, but do not boil. Add the remaining 1 tablespoon butter.

To assemble, slice the bread diagonally and place on ovenproof plates. Lay the sliced chicken on the toast and cover with the sauce. Top with 1 or 2 tomato slices, mushroom slices, and a bacon strip. Sprinkle with the Parmesan cheese and paprika. Place under the broiler until the sauce begins to bubble.

Makes 8 servings

Audrey Stover, Queen Old Biddie
Red Hat Hens and Chicks of Lancaster County, Heath
    Springs, South Carolina

Hot Turkey and Gravy for Sandwiches

For its long, slow baking, the turkey mixture can also cooked in a large slow cooker for three hours on high or five hours on low.

1   (14-pound) turkey

1   (10³/4-ounce) can cream of chicken soup

1   (10³/4-ounce) can cream of celery soup

1   (10³/4-ounce) can cheddar cheese soup

1   envelope (¹/3 cup) onion soup mix
    Salt and pepper to taste

Heat the oven to 350°. Roast the turkey in a large roasting pan for about 3¹/2 hours. (Loosely cover with foil after the bird is golden brown.) When the internal temperature reaches 180°, remove from the oven and let the turkey cool, reserving the liquid and drippings. Remove all the meat from the bones. Place the meat in a large roaster.

Preheat the oven to 350°. In a large bowl combine the soups and soup mix with the reserved turkey liquid and drippings. Season with salt and pepper. Pour the soup mixture over the turkey meat. Bake for 3 hours. The turkey and soup mixture can be frozen at this point and defrosted the day before you want to serve it.

Makes enough for about 60 sandwiches

LuAnn Dvorak, Her Royal Majesty Queen Baby
    Cakes
Czech Out the Divas, Montgomery, Minnesota

Magnolia Special

Update a BLT with a slice of fried green tomato, some fresh basil, and fresh mozzarella. Fresh mozzarella is usually sold as a large ball, or as jawbreaker-size balls in liquid. If you can't find it, part-skim mozzarella will do.

2   pounds green tomatoes (about 4 medium), sliced 1/4-inch thick
1/2 cup cornmeal
1   pound bacon, cooked until crisp (reserve 1/3 cup drippings)
1   pound fresh mozzarella, cut into 1/4-inch slices
24 fresh basil leaves, washed and dried
8   slices brioche or good sandwich bread

Preheat the broiler. Coat each slice of tomato on both sides with the cornmeal. Heat the reserved bacon drippings in a large skillet over medium-high heat. Fry the tomato slices in the skillet and cook 5 minutes on each side until golden. Transfer them to a paper-towel-lined plate to drain.

Arrange the bread on a baking sheet. Broil the bread 3 inches from the heat for about 2 minutes, toasting only one side. Make the sandwiches by layering on the untoasted bread sides the mozzarella, basil, tomato slices, and bacon. Top with another bread slice, untoasted side down, and serve.

Makes 4 servings

Diane Seibert, Diva Divina, QM
Divine Divas of the RHS, Lynchburg, Virginia

Italian Hero Sandwich

1   loaf French bread
1/4 cup sour cream
2   tablespoons yellow or Dijon mustard
1/8 teaspoon garlic powder
    Lettuce leaves
8   slices provolone cheese
8   slices bologna
    Tomato slices
8   slices Colby cheese
12 slices hard salami
8   slices Swiss cheese
    Sliced red onion rings

Cut the bread in half horizontally. In a small bowl combine the sour cream, mustard, and garlic powder; spread over the cut surfaces of the bread. Arrange the lettuce on the bottom half of the bread. Layer the provolone cheese, bologna, tomato slices, Colby cheese, salami, Swiss cheese, and onion rings. Cover with the top half of the bread. Cut into 8 serving portions.

Makes 8 servings

Lisa Katai, Queen Mum
Dallas Red Hat Flashes, Murphy, Texas

Connie Summer and Pat Wepprecht showing off
their Red Hat cookies

The Sunday Hat Sisterhood enjoying a day
with lunch and shopping in Aiken, South Carolina

Photo by Kevin Farrington

Photo courtesy of Diana Fuller, Dame Diana

Modoc Red Hot Hatters Marve Handley and Vickie Szutowicz are taking the food seriously

Photo courtesy of Queen Mum Lisa Katai

Dallas Red Hat Flashes Laurie Barnick and Angela Katai having a Pink Hat tea party

Photo courtesy of Chris Oliver of the Seneca Belles

Photo courtesy of Vice Queen Mum Karen Herget

The Tennessee Tootsies at a Women's Day luncheon in Arnold AFB, Tennessee

Purple Teas Erin and Rosemary (right) preparing for a formal tea

Rowdy Red Hat Momma Carol Park Coen making Key lime pie

Photo courtesy of Joyce Hack

One pink hat in a group of red enjoying a lunch on the town

Photo by Kevin Farrington

Photo courtesy of J. Frances Stielper

Rebecca Arnett, Alexix Stielper, and their
mother, Queen J. Frances Stielper at a
convention in Edgewood, Maryland

The Harbour Hatters about to enjoy a time of tea together

RoseAnn Rink, Mary Rose Sulger, and Shirlee Graham—all La Socíete Royale des Femmes aux Chapeaux Rouges—enjoying lunch at Torte Knox on Red Hat Day 2005.

Speedy, the unofficial member of the Red Roses in West Palm Beach, Florida

Rhinestone Rebels of Huntington Beach, California, having fun in the kitchen

Queen of Vice Jennie Helmantoler, Lady Greenthumb Shirley
Branthoover, and Countess Emerald Flasher Donna Strickler all
Fayettvill-Greene Mama Mias making omletes in a bag

Photo by Kevin Farrington

Photo courtesy of Lady Sabine Scanlon

Royal Rubies Lady Ruth and the
Queen Mother of Pearls having tea
at Tea Grannies and Friends

Photo courtesy of Queen Mother Beverly Carruthers

Barbara, Jean, and Maria of the Red Sails chapter on "Preserving Day"

Summer Sandwich

For a true summer pleasure, make this only when you can get homegrown tomatoes and cucumbers. A simple, seasonal joy for yourself or to share with a friend. This sandwich travels very well since there are no ingredients to spoil or make the bread soggy.

1 (8-ounce) package cream cheese, softened
12 slices pumpernickel bread
2 large tomatoes, sliced into 12 slices
2 to 3 avocadoes, sliced (optional)
1 large cucumber, sliced
   Guacamole
1 (6-ounce) container alfalfa sprouts
   Salt and pepper to taste (optional)

Spread the cream cheese on the bread slices. To 6 slices of bread each sandwich add 2 tomato slices, avocado, cucumber slices, and alfalfa sprouts. Spread some guacamole on the remaining—6 slices of bread. Season with salt and pepper if desired and then combine to make sandwiches.

Makes 6 sandwiches

Note: The sandwich is just as delicious without the avocado as it is with it.

Theresa Willoughby, Royal Member
Red Hat Merry Makers, Apex, North Carolina

Seafood Rangoon

A great way to stretch a single cup of seafood. Add a little grated fresh ginger to the mixture for extra zing.

Use defrosted seafood or chopped leftover seafood instead, if you have it on hand.

1 (8-ounce) package cream cheese, softened
2 to 3 green onions, sliced
1 (7-ounce) can crabmeat or baby shrimp, drained
1 teaspoon garlic powder
1 teaspoon black pepper
1 teaspoon Old Bay seasoning (optional)
1 teaspoon lemon juice or lemon pepper
   Peanut oil
1 (16-ounce) package wonton wrappers

Combine the cream cheese, onions, seafood, garlic powder, pepper, Old Bay, and lemon juice in a bowl. Beat with an electric mixer until well-blended and fluffy. Heat a skillet over a medium-high to high heat while you make the wontons. Put in a little oil to just cover the bottom. Lay out several of the wonton wrappers on a work surface. Moisten the edges of the wrappers with water. (This will help seal them once they are filled.) Place a scant teaspoon of filling in the center of each wrapper. Bring the two opposite corners together and press lightly with your fingers to seal. Place the wontons in the oil and sauté until browned on one side. Turn and cook the other side. Drain on paper towels.

Makes 45 to 50

Patti Gallagher, Queen Ritzy Glitzy Patti–FQM
Divas of Disorder (formerly Ruby Begonias), San Diego, California

Easy Ham Tortillas

2   (8-ounce) packages cream cheese, softened
1/4 cup each dill and sweet relish
2   tablespoons dry chives
1   tablespoon paprika
18 (6-inch) flour tortillas
18 thin slices ham

Mix the cream cheese, relishes, chives, and paprika together. Spread about 1 tablespoonful on each tortilla. Layer each tortilla with 1 ham slice, more cream cheese spread, another ham slice, more cream cheese spread, and finally another tortilla. This should make nine tortilla sandwiches. Using a pizza slicer, cut each tortilla into four pie-shape wedges.

Makes 36 pieces

TJ Chapman, Sister Fixer Upper
Sassy Sisters of Branson, Missouri, Branson, Missouri

Monte Cristo Sandwiches

3   large eggs
1/3 cup milk
4   tablespoons butter, softened
1   teaspoon prepared mustard
12 slices white bread
12 to 14 ounces shaved or sliced cooked ham
12 to 14 ounces shaved or sliced cooked turkey
12 slices Swiss, Cheddar, or American cheese

Preheat the oven to 425°. Beat together the eggs and milk. Blend the butter and mustard

together and spread on one side of each bread slice. Layer the ham, turkey, and cheese on half of the bread slices. Top with a second piece of bread, buttered side down.

Dip each sandwich in the egg mixture, and brown well on both sides on a lightly buttered griddle or large skillet on medium-high heat. Place on a baking sheet, and bake for 8 to 10 minutes.

Makes 6 servings

Jodi Guelzow, Princess Jodi—Lady of Likeness's
Rowdy Red Hat Mamas, Circle Pines, Minnesota

Chilled Vegetable Pizza

You've had it as an appetizer—what's to stop you from serving it at dinner?

2   (8-ounce) cans refrigerator crescent rolls
2   (8-ounce) packages cream cheese
3   tablespoons mayonnaise
1/4 teaspoon garlic powder
1/2 teaspoon dried basil (optional)
4   to 5 cups chopped fresh veggies: tomatoes, broccoli, onion, celery, mushrooms, cauliflower
1   cup salad croutons
1/2 cup Parmasan cheese (optional)

Preheat the oven to 350°. Unwrap and press the crescent rolls onto a lightly greased baking sheet, forming a small rolled edge. Bake for 10 to 12 minutes, or until lightly browned. Cool. Combine the cream cheese, mayonnaise, garlic powder, and basil. Spread this mixture evenly over the entire baked crust. Spread the chopped veggies over the cream cheese mixture. Top off with the croutons and Parmesan cheese, if using. Can be made ahead, wrapped, and refrigerated.

Makes 6 to 8 servings

Carol Park-Coen, Lady Carol-Countess of Conveance
Rowdy Red Hat Mamas of NW Wisconsin, Luck, Wisconsin

Asian-Style Lettuce Wraps

Lettuce stands in for bread here. Lots of flavor in an unusual wrap.

1   medium onion, finely chopped
1   teaspoon minced garlic
1/2 pound ground pork
1/2 pound ground veal
1   teaspoon soy sauce
1   tablespoon oyster sauce
2 1/2 cups bean sprouts
8   large lettuce leaves
1   tablespoon sesame seeds, toasted

In a large skillet over medium-high heat, sauté the onion, garlic, pork, and veal until browned, breaking up the large pieces. Stir in the soy sauce and oyster sauce. Cook uncovered for 5 minutes. Stir in the bean sprouts just before serving. Divide the meat among the lettuce leaves and sprinkle with the sesame seeds. Roll up and enjoy. One serving is two wraps.

Makes 4 servings

Kitty Botgia, Lady of the Palms
Sassy Sophistihats, Westtown, New York

Minnesota "Uff da" Tacos

Uff da is Norwegian for "ouch," "oops," "good grief." The fried circles are like tostadas and each person piles on goodies.

1   pound ground beef
1   (1.25-ounce) package taco seasoning mix
1   (16-ounce) loaf frozen bread dough, thawed

TOPPINGS

1/2 head lettuce, shredded
2   tomatoes, chopped
2   cups shredded cheese
1/4 cup chopped onions
1/2 cup sliced olives
1   (8-ounce) container sour cream
1   (8-ounce) bottle taco sauce

Brown the ground beef in a skillet over medium heat and drain. Add the taco seasoning mix and prepare according to package directions.

Cut the bread dough into 8 to 10 pieces and stretch each piece into a thin circular shape. Deep-fry the dough in vegetable oil until golden brown on both sides and the dough is done. Drain on paper towels. Top with spoonfuls of the meat mixture. Add the toppings you like.

Makes 8 to 10 servings

Jeannie Thorson, Queen
Sassy Sandhill Sweeties, Fertile, Minnesota

Beef and Bean Wraps

1   (15-ounce) can pinto beans
2   teaspoons chili powder
1   garlic clove, chopped
1   pound ground round
    Salt and pepper to taste
2   medium-size tomatoes, chopped
2   cups chopped lettuce
    Juice of half a lemon
1   cup grated mild cheddar cheese
1   small onion
6   to 8 flour tortillas

Mix the pinto beans, chili powder, and garlic in a pan with 1/2 cup water. Bring to a boil and simmer for 2 to 3 minutes, or until the beans cook down. Stir frequently. Brown the beef in a skillet. Drain the excess oil. Mix the tomatoes and lettuce in a bowl. Squeeze the lemon juice over the mixture. Wrap the tortillas in a clean kitchen towel and microwave until warm, about 30 seconds. Place each tortilla on a plate.

Line up the beans, beef, and lettuce mixtures. Have the cheese and onion in small bowls. Let each person layer the beans, beef, lettuce, cheese, and onion on a tortilla. Wrap the tortilla around the mixture.

Makes 6 to 8 servings

Betty Thomason, Lady Hyacinth
Winters Blizzards Red Hat Babes, Winters, Texas

Black Bean Pitas with Avocado Salsa

Chipotle peppers in adobo sauce are usually packed in a small can and are available at large supermarkets.

AVOCADO SALSA
1   avocado, pitted, peeled and diced
1 1/2 cups diced plum tomatoes
1/2   cup chopped green onion
2   tablespoons lime juice
2   tablespoons chopped fresh cilantro
1/2   teaspoon salt
1/2   teaspoon pepper
1/2   teaspoon ground cumin

FILLING
1   tablespoon olive oil
1   medium onion, chopped
1   garlic clove, crushed
1/2   teaspoon cumin
1   (16-ounce) can black beans, drained
1/4   teaspoon salt
1/4   cup mayonnaise
1   teaspoon chopped chipotle peppers in adobo sauce
4   pita rounds, cut into halves
1   cup chopped iceberg lettuce

For the avocado salsa, combine the avocado, tomatoes, onion, lime juice, cilantro, salt, pepper, and cumin in a medium bowl and mix well.

For the filling, heat the oil in a medium skillet over medium heat. Add the onion and cook for 2 minutes. Add the garlic and cumin and cook, stirring, for 1 minute. Add the beans and salt. Continue to cook until heated through, about 5 minutes. Lightly mash the mixture.

To assemble, combine the mayonnaise and chipotle peppers in a small bowl. Spread the mayonnaise mixture on the inside of each pita half. Spoon the bean mixture lightly into the pita about halfway. Fill with the chopped lettuce and top with the avocado salsa.

Makes 4 servings

Diane Seibert, Diva Divina, QM
Divine Divas of the RHS, Lynchburg, Virginia

Fish Tacos

A tester noted, "I didn't expect to like this, but it was delicious."

1/2 head green cabbage, shredded
1   bunch cilantro, chopped
1   medium onion, diced
3/4 cup mayonnaise
1/2 cup medium salsa
3   garlic cloves, minced
3/4 cup seasoned fish fry seasoning
2/3 cup plain dry bread crumbs
     Peanut oil
2   pounds any fish (cod fillets, halibut, shrimp, shark)

12   corn tortillas
     Mild to medium salsa

Combine the cabbage, cilantro, and onion in a bowl. In a separate bowl combine the mayonnaise, salsa, and garlic and mix well. Combine the fish fry seasoning and bread crumbs in a plastic bag. Heat the oil in a large skillet or deep fryer. Cut the fish into approximately 4 x 1-inch pieces. Toss the fish in the breadcrumb mixture. Fry the fish for 4 to 5 minutes, or until cooked through. Heat the corn tortillas in the microwave or wrapped in foil in a warm oven.

To assemble the tacos, place 1 piece of fish in a corn tortilla. Spoon 1 to 2 tablespoons sauce on the fish and top with the cabbage mixture. Top with additional salsa if desired. Repeat for the remaining fish pieces.

Makes 12 tacos, serving 2 to 3

Jeri Martin, Queen
Modoc Red Hot Hatters, Alturas, California

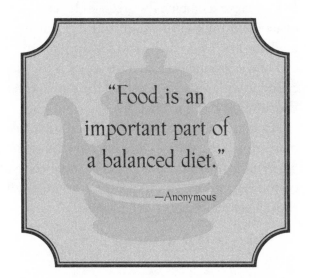

"Food is an important part of a balanced diet."

—Anonymous

Microwave Green Chile Enchiladas

Green chile sauce is sometimes labeled "salsa verde." If you prefer to make just two or three at one time, you can store green chile sauce in a jar and will keep in refrigerator for about a week.

1   pound ground beef
1   (1¼ ounce) package taco seasoning
2   cups shredded mozzarella cheese, divided
1   (16-ounce) can green chile sauce
1   (12-ounce) can evaporated milk
12 flour tortillas

Brown the ground beef in a large skillet until cooked through; drain. Add the taco seasoning and prepare according to the directions on the package. Add about ½ cup cheese to the mixture and cook until all the liquid is absorbed. Remove from the heat and cover to keep warm. In a saucepan combine the green chile sauce and evaporated milk until well blended. Heat over medium-low heat until warm. Spread about ¼ cup of the ground beef mixture on each tortilla. Sprinkle with some cheese. Fold the tortilla over the filling and roll to enclose.

Arrange the enchiladas on a microwaveable plate. Top each with several tablespoons of the green chile mixture. Sprinkle some more cheese on top. Microwave for about 1 to 2 minutes until the cheese melts. Serve immediately.

Makes up to 12 servings

Janie Bush, Lady of Leisure
Classie Lassies, Chivington, Colorado

Real Green Chile Enchiladas

4   tablespoons butter
¼   cup all-purpose flour
2   cups chicken broth
1   cup sour cream, plus extra for tortillas
5   (4 ounce) cans green chiles
¼   cup chopped green onions
    Flour tortillas
1   (16-ounce) package shredded cheddar cheese
1   (16-ounce) package shredded Monterey Jack cheese

For the sauce, melt the butter in a skillet or saucepan over medium-low heat and stir in the flour, mixing well. Stir in the chicken broth and simmer, stirring, until thick and smooth. Stir in 1 cup sour cream, the green chiles, and green onions.

Preheat the oven to 350°. Warm the flour tortillas, and divide the cheeses among them. Spread each tortilla with a little sour cream. Fold one side of the tortilla over the filling and roll to enclose. Arrange the tortillas folded side down in 13 x 9-inch baking dish. Spoon the green chile sauce over the enchiladas until all are covered. Bake for 25 to 30 minutes.

Makes 6 servings

Leah Stevens, Princess of Chocolate
Alizarin Czarinas, Davie, Florida

Almond Spinach Pizza

PIZZA CRUST

1   (1/4-ounce) package active dry yeast
1   cup warm water
13/4 plus 3/4 cups all-purpose flour (or more)
1   tablespoon vegetable oil
1   tablespoon sugar
1   teaspoon salt
1   egg, room temperature

TOPPINGS

1   (8-ounce) package feta cheese, crumbled
1   (10-ounce) bag fresh spinach, cooked
1   cup grated cheddar cheese
1   (8-ounce) package shredded mozzarella cheese
1   sliced almonds

For the crust, dissolve the yeast in the warm water, and add 13/4 cups flour (or enough to make a sticky dough) and mix well. Add the oil, sugar, salt, and egg; mix well. Add the remaining 3/4 cup flour (or enough to make a stiff dough) and mix well. Turn it out on a floured surface and knead in more flour until no longer sticky. Set it aside in a greased bowl to rise for about 1 hour. Punch down, roll out, and press the dough into two lightly greased pizza pans.

Preheat the oven to 450°. Divide the feta, spinach, cheddar cheese, mozzarella cheese, and almonds between the two crusts. Bake the pizzas for about 15 minutes, or until the cheese is melted and golden.

Makes 2 pizzas

Karen White, Queen Mum
Santo's Red Hats, The Villages, Florida

Upside-Down Pizza

1   pound sweet Italian sausage
1   pound ground round
1   (6 to 8-ounce) can mushroom stems and
    pieces
1   cup chopped bell pepper
1   (8-ounce) can tomato sauce
1/2 cup water
1   (1.2-ounce) package spaghetti sauce mix
2   cups shredded mozzarella cheese
1   cup biscuit mix
1   cup milk
2   eggs

Cook the Italian sausage in a large saucepan over medium heat until cooked through. Cut into rounds. In a medium skillet over medium heat, sauté the ground beef, mushrooms, and bell pepper. Cook until the beef is browned and crumbly. In a saucepan over medium heat, combine the tomato sauce, water, and spaghetti sauce mix. Simmer for 5 to 10 minutes. Add the Italian sausage and ground beef and mix well. Preheat the oven to 400°. Spoon the mixture into a greased 13 x 9-inch pan. Sprinkle the cheese over the meat mixture. In a bowl combine the biscuit mix, milk, and eggs. Pour over the cheese. Bake for 25 minutes, or until the biscuit mixture is set.

Makes 8 servings

Judy Kroesen, Queen Mum
Dames of Whinin' Roses, Lomita, California

Oops!

When Hurricane Agnes came through the Pocono Mountains in Pennsylvania in 1972, I was working at a resort in the Poconos. This particular resort was about one mile from the Pocono Racetrack. Because of damage from the hurricane, there were no food suppliers or grocery stores open in the area. Our available items on the menu were dwindling quickly.

Because we were so close to the racetrack, the drivers and their crews would come to our restaurant for lunch and dinner. I was waiting on Al and Bobby Unser, Mario Andretti, and members of their crews. They had ordered the last available cheeseburger platters. I brought everyone's plate out on a very large tray, sat the tray down on another table, took off the first platter, and—CRASH!—the rest of the platters went clattering to the floor! Everyone's eyes got really big, and I was soooooo embarrassed.

I think everyone had peanut butter and jelly sandwiches—on the house—for lunch that day!

Sue Stein
Hysterian
Hen–der–Hatters
Hendersonville, Tennessee

Quick Bubble Pizza

2   (10-count) cans refrigerated biscuits
1   pound ground beef
1   (15-ounce) can or jar pizza sauce
    Pizza toppings of your choice: sliced bell pepper, pepperoncini, mushrooms, pineapple, chopped ham, olives
1   (8-ounce) package shredded mozzarella cheese

Preheat the oven to 350°. Cut the biscuits in quarters and press into the bottom of a greased 13 x 9-inch pan. Brown the ground beef in a skillet over medium heat until no longer pink. Drain and add the pizza sauce. Spread over the biscuits. Bake for 20 minutes. Remove from the oven and top with your selection of toppings. Spread the cheese over the whole pizza. Bake for 10 minutes longer.

Makes 12 pieces

Mary Flanery, Queen
Stony Mermaids, Shelby, Michigan

Deep-Dish Broccoli Pizza

Not just broccoli, but all sorts of delightful goodies on a wholesome crust.

DOUGH

1   (1/4-ounce) package active dry yeast
3   cups warm water (105°)
4 1/2   teaspoons olive oil
1/4   cup rye flour
8   to 9 cups all-purpose flour
2   teaspoons salt

FILLING

8   sweet Italian sausages, casing removed
2   cups sliced fresh mushrooms
1/3   cup dry white wine
2   cups ricotta cheese
2   eggs
    Salt and pepper to taste
    Olive oil for greasing pans
    Cornmeal for pans
1 1/2   cups tomato sauce
2   bunches broccoli, cooked and drained
3   red bell peppers, roasted, skinned, seeded, and cut into strips
4 1/2   cups shredded mozzarella cheese
1   egg, beaten with water

For the dough, dissolve the yeast in the warm water in a large bowl. Stir in the oil. Combine the flours with the salt. Gradually add the flour mixture to the yeast mixture and slowly stir to make a moderately stiff dough. Cover and let rise 2 hours. Punch down and let rest for 10 minutes.

For the filling, brown the sausage in a skillet over medium-high heat. Transfer the sausage to a small bowl. Add the mushrooms and wine to the skillet. Cook gently to reduce the wine. Drain and set the mushrooms aside.

In a small bowl combine the ricotta cheese with the eggs and salt and pepper.

Preheat the oven to 400°. To assemble the pizza, brush a (14-inch) deep-dish pizza pan or two (10-inch) cake pans lightly with olive oil and dust with the cornmeal. Roll two-thirds of the dough to fit the bottom and sides of the selected pans. Fit the dough into the pans, overlapping the edges. Spread the tomato sauce over the dough. Layer the sausage, mushrooms, broccoli, roasted red peppers, ricotta cheese mixture, and mozzarella in any order to make a colorful presentation when sliced. Roll the remaining dough to make the top crust. Fit to the top of the pizza and fold the overhanging bottom crust up and over. Crimp to form a thick rim. Brush the top of the pizza with slightly beaten egg. Bake for 45 to 50 minutes. Remove from the oven and let stand 15 to 30 minutes to firm up. Turn out the pizza onto a cutting board and cut into wedges.

Makes 8 servings

Louise Carlotto, Contessa Cannoli
The Ladybugs RHS, Orwell, Vermont

Crazy Crust Pizza

A non-yeast crust whips up easily in a blender or mixer.

1   cup self-rising flour
1   teaspoon salt
1   teaspoon oregano
    Black pepper to taste
2   eggs
2/3 cup milk
1   cup cooked ground beef
    (or sausage)
1/4 cup chopped onion
6   ounces sliced fresh mushrooms
1   cup pizza sauce
1   cup shredded mozzarella cheese

Preheat the oven to 450°. Lightly grease and dust with flour a round 10-inch pizza pan. Combine the flour, salt, oregano, pepper, eggs, and milk; mix until smooth. Pour the batter into the pan and spread evenly to cover the pan. Arrange the beef, onion, and mushrooms on top. Bake on a low rack of the oven for 15 minutes, or until brown. Drizzle with the pizza sauce and sprinkle with the cheese. Return to the oven for 10 to 15 minutes.

Makes 12 to 14 servings

Linda Enrico, Lady Sewsalot
Red Hot Taters, Boise, Idaho

Tomato and Gorgonzola Pizza

Instead of a pizza shell, use refrigerated pizza dough to form your own crust.

1   (10-ounce) thin-crust pizza shell
1   tablespoon olive oil
6   plum tomatoes, thinly sliced
1   small red onion, thinly sliced and separated into rings
4   ounces Gorgonzola cheese, crumbled
1/4 cup sliced fresh basil

Preheat the oven to 425°. Put the pizza shell on a lightly greased baking sheet and spread with the oil. Top with tomatoes, onion, cheese, and basil. Bake for 8 to 9 minutes, or until the cheese melts. Cut into wedges and serve immediately.

Makes 3 to 4 servings

Charlene Chambers, Diva in the Kitchen
Scarlet O'Bearas, Ormond Beach, Florida

Chicken Fajita Pizza

1   tablespoon vegetable oil
2   chicken breasts, boned and cut into strips
1   garlic clove, minced
1/2 teaspoon chili powder
1/2 teaspoon salt
1   cup thinly sliced onion
1   cup thinly sliced bell pepper
1   (13-ounce) can refrigerated pizza dough
1/2 cup mild picante sauce
2   cups shredded Monterey Jack cheese

Heat the oil over medium-high heat in a skillet until hot. Add the chicken and stir fry until lightly brown. Stir in the garlic, chili powder, and salt. Add the onion and bell pepper. Stir fry an additional 2 minutes. Heat the oven to

425°. Unroll the pizza dough and fit it into a lightly greased 10 to 12-inch pizza pan. Bake for 8 to 10 minutes (dough won't be cooked through). Remove from the oven and top with the chicken mixture. Spoon the picante sauce over all. Sprinkle with the cheese. Bake 15 to 20 minutes, or until the crust is golden brown.

Makes 6 to 8 servings

Sharon Hutchison, Scrapbooker
Racy Reds, Kaufman, Texas

Malaysian Pizza

1/4   cup firmly packed brown sugar
3/4   cup rice wine or white vinegar
1/4   cup soy sauce
3   tablespoons water
1/2   cup peanut butter
1   tablespoon finely chopped fresh ginger
3/4   teaspoon crushed red pepper
4   garlic cloves, crushed
3   tablespoons lime juice
1/2   pound cooked, skinned, cut up chicken
1   (12-inch) pizza shell
3/4   cup shredded mozzarella cheese
1/4   cup chopped scallions
1/2   cup shredded carrots
1/3   cup finely chopped peanuts
1/3   cup finely chopped cilantro (optional)

Preheat the oven to 350°. In a saucepan combine the sugar, vinegar, soy sauce, water, peanut butter, ginger, red pepper, garlic, and lime juice. Cook over medium heat, stirring frequently, until slightly thickened. Stir in the chicken. Spread the sauce over the pizza shell. Sprinkle the cheese on top and bake for 25 minutes. Cool for 5 minutes. Sprinkle the scallions, carrots, peanuts, and cilantro over the pizza before serving.

Makes 4 to 6 servings

Kevann Lamkin, Queen Of Crop
Red Hattitudes, Fontana, California

Portobello Pizza

Giant portobello mushroom caps serve as the "crust" and are filled with cheese, tomatoes, and pepperoni. Serve with a tossed green salad for lunch.

4   portobello mushrooms, about 4 inches in diameter
1 1/4 plus 1/4 cups (about 6 ounces) grated Tex-Mex cheese mixture
6   ounces pepperoni, sliced very thin
4   plum tomatoes, sliced very thin

Remove the stems and scrape the gills from the portobello mushrooms. Peel the top, if you like. Preheat the oven to 350°. Place the mushrooms in an ovenproof baking dish, tops down. Layer 1/4 cup of the cheese mixture, then the pepperoni, then the tomatoes and finally the remaining 1 1/4 cups cheese. Bake for 20 minutes, or until the cheese is bubbly and the mushrooms are tender.

Makes 4 servings

Linda Cummings, Vice Mother
Red Hat'll Do Ya, Halifax, Nova Scotia, Canada

Four Favorites Pizza

If you have a bread machine, chewy, delicious homemade pizza crust is a snap.

CRUST

1	cup plus 2 tablespoons water
2	tablespoons olive oil or vegetable oil
3	cups bread flour
1	teaspoon sugar
1	teaspoon salt

TOPPINGS

1	(14-ounce) can chopped Italian-style tomatoes, drained
2	cups shredded mozzarella cheese
1/2	teaspoon Italian seasoning (or to taste)
1/2	teaspoon fennel seed (or to taste)
1	pound sweet Italian sausage, casings removed, cooked, crumbled
1	(13-ounce) can or jar artichoke hearts, drained, sliced
	Proscuitto, thinly sliced
1	(2-ounce) can sliced black olives
2	to 3 ounces shredded Parmesan cheese

For the crust, combine the water, oil, flour, sugar, and salt in a bread machine in the order listed. Select the white dough cycle. When the dough has finished, press the dough with oiled hands into a greased 10 to 12-inch pizza pan and spread evenly. Preheat the oven to 400°.

For the toppings, layer the tomatoes, mozzarella, Italian seasoning, fennel, sausage, artichoke hearts, prosciutto, and olives. Finish with a light sprinkle of the shredded Parmesan cheese. Bake for 18 to 20 minutes.

Makes 4 servings

Marka Gottlieb, Queen Mother
Grand Girls Gone Wild, Surprise, Arizona

Fresh Tomato Pizza with Pesto

1	(16-ounce) prebaked Italian bread or pizza shell
1/2	cup basil pesto
3	medium ripe tomatoes, thinly sliced
	Freshly ground black pepper to taste
1	(2-ounce) can sliced, pitted, ripe olives, drained
1	(8-ounce) package (2 cups) shredded Monterey Jack or mozzarella cheese

Preheat the oven to 425°. Place the pizza shell on a large pizza pan or baking dish. Spread the pesto evenly over the pizza shell. Arrange the tomato slices on top. Season with the pepper. Sprinkle the olives and cheese on top. Bake for 10 to 15 minutes, or until the cheese melts and the tomatoes are warm. Cut into wedges.

Makes 4 servings

Maria D. Oehler, Princess SS Maria
Sierra Sirens, Grass Valley, California

Grilled Pizza Margherita

An Italian classic. Good quality prepared pasta sauce stands in for pizza sauce, and the grilled taste is just terrific.

1   (12-inch) prebaked pizza crust
1   cup tomato and basil pasta sauce
    Sliced pepperoni
4   ounces thinly sliced mozzarella cheese
    Extra-virgin olive oil
    Chopped fresh basil leaves

Preheat the grill to medium. Place the pizza crust on the grill and spread the sauce evenly over the pizza crust. Layer the pepperoni slices on top and then the cheese. Close the cover and grill, rotating occasionally, for 10 minutes, or until the sauce is hot and the cheese is melted. Drizzle the olive oil over the pizza and sprinkle the basil on top. Serve immediately.

Makes 4 servings

Sallie Hudson, Queen Mother/Lady of the Lake
Dames of the Catawba, Winnsboro, South Carolina

Tomato-Onion Phyllo Pizza

Cut this pizza into smaller squares to serve as an appetizer.

5   tablespoons melted butter
7   sheets phyllo dough
1/2 cup grated Romano or Parmesan cheese
1   cup shredded mozzarella cheese
1   cup thinly sliced onion
7   to 9 plum tomatoes
1   teaspoon fresh oregano leaves or 1/2
    teaspoon dried oregano
    Salt and pepper to taste

Brush a 15 x 10-inch a jelly-roll pan with some of the melted butter. Lay a sheet of phyllo dough in the pan. (Keep the remaining dough covered with waxed paper or a damp paper towel to prevent drying out while layering.) Brush the dough with butter and sprinkle the Romano cheese on top. Repeat the layers five more times, folding in the edges to fit.

Preheat the oven to 375°. Brush the top layer with butter and sprinkle the mozzarella cheese. Arrange the onion and tomatoes over the cheese layer. Sprinkle the oregano, salt, and pepper and any remaining Romano cheese over the pizza. Bake for 20 to 25 minutes, or until the edges are golden in color.

Makes 2 to 4 servings

Paula Shaffer, The Royal Hynie
Scarlett Ladies of Littleton, Littleton, Colorado

Stromboli

Like a pizza, but with more of the chewy crust you love, and the filling is on the inside.

CRUST
1   (1/4-ounce) package active dry yeast
1/4   cup warm water
1/2   cup (1 stick) butter, melted
1   cup milk
2   tablespoons sugar
1   tablespoon salt
3   eggs, beaten
4 1/2   to 5 cups all-purpose flour

FILLING
2   cups shredded mozzarella cheese
1   pound sliced boiled ham or luncheon meat
1   (8-ounce) package sliced pepperoni
1   green bell pepper, sliced
1   onion, sliced
1   (8-ounce) package sliced mushrooms

Combine the dry yeast and the warm water; let stand for a few minutes and then stir. Add the melted butter and milk and mix well. Stir in the sugar, salt, and eggs. Add the flour. Beat into a soft dough. Knead until smooth and elastic in texture. Grease the sides and bottom of a very large mixing bowl, place the dough in the bowl, and let it rise until doubled in size.

Preheat the oven to 425°. Divide the dough into eight pieces and press each into a 4 to 6-inch circle. Cover half of the dough circle with the cheese, ham, pepperoni, bell pepper, onion, and mushrooms. Fold the dough over to enclose the filling. Press the edges together to seal. Bake for 15 minutes, or until golden brown. (The stromboli can be wrapped in foil before baking and frozen.)

Makes 8 servings

Jennie Helmantoler, Vice Queen Mama
Fayette-Greene Mama Mias, Carmichaels, Pennsylvania

Cocktail Pizzas

1   pound hot sausage
1   pound ground beef
1   cup chopped onion
2   cups grated sharp cheddar cheese
1 1/2   teaspoons oregano
1   teaspoon salt
1   (12-ounce) can tomato paste
3/4   cup water
4   to 5 (8-count) cans flaky biscuits
1/2   cup Parmesan cheese

Preheat the oven to 350°. Brown the sausage, beef, and onion in a skillet over medium-high heat and drain. Add the cheddar cheese, oregano, salt, tomato paste, and water to the sausage mixture and mix well. Separate the biscuits and press each into a mini crust on a lightly greased baking sheet. Top with the meat mixture and sprinkle with the Parmesan cheese. Bake for 15 minutes.

Makes 32 to 40 cocktail pizzas

Becky Keith, Communicator
Rolesville Red Hat Jewels, Rolesville, North Carolina

Stir-and-Roll Pizza Dough

Nothing beats homemade pizza dough. This one is simpler than average because it's made with baking powder rather than yeast.

2   cups all-purpose flour
2   teaspoons baking powder
1   teaspoon salt
2/3 cup milk
1/4 cup plus 2 tablespoons
    vegetable oil

Combine the flour, baking powder, and salt in a bowl and mix well. Add the milk and 1/4 cup oil and mix until combined. Form the dough into a ball and knead a few times. Divide the dough in half. On a floured surface roll each half into a 13-inch circle. Brush with the remaining 2 tablespoons oil. The dough is ready to top and bake, or prebake for 15 minutes.

Makes two 10 to 15-inch pizza shells

Nonie Weiland, Queen of Fishing
Purple Minded Sisters, Arlington, South Dakota

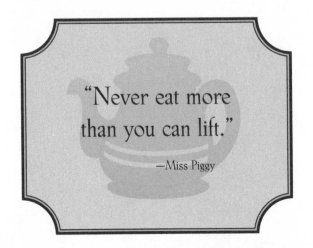

"Never eat more than you can lift."

—Miss Piggy

White Pizza

If you like, add a layer of steamed broccoli or cauliflower and thinly sliced green bell pepper before baking.

1   (15-inch) pizza crust
1   (15-ounce) container light ricotta cheese
1   cup shredded part-skim mozzarella cheese
1/2 cup shredded Romano cheese
1   tablespoon lemon juice
    Dash of cayenne pepper
1/2 teaspoon oregano
1   teaspoon minced fresh garlic
1/2 teaspoon freshly ground black pepper
3/4 cup sliced green onions
6   mushrooms, thinly sliced
8   to 10 ounces turkey sausage, cooked and drained

Preheat the oven to 450°. Fit the dough on a large greased pizza pan. In a bowl combine the ricotta and shredded cheeses. Add the lemon juice, cayenne, oregano, garlic, and black pepper and mix well. Spread the cheese mixture over the dough to within 1/2 inch of the edge. Distribute the green onions, mushroom slices, and turkey sausage evenly over the top. Bake for 15 to 20 minutes, or until the cheese is golden.

Makes 4 servings

Alisa Zimmerman, Lady in Pink
Colonie Red Hatters, Nassau, New York

Rice Pizza

*When you make rice, double the batch so you'll have
enough leftover to make this unusual meal.*

CRUST

3   cups cooked rice

2   beaten eggs

1   cup shredded mozzarella cheese

TOPPING

2   (8-ounce) cans tomato sauce

1/2   teaspoon oregano

1/2   teaspoon basil

1/2   teaspoon salt

1/4   to 1/2 teaspoon sugar

1   (4-ounce) package shredded mozzarella
cheese

3   ounces (6 tablespoons) grated Parmesan
cheese

Sliced or chopped cooked meat
(Italian sausage or ground beef)

Preheat the oven to 425°. For the crust, combine
the rice, eggs, and cheese in a bowl and mix well.
Press firmly into a 12-inch, greased, pizza pan. Bake
for 20 minutes.

For the topping, combine in a bowl the
tomato sauce, oregano, basil, salt, and sugar.
Spread the sauce over the baked rice crust. Top
with the cheeses and then the meat. Bake for
10 minutes longer.

Makes 2 to 3 servings

Roseann Hovey, Topaz
Red Hat Angels, Atkins, Iowa

TEN

‑❧ Big Deal Meals ❧‑

MEATS, FISH & POULTRY

"Hearty," "filling," "satisfying"…these are great words to use in describing the recipes in this section. These are the substantial dishes that have been said to "put some meat on your bones" or "hair on your chest." (Heaven forbid!) Put another way, these are the recipes that we pull out when we want to feed people in a way that will really satisfy their appetites—as well as tell them how much we care for them. While it is true that snacks and little delicacies can be very enjoyable, everyone appreciates a "real, home-cooked meal" at least once in a while.

When we were raising families, most of us put quite a bit of effort into preparing nurturing fare for our loved ones. Now that we have entered a different stage of life, we may cook such things less often. But, among us Red Hatters, we have pooled our caches of the best of these "substantial" dishes to share with others. That's because there are still times when we enjoy dazzling our families of even our chapterettes with a display of skill and love.

Grilled Chicken with White BBQ Sauce

2   cups vegetable oil
1   cup cider vinegar
3   tablespoons salt
1   teaspoon pepper
1   egg
1   teaspoon poultry seasoning
6   (8-ounce) boneless, skinless chicken breasts

Combine the oil, vinegar, salt, pepper, egg, and seasoning in a blender and process until smooth and thick. (The sauce can be refrigerated for at least a month.) Put the chicken in a zip-top bag. Pour enough sauce over the chicken to cover and marinate in the refrigerator at least 2 to 3 hours (overnight is best). Grill the chicken. Heat the remaining sauce in a saucepan over high heat for 5 minutes and serve as a dipping sauce.

Makes 6 servings

Dorothy Romanczuk, Queen Mum
Red Hot Zingers, Hamburg, New York

Big Pig Gig

Having a great big bash? A roast suckling pig is guaranteed to wow them. Testers rated this "fantastic" and "wonderful." Measure your oven and consult a butcher first to determine the size; often a 20-pound pig is the smallest available. Have the butcher or even the slaughterhouse put the wood block into the pig's mouth.

18   to 20-pound pig
     salt
1   pound bulk pork sausage
1   cup chopped celery
1/2 cup chopped onion
8   cups bread crumbs
1   tablespoon salt
1   teaspoon pepper
2   teaspoons sage
1/2 cup firmly packed brown sugar
1/2 cup honey
1   teaspoon lemon juice
     Small red apple, cherry tomatoes, fresh parsley and pineapple rings for garnish

Wash the pig all over, inside and out, and then dry with paper towels. Sprinkle the cavity with salt.

In a frying pan brown the sausage over medium heat. Remove the sausage from the pan and sauté the celery and onion in the drippings. Combine with the bread crumbs, cooked sausage, salt, pepper, sage, and enough water to moisten (about 2 cups). Put this stuffing in a cheesecloth and pack lightly in the cavity of pig.

Preheat the oven to 325°. Close the cavity by sewing or skewering. Set the pig in a roasting pan. Cover the ears and tail with foil while cooking. Insert a 4-inch wood block into mouth. Roast for 15 minutes per pound until a meat thermometer registers 185°.

For the glaze, combine the brown sugar, honey, and lemon juice in a saucepan or microwaveable dish. Heat in the microwave, stirring occasionally, until melted. Use the mixture to baste every hour. Remove the foil from the ears and tail during the

Big Pig Gig

I had invited twenty people to come and help celebrate my husband's sixty-fifth birthday. The highlight of the birthday feast was to be a roast suckling pig, a.k.a. Wilbur. Arrangements had been made with a butcher in a nearby town to have Wilbur ready for pickup on the morning of the big day.

When the day arrived, we received a phone call. Wilbur had arrived but would not fit in the cooler we had provided. He was, in fact, resting peacefully, stretched across the entire back seat of my son's car. The butcher had misunderstood and provided a pig ready for the barbeque spit, rather than my oven. Wilbur was also some six pounds heavier than we ordered, which compounded the problem. My dilemma was simple: a forty-eight inch pig and a thirty-inch range.

What to do? We had three hours before the cooking had to begin and, with people coming from out of town, postponing the feast was not an option.

No more attempts at secrecy—my husband was dispatched to search the town for foil roasting pans while I worked the phone, seeking large foil pans, better ideas, whatever.

No luck.

With two hours to go and out of options, out came the saw. Wilbur was subdivided: one portion to my mother's oven across town, the rest into mine. To make a long story short, Wilbur was a most welcome guest at our dinner. He was pronounced "delicious."

Eleanor Rowlandson
Boots
Happy Red Hatters
Oshawa, Ontario, Canada

last 30 minutes of cooking. When done, the skin will be dark brown. Allow to rest 15 minutes.

Transfer the pig to a large platter. Remove the wooden block and replace with a shiny red apple. Put cherry tomatoes or tomato halves in the eyes and garnish with parsley and pineapple rings.

Remove stuffing from cheesecloth and spoon back into cavity. Carve and serve warm.

Makes 18 servings

Eleanor Rowlandson, Boots
Happy Red Hatters, Oshawa, Ontaro, Canada

Ham in a Blanket

A show-stopper entrée doesn't need to be difficult, as this recipe shows. It's like a down-home beef Wellington.

4	to 5-pound fresh ham with skin on OR fresh rolled pork roast OR small whole precooked ham
2	(8-inch-long) loaves frozen bread dough, thawed completely

Preheat the oven to 350°. Arrange the ham in large pan and bake the fresh meat for 25 minutes per pound. The final meat thermometer reading should register 170°. If using a pre-cooked ham, cook for about 1 hour until heated through. Remove from the oven and gently pull to cut off the skin.

Spray two sheets of waxed paper, 2 feet long, with nonstick cooking spray. Place the dough between the sheets and roll out the bread dough, estimating how large to make the surface so that it will fit over the ham. Remove the top layer of the paper, place the ham in the middle, and pull the dough up and over like closing a bag so that the meat is completely covered. Place the meat on a greased baking pan with the seam side down. Increase the oven heat to 400° and bake for 30 minutes, or until the bread is nicely browned. To serve, slice through the bread and meat together. Use the pan drippings to make gravy, if desired.

Makes 10 to 14 servings

Note: Loaves will thaw in the refrigerator in about 8 to 10 hours or 4 to 7 hours at room temperature. For a quick thaw, heat the oven to 175°. Turn the oven off, place the loaves in a plastic bag, and leave it in the oven for approximately 1 hour until completely thawed.

Dixie Lulu, Queen Dixie
Red Hat Maw Maws, Orange, Texas

Gorgeous Grilled Pork Loin

Treat friends and family like royalty with a rolled-and-tied pork loin grilled over flames. Substitute a doubled sheet of heavy-duty aluminum foil for the foil roasting pan if you prefer.

1/4	cup olive oil
6	garlic cloves, minced
2	tablespoons snipped fresh basil
2	tablespoons snipped chives or chopped green onion
2	teaspoons chili powder or 1/4 teaspoon ground red pepper
1	teaspoon fresh sage or oregano
1	teaspoon salt
1/2	teaspoon pepper
1	(3 to 4-pound) boneless pork top loin roast, tied

In a zip-top plastic bag combine the oil, garlic, basil, chives, chili powder, sage, salt, and pepper. Add the roast to the bag and set the bag in a shallow dish. Close the bag and turn several times. Marinate in the refrigerator for 6 to 8 hours or overnight, turning occasionally.

Preheat a gas or charcoal grill to low. Remove the meat from the bag and discard the marinade. Insert a meat thermometer into the thickest part of the roast. Arrange in a foil roasting pan, poke a few holes in the bottom of the pan, and put the pan directly on the grill. Grill for approximately 2 hours, or until the meat thermometer registers 160°, turning once after 1 hour. Remove the roast and cover with foil. Let stand 15 minutes before carving to allow the roast to absorb its juices. Remove the strings and slice to serve.

Makes 12 servings

Lorraine Osbahr, Lady Lorraine
Classy Dames Sisterhood, Avoca, Iowa

Roast Pork Tenderloin

3   teaspoons sugar
2   teaspoons kosher salt
2   teaspoons coarse freshly ground black pepper
1   teaspoon coriander
1/2 teaspoon ground cloves
2   teaspoons olive oil
4   (12-ounce) pork tenderloins
2   tablespoons maple syrup

Preheat the oven to 325. Combine the sugar, salt, pepper, coriander, and cloves. Rub the olive oil on the tenderloins and place in a glass 13 x 9-inch pan. Rub the sugar mixture on both sides of each tenderloin. Roast for 20 minutes. Remove from the oven and brush with the maple syrup. Return to the oven and roast 20 minutes more, or until a meat ther-

mometer reaches 160°. Brush with the pan juices before serving.

Makes 12 to 16 servings

Mary Androff, Razzle Dazzle Member
Razzle Dazzle of Clinton Township, Warren, Michigan

Barbecued Pork Loin

3   to 5-pound pork loin roast
1   (10 3/4-ounce) can tomato soup
1/3 cup chopped celery
2   tablespoons light brown sugar
2   tablespoons Worcestershire sauce
4   drops hot pepper sauce
1/3 cup chopped yellow onion
1   garlic clove, minced
2   tablespoons lemon juice
2   tablespoons prepared yellow mustard

Preheat the oven to 325°. Put the roast in a greased 13 x 9-inch deep pan and bake for 1/2 hour per pound. A meat thermometer inserted into the thickest part should read 160° when done. Combine the soup, celery, brown sugar, Worcestershire sauce, pepper sauce, onion, garlic, lemon juice, and mustard. After 45 minutes, baste the roast with the drippings from the pan and pour the sauce over the meat. Continue roasting, basting every 15 minutes.

Makes 8 to 12 servings

Sheila Hannan, Queen
The Merry Madams of Merritt Island, Merritt Island, Florida

Peach and Ham Stir-Fry

Serve over rice, noodles, or deep-fried rice sticks.

1/2 cup orange juice
1   tablespoon cornstarch
2   tablespoon soy sauce
1   tablespoon sugar
1   tablespoon lemon juice
2   tablespoons vegetable oil
3/4 cup peanuts
1   teaspoon grated fresh ginger
1   onion, cut into thin wedges
2   zucchini, thinly sliced
2   cups cubed, cooked ham
1   (16-ounce) can sliced peaches, drained

Blend the orange juice into the cornstarch. Stir in the soy sauce, sugar, and lemon juice.

Heat a wok over high heat and add the oil. Stir-fry the peanuts for 2 to 3 minutes, or until toasted. Remove from the wok. Stir-fry the ginger for 30 seconds. Add the onion and stir-fry for 2 minutes. Add the zucchini and cook for 2 minutes. Remove the vegetables from the wok and add more oil if needed. Stir-fry the ham for 2 minutes and then pour in the orange juice mixture. Cook until thick and bubbly, about 2 minutes longer. Stir in the peaches, peanuts, and vegetables. Cover and cook for another 2 minutes. Serve over deep-fried rice sticks if desired.

Makes 4 to 6 servings

Sylvia North, Lady Syl
Swinging Mississippi Belles, Carriere, Mississippi

Cuban Roast Pork Loin

3/4 cup vegetable oil
1/2 cup soy sauce
1/4 cup Worcestershire sauce
1   tablespoon dry mustard
1/4 teaspoon salt
1/2 tablespoon pepper
1/4 cup white or cider vinegar
2   garlic cloves, crushed or minced
1/4 cup lemon juice
4   pork tenderloins

Combine the oil, soy sauce, Worcestershire sauce, mustard, salt, pepper, vinegar, garlic, and lemon juice in a large bowl or zip-top bag. Add the pork and marinate in the refrigerator for 4 to 5 hours, turning once.

Prepare a gas or charcoal grill to medium high. Grill approximately 7 to 10 minutes per side or to desired doneness. Discard marinade.

Makes 8 to 10 servings

Betty Swift, Princess Lazy Bones
Purple Passion Flowers, Greensboro, North Carolina

Pineapple Pork Loin Roast with Horseradish Sauce

2   cups firmly packed brown sugar
1   tablespoon lemon juice
4   garlic cloves, minced
     Salt and pepper to taste
1   tablespoon soy sauce

1 (8-ounce) can crushed pineapple, drained
1 (7-pound) pork loin roast
1 cup sour cream
2 tablespoons mayonnaise
   Dash of paprika
1 teaspoon horseradish sauce

4 garlic cloves, minced
1 teaspoon salt
1/2 teaspoon ground black pepper
2 (10-ounce) bottles sweet-and-tangy steak sauce
16 soft sandwich rolls, split

In a bowl combine the brown sugar, lemon juice, garlic, salt and pepper, soy sauce, and pineapple to make a paste that looks like oatmeal. Arrange the roast in a baking dish, fat side out. Spread the pineapple mixture on top. Cover and marinate in the refrigerator for at least 6 hours.

Preheat the oven to 250°. Bake the roast for 5 to 5 1/2 hours. If the roast becomes too brown before it is cooked to 160° inside, cover it with a tent of aluminum foil. For the sauce, combine the sour cream, mayonnaise, paprika, and horseradish in a small bowl and mix well. Slice the pork and serve with the sauce.

Makes 10 servings

Jackie Gabel, Chapterette
Swinging Mississippi Belles, Carriere, Mississippi

Half-Time Pulled Pork

1 (6 to 7-pound) bone-in pork shoulder
2 tablespoons vegetable oil
4 large onions, sliced (about 8 cups)

Brown the pork in the oil in a large ovenproof pot or roasting pan over medium-high heat, turning to brown all sides. Remove from the pot. Cook the onions in the same pot over medium heat until soft, about 10 minutes. Add the garlic and cook 5 minutes more.

Preheat the oven to 350°. Return the pork to the pot. Sprinkle both sides of the pork with the salt and pepper. Pour 1 bottle of the steak sauce over the pork. Cover tightly with a lid or foil and bake for 3 to 3 1/2 hours, or until very tender, basting with the pan juices every hour and adding a small amount of additional steak sauce or water if needed. Remove the meat to a carving board. Let stand for 15 minutes to cool. With two forks, pull the meat from the bone and shred the meat, discarding the fat and bone. Skim any excess fat from the onion and sauce mixture. Blend the meat into the sauce mixture. Serve hot in the rolls topped with the remaining bottle of steak sauce.

Makes 16 servings

Nancy Fugelberg, Queen
Vegas Vixens, Las Vegas, Nevada

Crown Pork Roast with Cranberry-Pear Sauce

ROAST

1   **7 to 8-pound crown roast of pork (about 18 ribs)**

    Salt and pepper to taste

1/3   **cup dry red wine**

1/4   **cup cranberry juice cocktail**

1/2   **cup honey**

CRANBERRY-PEAR SAUCE

1   **(14-ounce) can pear halves, drained**

1   **(16-ounce) can whole cranberry sauce**

1/2   **cup apricot preserves**

1/4   **cup cranberry juice cocktail**

1/4   **teaspoon salt**

1/4   **teaspoon cinnamon**

Preheat the oven to 325°. Arrange the roast, rib ends up, in a large shallow roasting pan (rack not necessary) and rub with salt and pepper. Insert a meat thermometer between two ribs in the center of the meat. Make sure the thermometer isn't touching the bone. Cover the rib ends with foil to keep from charring. Roast for 2 1/2 hours. Combine the red wine, cranberry juice, and honey. Baste the pork about four times with the liquid. Roast about 1 hour longer, or until the thermometer reads 160°.

For the cranberry-pear sauce, combine the pears, cranberry sauce, apricot preserves, cranberry juice, salt, and cinnamon in a saucepan. Bring to a boil, and then lower the heat to keep the sauce warm until ready to serve.

Serve the roast on a warm platter. Fill the center of the crown with your stuffing of choice and top with the hot cranberry-pear sauce.

Makes 12 to 18 servings

Beverly Johnson, Vice Queen

Tahoe REDS (Rowdy, Energetic, Diva Sisters), South Lake Tahoe, California

Roast Pork with Plum Sauce

For a gorgeous garnish, arrange canned plums and branches of rosemary around the roast.

PLUM SAUCE

2   **tablespoons butter**

3/4   **cup chopped onions**

1   **cup plum preserves**

2/3   **cup water**

1/2   **cup packed brown sugar**

1/3   **cup chili sauce**

1/4   **cup soy sauce**

2   **tablespoons prepared mustard**

3   **drops hot pepper sauce**

2   **tablespoons fresh lemon juice**

    Garlic salt to taste

ROAST

1   **(5-pound) pork loin roast**

2   **teaspoons salt**

2   **garlic cloves, minced**

2   **teaspoons dried rosemary or 4 teaspoons minced fresh rosemary**

1 1/2   **teaspoons dried oregano**

1 1/2   **teaspoons dried thyme**

1 1/2   teaspoons rubbed sage

1/4   teaspoon pepper

1/4   teaspoon nutmeg

For the plum sauce, melt the butter in a saucepan over medium-high heat. Add the onions and sauté them until tender. Add the preserves, water, brown sugar, chili sauce, soy sauce, mustard, pepper sauce, lemon juice, and garlic salt. Bring to a boil, reduce the heat to medium low and simmer for 15 minutes.

For the roast, preheat the oven to 325°. Rinse the roast to help hold the seasonings. In a small bowl stir together the salt, garlic, rosemary, oregano, thyme, sage, pepper, and nutmeg. With a sharp knife, make several rows of 1/2-inch-deep slits in the top of the roast. Press the seasoning mixture into the slits and rub the remainder all over the roast. Place the roast in a roasting pan and pour 1/2 cup plum sauce over it. Cover and bake for 2 1/2 hours, or to an internal temperature of 160°. Uncover the roast and baste it with additional plum sauce; bake for 30 minutes longer. Serve the remaining plum sauce on the side for a gravy or for dipping. Let the meat rest 15 minutes before slicing.

Makes 10 to 12 servings

Della Jackson, Queen of Leisure

Red Hatted Chicks and Pink Hatted Peeps, Petersburg, Illinois

Apple Pie Pork Dinner

3   to 4 pounds boneless pork roast or chops

6   cups applesauce

2   tablespoons apple pie spice

8   small red-skinned potatoes, left whole if small

6   carrots, peeled and cut into chunks

2   cups white pearl onions, peeled and left whole

2   firm tart apples, peeled, cored, and thinly sliced

Remove all visible fat from the pork and cut into large chunks (can also use boned pork chops). Spoon the applesauce into a large, heavy pot and sprinkle with the apple pie spice. Blend well and add the meat. Cover and cook on medium heat for 10 minutes. Reduce the heat to a low and simmer for 2 hours (or in a slow cooker for 4 hours). Add the potatoes, carrots, and onions and cook for 1 hour longer on the stovetop or 2 hours longer in a slow cooker. Ten to 15 minutes before serving, add the apple slices. Cook until just tender. Remove the meat, vegetables, and apples to a large serving platter. Spoon a little of the cooking liquid over the meat and vegetables and serve the rest in a gravy boat on the side.

Makes 6 to 8 servings

Marjorie Heil, Granniemom

Red Hat Bloomers, Bethel, Vermont

One Lump or Two?

When I was just a newlywed, I was making pork chops with mashed potatoes and gravy for dinner. The gravy turned out so lumpy that I decided to strain it in a colander in the sink. I forgot to put a bowl under the colander, and the gravy went down the drain. I had a colander full of lumps.

Cassandra DeAngelis
Queen
Charming Ladies with Hattitude
Mill Run, Pennsylvania

Ruby Sweet Pork Chops

Take advantage of fresh cranberries when they're in season.

4   to 6 pork chops, cut 1-inch thick
    Salt and pepper to taste
2   cups ground or chopped cranberries
1/4 to 1/2 cup honey
1/4 teaspoon ground cloves
1/4 teaspoon ground nutmeg
4   cups hot cooked rice

Preheat the oven to 300°. Trim the excess fat from the chops. Dice the fat and melt 1 table-spoon of it over low heat in a frying pan. Brown the chops in the fat, seasoning with salt and pepper. Transfer to a shallow baking dish. Combine the cranberries, honey, cloves, and nutmeg and pour over the chops. Bake for 30 to

45 minutes, or until the pork is just barely pink in the center. Serve with the rice.

Makes 4 to 6 servings

Joan Rodgers, Queen Mother
Onanole Red Hats, Onanole, Manitoba , Canada

Whiskey-Glazed Pork Chops

1/2 cup sour mash or bourbon whiskey
1/2 cup apple cider
2   tablespoons light brown sugar
1   tablespoon Dijon mustard
1/8 teaspoon cayenne pepper
1/2 teaspoon vanilla extract
2   plus 2 teaspoons cider vinegar
4   bone-in, center-cut pork chops, cut 1-inch thick
2   teaspoons vegetable oil
    Salt and pepper to taste
1   tablespoon unsalted butter

In a small bowl combine the whiskey, cider, brown sugar, mustard, cayenne, vanilla, and 2 teaspoons vinegar and whisk to blend. Transfer 1/4 cup of the whiskey mixture to a gallon-size zip-top plastic bag; add the pork chops, press the air out of the bag, and seal. Turn the bag to coat the chops with the marinade and refrigerate 1 to 2 hours. Reserve the remaining whiskey mixture separately.

Remove the chops from the bag, pat dry with paper towels, and discard the marinade. Heat the oil in large skillet over medium-high heat until just beginning to smoke. Season the chops with salt and pepper and cook for 3 to 4 minutes per side, or until well browned on both sides and pink in the middle. Transfer the chops to a plate and cover tightly with foil.

Add the reserved whiskey mixture to the skillet and bring to a boil, scraping up any browned bits with a wooden spoon. Cook for 3 to 5 minutes, or until reduced to a thick glaze. Reduce the heat to medium low and add to the skillet any juices that have accumulated around the chops, along with the remaining 2 teaspoons vinegar. Whisk in the butter and simmer the glaze until thick and sticky, 2 to 3 minutes. Remove the pan from the heat. Add the chops and let stand 5 minutes, turning once or twice to coat.

Makes 4 servings

Sandra S. Peebles, Queen Mum Blondie
Royal Divas, Belleville, Illinois

Beer Garden Pork Chops

1/4 cup plus 2 tablespoons olive oil
2 cups chopped onion
  Chicken seasoning
6 large, boneless, lean pork chops, cut 1 1/2-inches thick
1 to 2 (12-ounce) bottles beer
2 large onions, sliced
  Parsley for garnish

Heat 1/4 cup oil in a frying pan over medium heat. Cook the chopped onions until light brown. Move the onions to the sides of the pan. Rub seasoning on both sides of the chops to taste. Brown the chops in the pan with the onions. Add enough beer to cover the bottom of the pan. Cover, reduce the heat to low, and simmer for 1 hour, checking often and adding more beer if needed. In a separate pan sauté the sliced onions in the remaining 2 tablespoons oil over medium-high heat until browned. Serve over the chops and garnish with parsley.

Makes 6 servings

Kay Riley, Queen Mum Kay
Hunt for the Red Hats, Gainesville, Virginia

Sweet and Sour Stovetop Spareribs

Homemade sauce is the secret to deep layers of flavor.

1   pound boneless country-style spareribs
2   tablespoons vegetable oil
1/2 cup coarsely chopped onion
1/4 cup coarsely chopped green bell pepper
1/4 cup apple cider vinegar
1/2 cup firmly packed brown sugar
2   tablespoons cornstarch
1   cup water
1/2 cup ketchup
1/2 cup pineapple chunks
1   teaspoon salt
    Dash of pepper

Brown the ribs in the oil in a large skillet or Dutch oven with a lid over medium-high heat. Add the onion, green pepper, vinegar, and brown sugar. Cook until the vegetables are tender about 4 minutes. Reduce the heat to low. Combine the cornstarch and water and blend until smooth. Add the ketchup and pour the sauce over the ribs. Top with the pineapple and then add the salt and pepper. Cover and cook on low heat for 1 hour 15 minutes.

Makes 4 servings

Tine Grijalba, Red Hat Sister
Spiritfilled Hearts and Hats, Richmond, Kentucky

Baby Back Ribs with Java Sauce

When you plan to serve ribs, plan on one pound per person.

RIBS
2   large onions, quartered
4   celery stalks, broken in half
4   garlic cloves, peeled and smashed
3   chicken bouillon cubes
5   bay leaves
1   teaspoon salt
1/2 teaspoon red pepper flakes
6   slabs baby back pork ribs

JAVA SAUCE
1   tablespoon olive oil
1   large onion, chopped
2   garlic cloves, minced
2   cups strong black coffee (1/2 cup grounds per 2 cups water)
1/2 cup Worcestershire sauce
1   (14-ounce) bottle ketchup (1 1/2 cups)
1/2 cup lemon juice
4   teaspoons paprika
1   tablespoon chili powder
1/4 teaspoon cayenne
1/4 teaspoon hot red pepper sauce
1/8 teaspoon salt

For the Java Sauce, heat the oil in a saucepan over medium heat. Sauté the onion and garlic in the olive oil until soft but not brown. Add the coffee, Worcestershire sauce, ketchup, lemon juice, paprika, chili powder, cayenne, pepper sauce, and salt. Simmer, uncovered, for 60 minutes.

For the ribs, fill a very large pot (16 quarts or more in size) half full of water and add the onions, celery, garlic, bouillon, bay leaves, salt, and pepper flakes. Bring to a boil over high heat; reduce the heat to medium low and simmer, covered, for about 15 minutes. Add the ribs. There should be enough liquid to cover the ribs. Simmer, covered, until the meat is tender but not falling off the bones. Strain the broth and freeze for soups or dried beans. Refrigerate the ribs until grilling time or freeze for another day. Grill the ribs, basting often with the Java Sauce until nicely browned.

Makes 6 to 10 servings

Jennifer Johnson, Queen Mum
The Y–City Red Hat and Chocolate Lovers, Zanesville, Ohio

Maple-Glazed Ribs

Maple-glazed ribs might become your family's new favorite.

3   **to 4 pounds pork spare ribs, cut into serving portions**

Salt and pepper to taste
1   **cup maple syrup**
3   **tablespoons orange juice concentrate**
3   **tablespoons ketchup**
2   **tablespoons soy sauce**
1   **tablespoon Dijon mustard**
1   **tablespoon Worcestershire sauce**
1   **teaspoon curry powder**
1   **teaspoon garlic minced**
2   **green onions or 1 small onion, chopped**
1   **tablespoon sesame seeds**

Preheat the oven to 350°. Rub the ribs with salt and pepper and place them meaty side up in baking pan lined with heavy duty aluminum foil (for easy clean-up). Cover the pan tightly with foil and bake for 2 hours.

Combine the syrup, orange juice concentrate, ketchup, soy sauce, mustard, Worcestershire, curry powder, garlic, and green onions in a saucepan and bring to boil over medium heat. Simmer for 15 minutes, stirring occasionally. Drain the ribs, discarding the liquid. Cover generously with the sauce. Bake uncovered for 35 minutes, basting occasionally. Sprinkle with the sesame seeds just before serving. The ribs can be held in a very low oven for up to an hour.

Makes 4 to 6 servings

Michelle Koester, Queen Mum / Email Female
Rural Red Hatters, Duncombe, Iowa

Tender-to-the-Bone Spareribs in Quick Joe Sauce

1   cup brewed coffee
1/2 cup sugar
1   teaspoon salt
    Dash of pepper
1   cup ketchup
1/4 cup cider vinegar
1/4 cup chopped onion
4   pounds country style spareribs

Preheat the oven to 500°. Combine the coffee, sugar, salt, pepper, ketchup, vinegar and onion in a small saucepan; simmer for 10 minutes over medium heat. Place the ribs on a rack in a shallow greased pan. Bake for 10 minutes. Reduce the heat to 325° and bake for 1 1/2 hours. Brush frequently with the sauce.

Makes 4 servings

Ruthie Setterlund, Clearwater Red Hats
Red Hat Musical Notes, Clearwater, Florida

Kamahamaha Pork Spareribs

When you're serving a whole bunch, try this slightly Asian-flavored version.

8   pounds pork spareribs
    Salt and pepper to taste
6   whole cloves
6   bay leaves
6   branches fresh rosemary
6   branches fresh thyme
1   onion, diced
1   tablespoon minced garlic
2   (12-ounce) cans beer
    Water to completely cover the ribs
1 1/4 cups honey
1   (1-pound) package brown sugar
4   cups hoisin sauce
2   cups water
1/2 cup cornstarch

Place the ribs in a large greased roasting pan with a lid. Add the salt and pepper, cloves, bay leaves, rosemary, thyme, onion, garlic, beer, and water. Cover, bring to a boil, and then simmer for 1 hour. Remove the ribs from the liquid. Spread the honey over the hot ribs. Let the ribs cool. Cut into three-rib servings.

Mix the brown sugar, hoisin sauce, and water together in a saucepan and bring to a boil. Reduce the heat to medium low and whisk in the cornstarch. Cook until thick. Let cool. Heat the oven to 350°. Dip each rib into the sauce and place on a baking sheet and bake for 20 to 30 minutes.

Makes 24 three-rib servings

Joyce Davis, Duchess of What's Left Over
Steal Magnolias, Long Beach, California

Who Is Ruby Redhat?

Early in the year 2000, Andrea Reekstin (AKA Princess Daughter) made the acquaintance of (some say "invented") a little character, whom we quickly dubbed "Ruby Redhat." Making several appearances within this cookbook, she personifies the characteristics of a typical Red Hatter; she's adventurous, free-spirited, kind-hearted, and ready for fun! If she were Irish, Ruby might be called a leprechaun, because she is very small (about 10 inches tall) and sometimes difficult to see. As a matter of fact, some (humorless) people have suggested that she doesn't exist. But we know better! In her magical way, she embodies the best qualities of the little girl that survives—somewhere, somehow— within all women.

Ruby is very independent, and she flits from place to place, always seeking to join (or make) fun for herself. She always wears shade of purple and has something red on her head. She favors fuzzy pink slippers because she's "totally over" high heels and, besides, she needs to be fast on her feet, since she never knows where she might want to be off to next!

"Golf Balls" with Sauce

The ham is plenty salty, so there's no need to add any salt to the recipe. The sauce recipe makes enough for half of the ham balls. Freeze the other half for later, or double the sauce ingredients.

3   pounds ground ham
1   pound lean ground beef
4   eggs
1 1/3 cups milk
2   cups cracker crumbs
1   cup firmly packed brown sugar
1/2 cup prepared yellow mustard
1/4 cup cider vinegar

Preheat the oven to 350°. In a large bowl combine the ham, ground beef, eggs, milk, and cracker crumbs and mix well. Shape into 1 1/2-inch balls. (Use a 1/4-cup measure for uniformity.) Arrange the ham balls, 20 per pan, in two greased 13 x 9-inch baking dishes. In a bowl combine the brown sugar, mustard, and vinegar, and pour the sauce over the ham balls. Bake for 45 minutes to 1 hour.

Makes 40 to 50 balls

Note: The ham balls can be frozen after shaping. Spread them on a baking sheet and freeze; then transfer to a zip-top bag.

Peggy Giddens, Queen Mum Peg
Red Hot Red Hat Readers of Decatur, Ten Mile, Tennessee

Sausage-Stuffed Pepper Boats

6   large green bell peppers, halved lengthwise
4   hot sausages
4   sweet sausages
1   large onion, finely chopped
1   garlic clove, minced or pressed
1 1/4 pounds fresh mushrooms, chopped
1   cup dry Italian bread crumbs
1   egg, beaten
    Salt and pepper to taste
1   (4–6 ounce) can diced tomatoes, drained
1   teaspoon dried parsley
    Grated Parmesan cheese to taste

Preheat the oven to 425°. Cook the peppers in boiling water for 5 minutes. Remove the casings from the sausages and brown in a skillet over medium heat, stirring with a wooden spoon to break up any lumps. Add the onion and garlic and cook for about 5 minutes. Add the mushrooms. Cook for about 2 minutes and transfer the mixture to a mixing bowl. Let cool slightly; add the bread crumbs, egg, salt and pepper, tomatoes, and parsley. Blend well. Spoon the mixture into the pepper halves. Arrange in a buttered 13x9-inch baking dish and sprinkle with the cheese. Bake for 15 to 20 minutes, or until the cheese is lightly browned.

Makes 4 servings

Gail Safarikas, Vice Mother
Scarlet O'Hatters of Trinity (So Hot), Trinity, Florida

Slow-Cooker Kielbasa and Kraut

The alcohol cooks out of the beer, so it is safe to serve this meal to children.

1   (24-ounce) can sauerkraut
1   (8-ounce) jar applesauce
2   pounds kielbasa, cut into serving-size pieces
1   (12-ounce) can or bottle beer

Combine the sauerkraut and applesauce in a slow cooker. Arrange the kielbasa on top. Pour the beer over all. Cook on low for 7 to 8 hours or on high for 4 to 5 hours. Serve as a main dish with mashed potatoes or as a sandwich on hard rolls.

Makes 8 to 12 servings

Gerri Wood, Duchess of Dining Out
Ohio River Belles, Beaver, Pennsylvania

Little Swedish Meatballs

After the holidays, put that leftover ham to good use. Whip up a batch of meatballs and invite the girls over.

1 1/2 cups firmly packed brown sugar
1   teaspoon dry mustard
1/2   cup white or cider vinegar
1/2   cup water
1   pound ground ham
1 1/2 pounds ground pork
2   eggs
1   cup milk
2   cups dried bread crumbs

Preheat the oven to 275°. Combine the brown sugar, mustard, vinegar, and water in a bowl In a separate bowl combine the ham, pork, eggs, milk, and bread crumbs. Form meat mixture into balls and arrange loosely into a greased 13x9-inch casserole dish and pour the sauce over top. Bake for 1 1/2 hours.

Makes 6 to 8 servings

Janet Bloom, Princess Purple Plum
Scarlett Strutters, Carlsbad, New Mexico

Ham Loaf

A nice change from meatloaf, and ideal for using up extra ham. Omit the pineapple and juice if they aren't "you."

1 1/2 pounds ground pork
10   ounces ham, ground (about 2 cups)
2   eggs
1   cup corn flakes, crushed
1/8   to 1/4 cup firmly packed brown sugar
1   (8-ounce) can sliced or crushed pineapple (reserve some juice)

Preheat the oven to 400°. In a large bowl combine the pork, ham, eggs, corn flakes, and brown sugar and mix with your hands. Moisten the mixture with some of the pineapple juice if needed. Pack into a greased loaf pan or shape in a baking pan. Top with the pineapple. Bake for 1 hour. Top may get crunchy. Slice and serve like meatloaf.

Makes 6 to 8 servings

Pam Arcand, Lady Nascar
Lunch Bags of Orlando, Orlando, Florida

Plum Luscious Roast

Make sure you have wide, heavy-duty foil before you start this roast.

2   to 3 pounds rump or eye-of-round roast
     Salt and pepper to taste
2   envelopes (2/3 cup) onion soup mix
2   (15-ounce) cans purple plums, juice only

Preheat the oven to 325°. Trim all possible fat from the roast. Lay out two lengths of foil (about 2 feet each), crossing them. Turn up the edges of the upper foil to hold the liquid. Center the roast on the foil. Rub the roast with salt and pepper and the soup mix. Pour the juice from the cans of plums over the roast. Close the upper foil, sealing tightly so no juice escapes. Seal the outer layer of foil around all. Place the roast in a roasting pan with a lid and cover the pan. Bake for at least 4 hours. (If it's large, or you prefer your meat falling apart, you can cook 6 or more hours; but 4 will usually give nice slices.)

Makes 4 to 5 servings

Barbara R. Moon, Barb Moon
Scarlet Red Hatters, River City Foxy Ladies, Jacksonville, Florida

Peppery Beef

Lean beef eye-of-round has its own wonderful flavor and a whole eye-of-round roast feeds a crowd. The texture is a little chewy, though, so have it sliced very thin (or do it yourself with an electric knife).

1   (3-ounce) bottle seasoned meat tenderizer
1   (3-ounce) bottle unseasoned meat tenderizer
1 1/2 to 2 cups coarse black pepper
2   tablespoons garlic salt
1   (5 to 7-pound) eye-of-round roast

Combine the tenderizers, pepper, and garlic salt in a large plastic bag. Poke holes in the meat with a fork. Add the roast to the bag and rub the seasonings over the meat to completely coat. (Make sure the roast is well coated.) Remove the air from the bag, seal, and refrigerate for 8 to 12 hours, turning once or twice.

Preheat the oven to 350°. Place the roast in a large roasting pan and bake for 1 hour. Let stand 15 minutes then thinly slice the meat.

Makes 10 to 14 servings

Debbie Kapanoske, Duchess Debbie
Red Lite Ladies, Laurel, Maryland

Soda Pop Beef Brisket

Potato starch is traditional in this dish, but cornstarch works, too, to thicken the pan juices slightly.

2   tablespoons butter
1   onion, sliced
2   to 3 teaspoons brown sugar
1   teaspoon salt
1/2 teaspoon ground ginger
1/2 teaspoon garlic pepper
1   cup wine, preferably red
1   (12-ounce) can dark, carbonated soda

The Baked Ham

I was just married and starting my career as a professional nurse. My mom came to visit, and I wanted to take her to my hospital to show her around. I also wanted to impress my new husband with my multitasking abilities as a homemaker and a nurse, so . . . I put dinner in the oven before we left.

When we returned home and opened the front door, we got a face full of thick, black smoke. I felt dread welling up in me—I was sure I had set the house on fire.

When we entered the kitchen, the oven door was bent and lying on the floor. There were segments of metal embedded in the cupboards of the kitchen and the wire rack in the oven was bent. The lovely dinner ham looked like an explosion!

I learned something about cooking that day: you must open a canned ham before you put it in the oven.

Mayme Easton
Royal Granny Nanny
Red Hats of Oz
Olathe, Kansas

1   cup ketchup
1   teaspoon potato starch
1   (5-pound) beef brisket

Preheat the oven to 325°. Melt the butter in a saucepan over medium heat. Sauté the onion in the butter. Combine the sugar, salt, ginger, garlic pepper, wine, soda, ketchup, and potato starch into an oven bag. Add the onions and beef. Set the bag in a metal roasting pan. Bake for 2 hours. Remove the meat from the bag and slice.

Makes 6 to 8 servings

Sue Orosz, Queen Sue Lady Wolverine
Red Spicy Ladies, Stow, Oho

"Cooks By Itself" Brisket and Vegetables

Brisket is ideal for a cook with a busy life. It practically cooks itself, and it even cuts itself, since a well-cooked brisket falls into shreds.

1   cup chopped celery
1   cup chopped carrot
1   cup chopped onions
1/4 cup chopped fresh parsley
1   garlic clove, chopped
1   4 to 5-pound lean brisket
1 1/2 cups consommé
1/4 cup dry red wine
     Salt and pepper to taste
1   bay leaf

Preheat the oven to 450°. Arrange the celery, carrot, onions, parsley, and garlic in a well buttered roasting pan. Place the brisket on top and bake for 45 minutes, shaking the pan and turning the meat at 15 minutes intervals. Add the consommé, red wine, salt and pepper, and bay leaf. Cover the pan with a lid or aluminum foil, reduce the heat to 325°, and bake for 2 to 3 hours longer. Remove bay leaf before serving.

Makes 6 to 8 servings

Note: If you like, add potatoes, carrots, and small boiling onions for the last hour of the cooking.

Mary Woolsey, Marquisa De Martini
RHS Red Queens, Canoga Park, California

Flank Steak in Wine Sauce

1   pound flank steak
1   tablespoon Kitchen Bouquet*
2   tablespoons olive oil
1/2 cup diced onion
1   (6-ounce) can sliced mushrooms
1   (8-ounce) can tomato sauce
1/2 cup red wine
1/8 teaspoon black pepper
1/2 teaspoon sugar

Brush the steak all over with the Kitchen Bouquet. Heat the oil in a skillet over medium-high heat. Brown the steak on both sides. Add the onion and cook for about 5 minutes, or until tender. Drain the mushrooms and spread over the steak. Combine the tomato sauce, wine, pepper, and sugar and pour over the steak. Simmer for about 20 minutes, or until tender. Serve hot with egg noodles.

Makes 6 servings

Note: To make your own Kitchen Bouquet, cook 1/2 cup brown sugar in a saucepan over low heat until browned. Add 2 cups water and stir.

Irene Engel, Lady Angel
Ruby Gems of the Valley, Avon, Connecticut

Slow-Baked Dinner Steaks

2 cups all-purpose flour
1/2 teaspoon salt
1/4 teaspoon pepper
1 cup vegetable oil
6 to 8 beef cube steaks
1 envelope (1/3 cup) dry onion-mushroom or beefy-mushroom soup mix
1 (4-ounce) can sliced mushrooms, not drained
1 medium onion, sliced
1 (10-ounce) can beef gravy
1 gravy can (1 1/4 cups) water

Preheat the oven to 250°. Grease a 13 x 9-inch baking pan. Combine the flour, salt, and pepper in a plastic zip-top bag. Heat the oil in a pan over medium-high heat. Drop the steaks into the flour mixture and coat thoroughly. Lightly brown the steaks on both sides in the oil. Arrange the steaks in the prepared baking pan. Sprinkle the dry soup mix over the steaks. Cover with the mushrooms and their liquid. Layer the onions over the mushrooms. Mix the gravy and water and pour over the steaks. Do not stir. Cover tightly with aluminum foil. Bake for 3 to 4 hours.

Makes 6 to 8 servings

Debbie Anderson, Lady Scarlett
The Red Hot Flashes, Advance, North Carolina

Thocky

Also known as Beef Roulade, this traditional German entrée is also good as a hearty pick-up appetizer.

1 pound bacon, diced
1 onion, diced
1 3 to 4-pound round steak
Salt and pepper to taste
Flour for coating

In a skillet over medium heat cook the bacon and onion until the onion is tender. Drain into a bowl, reserving the bacon drippings. Pound the round steak until thin. Cut into 4-inch squares. Place a spoonful of the bacon mixture in the middle of each steak square. Roll to enclose the filling and secure with toothpicks. Season with salt and pepper. Coat with flour. Heat the reserved drippings in the skillet over medium-high heat and brown the beef rolls in batches. Drain on paper towels. Discard the drippings. Arrange the roll-ups in the skillet and cover with water. Bring to a boil and cover. Reduce the heat to low and simmer until tender. Use a little flour to thicken the pan juices for gravy.

Makes 8 to 10 servings

Dorothy Jensik, Dame DJ
Cyber, Woodbridge, Virginia

Baked Beef Stew

You can also cook this in a slow cooker for several hours.

1   to 1 1/2 pounds stewing beef, cut into cubes
1/2 cup Burgundy or other dry red wine
1   (10 3/4-ounce) can undiluted consommé
3/4 teaspoon salt
1/4 teaspoon pepper
1   medium onion, thinly sliced into rings
1/4 cup fine dry, bread crumbs
1/4 cup all-purpose flour

Preheat the oven to 300°. Combine the beef, wine, consommé, salt, pepper, and onion in a Dutch oven or heavy ovenproof casserole. Mix the bread crumbs with the flour and stir into the beef mixture. Cover and bake for about 3 hours, or until tender, stirring occasionally. Serve over noodles, rice, or mashed potatoes.

Makes 4 servings

Janie Bee, Queen
Scarlett O'Hatters of Howard County, Ellicott City, Maryland

Braised Short Ribs

2   pounds beef short ribs
1   garlic clove, halved
1/4 cup all-purpose flour
1   plus 1 teaspoons salt

1/4 plus 1/4 teaspoon pepper
1   teaspoon paprika
2   tablespoons olive oil
1   (28-ounce) can diced tomatoes
1   cup hot water
6   carrots, coarsely chopped
1   onion, coarsely chopped
1   bay leaf
     Hot cooked noodles

Rub the ribs all over with a cut edge of the garlic. Combine the flour, 1 teaspoon salt, 1/4 teaspoon pepper, and paprika in a bag and shake the ribs a few at a time to coat. (Reserve any extra flour mixture.) Heat the oil in a Dutch oven over medium-high heat. Brown the ribs one batch at a time, removing as they brown. Preheat the oven to 350°. Reduce the heat to medium low and add the reserved flour mixture to the Dutch oven and simmer, stirring well to make a roux. Add the tomatoes and hot water and mix well; increase the heat to medium high and bring to a boil. Add the carrots, onion, the remaining 1 teaspoon salt, the remaining 1/4 teaspoon pepper, the bay leaf, and short ribs. Cover tightly and bake for 2 to 2 1/2 hours, or until tender. Remove the bay leaf and any fat on the top and serve with the noodles.

Makes 4 servings

Karen Ridout, Dutchess of Desert
Red Hat Dollies of Calgary, Calgary, Alberta, Canada

Drunken Beef

This entrée is ideal for entertaining since it can be prepared the day before, leaving the hostess free to enjoy her guests.

4 pounds rolled rump beef roast
   (or a similar cut)
   Black pepper and oregano to taste
2 (10³/4-ounce) cans onion soup
1 (12-ounce) can beer
2 (2-ounce) jiggers brandy or whiskey

The day before serving, preheat the oven to 500°. Rub the beef roast with the pepper and oregano until well covered. Roast in an open pan for 1 hour. Remove and refrigerate for 8 to 10 hours, or until well-chilled.

Preheat the oven to 350°. Cut the chilled meat into thick slices for a roast, thin slices for sandwiches. Arrange in a roasting pan. Pour the soup, beer, and brandy or whiskey over the beef. Cover and bake for 4 hours. Serve as sandwiches or as an entrée with potatoes and vegetables.

Makes 8 servings

Elaine Kloepfel, Queen–E
Mad Red Hatters, Madison, Wisconsin

Corned Beef Extra

Corned beef is a St. Patrick's Day natural and good in cold weather. Adding pickling spices lends more of that great flavor you love in corned beef.

1   (3¹/2-pound) corned beef
    Water to cover
3   tablespoons sugar
3   tablespoons white or cider vinegar
1   tablespoon pickling spice
1   small cabbage
12 small red new potatoes

Place the corned beef in a large pot and cover with water. Bring to a boil over high heat. Reduce the heat to medium low and simmer for 5 minutes. Remove the beef and discard the water. Wipe out the pot. Put the beef back in the pot and cover with fresh water. Add the sugar, vinegar, and pickling spice. Bring to a boil. Reduce the heat and simmer for about 2 hours, or until the meat is fork tender. Remove the meat and wrap in foil. Strain the broth into a bowl. Return the broth to the pot and bring to a boil over medium heat. Add the cabbage and bring back to a boil. Cook for 30 minutes, or until tender. Add the potatoes after about 10 minutes and boil until potatoes are tender. Serve the sliced corned beef and boiled red potatoes on a platter.

Makes 6 servings

Patricia D. Barlow, Queen Mum Pat
The Belles of Bridgewater, Bridgewater, Connecticut

Salpicon

The name is French, but the dish is Latin American—go figure. This beef is usually served with chopped salad vegetables and dressing and wrapped in tortillas. Testers developed the lime vinaigrette to complement the flavor of the meat.

3   to 4 pounds brisket
     Water
1   (16-ounce) can diced tomatoes, not drained
3   garlic cloves, sliced
2/3 cup Italian salad dressing
1   (4-ounce) can chopped green chiles

SALAD
5   Roma tomatoes, chopped
3   avocados, sliced
1/2 cup chopped fresh cilantro
1/4 medium red onion, sliced

LIME VINAIGRETTE
3   tablespoons cooking liquid
1/3 cup chipotle chiles in adobo OR 1 minced pickled jalapeño
6   tablespoons extra-virgin olive oil
4   tablespoons fresh lime juice
2   tablespoons white vinegar
1   tablespoon ketchup
1   garlic clove, minced
     Salt and freshly ground black pepper to taste

Place the brisket in a slow cooker on high and add 1 to 2 inches water. Add the tomatoes with juice and the garlic. Cover and simmer for 5 hours or longer, or until the meat falls apart easily. Check often and add water as needed. Drain the meat thoroughly, reserving 3 tablespoons cooking liquid. Shred the meat by pulling apart with two forks. Add the Italian dressing and green chiles to the meat; mix well. Cover and allow to marinate overnight in the refrigerator.

For the salad, toss the tomatoes, avocadoes, cilantro, and onion in a large bowl. Top with the shredded meat.

For the vinaigrette, combine the reserved cooking liquid, chiles, oil, lime juice, vinegar, ketchup, garlic, and salt and pepper in a bowl or a jar with a tight-fitting lid and shake or blend well. Pour over the salad.

Makes 12 to 16 servings

Hazel Knowles, Queen Hazel
Twin Palm Red Hatters, Lubbock, Texas

Pennsylvania Dutch Beef and Noodles

8   meaty beef short ribs
1   large bay leaf
2   whole cloves
1   teaspoon whole peppercorns
6   quarts water
     Salt and pepper to taste
2   celery stalks, chopped
2   medium carrots, chopped

1   medium onion, chopped
1   (12 or 16-ounce) package bowtie pasta
1   tablespoon salt

Combine the ribs, bay leaf, cloves, pepper-corns, and water in a large pot. Bring to a boil. Reduce the heat and simmer for 15 minutes.

Preheat the oven to 350°. Lift the ribs from the pot and set the pot of broth aside. Arrange the ribs in a shallow greased baking dish (or line it with foil for easy cleanup). Season with salt and pepper and bake for 45 minutes

Meanwhile, add the celery, carrots, and onion to the reserved pot of broth. Bring to a boil over high heat and then reduce the heat and simmer for 30 minutes. Add the noodles to the vegetables and broth. Add 1 tablespoon salt and cook according to package instructions. Remove the ribs from the oven. Pour off the fat. Drain the noodles and vegetables and remove bay leaf arrange on a large platter. Top with the ribs to serve.

Makes 4 to 6 servings

Conchetta Ousey, Queen Mom
Scarlet O'Hatters, Columbus, Georgia

Chicken-Fried Steak

This traditional Texas favorite has an appealing crust outside and plenty of beefy flavor inside.

Vegetable oil
1/4   cup plus 3 tablespoons all-purpose flour

1/2   teaspoon salt
1/2   teaspoon pepper plus additional to taste
1   pound cubed beef steaks
1   egg, lightly beaten
1/2   cup plus 2 tablespoons milk
1   cup crushed crackers
1 1/4   cups chicken broth
      Dash of Worcestershire sauce
      Dash of hot pepper sauce

Fill a skillet with 1/2 inch of oil. Heat the oil over medium-high heat. Combine 1/4 cup of the flour, salt, and 1/2 teaspoon pepper and rub over the steaks. Combine the egg and 2 tablespoons milk. Dip the steaks in the egg mixture; coat in the crushed crackers. Brown the steaks in the hot oil. Cover, reduce the heat to medium low, and cook for 15 minutes, or until tender, turning occasionally. Drain on paper towels. Reserve 3 tablespoons drippings in the skillet. Stir in the remaining 3 tablespoons flour and cook over medium heat for 1 minute, stirring constantly. Add the chicken broth, the remaining 1/2 cup milk, Worcestershire sauce, and hot sauce. Cook, stirring constantly, until thickened. Serve the steaks with the gravy and additional pepper.

Makes 4 servings

Susan Duncan, Queen Susie Q
Derby City Ladybugs of Louisville, Kentucky, Louisville, Kentucky

Greek Beef Stew

3   pounds stewing beef, cut into cubes
3   tablespoons vegetable oil
4   large onions, cut into quarters
2   (15-ounce) cans diced tomatoes, not drained
1   tablespoon sugar
1   tablespoon salt
1   tablespoon pepper
2   teaspoons cinnamon
4   garlic cloves, minced
1   liter (750-milliliter bottle) dry red wine
    Hot cooked rice for serving

Brown the beef in the oil in a large pot over medium heat. Add the onions, tomatoes with liquid, sugar, salt, pepper, cinnamon, garlic, and red wine. Cover and cook on low heat for 4 hours. Remove the cover and cook for 1 more hour. Serve with the rice.

Makes 8 servings

Meg Ogilvie, Histerian
Newcastle Nifty Fifties, Newcastle, South Africa

Bar-B-Cups

Cute name and cute cups. Easy to eat on the go or take along for a party.

3/4   pound ground beef
1/2   cup barbecue sauce
1   tablespoon instant minced onion
2   tablespoons brown sugar
    Salt to taste

1   (8-ounce) can refrigerated biscuits
3/4   cup shredded cheddar cheese

Preheat the oven to 400°. In a skillet cook the ground beef over medium heat, breaking up until browned and crumbly. Drain well. Add the barbecue sauce, onion, brown sugar, and salt to the meat and mix well. Arrange the 12 biscuits in an ungreased muffin pan, pressing the dough up the sides to the edge of the cup. Spoon the meat mixture into the cups. Sprinkle the cheese over the top of the mixture. Bake for 10 to 12 minutes.

Makes 12 cups

Jenny Starling, Queen Shutter Bug Sue
Ooo-La-La Lee Girls, Princeton, North Carolina

Burgundy Beef Loaf with Burgundy Sauce

You've got to try it for that red, red flavor. Offer baked or boiled potatoes, buttered whole carrots, and sautéed mushrooms with the beef.

BEEF LOAF

1   cup Burgundy or other red wine
1/4   cup finely chopped celery
1   garlic clove
1   bay leaf
1   (2 1/2-pound) ground round or chuck
2 1/2   cups fresh bread crumbs
    (from about 5 slices bread)
1   large onion, finely chopped (1 cup)
1   tablespoon chopped fresh parsley

2 teaspoons salt
1/4 teaspoon chopped fresh rosemary
1/4 teaspoon chopped fresh thyme
1/4 teaspoon black pepper
2 eggs
1 (10 to 14-ounce) can condensed beef broth, divided
1 teaspoon Worcestershire sauce
1/4 cup water

BURGUNDY SAUCE

1 tablespoon chopped shallots or green onion
2 tablespoons butter or margarine
3 tablespoons all-purpose flour
1/2 cup Burgundy wine
1 teaspoon chopped fresh parsley

For the beef loaf, combine the wine, celery, garlic, and bay leaf in a small saucepan; bring to a boil over high heat. Lower the heat to medium low and simmer, uncovered, until the volume is reduced by half, about 10 minutes. Remove from the heat and discard the garlic and bay leaf; cool the wine mixture completely.

Preheat the oven to 350°. Combine the beef, bread crumbs, onion, parsley, salt, rosemary, thyme, and pepper in a large bowl. Add the wine mixture, eggs, 1/2 cup of the beef broth, and Worcestershire sauce. Mix until well blended. Shape into an oval loaf in a lightly oiled shallow metal baking pan. Bake for 1 hour 10 minutes, or until the loaf is a rich brown. Remove with two wide spatulas to a heated platter; keep warm. Add the remaining broth and the water to the drippings in the baking pan. Bring to a boil, stirring constantly to loosen the browned bits. Strain into a 1-cup measuring cup. (Add more water if needed to make 1 cup. This is for the sauce.)

For the Burgundy sauce, sauté the shallots in the butter in a medium saucepan over medium heat for about 2 minutes. Stir in the flour and gradually stir in the 1 cup reserved broth mixture. Add the wine. Cook for 2 minutes, stirring constantly, or until the sauce thickens and bubbles. Stir in the parsley.

To serve: Pour some of the sauce over the loaf and serve the remaining sauce in a small serving dish on the side. Makes about 1 1/2 cups.

Makes 8 to 10 servings

Donna DeGroff-Garber, La April Fool
Les Grande Dames of Cecil County, Elkton, Maryland

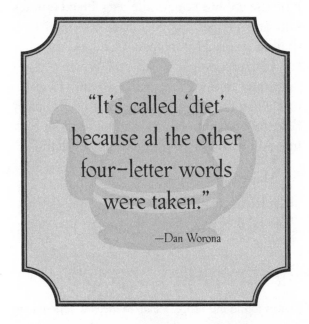

"It's called 'diet' because al the other four-letter words were taken."

—Dan Worona

Dill Pickle Meat Loaf

For a great-looking presentation that turns the dish into a meal, cut potatoes into wedges and arrange them around the loaf as it cooks.

1 1/2   pounds lean ground beef
1   medium onion, finely chopped
1   egg
1/2   cup soft bread crumbs
1/2   teaspoon salt
1/4   teaspoon pepper
1/2   cup chopped dill pickles
1/2   cup ketchup
1/4   cup water
2   tablespoons sugar
1   teaspoon Worcestershire sauce

Preheat the oven to 350°. In a large bowl combine the ground beef, onion, egg, bread crumbs, salt, and pepper. Shape into a loaf in a large shallow greased baking pan. Combine the pickles, ketchup, water, sugar, and Worcestershire sauce and mix well. Pour the mixture over the loaf. Bake for 40 minutes, basting occasionally. Bake for an additional 35 minutes without basting. Allow to rest 10 minutes before slicing.

Makes 6 servings

Julie Hudspeth, Email Female
Wanted: Red and Alive, Elgin, Texas

Microwave Beef Stroganoff

Testers found this recipe a snap to prepare. Microwave ovens vary, so your cooking times may be somewhat different.

1   pound sirloin steak
2   tablespoons all-purpose flour
1   teaspoon salt
1/2   teaspoon pepper
2   tablespoons butter
1/3   cup chopped onion
1   garlic clove, minced
1   (10 3/4-ounce) can cream of mushroom soup
1   (10 3/4-ounce) can cream of chicken soup
1   (4-ounce) can sliced mushrooms, drained
1/2   cup water
2   tablespoons tomato paste
1   cup sour cream
  Cooked rice or egg noodles

Trim the fat from the steak. Combine the flour, salt, and pepper in a bowl and pound into both sides of the steak with a mallet. Cut the meat into strips. Melt the butter in a 2-quart microwaveable casserole dish at 100 percent power for a few seconds, or until completely melted. Add the steak. Cook at 100 percent power for 5 to 6 minutes, or until no longer pink. Stir in the onion and garlic. Cook at 100 percent power for 2 or 3 minutes, or until the onion is tender. Stir in the soups, mushrooms, water, and tomato paste. Cook at 100 percent power for 8 to 10 minutes. Stir in the sour cream. Heat at 100 percent power for 1 minute. Serve over rice or noodles.

Makes 4 servings

Judy Derepentigny, Sassy Secretary
Tricia's Texas Treasures, San Antonio, Texas

Mexican Meat Loaf

1 1/2 pounds ground beef, turkey, chicken, or veal
3/4 cup old-fashioned rolled oats
1/2 cup tomato juice
1 egg, beaten
1 plus 1 teaspoons salt
1/4 teaspoon pepper
1 teaspoon chili powder
2 teaspoons dried minced onions
3 tablespoons butter or margarine
3 tablespoons all-purpose flour
1 1/2 cups milk
8 slices processed American cheese
1 (12-ounce) can Mexican-style whole kernel corn, drained
2 small green bell peppers, sliced in rings

Preheat the oven to 350°. In a large bowl combine the meat, oats, tomato juice, egg, 1 teaspoon salt, pepper, chili powder, and dried onions. Pack into a 9-inch square baking pan. Bake for 20 minutes. Drain the fat. Melt the butter in a skillet over medium heat. Add the flour and stir until smooth. Add the milk, a little at a time, cooking and stirring until thick. Add the remaining 1 teaspoon salt, the cheese, and corn and mix well. Cook until thick. Pour over the meatloaf. Arrange the green pepper rings on top. Bake another 20 minutes. Allow to rest 10 minutes before slicing.

Makes 8 servings

Soffia Taylor, Chapterette
Ruby Red Hatters, Richardson, Texas

French Onion Meatloaf

Leave it to a Red Hatter to figure out a way to avoid chopping and sautéing onions. This clever method uses the onions from a can of French onion soup.

1 (10 3/4-ounce) can French onion soup
1/2 cup herb-seasoned stuffing mix
1 pound ground beef
1 tablespoon minced fresh parsley
3 tablespoons grated Parmesan cheese
1 egg, slightly beaten
1 teaspoon salt
1/4 teaspoon pepper
1 (8-ounce) can tomato sauce
1 teaspoon oregano

Preheat the oven to 350°. Pour the soup through a strainer set over a bowl. Reserve only 1/2 cup of the liquid, setting aside the remainder for another use. Combine the 1/2 cup liquid and the onions with the stuffing mix in a large bowl, tossing until the stuffing is evenly moistened. Add the beef, parsley, cheese, egg, salt, and pepper and mix well. Pack into a loaf pan or shape into a loaf in a baking dish. Bake for 1 hour. Stir together the tomato sauce and oregano. Remove the meatloaf from the oven, drain, and pour the tomato sauce over top. Bake an additional 15 minutes. Allow to rest 10 minutes before slicing.

Makes 6 servings

Lois Small, Red Hatter
Classy Ladies, Denton, Texas

The Great Meatloaf Debacle

I had been married for only a few months when my new husband asked me to make meatloaf for dinner. I didn't care for meatloaf, so I had never made it before. I got out my trusted recipe book and found a recipe for meatloaf. I assembled all the ingredients and completed each step, religiously following every direction to the letter.

The meatloaf came out looking beautiful. My husband wasn't due home for another hour, so I decided to taste it to make sure that it was okay. I don't know where I went wrong, but it tasted ghastly.

I didn't want to waste the meat, and I sure wasn't going to feed it to my new husband, so I offered it to my dog. He came over, sniffed it, then turned up his nose and walked away. Normally that dog would eat anything, but the meatloaf was too disgusting even for him.

I took the meatloaf out to the trash can, but then reasoned that my husband might find it. I definitely didn't want to have to explain why it had been thrown away. I then came up with a brilliant idea. I went to the storage shed, got out a shovel, and buried it. My husband never did find out why he didn't have meatloaf that night.

Linda C. Brady
Princess Bargain Belle
Aurora Glorialis
Aurora, Colorado

Beef Stroganoff

1   (8-ounce) package egg noodles
1 1/2 pounds tenderloin or rib-eye steak
1   tablespoon paprika
1   tablespoon dry mustard
2   teaspoons garlic salt
1   teaspoon sugar
1   teaspoon black pepper
1/2   cup all-purpose flour
1   medium onion, diced
4   tablespoons butter
1   pound sliced fresh mushrooms

1   tablespoon olive oil

1 1/2   tablespoons Worcestershire sauce

1 1/2   cups chicken stock

3/4   cup Burgundy wine

3/4   cup sour cream

Fresh parsley, finely chopped

Prepare the noodles according to package directions. Cut the meat into 1/2-inch-thick slices; cut each slice into strips about 2 1/2 inches long and 1/4-inch wide. Combine the paprika, mustard, garlic salt, sugar, pepper, and flour in a plastic bag. Add the strips of beef and shake in the bag until all pieces are coated. In a large skillet sauté the onion in the butter over medium heat until soft but not brown. Raise the heat to medium high and add the mushrooms; simmer for 15 minutes uncovered. Remove from the skillet. Add the olive oil to the skillet and, using high heat, quickly brown the meat. Combine the Worcestershire sauce and stock and slowly add to the meat, stirring constantly to form a rich gravy. Reduce the heat to medium low and simmer for 15 minutes. Return the mushroom mixture to the skillet, mix well, add the red wine, and return just to a simmer. Remove from heat and stir in the sour cream. Adjust the seasoning to taste and serve immediately over the hot noodles. Garnish with parsley.

Makes 4 to 6 servings

Lucinda Denton, Founding Queen Mother (FQM)
Nonpareils, Knoxville, Tennessee

Italian Eggplant and Ground Chuck Casserole

2   tablespoons vegetable oil

1   pound ground chuck

1   medium eggplant

1/4   cup olive oil

1   teaspoon salt

Pepper to taste

1/3   cup all-purpose flour

2   (8-ounce) cans Italian tomato sauce

1/2   teaspoon Italian seasoning

1   tablespoon grated Parmesan cheese

1   cup shredded mozzarella cheese

Preheat the oven to 300°. Heat the vegetable oil in a large skillet over medium-high heat. Brown the ground chuck in the hot oil, breaking it up into pieces. Drain and remove from the skillet. Cut the eggplant into 2-inch-thick slices. Do not remove the skin. Heat the olive oil in the skillet over medium-high heat. Season the egg[plant slices with the salt and pepper to taste, coat with the flour, and brown in the olive oil. Arrange the cooked eggplant in a greased 13 x 9-inch baking dish. Top with the browned ground chuck. Cover with the tomato sauce. Sprinkle the Italian seasoning and Parmesan cheese over top. Add the shredded mozzarella cheese. Bake for 45 minutes.

Makes 6 servings

Claudia Huye, Maiden of Memories
GRITS (Girls Raised in the South), Montgomery, Texas

Reuben Meat Loaf

2   pounds lean ground beef
2   cups bread crumbs
1   egg, beaten
2   tablespoons ketchup
3/4   teaspoon salt
1   (8-ounce) can sauerkraut, rinsed and drained
3/4   cup plus 1/4 cup shredded Swiss cheese
3   to 4 ounces lean pastrami, chopped
1/4   cup sour cream
1   tablespoon prepared mustard

Preheat the oven to 350°. Combine the beef, bread crumbs, egg, ketchup, and salt in a medium bowl and mix lightly. Combine the sauerkraut, 3/4 cup cheese, pastrami, sour cream, and mustard in a separate bowl. Pat one-third of the beef mixture to form an oval 9 inches long in a greased 13x9-inch baking pan. Spread with half the sauerkraut mixture. Repeat the layers of meat and sauerkraut mixture. Use the remaining third of the meat for the top layer. Do not cover the sides where the sauerkraut shows. Loosely cover with aluminum foil. Bake for 60 to 70 minutes. Remove the foil and sprinkle the remaining 1/4 cup cheese on top of the loaf. Bake 5 minutes longer, or until the cheese is melted. Allow to rest 10 minutes before slicing.

Makes 6 servings

Patricia Fry, Lady of the Barnyard
Barnyard Chicks, Mohnton, Pennsylvania

Meat Puffs

Little individual meat loaves are just so adorable.

PUFFS
1/2   pound pork sausage
1   pound ground beef
1/2   cup minced onion
2   cups grated potatoes
2   cups grated carrots
2   eggs, beaten
2/3   cup evaporated milk
2/3   cup dry bread crumbs
1/2   teaspoon salt

SAUCE
2   tablespoons butter or margarine, melted
2   tablespoons white or cider vinegar
1   (10-ounce) can tomato soup, undiluted
1/2   cup water
2   tablespoons Worcestershire sauce
1/2   teaspoon salt
1/2   cup ketchup

For the puffs, combine the sausage, beef, onion, potatoes, carrots, eggs, milk, crumbs, and salt in a large bowl and mix well. When ready to cook, form into large balls and arrange on a lightly oiled baking pan.

For the sauce, combine the butter, vinegar, soup, water, Worcestershire sauce, salt, and ketchup in a bowl and mix well. (Both meat puffs and sauce can be made ahead of time and refrigerated.) When ready to cook, pour the sauce over the meat puffs. Cover with foil. Either cook for 1 hour at 350°, or 4 to 5 hours at 250°.

Makes 12 servings

Donna Frederick, Vice Queen
Red Hat Silver Belles, Ely, Nevado

Sicilian Meatloaf

Here's a meatloaf that encloses a layer of ham and cheese and slices up pretty enough for company.

2   pounds lean ground beef
2   eggs
2   tablespoons chopped fresh parsley
1/2 teaspoon oregano
3/4 cup soft bread crumbs
1   cup tomato juice
1   small garlic clove, diced
    Salt and pepper to taste
6   or 8 slices boiled ham
1   (8-ounce) package shredded mozzarella
    cheese

Preheat the oven to 350°. Combine the ground beef, eggs, parsley, oregano, bread crumbs, tomato juice, garlic, and salt and pepper. Mix well. On foil or waxed paper pat the mixture into a 12 x 10-inch rectangle. Arrange the ham on top of the beef, leaving an edge all around. Sprinkle the cheese on top of the ham. Roll and seal the edges and ends of the foil. Transfer to a 13 x 9-inch baking pan.

Bake for 1 hour 15 minutes. Allow to rest 10 minutes before slicing.

Makes 8 to 10 servings

Peggy Murtagh, Queen Mum
Crimson Hattitudes, Brockton, Massachusetts

Cheesy Meatloaf

1   egg
3/4 cup milk
1   (4-ounce) package grated cheddar cheese
1/2 cup quick-cooking oats
1/2 cup chopped onion
1   teaspoon salt
1   pound lean ground beef
2/3 cup ketchup
1/2 cup firmly packed brown sugar
1 1/2 teaspoons prepared mustard

Preheat the oven to 350°. In a large bowl mix the egg and milk. Stir in the cheese, oats, onion, and salt. Add the beef and mix well. Shape into eight small loaves and arrange in a greased 13 x 9-inch baking dish. Combine the ketchup, brown sugar, and mustard and spoon over the loaves. Bake for about 45 minutes, or until the meat reaches a temperature of 160° on a meat thermometer. Allow to rest 10 minutes before slicing.

Makes 6 to 8 servings

Dokie Bledsoe, Queen Ritzy Red Lady
Coleman County Texans, Valera, Texas

Impossibly Easy Cheeseburger Pie

2   teaspoons vegetable oil
1   pound extra lean ground beef
1   cup chopped onion
1/2 teaspoon salt
1   cup shredded fat-free cheddar cheese
1/2 cup reduced-fat baking mix
1   cup fat-free milk
2   eggs

Preheat the oven to 400°. Grease a 9-inch pie plate. Heat the oil in a skillet over medium heat. Sauté the beef and onion until the beef is cooked through and the onion is tender. Drain. Stir in the salt. Spread the meat mixture in the pie plate and sprinkle with the cheese. Combine the baking mix, milk, and eggs and stir until blended. Pour into the pie plate. Bake for 25 minutes, or until a knife inserted in the center comes out clean.

Makes 6 servings

Flo Henick, Fancy Flo
Santa Teresa Red Hots, San Jose, California

Quicker Beef Pastries

Portable and packable; so great for lunches and picnics.

2   (9-inch) refrigerated pie crusts
11/2 cups potatoes, finely diced
1   cup carrots, diced
1/2 cup onion, diced
1/2 teaspoon dried thyme
1/2 teaspoon salt
1/4 teaspoon freshly ground black pepper
1   can beef broth, reserve just enough to moisten mixture later
2   cups cooked ground sirloin
1   egg beaten with 1 teaspoon water

Preheat the oven to 350°. Divide each pie crust in half and roll out to about 4 inch circles to make the pastries. In a skillet over medium-low heat, combine the potatoes, carrots, onion, thyme, salt, pepper, and broth. Simmer until the vegetables are cooked but still firm. Drain. Spray a large baking sheet with olive oil or cooking spray. Lay each pastry round onto the baking sheet one at a time and fill the center of each with the beef mixture. Moisten the edges with the egg mixture. Pull up the sides, and press the edges together to form a sort of upright turnover. Brush the tops of the pastries with the egg mixture (or olive oil). Bake for 30 minutes, or until golden brown. Serve with gravy.

Makes 4 pastries

Sally Carbone, Lady-In-Waiting
Razzle Dazzle Red Hats of Colchester, Colchester, Connecticut

Summer Sausage

Excellent flavor, texture, and appearance, said our testers.

3	pounds ground beef
3	tablespoon Morton's Tender Quick Salt
1	cup cold water
1/2	teaspoon coarsely ground black pepper
1/8	teaspoon garlic powder
1 1/2	teaspoons mustard seeds
2	teaspoons liquid smoke

Combine the beef, salt, water, pepper, garlic powder, mustard seeds, and liquid smoke and mix well. Divide the mixture in half and shape each portion into an 11 x 2-inch roll. Wrap in aluminum foil and refrigerate for 24 hours. Roll the sausages on the counter a time or two during chilling to maintain a sausage shape.

Preheat the oven to 300°. Remove the sausages from the foil and bake on a rack in a roasting pan or in a large baking dish for 1 hour to 1 hour 15 minutes, or until the rolls reach an internal temperature of 170°. Cool, wrap in plastic wrap, and chill thoroughly. Cut into 1/4-inch to 1/3-inch-slices.

Makes 50 to 60 or more slices

Oleta Reinhart, Princess of Poultry
Kiwanis Manor Ramblin' Red Hatters, Tiffin, Ohio

Terry's Veal and Peppers

My mom, Terry, made the best Italian veal and peppers, and everyone was always asking for her recipe. She began the tradition of giving the recipe, its nonperishable ingredients, and a brand new cast iron frying pan, later an electric fry-pan, as a shower gift to her daughters, her nieces, and her nephews' fiancées. My sister and I continued this tradition with our daughters, other relatives, and friends. Now my daughter and niece continue on to the next generation. So there's no telling anymore how many people this recipe has touched.

1/2	cup olive oil
2	or 3 green bell peppers, chopped
1	pound veal cubes
1	garlic clove, chopped
1/2	cup dry white wine
1	chicken bouillon cube
1	cup hot water
1	(8-ounce) can tomato sauce
	Cooked rice or egg noodles

In a large skillet heat the oil over medium heat and sauté the peppers just until tender. Remove from the skillet. Brown the veal with the garlic, cooking until the skillet is nearly dry. Pour in the white wine. Dissolve the bouillon cube in the hot water and add to the skillet. Simmer for 10 minutes. Add the tomato sauce. Cover and simmer for 45 minutes. Return the peppers to the skillet for the last 15 minutes. Serve over rice or noodles.

Makes 2 servings

Johanna G. Capasso, Princess Grace
Red Hot Hattitudes, Columbus, New Jersey

Best Steak Marinade Ever

1/2   cup soy sauce

1/2   cup pineapple juice

1/4   cup olive oil

1   tablespoon brown sugar

2   teaspoons ground ginger

1   teaspoon garlic powder

1/2   teaspoon black pepper

Combine the soy sauce, pineapple juice, oil, brown sugar, ginger, garlic powder, and pepper in a saucepan. Simmer for 5 minutes, stirring occasionally. Let cool. Combine the marinade and steaks in a plastic bag. Refrigerate for at least 4 hours and up to 18. Discard the remaining marinade before grilling the meat.

Makes enough for 8 steaks

Sharon Phillips, Queen
Scarlett O'Hatters of Lansdale, Lansdale, Pennsylvania

Stuffed Cabbage Rolls

Sometimes you just need a little taste of tradition. Serve with mashed potatoes, corn, and rye bread.

1   pound ground beef or pork

1   teaspoon salt

1   teaspoon black pepper

3   tablespoons steak sauce

1   small onion, diced

3   garlic cloves, diced

3/4   cup cooked rice (whole grain)

12   cabbage leaves

1   (14-ounce) can sauerkraut

1   (8-ounce) can tomato sauce

1   teaspoon Splenda or sugar

Combine the ground meat, salt, pepper, steak sauce, onion, garlic, and rice in a large bowl. Steep the cabbage leaves in boiling water for 5 minutes and drain. Arrange 1/4 to 1/2 cup of the meat mixture on each cabbage leaf and roll up gently. Spread the sauerkraut over the bottom of a large pot or Dutch oven. Arrange the cabbage rolls on the sauerkraut. Pour the tomato sauce over the rolls, and sprinkle them with the Splenda. Cover with water. Simmer, covered, for 1 hour.

Makes 12 rolls

Louise Kubanda, Queen Louise
Blushing Red Hatters, San Diego, California

Veal with Lemon–Caper Sauce

Use a little of the caper juice to make it tangy, if you like.

1   pound veal scallopini

2   tablespoons all-purpose flour

1/2   teaspoon salt

1/8   teaspoon pepper

1/8   teaspoon paprika

1   tablespoon olive oil, divided
       Lemon-Caper Sauce

2/3   cup dry white wine

1/4   cup lemon juice

2   teaspoons drained capers

1   teaspoon butter
       Pasta or egg noodles

Pound the veal to 1/8-inch if necessary. Combine the flour, salt, pepper, and paprika on a plate. Coat the veal with the flour mixture. In a non-stick skillet heat 1/2 tablespoon oil over medium heat. Add half the veal pieces and cook 3 to 4 minutes, turning once. Remove and keep warm. Repeat with the remaining oil and veal.

For the sauce, add the wine and lemon juice to the skillet. Cook and stir until the browned bits are dissolved and the liquid thickens slightly. Remove from the heat; stir in the capers and butter. Spoon the sauce over the veal. Serve over pasta or noodles.

Makes 3 to 4 servings

Joanne Johnson, Queen JoJo 1st
Cats in the Hats in Annapolis, Annapolis, Maryland

Veal Paprikash

Paprika gives this entrée the right color for a celebration with friends.

1/4	cup all-purpose flour
1/2	teaspoon salt
1/4	teaspoon pepper
2	pounds veal, cubed
4	tablespoons safflower or corn oil
2	onions, sliced
2	teaspoons paprika
1	cup instant chicken bouillon granules
1/2	to 3/4 cup sour cream
	Hot cooked noodles

Place the flour, salt, and pepper in a bag. Shake the veal in the bag until lightly coated. Heat the oil in a large skillet over medium-high heat and brown the veal. Add the onions and cook until just tender. Stir in the paprika. Add the chicken bouillon, cover, and simmer gently for 20 minutes, or until the veal is tender. Just before serving, stir in the sour cream and heat through. Do not boil. Serve with the noodles.

Makes 4 servings

Ann Terry, Vice Mum
Crimson Cuties, Spring Hill, Florida

Roast Leg of Lamb

6	pounds boneless leg of lamb
1	teaspoon ginger
1	teaspoon garlic powder
1	teaspoon salt
1	teaspoon pepper
1	garlic clove, chopped
1	cup all-purpose flour
1	to 2 tablespoons rosemary

Preheat the oven to 350°. Rinse the lamb and pat dry. Mix together the ginger, garlic powder, salt, and pepper. Rub onto the lamb. Cut slits in the lamb and insert garlic pieces. Roll the meat in the flour. Sprinkle with the rosemary. Place in a roasting bag and roast in the oven for 3 hours.

Makes 10 servings

Anne Karn, Queen Mum
Lady Red Birds, Jones, Michigan

Chicken Asiago

The flavor here depends on good-quality cheese so splurge, you're worth it.

2   (14-ounce) cans chicken broth
1/2 cup water
2   pounds boneless chicken breast, cut in bite-size chunks
1   pound orzo
1   (8 ounce) bag frozen peas, thawed
3/4 plus 1/4 cup freshly grated Asiago cheese
1/4 teaspoon salt
1/4 teaspoon fresh oregano, minced
1/8 teaspoon freshly cracked black pepper

Bring the broth and water to a boil in a Dutch oven over high heat. Add the chicken and orzo. Reduce the heat to medium low and simmer until most of the liquid is gone. Add the peas, 3/4 cup Asiago, salt, oregano, and pepper. Mix well and cook for 5 more minutes, or until heated through. Sprinkle with the remaining 1/4 cup Asiago before serving.

Makes 4 servings

Sally Carbone, Lady-in-Waiting
Razzle Dazzle Red Hats of Colchester, Colchester, Connecticut

Chili Cheese Chicken

8   large skinless, boneless chicken breasts
1   (7-ounce) can chopped mild green chiles
1/2 pound Monterey Jack cheese, cut into 8 strips

1/2 cup bread crumbs
1/4 cup grated Parmesan cheese
1   to 3 teaspoons chili powder
1/2 teaspoon salt
1/4 teaspoon ground cumin
1/4 teaspoon black pepper
6   tablespoons butter, melted
1   (16-ounce) container mild salsa
    Sour cream for garnish

Preheat the oven to 400°. Pound the chicken breasts to an even thickness with a meat mallet. Spread each breast with 1 tablespoon chiles. Place a cheese strip on top of the chiles, roll up each breast and secure with a toothpick. Combine the bread crumbs, cheese, chili powder, salt, cumin, and pepper in a shallow dish. Dip each stuffed breast into the melted butter and then into the breadcrumb mixture. Place into a greased 13x9-inch baking dish, seam side down. Drizzle with the remaining butter. Bake for 40 minutes, or until cooked through. Serve with the salsa and garnish with sour cream.

Makes 8 servings

Barbara Sierra-Franco, Princess of Prussia
Purple Queens of Prussia, King of Prussia, Pennsylvania

Great Grilled Chicken

Something a little different from the usual patio fare.

1   cup white vinegar
1   cup vegetable oil
4   teaspoons salt
1   teaspoon pepper

3   to 4 teaspoons poultry seasoning
1   egg
1   fryer or 4 large chicken breasts

Mix the vinegar, oil, salt, pepper, poultry seasoning, and egg in a blender. Process until well
blended. Place the chicken in a bowl, pour the
sauce over the chicken and marinate in the
refrigerator for 1 to 2 hours. When ready, grill
the chicken, turning occasionally, basting pieces
with the sauce every time you turn them. Grill
until the chicken is thoroughly cooked.

Makes 4 servings

Peggy Hartzell, Queen Mum
Majestic Red Hatters, Pine Grove, Pennsylvania

Bacon & Tomato Chicken

8   slices bacon
1   medium onion, chopped
8   boneless, skinless chicken breast halves (or
    4 whole breasts cut in half)
    Salt and pepper to taste
1   (14-ounce) can stewed tomatoes
1   tablespoon sugar
3/4 cup Heinz 57 sauce
    Hot cooked rice

In a pan over medium-high heat, cook the bacon
until crisp. Remove from the pan and crumble.
In the same pan sauté the onion in the drippings
until tender. Remove from the pan. In same pan
brown the chicken breasts in the drippings.
Season with the salt and pepper. Drain the excess
fat. Combine the bacon and onions with the

tomatoes, sugar, and Heinz 57 sauce and add to
the chicken. Cover, reduce the heat to medium
low and simmer for 45 minutes, basting occasionally. Serve over the hot rice.

Makes 8 servings

Sharon Phillips, Queen
Scarlett O'Hatters of Lansdale, Lansdale, Pennsylvania

Celebration Chicken

4   slices dried beef
    Boiling water
4   boneless, skinless chicken breasts
4   slices bacon
1   (10 3/4-ounce) can cream of chicken soup
1   cup sour cream
1/4 cup Parmesan cheese
    Paprika

Preheat the oven to 275°. Separate the slices of
dried beef and pour boiling water over them to
reconstitute. Let stand for about 2 minutes.
Drain and pat dry. Arrange the beef in a
greased 9-inch glass baking dish. Wrap each
chicken breast with a slice of bacon and place
on the dried beef. Mix together the soup and
sour cream and spoon over the chicken. Bake
uncovered for 1 hour 45 minutes. Remove from
the oven and sprinkle with the Parmesan
cheese and paprika. Return to the oven and
bake 15 minutes longer.

Makes 4 servings

Fran Pritchert, Empress of Ebay
Scarlet Sophisticates, Woodbridge, Virginia

The Melting Turkey

In October of 2004, as the newly elected Queen of our chapter, I hosted the monthly luncheon. The ladies were each to bring some tasty treats for us all to enjoy.

My house was thoroughly decorated for Halloween, with decorations in the kitchen, dining room, and bathroom. However, since this was to be the last luncheon for one of our ladies for a while (she spends winters in Florida), I decorated the living room for Christmas, complete with a tree, lights, presents, and all the trimmings.

Looking everything over, I was quite proud of myself. But one detail remained: I knew that someone was certain to ask, "What happened to Thanksgiving?" Since the top part of my double oven had a glass partition in the oven door and the oven was not working properly anyway, I put a large plastic turkey in the oven for all to see. It looked completely real! I was very pleased with the results and knew that this would make a truly memorable day. Little did I know just how memorable it would be!

All the ladies arrived with their luncheon goodies and were delighted with the decorations. Just as I expected, someone did ask, "Whatever happened to Thanksgiving?" To which I answered, "The turkey's in the oven." We all had a good laugh. Just one guest was missing—a late arrival bringing an uncooked casserole that was then placed in the bottom oven.

My niece, Dawn, was with us on this day, demonstrating how to make cards as part of her business, called Stamping Up. As everyone was engrossed in the project, one of the ladies said, "Gosh, that turkey sure smells good." We all had a good laugh as I replied, "Oh yeah, plastic always smells good," and we continued working on our cards.

The aroma of food cooking made us all hungry, so as the others worked on their cards, I started putting the food out. Suddenly, someone said, "I think the food in the oven is ready." Black smoke was coming out of the top oven! Oh my gosh! Oh my gosh! The turkey was in there! "Guess who turned on the top oven instead of the bottom oven?!"

What a sight to see: the turkey in flames; Red Hatters scurrying around, waving their Red Hats at the smoke and flames; and Queen Mum, who works for an alarm company, on the phone telling the girls in the Central Station not to dispatch the fire department, as it was a false alarm—just another plastic turkey in the oven!

I guess you can call me a "real turkey"! Who else would ever put a plastic turkey in an oven? But I certainly did make an impression! This year we will all go out for a turkey dinner and entertainment, but I know that nothing will ever surpass the memory of our first "Red Hat Turkey Day"!

Ann O'Donnell
Queen Mum
The Rosa Capellas
Weymouth, Massachusetts

Berry Easy Red Chicken

It's not just the color that gives this entrée its name— it's the fantastic and unexpected combination (not to mention the extra-easy preparation). Testers called it the surprise hit of their tasting, with 10 of 11 testers giving it a score of "5." You can use the same mixture to top pork loin.

6 to 8 skinless, boneless halved chicken
   breasts *1½ to 2 lbs*
1 (16-ounce) can whole cranberry sauce
1 envelope (1/3 cup) onion soup mix
1 (7-ounce) bottle Catalina salad dressing
   Hot cooked rice

Preheat the oven to 350°. Arrange the chicken breasts in an ungreased 13 x 9-inch pan. In a medium-size bowl combine the cranberry sauce, dry soup mix, and Catalina dressing. Pour over the chicken and bake uncovered for 30 to 40 minutes. Serve over the rice.

Makes 6 to 8 servings

Note: The sauce mixture is very abundant— you could bake much more chicken or store excess uncooked sauce for later use.

Beth Grahl, Queen Bee
Red Hat Belles of Fenton, Fenton, Michigan

Garlic Fried Chicken Sesame Soy Glaze

1 cup soy sauce
1 cup sugar
1 tablespoon sesame oil
2 tablespoons brown sesame seeds, lightly toasted in a dry skillet over low heat (Be careful not to scorch.)
2 to 3 green onions, finely minced
3 or more garlic cloves, peeled and minced
1 chicken, cut into serving pieces (or 3 to 4 pounds fryer parts)
  Vegetable oil for deep frying
6 to 8 eggs, beaten
  All-purpose flour for dusting chicken
1 or more (10-ounce) bags Japanese dry bread crumbs (Panko)

For the glaze, in a medium-size, heat-proof bowl mix the soy sauce, sugar, sesame oil, sesame seeds, green onions, and garlic until the sugar is completely dissolved. Set aside while you prepare the chicken.

Rinse the chicken and pat dry with paper towels. Heat the oil in a pan for deep frying at a depth of two inches. Place the beaten eggs in a bowl. Place the flour in a separate bowl. Place the bread crumbs in a separate bowl. Dip the chicken parts into the flour, then the eggs, and lastly into the bread crumbs. Carefully place a few pieces of chicken at a time into the hot oil. Brown on one side; then turn and cook to an even golden brown on the other side. Immediately remove one piece at a time and dip directly into the sauce; turn in the sauce to coat evenly. Quickly remove from the sauce and place onto a deep pan tilted to one side. (Place a rolled-up kitchen towel under one side to hold the pan at an angle.) Arrange the chicken pieces on the higher end of the deep pan. This permits the excess sauce to drain off and keep the chicken crispy. Repeat with the remaining chicken pieces. Spoon the excess sauce that has drained to the bottom of the tilted pan back into the dipping bowl to use for cooking the remaining pieces of chicken.

Makes 4 to 6 servings

Jane Aita, Queen Mother
Alhambra Shopping Bag Ladies, Alhambra, Calfornia

Pineapple-Soy Sauce Chicken

1 cup all-purposeflour
1 teaspoon nutmeg (or to taste)
1 teaspoon celery salt (or to taste)
1/2 cup (1 stick) butter
1 pound skinless, boneless chicken breast halves
1/3 cup soy sauce
1 cup pineapple juice
  Hot cooked rice

Preheat the oven to 350°. Mix together the flour, nutmeg, and celery salt on a plate. Melt the butter in a skillet over medium-high heat. Coat the chicken with the flour mixture. Lightly brown the chicken in the skillet. Arrange the pieces in a shallow 8-inch baking pan. Mix the soy sauce and pineapple juice and pour over the chicken.

Bake uncovered for 30 minutes. Serve over hot cooked rice.

Makes 4 servings

Patricia Wick, Queen Mum
Wecandogals, Gowanda, New York

Cashew Nut Chicken

Dash of pepper
2 plus 1 teaspoons light soy sauce
1 skinless, boneless chicken breast, cut into small pieces
1 tablespoon cornstarch
Few drops of sesame oil
1/4 cup water
1 (8-ounce)can cashew nuts
1 medium onion, minced
6 slices fresh ginger
2 garlic cloves, chopped
1 cup sliced mushrooms
2 cups frozen mixed vegetables
1/4 teaspoon salt
Hot cooked rice

Combine the pepper and 2 teaspoons soy sauce in a bowl. Marinate the chicken in the soy sauce for 15 minutes. Combine the cornstarch with the remaining 1 teaspoon soy sauce, sesame oil, and water. Toast the cashew nuts in a little oil in a pan. Remove from the pan. In the same pan sauté the onion, ginger, and garlic on medium-high heat until nicely browned. Add the chicken and cook for 3 minutes. Add the mushrooms, frozen vegetables, and salt and cook for 5 minutes. Stir the cornstarch mixture and add to the pan. Cook, stirring, until thick. Stir in the toasted cashews. Serve with rice.

Makes 4 servings

Trudean Olson, Queen Mum
Red Hat Delta Divas, Delta, British Columbia, Canada

Mexican Citrus-Marinated Chicken

1/4 cup orange juice
2 tablespoons olive oil
2 teaspoons chili powder
1/4 teaspoon salt
1/2 small onion, chopped small
1/4 cup lime juice
2 tablespoons chopped fresh cilantro
1 teaspoon ground cumin
1/4 teaspoon hot sauce
3 pounds skinless, boneless chicken breast
Flour tortillas

Combine the orange juice, olive oil, chili powder, salt, onion, lime juice, cilantro, cumin, and hot sauce in a large bowl and mix well. Add the chicken, cover and refrigerate for at least 6 hours. Grill the chicken, brushing with the marinade and turning occasionally, until cooked through. Serve with flour tortillas or cut into slices for fajitas. Offer sautéed onions and bell peppers, cheese, and salsa, for a full meal. Or serve sliced on green salad with dressing.

Makes 6 servings

Susie Van Foeken, Queen
Hilmar Red Hat Readers, Hilmar, California

Crunchy Chicken

"Pretty on the table," raved testers. "Moist, crunchy, no grease."

1   (8-ounce) container sour cream
2   tablespoons lemon juice
1   tablespoon Worcestershire sauce
1   teaspoon paprika
1   tablespoon celery salt
    Pepper to taste
8   medium, skinless, boneless, chicken breasts halves (about 2 pounds)
1   (8-ounce) package herb seasoned stuffing mix (about 2 cups), coarsely crushed
1/4 cup (1/2 stick) butter, melted

Preheat the oven to 375°. In a shallow bowl combine the sour cream, lemon juice, Worcestershire sauce, paprika, celery salt, and pepper. Lightly pound the chicken to an even thickness, if desired. Dip the chicken into the sour cream mixture to coat and then roll it in the stuffing mix. Arrange the chicken in a large, shallow, greased 13x9-inch baking dish (pieces should not touch). Drizzle the melted butter over the chicken. Bake, uncovered, for 25 minutes, or until no longer pink (170°).

Makes 8 servings

Carolyn Knauss, Red Snapper
Red Cardinals, Tatamy, Pennsylvania

Crunchy Oven-Fried Chicken

Another irresistible, crunchy-crusted, chicken recipe. This one uses cutlets for quickest cooking.

3   tablespoons buttermilk
1 1/2 teaspoons fresh or bottled lime juice
1/4 teaspoon Dijon-style mustard
    Dash of garlic powder
    Dash of white pepper
    Dash of salt
2   thin chicken cutlets
1/2 cup plus 2 tablespoons crushed corn flakes
2   teaspoons vegetable oil, divided

Preheat the oven to 450°. In a small bowl combine the buttermilk, lime juice, mustard, garlic powder, white pepper, and salt. Mix well. Dip the chicken into the buttermilk mixture, coating both sides and using the entire mixture. Pour the crushed cornflake crumbs onto a sheet of waxed paper or a paper plate, and dip the chicken pieces into the crumbs, turning to coat both sides. Arrange the chicken on a nonstick baking sheet. Drizzle 1/2 teaspoon oil over each cutlet. Bake for 10 minutes, or until lightly browned. Turn, drizzle each cutlet with another 1/2 teaspoon oil, and bake until the chicken is tender and the coating is crisp, about 10 minutes longer.

Makes 2 servings

Joan Judd, Queen Mom
Pool Playmates, The Villages, Florida

Easy Chicken Dijon

For gals who like a sassy, tangy flavor.

4   boneless chicken breasts
    Salt and pepper to taste
2   tablespoons vegetable oil
1/3 cup chopped onion
1   garlic clove, minced
2/3 cup dry white wine
1   teaspoon cornstarch
2/3 cup chicken broth, divided
1   tablespoon Dijon mustard
2   teaspoons drained capers
    Fresh parsley for serving

Season the chicken with the salt and pepper. Brown in the oil over medium-high heat. Cook until done, about 10 minutes. Remove from the skillet. Sauté the onion and garlic until tender. Add the wine and simmer. Blend the cornstarch with 2 tablespoons of the broth. Add to the wine mixture. Add the remaining broth. Blend in the mustard and capers and heat through. Spoon over the chicken. Sprinkle with fresh parsley before serving.

Make 4 servings

Linda Pennington, Queen Mum
Sassy Hattitudes, Loganville, Georgia

Slow Cooker Chicken and Corn Bread Dressing

A smart cook knows how to feed a bunch with just three cups of chicken.

1   cup (2 sticks) butter
2   cups chopped onions
2   cups chopped celery
1   (13 x 9-inch) pan of corn bread
1   (10 3/4-ounce) can golden mushroom soup
1   (10 3/4-ounce) can cream of chicken soup
2   cups chicken broth
1   tablespoon poultry seasoning
1 1/2 teaspoons salt
2   teaspoons sage
1   teaspoon black pepper
3   cups chopped cooked chicken

Heat the butter in a saucepan over medium-high heat. Sauté the onions and celery in the butter. Crumble the corn bread into a large mixing bowl. Add the sautéed vegetables, mushroom soup, chicken soup, chicken broth, poultry seasoning, salt, sage, and pepper. Mix well and stir in the chicken. Pour into a slow cooker. Cook on high for 45 minues and then on low for 4 hours.

Makes 8 servings

Cindy Calahan, Queen Mother
YA–YA Hoopla Girls, Shelbyville, Tennessee

Herbed Chicken in Wine Sauce

Serve with French bread so none of the pan sauce goes to waste.

3   large chicken breast halves
1   teaspoon salt
1/4 teaspoon black pepper
1   tablespoon butter or margarine
1   (10³/4-ounce) can cream of chicken soup
3/4 cup dry white wine
3   ounces sliced mushrooms
2   teaspoons chopped green bell pepper
1/4 teaspoon thyme
1   teaspoon minced dried onions

Preheat the oven to 350°. Season the chicken with salt and pepper. Brown in the butter in a skillet over medium heat. Arrange the chicken in a baking dish. Blend the soup with the drippings in the pan. Stir in the wine slowly. Add the mushrooms, bell pepper, thyme, and onions and heat to boiling. Pour over the chicken and cover. Bake for 20 minutes. Remove the cover and bake 30 minutes longer.

Makes 4 servings

Carol Boshaw, Queen Mother
Fun Hatters of Holiday Acres, McHenry, Illinois

Honeymoon Special Chicken

Simple, easy, foolproof, good—the kind of recipe that reminds you why you like to cook in the first place.

1   fryer chicken, cut into serving pieces (or 3 to 4 pounds assorted chicken pieces)
2   teaspoons salt
2   tablespoons vegetable oil
1/2 cup honey
1   tablespoon prepared mustard
1   teaspoon lemon juice
1/2 teaspoon oregano

Preheat the oven to 350°. Arrange the chicken pieces in a single layer, skin side up, in a greased shallow baking pan. Mix the salt, oil, honey, mustard, lemon juice, and oregano. Pour the mixture over the chicken and bake, uncovered, for 1 hour, or until done. Baste with the sauce once or twice.

Makes 4 servings

Marie Zebrowski, Camping Queen
Redbuds of Bedford, Bedford, Virginia

Jalapeño-Lime Chicken for Fajitas

Sunny flavors.

4   boneless, skinless chicken breast halves
1   teaspoon grated lime zest
1   tablespoon lime juice
1   teaspoon ground cumin
1   jalapeño pepper, seeded and diced
1/4 teaspoon salt
1/4 teaspoon ground black pepper
2   to 3 garlic cloves, minced
1   tablespoon olive oil
     Flour tortillas

Mix the chicken, lime zest, lime juice, cumin, jalapeño, salt, pepper, garlic, and olive oil in a zip-top bag. Marinate for 30 minutes or up to 8 hours. Grill or sear in a nonstick pan. Slice for fajitas. Serve with flour tortillas and assorted garnishes.

Makes 4 servings

Brenda Hamlin–Lehmann, Queen Mum
  Laughs a Lot
Red Hat Dream Chasers, El Paso, Texas

Lemon Chicken

Prepare the chicken for baking; then refrigerate until ready to cook.

1/2 cup dry seasoned bread crumbs
1/2 teaspoon paprika
1/2 cup grated Parmesan cheese
     Salt and freshly ground pepper to taste
3   whole skinless, boneless chicken breasts, halved
2   eggs, beaten with 2 tablespoons water
1/4 cup (1/2 stick) butter or margarine
1   to 2 garlic cloves, minced
1/3 cup fresh lemon juice

Preheat the oven to 375°. Mix the bread crumbs, paprika, cheese, and salt and pepper in a large bowl. Dip the chicken breasts in the egg wash and then in the bread crumb mixture. Melt the butter in a large skillet over medium-high heat and brown the chicken breasts on both sides. Arrange in a greased 10 x 9-inch baking dish. Add the garlic and lemon juice to the skillet and cook for a few moments, scraping the bottom of the pan. Pour the liquid over the chicken. (Can be made ahead at this time and refrigerated. Allow to come to room temperature before baking.) Bake for 25 to 30 minutes.

Makes 6 servings

Bette Heide, Harborer of Hasty News
Sassy Classy Ladies, Chicago, Illinois

Two-Step Parmesan–Garlic Chicken

1/2 cup grated Parmesan cheese
1/2 teaspoon garlic powder
1   (1-ounce) envelope Italian salad dressing mix
6   boneless, skinless chicken breast halves (about 2 pounds)

Preheat the oven to 400°. Mix the cheese, garlic powder, and dressing mix together in a shallow dish. Moisten the chicken with water and coat with the cheese mixture. Arrange in a greased 13x9-inch baking dish. Bake for 20 to 25 minutes, or until done.

Makes 6 servings

Nancy Nix, Queen Mother
Dixie Dames, LaGrange, Georgia

Chicken Piccata

A restaurant classic, but easy enough to prepare at home.

- 4   tablespoons all-purpose flour
       Salt and pepper to taste
- 2   whole skinless, boneless chicken breasts,
       cut into strips
- 5   tablespoons olive oil
- 1/3 cup water
       Juice of 2 lemons
- 1/3 cup dry white wine
- 1   teaspoon freshly ground black pepper
- 1   lemon, thinly sliced
- 3   tablespoons drained capers
- 1/3 cup fresh parsley, chopped

Combine the flour with the salt and pepper to taste. Rinse the chicken and pat dry. Press each strip into the seasoned flour, coating completely. Heat the olive oil in a skillet over medium-high heat. Brown the chicken strips for approximately 3 minutes per side, or until the juices run clear. Remove the chicken to a plate and cover to keep warm. Add the water, lemon juice, wine, and freshly ground pepper. Bring to a boil, stirring constantly. Cook for 1 minute. Return the chicken to the skillet. Arrange the lemon slices over the chicken. Simmer for 5 minutes, or until the sauce thickens. Top with the capers and sprinkle with the parsley.

Makes 3 to 4 servings

Sue Southerland, Queen Mum
Sassy Bodacious Ladies, Greeneville, Tennessee

Mother's Potato Chip Chicken

Delight children (and the young at heart) with a platter of nuggets or breast strips coated with different flavors: sour cream and onion, barbecue, even dill pickle.

- 1/4 plus 1/4 cup (1 stick) butter, melted
- 6   to 8 skinless, boneless chicken breast halves
- 1   (11-ounce) bag potato chips, crushed to
       crumbs
       Paprika to taste
       Ranch dressing

Preheat the oven to 400°. Line a rectangular pan with foil. Coat the foil with 1/4 cup melted butter. Roll the chicken pieces in the chips and arrange in the pan. Dot the top of the chicken with the remaining 1/4 cup butter and sprinkle with paprika. Bake for 20 minutes; turn and bake 25 minutes longer, uncovered, watching closely so the coating doesn't burn. Remove the chicken to a platter. Serve with ranch dressing for dipping.

Makes 6 to 8 servings

Linda-Lee Parker, Princess Queen
Red Hots of Roswell, Roswell, Georgia

Purple Chicken with Plum Sauce

Just a few minutes of cooking from start to finish.

- 4   to 6 skinless, boneless chicken breasts
- 3   to 4 tablespoons olive oil

1   medium onion, diced

1   tablespoon (or more) minced garlic

1   to 2 zucchini, cubed

1   (8-ounce) can sliced water chestnuts, drained

1   (8-ounce) can bamboo shoots, drained

1   (7-ounce) jar plum sauce or hoisin sauce

    Hot cooked rice

Slice the chicken into bite-size pieces. In a wok or large frying pan heat the oil over medium-high heat. Sauté the chicken in the hot oil until browned. Add the onion and garlic. Cook for 1 to 2 minutes and add the zucchini pieces. Cook for 1 to 2 minutes. Add the water chestnuts, bamboo shoots, and plum sauce. Cook until warmed through. This recipe should take only 5 to 6 minutes to cook. Serve over the hot cooked rice.

Makes 4 to 6 servings

Mikayla DeRosier, Queen Mum of Sonoma
Le Chapeau Rouge D'Elegance, Sonoma, California

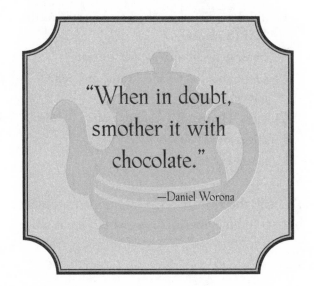

"When in doubt, smother it with chocolate."

—Daniel Worona

Chicken Sicilian

Serve over rice or pasta to make the most of the delicious pan juices.

2   tablespoons butter

2   tablespoons olive oil

    Salt and pepper to taste

4   to 6 skinless, boneless chicken breasts, cut into bite-size pieces

1/2   cup chopped onions

1   (4-ounce) jar mushrooms, drained

    Garlic salt taste

    Oregano to taste

1   (14-ounce) can artichokes, drained

2   tablespoons cooking sherry

2   tablespoons lemon juice

Melt the butter with the olive oil in a large pan over medium-high heat. Rub salt and pepper into the chicken breasts and add them to the pan. Cook the chicken for about 15 minutes, or until brown. Move to the side of the pan. Add the onions and mushrooms and sauté about 5 minutes. Add the garlic salt, oregano, artichoke hearts, sherry, and lemon juice. Mix well. Cook, covered, for about 5 minutes.

Makes 6 servings

JoAn Self, Queen Mum
Fine China Red Hatters of Saginaw, Saginaw, Texas

Chicken Marsala

3 to 4 pounds skinless, boneless chicken breasts
2 cups all-purpose flour (add more if necessary)
Salt and pepper to taste
1/2 cup (1 stick) butter
1 cup sliced fresh mushrooms
1 (10 1/2-ounce) can chicken broth
2 cups Marsala wine

Cut each chicken breast into three pieces. Mix the flour and salt and pepper on a plate. Press the chicken in the flour mixture, turning to coat completely. Melt the butter in a skillet over medium-high heat. Sauté the chicken for 15 to 20 minutes, or until browned, turning occasionally. Remove the chicken from the skillet. Sauté the mushrooms and add the chicken broth and Marsala wine. Return the chicken to the skillet, cover, and simmer until the liquid thickens, about 15 minutes.

Makes 4 servings

Pamela Kornick, Queen of Everything
The Red Madhatters, Windber, Pennsylvania

One-Dish Chicken and Rice Bake

Mild and mellow—guaranteed to please picky grandchildren.

1 (10 3/4-ounce) can cream of celery soup
3/4 cup uncooked white rice
1 cup water
1/4 teaspoon paprika plus more for sprinkling
4 skinless, boneless chicken breasts

Preheat the oven to 375°. In a greased 2-inch-deep baking dish, combine the soup, rice, water, and paprika. Arrange the chicken on top. Sprinkle with additional paprika. Cover with foil and bake for 45 minutes, or until the chicken is cooked through and the rice is tender.

Makes 4 servings

Note: For creamier rice, increase the water to 1 1/3 cups.

Mary Allred, Mistress Talks–a–Lot
Red Bonnet Sisters, Lakeland, Florida

Chicken Reuben

4 skinless, boneless chicken breasts, cut in half (8 pieces)
Seasoned salt and pepper to taste
1 (16-ounce) can sauerkraut, drained, squeezed dry
1 1/4 cups Thousand Island dressing, divided
8 slices Swiss cheese
8 slices rye bread

Preheat the oven to 325°. Pound the chicken breasts to an even thickness with a meat mallet.

College Appetite

When my daughter went to Lehigh University in Bethlehem, Pennsylvania, the college asked for recipes from home. I sent in my Chicken Reuben recipe. It was the first one chosen, and my daughter and four of her friends were invited to dine in the President's Dining Room, where they were served an elaborate candlelit dinner and treated like royalty. My daughter, Tamie Walters Swain, said that was the first time ever that there were no leftovers in the main dining hall.

Months later, we were eating at our neighbor's restaurant, The Depot, and I told him he should have my Chicken Reuben recipe. He said he already did. The chef who prepares the soup for his restaurant is also the chef at Lehigh University. He had excitedly told our neighbor about this Chicken Reuben recipe, saying he should use it for his restaurant. He was so surprised when he saw Tamie's name (his next-door neighbor) on the recipe card that he did use it, with great success, for his restaurant.

Nancy Walters
Queen Honey Bee
Cinnamon Cove Honey Bees
Fort Myers, Florida

Place the breasts in a greased 13x9-inch baking pan or casserole. Season with the seasoned salt and pepper. Combine the sauerkraut and 2 to 3 tablespoons Thousand Island dressing. Divide the sauerkraut mixture among the chicken breasts. Top with the Swiss cheese, and then spread generously with the remaining Thousand Island dressing. Cover the pan with foil. Bake for 45 minutes to 1 hour, or until the chicken is cooked through (juices will run clear when the meat is pierced with a knife). Serve on the bread.

Makes 6 to 8 servings

Nancy Walters, Queen Honey Bee
Cinnamon Cove Honey Bees, Fort Myers, Florida

Cajun Skillet Jambalaya

2   tablespoons vegetable oil
1   pound skinless, boneless chicken, cut into bite-size pieces
1   pound smoked sausage, cut into bite-size slices
1/2 cup chopped celery
1   medium onion, chopped
1/4 to 1/2 cup chopped bell pepper
1   (28-ounce) can diced tomatoes, not drained
3/4 cup water
1 1/2 cups instant rice (uncooked)
2   to 4 tablespoons Cajun seasoning

In a large skillet heat the oil over medium heat. Cook the chicken and the sausage in the oil for about 7 minutes, or until the chicken juices no longer run pink. Add the celery, onion, and bell pepper. Cook until the onion is transparent, about 2 minutes. Add the tomatoes with juice, water, rice, and Cajun seasoning. Bring the mixture to a boil, reduce the heat, cover, and simmer for about 20 minutes, or until the rice has cooked and absorbed the liquid. Let sit for about 5 minutes and serve.

Makes 6 servings

Shirley Lavender, Queen of the Bird House
Rolling Meadows Red Larks, Mountain Home, Arkansas

Chicken with Tarragon Cream Sauce

2   tablespoons unsalted butter
4   boneless, skinless chicken breast halves

1   cup chicken broth
1/4 cup dry white wine
1/4 cup chopped shallots
1   garlic clove, minced
1   cup whipping cream
1/2 cup sliced mushrooms
2   teaspoons chopped fresh tarragon
1   teaspoon fresh lemon juice
1/2 teaspoon freshly grated lemon peel
1/4 teaspoon salt
1/4 teaspoon pepper
     Lemon slices and fresh tarragon sprigs for garnish

In a large, heavy skillet over medium-high heat, melt the butter. Add the chicken and cook until light brown, about 2 minutes per side. Stir in the broth, wine, shallots, and garlic. Cover, reduce the heat to medium, and simmer for about 10 minutes. Transfer the chicken to a serving platter and cover to keep warm. Boil the broth mixture in the pan over medium-high heat for about 7 minutes, or until reduced to about half a cup. Remove from the heat and slowly add the cream, stirring constantly. Return to the heat and add the mushrooms and tarragon; cook about 5 minutes, stirring. Add the lemon juice, lemon peel, salt, and pepper. Pour the sauce over the chicken and garnish with the lemon slices and tarragon sprigs.

Makes 4 servings

Charlene Chambers, Diva in the Kitchen
Scarlet O'Bearas, Ormond Beach, Florida

Swiss & Cream Cheese Chicken Enchiladas

Creamy, cheesy, gooey satisfaction.

2   tablespoons butter
2   large Vidalia or other sweet onions, thinly
     sliced
1   garlic clove, minced or pressed
2   (3-ounce) packages cream cheese
2   cups diced cooked chicken
1/2 cup chopped pimientos or roasted red
     peppers
     Salt and pepper to taste
     Vegetable oil
12   corn tortillas
2/3 cup heavy whipping cream
2   cups shredded Swiss cheese
     Fresh cilantro and lime wedges for garnish

Melt the butter in a large frying pan over medium heat and sauté the onions and garlic until onions are soft and lightly brown. Remove from the heat, add the cream cheese, and mix with two forks until blended. Add the chicken and pimientos and mix lightly. Season with salt and pepper.

Heat 1 inch oil in a small frying pan over medium heat. When the oil is hot but not smoking, drop the tortilla into the oil for a few seconds, just long enough to begin to blister and become limp. Remove with tongs, drain briefly, and stack on a plate.

Spoon about 1/3 cup filling down the center of each tortilla and roll. Arrange the enchiladas seam side down in an ungreased 13 x 9-inch baking dish. At this point the enchiladas may be covered and refrigerated until the next day.

Preheat the oven to 375°. Immediately before baking, spoon whipping cream and Swiss cheese evenly over the enchiladas. Bake, uncovered, for 20 minutes, or until heated through. (If refrigerated, bake for a total of 30 minutes, 15 minutes covered and 15 uncovered.) Serve with garnish.

Makes 6 servings

Dr. L. Berry, Princess of the Kitchen
Ruby Begonias, Beaverton, Oregon

Teriyaki Grilled Chicken

4   boneless chicken breasts
1/2 cup soy sauce
1/2 cup real maple syrup
3   or more garlic cloves, smashed
2   green onions, sliced (green part only)

Wash and dry the chicken. Combine the soy sauce, maple syrup, garlic, and green onions in a large bowl. Mix well and add the chicken. Cover and refrigerate for at least 3 hours or up to 18. Bake or grill the chicken for 5 to 10 minutes on each side, or until the chicken is cooked through.

Makes 4 servings

Deborah Ford, Red Goddess
Teresa Red Hots, San Jose, California

Sour Cream Chicken

Lovers of dark chicken meat, this recipe is for you.

1   cup sour cream
2   tablespoons lemon juice
1   tablespoon Worcestershire sauce
1   teaspoon salt
1   teaspoon garlic salt
4   skinless, boneless chicken breasts
6   skinless, boneless chicken thighs
4   tablespoons butter, cut in small pats
2   cups dry bread crumbs
    Paprika

Mix the sour cream, lemon juice, Worcestershire sauce, salt, and garlic salt together in a large bowl. Add the chicken and marinate, refrigerated, for at least 6 hours and up to 18. When ready to bake, preheat the oven to 350°. Place the chicken in a buttered 13x9-inch baking dish, top each piece with a pat of butter; sprinkle with the bread crumbs and paprika. Bake for 45 minutes to 1 hour.

Makes 6 to 8 servings

Sue Hemphill, Queen Sue
Sassy Classy Red Hatters, San Leandro, California

Teriyaki Chicken

The contributor notes, "I've made this recipe for professional Japanese chefs and an owner of a Japanese restaurant. They all said it is the best Teriyaki they have ever eaten, or as good as what they make." The teriyaki mixture can also be used for fish and beef.

1   cup soy sauce
1/2 cup honey
1   garlic clove, minced
1   small onion, chopped
1   tablespoon grated fresh gingerroot
4   to 6 chicken breast halves

In a saucepan over medium heat, combine the soy sauce, honey, garlic, onion, and ginger. Heat to just before boiling. Reduce the heat to low and simmer for 5 minutes, stirring occasionally. Pour over the chicken and marinate in the refrigerator for at least 6 hours, turning once or twice. Preheat the oven to 350° and bake the chicken in a shallow baking dish, uncovered, for 20 to 30 minutes, or until cooked through.

Makes 4 to 6 servings

Mara Willick, Queen of SASCI
SASCI (Sexy Adventurous Sun City Instigators), Henderson, Nevada

Tequila–Lime Chicken

A grilled chicken meal bursting with sunny flavors.

2   teaspoons grated lime peel
1/4 cup lime juice
1/4 cup tequila
1   tablespoon olive oil
1   tablespoon orange liqueur
2   garlic cloves, minced
1/4 teaspoon salt
1/4 teaspoon pepper
6   skinless, boneless chicken breasts

In glass bowl, combine the lime peel, lime

juice, tequila, oil, liqueur, garlic, salt and pepper. Add the chicken, turning to coat. Cover and chill for 1 hour. Grill the chicken on an uncovered grill over medium heat for 5 minutes. Turn chicken and brush with the marinade. Grill for 7 to 10 minutes longer, or until the chicken is cooked through.

Makes 6 servings

Lorraine Sayas, Queen Mother Gem
Tidewaters Gems, Virginia Beach, VA

Chicken Vermouth

Here's a recipe for cooks who like it simple and on the mild side. Add mushrooms to the baking dish if it strikes your fancy.

4   skinless, boneless chicken breast halves
1   envelope onion soup mix
1/2   cup water
1/2   cup dry vermouth

Preheat the oven to 350°. Arrange the chicken in a greased 13x9-inch baking dish. Sprinkle the onion soup mix evenly over the top. Combine the water and vermouth and pour over the chicken. Cover and bake for 45 to 50 minutes.

Makes 4 servings

Marie Nightingale, The Royal Scribe
Red Hat'll Do Ya, Halifax, Nova Scotia, Canada

Baked Yogurt Chicken

Serve this as a mild, moist chicken, or jazz it up with more paprika, more mushrooms, and a tablespoon of chopped fresh thyme.

3   tablespoons olive oil
3   tablespoons butter or margarine
4   to 6 bone-in, skinless chicken breasts
2   tablespoons all-purpose flour
2   teaspoons paprika
1/2   cup plain yogurt
1/2   cup sliced fresh mushrooms
2   tablespoons fresh lemon juice
2   tablespoons chopped flat leaf parsley

Grease a 10-inch baking dish. Heat the oil in a large saucepan over medium-high heat. Add the butter. When the butter is melted add the chicken and cook for 5 minutes on each side, or until brown. Transfer the chicken to the prepared baking dish. Stir the flour and paprika into the pan drippings and cook for 2 minutes over medium heat. Add the yogurt and mix well. Pour the yogurt mixture over chicken.

Preheat the oven to 325°. Sauté the mushrooms in the lemon juice. Spoon over the chicken. Sprinkle with the parsley. Cover and bake for 1 hour 15 minutes.

Makes 4 to 6 servings

Grace Boehm, The Lady of Adventure
Classy Clarettes, Lake, Michigan

Lazy Chicken Cordon Bleu

The flavor of traditional cordon bleu, but much easier. Great for a potluck or covered dish event.

- 6 boneless, skinless chicken breasts (about 1 1/2 to 2 pounds) cut into 2-inch pieces
- 1/2 cup (1 stick) lightly salted butter, melted
- 2 cups dry Italian bread crumbs
- 1 pound sliced ham, diced
- 1 pound sliced Swiss cheese
  Juice of 1 lemon
- 1/2 cup dry white wine
- 1 (14.5-ounce) can beef broth
  Hot cooked rice or noodles

Preheat the oven to 375°. Grease a 13 x 9-inch glass ovenproof baking dish. Toss the cut-up chicken in the melted butter and then in the bread crumbs. Lay the coated chicken in the baking dish. Sprinkle the diced ham over the chicken. Lay the Swiss cheese slices over top. Combine the lemon juice, wine, and beef broth and pour on top of the cheese. Cover with foil and bake for 50 minutes. Serve over the buttered noodles or rice.

Makes 6 to 8 servings

Barbara Weinberg, Princess of Past and Present
Dusty Desert Roses, Cathedral City, California

Italian Baked Chicken

As we have all learned, the simplest things are often the best, but they depend on the smallest details. Use a mixture of chicken parts, not just breasts, for a deeper flavor. A naturally raised chicken will give superior results. And since cheese and olive oil are the main flavors here, skip the green can of cheese and instead select Parmegiano-Reggiano, Asiago or Romano cheese. Buy a block and grate it yourself for the best results.

- 1 cup dry Italian bread crumbs
- 1/2 cup grated Parmegiano, Asiago, or Romano cheese
- 2 eggs, well beaten
- 1/2 cup olive oil
- 1 fryer, cut up (or 3 pounds assorted fryer parts)
  Butter or margarine

Lightly grease a 13 x 9-inch baking dish. Preheat the oven to 375°. Combine the bread crumbs and cheese in a medium bowl. Combine the eggs and olive oil in another medium bowl. Dip the chicken pieces in the egg mixture, then in the crumb mixture. Arrange the chicken pieces in the prepared dish and dot each piece with butter. Bake for about 1 hour, or until the juices run clear when the meat is pierced with a knife.

Makes 4 servings

Sylvia North, Lady Syl
Swinging Mississippi Belles, Carriere, Mississippi

Prosciutto-Stuffed Chicken

Wonderfully delicate slices of prosciutto; add their succulent saltiness to these cheesy chicken rolls.

2   to 2 1/2 pounds chicken cutlets
8   slices prosciutto
8   slices provolone cheese
1/4   cup olive oil or corn oil
1   cup dry Italian-seasoned bread crumbs
1/2   teaspoon garlic powder
2   eggs, beaten with 2 tablespoons milk or water

Pound the chicken cutlets to an even thickness. Top each piece of chicken with a slice of prosciutto and a slice of provolone cheese. Fold the sides of the prosciutto over the cheese and roll the cutlet to enclose the filling. Secure with wooden picks at the open end. Heat the oil in a large saucepan over medium-high heat. Combine the bread crumbs and garlic powder. Dip the cutlets in the beaten egg mixture and then in the seasoned bread crumbs. Press the crumbs firmed onto the cutlets. Fry the prepared cutlets in the hot oil for about 5 to 6 minutes on each side. Remove to a warm platter and serve.

Makes 6 to 8 servings

JoAnn Porrello, Contessa JoAnn
Go for It Gals, Bayside, New York

Spinach-Stuffed Chicken Cutlets

Pretty and simple to make. Be sure to cut open the rolls to show the green filling.

6   skinless, boneless chicken breast halves
1   (10-ounce) package frozen spinach, thawed and squeezed dry
1   cup ricotta cheese
2   plus 1 eggs
2   tablespoons milk
    Dry bread crumbs

Preheat the oven to 350°. Grease a 10-inch baking dish. Pound the chicken to an even thickness. Combine the spinach, ricotta, and 2 eggs in a bowl. Beat the remaining 1 egg with the milk to make an egg wash. Dip the chicken in the egg wash. Coat the chicken on one side with bread crumbs. Arrange the coated chicken in the prepared dish. Spoon the ricotta mixture over the chicken, roll to enclose the filling, and secure with wooden toothpicks. Bake for 1 hour.

Makes 6 servings

Agnes Mancuso, The Italian Diva
Happening Ladies Of Hamilton, Lawrenceville, New Jersey

Mediterranean Chicken

Artichokes, mushrooms, pine nuts, lemon, and garlic are all classic ingredients found in many Mediterranean countries. They are easy to use, but give a gourmet taste. I have been making this chicken for forty years and always get rave reviews from my guests.

1³/4 cups water
1   plus 1 tablespoons butter
1   (6.3-ounce) package long grain and wild rice mix
1/4   cup pine nuts
1   (4 to 5-pound) whole chicken (roaster or fryer)
1   zest of medium lemon
1/4   teaspoon ground black pepper
1/2   teaspoon salt
4   garlic cloves, minced
1   (9-ounce) package frozen artichoke hearts, thawed
8   ounces fresh whole mushrooms, cleaned
10   pearl onions
      Juice of 1 medium lemon
1/3   cup dry white wine

Preheat the oven to 425°. In a saucepan over medium-high heat, bring the water and 1 tablespoon butter to a boil. Add the rice mix (including spice packet) and the pine nuts. Return to a boil. Reduce the heat to low, cover, and simmer for 25 minutes, or until the rice is done.

Remove the giblets and neck from the cav-ity and clean the chicken. Trim the fat from the tail area. Rinse the giblets and dice. Sauté the giblets in the remaining 1 tablespoon butter until browned. Stir into the cooked rice. In a small bowl combine the lemon zest, pepper, salt, and garlic. Arrange the chicken in a large baking dish. Stuff the rice mixture into the chicken. Rub the lemon zest mixture over the outside of the chicken. Brown, uncovered, in the oven for 25 minutes. Arrange the artichoke hearts, mushrooms, and onions around the chicken. Pour the lemon juice and white wine over the chicken. Cover with a securely fitting lid or aluminum foil. Reduce the oven heat to 375° and bake for approximately 1 hour, or until the chicken is cooked through.

Transfer the vegetables into a small covered serving dish. Transfer the rice stuffing into another covered serving dish. Carve the chicken and serve.

Makes 4 to 6 servings

Mara Willick, Queen of SASCI
SASCI (Sexy Adventurous Sun City Instigators), Henderson, Nevada

Chicken Thighs with Wine

For the family that prefers dark meat. Testers commented that it tastes like pot roast and suggested adding mushrooms.

5   tablespoons olive oil
1/2 cup (1 stick) butter
8   chicken thighs

All-purpose flour
1   large carrot, finely chopped
3/4   cup onion, finely chopped
1 1/2   celery stalks, finely chopped
3   garlic cloves, finely chopped
1 1/2   cups dry white wine
1/2   cup dry Marsala
1   teaspoon dried rosemary
4   basil leaves
1   teaspoon hot pepper oil (optional)
1/2   cup chicken stock
Salt and pepper to taste
Cooked rice

Heat the oil and butter in a skillet over medium-high heat. Coat the chicken with flour and fry in the skillet. Remove the chicken from the skillet and add the carrot, onion, celery, and garlic. Reduce the heat to medium and sauté for 15 minutes, or until soft. Return the chicken to the skillet and add the white wine, Marsala, rosemary, basil, pepper oil if using, chicken stock, and salt and pepper. Reduce the heat to low and cook for 1 hour. Serve the chicken with the sauce over rice.

Makes 4 servings

Judy Sausto, Dame Judy
Dames with a Par–Tea Hat–titude, Egg Harbor Township, New Jersey

Cuban Chicken and Rice (Arroz Con Pollo)

1   whole chicken, cut into 8 pieces (or 8 assorted fryer pieces)
1/2   cup olive oil
Salt and pepper to taste
4   garlic cloves, finely minced
1   medium onion, diced
2   celery stalks, chopped
1   cup long grain rice
1/2   cup small, pitted green olives (not stuffed)
1/4   cup drained capers
1   (15-ounce) can diced or crushed tomatoes
Water

Brown the chicken pieces in the oil in large skillet over medium-high heat. Transfer to a large bowl and season with salt and pepper. In the same skillet sauté the garlic, onion, and celery over medium heat until translucent. Add the rice and sauté, stirring constantly, until the rice begins to yellow. Add the olives, capers, and tomatoes. Add enough water to cover the rice. Adjust the salt and pepper to taste. Arrange the chicken pieces over the top. Cover, reduce the heat, and simmer slowly for 1 hour.

Makes 4 servings

Conchetta Ousey, Queen Mom
Scarlet O'Hatters, Columbus, Georgia

White Meatloaf

Serve with roasted root vegetables or mashed potatoes. Good with a chicken, herb, or country-style gravy, or just plain ketchup. Testers said it did not reheat as well as traditional meatloaf and didn't freeze well. So get it while it's hot.

3/4 cup rolled oats
1/2 to 3/4 cup broth, water, or milk
1 1/4 pounds ground turkey or chicken
1/2 to 3/4 pounds mild turkey or chicken Italian sausage
2 or 3 finely minced shallots or 1/2 cup finely minced onion
2 finely minced garlic cloves
1/2 cup finely chopped green bell pepper
1/2 cup finely chopped sun-dried tomatoes
1/2 cup finely chopped carrot, zucchini, celery, or mushrooms
1 large egg, beaten
1/2 to 3/4 cup grated Parmesan cheese
3 tablespoons finely chopped fresh parsley
Salt and pepper
1 tablespoon prepared horseradish (optional)
1 tablespoon Worcestershire sauce (optional)
1 tablespoon Dijon mustard (optional)

Preheat the oven to 350°. Soak the oats in the broth while preparing the loaf mixture. Place the meat in a large mixing bowl and combine with your hands. Add the shallots, garlic, bell pepper, sun-dried tomatoes, carrot (or other vegetables), oat mixture, egg, cheese, parsley, salt and pepper,

horseradish, Worcestershire sauce, and mustard. Blend well with your hands or two forks. Pack into a loaf pan, pressing down in the corners. Bake, uncovered, for approximately 1 hour. Let stand 5 to 8 minutes before draining off the excess juices and slicing.

Makes 8 servings

Linda Rose Thomsett, Divalicious LuLu
Ruby Royal Majes–"Teas," Port Townsend, Washington

Kentucky Duck

1 (4-pound) duckling
1 medium orange, zested and juiced
Additional orange juice to equal 1 cup
1/4 cup firmly packed brown sugar
1/2 cup bourbon

Preheat the oven to 350°. Make crisscross slits in the duck breast through the skin and fat layer. Immerse the duck in large pot of boiling water for 15 minutes. Remove the duck to a rack in a roasting pan with breast side up. In a saucepan over medium heat, cook the orange juice and brown sugar together to make a syrup. Remove from the heat and add the bourbon. Brush the duck with the syrup and sprinkle with the orange zest. Roast for 1 hour.

Makes 4 servings

Conchetta Ousey, Queen Mom
Scarlet O'Hatters, Columbus, Georgia

Gathering Together

We Red Hatters form our closest bonds with the women within our own chapters (whom we call "chapterettes"). These friendships form the solid bedrock of companionship and support. On a daily basis, wonderful stories pour into Hatquarters about the depth of the bonds that our members are developing. These will be the women who will be constants in your life.

But the bonding benefits within chapters are only the tip of the iceberg. We encourage our chapters to join forces with other chapters in their areas once in a while. Perhaps a chapter is planning a shopping day at the local mall and they decide to invite a dozen other groups to just show up at that mall, in their regalia, on the same day. When that day comes, there will be many opportunities to strike up conversations with other Red Hatters, and perhaps even join them for lunch.

Some of our chapters plan train "hoots," wherein bunches of chapters board the same train, at different stations, and meet at the same destination. Because our members are creative and because there are no rules, there are many ways that women can make new friends through participation in the Red Hat Society.

Several times a year "Hatquarters" plans large gatherings, open to all world chapters, and puts on big shindigs, packed with entertainment, events, and opportunities to expand our circles of friends. An international convention is held, once a year, in a major city; and regional conventions, slightly smaller in scope, are held at least three times a year. There are also several official cruises every year. We are determined to provide something for everyone!

Duck for Thanksgiving Dinner

My mother, my sister, and I were preparing Thanksgiving dinner at my mom's house. We had a large turkey, but we always like to also cook a duck or two. We went into Mom's freezer to get a duck, and we found one. It was unlabeled, but we could tell by the shape of the frozen bird that it was a duck, so we thawed it.

We started to prepare the duck and noticed that it didn't have much meat on the legs. It looked different from any of the other ducks we had cooked in the past, but we prepared it anyway.

When dinner was ready, my dad, a great hunter, cut up all the meat to be served. We prepared our plates, said our blessings, and started to eat. About halfway through the meal, my dad said, "I'm glad you cooked that raccoon in the freezer."

"Raccoon?" asked my mom. "We didn't cook any raccoon. This is that duck in the freezer."

"That wasn't a duck. It was a raccoon that you cooked," clarified Dad, helpfully.

We were all horrified, but to be truthful, it looked like a duck, and since we thought it was a duck, it tasted like a duck. If someone had asked any of us to cook a raccoon, we would have said, "No way!" But in reality, it was tasty.

Bookie Davis
Chapterette
Tyler Red Hat Roses and Gawdy Gals
Flint, Texas

Chicken Paprikash

This recipe came from a University of the Pacific professor and his Hungarian wife some forty years ago. Sweet and sour red cabbage is the ideal side dish.

4   to 6 tablespoons unsalted butter
1   cup all-purpose flour
    Salt and pepper to taste
8   to 10 pieces chicken (bone-in or boneless)
3   medium yellow onions, minced
1   large green bell pepper, minced

1   large ripe tomato, or 2 to 3 Roma
    tomatoes, chopped (or in a pinch, use 1
    cup canned)
2   to 3 tablespoons sweet Hungarian paprika
    (if you want this hotter, use hot paprika or
    combination)
1   cup chicken broth
1   cup sour cream
    Hot buttered noodles

6   flounder fillets (about 1 1/2 pounds)
1   (6.8-ounce) package Spanish rice mix
2   tablespoons olive oil
1 1/2 cups water
1   (14 1/2-ounce) can diced tomatoes
2   ounces tomato sauce
1/4 cup sliced ripe black olives
1/2 cup shredded Monterey Jack cheese
     Parsley (optional)

Melt the butter in a large skillet over medium-high heat. Combine the flour and salt and pepper in a bag. Coat the chicken pieces in the flour mixture and brown on both sides. Remove from the skillet. Sauté the onions and bell pepper until tender but not brown. Add the tomato and cook down. Add the paprika and broth, scraping up any bits from the bottom of the skillet. Add the chicken, coating well with the sauce. Cover, reduce the heat to low, and simmer for 40 minutes, or until tender (less for boneless meat).

Remove the chicken to a platter and keep warm. Add the sour cream and deglaze the skillet over low heat. Pour the sauce over the chicken and serve any extra on the side with the noodles.

Makes 8 to 10 servings

Linda Rose Thomsett, Divalicious LuLu
Ruby Royal Majes– "Teas," Port Townsend, WA

Southwestern Flounder

Choose any mild white fish fillets you prefer—tilapia, sole, perch, and orange roughy will all work.

Beginning at the narrow end, tightly roll up the flounder fillets. In a skillet prepare the rice mix according to the package directions, but using the olive oil instead of margarine for sautéing and 1 1/2 cups of water, the tomatoes, and tomato sauce for the cooking liquid. When the mixture begins to boil, arrange the rolled-up fish, seam side down, over the rice mixture in a circle around the pan. Cover, reduce the heat to low, and simmer for 15 minutes. Sprinkle the olives over the mixture in the skillet; cover, and continue cooking for about 3 to 5 minutes, or until the rice is cooked and the fish is tender. Remove from the heat. Sprinkle the shredded cheese over the fish; cover and let stand until the cheese begins to melt. Garnish with the parsley, if desired. Serve in the skillet along with salad and French bread.

Makes 6 servings

Dee Huber, Queen Bee Dee
Beach Plum Red Hatters of Long Neck, Long Neck, Delaware

Sole Meuniere with Baby Bella Mushrooms

Baby bella mushrooms are young portobello mushrooms. Cremini and white button mushrooms will work too.

12	ounces sole or tilapia fillets (or any flat fish)
1/4	cup all-purpose flour
	Salt and freshly ground black pepper to taste
	Olive oil spray
4	ounces sliced baby bella mushrooms
1 1/2	tablespoons butter
2	tablespoons chopped fresh parsley

Pat the fish fillets dry with a paper towel. Mix the flour with salt and pepper. Dip the fillets into the flour, coating both sides completely. Shake off any excess. Heat a nonstick skillet over medium-high heat. Spray with the olive oil. Cook the fish for 5 minutes (less if the fillets are under 1-inch thick); turn and cook for 5 minutes. Transfer to a plate. Turn the heat to high and add the mushrooms to the pan; sauté for about 1 minute and spoon over the fish. Add the butter to the skillet and cook until it just starts to brown. Pour over the mushrooms. Sprinkle the parsley on top.

Makes 2 servings

Mildred Ferreri, Duchess of Delight
Crimson Camellia Socialites, The Woodlands, Texas

Foil Dinner

Pretend you're back at summer camp with this fun dinner. Set out the ingredients and let each person make her own. Instead of fish, very thin, bite-size slices of pork or beef can be substituted.

4	(1/4-pound) fish fillets
8	thin slices sweet onion (about half an onion)
2	fresh tomatoes, sliced thick
12	button mushrooms, thinly sliced
16	fresh string beans, trimmed, microwaved 3 minutes
4	heaping tablespoons mayonnaise
4	teaspoons drained capers
1/2	cup white wine (optional)
	Seasoned salt and seasoned pepper to taste

For each fillet, spray a 2-foot square piece of heavy-duty aluminum foil with nonstick cooking spray. Arrange each fish fillet in the middle of a piece of foil. Top each fillet with 2 slices onion, 2 slices tomato, 3 mushrooms, and 4 beans in the order given. Spread the mayonnaise on top and divide the capers over each fillet. Add the wine if using and season with the salt and pepper. Bring the edges of the foil together at the top and fold over to close the ends so that the package is sealed.

Prepare a hot grill. Arrange the dinner packets side by side on the grill and cover. Cooking time will vary, but 15 to 20 minutes is about right. If you're in the great outdoors, place the packets directly on the embers of a campfire, but watch carefully because they will cook very quickly.

Makes 4 servings

Lucinda Denton, Founding Queen Mother (FQM)
Nonpareils, Knoxville, Tennessee

Halibut Parmesan

2 pounds halibut fillets
1 tablespoon olive oil or butter
1 small onion, sliced, rings separated
1 lemon
  Salt and pepper to taste
2/3 cup mayonnaise
1/2 cup grated Parmesan or Romano cheese

Preheat the oven to 425°. Trim the skin from the halibut. Pour the olive oil into a glass baking dish large enough to hold the fish. Arrange the onion rings in the dish. Cut the lemon in half and squeeze the juice of one-half into the dish. Remove any seeds. Season the onions with salt and pepper. Combine the mayonnaise and cheese in a bowl. Arrange the halibut fillets in the dish on top of the onions. Spread the mayonnaise mixture over the fish to cover. Squeeze the juice of the remaining lemon half onto the fillets. Bake for 15 minutes, or until the fish is opaque and flakes easily.

Makes 4 servings

Vikki McCoy, Eclectic Queen
Ruby's Red Hat Ramblers, Anchorage, Alaska

Crabby Tilapia

Use snapper, roughy, farm-raised catfish, or any other white fish fillet that's available.

2 cups crabmeat (imitation or canned is fine), flaked and drained
2/3 cup dry seasoned bread crumbs
4 tablespoons shredded Monterey Jack cheese
4 tablespoons butter, melted
1 tablespoon mayonnaise
1/4 teaspoon salt
1/4 teaspoon pepper
  Dash of cayenne pepper
4 (6-ounce) tilapia fillets
1/4 teaspoon paprika

Preheat the oven to 425°. In a bowl combine the crabmeat, bread crumbs, cheese, butter, mayonnaise, salt, pepper, and cayenne and mix well. Cut each fillet in half widthwise. Place two halves in a greased 13x9-inch baking dish. Press the crab mixture onto the fillets; top with the remaining halves. Sprinkle with the paprika. Bake uncovered for 22 to 26 minutes, or until the fish flakes easily with a fork.

Makes 4 servings

Joan Bacso, Chapterette
Red Hat Hautes, Mesquite, Nevada

Company Halibut

Halibut steaks are good-looking, and this creamy, cheesy crust gives them a restaurant quality.

4   **fresh halibut steaks, 1 to 1 1/2-inches thick**
     Juice of 1/2 a lemon
1   **pint sour cream**
1   **cup grated sharp cheddar cheese**

Preheat the oven to 325°. Pat the halibut dry with paper towels and arrange in an ungreased square glass baking dish. Pour the lemon juice over the top of the fish. Spread the sour cream over the halibut. Sprinkle the cheese over the top and press in lightly. Bake for 20 to 25 minutes.

Makes 4 servings

Nancy Ellis, Queen Mother
Desert Flowers, Palm Desert, California

Grilled Perch and Pine Nuts

If you have a cast-iron skillet, put it to use for this recipe

1/4 **cups pine nuts**
1/4 **cup butter or margarine**
2   **tablespoons chopped chives**
2   **lemons**
1 1/2 **pounds perch fillets**

Toast the pine nuts on a baking sheet in a single layer in a 350° oven for about 10 minutes, watching closely until they turn brown. Melt the butter in a skillet over medium heat. Add the toasted nuts and chives. Stir until the nuts are coated, then transfer to a serving bowl. Heat a skillet, griddle, or stovetop grill to medium-high heat. Slice the lemons and arrange on the hot surface. Arrange the fillets on top of the lemons and cook for 3 to 4 minutes. Do not turn; the fillets will turn opaque when they are done. Remove from the heat and serve with the pine nut sauce.

Makes 4 servings

Mary Jane Bristow, Princess Paranoid
Purple Passionattas, Painesville, Ohio

Marinated Tilapia

2   **tablespoons olive oil**
1   **tablespoon lemon juice**
4   **tilapia fillets**
1   **tablespoon dill weed**
1/8 **teaspoon Creole seasoning**

SAUCE
1/4 **cup mayonnaise**
1   **teaspoon prepared yellow mustard**
1/2 **teaspoon lemon juice**
2   **tablespoons dill weed**

In a large bowl or glass baking dish, combine the olive oil and lemon juice. Add the fish, cover, and marinate, refrigerated, for 2 to 4 hours, turning to coat both sides. Sprinkle with the dill and Creole seasoning. Grill over high heat for 5 minutes on each side. (Or use a broiler or a traditional grill with a sheet of heavy-duty aluminum foil.)

For the sauce, stir the mayonnaise, mustard, lemon juice, and dill weed together in a small bowl. Refrigerate until ready to serve. Serve the fish with the sauce on the side.

Makes 2 to 4 servings

Anne Carson, Queen Anne
Sassy Ladies of Lake Sinclair, Eatonton, Georgia

Pan-Seared Tilapia

2   to 4 tablespoons vegetable oil
4   to 8 tilapia fillets
    Salt and pepper to taste
5   tablespoons all-purpose flour
4   tablespoons butter
2   tablespoons chopped fresh parsley
1   tablespoon lemon juice

Heat the oil in a large skillet over medium-high heat. Season the fillets with salt and pepper and coat with the flour. Sear the fillets on each side for 4 minutes. In a glass bowl, heat the butter, parsley, and lemon juice in the microwave for 45 seconds. Stir with a whisk and pour over the cooked fillets. Serve immediately.

Makes 2 to 4 servings

Theresa Boughan, Duchess Cosmo
Lucky Sunshine Ladies, Newport News, Virginia

Panamanian Seviche

Fresh fish is the basis of a great seviche, *so make sure your fish is the freshest it can be. Whole fish stays fresher longer than fillets, so rather than purchasing fillets, buy whole fish, then have the seafood department fillet it for you. (Or invite some chapter mates over and do it yourself for an adventure.)*

1 1/2   pounds boneless, raw, skinned speckled sea trout or red snapper
3   quarts boiling water
1 1/2   cups finely chopped white onion
1 1/2   cups fresh or bottled lemon juice
1 1/2   cups fresh or bottled lime juice
2   teaspoons finely minced or crushed hot red pepper
2   teaspoons salt
2   garlic cloves, minced

Cut the fish in big, thick, bite-size pieces and put them in a colander. Slowly pour the boiling water over the fish, shaking and turning to scald all sides. Combine the onion, lemon juice, lime juice, red pepper, salt, and garlic in a crock or glass jar. Add the fish and mix well. The fish must be completely submerged. Cover and refrigerate for three days before serving.

Makes 6 to 8 servings

Patt Roberson, Countess of Chaos
Merry Maids of Mayhem, Baker, Louisiana

Whiskey–Soused Salmon

Serve with steamed, buttered asparagus and broiled, stuffed tomatoes.

4	slices onion
3	carrots, sliced
1	cup dry white wine
2	bay leaves
4	(5-ounce) salmon steaks or fillets
1/2	cup mayonnaise
2	tablespoons fresh lemon juice
2	tablespoons whiskey
	Several sprigs watercress (optional)

Place the onion, carrots, wine and bay leaves in a medium saucepan and bring to a boil. Boil for 5 minutes to make court-bouillon. Rinse the salmon and place it in the court-bouillon. The liquid should completely cover the salmon. Add water if needed. Bring to a simmer and gently cook for 5 minutes. The salmon will be opaque. Remove to individual plates. Whisk the mayonnaise, lemon juice, and whiskey together in a small bowl and spoon over the salmon. Garnish with the watercress.

Makes 4 servings

Mildred Ferreri, Duchess of Delight
Crimson Camellia Socialites, The Woodlands, Texas

Honey Salmon

2	tablespoons honey
2	tablespoons dry vermouth or white wine
1 1/2	teaspoons grated fresh gingerroot
1 1/2	teaspoons Dijon mustard
1/8	teaspoon salt
1/8	teaspoon freshly ground black pepper
4	(6-ounce) salmon fillets

In a small bowl combine the honey, wine, ginger, mustard, salt, and pepper. Place the salmon fillets on a baking sheet. Brush half the sauce on the fillets and let stand for 15 minutes. Broil, brushing with the remaining sauce, about 10 minutes per inch of thickness measured at the thickest part, or until done to your taste.

Makes 4 servings

Linda Hale, Chef Linda
Jolly Red Hatters, Centennial, Colorado

Fresh Albacore with Onion Marinade

4	plus 2 tablespoons olive oil
4	(6 to 8-ounce) fresh tuna steaks (preferably albacore)
2	large sweet onions, sliced
	Red wine vinegar

Heat 4 tablespoons olive oil in a saucepan over medium heat. Cook the tuna steaks 10 minutes per inch of thickness, or until the fish flakes. Remove from the pan. In a large skillet heat the 2 remaining tablespoons olive oil over medium heat and cook the onions until transparent. Add enough vinegar to cover all of the onions completely. Add the fish back to the pan, turning to coat both sides for just a few

A Fish Story

My husband asked if he could help me prepare our fish dinner, so I asked him to coat the fish with flour, which he did.

After I fried the fish, we sat down to our fish supper. Hmm. It tasted a little sweet, I told him. My husband agreed that it was unusually sweet for fried fish.

"Show me which flour you used," I asked. He went to the cupboard and pointed to the container.

"That's powdered sugar," I laughed. But either we were very hungry, or perhaps we discovered a new taste sensation, because we ate the fish anyway.

Mary Scarpino
Queenie
Blushing Red Hat Mamas
Waukee, Iowa

minutes until hot. Remove the fish, pour the marinade over the fish, and serve.

Makes 4 servings

Nina Alioto, Red Hot Mama
Red Hatters of Rancho Bernardo, San Diego, California

Dilled Red Salmon

Of course this recipe uses red sockeye salmon—what else, for a Red Hatter?

2   **pounds fresh sockeye salmon**
10 **to 12 stems fresh dill, chopped**
1/2 **cup (1 stick) butter**
    Juice of 1/2 lemon (reserve the other lemon half to slice and serve on the side)

Salt and pepper to taste
Hot cooked rice

Place the salmon skin side down on heavy-duty aluminum foil. Thickly cover the fish with the chopped dill. Slice the butter into pats to lay over the dill. Squeeze the lemon juice through a paper towel onto the fish. Season with salt and pepper. Loosely seal the foil and punch a couple of holes in the top. Place the package onto hot campfire coals or a hot grill and cook 15 to 20 minutes, or until the salmon easily flakes. Prepare the rice while the fish cooks. When the fish is done, pour the juices over the rice and serve with lemon slices.

Makes 4 servings

Vikki McCoy, Eclectic Queen
Ruby's Red Hat Ramblers, Anchorage, Alaska

Gingered Grilled Salmon

1 1/2 tablespoons butter

3   shallots, chopped

6   tablespoons fresh lemon juice

5   tablespoons brown sugar

1/2 teaspoon Tabasco

3   tablespoons fresh ginger, peeled and finely chopped

1/4 cup red wine vinegar

3   teaspoons soy sauce

3   teaspoons finely chopped fresh cilantro

4   (6 to 8-ounce) salmon fillets
    Parsley for garnish

Melt the butter in a small saucepan over medium heat. Add the shallots and sauté until softened. Add the lemon juice, sugar, Tabasco, ginger, vinegar, and soy sauce and stir until well combined. Remove from the heat and add the cilantro. Baste the salmon liberally with the sauce and cook on a grill over medium-high heat about 3 inches from the flame for 7 to 10 minutes per side. (The cooking time will depend on the thickness of the salmon. Fish can also be cooked under the broiler at the same timing.) Baste frequently while cooking. Remove from the grill and serve immediately. Garnish with fresh parsley and serve the remaining sauce on the side.

Makes 4 servings

Sally Cecil, The Countess of Cuisine
Rose's Rosebuds, Pittsburgh, Pennsylvania

Slow-Roasted Salmon with Wilted Spinach

6   (6-ounce) salmon fillets, skin removed

3   tablespoons olive oil
    Sea salt to taste
    Freshly ground black pepper to taste

3   tablespoons fresh oregano leaves, finely chopped

2   sprigs fresh rosemary

6   handfuls baby spinach leaves
    Lemon wedges for garnish

Preheat the oven to 200°. Place the salmon fillets side-by-side in a single layer in a greased 13x9-inch casserole dish. Drizzle with the olive oil, season with salt and pepper, and sprinkle with the oregano. Lay the rosemary over the fillets. Bake for 30 to 45 minutes until the fish just flakes when pressed with a fork. Bring about 1/4 cup water to a boil in a saucepan over medium heat. Add the spinach, cover, and simmer for 30 to 40 seconds, just until wilted. Drain and cover to keep warm. When the fish is done, serve over the spinach. Serve with lemon wedges for garnish.

Makes 6 servings

Fran Varnadore, Lady Red
Bodacious Beach Babes, Palos Verdes Estates, California

Chesapeake Bay Crab Cakes

One tester exclaimed, "These were better than any I've ever had in a restaurant, and I'm from Maryland."

1   pound back-fin crabmeat

1   cup crushed saltine crackers

1   egg

1/4 cup mayonnaise

1   tablespoon Worcestershire sauce

2   teaspoons dry mustard

1   teaspoon ground red pepper

1   rounded teaspoon black pepper

1   teaspoon parsley flakes

1   teaspoon baking powder

1   teaspoon sugar

1   tablespoon Old Bay seasoning

1   tablespoon vegetable oil for cooking
    Cocktail or horseradish sauce and parsley
    sprigs for garnish

Pick through the crabmeat and separate the chunks into fine threads. Add the crackers, egg, mayonnaise, Worcestershire sauce, mustard, peppers, parsley, baking powder, sugar, and Old Bay. Mix thoroughly with your hands. Form into 4 to 6 rounded, flat cakes (depending on desired size and thickness). Heat the oil in a skillet over medium heat. Cook the crab cakes for about 5 minutes on each side. Serve on buns, or in dishes with the cocktail or horseradish sauce. Garnish with the parsley.

Makes 4 to 6 servings

Deborah Grimm, Anti-Parlimentarian
Blessed Babes by the Bay, Norfolk, Virginia

Hampton Crab Cakes

These cakes may be frozen before cooking. Cook from frozen, adding a little extra time for cooking each side.

11/2 cups fine dry bread crumbs

1/2 teaspoon oregano

1/2 teaspoon basil

1/2 teaspoon salt

1   teaspoon dry mustard

1   teaspoon Worcestershire sauce

2   eggs

1/4 cup light salad dressing

1   pound crabmeat

4   tablespoons butter or margarine

In a bowl mix the bread crumbs, oregano, and basil. Measure 1 cup of the crumb mixture into a large bowl and add the salt, mustard, Worcestershire sauce, eggs, and salad dressing. Add the crabmeat to the egg mixture, and mix gently. Shape into 8 cakes. Roll the cakes in the remaining crumb mixture. Heat the butter in a skillet over medium heat and fry the crab cakes for 5 to 6 minutes per side until brown on both sides.

Make 4 servings

Shirley Stacey, Queen
Chapter Name: Lucky Sunshine Ladies, Hampton, Virginia

Scalloped Oysters

A holiday tradition in some parts of the country, and great any time.

3	dozen medium oysters
2	(10-ounce) boxes large oyster crackers, crushed
	Milk
	Salt and pepper to taste
2	to 3 tablespoons butter

Preheat the oven to 350°. In a large bowl combine the oysters plus their liquid and the crackers. Add enough milk to give the mixture a soupy texture. Season with salt and pepper. Pour into a greased 13x9-inch baking dish. Dot with the butter. Bake for 1 hour, stirring after 20 minutes. Serve warm.

Makes 12 servings

Carolyn Knauss, Red Snapper
Red Cardinals, Tatamy, Pennsylvania

Easy Crab Imperial

1	cup mayonnaise
2	teaspoons prepared mustard
2	teaspoons horseradish
1	pound back-fin crabmeat

Preheat the oven to 325°. Mix the mayonnaise, mustard, and horseradish. Reserve 1 tablespoon of the mixture for each crab serving. Add the crabmeat to the remaining mixture. Place in individual crab shells or serving containers and top with the reserved mixture. Bake for 10 to 15 minutes.

Makes 4 to 6 servings

Janet Gilbert, Royal Spinner
Red Hat Hotties, Newark, Delaware

Down-East Low Country Shrimp Boil

This traditional South Carolina feed is fun, but be sure to cover the table with newspaper and provide plenty of napkins and wet wipes.

1 1/2	gallons water
3	tablespoons Old Bay seasoning
3	tablespoons salt
2	pounds hot, smoked link sausages, cut into 2-inch pieces
12	ears freshly shucked corn, broken into 3 to 4-inch pieces
4	pounds large shrimp

Combine the water, Old Bay, and salt in a large stockpot and bring to a boil over high heat. Add the sausages and boil, uncovered, for 5 minutes. Add the corn and cook for 5 minutes. Add the shrimp and cook for 3 minutes. Don't wait for the liquid to return to a boil before timing the corn and the shrimp. Drain immediately, transfer the food to a platter, and serve. (Or just dump it into bowls on a newspaper-covered table.)

Makes 8 servings

Jean Hart, Co-Queen
Bodacious Belles of New Bern, New Bern, North Carolina

Crawfish Jambalaya in a Rice Cooker

Using a rice cooker yields nicely fluffed rice.

1/4 cup (1/2 stick) butter
1 small bell pepper, chopped
1 small onion, chopped
1 celery stalk, chopped
1 garlic clove, chopped
Salt and pepper to taste
1 (16-ounce) can whole tomatoes, not drained
1 pound crawfish, peeled
3/4 to 1 cup uncooked rice
1 cup water
1/2 cup green onion tops, chopped
1/2 cup chopped fresh parsley

Melt the butter in a large saucepan over medium heat. Sauté the bell pepper, onion, celery, garlic, and salt and pepper. Add the tomatoes with juice; simmer well. Add the crawfish, reduce the heat to low, and cook for 20 minutes. Add the rice, water, onion tops, and parsley; mix well and spoon or pour into the rice cooker. Cook as you would for rice.

Makes 5 servings

Joann McLemore, Vice Queen
The Red Brims with Purple Trims, Lafayette, Louisiana

Coquilles St. Jacques

An elegant dish for serving at an intimate dinner at home.

1/2 cup all-purpose flour
1 1/2 pounds sea scallops
2 tablespoons butter
1/2 cup finely chopped onion
2 tablespoons minced shallots
1 garlic clove, minced
3/4 cup dry white wine
1/8 teaspoon salt
1/8 teaspoon dried thyme
1/8 teaspoon ground white pepper
1 bay leaf
1/4 cup shredded Swiss cheese

Place the flour in a zip-top plastic bag; add the scallops. Seal and shake to coat. Remove the scallops from the bag, shaking off excess flour. Melt the butter in a large, nonstick skillet over medium heat. Add the onion and sauté for 3 minutes, or until lightly browned. Add the shallots and garlic and sauté for 1 minute. Add the scallops, wine, salt, thyme, white pepper, and bay leaf. Cover, reduce the heat, and simmer for 4 minutes. Uncover, bring to a boil, and cook 1 minute. Discard the bay leaf. Divide the scallop mixture evenly among four individual gratin dishes. Top each with 1 tablespoon cheese; broil for 30 seconds, or until the cheese melts. Serve immediately.

Makes 4 servings

Angel Grubb, High Mistress of Furry Four Footers
Lydia's Red Hatters of New Albany, Lewis Center, Ohio

Shrimp Creole

2   tablespoons vegetable oil
1   onion, chopped
3   celery stalks, chopped
1   garlic clove, minced
1   tablespoon all-purpose flour
1   teaspoon chili powder
1/2 teaspoon salt
1/4 cup water
1   can (14 1/2-ounce) diced tomatoes with
    basil, garlic, and oregano, not drained
1   pound shrimp, cooked, shelled,
    and cut in half
    Pinch of black pepper
1   (6.8-ounce) package Spanish rice

Heat the oil in a saucepan over medium heat. Sauté the onion, celery, and garlic. Cook for 10 minutes. Combine the flour, chili powder, and salt, and water in a small bowl. Add to the saucepan. Stir constantly. Add the diced tomatoes. Simmer for 10 minutes. Add the shrimp and pepper. Simmer for 10 minutes. Prepare the rice according to the package directions and serve the shrimp on a bed of rice.

Makes 3 or 4 servings

Wini Hamilton, Queen Bitchyboss
Cackling Crows, Woodbridge, Virginia

Shrimp for Tapas

Tapas is a sort of Spanish cocktail snack eaten late in the afternoon with a glass of wine or sherry.

2   tablespoons dried parsley
2   tablespoons lemon juice
1/2 teaspoon dried thyme
1/2 teaspoon crushed dried red pepper
1/4 teaspoon salt
1 1/2 pounds shrimp, shelled and deveined
3   tablespoons olive oil
2   garlic cloves
1   cup dry sherry
1   teaspoon Worcestershire sauce

Combine the parsley, lemon juice, thyme, red pepper, and salt. Add the shrimp, stirring to coat. Cover and refrigerate 2 hours, lightly stirring occasionally. Heat the oil in a skillet over medium heat; cook the garlic until golden. Add the shrimp and cook for about 3 minutes, stirring when the color is set. Add the sherry and Worcestershire sauce; bring to a boil. Reduce the heat and simmer for about 2 minutes. Serve as an appetizer in small bowls with crispy bread.

Makes 4 to 6 servings

Karen Ise, Queen
Le Chapeaux Rouge de Conejo, Westlake Village, California

Jalapeño-Stuffed Bacon-Wrapped Grilled Shrimp

Leave the tail on when grilling shrimp—it gives guests a "handle" for eating them.

Fresh jalapeño peppers, cut into very thin slices
4 to 5 pounds fresh cleaned large shrimp, shelled, deveined, tails on
Uncooked bacon slices
Celery salt to taste
Lemon pepper to taste
Garlic powder to taste
Melted butter, if needed

Place a toothpick-size sliver of fresh raw jalapeño inside the slit made when the shrimp are deveined. Press shut and wrap with a 1 to 2-inch piece of bacon. Run a barbecue skewer through the shrimp so that each shrimp is well secured on the skewer. Pack several shrimp snugly onto the skewer to hold them into place as they cook. Lay each skewer in a shallow dish and sprinkle with the celery salt, lemon pepper, and garlic powder. Grill the shrimp on a medium hot grill for about 10 to 15 minutes, or until the bacon is crisp. The lower tail sections may blacken. If the shrimp appear to be drying out too much during the grilling, baste the cooking shrimp with melted butter.

Makes 8 to 10 servings

Glenda Bonham, Countess of Confusion
Ruby Roadrunners, Fort Stockton, Texas

Easy Scampi

Scampi is so easy; add it to your mealtime repertoire.

1/4 cup finely chopped onion
4 garlic cloves, minced
4 sprigs fresh parsley, chopped
1/2 cup (1 stick) butter
2 pounds fresh medium shrimp, peeled and deveined
1/4 cup dry white wine
2 tablespoons lemon juice
Salt to taste
Freshly ground black pepper to taste
Hot cooked rice or angle hair pasta

Sauté the onion, garlic, and parsley in the butter until the onion is tender. Reduce the heat to low and add the shrimp. Cook for a couple of minutes, stirring frequently, until the shrimp turn pink. Add the wine, lemon juice, salt, and pepper to the mixture. Serve immediately over rice or angel hair pasta. Serve with French bread and a green salad.

Makes 4 servings

Sonja Sheffield, Queen Mother
Red Hatted Stepchild, Gulfport, Mississippi

Shrimp Etouffé

"This makes its own juice and is delicious," says the contributor.

2   to 3 pounds medium or large shrimp, peeled and deveined
2   teaspoons cayenne pepper
4   teaspoons white pepper
2   tablespoons Old Bay seafood seasoning
2   tablespoons garlic powder
2   teaspoons flavor enhancer (such as Accent)
1   cup chopped onion
1   cup chopped celery
1/2 cup (1 stick) butter
     Hot cooked rice

In a large bowl combine the shrimp with the cayenne pepper, white pepper, Old Bay seasoning, garlic powder, and flavor enhancer. Let stand for 30 minutes.

Sauté the onion and celery in the butter in a saucepan over medium heat. Add the shrimp. Cover and cook for 10 minutes. Stir once, then cover again, and simmer over low heat for 20 minutes. Serve over the rice.

Makes 4 to 6 servings

Kenni Shaw, Lady Sergeant in Gloves
My Lady Red Hats, Hagerstown, Delaware

Shrimp Over Rice

3/4 cup all-purpose flour
1/2 cup vegetable oil
2   medium onions, chopped
3   celery stalks, chopped
1   bell pepper, chopped
1   cup chopped green onions
3   pounds medium shrimp, cleaned and peeled
2   cups water
1/4 teaspoon salt
     Red, white, or black pepper to taste
1/4 cup white wine (optional)
6   cups hot cooked rice

In a Dutch oven brown the flour in the oil over medium-high heat until deep brown in color, stirring constantly. Add the onions, celery, bell pepper, and green onions. Cook over medium heat until the vegetables are tender. Add the shrimp and simmer for 30 minutes, stirring occasionally. Add the water and continue cooking for 30 minutes. Season with the salt and pepper. Add the wine if using. Heat through and serve over the rice.

Makes 6 servings

Betty Brogna, Queen Crazy as a Loon
Sashaying Scarlet Sisters, Chalmette, Louisiana

Shrimp Curry

Have a Dutch "rice table" by serving bowls of add-ons with this mild, creamy curry that was given high marks by testers. Let guests fix up their curries by adding their own pineapple, coconut, peanuts, and other ingredients.

1/2	cup finely chopped onion
5	tablespoons butter or margarine
1/3	cup all-purpose flour
2 1/2	teaspoons curry powder
1	teaspoon salt
1/4	teaspoon ground ginger
2	cups cream or evaporated milk
1	cup chicken broth
4	cups cooked shrimp or 2 (14-ounce) packages frozen shrimp, thawed
1	teaspoon lemon juice
	Hot cooked rice
	Pineapple chunks, peanuts, shredded coconut, bacon bits, sliced avocado for garnish

Cook the onion in the butter until tender. Blend in the flour, curry, salt, and ginger. Gradually add the cream and chicken broth, stirring constantly. Cook until thickened. Add the shrimp and lemon juice. Heat through, stirring frequently. Serve over rice with suggested side dishes of pineapple chunks, peanuts, shredded coconut, bacon bits, or sliced avocado.

Makes 4 large or 8 average servings

Lisa Katai, Queen Mum
Dallas Red Hat Flashes, Murphy, Texas

Shrimp and Grits

Grits enriched with cream and butter serve as a base for sherry-scented shrimp in this favorite from South Carolina and eastern Georgia.

2	cups uncooked grits
4	tablespoons milk
1	tablespoon cream
2	tablespoons butter
1	tablespoon chopped fresh parsley
1	pound cooked medium shrimp, peeled and deveined
	Garlic powder and lemon pepper
1	tablespoon ketchup
1	tablespoon cream sherry
	Dash of hot pepper sauce
1/2	teaspoon salt

Cook the grits in 5 cups water until thick and tender. Blend in the milk and cream.

In a large skillet melt the butter over medium heat; add the parsley and the shrimp. Season with the garlic powder and lemon pepper. Blend in the ketchup and sherry; add the hot sauce and salt. Simmer for 3 to 4 minutes, or until the shrimp are cooked through. Spoon the hot grits on a plate and top with the shrimp.

Makes 4 to 6 servings

Mitzi Wilson, QueenMumFunDames
Fun and Fantastic Dames, Charlotte, North Carolina

Curried Lobster Bake

1/2 cup chopped celery

1/2 cup diced onion

1/2 cup chopped green bell pepper

3 plus 1 tablespoons butter

1/2 teaspoon paprika

1 teaspoon curry powder
Dash of garlic powder
Dash of Tabasco sauce (optional)

4 tablespoons all-purpose flour

1 1/2 cups milk

3/4 cup evaporated milk

1/2 chicken bouillon cube mixed with 1
teaspoon water

1/2 to 3/4 teaspoon Worcestershire sauce

1/2 teaspoon brown sugar

1 1/2 cups long grain rice

2 (4-ounce) cans cold pack lobster
(or shrimp or scallops)
Bread crumbs for topping

Preheat the oven to 350°. Sauté the celery, onion, and bell pepper in 1 tablespoon butter. Add the paprika, curry, garlic powder and Tabasco if desired. Combine the remaining 3 tablespoons butter, flour, milk, and evaporated milk in a saucepan over medium heat. Cook until thickened. Add the bouillon mixture, Worcestershire sauce, brown sugar, rice, and seafood. Add the sautéed vegetables. Transfer the mixture to a greased 13x9-inch dish, cover with bread crumbs and dot with butter. Bake for 45 minutes.

Makes 4 to 6 servings.

Judy Beatty, Princess Excel
Chocolate River Cuties, Riverview, New Brunswick, Canada

ELEVEN

◦₃ More Marvelous ₃◦
Mainstays

MEATLESS ENTRÉES, CASSEROLES,
& MAIN DISH PASTA

Someone who consistently does the same thing, over and over, is said to be "in a rut." The Red Hat Society encourages its members to stay out of ruts as much as possible, challenging them to try new things. We aren't suggesting running off with the circus or anything (unless that sort of thing appeals to you). We suggest baby steps in this area.

It is so easy to get in a rut when we are planning meals. Many of us can automatically turn to certain, well-thumbed pages in our cookbooks to follow the old, tried and true recipes we have been following for years. Or we can mix together ingredients for our families' favorites without so much as glancing at the recipes—probably even in our sleep!

This chapter of our cookbook offers all of us help in taking some cooking "baby steps." Those who know about these things are constantly admonishing us to eat more vegetables and whole grains. Try these superb favorites, selected from hundreds of submissions, to see how pleasurable it can be to follow the admonishment of the food gurus—and climb out of your rut at the same time.

Sour Cream Noodle Bake

1   (8-ounce) package egg noodles
1   pound ground beef
1   tablespoon butter
1   teaspoon salt
1/4   teaspoon garlic salt
1/8   teaspoon pepper
1   (8-ounce) can tomato sauce
1   cup cottage cheese
1   cup sour cream
6   green onions, chopped
3/4   cup shredded cheddar cheese

Preheat the oven to 350°. Cook the noodles according to the package directions. Rinse and drain well. In a skillet over medium heat, brown the beef in the butter. Add the salt, garlic salt, pepper, and tomato sauce. Simmer for 5 minutes. Combine the noodles, cottage cheese, sour cream, and onions. Alternate layers of noodle mixture and meat in a greased 2-quart casserole dish, beginning with noodles and ending with meat. Top with the shredded cheese. Bake for 20 minutes, or until the cheese melts.

Makes 8 servings

Sherrill Cook, Kountess of the Kitchen
Scarlett O'Hatters, Powell, Wyoming

Shepherd's Pie

Think about how many great kids were raised on shepherd's pie—no wonder it's a taste of home-cooking for so many people.

1   pound ground beef
1   medium onion, sliced and sautéed until tender
    Salt and pepper to taste
1   beef bouillon cube
1/2   cup boiling water
2   heaping teaspoons Dijon mustard
4   to 5 large carrots, grated
1   pound potatoes, peeled, boiled, and mashed
    Grated cheese (optional)

Preheat the oven to 350°. Combine the ground beef and onion in a large microwaveable bowl, breaking up the beef into chunks. Microwave until the beef is no longer pink; drain. Break up the chunks and season to taste. Add the bouillon cube to the boiling water and stir in the mustard; pour the mixture over the beef. Cover with the grated carrots, mashed potatoes, and top with cheese in that order. Bake for 30 minutes. Broil for 5 minutes to brown the top.

Make 6 to 8 servings

Mary Clarke, Chapterette
Le-Val Scarlet Divas, Hellertown, Pennsylvania

Mexican Beef and Bean Casserole

     Tortilla chips
1 1/2   to 2 pounds ground beef
2   tablespoons taco seasoning
1   (15-ounce) can chili beans
1   (10 3/4-ounce) can cream of celery soup
    Shredded cheese
    Shredded lettuce
2   to 3 tomatoes, chopped

Preheat the oven to 350°. Crumble the tortilla chips in the bottom of a lightly greased 13 x 9-inch baking dish, enough to cover the bottom of dish. Cook the ground beef in a saucepan until browned. Drain and sprinkle with half of the taco seasoning. Stir in the chili beans and celery soup. Mix together and pour over the tortilla chips. Top with shredded cheese. Cover and bake for 30 minutes. Serve topped with shredded lettuce and the chopped tomatoes. Sprinkle a little more shredded cheese over the top.

Makes 8 servings

Bonnie Harris, Duchess Bonnie
Majestic Columbines, Longmont, Colorado

"Unstuffed" Cabbage Roll Casserole

All the great flavor of a cabbage roll, but without the rolling or stuffing.

2	pounds ground beef
1	cup chopped onion
1	(20-ounce) can tomato sauce
3 1/2	pounds cabbage, chopped
1	cup uncooked white rice
1	teaspoon salt
2	(14-ounce) cans beef broth

Preheat the oven to 350°. In a large skillet brown the beef over medium heat; drain. In a large mixing bowl combine the onion, tomato sauce, cabbage, rice, and salt. Add the cooked meat and mix well. Pour the mixture into a greased 13 x 9-inch baking dish. Pour the broth over the meat

mixture, cover, and bake for 1 hour. Stir, replace the cover, and bake for another 30 minutes.

Makes 5 to 8 servings

Vicki Haley, Baroness Haley
Purple Passion, Allen Park, Michigan

Microwave Spanish Rice

Starts on the stove top, finishes in the microwave. This rice is a good entrée as is, and also nice stuffed into green bell peppers, then baked.

1	pound lean ground beef
1	medium onion, chopped
1	teaspoon garlic powder
1	teaspoon parsley flakes
1	teaspoon seasoned salt
1	teaspoon pepper
1 1/2	teaspoons chili powder
4	cups cooked long-grain rice
1	(12-ounce) can tomato sauce
1	(6-ounce) can sliced mushrooms, drained

Brown the meat in a skillet over medium heat. Add the onion, garlic powder, parsley flakes, seasoned salt, pepper, and chili powder and cook until the meat is no longer pink. Drain and add the cooked rice, tomato sauce, and mushrooms and mix well. Spoon into a microwaveable 9-inch-square dish. Microwave for about 10 minutes, or until hot and bubbly. Serve hot.

Makes 4 to 5 servings

Donna Kilgore, Floosie
Floosie's Floosies, Lititz, Pennsylvania

Spicy Corn Bread Casserole

2   pounds ground beef
    Salt and pepper to taste
2   cups milk
1/2 cup canola oil
2   cups cornmeal
2   teaspoon salt
4   large eggs
2   teaspoons baking soda
2   (16-ounce) cans cream-style corn
1   large onion, chopped
3   small jalapeño peppers, finely chopped
1 1/2 cups shredded Mexican-blend cheese

Preheat the oven to 350°. Brown the ground beef in a skillet over medium heat. Season with salt and pepper. Drain well. Divide the browned beef in half. In a large bowl blend together the milk, canola oil, cornmeal, salt, eggs, baking soda, and corn. Coat a 13x9-inch dish with nonstick cooking spray. Layer half the browned beef, half the corn bread mixture, half the onion, half the jalapeño peppers, and half the cheese. Layer the remaining half of the browned beef over the cheese. Add the remaining ingredients in the same order as before. Bake for 45 minutes to 1 hour.

Makes 16 to 18 servings

Carolyn Holbrook, La Contessa of Love
GRITS with Hattitudes, Sherwood, Arkansas

Layered Reuben Bake

Bold flavors in an out-of-the-ordinary baked casserole.

10 slices rye or pumpernickel bread (or one small package party rye)
1   (14-ounce) can sauerkraut, well drained
1/2 pound thinly sliced corned beef (canned is fine)
1   pint sour cream
1   tablespoon Thousand Island dressing (optional)
1   small onion, chopped
1   (8-ounce) package shredded mozzarella cheese
1   (8-ounce) package shredded Swiss cheese
1/2 cup (1 stick) butter or margarine, melted

Preheat the oven to 350°. Lay half the bread on the bottom of a greased 13 x 9-inch pan. Layer the sauerkraut, corned beef, sour cream (mixed with the Thousand Island dressing, if desired), onion, and cheeses over the bread. Top with the remaining half of bread. Drizzle with the melted butter. Bake for 30 minutes.

Makes 8 to 10 servings

Linda Hendricks, Senorita Rosa Linda
Red Hot and Purple, Janesville, Minnesota

Texas Hash

The ingredients are simple and pure Texas: beef, rice, tomatoes, and spices. Testers just loved it, and many remembered it from their own childhood.

1   tablespoon olive oil
1   large onion, diced
1   pound ground beef
1/2 cup rice
1   teaspoon salt
1/2 teaspoon pepper
1   teaspoon chili powder
1   (16-ounce) can diced tomatoes
    Water to cover

Preheat the oven to 350°. Grease a 1 1/2-quart casserole dish. Heat the olive oil in a skillet over medium-high heat. Sauté the onion until golden brown. Add the ground beef and brown completely. Spoon the onion and cooked ground beef into the casserole dish. Add the rice, salt, pepper, and chili powder. Pour the diced tomatoes over all and add enough water to cover. Cover the dish and bake for 1 hour.

Makes 4 to 6 servings

Judy Binder, Queen Mum JB
Red Hot Red Hatters, Camarillo, California

Slow Cooker Pizza Casserole

Good for taking along to potlucks or for serving guests arriving at different times.

1   pound ground beef
1   (16-ounce) package macaroni
5   cups spaghetti sauce
3   cups sliced pepperoni
3   cups grated mozzarella cheese
    Grated Romano or Parmesan cheese to taste

Brown the ground beef over medium heat and drain, reserving the drippings. Cook the macaroni according to the package directions. Drain and toss with the meat drippings. In a slow cooker layer 1 cup sauce, one-third of the ground beef, 1 cup pepperoni, 1 cup mozzarella cheese, one-third of the macaroni, and Romano or Parmesan cheese.

Continue layering, and then top with the remaining 2 cups sauce, and any remaining mozzarella or Parmesan or Romano cheese. Heat through and keep warm in the slow cooker.

Makes 8 to 10 servings

Carol Wiles, Lady of Love, Luck, & Laughter
Rural Robust Red Hatters, Kittanning, Pennsylvania

What Goes Quack and Sits on a Plate?

When I was a little girl, my dad bought me a duck. I was thrilled. I would put a string around his neck and take him for walks on the sidewalk in front of our house. I know all the neighborhood kids were probably jealous. They only had a cat or dog, but I had a duck.

After a while, Ducky went to live with my aunt in the country. I remember being sad at first, but I kind of forgot about him, as an eight-year-old often does in the summertime.

That year we had Thanksgiving dinner at our house. As you may have guessed, Ducky was the main course, which I learned after I finished the meal. I went bawling away from the table and slammed the door to my room, convinced I had a bunch of barbarians in my family.

My dad's words still echo in my ears, "I told you not to tell her." Now I know why some recipes remain a family secret.

For Thanksgiving, I've tried plenty of things, including tofu "turkey," but please, never duck.

Dianne Gavin,
Thee Purple Princess
Crimson Tide Great Lakes,
Beach Park, Illinois

One, Two Sausage and Rice Bake

1   pound mild bulk pork sausage
1   pound hot bulk pork sausage
1   bag frozen chopped onions, thawed
1   bag frozen chopped bell peppers, thawed
3   cups cooked rice
1   (14-ounce) can chicken broth
1 1/2   broth cans of water

Preheat the oven to 350°. Brown the mild and hot sausages with the onions and bell peppers in a skillet over medium heat until the sausage is cooked through and crumbly; drain. In a large bowl combine the sausage, onions, peppers, rice, broth, and water. Mix well. Spray a 13x9-inch dish with nonstick cooking spray and add the sausage mixture. Bake for 30 to 40 minutes.

Makes 6 to 8 servings

Trish Newman, Lady 'Git-R-Done'
ShadyLadies of Jacksonville, Florida, Macclenny, Florida

Creamy Chicken and Stuffing Casserole

If you love a recipe that just calls for pouring everything into a baking dish, mark this one.

1	(16-ounce) package corn bread stuffing mix
3/4	cup (1 1/2 sticks) butter, melted
4	cups chopped cooked chicken
2	(10 3/4-ounce) cans cream of chicken soup
3 1/3	cups chicken broth or 2 (14-ounce) cans

Preheat the oven to 350°. Mix the stuffing mix and butter together in bowl. Spread half the mixture in 13 x 9-inch baking dish. Top with the chicken. Heat the soup and broth in a saucepan, stirring to blend. Pour the heated mixture over the chicken and stuffing. Sprinkle with the remaining stuffing mixture. Bake for 30 minutes.

Makes 12 servings

Sandra Selle, Royal Contessa to the Queen
Royal Purple Iris, Columbia, Tennessee

Slow Cooker Chicken and Dressing

2 1/2	cups crumbled corn bread
1	cup crumbled crusty white bread or biscuits
2	eggs
1/2	cup (1 stick) butter, melted
	Salt and pepper to taste
1	medium onion, chopped
	Pinch of sage (optional)
1	plus 1 (10 3/4-ounce) cans cream of chicken soup
1	medium chicken, cooked and boned, broth reserved

For the dressing mix the corn bread, white bread, eggs, butter, salt and pepper, onion, sage, and 1 can of soup (diluted with some of the chicken broth until mixture is moist). Spoon half the remaining can of soup into the bottom of a slow cooker. Alternate layers of chicken and dressing, ending with chicken. Top with the remaining half can of soup. Cook on low for 3 hours.

Makes 8 to 10 servings

Sandra Calhoun, Dutches of Bargins
Delightful Anderson Hattitude Sisterhood, Anderson, South Carolina

Crunchy Chicken Bake

A step or two more, an ingredient or two more than your average chicken casserole. Makes a big flavor impact.

2   tablespoons butter
2   small onions, finely chopped
3/4 cup diced celery
1   scant teaspoon salt
2   teaspoons lemon juice
1   (10 3/4-ounce) can cream of mushroom soup
1   (10 3/4-ounce) can cream of celery soup
1   cup mayonnaise
2   cups cooked chicken, diced
2   cups cooked rice
1/2 cup slivered almonds
4   hard-boiled eggs, chopped
1   to 1 1/2 cups frozen peas
2   cups crushed potato chips

Preheat the oven to 375°. Melt the butter in a skillet over medium heat. Add the onions and celery and sauté until soft. In a small bowl mix the salt and lemon juice together. In a greased 2-quart casserole combine the onion and celery mixture with the mushroom and celery soups, mayonnaise, and the lemon juice mixture. Mix well. Add the chicken, rice, almonds, eggs, and frozen peas. Sprinkle the top with the crushed potato chips and bake until hot and bubbly, 40 to 45 minutes.

Makes 6 to 8 servings

Jan Heighton, Highland Gal
Red Hat'll Do Ya, Halifax, Nova Scotia, Canada

Cheesy Chicken Vegetable Casserole

4   cups cooked noodles (macaroni, egg noodles, or shells)
1   pound cubed chicken
1   (10 3/4-ounce) can cream of chicken soup
1   (15-ounce) can mixed vegetables or 1 cup frozen mixed vegetables, thawed
1/2 cup whole kernal corn or 1/2 cup frozen corn, thawed
1   plus 1 cups grated cheddar and Monterey Jack cheese
     Seasoning salt and pepper to taste
     Dash of sweet basil

Preheat the oven to 350°. Cook the noodles according to the package directions; drain. In a saucepan, cook the chicken over medium heat until brown (and crispy, if you like) in a little oil or nonstick cooking spray. Combine the noodles, soup, mixed vegetables, corn, 1 cup cheese, salt and pepper, and basil with the chicken. Spread in a greased 13 x 9-inch pan; sprinkle the top with the remaining 1 cup cheese. Bake for 30 minutes.

Makes 6 to 8 servings

Donna Bass, Primadonna
Dial Tone Divas, Albany, Oregon

Hot Chicken Salad

For so many Hatters, this dish brings back memories of happy times back when. And the ladies still love it.

3 cups diced cooked chicken
1 cup chopped celery
1 cup cooked rice
1 cup drained sliced water chestnuts
3/4 cup mayonnaise or sour cream
1 teaspoon salt
1 teaspoon lemon juice
1/3 cup chopped onion
3 hard-boiled eggs, chopped
1 (10 3/4-ounce) can cream of chicken soup

TOPPING
1/2 cup (1 stick) butter or margarine, melted
1 cup cornflake crumbs
1/2 cup slivered almonds

Preheat the oven to 350°. In a large bowl combine the chicken, celery, rice, water chestnuts, mayonnaise, salt, lemon juice, onion, eggs, and soup. Spoon into a greased 13 x 9-inch baking dish. Prepare the topping by combining the butter, cornflake crumbs, and almonds. Spread the topping over the casserole and bake for 35 minutes.

Makes 8 servings

Nancy Fogleman, Honorable Gypsy
Little Red Hens, Asheboro, North Carolina

Southwest Hominy Casserole

For a handy, make-ahead dish, freeze the casserole before baking. Let it cool first, and then wrap with plastic wrap. To keep a casserole hot until serving time, set it in a 200° oven.

2 (14-ounce) cans yellow hominy, drained
1 medium onion, chopped
1 garlic clove, minced
2 tablespoons olive oil
1 pound ground beef
1 tablespoon all-purpose flour
1 teaspoon salt
1 teaspoon chili powder
1 (14-ounce) can petite cut tomatoes
1 (14-ounce) can chili beans (just beans in sauce)
1/4 pound cheddar or Colby/Jack cheese, shredded

Preheat the oven to 350°. In a nonstick skillet over medium heat, sauté the hominy, onion, and garlic in the olive oil until the onion is tender. Spoon the mixture into a greased 2-quart casserole dish. In the same skillet brown the ground beef, breaking it up. Drain all but 1 tablespoon drippings. Add the flour, salt, and chili powder to the beef, mixing well. Add the tomatoes and chili beans. Return the meat mixture to the skillet and bring to a boil over medium heat. If the mixture seems a little dry, add a little water or more tomatoes. Spoon into the casserole dish and top with the cheese. Bake until bubbly and the cheese melts, about 30 minutes.

Makes 6 servings

Note: Add a can of chopped green chiles if you like, and serve with a bottle of hot sauce.

Diana Fuller, Dame Diana
Modoc Red Hot Hatters, Alturas, California

King Ranch Chicken

How this Texas favorite got its name is a mystery. It seems to have originated somewhere besides the King Ranch in Kingsville, Texas.

1/4 cup (1/2 stick) butter
1   medium green bell pepper, chopped
1   medium onion, chopped
1   (10 3/4-ounce) can cream of mushroom soup
1   (10 3/4-ounce) can cream of chicken soup
1   (10-ounce) can tomatoes with green chiles
2   cups cubed cooked chicken
15   corn tortillas, torn into bite-size pieces
2   cups (8 ounces) shredded cheddar cheese

Preheat the oven to 350°. In a large saucepan, melt the butter over medium-high heat. Cook the bell pepper and onion until tender, about 5 minutes. Add the soups, tomatoes with chiles, and chicken, stirring until well blended. In a greased 13 x 9 x 2-inch baking pan, alternately layers of the tortillas, soup mixture, and cheese, repeating for three layers and ending with cheese. Bake for 40 minutes, or until hot and bubbling.

Makes 8 servings

Judy Sorenson, Queen Mother
Red Hat Ya-Yas, Rockdale, Texas

Wild Rice Chicken Casserole

Nice enough for company, but comforting too.

3   to 4 cups diced cooked chicken
1   cup chopped celery
2   tablespoons butter or margarine
2   (10 3/4-ounce) cans cream of mushroom soup
2   cups chicken broth
1   (4 1/2-ounce) jar sliced mushrooms, drained
1   (2-ounce) jar chopped pimientos, drained
1   small onion, chopped
1   cup uncooked wild rice, rinsed
1/4 teaspoon poultry seasoning
3/4 cup cashew pieces
     Chopped fresh parsley

Preheat the oven to 350°. In a skillet over medium heat, brown the chicken and celery in the butter. In a large bowl combine the soup and broth and mix until smooth. Add the mushrooms, pimientos, onion, rice, poultry seasoning, and chicken mixture. Pour into a greased 13 x 9-inch baking dish. Cover and bake for 1 hour. Uncover and bake for 30 minutes more. Stir; sprinkle with the cashews. Return to the oven for 15 minutes, or until the rice is tender. Garnish with parsley.

Makes 10 to 12 servings

Shirley Klinner, Queen Mother
Crimson C'Hatters, Medford, Wisconsin

Easy Chicken Enchilada Casserole

Green salsa is what gives this casserole its exceptional taste. Tangier than red salsa, it provides a wonderful foil for the richness of the cheeses and soup.

1   ($10^3/4$-ounce) can cream of chicken soup

4   ounces sour cream

1   (4-ounce) can diced chiles

1/4 cup green salsa
    (sometimes labeled "salsa verde")

1   (11-ounce) package corn tortillas,
    cut or torn in half

1   (12-ounce) can chicken; drained (or
    leftover chopped chicken)

4   green onions, chopped plus some for
    garnish

12 ounces shredded cheese

1   (8-ounce) can black olives, chopped plus
    some for garnish

Preheat the oven to 350°. Combine the soup, sour cream, diced chiles, and green salsa and mix well. Layer the tortillas, chicken, soup mixture, green onions, cheese, and olives in that order in a greased 13 x 9-inch casserole. Garnish with additional green onions and olives. Bake for 20 to 30 minutes, or until bubbly.

Makes 6 to 8 servings

Vickie West, Queen Vickie Lou
Fun and Fabulous, Lakewood, California

Taco Casserole

Many different versions of this dish arrived in our e-mail box. This one seemed to sum them all up.

$1^1/2$ pounds lean ground beef or turkey

1   (1.25-ounce) package taco seasoning

2   (8-ounce) cans or 1 (15-ounce) can
    tomato sauce

1   (16-ounce) can pinto beans, drained and
    rinsed

1   (11-ounce) can Mexican corn, drained

1   cup shredded cheddar cheese

1   cup coarsely crushed tortilla chips
    Sour cream, sliced green onions, shredded
    lettuce, chopped tomatoes for garnish

Preheat the oven to 400°. Brown the meat in a large skillet over medium-high heat; drain. Stir in the taco seasoning, tomato sauce, beans, and corn. Reduce the heat to medium low and simmer for 5 minutes. Spoon the mixture into a greased 2-quart baking dish. Top with the cheese and tortilla chips. Bake until the cheese is melted, 5 to 10 minutes. Garnish the casserole with sour cream and sliced green onions, and serve with the shredded lettuce and chopped tomatoes.

Makes 6 servings

Betty (Clara E.) Tisdale, Singing Betsy Wetsy
Red Hat–titudes, Tampa, Florida

Pepperoni Zucchini Casserole

A casserole with an Italian accent.

4   eggs, beaten
1/2 cup olive oil
1   cup chopped or cubed pepperoni
3   cups cubed zucchini
2   (4-ounce) cans mushroom pieces, undrained
1/2 green bell pepper, chopped
1/2 teaspoon parsley
1/2 teaspoon oregano
1   teaspoon onion salt
1/3 teaspoon black pepper
1/2 cup Parmesan cheese
1/3 teaspoon garlic salt
1   cup biscuit mix

Preheat the oven to 350°. Combine the eggs, oil, pepperoni, zucchini, mushrooms, bell pepper, parsley, oregano, onion salt, pepper, cheese, garlic salt, and biscuit mix. Stir until well mixed. Pour into an ungreased 13 x 9-inch baking dish. Bake for 25 minutes, or until brown.

Makes 6 servings

Jennie Helmantoler, Vice Queen Mama
Fayette–Greene Mama Mias, Carmichaels, Pennsylvania

Haddock Casserole

1   (12-ounce) can evaporated milk
1   (10 3/4-ounce) can cream of mushroom soup
1   (8-ounce) block Velveeta cheese, cubed

2   pounds haddock, cooked and flaked
1   sleeve buttery round crackers
1   cup (2 sticks) butter, melted

Preheat the oven to 350°. Combine the milk, soup, and cheese in a double boiler set over simmering water. Cook until the cheese is completely melted. Pour the sauce over the fish that has been placed in a greased 2-quart casserole dish. Crush the crackers to crumbs and add the butter; spread the crumbs over the casserole. Bake for 30 minutes, or until bubbly.

Makes 4 servings

Mickey Pearsall, General Chapterette
Old Babes in Red Hats, Garland, Maryland

Shrimp and Wild Rice Casserole

Another one for company, or just for celebrating.

1/2 cup thinly sliced onions
1/4 cup chopped green bell pepper
1/2 cup sliced mushrooms
1/4 cup (1/2 stick) butter
1   tablespoon Worcestershire sauce
     Few drops Tabasco (or to taste)
2   cups cooked wild rice
1   pound cooked shrimp

CREAM SAUCE
2   tablespoons butter
2   tablespoons all-purpose flour
2   bouillon cubes, dissolved in 1 cup hot water

Sauté the onions, bell pepper, and mushrooms in the butter in a large skillet over medium heat. Add the Worcestershire sauce, Tabasco, wild rice, and shrimp. Preheat the oven to 300°.

For the cream sauce, melt the butter in a small saucepan over medium heat and stir in the flour until well blended. Add the bouillon and cook until thickened. Combine the shrimp mixture with the cream sauce and pour into a buttered 13 x 9-inch casserole. Bake for 20 to 30 minutes, or until thoroughly heated.

Makes 4 to 6 servings

Frances Meder, Queen Mother
Bayou City Red Hats, Houston, Texas

Salmon Noodle Casserole

Economical and loaded with calcium.

1   (8-ounce) package egg noodles
1   (14.7-ounce) can salmon, drained
1 1/2   cups (12 ounces) sour cream
1/4   cup milk
1   (4-ounce) can sliced mushrooms, drained
1 1/2   teaspoons salt
1/4   teaspoon pepper
1/4   cup dry bread crumbs
1/4   cup grated Parmesan cheese
2   tablespoons butter, melted

Preheat the oven to 350°. Cook the noodles according to the package directions. Drain and return to the pan. Stir in the salmon, sour cream, milk, mushrooms, salt, and pepper. Pour into an ungreased 2-quart casserole. Combine the bread crumbs, Parmesan cheese, and butter and sprinkle over the casserole. Bake uncovered for 35 to 40 minutes, or until bubbly.

Makes 6 servings

Sadie Steinberg, Lady Gemini
Red Hot and Purple, Janesville, Minnesota

Poppy Seed Chicken

Rich flavor and pretty, polka-dotted look.

2   (10 3/4-ounce) cans cream of chicken soup
1   (8-ounce) carton sour cream
6   skinless chicken breasts, boiled in salted water, boned, and chopped
1   sleeve buttery round crackers, crushed
1/2   cup (1 stick) butter, melted
3   tablespoons poppy seeds

Preheat the oven to 350°. In a medium bowl combine the soup and sour cream. In a greased 13 x 9-inch pan layer the chopped chicken then the soup mixture. Top with the crushed crackers; pour the melted butter over the crackers. Sprinkle with the poppy seeds. Bake for 30 minutes.

Makes 8 to 10 servings

Jone Robertson, Duchess of Mail
Royal Sassies of Bowling Green, Bowling Green, Kentucky

Madame, S'il Vous Plaît, Guillotine the Turkey!

When I was in Paris on a year-abroad college program, my roommate and I lived with an elderly couple near Gare Saint Lazare. It was traditional for the American students to prepare a typical Thanksgiving repast for their French hosts, so I asked my mother to send recipes.

My roommate and I set out to gather our ingredients, but discovered the turkey had to be special-ordered from the butcher a week in advance. On the appointed day, we hiked up to the shop and collected our bird. When we later examined it in the kitchen, we discovered it was complete with neck attached, but the wings were cut off at the "elbow." Ugh!

We got the giggles and laughed till we cried. Neither one of us could bring ourselves to chop the neck off, so we finally had to ask our hostess, Madame Mielle, to do it for us. I'm sure she wondered if we'd ever manage to cook it if we couldn't even chop off its neck.

After a lot of trussing, we managed to get it stuffed, even without wings to hold the cavity shut. We never did find pecans in Paris, but the walnut pie we made was a passable substitute! Madame Mielle and her extended family, every last one of them, proclaimed our dinner the best American feast they'd ever had.

Wendy Works Gibson,
Queen Wendybird
Red Hat Readers Society,
Moneta, Virginia

Turkey Crunch Casserole

Sometimes the meals after Thanksgiving are as good as the big feast itself.

3　cups diced cooked turkey
2　hard-boiled eggs, chopped
1　(4-ounce) can sliced mushrooms, drained
3/4　cup diced celery
1/2　cup slivered blanched almonds
1　teaspoon chopped onion
1　(10 3/4-ounce) can cream of chicken soup
3/4　cup mayonnaise
　　Chow mein noodles or crushed potato chips

Preheat the oven to 350°. In a large bowl combine the turkey, eggs, mushrooms, celery, almonds, and onion. Stir the soup into the mayonnaise. Toss with the turkey mixture. Spoon into a greased 2-quart casserole. Sprinkle the noodles over the top. Bake for 30 minutes, or until the mixture is bubbly.

Makes 6 servings

Mary Drzal, Queen
Crimson Belles, Yonkers, New York

Five-Bean Casserole

The contributor notes that molasses brown bread is delicious with the beans.

1/2 cup dried kidney beans
1/2 cup dried garbanzo beans
1/2 cup dried baby lima beans
1/2 cup dried yellow-eyed beans
1/2 cup dried white (navy) beans
1 large onion, chopped
  Salt and pepper to taste
1/2 cup molasses
1/4 cup chili sauce
1/4 cup ketchup
1 tablespoon white or cider vinegar
1 tablespoon Worcestershire sauce
1 teaspoon dry mustard
1 pound bulk pork sausage, fried and cut up or 1/2 pound smoked ham, cubed

Soak the beans overnight. Boil for 20 minutes in the same water. Drain and place in a large bean pot or a greased 2-quart casserole dish.

Preheat the oven to 300°. Add the onion, salt and pepper, molasses, chili sauce, ketchup, vinegar, Worcestershire sauce, and dry mustard. Cover and bake for 3 to 4 hours, or until the beans are tender. Add the sausage when the beans are fully cooked; heat through.

Makes 6 to 8 cups

Helen Wilson, Dutchess of Snowbirds
Rockin' Mamas, St. John's, Newfoundland, Canada

Broccoli Bake

Toss in 1 cup diced cooked chicken or pork for a warm and wonderful meal from the oven.

2 cups cooked broccoli
2 eggs
1 (10 3/4-ounce) can cream mushroom soup, undiluted
1/2 cup mayonnaise
1 1/2 cups shredded medium cheddar cheese
2 tablespoons minced onion

Preheat the oven to 325°. In a large bowl combine the broccoli, eggs, soup, mayonnaise, cheese, and onion and mix well. Spoon into a greased 9-inch square baking dish. Bake for 40 minutes, or until the top becomes brown and crusty. Serve immediately or cover with foil and keep warm in a 200° oven.

Makes 8 servings

Shirley Sternberger, Queenie
Scarlet O'Hatters, Hershey, Pennslyvania

Utah Country White Beans

Serve this dish as a soup, or drain the liquid and serve as a vegetable side dish. Corn bread is a great accompaniment for this one-dish meal.

1	pound dried small white beans
2	teaspoons salt
1/2	teaspoon black pepper
1	garlic clove, minced
1	bay leaf
4	to 5 slices bacon, cut into small pieces
2	plus 2 tablespoons butter or margarine
2	medium yellow onions, finely chopped
3	medium firm tomatoes, chopped
1	medium green bell pepper, seeded and finely chopped
1/2	teaspoon oregano
1/4	cup chopped fresh parsley

Put the beans in a large saucepan and add enough water to cover. Bring the beans and water to a boil over high heat. Boil for 1 minute, remove from the heat, and let stand for 1 hour. Drain the beans and add fresh water to cover, about 5 cups. Add the salt, pepper, garlic, bay leaf, and bacon. Cover and bring to a boil over high heat. Reduce the heat to low and simmer for 2 hours, or until the beans are tender; drain.

Melt 2 tablespoons butter in a skillet over medium heat and sauté the onions for about 5 minutes. Add the tomatoes and bell pepper and cook for another 5 minutes. Stir in the oregano and parsley. Add this mixture and the remaining 2 tablespoons butter to the beans. Heat through. Remove bay leaf before serving.

Makes 6 to 8 servings

Sharron Wood, Top Hat
Desert Rouge Hattitudes of Hurricane Valley, LaVerkin, Utah

Calico Baked Beans

An old favorite because it's just so easy, and so economical.

1/2	pound ground beef
1/2	pound bacon, diced
1	medium onion, chopped
1	cup ketchup
1/2	cup firmly packed brown sugar
1	teaspoon white or cider vinegar
1	(16-ounce) can pork and beans
1	(16-ounce) can kidney beans, drained
1	(16-ounce) can butter lima beans, drained
1	(16-ounce) can northern white beans, drained

Preheat the oven to 350°. In a skillet over medium-high heat, brown the ground beef with the bacon, and onion; drain. Combine in a greased 13x9-inch baking dish with the ketchup, brown sugar, vinegar, and the beans. Bake for about 45 minutes.

Makes 15 to 20 servings

Linda Schaeffer, Queen
Curvaceous Babes, Fleetwood, Pennsylvania

Corn Casserole

Ideal with ham or fried chicken, and also nice with a little diced turkey stirred in.

1   (15-ounce) can whole kernel corn, drained
1   (15-ounce) can creamed corn
2   eggs, beaten
1/2 cup (1 stick) butter or margarine, melted
1   (8-ounce) container sour cream
1   (8-ounce) box corn bread mix

Preheat the oven to 350°. In a large bowl combine the corns eggs, butter, sour cream, and corn bread mix and blend well. Spoon into an ungreased 8-inch baking dish and bake uncovered for 1 hour.

Makes 10 servings

Karen Frahm, Queen Mother
Apache Redhats, Mesa, Arizona

Eggplant Casserole

1   medium eggplant, diced
1/2 cup sliced onion
2   tablespoons butter
1   egg
1/2 cup grated cheese
1   teaspoon salt
    Dash of pepper
1   cup dry bread crumbs

Cook the eggplant and onion in enough water to cover in a saucepan over medium heat for 20 minutes, or until tender; drain. Preheat the oven to 350°. Combine the eggplant and onion with the butter, egg, cheese, salt, and pepper. Spoon into a greased 1 1/2-quart baking dish. Top with the bread crumbs. Bake for 30 minutes.

Makes 8 to 10 servings

Bessie Williamson, Honey Pot
Sassy Ladies, Sumter, South Carolina

Squash or Eggplant Casserole

1   eggplant or about 2 pounds squash
1   (10 3/4-ounce) can cream of mushroom or celery soup
2   eggs, lightly beaten
1/2 cup chopped onion
1   cup grated American cheese
1/2 cup saltine cracker crumbs, divided
2   tablespoons butter, melted

Peel the eggplant and cut into cubes (or slice the squash). Boil in salted water until tender and then drain. Add the soup, eggs, and onion and mix well. Spoon half of this mixture into a greased 2 1/2-quart casserole dish. Preheat the oven to 350°. Add the cheese and half the cracker crumbs to the casserole. Cover with the remaining eggplant mixture and the remaining cracker crumbs. Pour the melted butter evenly over the top. Bake for about 45 minutes, or until lightly brown and bubbling hot.

Makes 8 to 10 servings

Mary Francinn Parker, Queen Mom of Grandyville
The Happy Hatters, Georgetown, Texas

Squash, Corn Bread, and Green Chile Bake

Good as a side dish or serve as a meatless entrée.

4   yellow squash, sliced
1   (14-ounce) can diced tomatoes with green chiles
1   (8-ounce) package corn bread stuffing mix
1   small white onion, diced
1   egg, beaten
1/4   cup milk
1   cup shredded cheddar cheese

Combine the squash with enough water to cover in a saucepan over medium-high heat. Cook the squash until tender and drain. Drain and reserve the juice from the tomatoes. Cook the stuffing according to the package directions, substituting the juice from the drained tomatoes for part of the water. Preheat the oven to 350°. While the stuffing is cooking, combine the tomatoes, onion, egg, milk, and cooked squash in a bowl. Add the stuffing and cheese. Spoon into a greased 2-quart casserole dish. Bake for 20 minutes, or until browned.

Makes 10 servings

Joy Jefferies, Web Mistress
The Red Hat Classy Chicks, Austin, Texas

Creamy Potato Bake

Rich enough to be a meatless entrée with a fruit or a mixed salad alongside. Or use it as a glorious side dish.

8   medium potatoes, chopped
3   carrots, shredded
1   onion, diced
2   tablespoons dried parsley
    Salt and pepper to taste
2   tablespoons butter or margarine
13/4   cups plus 1/4 cup grated cheddar cheese (8 ounces)
1/2   cup cream cheese (4 ounces)
1   (2-ounce) can chopped olives
    Chopped fresh parsley or green onions for garnish

Preheat the oven to 350°. Combine the potatoes, carrots, onion, parsley, and salt and pepper in a large pot; add just enough water to cover. Cook over medium-high heat until the potatoes are tender, about 20 minutes; drain. Add the butter, 13/4 cups cheese, and cream cheese. Adjust the seasonings to taste. Mix well and spoon into a greased 11/2–2 quart baking dish. Bake for 15 to 30 minutes, or until the cheese begins to bubble. Add the remaining 1/4 cup cheese and the olives on top. Garnish with the fresh parsley or green onions.

Makes 6 to 8 servings

Vickie West, Queen Vickie Lou
Fun and Fabulous, Lakewood, California

Zucchini Stuffing Bake

Chicken soup and stuffing give this the flavor and savor of meat.

2   pounds zucchini, chopped
1/4 cup diced celery
1/2 cup chopped onion
1/2 cup (1 stick) butter, melted
2   (8-ounce) boxes chicken-flavored stuffing mix
1   (10 3/4-ounce) can cream of chicken soup
1/2 cup sour cream
1   cup shredded cheddar cheese

Preheat the oven to 350°. Cook the zucchini, celery, and onion in a small amount of salted water in a saucepan over medium-high heat until the zucchini is tender. Drain, reserving the liquid. Combine the butter with the stuffing seasoning in a large bowl and then mix in the stuffing. It will be dry. Place half the stuffing mixture into a greased 13 x 9-inch baking pan. Mix the soup, sour cream, and cheese with the drained zucchini mixture and spread over the stuffing in the pan. Moisten the remaining stuffing with the reserved liquid and spread on top of the zucchini layer. Bake for about 45 minutes.

Makes 10 to 12 servings

Carol Schille, Paper Clips
Purple Sages, Springfield, Ohio

Depression Spaghetti

Hatters of a certain age may remember these days when spaghetti was 25 cents for 8 ounces, bacon was 13 cents per pound, onions were 4 cents per pound, sugar was 47 cents per pound, bread was 5 cents for a one-pound loaf, and butter was 24 cents per pound.

1   (8-ounce) package spaghetti (Mom used one package for two meals.)
3   slices of bacon, sliced thinly (cheaper way to use it)
2   medium-size onions, diced
1   (25-ounce) can diced tomatoes or tomato sauce (whichever was cheaper)
1   tablespoon sugar (if you had it!)

Cook the spaghetti according to the package directions. Cut the bacon into 2-inch pieces and fry in a large skillet over medium heat until crisp. Remove the bacon from the skillet and sauté the onions in the drippings for 5 minutes. Add the tomatoes or tomato sauce and sugar. (If using tomato sauce, add a small amount of water to the can. By doing this, Mom was allowed to use every last drop of the tomato sauce—she never wasted anything.) Simmer about 15 minutes. Add the cooked spaghetti, mix well, and cook 10 more minutes. Add the bacon, stir, and serve with bread and butter. It was rare that we had butter, but it was sure good when we did.

Makes 4 to 6 servings

Vanessa Luce, Queen of Vice
Johnson City Red Hatters, Johnson City, Texas

Zucchini Pie

Nice and easy, said the tester. Make it a side dish, or serve it as a light supper on a summer night (when you can practically hear the zucchini growing in the garden).

3   or 4 medium zucchini, sliced
1   medium onion, sliced
1   cup biscuit mix
1/2 cup vegetable oil
4   eggs
1/2 cup grated Parmesan cheese
1/2 cup shredded mozzarella cheese
1/4 teaspoon salt
1/2 teaspoon pepper

Preheat the oven to 350°. Combine the zucchini, onion, biscuit mix, oil, eggs, cheeses, salt, and pepper in a large bowl. Spoon into a greased 13 x 9-inch baking dish. Bake for 45 minutes, or until golden brown.

Makes 12 servings

Cara Rodgers, Queen Cara
Coral Springs Sweethearts, Coral Springs, Florida

Potluck Spaghetti

Oregano's flavor really blooms when you rub it between your fingers as you add it to the skillet.

1   cup chopped yellow onion
1   cup chopped green bell pepper
1   tablespoon butter

1   (4-ounce) can mushrooms, drained
1   (28-ounce) can whole tomatoes, not drained
1   (2-ounce) can sliced black olives
2   teaspoons oregano
1/2 pound ground beef, browned, drained
1/2 pound Italian pork sausage, browned, drained
1   (12-ounce) package spaghetti , cooked and drained
1   cup plus 1 cup shredded cheddar cheese
1   (10 3/4-ounce) can cream of mushroom soup
1/4 cup water
1/4 cup grated Parmesan cheese

Sauté the onion and bell pepper in the butter in a skillet over medium heat until tender. Add the mushrooms, tomatoes, olives, and oregano, breaking up the tomatoes. Add the beef and pork. Bring to a boil, reduce the heat to medium low, and simmer uncovered for about 10 minutes. Remove from the heat.

Spread half the spaghetti in a greased 13 x 9-inch baking pan. Top with half the meat sauce. Sprinkle with 1 cup cheddar cheese. Repeat the layers, sprinkling with the remaining 1 cup cheddar cheese. Mix the soup with the water and pour over the casserole. Sprinkle with the Parmesan cheese. Bake, uncovered, for 30 to 35 minutes, or until bubbly and heated through.

Makes 12 servings

Toni Garman, Queen Mum
Red Hat Honeys, Spokane, Washington

Spaghetti Sauce

It's hard to beat this family favorite.

1   medium onion, chopped
1   tablespoon butter, margarine, or vegetable oil
1   pound ground beef
    Salt, pepper, and oregano to taste
    Butter, margarine, or vegetable oil
1   (6-ounce) can tomato paste
1 1/2   cups (2 tomato paste cans) water
1   (14-ounce) can stewed tomatoes
2   bay leaves
2   tablespoons sugar
    Hot cooked spaghetti

Brown the onion in the butter in a large skillet over medium heat. Add the ground beef and season with salt, pepper, and oregano. Cook until the meat is browned and crumbly, breaking up the beef. Add the tomato paste, water, stewed tomatoes, bay leaves, and sugar. Bring to a boil, reduce the heat to low, and simmer for 2 1/2 to 3 hours, stirring occasionally. Remove bay leaves and serve over the cooked pasta.

Makes 6 servings

Sue Ellen Cooper, Exalted Queen Mother (Founder)
Fabulous Founders, Fullerton, California

String Pie

1   pound ground beef
1/2   cup chopped onion
1/4   cup chopped green pepper
1   (15-ounce) jar spaghetti sauce
1   (8-ounce) package spaghetti, cooked
1/3   cup grated Parmesan cheese
2   eggs, beaten
2   teaspoons butter (optional)
1   cup cottage cheese
1/2   cup shredded mozzarella cheese

Preheat the oven to 350°. Cook the beef, onion, and green bell pepper in a large skillet over medium heat until the beef is browned and crumbly; drain. Stir in the spaghetti sauce and mix well. In a large bowl combine the cooked spaghetti, Parmesan cheese, eggs, and butter. Spread over the bottom of 13 x 9-inch baking pan. Pour the spaghetti sauce mixture over the top of spaghetti mix. Spread the cottage cheese over the sauce. Sprinkle with the mozzarella cheese. Bake for 20 minutes.

Makes 12 to 15 servings

Charlotte Williams, Vice Queen
Lucky Sunshine Ladies, Hampton, Virginia

Mac and Texas Cheeses with Roasted Chiles

The roasted mild poblano chiles make this mac-and-cheese something special. Poblanos are the dark green, mild peppers used in Chile Rellenos. If you can't find poblanos, try Hatch or New Mexico peppers. They roast best when coated with a little oil—just toss them with oil in a clean plastic bag and then arrange them on the broiler rack.

4	poblano chile peppers
1	(16-ounce) package uncooked elbow macaroni
1/2	cup (1 stick) butter
1/2	cup all-purpose flour
2	cups whipping cream
1	cup milk
2 3/4	cups plus 1/4 cup shredded Monterey Jack cheese
1	(4-ounce) package goat cheese, crumbled
1	teaspoon salt
1/4	cup dry Italian bread crumbs
1/2	cup shredded Parmesan cheese

Spray the chile peppers with nonstick cooking spray. Broil the peppers on an aluminum foil-lined baking sheet 5 inches from the heat about 5 minutes on each side, or until the chiles look blistered. Place in a zip-top plastic bag, seal, and let stand 10 minutes to loosen the skins. Peel the chiles, remove and discard the seeds, and cut into strips. Cook the macaroni according to the package directions; drain.

Preheat the oven to 375°. Melt the butter in a Dutch oven over low heat and whisk in the flour until smooth. Cook for 1 minute, whisking constantly. Gradually whisk in the cream and milk. Cook over medium heat, whisking constantly, for 5 minutes, or until the mixture is thickened and bubbly. Stir in 2 3/4 cups Monterey Jack cheese, the goat cheese, and salt and cook until smooth. Stir in the roasted chiles and macaroni. Spoon mixture into a lightly greased 13 x 9-inch baking dish. Top evenly with the bread crumbs and Parmesan cheese. Bake for 40 minutes. Remove from the oven and sprinkle evenly with the remaining 1/4 cup Monterey Jack cheese. Broil for 3 to 5 minutes, or until the cheese is golden and bubbly.

Makes 8 servings

Janie Russell, Biker Goddess
Big D Regals, Garland, Texas

Yugoslavian Spaghetti Sauce

Slovenia, part of the former Yugoslavia, is just around the corner from Italy, with the same sunny slopes, sparkling shores, and similar food (with its own special touches).

1 1/2	pounds lean ground beef
2	onions, peeled and sliced
2	garlic cloves, peeled and quartered
1	tablespoon parsley
1	to 1 1/2 teaspoons cinnamon
1/2	to 1 teaspoon nutmeg
1	(8-ounce) can tomato sauce
4	to 5 cups (or tomato sauce cans) water
1 1/2	to 2 tablespoons red wine
	Pasta (shell macaroni, mostaccioli, or similar)

Grind the ground beef, onions, and garlic together in a meat grinder or food processor. Transfer to a Dutch oven or heavy pot with a little bit of canola oil. Sprinkle with the parsley. Brown over very low heat, stirring frequently. Season with the cinnamon and nutmeg. Add the tomato sauce, water, and wine. Let simmer over low heat for about 3 hours. Cook the pasta according to the package directions and drain. Toss with the sauce.

Makes 4 to 6 servings

Barbara Folkes, Princess Pom Mom
Red Hat Crafty Quilters, Maryville, Tennessee

Italian Gravy a la Rutigliano

"Italian gravy" was one term used to describe meat and tomato sauces for pasta. Make this over the weekend to serve during the week.

	Olive oil
1	pound eye of round (or rump roast), cubed
4	garlic cloves, minced
1	medium onion, minced
1	(12-ounce) can tomato paste
1 1/2	cups dry white wine
5 1/4	plus 3 cups water
1	(28-ounce) can tomato purée
1/2	teaspoon salt
1	teaspoon black pepper
1/2	tablespoon oregano
1	tablespoon chopped fresh or dried parsley
1	tablespoon chopped fresh or dried basil
	Hot cooked macaroni

In a 5-quart pot over medium heat, add enough olive oil to just cover the bottom. Brown the meat in the olive oil. Remove the meat. Sauté the garlic and onion in the oil. Increase the heat to medium high. Add the tomato paste, wine, and 3 cups water. Mix well. Add the tomato purée and the remaining 5 1/4 cups water. Mix well. Stir in the salt, pepper, oregano, parsley, and basil. Bring to a boil. Add the meat and cover. Reduce the heat to low and simmer for 3 hours, gently stirring occasionally. When ready to serve, skim off the fat. Serve over cooked macaroni.

Makes 6 servings

Linda Tarnowski, Red Hatter
Purple Perks, Jackson, New Jersey

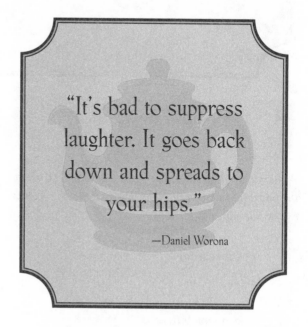

"It's bad to suppress laughter. It goes back down and spreads to your hips."

—Daniel Worona

Then vs. Now

Back in the early '60s, I was a single mother, and pennies were severely pinched. Meal preparation was limited to what our budget could manage. Appearing frequently on our table was a goulash dish comprised of the ubiquitous ground beef, macaroni, and tomatoes. This dish was a favorite of my beloved daughter and one she always requested when her little girlfriends came over for supper.

Some twenty-five years later, when she was married and in her own home, she called to request the recipe, reiterating that it was a favorite. I asked if she wanted the recipe the way I made it then or the way I make it now. Surprised, she asked what the difference was. I assured her that before it was half the hamburger and double the macaroni, and now it's double the hamburger and half the macaroni. Her beautiful reply was "Gee, Mama, I never knew the difference."

Judy Davenport,
Queen of Vice
Parkville Red Pepper Popsies,
Weatherby Lake, Missouri

Three-Cheese Macaroni and Cheese

A microwaved cream sauce—what a great idea. Since the power of microwave ovens varies so much, keep an eye on the sauce as it cooks.

3   cups macaroni

SAUCE
4   tablespoons butter
4   tablespoons all-purpose flour
1   teaspoon sugar

Dash of dry mustard
Dash of celery salt
2   cups milk
1   (16-ounce) container cottage cheese
2   cups grated aged cheddar cheese
2/3 cup sour cream or plain yogurt

TOPPING
1   cup grated medium cheddar cheese
1/2 cup dry bread crumbs

Cook the macaroni in a large saucepan according to the package directions. Drain well. Preheat the oven to 350°.

For the sauce, melt the butter in a 4-cup microwaveable bowl. Add the flour, sugar, mustard, and celery salt; cook on high for 30 seconds. Add the milk, stirring until well mixed. Microwave for 6 minutes, stirring every 2 minutes. When the sauce is thickened, stir in the cottage cheese. In a large bowl combine the macaroni, cheddar cheese, cream sauce, and sour cream. Mix well and spoon into a greased 13x9-inch baking dish or three small ones.

For the topping sprinkle the cheddar cheese and bread crumbs on top. Bake a large casserole for 1 hour or small ones for 45 minutes.

Makes 12 servings

Margaret Worth, Lady Margaret
Thousand Island Belles, Gananoque, Ontario, Canada

Feta Cheese Orzo

"Fun texture and lots of color in a good and unexpected combination of ingredients," raved testers. Marvelously meatless as it is, this dish can also be dressed up with shrimp or chicken. Makes a good side dish, too.

1   eggplant, chopped
1   red bell pepper, chopped
1   yellow bell pepper, chopped
1   orange bell pepper, chopped
1   cup plus 2 tablespoons olive oil
1   cup pine nuts
1   (16-ounce) box orzo
    Juice of 4 lemons (1/3 to 1/2 cup)
1   cup crumbled feta cheese (or to taste)
1   bunch green onions, sliced (or to taste)
1   bunch basil, chopped
    Salt and pepper to taste

Preheat the oven to 400°. Toss the eggplant and bell peppers with 2 tablespoons olive oil. Roast the vegetables on a baking sheet for about 30 minutes, or until tender, checking every 10 minutes. Toast the pine nuts in a skillet or on a baking sheet. Cook the orzo according to the package directions. Combine the lemon juice and the remaining 1 cup olive oil in a jar with a tight-fitting lid. Shake well to make a dressing. Combine the roasted vegetables with the cooked orzo, adding enough dressing to make the mixture is easy to stir. Add the feta cheese and green onions. Add the basil and pine nuts just before serving. Season with salt and pepper.

Makes 8 servings

Note: The mixture dries as it sits, so if you can't serve it right away, be prepared to add a tablespoon or two of water. Serve at room temperature.

Linda Gangemi, Queen
Red-E-or Nots, Stoughton, Massachusetts

Macaroni and Cheese Scallop

The real, homemade thing, dressed up with seashell pasta.

1   (4-ounce) package seashell macaroni
3   eggs, separated
1   cup grated medium or sharp cheddar cheese
3   tablespoons butter or margarine
3   tablespoons all-purpose flour (rounded)
1/2   teaspoon salt
     Pepper to taste
2   cups milk

Preheat the oven to 325°. Cook the macaroni in salted water according to the package directions; drain. Lightly beat the egg yolks and stir into the macaroni. Add the cheese and mix well. Melt the butter in a saucepan over medium heat. Stir in the flour, salt, and pepper. Add the milk slowly, stirring with a whisk. Cook until well blended and thick. Pour the sauce over the macaroni. Beat the egg whites until fluffy and fold them into the macaroni mixture. Pour the mixture into a well-greased 2 quart casserole dish. Bake for 30 minutes.

Makes 8 to 10 servings

Claudia Tatum, Queen Mum Pollyanna
Georgia Peachiz, Lilburn, Georgia

Never-Fail Macaroni and Cheese

2   cups macaroni or other pasta shape
4   teaspoons minced onion

3   plus 3 tablespoons butter or margarine
3   tablespoons all-purpose flour
2   cups milk
1   teaspoon Dijon mustard
     Salt and pepper to taste
2   cups (8 ounces) shredded extra sharp cheese (reserve some for top)
1/2   cup dry bread crumbs

Cook the pasta according to the package directions; drain. Preheat the oven to 350°. In a skillet over medium heat, sauté the onion in 3 tablespoons butter until translucent. Stir in the flour and mix well. Stir in the milk. Cook, stirring, over low heat until slightly thickened. Add the mustard, salt and pepper, and cheese; cook until the cheese is melted. Do not boil. (Mixture will curdle if the heat is too high.) Pour the mixture into a 3-quart casserole. Top with the reserved cheese and the bread crumbs and dot with the remaining 3 tablespoon butter. Bake for 20 minutes.

Makes 6 servings

Helen Warinsky, Countess of Reason
Feisty Red Hatters, Woodbury, Minnesota

Cheese Ravioli with Pumpkin-Sage Sauce

A restaurant-quality entrée for busy nights.

1/2   cup dry white wine
1/4   cup chopped shallots (or finely chopped white onion)

1   (10-ounce) container Alfredo sauce
1/2 cup packed pure pumpkin
1   teaspoon chopped fresh sage
2   (9-ounce) packages four-cheese ravioli
2   teaspoons chopped green onion
     Freshly grated Parmesan cheese
     Ground black pepper to taste

Cook the white wine and shallots in a medium saucepan over low heat, stirring occasionally, until reduced to 1 tablespoon. Stir in the Alfredo sauce, pumpkin, and sage. Cook, stirring occasionally, until the mixture is heated through; keep warm.

Prepare the cheese ravioli according to package directions; drain, reserving 1/4 cup cooking water. Stir the reserved cooking water into the sauce and toss with the ravioli. Sprinkle with the green onion and Parmesan cheese. Season with ground black pepper; serve immediately.

Makes 4 servings

Note: For another great topping for the ravioli, make caramelized walnuts. Melt 2 teaspoons butter with 1/4 cup brown sugar; stir in 1/2 to 3/4 cup walnuts. Bake on a cookie sheet until caramelized. Let cool before using.

Peggy Arntz, Queen Mum Pursalot
The Red Light Review Red Hatters, Waukesha, Wisconsin

Mama Mia Manicotti

Be sure not to overcook the shells; they're easier to stuff when they're firm.

1   (16-ounce) package jumbo manicotti shells
1   (15-ounce) container ricotta cheese
1 1/3 cups shredded mozzarella cheese
1/2   cup freshly shredded or grated Parmesan cheese
1   egg yolk
1   tablespoon minced fresh parsley
1   tablespoon mixed Italian herbs
1   (25-ounce) jar tomato-based pasta sauce

Cook the shells according to the package directions and drain. Mix the cheeses, egg yolk, parsley, and herbs together. Add a teaspoon of water if needed. Preheat the oven to 375°. Spread a small amount of the pasta sauce on the bottom of a greased 13x9-inch baking dish. Stuff the shells with the cheese mixture and place each shell into the baking dish, open side down. Pour the remaining pasta sauce over the shells. The sauce level should at least be even with the shells to keep the shells from drying out. Bake for about 25 minutes to heat through.

Makes 6 servings

Dot Evans, Vice Queen Mother & Princess of Purple Passion
Not Young & Not Restless, Piedmont, South Carolina

Slow-Cooker Macaroni and Cheese

Testers agreed on the good taste of this easy favorite.

1 (8-ounce) package elbow macaroni
1 (12-ounce) can evaporated milk
3 eggs, beaten
1/2 cup (1 stick) butter, melted
2 plus 1 cups grated sharp cheddar cheese

Cook and drain the macaroni according to the package directions. Combine the milk, eggs, butter, and 2 cups cheese in a bowl and mix well. Add the macaroni and mix well. Transfer to a slow cooker. Sprinkle the remaining 1 cup cheese on top. Cover and cook on low for 3 hours. Don't stir or remove the lid until time is up.

Makes 8 servings

Linda Denton, Queen
Chapeau Rouge, Richmond, Virginia

Pasta and Brie

Testers commented this would be a great, mid-summer, picnic dish to accompany bratwurst.

1 (24-ounce) package ziti (linguini works well too)
10 ounces brie cheese
3 to 4 medium-size fresh tomatoes, chopped
2 garlic cloves, chopped
3 tablespoons olive oil
1/2 cup torn fresh basil leaves
   Freshly ground pepper to taste

Bring a large pot of salted water to a boil, and cook the pasta until just tender. Drain the pasta and put in a large serving bowl. Cut the rind from the cheese and chop the cheese into bite-size pieces. In a medium-size bowl combine the cheese with the tomatoes, garlic, and olive oil. Stir to just blend. Add the cheese mixture to the pasta and mix well. Just before serving, add the basil and toss to blend. Grind some fresh pepper over the dish.

Makes 6 servings

Kathleen Franger, Queen Cost–Alot
Blushin' Belles, San Jose, California

Chicken-Stuffed Manicotti

No need to cook the manicotti before stuffing them; that's what makes this dish a keeper.

1/4 to 1/2 pound fresh mushrooms, sliced or chopped
   Vegetable oil
2 chicken breast halves, cooked and boned
1 (10-ounce) box frozen spinach, thawed and drained
1 egg
   Salt and pepper to taste
1 (16-ounce) package manicotti shells

Preheat the oven to 375°. Sauté the mushrooms in a little oil in a skillet over medium heat until tender. Combine with the chicken and spinach in a food processor fitted with the metal blade. Add the egg and salt and pepper. Process until combined. Stuff the shells with the chicken and spinach mixture and arrange them in a greased

13 x 9-inch baking dish. Add 1/2 cup water. Cover with foil and bake for 1 hour.

Makes 6 servings

Jacqueline Shucavage, Duchess of 4th Street
Milan Mad Red Hatters, Grants, New Mexico

Zesty Texan Chicken Alfredo

For easiest preparation, select cooked, seasoned, chicken strips or fillets.

1 (8-ounce) box spiral pasta (4 cups uncooked)
1 pint heavy whipping cream
1 (16-ounce) jar salsa
1 to 1 1/4 cups shredded cheddar cheese
3 (4-ounce) chicken breasts, cooked and diced (frozen fajita-seasoned chicken works well)
  Sour cream, diced tomatoes, diced avocado, shredded cheese for garnish

Cook the pasta according to the package directions and drain. In a large, nonstick pot heat the whipping cream and salsa over medium-low heat until hot. Add the shredded cheese and cook until thick. Add the diced chicken to the sauce and cook until heated through. Add the cooked pasta. Serve as is or with any or all of the suggested toppings.

Makes 4 to 6 servings

Susan Clark, Lady Sue
Laughter Hatters, Federal Way, Washington

Chicken Tetrazzini

The classic dinner party dish. It's nice to be reminded occasionally how good it is. Testers tinkered with it a little, and then gave it the thumbs-up.

1 (8-ounce) package spaghetti, cooked and drained
3 cubed cooked chicken
1 (6 1/2-ounce) can mushrooms, drained
1 to 1 1/2 cups crumbled cooked bacon
8 ounces Velveeta cheese, chopped

WHITE SAUCE
1/2 cup (1 stick) butter or margarine
1/4 cup all-purpose flour
4 teaspoons chicken bouillon granules (or 4 cubes)
  Dash of pepper
3 1/2 cups plus 1/2 cup milk
2 ounces sliced almonds for garnish

In a lightly greased 13 x 9-inch baking dish layer the spaghetti, chicken, mushrooms, bacon, and cheese. Preheat the oven to 350°.

For the white sauce, melt the butter in a medium-size pan over low heat; stir in the flour, bouillon, and pepper. Add 1/2 cup milk, stirring constantly to avoid lumps. Add the remaining 3 1/2 cups milk. Cook and stir over medium heat until thick and bubbly. Pour the white sauce over the chicken mixture. Bake for 45 minutes. Garnish with the sliced almonds.

Makes 8 to 10 servings

Dolores Sweezer, Queen Mother
Red Hot River Babes, Burlington, Iowa

Pasta with Sun–Dried Tomato Cream

Deemed "a tasty combination" of ingredients by testers. To roast the garlic, oil a whole bulb of garlic or just a few cloves. Wrap in aluminum foil and bake in a 350° oven for 20 minutes until browned. Keeps for two weeks in the refrigerator.

4 ounces bacon (4 to 5 slices)

4 roasted garlic cloves, smashed (or 2 cloves fresh garlic, chopped)

1/2 red onion, finely diced

1 pound skinless, boneless chicken breast, cubed

1/4 cup chopped fresh basil

2 ounces sun-dried tomatoes, hydrated in hot water for about 15 minutes, drained and chopped

3/4 cup dry white wine

1/2 cup chicken broth

1 cup heavy cream

1/4 cup freshly grated Parmesan cheese
   Salt and pepper to taste

1 (16-ounce) package pasta (penne, fusilli, or farfalle)

Cook the bacon in a skillet over medium heat until crisp. Remove from the skillet, drain, and crumble leaving 1 tablespoon of the drippings in the skillet. Cook the garlic and onion in the skillet until the onion is translucent. Transfer the garlic and onion to a paper towel-lined plate to drain. Cook the chicken in the bacon drippings over medium-high heat for about 3 minutes. Add the basil and sun-dried tomatoes and sauté for about 3 minutes. Add the crumbled bacon, onion, garlic, wine, and broth. Simmer until the liquid is reduced by half. Add the cream and Parmesan cheese. Cook until the sauce is reduced to a creamy consistency. Season with the salt and pepper.

Cook the pasta according to the package directions. Drain, reserving some of the pasta water. Add three-fourths of the pasta to the sauce. Heat and carefully fold together. Use some of the pasta water to thin the pasta mixture if it becomes too thick. Add the remaining pasta and mix well. Serve immediately with extra Parmesan.

Makes 6 to 8 servings

Karen Ise, Queen
Le Chapeaux Rouge de Conejo, Westlake Village, California

Chicken Chipotle Pasta

This dish gets its spicy nature from the chipotle chile, which is a ripe, smoked jalapeño. They are usually packed into cans or jars with a tangy marinade called adobo. Once opened, they keep for weeks in the refrigerator.

You will have extra mayonnaise mixture; serve it on the side, or store it for another batch of pasta (or try it as a spread for turkey sandwiches).

1/2 cup mayonnaise

1/4 teaspoon chicken bouillon granules

1/2 chipotle pepper

6 ounces boneless, skinless chicken breast, cut into strips

2 tablespoons olive oil

1/4 red bell pepper, cut into matchsticks

1/4 green bell pepper, cut into matchsticks

1/4 red onion, cut into matchsticks

1/2 teaspoon minced fresh cilantro

1/2 cup heavy whipping cream
1   (6-ounce) package fettuccine, cooked, drained

Combine the mayonnaise, chicken bouillon, and chipotle pepper. Purée in a blender or small bowl. (You will be using only a small amount of the mixture—the rest can be refrigerated for later use.)

In a large skillet, sauté the chicken strips in the olive oil over medium heat for 2 minutes. Add the bell peppers, onion, and cilantro; cook for 3 minutes. Add the heavy cream and 1 teaspoon of the mayonnaise mixture. Reduce the heat and cook an additional 2 minutes. Toss in the pasta and cook another minute or until the pasta is thoroughly heated. Serve immediately.

Makes 4 servings

Elaine Crum, Royal PITA
Red Hatters of Anthem, Anthem, Arizona

Pasta with Garlic and Oil

You know the old joke about garlic: When one person eats it, everyone has to eat it. Serve this restaurant classic with crusty bread and a tossed green salad.

1   (16-ounce) package spaghetti
3/4 cup extra virgin olive oil
1   tablespoon butter or margarine
8   to 12 garlic cloves, minced
1   teaspoon dried basil
2   teaspoon fresh oregano or 1 teaspoons dried oregano
1   tablespoon dried parsley
1/2 teaspoon black pepper
1   teaspoon red pepper flakes (optional)
     Grated Parmesan, pecorino, or Romano cheese to taste

Bring a large pot of salted water to a boil. Cook the pasta according to the directions on the package. In a large sauté pan heat the oil and butter over medium-high heat. Just before the smoking point, add the minced garlic, basil, oregano, parsley, black pepper, and red pepper flakes. Immediately turn off the heat. Drain the pasta well and add to the sauce. Toss to coat the spaghetti. Serve in pasta bowls, sprinkling with grated cheese.

Makes 4 servings

Rita Farmakidis, Lady Angel
Chapeaux Rouge, Cuyahoga Falls, Ohio

Garlic Parsley Spaghetti

If you can find flat-leaf parsley, choose it for its refined taste—after all, a Red Hatter is a lady of taste.

1   (16-ounce) package thin spaghetti
4   garlic cloves, minced
1/2 cup olive oil
1/2 cup minced fresh parsley
     Salt and pepper to taste

Cook the spaghetti according to the package directions; drain. In a large skillet lightly brown the garlic in the oil over medium heat. Add the drained spaghetti to the skillet. Sprinkle with parsley and salt and pepper. Toss to coat.

Makes 8 to 10 servings

Judy Peat, Duchess of Divine Delectibles
Rural Robust Red Hatters, Ford City, Pennsylvania

The Substitution Shuffle

She didn't have potatoes
So she used a cup of rice
She couldn't find paprika
So she used another spice
Tomatoes weren't in season
So she used tomato paste
The whole can, not a cup, dear,
She couldn't bear to waste!
And now she isn't speaking,
Convinced I pulled a fast one
So don't ask me for more recipes
That one was the last one!

Jetta Hanover,
Queen Jettapropulsion
Razzledazzle Boa Babes!,
Ocala, Florida

Pasta and Peas

2 tablespoons olive oil
1 white onion, diced
1 beef bouillon cube
1 (10-ounce) box frozen peas, thawed
   Black pepper, parsley, and paprika to taste
1 pound ditalini or other small pasta
   Parmesan cheese to taste

Heat the olive oil in a pan over medium heat; add the onion and brown. Add the boullion cube and peas with 1/2 cup water, and then add pepper, parsley, and paprika. Bring to a boil, reduce the heat to medium low. Cover and simmer for 15 minutes. In another pan cook the pasta until done and drain. Put the pasta in large bowl and top with the pea mixture. Sprinkle Parmesan cheese on top and serve. You can also serve it in individual bowls.

Makes 4 to 6 servings

Pam Arcand, Lady Nascar
Lunch Bags of Orlando, Orlando, Florida

Linguine with Roasted Peppers

2   large yellow bell peppers, roasted
2   large red bell peppers, roasted
3/4 cup virgin olive oil, divided
1/4 teaspoon hot pepper sauce
    Balsamic vinegar to taste
1 1/2 tablespoons minced garlic, divided
    Salt and pepper to taste
1   cup toasted pine nuts
1   cup kalamata olives, pitted and chopped
1   medium bunch fresh basil, julienned
1   (16-ounce) package linguine, cooked al dente
    Freshly grated Parmesan cheese to taste

Slice the roasted bell peppers into 1/2-inch-wide strips. In a bowl combine the bell peppers with 1 to 2 tablespoons of olive oil, the hot sauce, balsamic vinegar, half the garlic, and salt and pepper. Marinate for at least 20 minutes.

Combine the bell pepper mixture, the remaining olive oil, the remaining garlic, the pine nuts, olives, and basil with the cooked linguine. Adjust the seasonings to taste. Divide among four warm plates and sprinkle with Parmesan cheese.

Makes 4 servings

Sally Cecil, The Countess of Cuisine
Rose's Rosebuds, Pittsburgh, Pennsylvania

Shrimp Fettuccine

2   pounds unpeeled, medium fresh or frozen shrimp, thawed
3   plus 5 tablespoons (1 stick) butter or margarine
3   garlic cloves, minced
1/2 cup dry white wine
1   cup heavy whipping cream
1   cup grated Parmesan cheese
1/4 cup chopped fresh parsley or 1 tablespoon dried parsley
1/4 cup chopped fresh basil or 1 tablespoon dried basil
1   (8-ounce) package fettuccine, cooked

Peel the shrimp and devein. Sauté the shrimp in 3 tablespoons butter in a large skillet over medium-high heat for 3 to 4 minutes. Remove the shrimp with a slotted spoon. Melt the remaining 5 tablespoons butter in the skillet over medium-high heat. Add the garlic and sauté for 1 minute. Do not burn the garlic. Add the wine and cook for 4 minutes, or until the mixture is reduced by half. Stir in the cream and cook, stirring occasionally, for 4 to 5 minutes, or until slightly thickened. Add the shrimp, Parmesan cheese, parsley, and basil. Cook stirring occasionally until the cheese melts. Serve over the fettuccine.

Makes 4 to 6 servings

Carol Kennedy, Queen Red Beauty
Under-Aged Beauties, Van Alstyne, Texas

Shrimp and Sausage Penne

Rich and delicious and loaded with goodies—just the sort of thing to serve Hatters.

1/2 pound Italian sausage, removed from casing
2 garlic cloves, minced
1 tablespoon minced onion or shallot
1 teaspoon dried thyme
1 (15-ounce) can chopped tomatoes, not drained
1/3 cup heavy whipping cream
   Dash of chili paste (optional)
8 to 12 fresh shrimp (peeled, deveined, halved)
1 (8-ounce) package penne pasta, cooked and drained
1/4 cup grated Parmesan cheese

In a large skillet brown the sausage over medium heat. Drain on a paper towel, reserving 1 tablespoon of the drippings from the skillet. Add the garlic, onion, and thyme. Cook for 1 minute. Add the tomatoes (with juice), whipping cream, and chili paste. Stir and add the sausage. Simmer for 10 minutes, and then add the shrimp. Cook over low heat for 4 to 5 minutes, or until the shrimp are pink. Add the pasta, toss gently, and heat through. Pour the mixture into a large serving bowl and sprinkle with the grated Parmesan cheese.

Makes 6 to 8 servings

Ruth Bensmiller, Lady Merry Feather
Feathered Red Hatters of Northeast Iowa, Shellsburg, Iowa

Pasta with Pizzazz

Sausage, spinach, mushrooms, and feta cheese top bow-tie pasta.

1 to 2 tablespoons olive oil
   Lots of minced garlic
1 cup (or more) sliced fresh mushrooms
1 pound Italian sausage, sliced and cooked
1 bunch fresh spinach, washed
1 (12-ounce) package bow-tie or butterfly pasta, cooked and drained
1 (6-ounce) package feta cheese, crumbled
   Parmesan cheese to taste (optional)

Heat the olive oil in a large skillet over medium heat and sauté the garlic and mushrooms until barely cooked. Add the cooked sausage and spinach and cook until the spinach is limp. Add the cooked pasta and mix well. Add the crumbled feta cheese and allow the cheese to melt into mixture. Serve immediately on warm plates. Sprinkle with freshly grated Parmesan cheese if desired.

Makes 3 to 6 servings

Carol Betush, Rebel Queen
Rebellious Elegant Dames, Redding, California

Sausage and Peppers over Pasta

1 package sweet Italian turkey sausages (about 6 links)
1 tablespoon olive or canola oil
1 red bell pepper, cut into strips

1 yellow bell pepper, cut into strips

1 green bell pepper, cut into strips

1 medium onion, cut into vertical quarters

2 to 3 garlic cloves, minced

1/2 teaspoon seasoned salt

1/2 teaspoon seasoned pepper

1 teaspoon Italian herbs

1 (14-ounce) can diced tomatoes, not drained

1/2 cup dry white wine

1 (16-ounce) package spaghetti or linguini, cooked

Grated Parmesan cheese to taste (optional)

Coat a nonstick skillet with nonstick cooking spray, and cook the sausages for about 5 minutes over medium heat, turning frequently to brown. Transfer to a paper towel-lined plate. Heat the oil in the skillet. Add the bell peppers, onion, and garlic; cook about 5 minutes, stirring frequently. Add the seasoned salt, pepper, herbs, tomatoes, wine, and the sausages to the skillet; stir to blend. Cook for 10 to 15 minutes, stirring frequently. Serve over the pasta. Top with grated cheese if desired.

Makes 3 to 4 servings

Joanne Johnson, Queen JoJo 1st

Cats in the Hats in Annapolis, Annapolis, Maryland

Seafood Pasta

Freshly cooked seafood has the best flavor and texture, so serve this right away. Otherwise, the scallops and shrimp can toughen and lose their flavor.

1 (16-ounce) package linguini

2 tablespoons butter

1 pound fresh scallops

1 pound fresh shrimp, peeled and deveined

1/4 cup olive oil

1/4 cup dry white wine

2 cups heavy cream

8 garlic cloves, finely chopped

Salt and pepper to taste

2 dashes soy sauce

1 teaspoon Old Bay seasoning

Cook the linguini according to the package directions. Drain and stir in the butter.

Mix the scallops and shrimp in a colander, rinse, and drain. In a large saucepan combine the oil, wine, cream, garlic, salt and pepper, soy sauce, and Old Bay and bring to a simmer over low heat. Add the drained seafood mixture. Cook over low heat, stirring gently, until the seafood is done and the sauce has a creamy consistency, about 10 minutes. Add the linguini to the mixture and heat to serving temperature over low heat, stirring constantly. Serve immediately.

Makes 6 to 8 servings

Charla Jordan, Queen of Quite a Lot

Brandon's Bodacious Babes, Brandon, Mississippi

Tuscan-Style Shrimp and Linguine

Here's one to love—just 350 calories per serving—and the testers raved over the moist texture and bold flavor.

1   pound shrimp, peeled and deveined
1   (8-ounce) package dried linguine
2   tablespoons extra virgin olive oil
4   garlic cloves, minced
1   (14-ounce) can Italian-style diced tomatoes
    Salt and pepper to taste
    Juice of 1/2 fresh lemon

Pat the shrimp dry. Cook the linguine according to the package ingredients. Heat the olive oil in a large skillet over low heat and sauté the garlic for 1 minute, but do not brown. Increase the heat to medium. Add the shrimp, and cook for 2 minutes, or until the shrimp are pink. Add the diced tomatoes and cook an additional 5 minutes. Add salt and pepper. Sprinkle the lemon juice over the top. Toss with the cooked pasta.

Makes 4 servings

Fran Pritchert, Empress of Ebay
Scarlet Sophisticates, Woodbridge, Virginia

Pasta with Marinated Tomatoes

Nicely ripe, fresh, plum tomatoes are a good choice in season. Testers rated this above average in flavor.

6   canned plum tomatoes, chopped
6   whole sun-dried tomatoes in oil, chopped
2   garlic cloves, minced

1/2   cup extra virgin olive oil
      Salt and pepper to taste
1   (16-ounce) package penne pasta
1   cup loosely packed fresh basil leaves

Marinate the plum tomatoes, sun-dried tomatoes, garlic, and olive oil in a serving bowl. Cook the pasta according to the package directions; drain. Add to the bowl with the tomato mixture. Add the basil leaves and toss well. May be served immediately or at room temperature.

Makes 6 servings

Thelma Montecalvo, Queen Supreme
Little Rhody Red Hens, Woonsocket, Rhode Island

Shrimp and Fresh Tomato Pasta

Twenty minutes of prep, but just five minutes of cooking until dinner is ready.

1   pound medium-size fresh shrimp, peeled and deveined
3   tomatoes, peeled and chopped
6   to 8 fresh mushrooms, sliced
2   green onions, sliced
1/4   cup sliced ripe olives
1/4   cup dry white wine
1   tablespoon mixed Italian herbs
1   tablespoon olive oil
1/4   teaspoon salt
1/4   teaspoon lemon pepper
1/4   teaspoon black pepper
1/4   teaspoon drained minced capers
1/8   teaspoon ground red pepper

1 (10-ounce) package lemon pepper
  fettuccine, cooked
2 tablespoons grated Parmesan cheese

In a large skillet combine the shrimp, tomatoes, mushrooms, onions, olives, wine, herbs, olive oil, salt, lemon pepper, black pepper, capers, and red pepper and bring to a boil over medium-high heat. Reduce the heat to low and simmer, stirring occasionally, for 5 minutes, or just until the shrimp turn pink and the sauce is slightly thickened. Serve over the pasta; top with the Parmesan cheese.

Makes 4 to 6 servings

Sue Southerland, Queen Mum
Sassy Bodacious Ladies, Greeneville, Tennessee

Shrimp or Clam Marinara Pasta

2 anchovies (optional)
2 tablespoons chopped garlic
3 tablespoons olive oil
1 (14-ounce) can tomatoes
2 tablespoons dried oregano
1/4 cup chopped fresh parsley or 2
  tablespoons dried
1 pound or more fresh or thawed canned
  shrimp and/or fresh or canned clams
1 (8-ounce) package pasta, cooked and
  drained

In a large skillet over medium heat, sauté the anchovies and garlic in the olive oil until the anchovies dissolve. (Or omit the anchovies and add a teaspoon of salt to the garlic.) Purée

the tomatoes in a blender or food processor. Add the tomatoes, oregano, and parsley to the skillet. Cook for 20 minutes; then add the shrimp and/or clams. Cook until the shrimp turn pink, fresh clams open, or canned clams are hot. Sprinkle with additional parsley and serve over hot pasta.

Makes 4 servings

Barbara Beauchemin, Queen
Chapeaux Rouge of RI, Greene, Rhode Island

Ravioli Lasagna

Quick, good, and a bit out of the ordinary.

1 pound ground beef, divided
1 (28-ounce) jar spaghetti sauce, divided
1 (25-ounce) package frozen sausage or
  cheese ravioli, thawed and divided
1 1/2 cups (6 ounces) shredded mozzarella
  cheese, divided

Preheat the oven to 400°. Cook the ground beef over medium heat in a large skillet until browned and crumbly; drain. In a 2 1/2-quart greased baking dish, layer one-third of the spaghetti sauce, one-half the ravioli and beef, and 1/2 cup cheese; repeat the layers. Top with remaining one-third of the sauce and the remaining 1/2 cup cheese. Cover and bake for 40 to 45 minutes, or until heated through.

Makes 6 to 8 servings

Jeannette White, Princess Jaycee
Red Hat Mommas of Western Maine, Dixfield, Maine

Spinach Ziti

Here's a handy idea for a quick, from-the-freezer lunch or dinner. Cool, then chill leftover spinach ziti. When it's cold, cut it into serving portions. Individually wrap each square, place in a zip-top bag, and freeze.

1   (32-ounce) jar marinara sauce (4 cups), divided
1   (16-ounce) package ziti, cooked and drained
1   (16-ounce) package shredded mozzarella cheese, divided
1   (10-ounce) package frozen chopped spinach, thawed and drained
1   (16-ounce) container ricotta cheese
     Salt and pepper to taste
1/4 plus 1/4 cup grated Parmesan cheese

Preheat the oven to 350°. Spray a 13 x 9-inch glass baking dish with nonstick cooking spray. In a large mixing bowl combine 2 cups marinara sauce with the ziti. Add 1 cup mozzarella cheese, the spinach, ricotta cheese, salt and pepper, and 1/4 cup Parmesan cheese. Mix well. Pour 1/3 cup of the marinara sauce into the baking dish. Then evenly spread the ziti mixture on top. Spoon 1/4 cup of the sauce over the ziti and sprinkle with the remaining 1/4 cup Parmesan cheese. Bake for 25 minutes. Sprinkle with the remaining mozzarella cheese and bake another 10 to 15 minutes. Serve hot.

Makes 9 to 12 servings

Roslyn Katz, Mistress of Memories
Coral Springs Sweethearts, Coral Springs, Florida

Spaghetti with Tuna Sauce

Serve with salad and garlic bread, and . . . maybe a nice glass of wine too.

2   large onions, chopped
2   garlic cloves, minced, or 1/2 teaspoon garlic powder
2   tablespoons olive oil
2   (6-ounce) cans tuna packed in oil
1   (28-ounce) can crushed tomatoes or tomato purée
1   tablespoon crushed dried basil
     Pinch of oregano
     Salt and pepper to taste
1   (8-ounce) package thin spaghetti
     Grated Parmesan cheese for serving

In a 4 to 6-quart saucepan over medium heat, sauté the onions and garlic with the olive oil until translucent. Add the tuna. (Drain it if you like, but the dish has more flavor if tuna isn't drained.) Break up the tuna with a fork. Add the tomatoes, basil, oregano, and salt and pepper. Simmer for about 20 minutes. Cook the spaghetti according to package directions. Drain the spaghetti and put it into a serving bowl. Spoon half the sauce on top of the spaghetti and fold it in. Serve with extra sauce on the dinner plate if needed. Sprinkle with the grated cheese.

Makes 2 to 4 servings

Dawna Lee Ursillo, Duchess Dawna
Chapeaux Rouge, Narragansett, Rhode Island

Lasagna Roll–Ups

Delight children (of all ages) with this novel presentation.

1   (16-ounce) package lasagna noodles
1   (16-ounce) container ricotta cheese
1   egg
1   (12-ounce) package shredded mozzarella cheese, divided
1   (9-ounce) package frozen chopped broccoli, thawed and drained
1   (26-ounce) jar spaghetti sauce (or use homemade)
    Parmesan cheese to taste

Cook the lasagna noodles according to the package directions. Drain well. In a large bowl combine the ricotta cheese, egg, and half the shredded mozzarella cheese. Add the broccoli and mix well. Preheat the oven to 350°. Spread the broccoli mixture thinly on the lasagna noodles. You probably can cover only about 10 noodles. Roll the noodles and place in a baking pan, seam side down. Cover with the spaghetti sauce and the remaining mozzarella cheese. Sprinkle with Parmesan cheese. Cover with foil and bake for about 30 minutes. Remove the cover and continue baking until the cheese is melted and the sauce is bubbly. Serve with meatballs and/or sausage if desired.

Makes 10 servings

Marilyn Barr, Queen Marilyn
Red Hot Royals of Roxbury, Ledgewood, New Jersey

Spinach Lasagna

Take a shortcut with no-cook lasagna noodles.

1   pound ricotta cheese
1   egg
1   teaspoon salt
1   teaspoon pepper
3/4 teaspoon oregano
1   (10-ounce) box frozen spinach, thawed
1   (8-ounce) package shredded mozzarella cheese, divided
1   (32-ounce) jar tomato-based spaghetti sauce, divided in half
1   (8-ounce) package uncooked lasagna noodles, divided in half
1   cup water

Preheat the oven to 350°. In a large bowl combine the ricotta cheese, egg, salt, pepper, oregano, spinach, and 1 cup mozzarella. In a greased 13 x 9-inch pan, layer one-half of the sauce, one-half of the noodles, and one-half of the cheese mixture. Repeat the layers. Top with the remaining 1 cup mozzarella. Pour the water around the edges. Cover tightly with foil. Bake for 45 minutes. Remove the foil and bake 30 minutes more, or until bubbly.

Makes 8 to 10 servings

Rosanne Bridges, Vice Mother
Ruby Hatters, Bethlehem, Pennsylvania

Red Pepper Lasagna

The contributor notes that if you're serving hungry boys, you may get only six servings.

RED PEPPER SAUCE

1   (12-ounce) jar roasted red peppers, chopped
1   tablespoon olive oil
1   (28-ounce) can crushed tomatoes
1/4   cup chopped fresh parsley
4   to 5 garlic cloves, minced
1/2   teaspoon black pepper

NUTMEG SAUCE

1/3   cup butter
1/3   cup all-purpose flour
1/4   teaspoon salt
1/2   teaspoon nutmeg
3   cups milk
     Lasagna noodles, cooked
1   cup grated Parmesan cheese
1   (8-ounce) package sliced mozzarella cheese

For the red pepper sauce, mix together in a saucepan the peppers, oil, tomatoes, parsley, garlic, and black pepper; simmer over medium-low heat for 20 minutes, stirring often.

For the nutmeg sauce, melt the butter in a separate saucepan over medium heat. Stir in the flour, salt, and nutmeg. Cook, stirring, until smooth. Slowly add the milk and cook until thickened and bubbly.

Preheat the oven to 350°. Layer the ingredients as follows: one-third noodles, one-third red pepper sauce, one-third nutmeg sauce, 1/3 cup Parmesan cheese. Repeat two more times. Top with the sliced mozzarella cheese. Bake for 30 to 35 minutes.

Makes 6 to 8 servings

Peggy Krickbaum, Princess Knit Wit
Flashy Sassies, Montrose, Colorado

Seafood Lasagna

When you want to go all-out, flex your wallet for this deluxe lasagna.

8   lasagna noodles
1   onion, chopped
2   tablespoons butter
1   (8-ounce) package cream cheese, softened
1 1/2 cups creamed cottage cheese
1   egg, beaten
2   tablespoons dried basil, crushed
1 1/2 teaspoons salt
1/2   teaspoon pepper
2   (103/4-ounce) cans cream of mushroom, shrimp, or celery soup
1/3   cup milk
1/3   cup white wine
1   pound shrimp, cooked, peeled, and halved
1/2   pound fresh crabmeat, if available (or substitute canned crabmeat)
1/4   cup grated Parmesan cheese
1/2   cup shredded cheddar cheese

Cook the lasagna noodles and drain well. Arrange four noodles to cover the bottom of a greased 13 x 9-inch baking dish. In a medium saucepan over medium heat cook the onion in the butter until tender but not brown. Blend in the cream cheese. Stir in the cottage cheese, egg, basil, salt, and pepper. Spread half the mixture on top of the four noodles.

Preheat the oven to 350°. Combine the soup, milk, and wine. Stir in the shrimp and crabmeat. Spread half over the cottage cheese layer. Repeat the layers of noodles, cheese mixture, and seafood mixture. Sprinkle with the Parmesan cheese. Bake, uncovered, for 45 minutes. Top with the shredded cheddar cheese. Bake an additional 3 to 4 minutes, or until the cheese melts. Let stand 15 minutes before serving.

Makes 12 servings

Marianne Wood, Queen Mother
Royal Rubies, Columbia, Maryland

Pierogies

Ideal for a group project, or for showing a beloved child how old-fashioned homemade food was prepared (and how delicious even simple ingredients can be when made with loving hands).

DOUGH
3 1/2 to 4 cups all-purpose flour
1 teaspoon salt
3 eggs
 Water as needed

FILLING
1 (16-ounce) container small-curd cottage cheese
1 (16-ounce) container ricotta cheese
3 large eggs
 Salt and pepper to taste
 Vegetable oil

For the dough, combine the flour and salt in a large bowl. Make a well in the center and break the eggs into it. Mix until crumbly; then add enough water to make the mixture stick together in a ball. Chill for about 8 hours.

For the filling, Combine the cottage cheese and ricotta cheese in a bowl. Add the eggs and salt and pepper and beat well.

Roll out the dough and cut into 4 or 5-inch squares or rounds. Spoon 1 generous tablespoon of filling on each dough square. Brush the edges with water, fold the dough over the filling and press to seal. Cook the pierogies in boiling water for about 10 minutes. Remove, drain, and fry them in oil over medium-high heat until lightly browned on both sides. Serve plain as a side dish or with sauces as desired.

Makes 6 to 10 servings

Note: Depending on the size of your dough squares, you may have to adjust your filling amount. You may also choose other fillings such as beef and onion, shredded cooked chicken, or mashed potatoes and sauerkraut.

Margaret Ramage, Lady Email
Hoptown Happy Hatters, Hopkinsville, Kentucky

Iced Tee

One of my favorite ways to gather with friends and family in the summer is the themed cookout party that I throw each year. Themes we've had were Toga, Hillbilly, Hawaiian, and so forth. Everyone dresses to the theme and brings a covered dish (which is a great way to try different recipes).

Our "Kids' Pajama Party" themed cookout started with my Southern-cooked pork barbecue, and included many different covered dishes and desserts—even homemade ice cream. The food is usually the highlight of the day, but this time, one of my games topped even that.

The guests put their names on a slip of paper, and I drew three names without anyone knowing what those three lucky people would be doing. After the three were picked, I handed each of them a folded white T-shirt that had been soaked in water and put in the freezer for a week. To win the prize, you had to be the first to get the T-shirt on. Rules: No dipping in the pool or soaking with any liquid.

The race was on! Those three (and they're wearing pajamas, remember) did all they could to melt the icy tees, from sitting on them to placing them on hot rocks. Good thing there wasn't a grill around!

Lorraine Sayas,
Queen Mother Gem
Tidewaters Gems,
Virginia Beach, Virginia

Baked Noodle Cups

Serve this mild-flavored side dish with meat entrées with gravy as a change from potatoes. The cups are ready to eat when the mixture is set. Testers found the texture too dry with long cooking, so begin testing for doneness after 1 hour.

2 bouillon cubes or granules
1 (12-ounce) package small pasta shapes (ABCs, orzo, or other small shape)
4 eggs
3 1/2 to 4 cups milk
   Pepper to taste
   Paprika to taste

Preheat the oven to 300°. Bring 6 to 8 cups water to a boil with the bouillon cubes. Cook the pasta in the water. All the liquid should be absorbed. (This method gives the noodles a meaty flavor.) Beat the eggs with the milk, pepper, and paprika. Fill greased custard cups or ramekins with the noodle mixture. Add the milk mixture to fill the cups. Bake for 1 to 2 hours. Unmold to serve. The mixture can be baked in a casserole dish, but individual dishes yield a nice, crusty, crispy outside.

Makes 12 servings

Win Larsen, Countess of Cookery
Purple Rosettes, Ft. Myers, Florida

Cheese Soufflé

1/2 pound medium or sharp cheddar cheese, finely grated (about 2 cups)
1/2 cup (1 stick) butter
4 eggs, beaten
2 cups milk
10 slices fresh white bread, crusts removed, bread cut in cubes

Melt the cheese and butter in the top of a double boiler, or in the microwave. Beat the eggs and milk together. In a greased casserole or soufflé dish, alternate the layers of bread cubes and cheese mixture. Pour the egg and milk mixture over the bread and cheese, and refrigerate, covered, 6 to 8 hours or overnight.

Preheat the oven to 325°. Place the casserole or soufflé dish in a shallow pan of cold water and bake for 1 hour, covered. Reduce the heat to 300° and bake, uncovered, for 1 hour longer.

Makes 6 to 8 servings

Kathleen Smith, Queen Kate au Contraire
Steel Magnolias, Ancaster, Ontario, Canada

Dutch Tart

Looks and tastes great, declare testers.

10 ounces Gouda cheese (domestic is better for this)
1/4 cup (1/2 stick) melted butter, plus more for drizzling
1 cup bread crumbs
    Salt and pepper to taste
3 medium tomatoes, sliced 1/4-inch thick
1 tablespoon chopped fresh parsley
8 medium mushroom caps

Preheat the oven to 375°. Shred enough of the cheese to make 1 cup. Slice the remaining cheese into 1/4-inch-thick slices. With a fork, or in a food processor, mix the shredded cheese and 4 tablespoons butter with the bread crumbs. Add salt. Press the mixture over the bottom and up the side of a pie pan with your fingers. Spread the sliced cheese on the bottom and cover with the tomato slices. Sprinkle with salt and pepper and the parsley. Add the mushroom caps and drizzle with melted butter. Bake 15 to 20 minutes.

Makes 4 servings

Sheila Cassella, Marchioness of Mirth
Purple Passion Majesties, Chicago, Illinois

California Casserole

1/4   cup (1/2 stick) butter

1   cup chopped onion

4   cups cooked rice

2   cups sour cream

1   cup cottage cheese

1   large bay leaf crumbled

1/2   teaspoon salt

1/4   teaspoon pepper

3   (4-ounce) cans green chiles, divided in half

1   plus 1 cup sharp cheddar cheese

      Chopped fresh parsley for garnish

Preheat the oven to 350°. Melt the butter in a skillet over medium-high heat. Sauté the onion in the butter until golden brown. Remove from the heat. Stir in the cooked rice, sour cream, cottage cheese, bay leaf, salt, and pepper and toss well. Layer half the rice mixture in the bottom of a greased 1 1/2 quart baking dish. Top with half the chiles, then 1 cup cheese; repeat with the remaining chiles and the remaining 1 cup cheese. Bake, uncovered, for 25 minutes, or until hot and bubbly. Sprinkle with the parsley.

Makes 8 servings

Rae Castro, Grand Duchess de Champagne
Ruby Redhat's Ramblers, Escondido, California

Cake-Pan Cheese Soufflé

The tester gave this a "5," calling it a good alternative to quiche, and less eggy.

2   (4-ounce) cans chopped green chiles

1   pound Monterey Jack cheese, grated

1   pound cheddar cheese, grated

4   eggs, separated

2/3   cup evaporated milk

1   tablespoon all-purpose flour

      Salt and pepper to taste

2   medium tomatoes, each cut into six slices

Preheat the oven to 325°. Grease a 13 x 9-inch baking pan or 2-quart casserole. Toss the chiles and cheeses in a bowl and spread over the bottom of the pan. Beat the egg whites in a small, metal or glass bowl with an electric mixer at high speed until stiff. In a separate bowl combine the egg yolks, milk, flour, and salt and pepper and blend well. Fold in the egg whites carefully and pour over the cheese and chiles. Use a fork to mix gently. Bake for 30 minutes. Place the tomato slices carefully on the half-baked soufflé and return to oven for another 30 minutes. Cut and serve. (Leftovers warm nicely in a microwave on low.)

Makes 12 servings

Jackie Tarpinian, Queen Mother
Jewels of the Prairie, Jamestown, Nevada

Fresh Tomato Tart

1   refrigerated piecrust

1   plus 1 cup mozzarella cheese

5   plum tomatoes, sliced

1/2   cup mayonnaise

1/4   cup grated Parmesan cheese

1/2   teaspoon ground black pepper

      Chopped fresh basil (optional)

Preheat the oven to 425°. Unfold the piecrust onto a lightly greased baking sheet. Brush the outer inch of the crust with water and crimp the edge. Prick the bottom of the crust with a fork to prevent bubbles. Bake for 8 to 10 minutes. Remove from the oven. Sprinkle with 1 cup mozzarella cheese; cool 15 minutes. Arrange the tomato slices over the cheese. Stir together the remaining 1 cup mozzarella, mayonnaise, Parmesan cheese, and pepper. Spread over the tomato slices. Reduce the oven temperature to 375° and bake for 20 to 25 minutes. Sprinkle with the chopped basil if using.

Makes 4 main-dish servings, 8 appetizer servings

Susan Thomas, Vice Queen
Divine Divas, San Antonio, Texas

Vegetable Strata

Great for brunch, and also a good meatless dinner entrée. Testers note that they preferred a firmer strata and used the lesser amount of milk.

1	tablespoon olive oil
2	tablespoons butter
1	cup chopped red onion
1	green bell pepper, chopped
1	red bell pepper, chopped
8	ounces sliced mushrooms
1	cup seeded and chopped Roma tomatoes
	Salt and pepper to taste
1	large loaf stale Italian bread, cubed (about 8 to 9 cups)
1/2	plus 1/2 cup Parmesan cheese
2	cups shredded sharp cheddar cheese
9	to 10 large eggs, beaten
2	to 3 cups milk
2	to 3 tablespoons Dijon mustard

In a large skillet heat the olive oil over medium-high heat. Melt the butter in the oil and add the onion and bell peppers. Sauté until tender and caramelized. Add the mushrooms and tomatoes and heat through. Season with salt and pepper. Set aside to cool.

In the bottom of a greased 13 x 9-inch glass baking dish, arrange a layer of bread cubes. Carefully distribute about half the vegetable mixture over the bread cubes. Sprinkle 1/2 cup Parmesan cheese over the vegetables. Add the remaining bread cubes and top with the remaining vegetables and the remaining 1/2 cup Parmesan cheese. Top with the cheddar cheese. In a large bowl blend the eggs, milk, mustard, and 1 teaspoon each of salt and pepper. Whisk by hand or use mixer until frothy and well combined. Pour over the bread mixture, making sure to cover all the bread. Cover with plastic wrap and refrigerate at least 5 to 6 hours or overnight.

When ready to bake, remove the dish from the refrigerator and allow to stand at room temperature for 20 to 30 minutes. Preheat the oven to 350° and bake for 45 to 60 minutes, or until golden and puffy. Let stand 5 to 10 minutes before serving.

Makes 8 to 10 generous servings

Paula Vander Meulen, Queen Mother
Ramblewood Red Hatters, Wyoming, Michigan

Vegetarian Chili Corn Bread Casserole

The original called for two (28-ounce) cans of beans, which testers found to be too many for the pan, but if it suits you, give it a try.

CHILI

1	onion, chopped
1	zucchini, chopped
1	green bell pepper, chopped
2	carrots, chopped
3	celery stalks, chopped
8	garlic cloves, minced
1	teaspoon oregano
1	teaspoon ground cumin
2	teaspoons chili powder (optional)
1	(28-ounce) can tomato sauce
1/4	cup tomato paste
1	(28-ounce) can and 1 (15-ounce) can kidney or pinto beans

TOPPING

1	cup cornmeal
1	cup all-purpose flour
2	teaspoons baking powder
1	teaspoon brown sugar
1/2	teaspoon salt
13/4	cups water
1	tablespoon vegetable oil

For the chili, place the onion, zucchini, bell pepper, carrots, celery, and garlic in a skillet with 1/2 cup water and cook until the onions start to brown, adding a little oil if needed to prevent the onion from burning. Add the oregano, cumin, chili powder, tomato sauce, and tomato paste. Simmer until the vegetables are tender. Drain the beans, reserving the liquid. Add the beans to the vegetables and enough juice to make the mixture slightly liquid. Simmer 10 minutes, or until most of the liquid is evaporated. Pour into a greased 13 x 9-inch glass casserole dish (you may need an extra dish for the overflow).

Preheat the oven to 350°.

For the topping, combine the cornmeal, flour, baking powder, brown sugar, and salt in a medium bowl and mix well. Stir in the water and oil. Stir and pour the mixture over the chili. Bake for 25 to 30 minutes, or until the corn bread is set.

Makes 8 to 10 servings

Gay Mentes, Growl Tigggerr X Pinky
Red Hot Jazzy Ladies, Kelowna, British Columbia, Canada

Green and Gold Casserole

Vegetables and cheese with a gratin topping.

1	pound small zucchini
11/2	cups cottage cheese
2	tablespoons sour cream
2	eggs, beaten
1	tablespoon finely chopped onion
2	tablespoons all-purpose flour
1/2	teaspoon salt

Dash of white pepper

1   (15-ounce) can corn niblets, drained or 12 ounces frozen corn niblets, thawed and drained

1/2   cup grated sharp cheddar cheese

1/2   cup dry bread crumbs

Preheat the oven to 350°. Butter a shallow 1 1/2-quart baking dish. Slice each zucchini in half, then slice each half into 1/2-inch slices. Steam just until crisp tender. Drain and plunge into cold water to stop the cooking; then drain well in a colander or strainer. In a large mixing bowl combine the cottage cheese, sour cream, eggs, and onion and stir until well mixed. Sprinkle the flour, salt, and white pepper over the surface of the cottage cheese mixture and mix well. Fold in the zucchini and corn. Pour the mixture into the baking dish. Sprinkle the cheese and bread crumbs evenly over the surface. Bake for 40 to 45 minutes, or until the center is bubbly and the crumbs and cheese are browned. Remove from the oven and cool on a rack for 10 minutes, or until set.

Makes 4 main-dish servings or 6 side-dish servings

Kay Wright, Condessa
The Happy Hatters, Columbia, Missouri

Feta-Spinach Pie

The pie puffs as it bakes and will fall slightly as it cools, but don't worry—it's still delicious.

1   (9-inch) unbaked piecrust, frozen or homemade

2   tablespoons grated Parmesan cheese

1   (8 to 10-ounce) package frozen spinach, thawed, drained, and squeezed dry

1/4   cup crumbled feta cheese

3   large eggs

1/4   cup mayonnaise

4   ounces low-fat sour cream

4   ounces ricotta cheese, low-fat or whole milk

1   teaspoon garlic powder

1/2   teaspoon black pepper

1/4   teaspoon nutmeg

Preheat the oven to 350°. Bake the piecrust for 5 minutes; then cool slightly. Sprinkle the Parmesan cheese on the bottom of the crust. Evenly distribute the spinach and feta cheese over the crust. In a medium bowl lightly beat eggs. Add the mayonnaise, sour cream, ricotta cheese, garlic powder, black pepper, and nutmeg; mix thoroughly. Pour over the spinach and cheese. Bake in the center of the oven for 45 minutes, or until medium brown and the center has risen. Cool on a rack for 10 minutes before cutting.

Makes 4 main-dish servings or 8 appetizer servings

Rosa West, Queen Bee
Red Hat Seagalls, Hudson, Florida

Vegetable Kabobs

1   tablespoon chopped garlic

2   tablespoon olive oil

1   teaspoon rosemary, rounded

1   lime, juiced

1   teaspoon salt

16 cherry tomatoes

12 small red-skin potatoes, parboiled, cooled

12 mushrooms, trim stems

1   small red onion, peeled, cut into 1/2 inch wedges

Preheat a grill. Combine the garlic, oil, rosemary, lime juice, and salt in a bowl and mix well. Slide alternating pieces of tomatoes, potatoes, mushrooms, and onion on skewers until full. Arrange on a plate and baste with marinade mix. Cook on the grill over medium-low heat until lightly charred, about 4 minutes for each quarter turn, basting with the marinade.

Makes 4 servings

Teresa Smith, Queen Mother
Sassy Southern Sisters, Shelby, North Carolina

TWELVE

~ Embellishments ~ & Additions

VEGETABLES, SIDE DISHES, PICKLES, RELISHES, & SAUCES

One of the watchwords of the Red Hat Society is "accessorize." When a brand new Red Hatter starts or joins a chapter, the first thing on her "to do" list is to gather her purple and red regalia items. No self-respecting Red Hatter would be caught dead at an official event wearing anything but purple clothing and a red hat. Suitably attired in clothes in our colors, she is instantly identifiable as "one of us."

But very little time passes before most of our members develop an urge to embellish their basic outfits. A purple pants suit and a red hat are good. But how much better it is to sashay into a room wearing the purple pants suit, a red hat, a lavishly-feathered red or purple boa—perhaps even fishnet stockings—and lots of "bling!" One of the areas in which we play is that of clothing.

Basic meals can be much like basic attire—sufficient, but not terribly interesting. This is where such things as pickles, relishes, and sauces come in. They may not make a complete statement by themselves, but they can add a lot of zing to a meal. And we Red Hatters can be very big indeed on zing.

Enhanced Black Beans

For a milder garlic taste, leave the garlic cloves whole, and remove them before serving. These beans are great with steaks.

2   (16-ounce) cans black beans
3   garlic cloves, pressed or minced
2   cups chopped ham
2   tablespoons red wine vinegar
    Yellow rice and chopped onions for serving

Combine the beans and garlic in a large saucepan. Add the ham and bring to a simmer. Simmer for about 20 minutes. Add the vinegar and mix well. (This gives the beans a home-made taste.) Serve with the yellow rice, offering the chopped onions as a garnish.

Makes 4 to 8 servings

Sharon Simpson, Queen Mom
Ladies of the Lake, Abbeville, Alabama

Kahlua Baked Beans

4   (15-ounce) cans oven-baked beans, drained
1   cup Kahlua
1/4 cup chili sauce
1   tablespoon prepared yellow mustard
1   tablespoon molasses

In a large greased baking pan or 13 x 9-inch casserole, combine the beans, Kahlua, chili sauce, mustard, and molasses. Refrigerate for at least 4 hours to blend flavors. Bake in a preheated 375° oven for 50 to 60 minutes.

Makes 8 to 10 servings

Pamela Murphy, Queenette
Supreme Queens of Elegance, Virginia Beach, Virginia

Sweet Red Beets

1   (15-ounce) can pineapple chunks, drained, reserving 2 tablespoons juice
2   tablespoons cornstarch
2   cups canned beets, drained, reserving 3/4 cup beet juice
1   tablespoon white or cider vinegar
3/4 teaspoon salt (optional)
1   tablespoon butter or margarine

In a large saucepan combine the 2 tablespoons pineapple juice with the cornstarch and 3/4 cup beet juice. Blend until smooth. Cook over low heat until thick, stirring constantly. Add the pineapple chunks, beets, vinegar, salt, and butter to the juice mixture and heat thoroughly.

Makes 6 to 8 servings

Judy Hulsey, Founding Queen Mother
Primarily Purple (PP) Girls, Lavonia, Georgia

Smoky Baked Beans

Very good, said tasters, who also noted that some cooks may wish to cut back on the chipotles for a milder result.

6 bacon slices

1 1/2 cups chopped onions

1 1/4 cups barbecue sauce

3/4 cup dark beer

1/4 cup mild flavored (light) molasses

3 tablespoons Dijon mustard

2 tablespoons Worcestershire sauce

1 tablespoon soy sauce

4 to 6 teaspoons minced, canned, chipotle peppers

6 (15 to 16-ounce) cans great Northern beans, drained

Chopped fresh parsley for garnish

Preheat the oven to 350°. Cook the bacon in a large skillet over medium heat until crisp. Transfer to paper towels and drain. Transfer 2 1/2 tablespoons bacon drippings from the skillet to a large bowl. Finely crumble the bacon and add it to the bowl. Add the onions, barbecue sauce, beer, molasses, mustard, Worcestershire sauce, and soy sauce to the bowl and blend. Stir in 4 to 6 teaspoons chipotle peppers, depending on spiciness desired. Stir in the beans. Transfer the mixture to a greased 13 x 9-inch glass baking dish. Bake uncovered until the liquid bubbles and thickens slightly, about 1 hour. Cool for 10 minutes. Sprinkle with the parsley before serving.

Makes 8 to 10 servings

Dorothy Williams, Queen Mother
No Stopping Us Now, Richmond, Virginia

Scalloped Cabbage

For cold nights when the family is gathered for a good ole home-cooked meal.

1 medium head cabbage, chopped

1 teaspoon sugar

Pinch of salt

1 cup water

4 tablespoons plus 3 tablespoons butter

3 tablespoons all-purpose flour

1 cup milk

1/2 teaspoon salt

4 to 5 slices of Velveeta cheese

1 cup dry bread crumbs

Preheat the oven to 350°. In a large saucepan combine the cabbage with the sugar, salt, and water. Cook over medium heat for 8 minutes and then drain. Transfer the cabbage to a 2-quart greased casserole. Melt 3 tablespoons butter in a large saucepan over medium heat and stir in the flour. Whisk in the milk and salt gradually and cook for 1 minute. Add the cheese and cook, stirring, until melted. Pour the sauce over cabbage. In a small skillet melt the remaining 4 tablespoons butter and add the bread crumbs, tossing to coat. Sprinkle the crumbs on top of the casserole. Bake for 35 minutes, or until the casserole is bubbly and the bread crumbs are brown.

Makes 8 servings

Bonnie Streif, Lady of Comedy
Feathered Red Hatters of Northeast Iowa, Springville, Iowa

Garlic Broccoli

Don't be fooled by the short ingredient list. The garlic and olive oil really make a flavor impact on broccoli.

2   bunches broccoli, cut into stalks and florets
1/4   cup olive oil
4   large garlic cloves (or to taste), minced
    Salt and pepper to taste

In a large pan boil the stalks of broccoli for 20 minutes. Add the florets and continue to boil for another 20 minutes. Drain. Heat the oil in a saucepan over medium heat. Sauté the minced garlic in the oil until just beginning to color. Pour the oil over the broccoli and season with salt and pepper. Mix well.

Makes 5 to 10 servings

Vicki Haley, Baroness Haley
Purple Passion, Allen Park, Michigan

Brussels Sprouts Gratinée

1/2   pound small, fresh Brussels sprouts
2   teaspoons butter or olive oil
1   garlic clove, minced
1/4   cup shredded cheddar cheese
    Parmesan cheese to taste
    Dry Italian bread crumbs to taste

Parboil the Brussels sprouts until tender but not mushy. Transfer to a greased 1 quart shallow casserole dish. Melt the butter in a skillet over medium heat. Sauté the minced garlic in the butter until tender. Mix the garlic with the Brussels sprouts in the casserole dish. Sprinkle with the cheddar cheese and Parmesan cheese. Top with bread crumbs. Broil until browned.

Makes 4 servings

Marlene Lawton, Queen Ruby M
Ruby Jewels of the Beach, Ipswich, Massachusetts

Carrot Soufflé

Puffy and sweet, almost "dessert-y" and "a big hit," said tasters. "Children like it if you don't tell them it's carrots," wrote one taster. A wonderful accompaniment to roasted meats, or as part of a meatless meal.

2   pounds fresh carrots, sliced
6   large eggs
2/3   plus 1/3 cup sugar
1/3   cup matzo meal
1/2   plus 1/4 cup (1 1/2 sticks) butter or margarine, melted
1/4   teaspoon salt
1/8   teaspoon ground nutmeg
2   teaspoons vanilla extract
1   cup chopped walnuts

Cook the carrots in water to cover in a large saucepan over medium-high heat 20 to 25 minutes, or until very tender; drain well. Preheat the oven to 350°. Process the carrots and eggs in a blender or food processor until smooth, stopping to scrape down the sides. Add 2/3 cup sugar, the matzo meal, 1/2 cup butter, the salt, nutmeg, and vanilla; process until smooth. Pour the mixture into a lightly greased 13 x 9-inch baking dish. Bake for 40 to 45 minutes, or until set. Combine the remaining 1/3 cup sugar, 1/4 cup butter, and walnuts. Top the soufflé with the walnut mixture; bake 5 to 10 more minutes.

Makes 8 to 10 servings

Maryanne Whatley, Queen Mother
Red Hatters of Rincon, Rincon, Georgia

Apricot Carrot Mélange

The rich orange hue tells the story—this is loaded with Vitamin A.

1	pound carrots
1/2	cup (1 stick) butter
1	(8-ounce) container dried apricots
1/2	cup raisins
1	teaspoon ground cinnamon
1	teaspoon ground nutmeg
1/2	cup water

Peel the carrots and cut into thirds diagonally. Melt the butter in a heavy iron skillet. Add the carrots, apricots, raisins, cinnamon, and nutmeg. Sauté for about 3 minutes over medium heat. Add the water, cover, and cook on low heat for 30 to 45 minutes. Make sure water does not totally evaporate but cooks to the point that the apricots absorb it.

Makes 8 servings

Betty Swift, Princess Lazy Bones
Purple Passion Flowers, Greensboro, North Carolina

Swedish Cauliflower

For the home crowd, a wholesome and humble meal.

3	pounds cauliflower
4	tablespoons butter, melted
1	tablespoon lemon juice
1/4	cup whole wheat bread crumbs
1/4	cup wheat germ
1/4	teaspoon salt
1/3	teaspoon nutmeg
2	tablespoons butter
3	hard-boiled eggs, cut in wedges for garnish
1	teaspoon chopped fresh parsley for garnish

Wash and trim the cauliflower, but leave it whole. Steam the cauliflower for 6 to 8 minutes, or until the cauliflower is tender-crisp. Remove; keep warm on a platter. Combine 4 tablespoons melted butter with the lemon juice. Combine the bread crumbs, wheat germ, salt, and nutmeg. In a saucepan over medium heat, melt the 2 tablespoons butter. Add the crumb mixture and brown, stirring frequently. Sprinkle over the cauliflower. Garnish with the eggs and parsley.

Makes 6 to 8 servings

Margaret Thomas, Queen Peg o' My Hat
Red-Crested Purple-Breasted Beauties, Clemson, South Carolina

Copper Pennies

Sweet and tart and great at room temperature—an ideal take-along for picnic and potluck.

2   pounds carrots, peeled and sliced
1/2   cup corn oil
1/2   cup white or cider vinegar
1/2   cup sugar
1   (10 3/4-ounce) can condensed tomato soup
1   medium onion, chopped
1/2   green bell pepper, chopped

In a large saucepan simmer the carrots in salted water for 10 minutes. Drain well.

In a small saucepan bring the oil, vinegar, sugar, and soup to a boil over medium-high heat. Reduce the heat to low and simmer for 5 minutes. Layer one-third of the carrots, one-third of the onion, and one-third of the pepper in a large mixing bowl. Repeat the layers, ending with carrots. Pour the soup mixture over the carrots and marinate for 24 hours. Will keep for several weeks.

Makes 20 servings

FloyAnne McKenzie, Vice Queen Mum
Panama Red Hats, Panama City, Florida

Micro-Scalloped Corn

1   (15-ounce) can cream-style corn
1   (15-ounce) can whole kernel corn, drained
1   (4-ounce) can mushroom stems and pieces, drained

1   cup crushed crackers
1/2   to 3/4 cup milk

Coat a microwave safe casserole dish with non-stick cooking spray. Combine both cans of corn, mushrooms, and crackers in the dish and mix well. Add 1/2 cup milk and mix well. If the mixture seems thick, add more milk but not so much that the consistency is soupy. Microwave 15 minutes; stir well. Cook for 10 to 15 minutes longer. If you prefer, the mixture can be baked at 375° for 30 to 35 minutes. Garnish around the edge of the dish with a small amount of crushed crackers.

Makes 6 to 8 servings

Patti Farley, Lady Godiva
Majestic Myrtles, Yorktown, Texas

Corn Soufflé

Corn and cornmeal make a side dish with substance.

1   plus 1 cup corn kernels
1/2   cup (1 stick) butter, melted
2   eggs
1   cup sour cream
1   cup diced Monterey Jack cheese
1/2   cup yellow cornmeal
1 1/2 teaspoons salt

Preheat the oven to 350°. Grease a 2-quart casserole or 13x9-inch baking dish. In a blender or food processor purée 1 cup corn with the melted butter and eggs. Pour into a large bowl and add the remaining 1 cup corn, the sour cream, cheese, cornmeal, and salt. Pour into the casserole and bake for 50 to 60 minutes, or until the top is light brown and the soufflé is firm.

Makes 10 to 12 servings

Robin Yancey, Lady of Stroll
Ruby Red Hats of Joy, San Ramon, California

Corn Fritters

You can substitute an equal amount of chopped apple in this flexible batter.

2/3   cup all-purpose flour
1 1/2   teaspoons sugar
1   teaspoon baking powder
1/4   teaspoon salt
1/3   cup milk
1   egg, beaten
2   cups corn kernals
  Vegetable oil for frying

In a large bowl the mix flour, sugar, baking powder, and salt. Combine the milk and egg and stir into the flour mixture. Add the corn and stir until the mixture is moist. Add a half inch of oil to a large skillet over medium-high heat. Drop tablespoonfuls of the corn mixture into the hot oil and fry for 3 to 4 minutes on each side, or until golden brown.

Makes 2 to 3 servings

Evelyn Godfrey, Red Hatter
Steel Magnolias of Magnolia, Magnolia, Delaware

Creamy Slow Cooker Corn

1   (20-ounce) bag frozen corn
1   (8-ounce) package cream cheese
4   tablespoons butter
2   tablespoons sugar
6   tablespoons water

Combine the corn, cream cheese, butter, sugar, and water in a slow cooker. Cook on low for 4 hours, stirring every hour.

Makes 4 to 6 servings

Doris Taylor, Duchess of Quilts
Red Hot Red Hat Readers of Decatur, Ten Mile, Tennessee

Fresh Fried Corn

3   cups corn kernels, cut from 4 to 6 cobs
1/2   teaspoon all-purpose flour
3   tablespoons milk
1   teaspoon sugar
  Salt and pepper to taste
2   tablespoons olive oil

With the edge of a spoon scrape any remaining corn off the cob. Combine the corn, flour, milk, sugar, and salt and pepper. Add the oil to a skillet over medium heat. Fry the corn mixture until golden yellow, about 3 to 5 minutes.

Makes 2 to 4 servings

Pauline Banks, Esteemed Queen Bee
The Burnet Road Beauties, Austin, Texas

Flammable Corn, Do Not Eat!

Last summer my husband, Mike, and I were entertaining friends at a barbecue. My grown son had sent me a delicious recipe for corn on the grill. I had prepared about eighteen ears of corn, and they were beautiful. I had tied up the husks and had them in a bowl almost ready for barbecuing. Just before grilling, they were to be sprayed with nonstick cooking spray. I sprayed those beautiful ears and immediately noticed a strange smell. I realized that my husband had taken the cooking spray to the grill. Sitting near where I kept it was a similar can. Both cans had bright red lids. I had just sprayed my beautiful corn with OOPS, an adhesive remover. Not only did I almost poison my friends, but if that corn had reached the hot grill, my husband might have been blown sky high.

Well, the guys saved the day by going to the nearest town and buying fresh corn, and we all had a corn husking party. The corn was delicious, and to this day I am often called the Queen of OOPS.

Jean Washick,
Queen Jean
Twister Sisters,
Monett, Missouri

Eggplant Timbale

Sort of a savory custard or pudding. Great for an all-vegetable meal.

1   large eggplant, about 1 1/4 to 1 1/2 pounds
4   eggs
1/8   teaspoon white pepper
1   cup light cream or half-and-half
1/4   teaspoon minced fresh dill
2   tablespoons butter
1/4   cup finely minced parsley

1/2   teaspoon salt
Pinch of freshly ground nutmeg

Preheat the oven to 325°. Peel the eggplant and cut into 1-inch cubes. Bring 1 1/2 inches salted water to a boil in a 4-quart casserole and add the eggplant. Cover and cook for 8 minutes, or until tender, stirring occasionally. Drain well. Transfer the eggplant to a large bowl and whip until smooth. Add the eggs, white pepper, cream, dill, butter, parsley, salt, and nutmeg; beat until light and fluffy. Pour the mixture into a greased, shallow 1 1/2-quart baking dish. Bake, uncovered, for 35 minutes, or until set. Serve immediately.

Makes 6 to 8 servings

Audi Reinthaler, La Reine Maman (QM)
Cascade Contessas, Leavenworth, Washington

Corn & Zucchini Gratin

3   or 4 zucchini, cut into 1-inch slices
1   tablespoon plus 1 tablespoon butter
1/4   cup chopped onion
2   eggs, beaten
1   (10-ounce) package frozen corn, cooked
1   cup grated Swiss cheese
1/4   teaspoon salt
1/4   cup dry bread crumbs
2   tablespoons Parmesan cheese

Preheat the oven to 350°. Cook the zucchini in a small amount of salted water until very tender. Drain and mash. Melt 1 tablespoon butter in a skillet over medium heat. Sauté the onions for 5 minutes, or until translucent. Combine the eggs, zucchini, onion, corn, cheese, and salt in a greased 1-quart casserole. Combine the bread crumbs, Parmesan cheese, and the remaining 1 tablespoon butter. Sprinkle the bread crumb mixture over the casserole. Bake for 25 to 30 minutes, or until a knife comes out clean. Let stand 5 to 10 minutes before serving.

Makes 6 to 8 servings

Merna Price, Queen Mother
Thousand Island Belles, Gananoque, Ontario, Canada

Sweet-and-Sour Green Bean Casserole

A good treatment for canned green beans.

2   (14-ounce) cans French-cut green beans
1   medium red onion, cut in thin rings, separated
8   strips bacon, cut in small pieces
1/2   cup slivered almonds (optional)
6   tablespoons sugar
6   tablespoons white or cider vinegar

Drain the beans and arrange them in a greased 1 1/2-quart casserole dish. Arrange the onion slices over the beans. Fry the bacon in a skillet over medium heat until brown and crisp. Drain on paper towels and crumble, reserving the drippings in the skillet. Sprinkle the bacon over the casserole and top with the almonds, if using. Add the sugar and vinegar to the bacon drippings and heat until the sugar is dissolved. Pour over the casserole and marinate for several hours in the refrigerator or overnight. When ready to cook preheat the oven to 350° and bake for 45 minutes, or until bubbly. May be made a day ahead.

Makes 10 to 12 servings

Brenda Bieth, Ten Times a Lady
The Mad Red Hatters, St. Clairsville, Ohio

Barbecued Green Beans

3   (1-pound) cans green beans
3/4 cup firmly packed light brown sugar
1/2 cup ketchup
1/3 cup dark corn syrup
1   teaspoon liquid smoke
1   medium onion, finely chopped
6   to 8 slices cooked bacon, crumbled

Preheat the oven to 325°. Combine the beans, sugar, ketchup, corn syrup, liquid smoke, and onion in a greased 2-quart casserole. Top with the crumbled bacon. Bake, uncovered, for 1 hour.

Makes 8 to 10 servings

Patti Waszak, Queen
Red Tarts of SBC CSS, Cudahy, Wisconsin

Confetti Corn Scallop

1   egg
2/3 cup milk
1/2 cup (1 stick) butter or margarine, melted and cooled
1   (15-ounce) can whole kernel corn, drained
1   (15-ounce) can cream-style corn
1   medium onion, chopped
1/4 cup chopped green and red bell pepper (optional)
2   tablespoons sugar
1   cup grated cheddar cheese
1   cup crushed soda crackers or unseasoned Dry bread crumbs

Preheat the oven to 350°. Lightly beat the egg in a large bowl. Add the milk and butter and mix well. Add the corns, onion, peppers, sugar, cheese, and crackers. Spoon into a greased 2-quart round baking dish. Bake for 35 to 40 minutes.

Makes 6 to 8 servings

Ann Burns, Lady Astor
Red Hot Hatters of Euless, Euless, Texas

Farmer's Green Beans

4   thick bacon slices, chopped
1   pound green beans, snapped (about 4 cups)
2   medium onions, sliced
3   medium tomatoes, peeled and chopped (2 cups)
1/4 cup water
     Dash of black pepper
     Salt

Cook the bacon, drain, and reserve 3 tablespoons drippings. In a medium saucepan combine the beans, onions, tomatoes, water, and pepper. Bring to a boil. Cover, reduce the heat, and simmer for 20 to 25 minutes, or until the beans are tender. Stir in the reserved bacon drippings and season to taste with the salt. Transfer to a serving bowl and top with the bacon pieces. Mix well.

Makes 8 servings

Ann Terry, Vice Mum
Crimson Cuties, Spring Hill, Florida

Green Bean & Swiss Cheese Casserole

Smooth white sauce makes green beans just disappear. Tasters loved this side dish—the Swiss cheese makes it.

WHITE SAUCE
2   tablespoons butter
3   tablespoons all-purpose flour
1/2 teaspoon sugar
1/4 teaspoon pepper
1   cup milk
1/2 cup sour cream

CASSEROLE
2   (14.5-ounce) cans French-style green beans
1 1/2 cups grated Swiss cheese
1/3 cup corn flake crumbs
    (or dry bread crumbs)
1   tablespoon butter, melted

For the white sauce, melt the butter in a saucepan over low heat. Add the flour, sugar, and pepper; mix well. Add the milk and mix well with a whisk. Cook for about 1 minute, remove from the heat, and stir in the sour cream.

Preheat the oven to 350°. Heat the green beans in a saucepan over medium heat for 5 minutes and drain. Mix the beans with the white sauce. Layer the beans alternately with the Swiss cheese in a greased 1 1/2-quart casserole dish, ending with the cheese on top. Combine the corn flakes with the butter and spread on the top layer of the cheese. Bake for 40 minutes.

Makes 6 to 8 servings

Joann Heisch, Truffle Queen
Home & Heartstrings Red Hatters, Auburn, California

Onion Tart

Side dish or meatless meal? You decide.

1   (8-ounce) can crescent rolls
6   bacon slices, diced
2   large Vidalia onions, sliced
1/4 teaspoon cumin
1/2 teaspoon salt
1/2 teaspoon black pepper
3   eggs
2   cups sour cream
1/4 cup grated fresh Parmesan cheese

Preheat the oven to 400°. Spray a medium-size tart pan or casserole dish with nonstick cooking spray. Arrange the crescent rolls evenly on the bottom and up the side of the pan. Fry the bacon in a skillet over medium heat until crisp and transfer to a medium-size bowl, leaving the drippings in the skillet. Sauté the onions in the bacon drippings over medium heat until tender but not brown. Combine the sautéed onions, cumin, salt, pepper, eggs, sour cream, and bacon and mix. Pour on top of the crescent roll dough in the casserole dish. Sprinkle with the Parmesan cheese and bake for 30 minutes.

Makes 6 servings

Carol A. Kinelski, Husband's Royal Pain
Cats in the Red Hat, Richmond, Kentucky

Sesame Snap Peas

4 teaspoons vegetable oil

1 tablespoon sesame seeds

1 pound fresh or frozen sugar snap peas, thawed

1/2 cup water

1 tablespoon butter

1 garlic clove, minced

3/4 teaspoon lemon pepper

1/4 teaspoon salt

Heat the oil in a small skillet over low heat; add the sesame seeds and cook until light brown, stirring frequently. Set aside. Combine the peas and water in a separate skillet and bring to a boil over high heat; reduce the heat to medium low, cover, and cook for 7 to 8 minutes. Drain and add the butter, garlic, lemon pepper, and salt. Cook for 2 minutes, stirring frequently. Remove from the heat and top with the sesame seeds.

Makes 4 servings

Nancie Day, The Happy Cooker
Red Hat Hotties, Fort Worth, Texas

Candied Lima Beans

Testers called this "the biggest surprise of all" in their tastings—"outstanding," "wonderful," and "great for pot luck." The original called for two sticks of butter and two cups brown sugar for one pound of beans. Testers found that you could cook twice as many beans in that amount of butter and sugar (or halve the butter and sugar for one pound of beans).

1 to 2 pounds large lima beans

4 cups (2 sticks) butter (no substitutes)

2 cups firmly packed brown sugar

Salt and pepper to taste

In a large saucepan, cover the beans with plenty of water and bring to a boil over high heat. Reduce the heat to low and simmer for 1 hour. Partially drain the beans, leaving a little water. Preheat the oven to 350°. Pour the beans into a lightly greased 13 x 9-inch baking dish. Stir in the butter and brown sugar. Bake for 1 hour, uncovered.

Makes 6 to 8 servings

Alda Powell, Royal Scribe
Rural Robust Red Hatters, Templeton, Pennsylvania

Holiday Scalloped Onions

8 large onions, peeled and cut into quarters

2 tablespoons butter

2 tablespoons all-purpose flour

1 cup milk

1 cup shredded American cheese

1/2 cup dry bread crumbs

Place the onion quarters in a large saucepan and cover with water. Cook the onions over medium-high heat for 10 minutes, or until tender crisp; drain.

Preheat the oven to 350°. In a glass mixing bowl melt the butter in the microwave on half power for about 45 seconds. Add the flour and stir to mix well. Whisk in the milk. Return the bowl to the microwave and cook until thickened, about 2 minutes. Add the cheese and mix well. Arrange the onions in a 1½-quart casserole dish. Pour the cheese sauce over the onions and top with the bread crumbs. Bake for 30 to 40 minutes, or until hot and bubbly.

Makes 8 to 10 servings

Note: You can make the cheese sauce in a saucepan on the stove over medium heat. It will take about 15 minutes instead of 2½ to 3 minutes in the microwave.

Cynthia West, Queen Cookie
Traveling Cooks with Hattitude, Marshalltown, Iowa

Green Bean Bundles

2   pounds fresh green beans, steamed crisp-tender

6   strips bacon, partially cooked and halved
     Garlic salt to taste

4   tablespoons butter, melted

3   tablespoons packed light brown sugar

Preheat the oven to 350°. Gather 6 to 10 beans in bundles and wrap half a slice of bacon around the center of each bundle. Place the bundles in a 12 x 8-inch baking dish. Sprinkle garlic salt, melted butter, and brown sugar on top. Bake for 15 to 20 minutes, or until the bacon is cooked.

Makes 6 to 8 servings

Lynne Wixom, Gray Fox
Red Hat TeasHers, Silver Spring, Maryland

Balsamic Onions with Honey

3   large red onions (about 3 pounds), peeled and quartered

1/4   cup plus 1 tablespoon water

6   tablespoons honey

1/4   cup balsamic vinegar

3   tablespoons butter, melted

1   teaspoon paprika

1/2   teaspoon curry powder

1/2   teaspoon salt

1/8   teaspoon ground black pepper

Preheat the oven to 350°. Arrange the onions in a greased 1 quart shallow baking dish. Sprinkle with 1 tablespoon water and cover with a lid or foil. Bake for 30 minutes. Combine the honey, vinegar, the remaining 1/4 cup water, butter, paprika, curry, salt, and pepper in a small bowl. Remove the onions from the oven and turn them over. Spoon half the honey mixture over the onions. Bake, uncovered, 15 minutes more. Baste with the remaining honey mixture, and then bake another 15 minutes, or until tender.

Makes 4 to 6 servings

Barbara Schutz, The Lady of Roseville
Feisty Dynamites, Roseville, California

Make-Ahead Mashed Potatoes

Here's a recipe to delight the heart of the busy hostess. Tasters wrote, "We all loved this recipe."

3   pounds white potatoes (about 9 medium)
1 1/2 cups sour cream
1/4   cup (1/2 stick) butter
1   teaspoon salt
1/4   teaspoon black pepper
1/4   cup dry bread crumbs
1   tablespoon butter, melted

Peel potatoes and cut into quarters. Cook the potatoes in boiling water over high heat until tender, about 15 minutes. Drain. Preheat the oven to 325°. Combine the potatoes with the sour cream, butter, salt, and pepper in large bowl. Beat at low speed with an electric mixer until blended. Increase the speed to high and beat until light and fluffy. Transfer to a lightly buttered, 2-quart casserole. (At this point, the potatoes can be covered and refrigerated for 12 to 16 hours or frozen for several days.) Bake, covered, for at least 1 hour (or longer if frozen). Toss the bread crumbs with the melted butter and sprinkle over the potatoes. Continue baking for 30 minutes.

Makes 8 servings

Carolyn Knauss, Red Snapper
Red Cardinals, Tatamy, Pennsylvania

Potatoes Smashed with Olives

Potatoes are often cooked and served with olives in the Mediterranean. You'll agree it's a good combination.

2   pounds Yukon gold potatoes
1/3   to 1/2 cup extra virgin olive oil, warmed over low heat
2/3   cup black olives, pitted and coarsely chopped (I prefer Kalamatas)
     Sea salt and freshly ground black pepper to taste

Steam the potatoes in a vegetable steamer set over simmering water in a covered pot until tender, 25 to 30 minutes. Peel the potatoes immediately. Place the hot potatoes in a medium-size mixing bowl and coarsely mash them with a potato masher. Gradually incorporate the warmed olive oil. Gently fold in the olives and season the mixture with the salt and pepper. Serve immediately.

Makes 4 to 6 servings

Bette Heide, Harborer of Hasty News
Sassy Classy Ladies, Chicago, Illinois

Hidden Valley Potatoes

Testers said this dish has plain-Jane looks, but tastes delicious.

2   bags frozen hash browns (24 ounces each), semi-thawed
2   packages cream cheese (8 ounces each), softened
2   (.4-ounce) envelopes ranch dressing mix
2   (10 3/4-ounce) cans cream of potato soup

Arrange the hash browns in a large slow cooker sprayed with nonstick cooking spray. Mix the cream cheese, dressing mix, and potato soup in a bowl and add to the hash browns. Mix well. Cook on low in the slow cooker for 7 to 9 hours. Stir before serving.

Makes 12 to 15 servings

Betty Weldon, Sparkle Plenty
Vancouver Belles, Longview, Washington

Dilly Mashed Idaho Potatoes

Fresh dill transforms mashed potatoes into a fragrant herbed pleasure. Mix leftovers with a little flour and an egg, and then make potato cakes to fry.

6   medium Idaho potatoes
1/2 cup milk
1   cup sour cream
2   tablespoons minced fresh dill or 2 teaspoons dried dill weed
1   tablespoon dried minced onion
3/4 teaspoon seasoned salt
1/4 teaspoon pepper

In a saucepan cover the potatoes with water and cook over medium-high heat until very tender; drain. Peel the potatoes while warm and cube. Mash in a mixing bowl with a potato masher or fork. With an electric mixer beat the potatoes with the milk; add the sour cream, dill, onion, salt, and pepper and mix well.

Makes 6 to 8 servings

Mary Servatius, Lady in Waiting
Red Hot Taters, Meridian, Idaho

Little Baby Reds

8   to 10 small red potatoes
1   tablespoon vegetable oil
    Salt and pepper to taste
    Grated Parmesan cheese to taste

Preheat the oven to 350°. Cut the potatoes into thin slices. Grease a 13 x 9-inch baking dish with the vegetable oil. Add the potatoes. Season with salt and pepper and sprinkle with cheese. Bake for 35 to 40 minutes. Serve immediately.

Makes 4 servings

Evelyn Agee, Queen Mother
Sugar Plum Girls, Lebanon, Tennessee

Cheesy New Potatoes

12   to 14 medium new potatoes, washed and quartered
2   cups grated cheddar cheese
12   bacon slices, cooked and crumbled
1/2 cup (1 stick) butter, melted
    Salt and pepper to taste
1/2 cup chopped fresh parsley (optional)

Cook the potatoes in boiling water until done, about 20 minutes. Preheat the oven to 350°. Grease a 13 x 9-inch casserole dish. Layer the potatoes, cheese, bacon, butter, salt and pepper, and the parsley in the dish. Bake for 15 minutes.

Makes 6 to 8 servings

Betty Spencer, Queen
Scarlet Divas, Atoka, Tennessee

Dirty Potatoes

A few days after our wedding, my husband accompanied me to the grocery store. When I picked up a bag of potatoes, he whispered, "Don't buy those." I told him that we were out of potatoes, and we needed to buy some. Again, he said, "Don't buy those." Puzzled, I pressed him for a reason. He reluctantly responded, "They're dirty." Suppressing my laughter, I realized that he must have missed the grade-school science lesson where we're taught that potatoes grow in the dirt. I assured him they were OK, saying, "That's why we wash them."

Janet Meyer,
Princess Flying Tutu
West County Gals,
Ballwin, Missouri

Italian Potatoes

Call it a warm potato salad and enjoy the bold flavors.

15   large red potatoes (about 5 pounds)
1/2   cup chopped fresh parsley leaves
1/2   cup chopped green onions
3   large garlic cloves, thinly sliced
1   heaping teaspoon salt
    Black pepper to taste
1/2   teaspoon dry mustard
1   scant tablespoon sugar
1   tablespoon Worcestershire sauce
1   cup olive oil
1/2   cup tarragon vinegar

Place potatoes in a large pot and cover with water. Bring to a boil, generously salt the water, and boil the potatoes until tender, approximately 30 to 40 minutes. Drain and let stand until cool enough to handle. Peel potatoes, if desired and cut into 1-inch chunks. Place cut potatoes in a large bowl. Sprinkle the parsley and green onions over the potatoes. Make the sauce by combining the garlic, salt, pepper, mustard, sugar, Worcestershire sauce, olive oil, and vinegar. Mix well. Pour the sauce over the potatoes. Stir well. Let stand for at least for 4 hours, stirring every hour. Serve at room temperature.

Makes 16 servings

Jeannette Batjer, Queen Mother
J&J Purple Hatters of Irondequoit, Rochester, New York

Spirited Sweet Potato Bake

In parts of the country, orange-flesh sweet potatoes are sometime labeled "yams," especially the canned and frozen varieties. They are more moist and sweeter than the white-fleshed variety. A true yam is a tropical vegetable rarely seen in the States.

6	ounces Cointreau liqueur
6	ounces banana liqueur
1	(16-ounce) package brown sugar
1/2	cup (1 stick) butter
1	(20-ounce) bag frozen sliced sweet potatoes

Mix together the liqueurs, brown sugar, butter, and sweet potatoes in a saucepan and cook over medium heat until the potatoes are tender.

Makes 6 servings

Alta Kuzma, Queen
Stat Code Red Hats, McKeesport, Pennsylvania

Quick Squash Stir-Fry

You can serve the recipe as written, or at the last minute toss in a 14 1/2-ounce can chopped tomatoes (or the equivalent of fresh tomatoes) for a different taste.

1	tablespoon olive oil
1	pound zucchini or other summer squash, sliced about 1/8-inch thick
1	medium onion, coarsely chopped
	Salt and pepper to taste
	Garlic powder to taste

Heat the olive oil in a skillet over medium heat. Sauté the zucchini and onion with salt and pepper and garlic powder until just tender; do not overcook.

Makes 4 servings

Rosalie Hunt, Queen Mother
Hoosier Honeys, Fortville, Indiana

Crazy Potatoes

10	potatoes, washed and cubed
8	bacon strips
1	(.4-ounce) package ranch dressing mix
2	cups mayonnaise
1	cup milk
3/4	pound sharp cheddar cheese, grated

Cook the potatoes in boiling, salted water until tender. Drain and place in a greased 13 x 9-inch baking dish. Cook the bacon in a skillet over medium-high heat until crisp; drain on paper towels, cool, and crumble. Preheat the oven to 375°. Mix together the ranch dressing mix, mayonnaise, and milk. Add the grated cheese and mix. Pour over the potatoes. Sprinkle the bacon over the top. Bake for 30 minutes.

Makes 12 to 16 servings

Judy Schloff, Queen Mum
Happy Trails, Chesapeake, Virginia

Timber Lodge Hash Browns

Good for a crowd, and useful for brunch, lunch, or supper.

40 ounces refrigerated or frozen shredded hash browns
1/3 cup chopped onion
1 cup shredded Monterey Jack cheese
1 cup shredded cheddar cheese
1/2 teaspoon salt
1/2 teaspoon black pepper
1 (103/4-ounce) can cream of chicken soup
1/2 cup (1 stick) butter or margarine

Preheat the oven to 450°. Combine the hash browns, onion, cheeses, salt, and pepper. In a small saucepan warm the soup and butter over medium heat until the butter is mostly melted. Combine this with the potato mixture. Spread the mixture evenly in a greased 13 x 9-inch pan; do not pack down. Bake for 1 hour on the top rack of the oven, or until golden brown, rotating the pan to brown the hash browns evenly. Let stand 4 minutes before serving.

Makes 12 servings

Deanna Riley, Queen
Razzler–Dazzlers, Chatfield, Minnesota

Praline-Top Sweet Potatoes

POTATOES
2 pounds sweet potatoes, cubed
1/2 teaspoon salt
1/2 teaspoon black pepper
2 tablespoons brown sugar
1 egg yolk
1 tablespoon butter or margarine

TOPPING
2 tablespoons butter or margarine, melted
3 tablespoons brown sugar
1/4 cup chopped pecans
1/4 teaspoon nutmeg

Cook the sweet potatoes in boiling water until tender. Drain, cool, and peel. Mash or process the potatoes until smooth. Mix in the salt, pepper, brown sugar, egg yolk, and butter. Beat until light. Spoon into an 8-inch square baking dish. Preheat the oven to 350°.

For the topping, combine the butter, brown sugar, pecans, and nutmeg. Spread over the sweet potatoes. Bake for 35 to 40 minutes. Let sit for a few minutes before serving.

Makes 6 servings

Carol Boshaw, Queen Mother
Fun Hatters of Holiday Acres, McHenry, Illinois

Two-Squash Bake

1 small onion, chopped
2 tablespoons olive oil
1 medium yellow squash, coarsely chopped
2 medium zucchini, coarsely chopped
1/2 teaspoon salt
1/4 teaspoon black pepper
1/2 cup shredded cheddar cheese
3/4 cup shredded mozzarella cheese
1/2 (2.8-ounce) can french-fried onions

Preheat the oven to 350°. Spray a 1½-quart casserole dish with nonstick cooking spray. In a medium skillet over medium heat sauté the onion in the oil until transparent. Add the yellow squash and cook for 5 minutes. Add the zucchini and cook 5 more minutes. Stir in the salt, pepper, and cheeses and pour into the prepared dish. Sprinkle the french-fried onions on top. Bake for about 15 minutes, or until the cheese bubbles.

Makes 3 to 4 servings

Bessie Moreland, Queen Mother
Cavanal Gems Red Hat Society, Poteau, Oklahoma

Butternut Squash Bake with Snap-Crackle-Pop Topping

1/3 cup butter or margarine, softened
3/4 cup granulated sugar
2 eggs
1 (5-ounce) can evaporated milk
1 teaspoon vanilla extract
2 cups cooked butternut squash, mashed

TOPPING
1/2 cup crisp rice cereal
1/4 cup packed brown sugar
1/4 cup chopped pecans
2 tablespoons butter or margarine, melted

Preheat the oven to 350°. In a large mixing bowl beat the butter and sugar together. Beat in the eggs, milk, and vanilla. Stir in the squash (mixture will be thin). Pour into a greased, 11

x 7-inch baking pan. Bake, uncovered, for 45 minutes, or until almost set.

For the topping, combine the cereal, brown sugar, pecans, and butter and sprinkle over the casserole. Return to the oven for 5 to 10 minutes, or until bubbly.

Makes 6 to 8 servings

Barbara Diemler, Queen
Classy Red Hatters, Jefferson City, Missouri

Baked Dijon Tomatoes

Easy and elegant. Every recipe collection needs more recipes like this.

1 tablespoon light mayonnaise
1 tablespoon Dijon mustard
1/4 cup seasoned dry bread crumbs
1 tablespoon chopped parsley
1 tablespoon Parmesan cheese
4 tomatoes

Preheat the oven to 350°. In a small bowl combine the mayonnaise and mustard. In another small bowl combine the bread crumbs, parsley, and Parmesan cheese. Cut each tomato in half and place on a lightly greased baking sheet. Spread the mayonnaise mixture on top of each half; then sprinkle with the bread crumb mixture. Bake for 20 minutes.

Makes 4 servings

Bonnie Mischo Allinger, Queen
Bonnet Rouge, Wilton, California

Stuffed Tomatoes

5   medium tomatoes
1   cup diced celery
1   cucumber, peeled and diced
1   tablespoon finely chopped onion
    Salt and pepper to taste
1/3 cup ranch or Italian salad dressing

Wash the tomatoes. Cut out the stems. Scoop out and reserve the centers. Refrigerate the tomatoes while preparing the filling. In a mixing bowl combine the reserved tomato centers, celery, cucumber, onion, salt, and pepper. Toss lightly. Add the dressing. Stuff the chilled tomatoes with the filling.

Makes 5 servings

Jenny Starling, Queen Shutter Bug Sue
Ooo-La-La Lee Girls, Princeton, North Carolina

Fried Green Tomatoes

Crisp outside, firm and tangy inside—the perfect combination for a side dish, or even as part of a meatless, mid-summer meal.

    Vegetable oil
1   cup all-purpose flour
    Black pepper to taste
    Salt to taste
4   green tomatoes, cut into 1/2-inch slices

Heat about 1/4-inch vegetable oil in a large skillet over medium-high heat. Mix the flour, pepper, and salt together on a plate or piece of waxed paper. Dip the tomatoes into the mixture. Fry in the hot oil until browned. Turn and brown the other side. Drain on paper towels before serving.

Makes 4 servings

Frances Piper, Lady Godiver
Elite Ladies of the Hat, Franklinton, North Carolina

Turnip & Carrot Casserole

1   medium turnip, peeled and chopped
8   to 10 carrots, peeled and chopped
2   cups cubed Velveeta cheese
4   tablespoons plus 2 tablespoons butter, melted
1/2 cup fine dry bread crumbs

Preheat the oven to 350°. In a large pot cover the turnip and carrots with water and bring to a boil over medium-high heat. Cook for 20 to 30 minutes, or until very tender. Drain and mash thoroughly. Add the cubed cheese and 4 tablespoons butter. Mix well and spoon into a buttered 6-cup casserole. Mix the remaining 2 tablespoons butter with the bread crumbs and sprinkle on top. Bake for 40 minutes, or until the crumbs are browned and the casserole is hot.

Makes 8 servings

Nancy MacNeil, E-mail Lady
Saay Lassies–Burlington, Burlington, Ontario, Canada

Cheesy Baked Apples

The contributor notes that she loves the topping so much that she doubles the quantities for it.

APPLES
8 medium Granny Smith apples
2 tablespoons lemon juice
1 tablespoon sugar
2 tablespoons water

TOPPING
6 tablespoons butter, softened
1 cup all-purpose flour
   Pinch of salt
1/2 cup sugar
1 cup grated sharp cheddar cheese

Preheat the oven to 350°. Slice the apples and toss with the lemon juice, sugar, and water. Place in a greased 13 x 11-inch casserole dish.

To prepare the topping, cut the butter into the flour and then add the salt, sugar, and cheese. Sprinkle the topping over the apples. Bake for about 1 hour, checking after 30 minutes. Spread some butter on any dry spots that appear on the dough. You may need to add some water if the apples look dry.

Makes 12 servings

Sherry Rice, Lady of the Loot
Legally Red, Jacksonville, Florida

Zucchini Cheese Puff

A good way to turn squash into a side dish the family will eat. Testers found the dots of cottage cheese in the baked result a little homely—you may wish to use ricotta cheese instead, or purée the cottage cheese if you want a more attractive dish.

6 medium zucchini or summer squash or a combination, sliced
1 cup small curd cottage cheese
1 cup grated Monterey Jack cheese
2 eggs
3/4 teaspoon dill weed or 1 1/2 teaspoons chopped fresh dill
1/2 teaspoon salt (or to taste)
1/2 teaspoon white or other pepper
1/2 cup soft bread crumbs (from day-old bread)
1 tablespoon butter or margarine, melted

Preheat the oven to 350°. In a large pot, cover the zucchini with water and bring to a boil over high heat and cook for 5 minutes. Drain well and transfer to a shallow, buttered 1 1/2-quart baking dish. In a bowl combine the cheeses, eggs, dill, salt, and pepper and mix well. Spoon over the squash. Bake, uncovered, for 15 minutes. Mix the bread crumbs and melted butter and sprinkle over the squash. Bake for another 15 minutes.

Makes 10 to 12 serving.

Lee Smith, Princess of Prose
Saline Salty Sexy Sirens, Tecumseh, Michigan

Zucchini (Crab) Cakes

A great way to use that zucchini from the summer garden, the tester noted.

2 1/2 cups shredded zucchini
1   egg, lightly beaten
2   tablespoons chopped onion
1   tablespoon butter, melted
1   teaspoon prepared mustard
1   teaspoon Old Bay seasoning
1   cup seasoned dry bread crumbs
2   tablespoons vegetable oil

In a bowl combine the zucchini, egg, onion, butter, mustard, and Old Bay seasoning. Mix in the bread crumbs and mix well. Shape into patties. Add another egg if you are not able to shape into patties. Heal the oil in a skillet over medium-high heat, and fry 4 minutes on each side, or until golden brown. Drain well.

Makes 12 three-inch cakes

Barbara Simpson, Assistant Queen Mother
Highbanks Hatters, DeBary, Florida

Vegetable Kabobs

A shish kabob without the meat is a fun way to prepare a side dish, or a clever way to get guests to prepare their own.

1   tablespoon chopped garlic
2   tablespoons olive oil
1   teaspoon rosemary, chopped
1   lime, juiced
1   teaspoon salt
16 cherry tomatoes
12 small red-skin potatoes, parboiled, cooled
12 mushrooms, trim stems
1   small red onion, peeled, cut into 1/2-inch wedges

Combine the garlic, oil, rosemary, lime juice, and salt in a bowl; blend well. Pierce alternating pieces of tomatoes, potato, mushrooms, and onion with skewers until full. Arrange on a plate and baste with the oil mixture. Grill the kabobs on a medium hot grill until lightly charred, about 4 minutes for each quarter turn, basting with the marinade.

Makes 4 servings

Lorraine Sayas, Queen Mother Gem
Tidewaters Gems, Virginia Beach, Virginia

Roasted Vegetables

Roasting brings out the mellow sweetness in vegetables, caramelizing their sugars and utterly transforming their flavors. It's best if vegetables are in a single layer—use two pans if needed.

2   zucchini, chopped
2   yellow crookneck squash, chopped
    Mushrooms, as many as you like, sliced in half
20 garlic cloves, peeled and left whole (yes, 20-about 3 whole bulbs)
1   or 2 red bell peppers, chopped
1   or 2 (14-ounce) jars marinated artichoke hearts; undrained and sliced in half if large

1 red onion, coarsely chopped

2 Roma tomatoes, chopped

2 Asian eggplants with skin on, sliced but not too thinly

2 to 4 teaspoons garlic-flavored (or plain) olive oil plus more for baking

Chopped fresh or dried parsley to taste

Dried Italian herbs to taste

Fresh or dried basil to taste

Combine all the vegetables in a bowl. Add the reserved artichoke marinade and olive oil and mix well to coat. Preheat the oven to 450°.

When ready to cook, drain the oil from the vegetables. Put a small amount of olive oil in the bottom of a 13 x 9-inch glass baking dish. Arrange the vegetables in the baking dish, keeping them in a single layer if possible. Drizzle a small amount of olive oil over the vegetables. Season with parsley, Italian herbs, and basil. Bake, uncovered, in the oven for 25 minutes. Leftovers are even tasty over a bowl of white rice with a tiny amount of soy sauce.

Makes 10 servings

Note: Change out your vegetables as seasons change.

Carol Ann Wilshusen, Queen Mum
Sassy Sisters, Grass Valley, California

Herb-Baked Veggies

A carefree side dish featuring the full flavor of baked vegetables.

4 to 6 medium red potatoes, chopped

2 carrots, chopped

1 plus 1/2 teaspoon rosemary

1 plus 1/2 teaspoon basil

1 plus 1/2 teaspoon thyme

1 plus 1/2 teaspoon salt

1 plus 1/2 teaspoon oregano

Olive oil

2 parsnips, peeled and coarsely chopped

1 to 2 zucchini squash, coarsely chopped

1 yellow squash, coarsely chopped

1 to 2 bell peppers, sliced

1 onion, coarsely chopped or cut into wedges

Preheat the oven to 400°. In a large zip-top bag combine the potatoes and carrots with 1/2 teaspoon each of rosemary, basil, thyme, salt, and oregano. Shake the bag to coat. Add a tablespoon or two of olive oil and shake again to coat the pieces. Mix well. Spray a baking sheet with sides with nonstick cooking spray. Arrange the potatoes and carrots on the baking sheet and bake for 20 minutes.

Combine the parsnips, zucchini, yellow squash, peppers, and onion in the zip-top bag. Add more olive oil to coat well and the remaining 1 teaspoon of each of the herbs. Mix well. After the potatoes have baked for 20 minutes, add the remaining veggies to the baking sheet and continue baking for another 20 minutes. You may want to stir a couple of times to be sure all veggies are coated well so they won't dry out.

Makes 4 to 6 servings

Darlene Minor, Queen Mother
Sassy Bowlers, New Braunfels, Texas

Apple Sauce

As a twenty-one-year-old bride, I had a mother-in-law who was a wonderful cook. One day she presented me with a large sack of apples and said I should make some applesauce for my new husband. I didn't have a clue how to make applesauce, but I still took the apples home and cooked and cooked and cooked them. Of course, I ended up with a watery mess. So while my husband was still at work, I rushed to the grocery store and bought Mott's Apple Sauce. I rushed home, repackaged my purchase in Ball jars, and trashed the evidence. My husband thought my applesauce was wonderful, and after all this time, I still have never told him the secret. I guess it's time I confess—especially before this comes out in print!

Shirley Duffer,
Historian
Ya-Ya Purplehood,
Fishers, Indiana

Squash Pie

A nice looking side dish, said testers. Good at room temperature and travels well since it doesn't slosh or spill.

3   cups thinly sliced zucchini squash or yellow squash (2 medium)
1/2 cup chopped onion
1/2 cup grated sharp cheddar cheese
4   eggs, beaten
1/2 cup vegetable oil
3   tablespoons chopped fresh parsley
1   cup biscuit mix
     Salt and pepper to taste

Preheat the oven to 350°. In a large bowl combine the zucchini, onion, cheese, eggs, oil, parsley, biscuit mix and salt and papper. Mix well. Pour into a greased 9-inch pie plate. Bake for 30 minutes, or until the top is golden. Let stand several minutes to firm up before slicing.

Makes 6 servings

Jeanette M. Ganio, Lady Eliza
Holly Hatters, Vineland, New Jersey

Mighty Vegetable Casserole

Look at all those powerhouse vegetables.

2   cups plum tomatoes
1 1/2 cups chopped onions
1 1/2 cups sliced carrots (pre-cooked slightly)
3/4   cup sliced green bell pepper
1/4   pound snow peas
1   cup chopped cauliflower
1   cup chopped broccoli
1 1/2 cups sliced celery
1   can sliced water chestnuts, drained
4   tablespoons butter
3   tablespoons granulated tapioca
1 1/2 teaspoons salt
1/2   teaspoon black pepper
1   tablespoon sugar
     Pinch of sweet basil

Preheat the oven to 350°. Mix the tomatoes, onions, carrots, bell pepper, peas, cauliflower, broccoli, celery, and water chestnuts together in a greased 13x9-inch baking dish. Melt the butter in a saucepan over low heat. Stir in the tapioca, salt, pepper, sugar, and basil. Pour over the vegetables. Bake for about 30 minutes.

Makes 8 to 10 servings

Dianne Crawford, Queen Mother
Ajijic Red Hat Mamas, Ajijic, Mexico

Ratatouille (Summer Veggie Medley)

1/4   cup olive or vegetable oil
1   medium eggplant, chopped
1   medium to large green bell pepper, chopped
1   large sweet onion, chopped
2   small zucchini squash, sliced
2   small yellow summer squash, sliced
1   tablespoon minced garlic (optional)
2   teaspoons salt (kosher, if available)
1/4   teaspoon black pepper

Heat the oil in a 10-inch skillet over medium heat. Add the eggplant, bell pepper, and onion and sauté for 10 minutes. Add the zucchini squash, yellow squash, garlic, salt, and pepper. Cover and simmer until the vegetables are cooked through, 5 to 10 minutes. Remove the lid and simmer 2 to 3 minutes longer to reduce the liquid, or drain the liquid, if you prefer. Serve hot, at room temperature, or cold. Keeps for up to 3 days when refrigerated.

Makes 4 generous servings

Judith Lewis, Empress of Events/ViceQueenMother
Les Chapeaux Rouges of Bristol Village, Waverly, Ohio

Cranberry Swirl Salad

Sweet, tangy, creamy, and great-looking on a holiday buffet.

1   (6-ounce) package raspberry gelatin
2   cups boiling water
2   cans whole cranberry sauce
1   cup walnuts
2   cups sour cream

Dissolve the gelatin in the boiling water. Pour into a 13 x 9-inch glass dish. Chill until slightly thickened. Break up the cranberry sauce with a fork. Fold into the gelatin along with the nuts. Add the sour cream to the mixture and mix just enough for a pretty swirl affect. Refrigerate until set.

Makes 8 servings

Nancy Rosi, Queen Mother
Jolly Red Hatters, Denver, Colorado

Escalloped Pineapple

Is it pudding or a side dish? Whichever it is, it appeals to many of you—we received many versions of this dish.

6   slices white bread, cubed
1   cup sugar
1/2 cup (1 stick) butter or margarine, melted
2   eggs
1/2 cup milk
1   (20-ounce) can juice-packed pineapple tidbits, drained

Preheat the oven to 350°. Layer the bread in the bottom of a 2-quart casserole dish. Sprinkle the sugar on top and pour the melted butter over the sugar. Beat the eggs with the milk and pour over the bread mixture. Top with the pineapple and toss lightly. Bake for 45 minutes to 1 hour, or until brown and crusty.

Makes 6 to 8 servings

Judy Laughter, Lady Joy
Bridge Divas of Vandalia, Vandalia, Ohio

Hot Sherried Fruit

1   (15 1/2-ounce) can pineapple chunks, drained
1   (15-ounce) can sliced pears, drained
1   (24-ounce) jar cling peaches, drained
1   (14-ounce) jar apple rings, drained
1/4 cup (1/2-stick) butter
1/2 cup sugar
2   tablespoons all-purpose flour
1   cup dry sherry

Pour the fruit into a lightly greased 1 1/2-quart casserole dish. In the top of a double boiler over simmering water, combine the butter, sugar, flour, and sherry. Heat, stirring, until thick; then pour the mixture over the fruit. Refrigerate for at least 6 hours.

When ready to bake, preheat the oven to 350°. Bake the fruit for 30 minutes, or until bubbly. Cool and serve.

Makes 6 to 8 servings

Mitzi Wilson, QueenMumFunDames
Fun and Fantastic Dames, Charlotte, North Carolina

Corn Bread Bake

*This recipe was one of the most-submitted recipes—
Red Hatters love it.*

1/2 cup (1 stick) butter
1   cup (8 ounces) sour cream
1   (15-ounce) can cream-style corn
1   (15-ounce) can whole corn, drained
1   egg
1   cup corn bread mix

Preheat the oven to 350°. Melt the butter in a 2-
quart round, glass baking dish. Add the sour
cream, corns, egg, and corn bread mix. Mix well.
Bake for 45 minutes to 1 hour. The bread is done
when a knife inserted in the center comes out
with a little moisture on it but not sticky.

Makes 8 to 10 servings

Mari Walther, Queen Mother
Foxy Divas of Okee, Okeechobee, Florida

Baked Rice

*You may also use chicken broth in place of the beef
broth, and add some chicken to it to make an entrée.*

1   cup uncooked rice
1   (4-ounce can) mushrooms, not drained
1   (10 1/2-ounce) can French onion soup
1   (14-ounce) can beef broth

Preheat the oven to 350°. Put the rice into a 2-
quart casserole dish. Add the mushrooms with
liquid, soup, and broth. Don't drain any of
them. Cover and bake for 1 hour, or until the
liquid is absorbed and the rice is tender.

Makes 8 servings

Elaine McCurry, Email Female
Regal Rubies, Renwick, Iowa

Wild Rice Casserole

1/2 cup sliced almonds
1/2 cup (1 stick) butter
1   cup wild rice or 1/2 cup wild rice and 1/2
     cup brown rice
3   tablespoons chopped green onion
1   pound sliced fresh mushrooms
3   cups low-sodium chicken broth

Place the almonds in a skillet over medium
heat, and sauté for about 3 minutes. In a heavy
skillet over medium heat combine the butter,
rice, onion, toasted almonds, and mushrooms.
Sauté for 8 to 10 minutes, stirring almost constantly. Preheat the oven to 325°. Transfer the
skillet mixture to a buttered 2-quart casserole.
Add the broth. Cover tightly and bake for 1 1/2
to 2 hours.

Makes 8 servings

JoAnne Montgomery, Queen
Red Hot Mamas of the Pines, Magalia, California

Fragrant Curried Rice

Buttery, with a bold curry flavor, this wonderful side dish complements chicken, lamb, or pork.

2   cups brown or regular instant rice
1/2 cup (1 stick) butter or margarine
1/2 onion, chopped
1/2 green bell pepper, chopped
6   to 8 sliced fresh mushrooms
2   tablespoons curry powder

Cook the rice according to the package directions. In a skillet melt the butter or margarine over medium-high heat and sauté the onion, bell pepper, and mushrooms until the onion is translucent. Stir in the curry powder. Add the rice and mix well.

Makes 6 servings

Diana Blazek, Queen Mum
The Red Hot Grand Hatters, Surprise, Arizona

Noodle Kugel

This traditional Jewish side dish is as sweet as a dessert and very rich. It's usually served as a side dish, but it's also great for a breakfast that's definitely not your usual fare. Note that this recipe makes a big batch.

1   (16-ounce) container cottage cheese
2   (8-ounce) packages cream cheese, softened
2   cups milk
6   eggs
1 1/2 cups sugar

2   teaspoons vanilla extract
2   cups sour cream
1   cup (2 sticks) butter, melted
1   cup raisins (optional)
1   (16-ounce) package fine egg noodles, cooked and rinsed in cold water
1   package graham crackers, finely crumbled

Preheat the oven to 350°. Combine the cottage cheese, cream cheese, and milk. Beat until smooth. Combine the eggs, sugar, vanilla, sour cream, melted butter, and raisins and add to the milk mixture. Add the cooked noodles and mix. Pour into two 13 x 9-inch pans or one 18 x 14-inch pan coated with nonstick cooking spray. Top with the graham cracker crumbs. Bake for 1 hour. To make ahead, bake for 30 minutes, cool, then freeze. Defrost and bake for another 30 minutes.

Makes 20 servings

Ruth Harris, Queen Mother Candy Grammy
The Royal Order of the Yada Yada Red Hatters, Sunrise, Florida

Kentucky Derby Grits

After the meal, there won't be any grits left, as any Southern hostess can tell you. This recipe easily doubles and triples for parties.

3   cups water
1   cup white quick grits
1   teaspoon salt (or more to taste)
4   tablespoons butter, melted

4   eggs, beaten
1   cup milk
1   cup grated sharp cheddar cheese
    Black pepper to taste
    Cayenne pepper to taste

Preheat the oven to 350°. Cook the water, grits, and salt in a saucepan over medium-high heat until slightly thickened. Combine the butter, eggs, milk, cheese, black pepper, and cayenne pepper. Add the grits to the milk mixture. Mix well and pour into a greased 12 x 9-inch glass baking dish. Bake for 30 to 40 minutes, or until golden brown on top and the mixture is set.

Makes 6 to 8 servings

Pam Burke, Queen Mum
Ruby Mermaids, Sanibel, Florida

Rice Pilaf

3   tablespoons butter
1/2   cup minced onion
1/2   cup minced celery
3 1/2 cups (28 ounces) chicken broth
1 1/2 cups long grain rice
1   tablespoon chopped fresh parsley
       (optional)

Preheat the oven to 350°. Melt the butter in a skillet over medium-high heat. Sauté the onion and celery in the butter until tender, about 5 minutes. Transfer to a 1 1/2-quart casserole dish or a 9-inch-square pan. Add the chicken broth and rice. Cover tightly with foil. Bake for 40 minutes. Uncover, sprinkle with the parsley, and bake 10 minutes longer, or until the liquid is absorbed and the rice is tender.

Makes 6 to 8 servings

Jan Hansen, Lady
Wasatch Good Golly Dollys, Holladay, Utah

Brown Rice Pilaf

4   bacon slices
1/2   cup chopped onion
1/2   cup chopped celery
3   cups beef broth
1   cup uncooked brown rice
1/2   cup dry white wine
1/4   cup toasted slivered almonds
1/2   teaspoon salt

Preheat the oven to 350°. In a large skillet cook the bacon until crisp; drain, reserving 2 tablespoons drippings. Crumble the bacon. Cook the onion and celery over medium-high heat in the drippings until tender but not brown. Stir in the broth, rice, wine, almonds, salt, and bacon. Heat to boiling. Transfer to a 1 1/2-quart casserole sprayed with cooking spray. Bake, covered, for 1 hour.

Makes 6 to 8 servings

Peggy Giddens, Queen Mum Peg
Red Hot Red Hat Readers of Decatur, Ten Mile, Tennessee

"Brown" Rice

Beef broth gives the rice its appealing color and delicious aroma.

4   tablespoons butter or margarine, melted
1   medium onion, diced
1   cup rice
1   (10 3/4-ounce) can beef broth
1   (10 3/4-ounce) can beef consommé

Preheat the oven 350°. Coat a 2-quart round glass casserole dish with nonstick cooking spray for easy cleanup. Melt the butter in a skillet over medium heat. Sauté the onion in the butter. Add the rice, broth, and consommé. Cover the casserole dish. Cook for 45 minutes to 1 hour.

Makes 6 to 8 servings

Helen Bates, Hatterett
Rowdy Red Hatters, North Augusta, South Carolina

Savory Heartland Poultry Stuffing

1   pound bulk pork sausage
1   cup chopped onion
1   cup chopped celery
1   loaf crusty (or day-old) bread, torn or cut into cubes
1   teaspoon sage
1   teaspoon poultry seasoning
2   (10 to 14-ounce) cans chicken broth

Preheat the oven to 350°. In a skillet brown the sausage over medium heat until cooked through, breaking up the chunks. Remove the sausage from the skillet with a slotted spoon, leaving the drippings. Sauté the onions and celery in the drippings. Combine the bread with the sausage, onion, celery, drippings, sage, poultry seasoning, and broth in a large bowl. Mix well. (It's okay to use your hands for this; cover them with plastic bags if you like.) Spoon the mixture into a greased 8-inch-square glass baking dish. Bake for 2 hours.

Makes 8 servings

Harriette Milburn, Laughing Mama
Blushing Red Hat Mamas, Des Moines, Iowa

Oysterless Turkey Dressing

Not exactly a picnic to make, but you can guarantee people will love it, and good times will follow. You can make the dressing a day ahead, refrigerate it in the roasting pan overnight, and bake it when ready to serve. If you don't have a roasting pan, use a 13 x 9-inch pan and a 1 1/2-quart casserole dish.

2   turkey wings, roasted until well browned (reserve 1/8 to 1/4 cup drippings)
     Turkey drippings
1   (16-ounce) package sage-flavored bulk pork sausage
1   (16-ounce) package spicy bulk pork sausage
2   medium onions, chopped
1   whole bunch celery, chopped
6   bunches green onions, chopped

2 (8-ounce) packages sliced fresh
mushrooms
1 (8-ounce) package herb bread stuffing
Salt and black pepper to taste
Red pepper flakes to taste
Sage to taste (optional)
2 (14-ounce) cans chicken broth

Put the turkey wings in a pot with enough water to cover and boil until the meat begins to fall off the bones. Remove from the pot, cool, and remove the turkey meat from the bones. Cut the turkey meat into bite-size pieces and return to the broth. You should have about 3 cups of broth.

In a large pot brown the pork sausages over medium heat until no longer pink. Add the onions and celery and cook until the celery begins to soften. Add the green onions and cook until wilted, stirring frequently. Add the mushrooms and cook until tender.

Stir the turkey pieces and their broth into the vegetable mixture. Add some of the turkey drippings. Stir in the stuffing. Allow to sit for 10 to 15 minutes to allow the stuffing to absorb the broth. Add salt and pepper, red pepper flakes, and sage if you like. The dressing should be very wet. If not, add 1 or both cans of chicken broth.

Preheat the oven to 350°. Pour the dressing into a greased medium-size roasting pan. Bake until the top of the dressing is brown.

Makes 10 to 12 servings

Patricia Terrell, Grandame Gadfly
Right Royal Red Hatters, Long Beach, Mississippi

Cranberry Marmalade

Think of this on a nice hot scone . . . mmmmm.

2 medium oranges
1 medium lemon
1 pound cranberries
1 1/2 cups water
1/8 teaspoon baking soda
6 1/2 cups sugar
1/2 (8-ounce) bottle liquid pectin or Certo

Prepare the fruit as follows: Cut the unpeeled oranges and lemon into quarters and remove any seeds. Chop or finely grind the oranges, lemon, and cranberries. (You should have 5 cups of fruit.) In a large pot combine the fruit with the water and baking soda. Bring to a boil and simmer, covered, for 20 minutes, stirring occasionally. Add the sugar and mix well. Over high heat boil hard for 1 minute, stirring constantly. Remove from the heat and stir in the pectin at once. With a metal spoon, ladle off the foam, stir, and skim for 5 minutes. Spoon into hot, sterilized jars, leaving 1/4-inch head space. Top with hot, sterilized lids and rings. Process 5 minutes in a boiling water bath.

Makes 6 pints

Marie Salter, Queen Mother
Women on Wheels, Fredericton, New Brunswick, Canada

My Mom's Homemade Applesauce

Hot or cold, this is delicious. It's even good on toast.

8   Granny Smith apples, peeled, cored, sliced
1   cup sugar
2   or 3 teaspoons cinnamon to taste

Put the apples in a 2 or 3-quart pot and cover with water. Cover the pot and bring to a boil over high heat. Reduce the heat to medium and cook until the apples are soft and smell delicious. Add the sugar and several teaspoons cinnamon. Stir until the apples fall apart into a lumpy sauce. Serve in a pretty glass bowl. Refrigerate leftovers.

Makes about 6 cups

Sara Szydlik, Queen Mum
Hell's Belles in Red, Brackenridge, Pennsylvania

Raise-a-Toast Turkey Dressing

Wine and a lot of eggs give this dressing its sophisticated flavor. The mixture will be thin, but the contributor assures us it firms up with cooking, adding "Don't let it scare you—it's delicious."

Turkey giblets
2   to 3 cups chopped celery
2   to 3 onions, chopped
4   cups white wine (light sauterne is a good choice)
2   pounds bread, cubed
2   cups (4 sticks) butter, melted
12 eggs, lightly beaten
2   tablespoons salt
2   tablespoons poultry seasoning

In a saucepan cover the turkey giblets in water to cover and cook over medium-high heat until the giblets are tender. Cool and chop, reserving some of the cooking liquid. In another saucepan simmer the celery and onions in the wine until tender, about 7 minutes. Pile the bread into a large bowl and add the butter, eggs, salt, poultry seasoning, giblets, onions, celery, and wine. The dressing will be very thin. Stuff part in the turkey and roast for 25 minutes per pound. Pour the remaining stuffing into a greased roasting pan and bake for 1 hour at 350°.

Makes 10 to 12 servings

Note: Halve the recipe for a small turkey or chicken.

Peggie Voorhees, Queen
Red Hat Roundabouters, Port Orchard, Washington

Spiced Cranberry-Orange Sauce

1/2 cup orange juice
1/2 cup water
1   cup sugar
1   (12-ounce) package fresh cranberries
1   tablespoon grated orange peel
1   tablespoon ground cinnamon
5   whole cloves
1   teaspoon nutmeg
2   tablespoons brandy

In a large saucepan combine the orange juice, water, and sugar. Bring to a boil over high heat. Add the cranberries, orange peel, cinnamon, cloves, nutmeg, and brandy. Bring back to a boil, reduce the heat to medium low, and simmer until the cranberries start breaking apart, 15 to 30 minutes.

Makes 8 to 12 servings

Note: The cranberry sauce will thicken as it cools. Refrigerate for 12 hours or more.

Mara Willick, Queen of SASCI
SASCI (Sexy Adventurous Sun City Instigators),
   Henderson, Nevada

Pineapple & Black Bean Salsa

Great as an accompaniment to meats or fish.

3   (15-ounce) cans crushed pineapple in
      heavy syrup
4   (15-ounce) cans black beans, drained and
      rinsed
2   (10-ounce) cans diced tomatoes with lime
      juice and cilantro
3   (14.5-ounce) cans diced tomatoes with
      green chiles
3   garlic cloves, finely minced
2   large white onions, finely chopped
2   cups firmly packed light brown sugar
1/2 cup cider vinegar
2   heaping teaspoons chili powder
1   teaspoon salt

Combine the pineapple, black beans, both diced tomatoes, garlic, onions, brown sugar, vinegar, chili powder, and salt in a heavy, very large kettle. Mix together well and cook over medium-low heat for 3 hours, or until thick.

Makes about 8 pints

Norma Vaughn, Queenie
Red Hat Senior Mamas, Tina, Missouri

Carrot Marmalade

Shred the carrot on the smallest holes of the grater or the cooking time can be quite long, according to testers. The tester had a higher yield than indicated, so have a few extra jars ready in case you do too.

2   pounds carrots, peeled and shredded
1   (20-ounce) can crushed pineapple, well
      drained
7   cups sugar
3/4 cup lemon juice
1   (1 3/4-ounce) box powdered pectin

In a large pot boil the carrots over medium-high heat until tender, about 15 minutes; drain. In a large saucepan combine the carrots with the pineapple, sugar, lemon juice, and pectin. Cook over high heat for 1 minute, or until the syrup is thickened. Skim off the foam and ladle into hot, sterilized jars, leaving 1/4-inch head space. Top with hot, sterile lids and rings. Process the jars in boiling water for 10 minutes.

Makes about 4 pints

Celia Cloud Walker, La Chef de Hattitude
Pink & Purple Pampered Prissies, Dothan, Alabama

Freezer Pickles

Testers declared these to taste quite "oniony"—great if you love pickled onions on a sandwich.

2   quarts sliced cucumbers, about 15 (5-inch) pickling cucumbers
2   medium onions, peeled and sliced
2   tablespoons pickling salt
1 1/2 cups sugar
1   cup cider vinegar
1   teaspoon celery seed

Combine the cucumbers and onions with the salt. Mix well. Cover the bowl and let stand for 3 hours. Rinse the vegetables with cold tap water and drain thoroughly. Mix the sugar, vinegar, and celery seed. Pour the brine over the vegetables, mix, and cover. Refrigerate for at least 8 hours.

Pack the pickles into straight-sided jars. Cover with the brine, leaving 1 inch of head space. Seal. Freeze. Defrost in refrigerator for 8 hours before serving.

Makes 4 pints

Christine Austin, Royal Sunshine
Sassy Squaws of Seminole Lakes, Punta Gorda, Florida

Seven-Day Sweet Pickles

Declared a good recipe by testers, worth all the steps.

7   pounds medium cucumbers
1 1/2 to 2 gallons boiling water
1   quart (4 cups) cider vinegar
8   cups sugar
2   tablespoons salt
    Pickling spices to taste

Wash the cucumbers, leaving them whole; in a large bowl or stone crock, cover them with boiling water. Let stand 24 hours.

On the second, third, and fourth days, drain the water each day. Cover with fresh boiling water.

On the fifth day, drain the cucumbers and cut them into 1/4-inch slices. In a saucepan combine the vinegar, sugar, salt, and spices. Bring to a boil and pour over the sliced cucumbers. Let stand 24 hours.

On the sixth day, drain the syrup into a saucepan. Bring to a boil and pour back over the cucumbers.

On the seventh day, again drain the syrup into a very large pan and bring to a boil. Add the cucumber slices and bring to the boiling point. Pack into hot, sterilized jars; and top with hot, sterilized lids. Seal, then process in a boiling water bath for 20 minutes.

Makes 9 pints

Evelyn Garrett, Milkmaid
Happy Red Hatters of Somerset, Somerset, Kentucky

Green Tomato Jam

A big surprise, said the tester, and a pleasant one. "No one will believe that this jam is based on green tomatoes. Worth the effort."

10   large green tomatoes, washed and cored

5   cups sugar

1   (6-ounce) package raspberry gelatin

Preheat the oven to 350°. Roast the tomatoes until soft then transfer to a blender and process until mushy. You should have about 5 cups pulp. Bring the pulp and sugar to a rolling boil and let boil for 10 minutes. Remove from the stove. Add the gelatin and stir until it is completely dissolved. Spoon the jam into hot, sterilized jars, leaving 1/4-inch headspace and seal with hot, sterilized lids. Process 5 minutes in a boiling water bath.

Makes 8 pints

Lena Caswell, Madam Cracker
Traveling Cooks with Hattitude, Greenfield, Indiana

Pineapple–Kiwi Microwave Jam

The contributor recommends this on toasted English muffins.

4   ripe kiwifruit, peeled and sliced 1/8 to 1/4-inch thick

3   cups sugar

1/4   cup lime juice

1   (8-ounce) can crushed pineapple, undrained

1   (3-ounce) package liquid pectin

3   drops green or yellow food coloring

In a 2-quart microwave-safe bowl, combine the kiwi slices, sugar, lime juice, and pineapple. Microwave on high for 12 to 16 minutes, or until the mixture comes to a full rolling boil; stir every 2 minutes. Mix in the liquid pectin. Microwave on high for 3 to 4 minutes, or until the mixture comes back to a full rolling boil. Remove from the microwave and skim any foam from the top. Stir in the food coloring. Spoon the mixture into hot, sterilized jars, leaving 1/4-inch headspace at the top. Cover with sterile lids and rings. Process 5 minutes in a boiling water bath.

Makes 5 (8-ounce) jars

MJ Lawrence, Duchess of Many Hats
Scarlett Strutters, Carlsbad, New Mexico

Herb Butter

1/2   cup (1 stick) butter, softened
1/2   cup mayonnaise
1/2   teaspoon poultry seasoning
1   tablespoon dried onion flakes
1/4   teaspoon black pepper
1/4   teaspoon garlic salt
1   tablespoon prepared yellow mustard

Combine the butter, mayonnaise, poultry seasoning, onion flakes, pepper, garlic salt, and mustard and mix well. Refrigerate overnight to allow all the flavors to mingle. Spread on your choice of bread (party rye is our favorite) and turkey for a delicious sandwich. Great to use the leftovers after a big turkey dinner.

Makes about 2 cups spread

Peggy Noe, Assistant Queen
Northside Indy Red Hats, Indianapolis, Indiana

~&~ Part III ~&~
—Dinner for One or Two—
Well Worth Making!

We Red Hat Society women value friendship, fun, and frivolity. We also value each other—deeply and sincerely. At Hatquarters we hear often from Red Hatters who extol their chapterettes with such comments as, "No blood sisters could mean more to me."

While we usually acknowledge how much other people mean to us, it seems to be more difficult to acknowledge our own value. Sometimes we might think that treating ourselves with respect is a sign of conceit or self-absorption. But we know better! We know that when you treat yourself as if you are valuable you will absorb some of that "warm fuzzy" stuff. This will increase your self-esteem and your pleasure in living.

So what if it's just you dining by yourself tonight? Why not take a few minutes to prepare something nutritious, tasty and appealing? Pour yourself a glass of wine in a crystal goblet. Set the table attractively. You are worth a bit of extra care. Live the life you have—and live it well!

DESSERT FIRST!

Apple Crunch

A peach, a pear, or 3/4 cup blueberries all substitute nicely for the apple.

1   apple, peeled and sliced
2   tablespoons sugar
1   tablespoon all-purpose flour or oatmeal
1/4 teaspoon cinnamon
1   tablespoon chopped nuts
1   teaspoon butter or margarine, melted

Put the apple into a small, glass casserole dish. In a small bowl combine the sugar, flour or oatmeal, cinnamon, and nuts and mix well. Sprinkle over the apples. Dot with the butter. Microwave, uncovered, on high for 2 to 2½ minutes, or until the apples are tender. Serve with whipped cream if desired.

Makes 1 serving

Vicky Heuer, Countess
Red Hot, Red Hats Too, Park Ridge, Illinois

Bread Pudding for Two

1   cup soft bread crumbs
1   egg
2/3 cup milk
1   tablespoon brown sugar
1   tablespoon butter or margarine, melted
1/2 teaspoon ground cinnamon
1/4 teaspoon ground nutmeg

Dash of salt
1/3 cup raisins
Vanilla ice cream

Preheat the oven to 350°. Place the bread crumbs in a greased 1-quart baking dish. In a bowl whisk together the egg and milk. Stir in the brown sugar, butter, cinnamon, nutmeg, and salt. Pour the mixture over the bread crumbs and sprinkle with the raisins. Bake, uncovered, for 30 to 35 minutes, or until a knife inserted near the center comes out clean. Serve warm with the ice cream.

Makes 2 servings

Mary R. Roddy, Duchess of Corpus
Sister Hood, Corpus Christi, Texas

Little Lemon Meringue Pies

"My husband thinks he is in 'hog heaven' when I make these," says the contributor.

CRUST
1/3 cup all-purpose flour
1/8 teaspoon salt
1   tablespoon shortening
1   tablespoon cold butter (no substitutes)
1   teaspoon cold water

FILLING
1/3 cup sugar
1   tablespoon cornstarch

1/8   teaspoon salt

1/2   cup cold water

1   egg yolk, beaten

2   tablespoons lemon juice

1   tablespoon butter

MERINGUE

1   egg white

1/8   teaspoon cream of tartar

2   tablespoons sugar

For the crust, preheat the oven to 425°. Combine in a bowl the flour and salt; cut in the shortening and butter until crumbly. Gradually add the water, tossing with a fork until the dough forms a ball. Divide the dough in half. Roll each portion into a 5-inch circle. Transfer to two 10-ounce custard cups. Press the dough 1 1/8 inches up the sides of the cups. Place on a baking sheet. Bake for 7 to 10 minutes, or until golden brown.

For the filling, combine in a saucepan the sugar, cornstarch, and salt. Gradually stir in the cold water until smooth. Cook and stir over medium heat until thickened and bubbly. Reduce the heat; cook and stir 2 minutes more. Remove from the heat. Stir half the hot filling into the egg yolk; return all to the pan. Bring to a gentle boil; cook and stir for 2 minutes. Remove from the heat; stir in the lemon juice and butter. Pour the mixture into the pastry shells.

Reduce the oven temperature to 350°.

For the meringue, beat the egg white and cream of tartar in a small mixing bowl on medium speed until soft peaks form. Gradually beat in the sugar, 1 tablespoon at a time, on high until stiff peaks form. Spread the meringue evenly over the hot filling, sealing edges to the crust. Bake for 15 to 20 minutes, or until the meringue is golden brown. Cool on a wire rack for 1 hour. Refrigerate for at least 3 hours before serving.

Makes 2 pies

Carol Thompson, Contessa of Loquacious
Rowdy Red Hat Mamas, Frederic, Wisconsin

Baked Pear

1   pear

1/2   to 1 teaspoon turbinado (or raw sugar) or brown sugar

1/4   teaspoon butter
       Pinch of powdered ginger

Preheat the oven to 350°. Peel the pear and cut into slices. Arrange in a small greased baking dish. Sprinkle with the sugar and dot with butter. Top with the ginger. Bake for about 20 minutes.

Makes 2 servings

Laurie L. Anderson, Queen Mum Hannah
Visions in Red, Eagan, Minnesota

Chilled Strawberry Cream

Lightly sweetened strawberries and cream are simply delicious together, and pretty enough for a special occasion.

2 cups frozen unsweetened whole strawberries, thawed
1/4 cup confectioners' sugar
1/2 cup heavy whipping cream

Combine the strawberries and sugar in a food processor or blender; cover and process until finely chopped. In a small mixing bowl beat the cream until stiff peaks form. Fold into the berries. Pour into serving dishes. Refrigerate or freeze for 25 minutes.

Makes 2 servings

Joyce Lauer, Princess Laffing Hatter
Ms. Aster's Disasters, Corpus Christi, Texas

BREAD AND BRUNCH

Apple Oven Pancake

For breakfast, brunch, or lunch, try this light, puffy pancake topped with a spicy apple jelly sauce.

PANCAKE
2 large eggs
1 tablespoon butter, melted
1/2 cup all-purpose flour
1/8 teaspoon salt
1/2 cup milk

APPLE TOPPING
1 medium Granny Smith apple, peeled and finely chopped
1/2 cup apple jelly
1/4 teaspoon cinnamon
1/8 teaspoon nutmeg

Preheat the oven to 400°. For the pancake, beat the eggs for 3 minutes in a mixing bowl until thick and lemon colored. Stir in the melted butter. In another bowl whisk together the flour and salt. Add to the egg mixture along with the milk. Pour into a greased, 8-inch round baking pan. Bake for 20 to 25 minutes, or until lightly browned.

For the topping, combine the apple, jelly, cinnamon, and nutmeg in a saucepan. Cook, stirring, over medium heat until the jelly is melted. Pour into a serving boat. Cut the pancake into four wedges. Place two pieces on each plate. Top with the apple mixture.

Makes 2 servings

Carolyn Gass Hardimon, The Recipe Lady
Recipe Ladies, Belleville, Illinois

Migas for One

1/4 to 1/2 small onion, chopped
1 teaspoon vegetable oil
3 corn tortillas, cut into bite-size pieces
1 egg, lightly beaten
Salt to taste
1/4 cup shredded cheddar cheese
Salsa or picante sauce

In a small skillet sauté the onion in the oil over medium heat until tender. Add the tortillas and sauté until the tortillas soften. Add the egg and salt. Add the cheese and cook, stirring, until the egg is cooked and the cheese is melted. Remove from heat and serve with salsa or picante sauce.

Sandra Morales, The Traveling Contessa
New Braunfels Colleens, Wimberley, Texas

Crunchy-Top Coffee Cake

Tender cake and crunchy topping in just the right proportions for two servings.

CAKE
1 cup baking mix
1 tablespoon granulated sugar
1 egg
1/3 cup milk
1/4 cup finely chopped dried fruit (apricots, cherries, cranberries, or peaches)

TOPPING
3 tablespoons baking mix
2 tablespoons brown sugar
1/4 teaspoon ground cinnamon
2 tablespoons chopped pecans
1 tablespoon butter

Preheat the oven to 350°. Grease a 5-inch round baking dish or two 8-ounce custard cups. For the cake, stir together the baking mix and granulated sugar in a bowl. In another bowl beat the egg with the milk. Stir the dry ingredients into the liquid ingredients just to combine. Fold in the dried fruit and pour into prepared pan.

For the topping, combine the baking mix, brown sugar, cinnamon, and pecans in a bowl. Cut in the butter with a pastry blender until the mixture is crumbly. Sprinkle evenly over the cake batter. Bake for 15 minutes, or until a toothpick inserted in the center comes out clean. Let stand for 5 minutes before serving.

Makes 2 servings

Sarah Carolyn Hardimon, The Creative Gourmet
Belleville Elegant Swans, Belleville, Illinois

Oven Puff Pancake

Make sure the butter gets really hot so the pancake puffs up. You can fill the center with jam or fruit or even creamed meat or vegetables.

2	tablespoons butter
1	egg
1/4	cup all-purpose flour
1/4	cup milk
1/4	teaspoon salt
	Lemon juice
	Confectioners' sugar

Preheat the oven to 425°. Melt the butter in an 8-inch skillet with an ovenproof handle or a pie plate. In a small bowl beat the egg with the flour, milk, and salt. Pour the egg mixture into the hot butter. Bake for 25 minutes. Squeeze a little lemon juice over the puff and sprinkle with the confectioners' sugar.

Makes 1 serving

Mary Louise Moore, Queen Mama
Fayette-Greene Mama Mia's, Uniontown, Pennsylvania

Prunacolada

If you drink prune juice every day, use this idea from a fellow hatter to shake up its flavor.

1	cup (or less) prune juice
1	shot piña colada drink mix

Combine the prune juice and piña colada mix in a drinking glass and mix well.

Makes 1 drink

Barbara Tiffany, Queen Mother
La Tea Dolls, Somerset, Pennsylvania

Broccoli Ham Muffins

A real help for single queens living alone. Grab one from the freezer on the way out the door any time you don't have time for a meal. They're also a good side dish for soup or salad.

11/2	cups chopped cooked broccoli or 10 ounces thawed frozen broccoli
11/2	cups chopped cooked ham
1	medium onion, chopped
1/2	cup grated cheddar cheese
6	eggs
1/2	cup vegetable oil
1/4	cup all-purpose flour
1	tablespoon baking powder
1	teaspoon oregano
1	teaspoon parsley
1/2	teaspoon salt
1/4	teaspoon thyme
1/4	teaspoon garlic powder

Preheat the oven to 375°. In a large bowl combine the broccoli, ham, onion, and cheese. Mix well. In another bowl beat the eggs until foamy. Add the oil, flour, baking powder, oregano, parsley, salt, thyme, and garlic powder. Beat until smooth. Stir into the broccoli mixture and mix just until blended. Spoon the mixture into greased muffin tins, filling them about two-thirds full. Do not use paper liners because the muffins will stick.

Bake for 20 to 25 minutes, or until golden.

Makes 12 to 15 large muffins

Evelyn Sharman, Queen
Mad Hatters of Saskatoon, Saskatoon, Saskatchewan, Canada

PeachRazNana Smoothie

Not a big breakfast eater? A shake might be just right in the morning.

1   (81/2-ounce) can juice-packed peaches, chilled
1   peeled banana
1/4   cup nonfat dry milk
1   (8-ounce) container vanilla yogurt
1   teaspoon vanilla extract
1/4   cup frozen or fresh raspberries
      Dash of nutmeg
1/4   to 1/2 cup milk
2   ice cubes

In a blender combine the peaches, banana, dry milk, yogurt, vanilla, raspberries, nutmeg, milk, and ice cubes. Cover and blend. Use strawberries instead of raspberries if desired.

Makes 1 serving

Laurie L. Anderson, Queen Mum Hannah
Visions in Red, Eagan, Minnesota

Southern-Style Corn Sticks

If you don't have a cornstick pan (a cast-iron baking pan with corn molds), try muffin cups or ramekins.

1/4   cup all-purpose flour
1/4   cup yellow cornmeal
1/2   teaspoon baking powder
1/8   teaspoon salt
2   teaspoons sugar
1/4   cup skim milk
11/2   teaspoons vegetable oil
1   egg white, lightly beaten

Preheat the oven to 425°. Coat four molds of a cast-iron cornstick pan with nonstick cooking spray, and place in the oven for 3 minutes, or until hot. In a small bowl combine the flour, cornmeal, baking powder, salt, and sugar. Make a well in the center of the mixture. In another bowl combine the milk, oil, and egg white; add to the dry ingredients, stirring just until ingredients are moistened. Remove the pan from the oven, and spoon the batter evenly into four molds, filling each three-fourths full. Bake for 14 minutes, or until golden.

Makes 4 corn sticks

Joan Collier, Empress Jo-So-Fine
The Red Hat Hotties, Franklin, Tennessee

Sour Cream Muffins

1   cup self-rising flour
1/2 cup (1 stick) butter, melted
1/2 cup sour cream

Preheat the oven to 350°. Combine the flour, butter, and sour cream and spoon the mixture into small, ungreased muffin tins. Bake for 20 to 30 minutes.

Makes 4 muffins

Joyce Barkel, Queen Mudder
Fun Lovin' Ladies, Zeeland, Michigan

Baja Turkey Wrap

A great light supper that makes something new of turkey cold cuts. Burrito veterans can probably manage eating this by hand, but you may have to resort to a fork.

1/4 cup guacamole
1/4 cup salsa
     Soft flour tortilla
2   to 3 turkey slices
2   bacon slices, cooked
     Lettuce
2   slices tomato
     Sour cream

Spread the guacamole and salsa on one side of the tortilla. Top with the turkey, bacon, lettuce, and tomato. Fold one side over the filling; then roll to enclose. Top with more guacamole and salsa and some sour cream. Eat with a fork.

Makes 1 serving

Betsy Sprenkle, Queen
Nipomo Nifties, Nipomo, California

WARM AND COZY, COOL AND CRISP

Sweet Potato Soup for Two

This pretty orange soup is packed with Vitamin A and beta-carotene. And it's a cozy soup for dinner with your "sweet potato." Add a dusting of nutmeg, testers recommended.

1   tablespoon butter
1/4 cup diced onion
1 1/2 tablespoons all-purpose flour
1   (14-ounce) can low-sodium chicken broth

1/2 cup dry white wine
1   large sweet potato, peeled and diced
1/2 teaspoon ground ginger
1/2 teaspoon salt
2/3 cup evaporated milk
1   tablespoon lime juice
2   tablespoons dried cranberries
     Lime wedges for garnish

Melt the butter in a medium saucepan over medium heat and sauté the onion until tender.

Sprinkle the flour over the onion and cook over low heat, stirring, for 1 minute. Gradually add the chicken broth and wine, stirring until smooth. Cook over medium heat, stirring constantly until the mixture is thick and bubbly. Stir in the sweet potato, ginger, and salt. Reduce the heat and simmer, uncovered, for 30 minutes, or until the potato is tender. Stir in the milk. Transfer the mixture to a blender, add the lime juice, and process until smooth. Ladle into two soup bowls and top each with 1 tablespoon dried cranberries. Serve with a slice of lime.

Makes 2 servings

Jane Speer, Vice QM
Vintage Roses, Warner Robins, Georgia

Shrimp Bisque

Made with reduced-sodium bouillon, a 1-cup serving has 325 calories, 24 grams fat, 180 milligrams cholesterol, 201 milligrams sodium, and 11 grams carbohydrate.

1/2 cup chopped onion
2   garlic cloves, minced
1   tablespoon olive oil
1   tablespoon all-purpose flour
1   cup water
1/2 cup heavy whipping cream
1   tablespoon chili powder
2   teaspoons chicken bouillon granules
1/2 teaspoon ground cumin
1/2 teaspoon ground coriander

1/2 **pound medium shrimp, peeled and deveined**
1/2 **cup sour cream**
     Fresh cilantro for garnish (optional)

In a large saucepan over medium-high heat, sauté the onion and garlic in the oil until tender. Stir in the flour and mix until no streaks of dry flour remain. Stir in the water, cream, chili powder, bouillon, cumin, and coriander. Bring to a boil. Reduce the heat to medium low, cover, and simmer for 5 minutes.

Cut the shrimp into bite-size pieces and add to the soup. Simmer 5 minutes longer, or until the shrimp turn pink. Gradually stir 1/2 cup of the hot soup into the sour cream; then return all to the pan, stirring constantly. Heat through, but do not boil. Garnish with the cilantro if desired.

Makes 3 cups

Jo McKeown, Queen Mum
Forever Young, The Villages, Florida

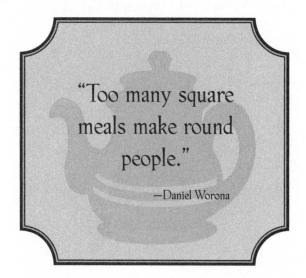

"Too many square meals make round people."

—Daniel Worona

Orange & Bermuda Onion Salad

SALAD
1 orange, peeled
1 Bermuda onion

RUBY RED DRESSING
1/2 cup currant jelly
1/4 cup vegetable oil
2 tablespoons lemon juice
Dash of salt
Few drops of onion juice

For the salad, cut the orange into rounds. Slice the onion paper thin. Alternate the slices of orange and onion on a salad plate.

For the dressing, beat the jelly with a fork until smooth. Add the oil, lemon juice, salt, and onion juice. Beat again until smooth. Pour dressing over salad. Refrigerate any leftover dressing.

Makes 3/4 cup

Margie Nolan Cowles, Mistress Margie Lady in Waiting
The Virginia Vamps, Richmond, Virginia

Fish Chowder

Thick, hearty soup for one hungry person, maybe two as an appetizer. A perfect little meal when served with buttered French or sourdough bread, green salad, and a glass of white wine.

6 ounces fresh fish fillet, cut into 1-inch chunks
1 potato, peeled and cubed
1/4 medium onion, diced
1/4 teaspoon garlic salt
Salt and pepper to taste
Water to cover
1 cup whole milk
2 tablespoons minced fresh parsley or 2 teaspoons dried parsley
2 tablespoons chopped fresh or 2 teaspoons dried chives

In a saucepan combine the fish, potato, onion, garlic salt, and salt and pepper. Pour in enough water to cover and bring to a boil over high heat. Reduce the heat to medium and simmer, covered, for 20 minutes, or until the potatoes are tender. Add the milk, parsley, and chives and bring back to a simmer for 3 minutes.

Makes 1 to 2 servings

Lucinda Denton, Founding Queen Mother
Nonpareils, Knoxville, Tennessee

Italian Tomato Soup for Two

1   tablespoon butter
2   celery stalks, diced
1/2 onion, chopped
1/2 green bell pepper, diced
1   (14-ounce) can chicken broth
1   (28-ounce) can stewed tomatoes, crushed
1   teaspoon basil
1   teaspoon oregano
    Salt and pepper to taste

Heat the butter in a skillet over medium-high heat and sauté the celery, onion, and bell pepper until soft. Combine the broth and tomatoes in a saucepan. Add the sautéed vegetables, basil, oregano, and salt and pepper. Heat through.

Makes 2 servings

Note: Brown 1/2 pound ground beef and add along with 1/2 cup small pasta shapes, for a hearty soup.

Toni Garman, Queen Mum
Red Hat Honeys, Spokane, Washington

SINGLE SUPPERS AND DOUBLE DINNERS

Slow-Cooker Stew for Two

Our contributor calls her stew "She's Out Shopping Supper" because it's handy for the days when her calendar is full of Red Hatting.

1   pound stew beef or venison
1   small onion, diced
6   small potatoes, diced
2   carrots, sliced
1   (10³/4-ounce) can beef broth
1   (10³/4-ounce) can chicken rice soup
1   tablespoon vegetable oil
    Salt and pepper to taste
1   teaspoon seasoned salt

Combine the beef, onion, potatoes, carrots, broth, soup, oil, salt and pepper, and the seasoned salt in a slow cooker. Cook for about 8 hours on low or 4 hours on high. Serve with hot rolls.

Makes 2 to 4 servings

Linda Glenn, Mistress of Mischief & Merriment
Rowdy Red Hat Mamas of N.W. Wisconsin, Luck, Wisconsin

Soy-Sizzled Sirloin Strips

The flavor of Chinese-American cooking, minus most of the chopping.

2   tablespoons butter
3/4 pound sirloin steak (1/2-inch thick), cut into 2-inch by 1/2-inch strips
2   tablespoons soy sauce
1 1/2 cups chopped celery
1   tablespoon cornstarch
    Hot rice

Heat the butter in a large skillet over high heat and brown the steak strips on all sides very briefly, about 2 minutes. Combine the soy sauce with enough water to measure 1/8 cup. Add to the meat along with the celery. Simmer, covered, until the meat and celery are tender. Blend the cornstarch with 2 tablespoons water until smooth. Gradually add to the meat mixture and cook, stirring, until thickened and glossy. Serve over hot rice.

Makes 2 servings

Susie Courington, Queen
The Crimson Jewels, The Woodlands, Texas

Ground Beef Mix

Make one mixture and use it for several dinners. A hatter-developed recipe turns into four different mini meals.

2   eggs
1/4 cup ketchup

1/4 cup water
1/2 cup minced onion
1   tablespoon Worcestershire sauce
1   teaspoon salt
1   cup soft breadcrumbs, lightly packed
1   pound lean ground beef

In a large bowl beat the eggs. Blend in the ketchup, water, onion, Worcestershire sauce, and salt. Mix in the bread crumbs. Add the ground beef and mix with a fork. Divide into four, single-serving portions. Place the portions in plastic bags or containers and freeze. Thaw or defrost in the microwave to use in the following recipes.

Makes 4 portions

Linda Roberts, Queen of Queries
Nonpareils, Knoxville, Tennessee

Meatballs for One

1   portion Ground Beef Mix, see above

Preheat the oven to 400°. Shape the beef mix into 1-inch meatballs. Arrange on a shallow baking sheet and bake for 15 minutes.

Makes 1 serving

Note: To freeze cooked meatballs, place in a plastic bag and squeeze the air out.

Linda Roberts, Queen of Queries
Nonpareils, Knoxville, Tennessee

Spaghetti and Meatballs for One

4   ounces spaghetti
2   cooked meatballs
1   cup spaghetti sauce
1/2 cup sliced mushrooms (optional)
    Minced garlic to taste (optional)

Cook the spaghetti according to the package directions. Drain. Combine the meatballs and spaghetti sauce in a saucepan over medium heat. Add the mushrooms and minced garlic if desired. Cook for 5 minutes to heat through. Pour over the spaghetti.

Makes 1 serving

Linda Roberts, Queen of Queries
Nonpareils, Knoxville, Tennessee

Meatloaf in a Mug

Meatloaf for one and no pan to wash—another innovation for solo queens.

1/4 pound ground beef
2   tablespoons oatmeal
2   teaspoons milk
1   tablespoon ketchup
1   teaspoon dry onion mix or minced onion

In a medium bowl combine the beef, oatmeal, milk, ketchup, and onion. Pack the mixture into a microwave-safe coffee mug. With the handle of a wooden spoon, make a hole in the center of the meat mixture. Microwave for 6 to 10 minutes on 50 percent power. Drain and let rest for 2 minutes.

Makes 1 serving

Kathryn Neidy, Madam Red Purse
Feathered Red Hatters of NE Iowa, Independence, Iowa

Cube Steak and Potatoes for Two

2   tablespoons olive oil
2   (8-ounce) cube steaks
2   large potatoes, cut into thin slices
3   tablespoons butter or margarine, divided
2   onions, cut into thin slices
    Salt and pepper to taste

Preheat the oven to 400°. Heat the oil in a skillet over high heat. Brown the cube steaks in the oil. Grease a large sheet of aluminum foil, and arrange the cube steaks in the center. Arrange 1 sliced potato over the steaks. Dot with 1 tablespoon butter. Arrange the onions over the potatoes and steak. Dot with 1 tablespoon butter. Arrange the remaining potatoes on the onions. Dot with the remaining 1 tablespoon butter. Season with salt and pepper. Fold the foil and seal to enclose the steaks. Wrap the package in a second piece of foil. Bake (or grill on a medium hot grill) for 40 minutes.

Makes 2 servings

Joyce Dillow, Queen Mother
Red Hot Rockettes, Florissant, Missouri

Stuffed Peppers

1   large green bell pepper
1   portion Ground Beef Mix (see page 536)
1/4 cup tomato or spaghetti sauce

Preheat the oven to 350°. Trim a small slice from the bottom of the pepper if needed so it stands level. Cut the top from the pepper and remove all seeds and white membranes. In a small saucepan over medium-high heat, combine the pepper and enough water to cover. Cook for 5 minutes. Drain and fill the pepper with the beef mix. Place in a 10-ounce custard cup or pot-pie pan. Top with the spaghetti sauce. Bake for 40 minutes.

Makes 1 serving

Note: To freeze before baking, cool the green pepper and fill. Place in a foil pan, add sauce, and wrap in foil.

Linda Roberts, Queen of Queries
Nonpareils, Knoxville, Tennessee

Green Bean & Ground Beef Casserole

1/2 pound ground beef
1   (8-ounce) can green beans, drained
1/2 (10 3/4-ounce) can tomato soup
     Salt and pepper to taste
2   large potatoes, peeled, quartered, and cooked
2   slices cheese (optional)

Preheat the oven to 300°. In a skillet over medium-high heat, brown the ground beef and drain. Transfer to a 1-quart baking dish. Add the green beans, soup, and salt and pepper and mix well. Mash the potatoes, and spoon them over the beef mixture. Top with the cheese. Bake for 25 minutes.

Makes 2 servings

Joyce Dillow, Queen Mother
Red Hot Rockettes, Florissant, Missouri

Individual Meat Loaf

2   tablespoons ketchup
1   teaspoon brown sugar
1/2 teaspoon prepared mustard
1   portion Ground Beef Mix (see page 536)

Preheat the oven to 350°. Combine the ketchup, brown sugar, and mustard in a bowl and mix. Shape the beef mix into a small loaf. Place in a small, shallow baking dish and cover with the ketchup sauce. Bake for about 30 minutes, or until cooked through.

Makes 1 serving

Note: To freeze the loaf before baking, wrap it in foil without the sauce.

Linda Roberts, Founding Queen Mother
Nonpareils, Knoxville, Tennessee

Stuffed Zucchini

This recipe can be halved for one person or smaller appetites.

2   large zucchini
1/2 pound ground beef
1/4 cup mayonnaise
2   teaspoon dehydrated onion flakes
2   teaspoons dried parsley
1   teaspoon dried oregano
1   teaspoon lemon juice
1   teaspoon salt
1/4 teaspoon black pepper
2/3 cup spaghetti sauce

Preheat the oven to 350°. Cut the zucchini into half lengthwise and scoop out the centers, leaving a 1/4-inch shell. Arrange in a shallow baking dish. Coarsely chop the scooped-out flesh. In a bowl combine the chopped zucchini with the beef, mayonnaise, onion flakes, parsley, oregano, lemon juice, salt, and pepper. Spoon the mixture into the zucchini shells and top with the spaghetti sauce. Bake for 30 minutes.

Makes 1 to 2 servings

Barbara Nilson, Queen Mum
Red Hat Hussies, Renton, Washington

Pan-Fried Liver with Thyme

Use either calf's liver or lamb's liver for this easy, low-fat entrée.

2   slices liver
1   tablespoon all-purpose flour
     Salt and pepper to taste
1   teaspoon vegetable oil
1   tablespoon butter or margarine
2   tablespoons white wine
1/2 teaspoon chopped fresh thyme or large pinch of dried thyme
     Pinch of lemon zest
2   teaspoons lemon juice
1   teaspoon drained capers
1   to 2 tablespoons light cream (optional)

Trim the liver if necessary and toss it with the flour and salt and pepper until evenly coated. Heat the oil and butter in a skillet over medium heat. When the oil is foaming, add the liver and cook for 2 to 3 minutes on each side until well seared and just barely cooked through. Take care not to overcook or the liver will become tough and hard. Transfer the liver to a plate and keep warm. Add the wine to the pan juices along with 1 tablespoon water, the thyme, lemon zest, lemon juice, and capers and heat until bubbling. Add the cream and reheat gently. Adjust the seasoning to taste and spoon the sauce over the liver.

Makes 1 serving

Norma Washington, Queen
The Precious Red Crowns and Brims, Tallahassee, Florida

Mini Meat Loaf for Two

3/4 pound ground beef
1 medium banana, mashed
2 tablespoons finely chopped onion
2 teaspoons prepared mustard
3/4 to 1 cup dry bread crumbs or crushed cornflakes
1 teaspoon salt
Dash of pepper, optional

Preheat the oven to 350°. In a large bowl combine the beef, banana, onion, mustard, breadcrumbs, and salt and pepper to taste and mix well. Add more crumbs if necessary to hold the meat together just enough to shape into a small loaf. Place in an open roasting pan or baking dish. Bake for 45 to 50 minutes.

Makes 2 to 3 servings

Note: To use a food processor, mash the banana first and then add the remaining ingredients using an "off and on" method until it forms a ball.

Betty Lupton, Red Hottie Betty
Sexy Broads, Grass Valley, California

Baked Pork Chops with Apples

1 tablespoon vegetable oil
1/2 teaspoon seasoned salt
2 thick-cut pork chops
1 small onion, chopped
2 apples, any kind will work

1/2 cup warm water
1/2 teaspoon yellow mustard
2 tablespoons brown sugar
1/4 teaspoon ground cloves

Lightly grease a 1-quart baking dish. Heat the oil in a skillet over medium-high heat. Add the seasoned salt and cook the pork chops and onion in the hot oil for 5 minutes, turning the pork chops once. Place the browned pork chops into the prepared baking dish. Preheat the oven to 375°. Peel, core, and slice the apples and layer them on top of the pork chops. Mix together the warm water, mustard, brown sugar, and cloves. Pour the mixture over the pork chops and apples. Bake, covered, for about 45 minutes. Uncover and continue baking for 15 to 20 minutes. Wonderful served with white rice.

Makes 2 servings

Linda Glenn, Mistress of Mischief & Merriment
Rowdy Red Hat Mamas of N.W. Wisconsin, Luck, Wisconsin

Ham 'n' Cheese Mashed Potatoes

Make a meal from leftover mashed potatoes, or use those wonderful, frozen mashed potatoes for a real shortcut.

1 cup mashed potatoes
2/3 teaspoon garlic salt
1/2 cup diced cooked ham
1/2 cup (4 ounces) shredded cheddar cheese
1/4 cup whipping cream, whipped

Preheat the oven to 450°. In a bowl combine the potatoes and garlic salt. Spread into a greased 1 quart baking dish. Sprinkle with the ham. Fold the cheese into the whipped cream and then spoon the mixture over the ham. Bake, uncovered, for 15 minutes, or until golden brown.

Makes 2 to 3 servings

Joyce Barkel, Queen Mudder
Fun Lovin' Ladies, Zeeland, Michigan

Almond-Crusted Chicken with Caramelized Pear and Brie Cream Sauce

You can double the amount of chicken; there will be plenty of sauce to cover it. Serve with mushroom risotto and a leafy green salad.

FOR THE PEARS
1/2   cup balsamic vinegar
2   tablespoons brown sugar
1   whole pear, peeled, sliced in half lengthwise, core removed

FOR THE CHICKEN
2   (6-ounce) skinless, boneless chicken breast halves
1/2   cup chopped toasted almonds
1   tablespoon garlic butter

FOR THE SAUCE
2   tablespoons butter
2   tablespoons all-purpose flour

1/4   cup dry white wine
1   cup heavy cream
2   tablespoons chopped Brie cheese (or Gorgonzola or crumbled goat cheese)

Prepare the pears one day ahead of time by combining the balsamic vinegar and brown sugar in a saucepan over medium heat. Simmer the pear halves for about 5 minutes per side, or until tender but not mushy. Transfer the pear halves to a bowl, cover with plastic wrap, and refrigerate until needed.

Preheat oven to 350°. To prepare the chicken, line a roasting pan with parchment paper. Roll the chicken breasts in the almonds and arrange on the roasting pan. Dot each chicken breast with the garlic butter. Bake for 15 minutes, or until the chicken is cooked through. Warm the poached pear halves in the oven for about 5 minutes.

For the sauce, melt the butter in a saucepan over medium heat. Whisk in the flour; cook, stirring, to make a light-brown roux. Add the wine and cream and simmer until thickened, whisking constantly. Finally, add the cheese and cook, stirring, to melt the cheese into the sauce.

To assemble the dish, place the chicken on a plate. Top with the sauce and halved poached pear.

Makes 2 servings

Arvilla Shouldice, Empress of Elegant Red Hattin' Grandmas
Positively Meno-Positive, Ottawa, Ontario, Canada

Tropical Pork Chops

1   firm banana
1   teaspoon plus 1 teaspoon vegetable oil
2   lean pork chops, cut 1/2-inch thick
1   garlic clove, finely chopped
1/4   teaspoon ground ginger
2   tablespoons raspberry jelly or honey
2   teaspoons prepared mustard
1/2   cup water

Cut the banana in half crosswise, then length-wise into four pieces. Heat 1 teaspoon oil in a nonstick skillet over medium heat. Sauté the banana in the oil until browned, adding more oil if needed. Transfer the browned bananas to a warm plate. Rub the pork chops with the garlic and ginger. Add the remaining 1 teaspoon oil to the skillet. Brown the chops on both sides and transfer to a warm platter. Melt the jelly or honey in the skillet; add the mustard and water. Stir to blend. Return the chops to the skillet; spoon the sauce over them. Cover and simmer for 8 to 10 minutes, or until thoroughly cooked. Transfer the pork chops to dinner plates and top with the bananas. Spoon the remaining sauce from the skillet over the pork chops. Serve with green and yellow beans. Garnish with raspberries and thyme if desired.

Makes 2 servings

Vicky Millwood, Chapterette
Girls of the Pearl, Whitmire, South Carolina

Simple Cordon Blue

This is a simple, tasty, not-breaded Cordon Blue. The recipe can easily be adapted to serve as many people as you like.

1   tablespoon vegetable oil
1   (4-ounce) skinless, boneless chicken breast
1   ounce thinly sliced deli ham
1   slice baby Swiss or Asiago cheese
2   tablespoons blue cheese dressing

Heat the oil in a skillet over medium heat. When hot, brown the chicken breast on both sides. Reduce the heat to low, cover the skillet, and cook for about 10 minutes, turning once. Butterfly the chicken breast by slicing it not quite completely through horizontally, so you can open it like a book. (If the meat is not cooked completely, place the "inside" of the breast on the skillet, cover, and cook a 2 to 3 more minutes, or until thoroughly done but not dry.) Place the ham on one-half of the chicken breast. Place the cheese on top of the ham and fold the other half of the chicken breast over the ham and cheese. Drizzle the blue cheese dressing over the top. Return the chicken to the skillet, cover, and cook for an additional 5 minutes, or until the ham is warmed and the cheese is melted.

Makes 1 serving

Mare McKim, Crimson Queen Mare
Canyon Country Crimson Cappers, Hatch, Utah

Lemon Chicken Pilaf

1 tablespoon butter or vegetable oil

1/3 cup regular uncooked rice

1 skinless, boneless chicken breast half, chopped

1/2 cup diced onion

1/2 cup diced green bell pepper

2/3 cup chicken broth, water, or white wine

1 tablespoon lemon juice

1 teaspoon dried basil (optional)

In a skillet with a tight-fitting lid, heat the butter or oil over medium-high heat. Add the rice to the hot oil and stir until all the grains are coated. Add the chicken, onion, pepper, broth, lemon juice, and basil. Mix well. Cover, reduce the heat to low, and cook for 15 minutes. No peeking. Turn off the heat and let the covered pan stand for another 5 minutes before serving.

Makes 1 serving

Note: Other vegetables such as sliced tomatoes, beans, or even olives can also be used to vary the dish.

Linda Roberts, Queen of Queries
Nonpareils, Knoxville, Tennessee

Turkey Piccata for Two

Puckery with lots of lemon, this is one easy dish with gourmet flavor.

2 lemons

1/3 cup all-purpose flour

1/2 teaspoon salt

1/2 teaspoon freshly ground black pepper

2 turkey cutlets (about 1/2 pound)

1 teaspoon olive oil

1 garlic clove, minced

1/4 cup chicken broth

1/2 tablespoon drained capers

1 teaspoon butter

Cut the peel and white pith from the lemons and discard. Cut the lemon segments from the surrounding membranes. Chop the segments coarsely and reserve with the juice. Combine the flour, salt, and pepper in a shallow dish. Lightly coat the cutlets with the flour mixture, shaking off the excess. Heat the oil in a large skillet over medium-high heat and sauté the cutlets until the outside is golden brown and the interior is no longer pink, 2 to 3 minutes per side. Transfer to a plate and cover to keep warm. Add the garlic to the skillet and cook, stirring, for several seconds. Pour in the chicken broth and bring to a boil. Cook for 1 minute. Add the lemon segments, reserved lemon juice, and capers and cook 30 more seconds. Add the butter, swirling the skillet to melt and blend in. Spoon the sauce over the turkey.

Makes 2 servings

Linda Roberts, Queen of Queries
Nonpareils, Knoxville, Tennessee

Honey Mustard Chicken

1   cup honey
1/4 cup prepared yellow mustard
1   to 2 boneless, skinless chicken breast
    halves, cut in half

In a medium nonstick skillet over medium-high heat, combine the honey and mustard and mix well. Adjust the amounts to taste. Add the chicken and let the sauce come to a boil. Reduce the heat to medium and cook uncovered for 15 minutes, turning the chicken every few minutes for even browning. As the honey caramelizes the sauce will thicken and the chicken will start getting a golden-brown look.

Makes 1 serving

Martha Caldwell, Duchess of Pastry
Red Hat Ramblers, Hollywood, Florida

Simple Asian-Style Chicken or Chop

You could also make the chop with conventional milk, all-purpose flour, and saltines, for a more traditional flavor. Serve with a baked sweet potato and a green salad or vegetable.

1/4 cup unsweetened soymilk
1/4 cup soy flour or ground garbanzo beans
1   large egg, beaten
1/2 cup crushed rice crackers (try flavored ones such as tamari-seaweed)
1   tablespoon peanut or other cooking oil

    (not olive oil)
2   (4 to 6-ounce) butterfly pork chops
1   to 2 tablespoons duck sauce or sweet and sour sauce

Near the stove set out four plates or shallow bowls big enough to hold a single chicken breast or pork chop. Arrange the ingredients in the plates in this order: soymilk, flour, egg, cracker crumbs. Heat the oil in a saucepan over medium-high heat. Place a pork chop in the soymilk and turn to coat. Press into the flour, shaking off the excess. Dip into the beaten egg and turn to coat evenly and then roll in the cracker crumbs, pressing so they adhere. Place the pork chop in the hot oil. Repeat the process with the remaining pork chop. Sauté the pork chops until light golden brown on each side and reduce the heat to low. Cook just until no longer pink in the center. Just before serving, spoon the duck sauce or sweet and sour sauce over the chops and heat until the sauce is warm.

Makes 2 servings

Dot Boutwell, Fairy Queen of Delirious Delight
Fairy Mad Hatters, Wichita, Kansas

Korean-Style Chicken in a Lettuce Leaf

A "hands on" meal for two. This recipe can be adapted easily to serve more people and is just right with a bowl of won ton or noodle soup.

1   large boneless, skinless whole chicken breast

2   tablespoons soy sauce

2   tablespoons lemon juice
     Freshly ground black pepper to taste

6   large outer iceberg lettuce leaves

3   green onions, cut lengthwise in strips

1   cup grated daikon or raw carrot

1   (7-ounce) jar hoisin sauce or duck sauce

Marinate the chicken breast in a mixture of the soy sauce and lemon juice. Microwave on high for 8 minutes. Turn and microwave for another 8 minutes, or until cooked through. (You can broil the chicken for about 25 minutes instead.) Cut crosswise into 1/2-inch strips. Grind the pepper on top.

To serve, arrange the lettuce leaves, green onion strips, and grated daikon or carrot on a serving dish beside the chicken. The hoisin sauce can be placed in a small bowl in the center with a spoon for serving. To eat spread about a teaspoon of hoisin or duck sauce on a lettuce leaf, place a few strips of chicken and green onions and a hefty pinch of grated vegetable on top, and then roll it like a fat cigar. It is eaten with the fingers like a hot dog in a roll.

Makes 2 servings

Linda Denton, Queen
Chapeau Ridge, Richmond, Virginia

Chicken Basilico

Just two for dinner? Or one for you, two nights?
Enjoy this flavorful meal-in-one.

2   tablespoons plus 1 teaspoon olive oil

1/4 cup chopped scallions

1/4 to 1/3 cup (or more) zucchini, cut into matchsticks

2   tablespoons chopped fresh basil

1/2 teaspoon minced garlic

1/4 cup shredded mozzarella

2   boneless, skinless chicken breasts
     Salt and pepper to taste

1/2 cup all-purpose flour

Heat 1 teaspoon olive oil over low heat and sauté the scallions, zucchini, basil, and garlic for 5 minutes. Cool and blend in the mozzarella.

Preheat the oven to 350°. Pound the chicken breasts between two sheets of plastic wrap. Spoon half the zucchini mixture on each breast. Roll up tightly and secure with toothpicks. Season with salt and pepper. Coat with the flour. Heat the remaining 2 tablespoons oil in a skillet over medium-high heat. Sauté the chicken in the hot oil, seam side down. Turn to brown on all sides. Transfer to a greased 1 quart casserole dish and bake for 15 to 20 minutes. Serve on a bed of spaghetti with a chunky-style tomato marinara sauce.

Makes 2 servings

Ginger Stanton, Reina Madre
Red Hat Pack with Hattitude, Goodyear, Arizona

Bob Hope's Favorite Chicken Hash

A fine meal from a gentleman whose wit is fondly remembered by many Hatters.

2   skinless, boneless chicken breasts, broiled
2   bacon strips, crisply cooked
1/2   small onion, chopped
2   tablespoons butter
1/2   teaspoon lemon juice
    Salt and pepper to taste
1   teaspoon sherry
2   tablespoons sour cream

Cut the chicken into fine strips. Crumble the bacon and combine with the sliced chicken, onion, butter, lemon juice, and salt and pepper. Sauté the mixture in a skillet over medium heat until thoroughly heated. Shortly before serving add the sherry and sour cream. Heat through.

Makes 2 servings

Linda Fraley, E-mail Female
Mermaids, Millington, Tennessee

Chicken-Stuffed Acorn Squash

A complete meal that looks and tastes great.

1   acorn squash
1   tablespoon vegetable oil for sautéing
1   small onion, chopped
1/2   pound ground chicken
1   medium tomato, chopped
1/4   teaspoon salt
    Brown sugar to taste

Preheat the oven to 375°. Cut the squash in half lengthwise (see note below). Scoop out and discard the seeds. Bake the squash halves on a foil-lined baking sheet for 45 minutes, or until tender. In a medium skillet heat the oil and sauté the onion until cooked through but not browned. Add the chicken, tomato, and salt; cook 5 more minutes (the tomato will give it just enough moisture). Remove the cooked squash from the oven and generously mound the chicken mixture into the center of each squash half. Sprinkle brown sugar over each squash and put it under the broiler until the sugar is melted and the filling is slightly crunchy.

Makes 2 servings

Note: Raw acorn squash can be tough to cut, so place on a paper towel and microwave 10 to 12 minutes to soften before cutting.

Sharon Steinhoff, Queen I 4 GET
The Red Hat Breakfast Club of Highland Heights, Highland Heights, Ohio

Sun-Drenched Cod

To keep the kitchen cool, use the microwave to cook the cod.

1   pound fresh or frozen cod fillets
2   whole oranges
1/2   tablespoon butter, melted

Pinch of salt

Pinch of white pepper

1 1/2 teaspoons chopped fresh parsley (optional)

Preheat the oven to 350°. Pat the cod fillets dry. Coat a 1-quart baking dish with nonstick cooking spray. Lay the fillets in the dish. From 1 of the oranges peel half the zest and squeeze the juice into a bowl. Add the orange zest, butter, salt, and pepper. Pour the mixture over the fillets. Bake, uncovered, for 20 to 25 minutes, or until the fish flakes easily with a fork. Slice the remaining orange into 1/4-inch slices. Arrange the fillets on a serving plate, sprinkle with the parsley if using, and garnish with the fresh orange slices if desired.

Makess 2 generous servings

Nadia Giordana, Queen Mum
Merry Mad Hatters, Dayton, Minnesota

Chicken Supreme

2   boneless, skinless chicken breast halves

4   ounces mozzarella cheese, sliced

1   small onion, chopped

1   (10 3/4-ounce) can cream of mushroom soup
     Enough milk to make gravy

1/4 cup dry bread crumbs

4   tablespoons butter, melted

Preheat the oven to 350°. Place the chicken in 9-inch square pan and top each piece with a cheese slice. In a bowl combine the onion, soup, and enough milk to thin the soup to gravy con-

sistency. Pour over the chicken. Sprinkle with the bread crumbs and drizzle with the melted butter. Bake for 1 hour.

Makes 1 to 2 servings

Pat Finney, Queen
Sassy Classy Ladies of Walker, Walker, Minnesota

Grilled Tuna with Honey-Mustard Marinade

Flake the tuna to serve over a green salad, or serve with hot cooked rice.

1   to 1 1/2 pounds tuna medallions or steaks

2   tablespoons Dijon honey mustard

1   tablespoon olive oil

2   teaspoons low-sodium soy sauce

2   tablespoons rice wine vinegar or white vinegar

About 1 to 2 hours before grilling, place the tuna in a glass bowl. Combine the mustard, olive oil, soy sauce, and vinegar and pour over the tuna. Turn to make sure all pieces are well coated. Cover the bowl with plastic wrap and refrigerate until ready to grill.

When ready to grill, spray a clean grill or grilling container with nonstick cooking spray. Grill the tuna over hot coals for 5 to 7 minutes, or until nicely charred on the outside and still a bit pink in the middle.

Makes 2 servings

Janet Richardson, Red Hot Mamma
Ruby Redhats Ramblers, San Diego, California

Blackened Ahi Tuna with Horseradish Vinaigrette

CAJUN BLACKENING SPICE
1/2 teaspoon sea salt
1/2 teaspoon garlic powder
1/2 teaspoon paprika
1/2 teaspoon onion powder
1/4 teaspoon freshly ground black pepper
1/2 teaspoon dried thyme
1/8 teaspoon cayenne pepper
1/8 teaspoon dried oregano

HORSERADISH VINAIGRETTE
1 tablespoon prepared horseradish
1 tablespoon water
1/4 teaspoon grated fresh ginger root
1/4 teaspoon minced fresh garlic
1 tablespoon white wine vinegar
1/4 cup olive oil
2 (4-ounce) center-cut, sushi-grade, Ahi tuna fillets

Prepare the Cajun Blackening Spice. Mix together in small bowls the sea salt, garlic powder, paprika, onion powder, black pepper, thyme, cayenne, and oregano. Mix well and place on a plate.

Prepare the vinaigrette. Combine the horseradish, water, ginger, garlic, and vinegar in a blender and process on medium speed. Slowly drizzle in the oil on high speed.

Preheat a cast-iron skillet on medium-high heat. Rub the tuna fillets on both sides with the Cajun Blackening Spice. Sear in the skillet for 2 minutes on each side, or longer to taste. Serve the fillets on heated plates and drizzle with the Horseradish Vinaigrette.

Makes 2 servings

Sarah Carolyn Hardimon, The Creative Gourmet
Belleville Elegant Swans, Belleville, Illinois

Baked Orange Roughy with Veggies

3/4 teaspoon lemon-pepper seasoning
1/8 teaspoon salt
2 (6-ounce) fresh or thawed orange roughy fillets
1/2 cup sliced fresh mushrooms
1/4 cup thinly sliced green onions
2 tablespoons butter or margarine, melted
1 1/2 teaspoons orange juice
1 cup hot cooked rice
4 1/2 teaspoons grated Parmesan cheese (optional)

Preheat the oven to 350°. Combine the lemon-pepper and salt and sprinkle over both sides of the fillets. Place in a greased, 11 x 7-inch baking dish with the mushrooms and green onions. In a small cup combine the butter and orange juice. Pour over the fish and vegetables. Cover and bake for 20 to 25 minutes, or until the fish flakes easily with a fork. Serve over the rice with a sprinkling of Parmesan cheese if using.

Makes 2 servings

Chris J. Cowley, FQM "Madame Rozalie"
Alpha Red Hat Ramblin' Gypsies, Madison, Alabama

LITTLE FEASTS

Spinach Soufflé

The recipe makes 5 to 6 small soufflés. Three of them make a hearty meal, says the contributor.

1   (12-ounce) package spinach or 1 bunch fresh spinach, washed and trimmed
3   tablespoons butter (no substitutes)
4   tablespoons all-purpose flour
1   cup evaporated milk
1/2 teaspoon salt
    Dash of cayenne pepper
3   eggs, separated
1   cup grated cheddar cheese (or more to taste)

Cook the spinach in a microwave for about 7 minutes. Preheat the oven to 350°. Melt the butter in a small saucepan over medium heat. Stir in the flour. Whisk in the milk, salt, and cayenne pepper. Cook, whisking occasionally, until thickened. Add the drained spinach and the egg yolks and mix well. Let cool for a few minutes. Beat the egg whites until very stiff. Add the cheese to the spinach mixture, and fold in the stiff egg whites. Pour into greased ramekins (small ovenproof bowls), set them in a pan of water, and bake for 40 to 45 minutes. They should come out browned and puffed-up beautifully. Serve immediately.

Makes 5 to 6 ramekins, 2 generous servings

Anita Tepper, Queen Muddah
Funny Old Gals (FOG's), Kailua-Kona, Hawaii

Pasta Fagioli

2   tablespoons vegetable oil
3   garlic cloves, minced
1   large carrot, chopped
1   small onion, chopped
1   celery stalk, chopped
1   to 2 teaspoons chopped basil
1   teaspoon salt
1/2 teaspoon black pepper
1   (14-ounce) can chickpeas or white (cannellini or navy) beans, drained, rinsed
1/2 cup uncooked small pasta (fusilli or rotini)
2   cups chicken stock or water
    Juice of 1 lemon
    Grated Parmesan cheese

Heat the oil in a large saucepan over medium-high heat and sauté the garlic, carrot, onion, celery, basil, salt, and pepper for 3 minutes, or until tender. Add the chickpeas, pasta, and stock. Bring to a boil and reduce the heat to low. Simmer for 20 minutes, or until the pasta is tender and the soup is nice and thick. Stir in the lemon juice. Serve sprinkled with Parmesan cheese.

Makes 2 servings

Claire Knodell, Munkus the Brat
Red Hot Jazzy Ladies, Kelowna, British Columbia, Canada

Green Bean Casserole

Yearning for that great flavor of green bean casserole? Here's a miniature version.

1   (4.5-ounce) package herb and butter pasta mix
1   (14-ounce) can French-cut green beans, drained
1   (2.8-ounce) can French-fried onions
1   cup shredded cheddar cheese

Cook the pasta in boiling salted water according to the package directions. Add the beans to the noodles and mix well. Add half the onions and mix well. Spoon the mixture into a small baking dish. Top with the remaining onions and the cheese. Bake or microwave until the cheese melts.

Makes 2 generous servings

Janelle Ford, Lady Toodles
50 and Loving It, Kansas City, Kansas

Swiss Cheese Soufflé

Treat yourself to a soft, puffy soufflé.

1   tablespoon grated Parmesan chase, divided
1   tablespoon unsalted butter, melted
2   teaspoons all-purpose flour
1/2 cup whole milk
1/8 teaspoon Worcestershire sauce
1/8 teaspoon salt
1/8 teaspoon white pepper
1   large egg, separated
1/3 cup finely shredded Swiss cheese

Preheat the oven to 375°. Grease a soufflé ramekin or small ovenproof bowl. Sprinkle with 1 teaspoon Parmesan cheese. In a small, nonstick saucepan whisk together the butter, flour, and milk. Whisking constantly, bring the mixture to a boil and cook until slightly thickened. Remove from the heat and stir in the Worcestershire sauce, salt, and pepper. Beat the egg yolk in a small bowl. Whisk in 1 tablespoon of the milk mixture to temper the egg. Add the egg yolk to the saucepan. In a clean bowl with an electric mixer, beat the egg white until stiff peaks form. Fold half the beaten white into the egg yolk mixture. Fold in the Swiss cheese and then the remaining beaten egg white. Pour into the prepared baking dish. Sprinkle with the remaining Parmesan cheese. Place on a small baking sheet and bake for 20 to 25 minutes, or until set and lightly browned. Remove from the oven and let stand for 2 minutes to complete baking. Serve immediately.

Makes 1 serving

Sarah Carolyn Hardimon, The Creative Gourmet
Belleville Elegant Swans, Belleville, Illinois

Mushroom Risotto

Any extra risotto keeps well in the refrigerator for several days. It makes delicious little rice cakes like you might get at a fine restaurant (see Variation).

1 tablespoon butter

4 ounces mushrooms, diced

2 tablespoons olive oil

1 red onion, diced

1 tablespoon garlic, chopped

1 cup Arborio rice

1 1/2 cups white wine

1 1/2 cups vegetable or chicken stock

3 tablespoons grated Parmesan cheese

Freshly ground black pepper to taste

In a medium-size saucepan over medium heat, melt the butter and sauté the mushrooms for about 4 or 5 minutes, or until the mushrooms have released their juices. In a second saucepan heat the olive oil over medium heat and sauté the onion until translucent but not browned, about 2 minutes. Add the garlic and sauté briefly; then add the rice and cook for 1 minute, stirring with a wooden spoon. In a third saucepan or using a microwave, combine the wine and stock. Bring to a simmer; reduce the heat, cover, and keep at a bare simmer.

Add to the rice 1 cup at a time, stirring constantly until each addition of liquid is absorbed. Continue adding the hot liquid until the rice is creamy and al dente. Then fold in the mushrooms, grated Parmesan, and pepper.

Makes 4 servings

Variation: Make the risotto a day ahead, and then refrigerate. When cold, form into patties with your hands. Coat with dry bread crumbs, top with garlic butter, and bake in a preheated oven at 350° for about 10 minutes. Flip over, bake another 5 minutes, and serve. The whole batch will make 12 patties.

Arvilla Shouldice, Empress of Elegant Red Hattin'
Grandmas
Positively Meno-Positive, Ottawa, Ontario, Canada

Pizza for One

Forget expensive individual pizza shells—a tortilla is just right.

1 (8-inch) flour tortilla

1/4 cup pizza sauce

1/2 cup shredded mozzarella cheese

4 tomato slices

1/4 cup chopped onion

1/4 cup chopped green bell pepper

1/4 cup sliced fresh or canned mushrooms

Italian seasoning or dried oregano to taste

Preheat the oven to 350°. Lay the tortilla on a baking sheet. Spread the pizza sauce over the tortilla. Add the cheese, tomatoes, onion, bell pepper, and mushrooms. Season with the Italian seasoning. Bake for 15 to 20 minutes, or until the flour shell is nicely crisped.

Makes 1 serving

Pat Lutes, Chief Cook-A-lot
Desert Babes, Meadview , Arizona

Linguine with Shrimp and Mushrooms

Just add salad and breadsticks and you've got a meal to rival one in a great little Italian place.

- 3   tablespoons butter
- 8   ounces sliced mushrooms
- 1   medium garlic clove, minced
- 1/4   teaspoon dried oregano
- 1/8   teaspoon freshly ground black pepper
- 1/2   cup heavy whipping cream
- 1/2   pound fresh shrimp, peeled, deveined, and rinsed
- 4   ounces dried linguine
- 1/3   cup shredded mozzarella cheese
      Salt to taste
      Minced fresh cilantro to taste

Melt the butter in a large, heavy sauté pan over medium heat. Sauté the mushrooms, garlic, oregano, and pepper for 5 minutes, stirring occasionally, until tender. Add the cream and shrimp and bring the mixture to a simmer. Simmer for about 3 minutes, or until slightly thickened.

In the meantime, cook the linguine in large pot of boiling, salted water according to package directions. Drain well. Add the linguine and shredded cheese to the sauce and stir until the cheese melts. Season with salt and minced cilantro.

Makes 2 servings

Joyce A. Bacon, Queen of Tarts
The Elderberry Tarts, Baltimore, Maryland

LITTLE FEASTS

Asparagus with Fresh Cheese

The cheese turns brown and crisp as the asparagus roasts.

- 1   pound fresh asparagus
- 1   tablespoon chopped garlic
- 4   tablespoons freshly shredded Parmesan cheese

Preheat the oven to 350°. Grease an ovenproof 1 1/2 quart glass baking dish. Trim the asparagus and arrange in a single layer. Spray with non-stick cooking spray and then sprinkle with the garlic. Sprinkle with the Parmesan cheese. Bake for about 20 minutes.

Makes 2 servings

Connie Hausenfleck, Vice Mum
The Good-Time Red Hatters, North Canton, Ohio

One Potato

1   large baking potato
2   tablespoons olive oil or butter, melted
1/4 cup grated Parmesan cheese
1/4 teaspoon paprika

Preheat the oven to 350°. Slice the potato in half lengthwise. Brush the cut sides with the olive oil. Mix the Parmesan cheese and paprika together. Dip the sliced sides in the cheese mixture. Place the potato, cut sides down, on a greased baking sheet, and bake for 1 hour.

Makes 1 large or 2 small servings

Note: Romano cheese or grated Asiago cheese can be used in place of Parmesan.

K. Mortensen, Baroness of Blunt
Hub City Honeys, Petal, Mississippi

~ Index ~

INDEX OF NAMES

ALABAMA

Burns, Dana, Mystical Dixie Pixies (Oxford), 95, 189

Cloud Walker, Celia, Pink & Purple Pampered Prissies (Dothan), 331, 519

Cowley, Chris J., Alpha Red Hat Ramblin' Gypsies (Madison), 546

Jones, Pam, Rose-Mary Virtuous Divas (Birmingham), 222

Rudd, Gayle, Red Chicks (Springville), 140–141

Simpson, Sharon, Ladies of the Lake (Abbeville), 488

Wallace, Marylin, Sophisticated Ladies (Centre), 175

ALASKA

McCoy, Vikki, Ruby's Red Hat Ramblers (Anchorage), 425, 429

ARIZONA

Blazek, Diana, The Red Hot Grand Hatters (Surprise), 203, 514

Crum, Elaine, Red Hatters of Anthem (Anthem), 295, 468–469

Frahm, Karen, Apache Redhats (Mesa), 455

Goodell, Mary, Razzle Dazzle Darlins' (Sun City West), 45

Gottlieb, Marka, Grand Girls Gone Wild (Surprise), 356

Hansen, Brenda, Happy Red Hatters (Youngtown), 158–159

Lee, Ina, Scarlett Sugars (Mesa), 248

Lutes, Pat, Desert Babes (Meadvie), 549

Parker, Brenda, Sun City Grand Dames (Surprise), 280–281

Sanders, Mary, Royal Tea Red Hatters (Peoria), 196

Sharkey, Nancy, The Budding Red Roses of Arizona (Glendale), 130

Shaw, Doris, The Red Fedora Flora Doras of Gilbert, Arizona (Mesa), 131

Sheaver, Sharon, Red Hats of the Purple Stage (Hereford), 40

Siatt, Linda, Rio Red Hots (Sun City West), 258–259

Snowden Crosman, Anne, Curvaceous Cuties (Sedona), 175, 290–291

Sperry, Billie, Desert Darlins (Mesa), 207

Stacey, Judy, Vim, Vigor and Vitality Gals (Surprise), 314

Stanton, Ginger, Red Hat Pack with Hattitude (Goodyear), 543

Thill, Joanne, London Bridge Red Hots (Lake Havasu City), 103, 227

Wright, Shirley, Super Sun Sweeties (Apache Junction), 74

ARKANSAS

Davis, Gail, Sassy Survivors (A Group for Breast Cancer Survivors) (Fort Smith), 156

Gauthier, Gloria, Growing Up Gawdy, The Gawdy Girls (Conway), 130

Holbrook, Carolyn, GRITS with Hattitudes (Sherwood), 442

Holmes, Melba, The Red Hatters of The Lakes (West Memphis), 6

Horton, Tony, Crawford County Cuties (Van Buren), 23

Lavender, Shirley, Rolling Meadows Red Larks (Mountain Home), 412

Murphy, Cathi, Growin' Up Gawdy (Conway), 176–177

Ramer, Judy, Dazzling Diamond Divas (North Little Rock), 71

Smith, Cathy, Crawford County Cuties (Charleston), 312

Turner, Darlene, Red Hat Chile Peppers (Kodiak), 211

AUSTRALIA

Atkinson, Colleen, Red Hat Dames Down Under (Adelaide), 146

Burgess, Karen, Sydney RHS (Gladesville, New South Wales), 126

Kelly, Joann, Hobart Scarlett O'Hatters (West Hobart, Tasmania), 38–39

CALIFORNIA

Aita, Jane, Alhambra Shopping Bag Ladies (Alhambra), 402

Alioto, Nina, Red Hatters of Rancho Bernardo (San Diego), 428–429

Ausmus, Judith, Purple Plumes (Santa Ana), 40

Bauder, Jackie, A Gathering of Hats (West Hills), 241

Becker, Roxie, Foxy Roxy's (Fullerton), 178–179, 205

Beidelman, Vicki, Foxy Roxys (Fullerton), 82

Betush, Carol, Rebellious Elegant Dames (Redding), 472

Binder, Judy, Red Hot Red Hatters (Camarillo), 442–443

Bobo, Carol, Heavenly Hatters (Santa Cruz), 161

CALIFORNIA (*continued*)

Borg, Lynn, The Grateful Red Hatters (Encinitas), 48

Boxold, Barbara, Notorious Tacky Hatters of Norco (Riverside), 269

Boyd, Donna, Crazy Daiseys (Palm Desert), 310, 342

Brown, Gladys, Red Hat Gems (San Diego), 226–227

Brune, Gayle, Bodacious Biddies (La Quinta), 284

Busby, Elaine, Flaming Fedoras (Rancho Palos Verdes), 214–215

Camp, Jeanette, Red Hot Hens (Hemet), 69

Castro, Rae, Ruby Redhat's Ramblers (Escondido), 482

Coombs, Diane, Belles of Sun City (Sun City), 27

Cooper, Sue Ellen, The Fabulous Founders (Fullerton), 156, 459

Crawford, Gwendolyn, Ladie Gone Purple (Victorville), 336

Davenport, Lana, California Central Coast Femme Fatales (Vandenberg AFB), 286

Davis, Joyce, Steal Magnolias (Long Beach), 374

Davison, Judy, Ladybugs (Dana Point), 314

Dawes, Rose Marie, Camarillo Red Hatters (Camarillo), 246

DeRosier, Mikayla, Le Chapeau Rouge D'Elegance (Sonoma), 306–307, 408–409

Eidam, Erika, Naples Knoties (Long Beach), 183

Ellis, Nancy, Desert Flowers (Palm Desert), 135, 268, 426

Ford, Deborah, Teresa Red Hots (San Jose), 413

Foster, Patricia, Dusty Desert Roses (Desert Hot Springs), 14

Franger, Kathleen, Blushin' Belles (San Jose), 466

Fuller, Diana, Modoc Red Hot Hatters (Alturas), 155, 282, 447

Gabel, Betty, La Vida Real Red Hats (El Cajon), 229

Gallagher, Patti, Divas of Disorder (formerly Ruby Begonias) (San Diego), 345

Garfield, Lois, Jen Jo's Crown Jewels (San Diego), 89

Gerstley, Caroline, Radical Fringe Red Hatters (Santa Monica), 128

Giboney, Cyntra, Ruby Red Girls of Martinez (Pleasant Hill), 160–161

Gilio, Debbie, Coastal Rose Buds (Pismo Beach), 182

Grisaffi, Mary, Spicy Red Hats of Santa Clarita Valley (Valencia), 87

Heisch, Joann, Home & Heartstrings Red Hatters (Auburn), 161, 497

Hemphill, Sue, Sassy Classy Red Hatters (San Leandro), 330–331, 414

Henick, Flo, Santa Teresa Red Hots (San Jose), 394

Hosford, Virginia, Santa Teresa Red Hots (San Jose), 28

Huitt, Judy Emily, Norby's Red Rowdies (Anaheim), 251, 273

Huston, Kay, Santa Teresa Red Hots (San Jose), 304

Ise, Karen, Le Chapeaux Rouge de Conejo (Westlake Village), 434, 468

Jameson, Bonnie, Bloomin' Tea Roses (San Dimas), 192

Johnson, Beverly, Tahoe REDS (Rowdy, Energetic, Diva Sisters) (South Lake Tahoe), 239, 368

Keas, Shirley, South Bay Babes (Torrance), 107

Kidder, Glennis, Red Hatters of the Orestimba (Newman), 34

King, Emma, Roses on the Go (Jamul), 294

Kroesen, Judy, Dames of Whinin' Roses (Lomita), 351

Kubanda, Louise, Blushing Red Hatters (San Diego), 396

Lamkin, Kevann, Red Hattitudes (Fontana), 355

Lancer, Violet, Fuschia Fillies (Dublin), 91

Lupton, Betty, Sexy Broads (Grass Valley), 538

Martin, Jeri, Modoc Red Hot Hatters (Alturas), 349

Maylasang, Monica, Der Tahs of Orange County (Tustin), 308

McGrath, Connie, Last of the Red Hat Mommas (Riverside), 62–63

Mischo Allinger, Bonnie, Bonnet Rouge (Wilton), 505

Montgomery, JoAnne, Red Hot Mamas of the Pines (Magalia), 513

Nunes, Jackie, Scarlet Ribbons (Elk Grove), 36–37

Oehler, Maria D., Sierra Sirens (Grass Valley), 356

Pell, Sherry, West Coast Sisterhood of The Red Hat Society (Huntington Beach), 202

Pitts, Carolyn, Razzle Dazzle Dames of Pasadena (Azusa), 32, 286–287

Richardson, Janet, Ruby Redhats Ramblers (San Diego), 545

Roe, Susan, Heavenly Hatters (Seal Beach), 191

Rogers, Lyn, The Victorian Roses (San Jose), 162

Schutz, Barbara, Feisty Dynamites (Roseville), 499

Shank, Loretta, Santa Teresa Red Hots (San Jose), 127

Simmons, Jewel, High Hatters (Santee), 75

Sitton, Kali, Rhat Pacque (Canyon Country), 82, 216–217, 269

Snow, Rose Marie, Blushing Bells (Campbell), 224

Souza, Phyllis, Red Hot Hatter's of San Jose (San Jose), 254–255

Sprenkle, Betsy, Nipomo Nifties (Nipomo), 530

Tarvin, Linda, The Stinkin' Red Roses (Morgan Hill), 184, 290

Van Der Linden, Sandy, Vintage Valley Girls (Hemet), 154

Van Foeken, Susie, Hilmar Red Hat Readers (Hilmar), 168, 403

Varnadore, Fran, Bodacious Beach Babes (Palos Verdes Estates), 430

Varnadore, Fran, Radical Fringe Red Hatters (Palos Verdes Estates), 36

Weinberg, Barbara, Dusty Desert Roses (Cathedral City), 90, 184, 416

West, Vickie, Fun and Fabulous (Lakewood), 449, 456

Wilshusen, Carol Ann, Sassy Sisters (Grass Valley), 508–509

Woolsey, Mary, RHS Red Queens (Canoga Park), 138, 318–319, 380

Wunderlich, Dee, PARFF—Purple And Red For Fun (Napa), 211

Yancey, Robin, Ruby Red Hats of Joy (San Ramon), 102, 492–493

CANADA

Beatty, Judy, Chocolate River Cuties (Riverview, New Brunswick), 438

Beer, Linda, Red Hot Super Chicks (Bethany, Ontario), 138

Bryson, Joy, Red-Red Robins (Winnipeg, Manitoba), 70–71

Buchanan, Sharon, Celtic Bells Red Hatters (Baddeck, Nova Scotia), 62

Caldwell, Virginia, Delta Gals (Delta, British Columbia), 280

Cummings, Linda, Red Hat'll Do Ya (Halifax, Nova Scotia), 355

Fallahay, Sylvia, Just 14 Ladies, (Elliot Lake, Ontario), 25

Godard, Laurette, Tuesday Linedancers (Winnepeg, Manitoba), 301, 321

Heighton, Jan, Red Hat'll Do Ya (Halifax, Nova Scotia), 446

Hendrickson, Marsha, Red Roses of Brampton (Brampton, Ontario), 42–43

Hofer, Ann, Kootenay Red Belles (Castlegar, British Columbia), 132

Hollis, Yolande, The Fiddle-Reds (Shelburne, Ontario), 73

Knodell, Claire, Red Hot Jazzy Ladies (Kelowna, British Columbia), 547

Lawson, Candice, Cinnamon Hearts (Winnipeg, Manitoba), 148–149

MacNeil, Nancy, Saay Lassies-Burlington (Burlington, Ontario), 506

MacVicar, Janet, Jubilee Jewels (Montreal, Quebec), 278

MacVicar, Mary Jane, Scarlett Shady Ladies (Leamington, Ontario), 226, 332

Marks, Carol, Silver Star Jewels (Vernon, British Columbia), 178

McClelland, Joan, Niagara Hatties (St. Catharines, Ontario), 74

McDermott, Maureen, Delta Gals (Delta, British Columbia), 111

McDowell, Lorna, Scarlett O'Haras (Garson, Ontario), 164

Mentes, Gay, Red Hot Jazzy Ladies (Kelowna, British Columbia), 484

Nevills, Ruth, Red Hat'll Do Ya (Halifax, Nova Scotia), 289

Nightingale, Marie, Red Hat'll Do Ya (Halifax, Nova Scotia), 415

Nowlan, Betty, Chocolate River Cuties (Moncton, New Brunswick), 226

Olson, Trudean, Red Hat Delta Divas (Delta, British Columbia), 403

O'Malley, Marlene, Ruby Revellers (Dartmouth, Nova Scotia), 158

Price, Merna, Thousand Island Belles (Gananoque, Ontario), 495

Ridout, Karen, Red Hat Dollies of Calgary (Calgary, Alberta), 106–107, 142–143, 382

Rodgers, Joan, Onanole Red Hats (Onanole, Manitoba), 370

Ross, Judy, Celtic Bells Red Hatters (Baddeck, Nova Scotia), 266

Rowlandson, Eleanor, Happy Red Hatters (Oshawa, Ontario), 362–363

Salter, Marie, Women on Wheels (Fredericton, New Brunswick), 517

Sandahl, Millie, Red Baronettes (Sechelt, British Columbia), 77

Sharman, Evelyn, Mad Hatters of Saskatoon (Saskatoon, Saskatchewan), 528–529

Shouldice, Arvilla, Positively Meno-Positive (Ottawa, Ontario), 539, 548–549

Smith, Kathleen, Steel Magnolias (Ancaster, Ontario), 76, 308, 481

Wilson, Helen, Rockin' Mamas (St. John's, Newfoundland), 453

Wollaston, Elsie, Red Snappers (Vancouver, British Columbia), 120–121

Worth, Margaret, Thousand Island Belles (Gananoque, Ontario), 462–463

COLORADO

Boyes, Dee, Lusty Ladies in Red of Loveland (Loveland), 163, 325

Brady, Linda C., Aurora Glorialis (Aurora), 390

Bush, Janie, Classie Lassies (Chivington), 350

Hale, Linda, Jolly Red Hatters (Centennial), 428

Harris, Bonnie, Majestic Columbines (Longmont), 440–441

Helgerson, Colleen, Red Hatters and That's What Matters (Aurora), 159

COLORADO (continued)

Holdren, Paula, Scarlett Ladies of Littleton (Littleton), 260–261

Johnson, Patricia, Cugini Bei (Aurora), 152

Konken, Marsha, Red Raspberry Tarts (Sterling), 299

Krickbaum, Peggy, Flashy Sassies (Montrose), 60, 169, 478

Palmer, Mary Beth, Columbine Cuties (Colorado Springs), 98

Rosi, Nancy, Jolly Red Hatters (Denver), 324, 512

Shaffer, Paula, Scarlett Ladies of Littleton (Littleton), 357

CONNECTICUT

Barlow, Patricia D., The Belles of Bridgewater (Bridgewater), 257, 383

Carbone, Sally, Razzle Dazzle Red Hats of Colchester (Colchester), 122, 394, 398

Engel, Irene, Ruby Gems of the Valley (Avon), 380

Flynn, Mary, Scarlet Splashers (Torrington), 160, 256

Fossati, Eleanor, Scarlet Splashers (Torrington), 259

Shirlock, Susanna, Scarlet Splashers (Goshen), 178

Warner, Maureen, The Belles of Bridgewater (Bridgewater), 218

DELAWARE

Gilbert, Janet, Red Hat Hotties (Newark), 56, 432

Godfrey, Evelyn, Steel Magnolias of Magnolia (Magnolia), 493

Huber, Dee, Beach Plum Red Hatters of Long Neck (Long Neck), 423

Schultz, Jo Anne, The Red Hat Hoydens (Delmar), 72

Shaw, Kenni, My Lady Red Hats (Hagerstown), 436

FLORIDA

Adams, Bonnie, Red Bonnet Sisters (Lakeland), 117

Allred, Mary, Red Bonnet Sisters (Lakeland), 410

Anderson, Connie, Bodacious Babes Of Belvedere (The Villages), 15

Arcand, Pam, Lunch Bags of Orlando (Orlando), 377, 470

Austin, Christine, Sassy Squaws of Seminole Lakes (Punta Gorda), 88, 324–325, 520

Beasley, Charlotte, Southern Belles of Boca Raton (Boca Raton), 129

Bloss, Judy, Vintage Gals (Alachua), 283, 302

Burke, Pam, Ruby Mermaids (Sanibel), 105, 514–515

Caldwell, Martha, Red Hat Ramblers (Hollywood), 542

Carver, Phyllis, Red Bonnet Sisters (Lakeland), 177

Chambers, Charlene, Scarlet O'Bearas (Ormond Beach), 306, 354, 412

Chiocchi, Mary, Red Hat Rebels (Port Charlotte), 131

Cowan, Barbara, Hacienda Red Hatters (Seven Springs), 264–265

Cummings, Connie, Red Hatter Chatters (Silver Springs), 209

Dill, Lois, River Red Hatters (DeBary), 30–31

Eaton, Faith, Jamaica Bay YaYas (Fort Myers), 260

Ferlita, Connie, Late Bloomers w/ Red Hattitude (Cocoa), 293

Fulford, Anna Belle, West Orange Red Hat Society (Winter Garden), 275

Gerber, Marsha, Marsha, Marsha, Marsha and her Marvelous Mates (Parkland), 158

Godoy Gonino, Jean, Sassy Scarletts of St. Augustine (St. Augustine), 29

Gurdgiel, Janet, Ladies of Grace (Merritt Island), 282–283

Haizelden, Sue, Preemie Donnas of Jacksonville (Jacksonville), 116

Hannan, Sheila, The Merry Madams of Merritt Island (Merritt Island), 101, 365

Hanover, Jetta, Razzledazzle Boa Babes! (Ocala), 470

Harris, Ruth, The Royal Order of the Yada Yada Red Hatters (Sunrise), 514

Horsfield, Delilah, The Villages 1st Red Hatters (The Villages), 238

Jimmerson, Elaine, The Valley Girls (of Apopka) (Apopka), 9, 121

Judd, Joan, Pool Playmates (The Villages), 32, 404

Kania, Joan, Hat'Attudes of Safety Harbor (Clearwater), 216

Katz, Roslyn, Coral Springs Sweethearts (Coral Springs), 476

Kiernan, Carol, Scarlett O'Hatters of Trinity (So Hot) (Trinity), 63

Larsen, Win, Purple Rosettes (Ft. Myers), 480–481

LeRoy, Margaret, Red Flamingos of Grandezza (Estero), 41

McElroy, Donna, Rosebud Hues (Venice), 169

McKenzie, FloyAnne, Panama Red Hats (Panama City), 492

McKeown, Jo, Forever Young (The Villages), 531

Moon, Barbara R., Scarlet Red Hatters, River City Foxy Ladies (Jacksonville), 378

Newman, Trish, Shady Ladies of Jacksonville, Florida (Macclenny), 444

Pillitteri, Joyce, Reddy Set Goes (Jacksonville), 288

Pritchard, Marge, Scarlet Dames at Tea (Hudson), 246

Ramby, Shirley, Red Hat Divas Too (Spring Hill), 194

Rice, Sherry, Legally Red (Jacksonville), 507

Rodgers, Cara, Coral Springs Sweethearts (Coral Springs), 206, 458

Russo, Suzanne, Sizzlin' Sisters (Melbourne), 225

Safarikas, Gail, Scarlet O'Hatters of Trinity (So Hot) (Trinity), 376

Sendall, Barbara, Red Hot Dollies (Port Charlotte), 272–273

Setterlund, Ruthie, Red Hat Musical Notes (Clearwater), 374

Simpson, Barbara, Highbanks Hatters (DeBary), 147, 508

Smith, JoEllen, Scarlett Darlings (Clearwater), 134, 207

Stevens, Leah, Alizarin Czarinas (Davie), 350

Szczerbicki, Ann, Nine to Fivers (Jupiter), 64

Terry, Ann, Crimson Cuties (Spring Hill), 397, 496

Tisdale, Betty (Clara E.), Red Hat-titudes (Tampa), 449

Tollefson, Lorraine, Chapeau Rouge of Crystal River (Crystal River), 91, 163

Tuisku, Dee, Hat'attudes of Safety Harbor (Safety Harbor), 252

Walters, Nancy, Cinnamon Cove Honey Bees (Fort Myers), 410–411

Walther, Mari, Foxy Divas of Okee (Okeechobee), 513

Washington, Norma, The Precious Red Crowns and Brims (Tallahassee), 537

West, Rosa, Red Hat Seagalls (Hudson), 95, 485

White, Karen, Santo's Red Hats (The Villages), 228, 351

GEORGIA

Battle, Sally, Shamrock Red Hatters (Dublin), 186

Carson, Anne, Sassy Ladies of Lake Sinclair (Eatonton), 426–427

Ganaway, Z., Radiant Redhats of Georgia (Atlanta), 5

Giedd, Barbara, Brair Patch Hattitudes (Eatonton), 28–29, 337

Hulsey, Judy, Primarily Purple (PP) Girls (Lavonia), 488

Jones, Joy T., Le Rouge Chapeaux of Rockdale (Conyers), 305

Kerr, Edel, Sensuous Hens (Lilburn), 309

Mace, Cil, Vintage Roses (Warner Robins), 190–191

Moxley, Brenda, Bold 'N Classy (Macon), 235

Nix, Nancy, Dixie Dames (LaGrange), 407

Ousey, Conchetta, Scarlet O'Hatters (Columbus), 385, 419, 420

Parker, Linda-Lee, Red Hots of Roswell (Roswell), 408

Pennington, Linda, Sassy Hattitudes (Loganville), 169, 405

Preston, Marie, Vintage Roses (Perry), 307

Ranieri, Carol, Belles of the Hooch (Columbus), 248–249

Smith, Maggie, The Hart Throb and Socialites of Hartwell (Buford), 170, 251

Speer, Jane, Vintage Roses (Warner Robins), 530–531

Tatum, Claudia, Georgia Paechiz (Lilburn), 464

VanAtta, Mary, Vintage Roses (Warner Robins), 322

Whatley, Maryanne, Red Hatters of Rincon (Rincon), 490–491

Wheeler, Beth, Scarlett's Starlets (Jonesboro), 188

HAWAII

Ching, Winnie, Wiki Papa O Ka Papale Ulaula Ahahui (Kaneohe), 303

Freitas, Roxie, Big Island Beauties (Kailua-Kona), 140, 245

Pettersen, Judy, Big Island Beauties (Kailua-Kona), 274

Tepper, Anita, Funny Old Gals (FOG's) (Kailua-Kona), 547

IDAHO

Enrico, Linda, Red Hot Taters (Boise), 289, 354

Fitzsimmons, Karen, Red Hot Taters (Meridian), 335

Servatius, Mary, Red Hot Taters (Meridian), 501

ILLINOIS

Boshaw, Carol, Fun Hatters of Holiday Acres (McHenry), 180, 406, 504

Cassella, Sheila, Purple Passion Majesties (Chicago), 182, 214, 481

Cravens, Tove, Red Hatters, Fun and Chatters (Orion), 160

Dzwonkiewicz, Linda, Bloom Violets (Mundelein), 174

Gass Hardimon, Carolyn, Recipe Ladies (Belleville), 526

Gavin, Dianne, Crimson Tide Great Lakes (Beach Park), 444

Hardimon, Sarah Carolyn, Belleville Elegant Swans (Belleville), 527, 546, 548

Heide, Bette, Sassy Classy Ladies (Chicago), 407, 500

Heuer, Vicky, Red Hot, Red Hats Too (Park Ridge), 524

Jackson, Della, Red Hatted Chicks and Pink Hatted Peeps (Petersburg), 368–369

Kirbach, Linda, Fiesty Femmes (Jacksonville), 89

ILLINOIS *(continued)*

Koscielski, Delora Jo, Red Hot Hatters (Quincy), 171

Lis, Rogene, Sassy Classy Ladies (Roselle), 92–93

Lytle, Millie, Red Hats On To You (Carol Stream), 24, 170

Mans, Nancy, Sassy Classy Ladies (Roselle), 109, 142

Peebles, Sandra S., Royal Divas (Belleville), 370–371

Swip, Mary Ann, Heartland Red Hat Doll Society (Collinsville), 229

Tisdale, Sue, Red Hat Society Crones and Cronies (Pekin), 253

Warriner, Peg, Red Hat Divas (Villa Grove), 43

Wheeler, Linda, Tazwell Scarlett Ladies (Creve Coeur), 140

Whitledge, Paula, Ruby and Amethyst Jewels (Bartonville), 120

Widby, Sally, Sassy Lassies (Pekin), 208

INDIANA

Caswell, Lena, Traveling Cooks with Hattitude (Greenfield), 51, 520–521

Duffer, Shirley, Ya-Ya Purplehood (Fishers), 510

Hunt, Rosalie, Hoosier Honeys (Fortville), 503

Martin, Marilyn, The Royal Court of Live a Lot (Avon), 288

Noe, Peggy, Northside Indy Red Hats (Indianapolis), 521

Noll, Joy, Country Girls (Paoli), 11

Pickett, Karen, Young @ Hearts, Racy Reds & Perky Pinks (Evansville), 268

Robb, Vickie, Friends of The Red Hatters (Springville), 139, 250

Schmedel, Beverly, Purple Posies (Indianapolis), 49

Snedegar, Sydney, Real Extraordinary Dames (Rushville), 249

West, Cynthia, Traveling Cooks with Hattitude (Marshalltown), 39

IOWA

Bensmiller, Ruth, Feathered Red Hatters of Northeast Iowa (Shellsburg), 472

Carter, Cindi, Monroe Hotsy Totsys (Monroe), 54, 223

Espy, Paula Rae, Red Hot River Babes (Burlington), 133

Hauck, Louise, Red Hat Rockers (Humboldt), 212–213

Holtz, Brenda, Vintage Vines of Kingsley, Iowa (Kingsley), 78

Hovey, Roseann, Red Hat Angels (Atkins), 360

Keiper, Betty, Red Hat Angels (Atkins), 201

Koester, Michelle, Rural Red Hatters (Duncombe), 373

McCurry, Elaine, Regal Rubies (Renwick), 513

Metz, Margaret, The Hottie Red Hatters of Coralville (Coralville), 335

Milburn, Harriette, Blushing Red Hat Mamas (Des Moines), 516

Neidy, Kathryn, Feathered Red Hatters of NE Iowa (Independence), 535

Osbahr, Lorraine, Classy Dames Sisterhood (Avoca), 12, 364–365

Scarpino, Mary, Blushing Red Hat Mamas (Waukee), 429

Streif, Bonnie, Feathered Red Hatters of Northeast Iowa (Springville), 489

Sweezer, Dolores, Red Hot River Babes (Burlington), 467

West, Cynthia, Traveling Cooks with Hattitude (Marshalltown), 155, 498–499

KANSAS

Boutwell, Dot, Fairy Mad Hatters (Wichita), 542

Easton, Mayme, Red Hats of Oz (Olathe), 100, 379

Ford, Janelle, 50 and Loving It (Kansas City), 548

Houdyshell, Virginia, Serendipity Reds (Pratt), 219

Newberry, Roseanna, The Fort Scott Ladies of Oz (Fort Scott), 273

KENTUCKY

Duncan, Susan, Derby City Ladybugs of Louisville, Kentucky (Louisville), 162–163, 196, 385

Fothergill, Elizabeth, Bluegrass (Lexington), 11

Garrett, Evelyn, Happy Red Hatters of Somerset (Somerset), 257, 520

Grijalba, Tine, Spiritfilled Hearts and Hats (Richmond), 372

Kinelski, Carol A., Cats in the Red Hat (Richmond), 186–187, 497

Ramage, Margaret, Hoptown Happy Hatters (Hopkinsville), 479

Robertson, Jone, Royal Sassies of Bowling Green (Bowling Green), 451

LOUISIANA

Beene, Claudia, Scarlett O'Hatters (Bossier City), 97, 164

Bendily, Mary Ann, Red Hat Flamingal's (Denham Springs/Walker), 5

Brogna, Betty, Sashaying Scarlet Sisters (Chalmette), 436

Cooper, Pat, Red Hatter Sweethearts (Shreveport), 220

Findorff, Irene, Red Hat Divas of Metairie (Metairie), 200–201

Hemenway, Fran, Creole Red Hat Divas (River Ridge), 150

Herzog-Pope, Lynda, Herzog's Hilarious Hellyun Hairdressers and Healthcare Heifers of Haughton (Haughton), 222

McLemore, Joann, The Red Brims with Purple Trims (Lafayette), 433

Roberson, Patt, Merry Maids of Mayhem (Baker), 427

MAINE

Androff, Mary, Razzle Dazzle of Clinton Twp. Maine (Clinton Township), 148

Cunningham, Rita, Red Hat Mommas of Western Maine (Dixfield), 300–301

Dobens, Mary, Red Hat Tomatoes (Poland), 69

Donovan, Brenda, Northern Maine Classie Lassies (Presque Isle), 136–137

Hodnett, Barbara, Clinton Fairlaydes (Clinton), 244

White, Jeannette, Red Hat Mommas of Western Maine (Dixfield), 475

MARYLAND

Bacon, Joyce, The Elderberry Tarts (Baltimore), 42, 550

Bee, Janie, Scarlett O'Hatters of Howard County (Ellicott City), 210, 382

Buss, Gail, The Scarlette Bells (Westminster), 4–5, 98–99

Corbett, Winnie, Les Grande Dames of Cecil County (North East), 183

Deeter, Elizabeth Ann, Gettys Garnets (Thurmont), 106

DeGroff-Garber, Donna, Les Grande Dames of Cecil County (Elkton), 386–387

Frederick, Pat, Spiffy with Hattitude (Clarksville), 210

Jantz, Cecile, Queen Anne Red Hat Swingers (Queenstown), 338

Johnson, Joanne, Cats in the Hats in Annapolis (Annapolis), 396–397, 472–473

Kapanoske, Debbie, Red Lite Ladies (Laurel), 378

Killett, Joyce, Spiffy with Hattitude (Sykesville), 135

Kozlowski, Dee, Scarrlett Harlotts (Edgewood), 145

Maurer, Fran, Chesapeake Bay Red Hatters of Baltimore (Baltimore), 173

Ostrander, Barbara, Crimson Croonies (Lexington Park), 148

Pearsall, Mickey, Old Babes in Red Hats (Garlan), 450

Seppy, Jackie, Scarlet O'Hatters (Gaithersburg), 255

Tomlinson, Polly, Red Hat Chili Peppers (Randallstown), 52

Wixom, Lynne, Red Hat TeasHers (Silver Spring), 300, 499

Wood, Marianne, Royal Rubies (Columbia), 478–479

MASSACHUSETTS

Bennett, Shirley, Red Hot Ladies (Franklin), 234

Buckley, Dolores R., #1 Low-Fat Red Hatters (Worcester), 62

Gangemi, Linda, Red-E-or Nots (Stoughton), 463

Harding, Ruth, Classy Lady Red Hats of Worcester (Worcester), 232

Lawton, Marlene, Ruby Jewels of the Beach (Ipswich), 490

Murtagh, Peggy, Crimson Hattitudes (Brockton), 33, 393

O'Donnell, Ann, The Rosa Capellas (Weymouth), 400–401

Scott, Sue, Over The Seven Hills of Marlborough Red Hat Society, (Marlborough), 109

MEXICO

Crawford, Dianne, Ajijic Red Hat Mamas (Ajijic), 511

MICHIGAN

Adams, Judy, B Watcha Wanna Bee Red Hatters (Shepherd), 32–33

Androff, Mary, Razzle Dazzle of Clinton Township (Warren), 365

Barkel, Joyce, Fun Lovin' Ladies (Zeeland), 530, 538–539

Boehm, Grace, Classy Clarettes (Lake), 415

Bono, Dorothy, Silly Sassy Shelby Sisters (Washington Twp.), 265, 340

Denny, Diane, Berlin Center Red Hat Floozies (Saranac), 16

Dickerson, Joann, Classy Clarettes (Clare), 231

Flanery, Mary, Stony Mermaids (Shelby), 352

Gowans, Barbara, Birmingham Red Hat Belles (Waterford), 254

Grahl, Beth, Red Hat Belles of Fenton (Fenton), 331, 401

Haley, Vicki, Purple Passion (Allen Park), 441, 490

Hudson, Judy, Red Mint Hatters (Sturgis), 200

Joseph, Sylvia, Kool Katz's (Warren), 248

Kangas, Sandy, Red Hatters of the North (Menominee), 334

Karn, Anne, Lady Red Birds (Jones), 397

McGovney, Marge, The Red Hattitudes (DeWitt), 54

Mills, Helene, Birmingham Red Hat Belles (Birmingham), 250–251

Rouston, Joann, Hats Amore (Northville), 288–289

Saint, Mary Ann, The Happy Hatters (Plymouth), 99

Smith, Lee, Saline Salty Sexy Sirens (Tecumseh), 507

MICHIGAN (*continued*)

Smith, Reyes, Carefree Crimson Court of Coventry (Royal Oak), 311, 339

Suminski, Wanda, Classy Clarettes (Lake), 231

Vander Meulen, Paula, Ramblewood Red Hatters (Wyoming), 483

Vander Ploeg, Mary, Rivertown Belles (Wyoming), 153

Van Sickle, Tillie, Western Wayne County Red Hat Society (Westland), 181

Verkennis, Carol, Ruby Red Hat's Ramblers (Westland), 236

Waynick, Della, The Hot Foxy Ladies (Warren), 270, 272

MINNESOTA

Anderson, Laurie L., Visions in Red (Eagan), 525, 529

Benassi, Gerry, Red Hatted League of Duluth (Duluth), 37, 81

Dvorak, LuAnn, Czech Out the Divas (Montgomery), 343

Erickson, Rubye, Red Hat Adventurers (Edina), 181

Finney, Pat, Sassy Classy Ladies of Walker (Walker), 545

Fischer, Rose Marie, Red Hot Roses (South St. Paul), 47

Giordana, Nadia, Merry Mad Hatters (Dayton), 544–545

Guelzow, Jodi, Rowdy Red Hat Mamas (Circle Pines), 346

Hendricks, Linda, Red Hot and Purple (Janesville), 442

Huovinen, Lynette, Babbitt Just-for-Fun Red Hatters (Babbitt), 323

Kneeland, Sheryl, The Razzle Dazzlers (Elmore), 18, 293

Layer, Stephanie, The Red Cosmopolitans (Maplewood), 151, 195

McWilliams, Kristen, Red Hot Raspberries (Richfield), 316

Preston, Marilyn, Red Ladyslippers (Maplewood), 262

Riley, Deanna, Razzler-Dazzlers (Chatfield), 225, 504

Sauer, Linda, Crimson Cruisers/Wells Belles (Wells), 219

Schmoll, Deb, The Purple Apron Gals (Champlin), 51

Schoen, Sylvia M., Perky Purple Pixies of Minnesota (Minneapolis), 229, 284

Shaw, Verla, Breezy Belles in Bonnets (Pequot Lakes), 98

Steinberg, Sadie, Red Hot and Purple (Janesville), 451

Taylor, Esther, Frolicking Fuchsias (Lakeville), 198

Thorson, Jeannie, Sassy Sandhill Sweeties (Fertile), 347

Warinsky, Helen, Feisty Red Hatters (Woodbury), 464

Warta, Fay, Pearls & Red Hat Society (Delano), 205

MISSISSIPPI

Barwick, Lucy, Ladies of the Lake (Vicksburg), 328

Chedotal, Jeanette, Classy Sassy Ladies (Gulfport), 299, 304

Damiens, Camilla, Swinging Mississippi Belles (Carriere), 123

Gabel, Jackie, Swinging Mississippi Belles (Carriere), 366–367

Graves, Rhonda, Red Hot Hatters of Mid-Mississippi (Ridgeland), 174–175

Jordan, Charla, Brandon's Bodacious Babes (Brandon), 318, 473

Lemmuler, Joan, Swinging Mississippi Belles (Picayune), 237

Mortensen, K. Hub City Honeys (Petal), 551

North, Sylvia, Swinging Mississippi Belles (Carriere), 366, 416

Sheffield, Sonja, Red Hatted Stepchild (Gulfport), 171, 435

Smith, Paula, Red Hot Hatters of Mid-Mississippi (Ridgeland), 310

Strickland, Tammy, Osyka Red Hat Society (Osyka), 124

Terrell, Patricia, Right Royal Red Hatters (Long Beach), 516–517

Trahan, Beverly, Swinging Mississippi Belles (Carriere), 164

Wilson, Kathy T., Fondrem Femme Fatales (Jackson), 297

Yates, Betty, Willowing Mad Hatters (Steens), 170

MISSOURI

Asigner, Kathi, Red Hot Flashes (St. Ann), 168

Chapman, TJ, Sassy Sisters of Branson, Missouri (Branson), 346

Davenport, Judy, Parkville Red Pepper Popsies (Weatherby Lake), 462

Davis, Saima, Gateway Red Hatters (St. Louis), 208

Diemler, Barbara, Classy Red Hatters (Jefferson City), 70, 505

Dillow, Joyce, Red Hot Rockettes (Florissant), 535, 536

Fleeman, Marlene, Simply Red (Kingsville), 87, 287

Gideon, Betty, Classi Lassies (Lamar), 220–221

Graf, Betty, O'Really Reds (Nixa), 253

Hobson, Sue, Classi Lassies (Lamar), 237

Kickham, Leeann, Red Hat Prospects (Wentzville), 35

Meller, Sandy, California Reds (Lohman), 34, 93, 171

Meyer, Janet, West County Gals (Ballwin), 502

Miller, Karen, Diamond Lil's Red Hot Hatters (Kansas City), 298–299

Murray, Naomi, Scarlet O'Hatters of the Ozarks (Springfield), 4

Page, Mary, Lovely Ladies of Pevely (Pevely), 230

Phelps, Dottie, Les Dames aux Chapeaux Rouges (Malden), 319

Ross, Jane, High Steppin' Red Hatters (Carrollton), 195

Vaughn, Norma, Red Hat Senior Mamas (Tina), 519

Washick, Jean, Twister Sisters (Monett), 494

Witges, Barb, LuLu's Scarlet Ladies (Wentzville), 94

Wright, Kay, The Happy Hatters (Columbia), 484–485

Wright, Sandy, Simply Red (Pleasant Hill), 104

MONTANA

Byford, Marge, Titian Queens & Ladies-in-Waiting (Helena), 96

NEBRASKA

Glansdorp, Cynthia, Carolina Crimson Camellias (Pinehurst), 309

Jensen, Dorothy, Red Hat Honeys (Randolph), 261

Kudron, Patt, Raspberry Tarts (Lincoln), 213

Noakes Aldrich, Barbara, Tootee Flutee Red Hats (Omaha), 40–41, 122

Rose, Dolores, Isle de Grand Red Hat Divas (Grand Island), 159

Shaw, Bonita, Cardinal Hattitudes (Roseland), 116

Smith, Sharon, Ruby Rebels with Purple Passion (Palmyra), 193

Spader, Elaine, Red Hat Honeys (Randolph), 196

Sturgill, Phyllis, Red Hatted Faithful Few (Omaha), 104–105, 247, 292

Walters, Joann, Husker Honeys (Omaha), 336

Zavadil, Willma, Star City Gladabouts (Lincoln), 23

NEVADA

Bacso, Joan, Red Hat Hautes (Mesquite), 425

Chris, Carmella, Divine Desert Divas of Las Vegas (Las Vegas), 252

Duvall, Alice, Red Hat Valley Chicks (Minden), 214, 296–297

Frederick, Donna, Red Hat Silver Belles (Ely), 392–393

Fugelberg, Nancy, Vegas Vixens (Las Vegas), 367

Tarpinian, Jackie, Jewels of the Prairie (Jamestown), 482

Willick, Mara, SASCI (Sexy Adventurous Sun City Instigators, (Henderson), 271, 414, 418, 519

NEW HAMPSHIRE

McGee, Mary, Scarlet Women of Portsmouth (Portsmouth), 144–145

Payne, L. E., Red Hat Chilly Peppers (Epson), 265

NEW JERSEY

Barr, Marilyn, Red Hot Royals of Roxbury (Ledgewood), 184–185, 477

Capasso, Johanna G., Red Hot Hattitudes (Columbus), 395

Clapp, Maria, Hats 'R' Us (Williamstown), 7

Clark, Vonnie, Dames with a Par-tea Hat-titude (Absecon), 189

Da Petrillo, Mahel, Newton Redglows (Newton), 244

Fiori, Dolores, Tea-lightful Red Hatters (Hammonton), 56

Ganio, Jeanette M., Holly Hatters (Vineland), 510

LoPresti, Linda, Bergen Beauties (Paramus), 183

Mancuso, Agnes, Happening Ladies of Hamilton (Lawrenceville), 9, 76–77, 417

Salvesen, Alice, My Fair Ladies of Lakewood (Lakewood), 18–19

Sausto, Judy, Dames with a Par-Tea Hat-titude (Egg Harbor Township), 179, 418–419

Shannon, Janet, Crafty Cats In Crimson Hats (Tom's River), 328

Tarnowski, Linda, Purple Perks (Jackson), 461

Tucci, Mildred, Dazzling Damzels (Lodi), 149

Werlock, Eletta, Crafty Cats in Crimson Hats (Tom's River), 154

NEW MEXICO

Bloom, Janet, Princess Strutters (Carlsbad), 377

Jackson, Diane, Glitz & Glamour (Albuquerque), 168

Lawrence, MJ, Scarlett Strutters (Carlsbad), 311, 521

Sample, Ann, Jewels of the Desert (Albuquerque), 202–203

Shucavage, Jacqueline, Milan Mad Red Hatters (Grants), 466–467

NEW YORK

Andrews, Irene, The Ruby Red Hats (Lakewood), 277

Batjer, Jeannette, J&J Purple Hatters of Irondequoit (Rochester), 502

Beadle, Sharon, Sassy Sophistihats (Wallkill), 240

Botgia, Kitty, Sassy Sophistihats (Westtown), 347

Cassidy, Theresa, REDucators R Us (Forestburgh), 187

NEW YORK (*continued*)

Claydon, Sally, Glad Abouts (Gasport), 333

Drzal, Mary, Crimson Belles (Yonkers), 452–453

Eckart, Deborah, Bronx Bombshells (Bronx), 297

Ferris, Marian, The Rural Red Hats (Attica), 321

Finley, Mary, Violettas (Albany), 110

Gonzalez, Yvonne, The Sunshine Girls (Massapequa Park), 332–333

Harter, Joanne, Hot Tamales of Watertown (Harrisville), 79, 322

Hinkson, Elsie, Red Hatters of Bay Ridge (Brooklyn), 232–233

Howard, Judy, Retro Rubies (Penfield), 35

McAfee, Dolly, Sassy Sophistihats (Highland), 24

Menke, Sara, Rosie Red Hats (Wellington), 111

Porrello, JoAnn, Go for It Gals (Bayside), 417

Raymond, Susan, Brewster Wild Flowers (Pawling), 259

Romanczuk, Dorothy, Red Hot Zingers (Hamburg), 291, 362

Saulsbery, Joanne, Violettas (Colonie), 101

Sheppard, Judy, Hunnies with Hattitude (Hornell), 291

Wick, Patricia, Wecandogals (Gowanda), 113, 402–403

Winkes, Gloria, Sassy Sophistihats (Montgomery), 29

Zimmerman, Alisa, Colonie Red Hatters (Nassau), 359

Zimmerman, Lani, Colonie Red Hatters (Nassau), 198

NORTH CAROLINA

Anderson, Debbie, The Red Hot Flashes (Advance), 24–25, 381

Bragg, Louise, Elite Ladies of The Hat (Franklinton), 124, 173

Callicutt, Pat, Little Red Hens (Seagrove), 276–277

Fain, Jo Ann, Red Hats and Ready Hearts (Hendersonville), 52–53

Fogleman, Nancy, Little Red Hens (Asheboro), 446–447

Fuller, Lucy, Elite Ladies of The Hat (Franklinton), 19

Hart, Jean, Bodacious Belles of New Bern (New Bern), 432

Inman, Marjorie, Jazzy Belles (Chocowinity), 152–153

Jenkins, Phyllis, The Durham Dillies (Durham), 14–15

Jones, Phyllis, Carolina Belles (Charlotte), 6

Keith, Becky, Rolesville Red Hat Jewels (Rolesville), 358

Kirk, Elizabeth, Rocking Red Hatters (Lumberton), 46–47

Macomber, Patricia, Tickled Pink (Hertford), 132–133

Piper, Frances, Elite Ladies of the Hat (Franklinton), 65, 506

Reed, Sally, Tarheel Red Hat Club of Clemmons (Clemmons), 8–9, 90

Rivest, Kathleen, Sassy Red Hatters (Winston-Salem), 185, 302

Smith, Teresa, Sassy Southern Sisters (Shelby), 486

Spencer Robinson, Yvonne, 2 Many Foxy Red Hat Divas with Hattitude (Rockingham), 262

Starling, Jenny, Ooo-La-La Lee Girls (Princeton), 386, 506

Swift, Betty, Purple Passion Flowers (Greensboro), 366, 491

Tidy, Evelyn, Siler City Royal Belles (Siler City), 172

Wall, Joan, Randleman Red Hat Darlin's (Randleman), 68

Willoughby, Theresa, Red Hat Merry Makers (Apex), 344–345

Wilson, Mitzi, Fun and Fantastic Dames (Charlotte), 46, 437, 512

Wright, Leah, Elite Ladies of the Hat (Franklinton), 64, 129, 192

Yarbrough, Mary, Elite Ladies of The Hat (Franklinton), 145

Yost, Barbara, Bodacious Floozies (Jacksonville), 53

Young, Linda, HmmmDingers (Cedar Mountain), 72

NORTH DAKOTA

Glandt, Illa, Dakota Wild Roses (Valley City), 31

Hayes, Carole, Jewels of the Prairie (Jamestown), 43

Ouhl, Audrey, Prairie Dames of Elgin (Elgin), 114

Reid, Arlene, Dakota Wild Roses (Valley City), 206

Tarpinian, Jackie, Jewels of the Prairie (Jamestown), 215, 233

OHIO

Bibbee, Pamela, Springfield Globetrotters (Springfield), 128

Bieth, Brenda, The Mad Red Hatters (St. Clairsville), 495

Bristow, Mary Jane, Purple Passionattas (Painesville), 426

Buehrer, Dianne, Ramblin' Red Rose (Canton), 190

Farmakidis, Rita, Chapeaux Rouge (Cuyahoga Falls), 469

Gayer, Tina, The Water Lilies (Strongsville), 177

Grubb, Angel, Lydia's Red Hatters of New Albany (Lewis Center), 433

Hausenfleck, Connie, The Good-Time Red Hatters (North Canton), 550

Johnson, Jennifer, The Y-City Red Hat and Chocolate Lovers (Zanesville), 372–373

Laughter, Judy, Bridge Divas of Vandalia (Vandalia), 512

Lewis, Judith, Les Chapeaux Rouges of Bristol Village Ohio (Waverly), 285, 511

Myers, Anita, Kiwanis Manor Ramblin' Red Hatters (Tiffin), 26

Orosz, Sue, Red Spicy Ladies (Stow), 378–379

Pickering, Jacqueline, Queen City Crimson Belles (Cincinnati), 216

Reinhart, Oleta, Kiwanis Manor Ramblin' Red Hatters (Tiffin), 157, 395

Rennels, Rita, Ravishing Red Hatters (Westfield Center), 218

Schille, Carol, Purple Sages (Springfield), 457

Schlemmer, Darlene, Red Rovers (Kent), 65

Schweinhagen, Sherry, Tri-County Reds (Archbold), 235

Steinhoff, Sharon, The Red Hat Breakfast Club of Highland Heights (Highland Heights), 544

Wachter, Barbara, Regal Red Hatters of Germantown (Germantown), 10

Wagner, Sylvia, Red Bonnet LB Chapter (Cincinnati), 224

OKLAHOMA

Allen, Dolores, Awesome Sisters McAlester Red Hatters (McAlester), 77

Bougher, Sheila, Holy Rollers (Owasso), 268–269

Cannon, Eileen, Crimson Chapeau Club (Tulsa), 125

Divine, Debbie, Divine Dames (Wagoner), 83, 213

Hampshire, Hisako, Sassy Silly Sisters (Lawton), 185

Heldenbrand, Lola, Red Bud Belles (Bethany), 123

Kersey, Karen, Diamond Valley Divas (Cushing), 341

Moreland, Bessie, Cavanal Gems Red Hat Society (Poteau), 504–505

Morrison, Josephine, Purple Playground Ladies (Sand Springs), 8

OREGON

Bass, Donna, Dial Tone Divas (Albany), 446

Berry, L., Ruby Begonias (Beaverton), 413

Davis, Jill, Crimson Crones (Beaverton), 324

Kockx, Judith C. (Judy), Red Chalice Chicks (Medford), 261

Wolf, Evelyn, Crimson Bonnets (Sublimity), 217

PENNSYLVANIA

Ashbee, Gayla, Fun Buddy Babes (West Chester), 17

Branthoover, Shirley, Fayette-Greene Mama Mias (Alverton), 310–311

Bridges, Rosanne, Ruby Hatters (Bethlehem), 301, 477

Cannella, Marland, Falls-Overfield Scarlet Sages Injoying Lotsa Silliness (FOSSILS) (Falls), 134–135

Cecil, Sally, Rose's Rosebuds (Pittsburgh), 316–317, 430, 471

Christian, Joyce, Chester County's Classy Chassis (Downingtown), 149

Clarke, Mary, Le-Val Scarlet Divas (Hellertown), 440

Corrado, Kathy, Red Hat Chicks (Pittsburgh), 334

DeAngelis, Cassandra, Charming Ladies with Hattitude (Mill Run), 60–61, 370

Fabian, Judy, Rural Robust Red Hatters (Ford City), 47

Fiocca, Kathleen, Red Hat Philly Beach Babes (Langhorne), 94

Fry, Patricia, Barnyard Chicks (Mohnton), 392

Guilbeaux, Sandy, Shrewd Hatters of Shrewsbury (Stewartstown), 263, 319

Hartzell, Peggy, Majestic Red Hatters (Pine Grove), 398–399

Helmantoler, Jennie, Fayette-Greene Mama Mias (Carmichaels), 358, 450

Hofecker, Beverly, Red Hat Hotties (Johnstown), 112–113

Kilgore, Donna, Floosie's Floosies (Lititz), 441

Knauss, Carolyn, Red Cardinals (Tatamy), 404, 432, 500

Kornick, Pamela, The Red Madhatters (Windber), 410

Kriner, Joan L., The Red Hat Society of Shippensburg (Shippensburg), 23, 49, 198

Kuzma, Alta, Stat Code Red Hats (McKeesport), 503

Lengel, Lynn, Red Hat Cardinals (Nazareth), 96–97

McCollum, Grace, Red Hat Twisted Sisters Of Brotherly Love (Philadelphia), 71

Moore, Mary Louise, Fayette-Greene Mama Mia's (Uniontown), 528

Peat, Judy, Rural Robust Red Hatters (Ford City), 469

Phillips, Sharon, Scarlett O'Hatters of Lansdale (Lansdale), 396, 399

Plitt, Joan, The Cats in the Hats (York), 46

Powell, Alda, Rural Robust Red Hatters (Templeton), 498

Royal Raspberry Tarts, Chapter 60487 (Levittown), 244

Schaeffer, Linda, Curvaceous Babes (Fleetwood), 454

PENNSYLVANIA (*continued*)

Schonebaum, Letitia, Red Hot To Trots (Honey Brook), 96, 112

Shaeffer, Mildred, Rural Robust Red Hatters (Ford City), 19

Sierra-Franco, Barbara, Purple Queens of Prussia (King of Prussia), 398

Skibinski, Barbara, The Lake Side Red Hatters (Erie), 317

Sternberger, Shirley, Scarlet O'Hatters (Hershey), 453

Szydlik, Sara, Hell's Belles in Red (Brackenridge), 518

Tiffany, Barbara, La Tea Dolls (Somerset), 528

White, Diana, Royal Raspberry Tarts (Levittoun), 244

Wilcox, Bobbee, Foxy Red Hatters (Canton), 182

Wiles, Carol, Rural Robust Red Hatters (Kittanning), 443

Wilson, Susan, Iron Butterflies (Mont Alto), 86

Wood, Gerri, Ohio River Belles (Beaver), 377

RHODE ISLAND

Beauchemin, Barbara, Chapeaux Rouge of RI (Greene), 475

Montecalvo, Thelma, Little Rhody Red Hens (Woonsocket), 329, 474

Ursillo, Dawna Lee, Chapeaux Rouge (Narragansett), 476

SOUTH AFRICA

Ogilvie, Meg, Newcastle Nifty Fifties (Newcastle), 386

SOUTH CAROLINA

Bates, Helen, Rowdy Red Hatters (North Augusta), 516

Brooke, Trish, Sassy But Classy Carolina Girls (Sumter), 342

Calhoun, Sandra, Delightful Anderson Hattitude Sisterhood (Anderson), 218–219, 445

Davis, Mary, Red Hat Vintage Belles (West Columbia), 55

Evans, Dot, Not Young & Not Restless (Piedmont), 303, 312, 465

Hudson, Sallie, Dames of the Catawba (Winnsboro), 357

Kann, Aleene, Princesses of the Pines (Summerville), 315

Kicklighter, Nancy, Duchesses of Dorchester (Dorchester), 20, 66

Millwood, Vicky, Girls of the Pearl (Whitmire), 540

Morey, Diane, Secret Society of Southern Scarlet Sisters (Hardeeville), 157, 247

Parker, Linda, Carolina Jessamines (Chapin), 6–7

Stover, Audrey, Red Hat Hens and Chicks of Lancaster County (Heath Springs), 342–343

Thomas, Margaret, Red-Crested Purple-Breasted Beauties (Clemson), 491

Williamson, Bessie, Sassy Ladies (Sumter), 455

SOUTH DAKOTA

Fiedler, Sylvia, Bowdle WOWS (Bowdle), 103

Grosz, Diana, Platinum Valley Plum Tarts (Sioux Falls), 64–65, 193

Kiebach, Pat, Sweet T.A.R.T.S. (Harrisburg), 146, 192

Roth, Judy, Rockin Red Hatters (Warner), 332

Shaffer, Anna Marie, Red Hat Tamales of Many Towns (Sioux Falls), 10

Telkamp, Barbara, Le Chapeau Rouge (Brookings), 330

Weiland, Nonie, Purple Minded Sisters (Arlington), 359

TENNESSEE

Agee, Evelyn, Sugar Plum Girls (Lebanon), 501

Burnett, Nancy, Red Hat Chicks of Murfreesboro (Smyrna), 66

Calahan, Cindy, YA-YA Hoopla Girls (Shelbyville), 405

Caldwell, Jo Ann, Red Hat Jezebels (Brentwood), 220

Childress, Sheila, Bonnett Belles of Blountville (Blountville), 144

Clowers, Sally, Tennessee Tootsies (TNTs) (Tullahom), 114

Collier, Joan, The Red Hat Hotties (Franklin), 529

Cunningham, Tiffany, Sugar Plum Girls (Lebanon), 192–193

Deaton, Donna, Happy Hatters (McMinnville), 222–223

Denton, Lucinda, Nonpareils (Knoxville), 67, 270, 390–391, 425, 532

Flannery, Jeani, Devine Divas of Algood (Algood), 286

Folkes, Barbara, Red Hat Crafty Quilters (Maryville), 460–461

Forrest, Diana, Fab 50s (Athens), 258

Fraley, Linda, Mermaids (Millington), 544

Giddens, Peggy, Red Hot Red Hat Readers of Decatur (Ten Mile), 271, 376, 515

Jackson, Melonee, Donelson Red Hat Honeys (Nashville), 157

Kirk, Vera, Sugar Plum Girls (Lebanon), 13

Roberts, Linda, Nonpareils (Knoxville), 534–535, 536, 541

Rogers, Carolyn, Royal Reds (Knoxville), 22

Russell, Alice, Sassy Bodacious Ladies (Greeneville), 337

Selle, Sandra, Royal Purple Iris (Columbia), 445

Southerland, Sue, Sassy Bodacious Ladies (Greeneville), 274–275, 408, 474–475

Spencer, Betty, Scarlet Divas (Atoka), 212, 501

Stacy, Elsie, Red Hot Red Hat Readers of Decatur (Decatur), 212, 338

Stein, Sue, Hen-der-Hatters (Hendersonville), 187, 352

Taylor, Doris, Red Hot Red Hat Readers of Decatur (Ten Mile), 493

Tinch, Bonnie, Cathie's Cuties (Cookeville), 143

Tucker, Ronda, Red Hot Red Hat Readers of Decatur (Ten Mile), 61

Williams, Shirley, The Red Hat Mermaids (Knoxville), 44–45

Youngstead, Natalie, The Nonpareils (Loudon), 258

Ziegler, Judy, Farragut Classy Red Hots (Knoxville), 81

TEXAS

Banks, Pauline, The Burnet Road Beauties (Austin), 493

Barker, Lynda, Texas Red Bonnets (Mansfield), 233

Bledsoe, Dokie, Coleman County Texans (Valera), 73, 108–109, 393

Bohrer, Doreen, The Red Razzle Dazzles (Wimberley), 186

Bonham, Glenda, Ruby Roadrunners (Fort Stockton), 435

Burgess, Joan, Red Topped Texas Tornadoes (Branch), 21

Burns, Ann, Red Hot Hatters of Euless (Euless), 177, 496

Burns, Helen, Sassy Angels (Houston), 239

Burns, Maida, Houston Heights Red Hat Honeys (Houston), 238

Christian, Rita, Yesterday's Teens (Wake Village), 79

Clemons, Nancy, Luscious Ladies of League City (League City), 12–13, 16–17, 88, 277

Courington, Susie, The Crimson Jewels (The Woodlands), 534

Davis, Brookie, Tyler Red Hat Roses and Gawdy Gals (Flint), 422

Day, Nancie, Red Hat Hotties (Fort Worth), 498

Day, Wilma, Daring Audacious Yakety-Yaks (Oak Ridge North), 172

Derepentigny, Judy, Tricia's Texas Treasures (San Antonio), 388

Dobbs, Linda, Red Hat Ya-Yas (Beaumont), 68

Dudley, Marilyn, La Feria Femmes in Red Hats (Harlingen), 230

Farley, Patti, Majestic Myrtles (Yorktown), 492

Ferreri, Mildred, Crimson Camellia Socialites (The Woodlands), 424, 428

Goos, Rosemarie, Nine to Five Divas (Kingwood), 298

Griffin, Katie, Women in Time (Houston), 190

Grimes, Maryellen, Glamorous Gallavanting Gals (Fort Worth), 173

Hamlin-Lehmann, Brenda, Red Hat Dream Chasers (El Paso), 406–407

Hendon, Carol, Red Toppers (Katy), 141, 162

Hoyt, Doris, Red Hatted Ya Yas (Houston), 276

Hudspeth, Julie, Wanted: Red and Alive (Elgin), 388

Hutchison, Sharon, Racy Reds (Kaufman), 354–355

Huye, Claudia, GRITS (Girls Raised in the South),(Montgomery), 340–341, 391

James, Jowanna, Sweeny Hatters (Sweeny), 228

Jefferies, Joy, The Red Hat Classy Chicks (Austin), 456

Katai, Lisa, Dallas Red Hat Flashes (Murphy), 344, 437

Keefner, Nancy, Red Hatted Ya Yas (Richmond), 296

Keith, Edith, Betty's Bonnets (Fort Worth), 121

Kennedy, Carol, Under-Aged Beauties (Van Alstyne), 106, 471

Kiker, Martha, The Heavenly Hatters of Cedar Hill (De Soto), 100

Knowles, Hazel, Twin Palm Red Hatters (Lubbock), 384

Koehler, Dottie, Sassy Angels (Houston), 246

Lauer, Joyce, Ms. Aster's Disasters (Corpus Christi), 526

Lewis, Stella, Antique Rose Hatters (Farmers Branch), 314–315

Luce, Vanessa, Johnson City Red Hatters (Johnson City), 457

Lulu, Dixie, Red Hat Maw Maws (Orange), 364

Meder, Frances, Bayou City Red Hats (Houston), 450–451

Miller, Gaylene, The Red Hattitudes of Galveston (Ticki Island), 188

Minor, Darlene, Sassy Bowlers (New Braunfels), 509

Morales, Sandra, New Braunfels Colleens (Wimberley), 263, 527

Moseley, Bessie, Sassy Angels (Houston), 247

Ogletree, Irvaleen, Alpine Red Hat Society (Alpine), 254

Parker, Mary Francinn, The Happy Hatters (Georgetown), 179, 240, 264, 455

Ralls, Edith, Sassy Angels (Houston), 126

Rock, Roxy, Spring Elite Red Hatters (Tomball), 280

Roddy, Mary R., Sister Hood (Corpus Christi), 524

TEXAS (*continued*)

Russell, Janie, Big D Regals (Garland), 30, 460

Self, JoAn, Fine China Red Hatters of Saginaw (Saginaw), 409

Silva, Jo Anne, El Paso Red Hat Border Babes (El Paso), 57, 194

Sinast, Evelyn, Taft Red Hat Ladies (Taft), 336

Small, Lois, Classy Ladies (Denton), 389

Sorenson, Judy, Red Hat Ya-Yas (Rockdale), 448

Steines, Marilyn, Bodacious Bastrop Belles (Bastrop), 285

Taylor, Soffia, Ruby Red Hatters (Richardson), 389

Thomas, Susan, Divine Divas (San Antonio), 482–483

Thomason, Betty, Winters Blizzards Red Hat Babes (Winters), 348

Walls, Gena, The BEARables (Richmond), 188, 282

Wetherby, Carolyn, Regal Foxie Fillies (Cumby), 264

UTAH

Dolge, Pam, Sophisticated Sisters (St. George), 284–285

Haney, Marie, The Cats in the Hats (Ogden), 48–49

Hansen, Jan, Wasatch Good Golly Dollys (Holladay), 515

McKim, Mare, Crimson Canyon Country Crimson Cappers (Hatch), 540

Wood, Sharron, Desert Rouge Hattitudes of Hurricane Valley (LaVerkin), 454

VERMONT

Carlotto, Louise, The Ladybugs RHS (Orwell), 281, 353

Davidson, Sally, Purple Pips (Northfield), 92

Heil, Marjorie, Red Hat Bloomers (Bethel), 369

VIRGINIA

Baker, Diana, ParTeaGals (Burke), 153

Boughan, Theresa, Lucky Sunshine Ladies (Newport News), 427

Bullock, Dale, The Hummingbirds (Glen Allen), 136

Denton, Linda, Chapeau Rouge (Richmond), 38, 466, 543

Finger, Tonia, His Glorious Gals (Rustburg), 172

Fletcher, Gloria, First of The Red Hat Mammas (Charlottesville), 127

Goodwin, Dell, Crabtown Ladies (Hampton), 102–103

Grimm, Deborah, Blessed Babes by the Bay (Norfolk), 430–431

Hamilton, Wini, Cackling Crows (Woodbridge), 434

Jackson, Shirley, Totally Eccentric Adventurous Red Hatters of Vienna (Vienna), 262–263

Jensik, Dorothy, Cyber (Woodbridge), 381

Joye, Valerie, Rouge Chapeau Divas (Richmond), 27, 151

McCoy, Sherry, Star City Scarlett O'Hatters (Roanoke), 174

Mickley, Patricia, Redbuds of Bedford (Thaxton), 202

Mitchell, Barbara, Royal, Regal, Red Hat Rounders (Mechanicsville), 333

Monroe, Betty, Scarlet Sophisticates (Fredericksburg), 15

Murphy, Pamela, Supreme Queens of Elegance (Virginia Beach), 488

Nolan Cowles, Margie, The Virginia Vamps (Richmond), 532

Parkhurst, Nancy, Feathers and Flowers (Bedford), 58, 330

Praino, Dawn, Red Hot Colonial Sister (Dumfries), 256

Pritchert, Fran, Scarlet Sophisticates (Woodbridge), 338–339, 399, 474

Riley, Kay, Hunt for the Red Hats (Gainesville), 306, 371

Sayas, Lorraine, Tidewaters Gems (Virginia Beach), 143, 414–415, 480, 508

Schloff, Judy, Happy Trails (Chesapeake), 503

Scriven, Roma, Star City Scarlett O'Hatters (Roanoke), 208–209

Seibert, Diane, Divine Divas of the RHS (Lynchburg), 344, 348–349

Sensi, Judy, Ladies with HATtitude, Reston (Springfield), 328–329

Stacey, Shirley, Lucky Sunshine Ladies (Hampton), 431

Waters, Mary, Red Hat Divas (Moseley), 191

Williams, Charlotte, Lucky Sunshine Ladies (Hampton), 459

Williams, Dorothy, No Stopping Us Now (Richmond), 488–489

Works Gibson, Wendy, Red Hat Readers Society (Moneta), 56–57, 452

Zebrowski, Marie, Redbuds of Bedford (Bedford), 406

WASHINGTON

Botelho, Sami, Sleepless in Seattle Sassy Scarlet Sisterhood (Seattle), 194–195

Clark, Susan, Laughter Hatters (Federal Way), 467

Dutton, Cherie, Red Hot Tea Bags of Shoreline (Shoreline), 234

Eason, Jan, Windy Hat Snatchers (Ellensburg), 236

Garman, Toni, Red Hat Honeys (Spokane), 458, 533

Harris, Sabrena, Red Hat Jazzers (Kirkland), 26–27

Kauno, Kathy, Lynnwood Red Hat Flashes (Mountlake Terrace), 292

McIntyre Walker, Catie, Les Merlot Chapeaux (Walla Walla), 74–75, 110–111

Mitchell, Glenda, Red Hat Wine Mamas (Darrington), 221

Nilson, Barbara, Red Hat Hussies (Renton), 537

Reinthaler, Audi, Cascade Contessas (Leavenworth), 494–495

Shiflett, Linda, San Carlos She Shells (Liberty Lake), 290

Thomas, Paula, Red Hat Honeys (Spokane), 313, 323

Thomsett, LuLu (Linda-Rose), Ruby Royal Majes-"Teas" (Port Townsend), 108, 176, 313, 420, 422–423

Voorhees, Peggie, Red Hat Roundabouters (Port Orchard), 518

Weldon, Betty, Vancouver Belles (Longview), 500–501

WEST VIRGINIA

Gibb, Linda, Red Hat Roadrunners (Marlinton), 339

WISCONSIN

Aremka, Judy, Purple & Proud (Kenosha), 146–147

Arntz, Peggy, The Red Light Review Red Hatters (Waukesha), 464–465

Brown, Sharon, The Saintly Red Germain-iums (St. Germain), 278

Fritsche, Jeanne, Classie Lassies (Elkhorn), 68–69

Glenn, Linda, Rowdy Red Hat Mamas of N.W. Wisconsin (Luck), 39, 137, 533, 538

Herbers, Nancy, Ruby Fashionettes (Holmen), 180

Ingli, Patti, Ellsworth Red Hatters (Ellsworth), 276

Klinner, Shirley, Crimson C'Hatters (Medford), 180–181, 294, 448

Kloepfel, Elaine, Mad Red Hatters (Madison), 383

Lovas, Dawn, Red Tarts of SBC CSS (Cudahy), 174

Niesen, Maryanne, Red Hot Cheesy Chicks (Whitefish Bay), 112

Park-Coen, Carol, Rowdy Red Hat Mamas of NW Wisconsin (Luck), 295, 346–347

Rubietta, Marie, Red Hat Sweethearts for Atkinson (Jefferson), 245

Sykora, Gail K., Magenta Madames (Meno. Falls), 272

Taddey, Marcia, Damsels in Dis-Order (West Allis), 139

Thompson, Carol, Rowdy Red Hat Mamas (Frederic), 524–525

Waszak, Patti, Red Tarts of SBC CSS (Cudahy), 305, 496

Wierzbinski, Laura Lee, Raspberry Preserves (New Berlin), 86–87

Ziltener, J. Sue, Sassy Society Sisters (Janesville), 55

WYOMING

Cook, Sherrill, Scarlett O'Hatters (Powell), 440

Index of Recipes

Recipes for one or two servings are indicated by SMALL CAPS

ACORN SQUASH
Acorn Squash Soup, 295
CHICKEN-STUFFED ACORN
    SQUASH, 544

ALMONDS
Almond Butter Crunch, 158
ALMOND-CRUSTED CHICKEN WITH
    CARAMELIZED PEAR AND BRIE
    CREAM SAUCE, 539
Almond Joy Cake, 28
Almond Lovers' Cake, 48–49
Almond-Sesame Bars, 88
Almond Spinach Pizza, 351
Apple-Almond Chicken
    Sandwiches, 259
Christmas Cake Cookies, 106
Dream Bars, 246
Fruitcake Cookies, 105
Red Hat Venetians for Teatime, 255
Scandinavian Almond Tea, 193
Toasted Almond Dessert, 121

AMARETTO
Amaretto Apricot Chews, 253
Amaretto Cookies, 92–93
Easy Amaretto Flan, 120–121
Toasted Almond Dessert, 121

APPETIZERS AND SNACKS.
    See also Dips
Asian-Style Lettuce Wraps, 347
Asparagus Lovelies, 258–259
Asparagus Rolls, 259
Bacon Roll-Ups, 184–185
Baked Cheese Bundles, 182
Bitty Beef Calzones, 181

BLT Bites, 183
Bonna's Tipsy Tomatoes, 188
Bruschetta Sauce, 328
Caviar Pie, 178
Cheese and Pesto Spread, 178
Cheese Bombay, 169
Cheesy Artichoke Hearts Appetizer,
    180–181
Chilled Vegetable Pizza, 346–347
Chocolate Chip Cheese Ball, 169
Corned Beef Pâté, 168
Cowboy Caviar, 177
Drunken Hot Dogs, 183
Flat and Uglies, 178–179
Fresh Tomato Tart, 180
Garlic Mushrooms Morgan Hill, 184
Gougères, 181
Hot Peanuts, 187
Hot Sweet Little Sausages, 186
Joyce Moore's Crab Crunch, 171
Oh-So-Easy Sweet Kielbasa, 182
Pecan-Tuna Crunch Spread, 264
Pepperoni Loaf, 183
Pickled Shrimp, 185
Pineapple Cheese Ball, 173
Port Wine Cheese Spread, 247
Reuben Spread, 174
Roasted Red Pepper Cheesecake, 179
Sausage Balls, 182
Sausage Stars, 212
Seafood Rangoon, 345
Shrimp for Tapas, 434
Shrimp Puff Oriental, 185
Slumguneon, 264–265
Smashed Green Olives, 187
Spiced Pecan Halves, 188

Spinach Florentine Antipasto,
    186–187
Spinach Things, 190
Stuffed Mushrooms, 184
Taco Tartlets, 180
Texas Crab Grass, 172
Thocky, 381
Tortilla Rollups, 186
Tuna Spread, 179
Zesty Brussels Sprouts, 177

APPLES
Apple-Almond Chicken
    Sandwiches, 259
Apple Brownies, 86–87
APPLE CRUNCH, 524
Apple Dumplings, 121
Apple Loaves, 252
APPLE OVEN PANCAKE, 526
Apple Pie Pork Dinner, 369
Apple Slices, 245
Apple-Stuffed French Toast with
    Praline Topping, 208–209
APPLE TOPPING, 526
Autumn Treasure Green Salad, 293
BAKED PORK CHOPS
    WITH APPLES, 538
Brown Bag Apple Pie, 60
Caramel Apple Salad, 268
Cheddar-Apple Breakfast Lasagna,
    222–223
Cheesy Baked Apples, 507
Cranberry Apple Crisp, 138
Flowerpot Apple Muffins, 245
Fresh Apple Cake, 9
Fresh Fruit Salad Pita, 206
Grandma's Apple Pot Pie, 60–61

APPLES (continued)
Jewish Apple Cake, 9
Peach & Cranberry Pie, 73
Pomegranate Salad, 284–285
Sally's Apple and Nut Bread
  Pudding, 122
Stack Cake, 10

APPLESAUCE
Applesauce Cake, 250–251
My Mom's Homemade
  Applesauce, 518

APRICOTS
Amaretto Apricot Chews, 253
Apricot Carrot Mélange, 491
Apricot Cream Cheese Pound
  Cake, 4
Apricot Fold-Ups, 93
Apricot Nectar Cake, 11
Hot Fruit Casserole, 219
Viennese Apricot Jam Macaroons, 91

ARTICHOKE HEARTS
Artichoke Bake, 220
Artichoke Chicken Pasta Salad, 268
Big-Hearted Salad, 280
Cheesy Artichoke Hearts Appetizer,
  180–181
Chicken Sicilian, 409
Four Favorites Pizza, 356
Mediterranean Chicken, 418

ASPARAGUS
Asparagus Lovelies, 258–259
Asparagus Raspberry Salad, 269
Asparagus Rolls, 259
ASPARAGUS WITH FRESH
  CHEESE, 550
Lemon Asparagus Soup, 295
Marinated Asparagus Salad, 268–269

AVOCADOS
Avocado Cocktail, 269
Avocado Quick Bread, 227
Avocado Salsa, 348–349
Black Bean Pitas with Avocado Salsa,
  348–349
Salpicon, 384

BACON
Asparagus Lovelies, 258–259
Bacon & Tomato Chicken, 399
Bacon Roll-Ups, 184–185
Baked Cheese Bundles, 182
BLT Bites, 183
BLT Dip, 168
Broccoli Bacon Salad, 270
Calico Baked Beans, 454
Jalapeño-Stuffed Bacon-Wrapped
  Grilled Shrimp, 435
Magnolia Special, 344
Mississippi Sin Dip, 174–175
Old-Fashioned German-Style Potato
  Salad, 285
Popcorn Salad, 284
Thocky, 381

BANANAS
Aloha Loaf, 231
Banana Blueberry Bread, 228
Banana Butter, 247
Banana Cream Coffeecake, 223
Banana Cream Salad, 276
Banana Glaze, 15
Banana-Nut Cake, aka Grammy
  Cake, 16–17
Banana Split Dessert, 122
Blue Ribbon Banana Coconut
  Cake, 12–13
Delicious Spice Cake, 15
Frozen Fruit Cups, 219
Honey-Sweet Banana-Nut Bread, 228

Kiwi-Banana Kuchen, 140
PEACHRAZNANA SMOOTHIE, 529
Pineapple Boat Salad, 282–283
Pomegranate Salad, 284–285
Strawberry and Caramel-Banana
  Trifle, 150

BARLEY
Chicken Barley Soup, 306

BARS AND SQUARES
Almond-Sesame Bars, 88
Cherry Coconut Tea Dainties, 252
Choco-Cherry Bars, 90
Coconut Mounds Bars, 98
Crescent Cream Squares, 151
German Chocolate Luscious Bars, 87
Honey Bars, 108–109
No-Bake Bars, 116
Peanut Butter Squares, 56
Pecan-Topped Pumpkin Pie
  Squares, 78
Piña Colada Squares, 111
Red Hat Venetians for Teatime, 255
Refrigerator Fruit Cake, 117
Rich Nut and Jam Squares, 254
Sweet Maria Bars, 116

BEANS. See also Black beans;
  Garbanzo beans
baked beans
    Calico Baked Beans, 454
    Kahlúa Baked Beans, 488
    Smoked Baked Beans, 488–489
Beef and Bean Wraps, 348
Colby Bean Dip, 168
Escarole and Bean Soup, 309
Five-Bean Casserole, 453
Layered Nacho Dip, 172
Mexican Beef and Bean Casserole,
  440–441

Pantry Soup, 298
Special Red Bean Recipe, 299
Tuscan Soup, 319
Utah Country White Beans, 454

BEEF
Baked Beef Stew, 382
Bar-B-Cups, 386
Beef and Bean Wraps, 348
Beef Stroganoff, 390–391
Beefy Picadillo Dip, 169
Best Steak Marinade Ever, 396
Bitty Beef Calzones, 181
Braised Short Ribs, 382
burgers and sandwiches
  Beef and Chile Cheese Rolls, 330–331
  Beef Barbecue for a Bunch, 336
  Beef-Stuffed French Loaf, 332
  Dynamites, 329
  Gourmet Gingerburgers, 328
  Memories of Philly Burgers, 330
  The Ol' Ball Game Hot Dog Chili, 333
  Pizza Burgers, 331
  Pizza-wiches, 336
  Red Hot Topper, 333
  Sirloin French Dip, 334
  Slow Cooker Italian Sandwich Beef, 335
casseroles
  Calico Baked Beans, 454
  GREEN BEAN & GROUND BEEF CASSEROLE, 536
  Mexican Beef and Bean Casserole, 440–441
  Microwave Spanish Rice, 441
  Potluck Spaghetti, 458
  Ravioli Lasagna, 475
  Shepherd's Pie, 440
  Slow Cooker Pizza Casserole, 443

Sour Cream Noodle Bake, 440
Southwest Hominy Casserole, 447
Spicy Corn Bread Casserole, 442
String Pie, 459
Taco Casserole, 449
Texas Hash, 442–443
"Unstuffed" Cabbage Roll Casserole, 441
Chicken-Fried Steak, 385
Cocktail Pizza, 358
"Cooks By Itself" Brisket and Vegetables, 380
Crazy Crust Pizza, 354
CUBE STEAK AND POTATOES FOR TWO, 535
Drunken Beef, 383
Flank Steak in Wine Sauce, 380
"Golf Balls" with Sauce, 376
Greek Beef Stew, 386
Green Chili Stew, 314
GROUND BEEF MIX, 534, 536
Hamburger Noodle Soup, 302
Impossibly Easy Cheeseburger Pie, 394
Italian Eggplant and Ground Chuck Casserole, 391
Italian Gravy a la Rutigliano, 461
Italian Pasta Fazool, 296
MEATBALLS FOR ONE, 534
Meatball Soup, 304
meat loaf
  Burgundy Beef Loaf with Burgundy Sauce, 386–387
  Cheesy Meatloaf, 393
  Dill Pickle Meat Loaf, 388
  French Onion Meatloaf, 389
  INDIVIDUAL MEAT LOAF, 536
  MEATLOAF IN A MUG, 535
  Meat Puffs, 392–393
  Mexican Meat Loaf, 389
  MINI MEAT LOAF FOR TWO, 538

Reuben Meat Loaf, 392
  Sicilian Meatloaf, 393
Microwave Beef Stroganoff, 388
Minnesota "Uff da" Tacos, 347
PAN-FRIED LIVER WITH THYME, 537
Pantry Soup, 298
Pennsylvania Dutch Beef and Noodles, 384–385
Peppery Beef, 378
Plum Luscious Roast, 378
Quick Bubble Pizza, 352
Quicker Beef Pastries, 394
Red Hot Taco Soup, 310
Rowdy Red Chili, 306–307
Salpicon, 384
Slow-Baked Dinner Steaks, 381
SLOW-COOKER STEW FOR TWO, 533
Soda Pop Beef Brisket, 378–379
SOY-SIZZLED SIRLOIN STRIPS, 534
SPAGHETTI AND MEATBALLS FOR ONE, 535
Steak Lovers' Soup, 298–299
Stuffed Cabbage Rolls, 396
STUFFED PEPPERS, 536
Summer Sausage, 395
Taco Dip, 174
Taco Tartlets, 180
Thocky, 381
Upside-Down Pizza, 351
Yugoslavian Spaghetti Sauce, 460–461

BEER
Beer Garden Pork Chops, 371
Drunken Beef, 383
Slap-It-Together Beer Cheese Soup, 305

BEETS
Curried Beet Salad, 272–273
Czarina's Cranberry Borscht Salad with Horseradish Dressing, 278

BEETS (*continued*)
Rollicking Red Beet Cake, 10
Sweet Red Beets, 488

BEVERAGES
Bloomer Droppers, 196
Brandy Slush, 193
Coffee Punch, 190
Coronation Citrus Tea Punch, 244
Cosmotini, 195
Eggnog, 190–191
Fresh Strawberry Daiquiri, 198
Gin Julep, 195
Holiday Wassail Punch, 198
Holiday Wine Coolers, 198
Homemade Kahlúa, 194
Hot Mulled Apple Cider, 189
Orange Eggnog, 191
Peach Iced Tea, 192
PEACHRAZNANA SMOOTHIE, 529
Pink Hatter Lemonade, 192–193
PRUNACOLADA, 528
Red Hat Diva Holiday Tea, 191
Red Head's Irish Cream, 194–195
Rhubarb Slush, 192
Scandinavian Almond Tea, 193
Snowman Soup, 192
Strawberry and Cream Cooler, 196
Strawberry Champagne Fancy
    Schmancy Drink, 196

BISCOTTI
Cranberry-Pistachio Biscotti, 101

BISCUITS
Cheese Biscuits, 239
Omelet Biscuit Cups, 224
Pineapple Upside-Down Biscuits, 147
Queen Mom Angel Biscuits, 240

BLACK BEANS
Black Bean Pitas with Avocado Salsa,
    348–349
Enhanced Black Beans, 488
Mexican Kitchen Black Bean and
    Sausage Posole, 296–297
Pineapple & Black Bean Salsa, 519

BLACK-EYED PEAS
Black-Eyed-Pea Salad, 270
Cowboy Caviar, 177
Shoe Peg Salsa, 175

BLUEBERRIES
Banana Blueberry Bread, 228
Blueberries and Cream Dessert, 124
Blueberry Bread Pudding with
    Caramel Sauce, 123
Blueberry Cake, 13
Blueberry Nut Crunch, 124
Blueberry Pound Cake, 5
Double Berry Multi-Grain
    Pancakes, 208
Fresh Fruit Salad Pita, 206
Gridiron Blueberry Muffins, 230
Nova Scotia Blueberry Cream Cake, 25
Red Hat Berry Cream Pie, 79
Three Sisters Pie, 61
Unbaked Fresh Blueberry Pie, 62

BLUE CHEESE
Baby Blue Salad, 274–275
Roquefort Dressing, 288–289
Tomato and Gorgonzola Pizza, 354

BOLOGNA
Bologna Sandwich Spread, 336
Italian Hero Sandwich, 344
Meal in a Bun, 330

BOURBON
Bourbon Balls, 157
Bourbon Pecan Pie, 75
Drunken Hot Dogs, 183
Eggnog, 190–191
Whiskey-Glazed Pork Chops,
    370–371
Whiskey-Soused Salmon, 428

BREAD PUDDINGS AND
    STRATAS
Apple-Stuffed French Toast with
    Praline Topping, 208–209
Blueberry Bread Pudding with
    Caramel Sauce, 123
Bread Pudding, 207
BREAD PUDDING FOR TWO, 524
Cheese Soufflé, 481
Cinnamon-Raisin French Toast
    Soufflé, 206
Crab Soufflé, 211
Creamy Sausage Brunch Soufflé, 214
Doughnut Bread Pudding with Butter
    Rum Sauce, 126
Ham and Egg Strata, 216
Pajama Party Breakfast Bake, 209
Sally's Apple and Nut Bread
    Pudding, 122
Sausage and Rye Brunch Bake, 218
Sausage Fondue, 216
Vegetable Strata, 483

BREADS AND ROLLS
Cloverleaf Dinner Rolls, 234
corn bread
    Cake Corn Bread, 238
    Corn Bread Bake, 513
    Corn Bread Salad, 275
    Hot Hot Jalapeño Corn
        Bread, 238

SOUTHERN-STYLE CORN STICKS, 529
Texican Corn Bread, 237
Cottage Dill Bread for Bread Machine, 236
Crescent Caramel Swirl, 226–227
French Baguettes, 237
Land-Of-Nod Cinnamon Buns, 226
Monkey Bread, 202
Oat Cakes, 266
Oatmeal Bread, 235
Onion Bread, 241
Pecan-Cinnamon Tea Ring, 249
Quick and Easy Rolls, 235
quick breads
    Aloha Loaf, 231
    Apple Loaves, 252
    Avocado Quick Bread, 227
    Banana Blueberry Bread, 228
    Carrot-Date-Nut Bread, 229
    Cherry Bread, 229
    Chocolate Zucchini Bread, 253
    Date-Nut Bread, 232–233
    Green Tomato Bread, 240
    Honey-Sweet Banana-Nut Bread, 228
    Pumpkin Spice Bread, 234
    Pumpkin Tea Bread, 258
    Red Jewel Bread, 230
    Strawberry Bread, 258
    Weathervane Inn Irish Soda Bread, 257
Sheepherder's Bread, 236
Shortcut Cinnamon Rolls, 225
Sunday Yeast Rolls, 233

BREAKFAST AND BRUNCH DISHES. See also Bread puddings and stratas; Coffeecakes and pastries; Pancakes
Artichoke Bake, 220
Baked Cheese, 213

Baked Eggs Dijon, 214
Breakfast Burrito Bar, 214–215
Cheddar-Apple Breakfast Lasagna, 222–223
Country-Style Sausage Gravy, 220–221
Crème Brulée French Toast, 210
Elephant Ears, 200
English Toad in the Hole, 213
Fresh Fruit Salad Pita, 206
Frozen Fruit Cups, 219
Grits Soufflé, 218–219
Hot Fruit Casserole, 219
Kodiak Waffles, 211
MIGAS FOR ONE, 527
Morning Potatoes, 222
Omelet Biscuit Cups, 224
Omelets in a Bag, 222
Raised Czech Dumplings, 203
Rice Croquettes, 220
Sausage-Rice Brunch Casserole, 212–213
Sausage Stars, 212

BROCCOLI
Broccoli Bacon Salad, 270
Broccoli Bake, 453
BROCCOLI HAM MUFFINS, 528–529
Corn Bread Salad, 275
Cream of Fresh Broccoli Soup, 297
Deep-Dish Broccoli Pizza, 353
Garlic Broccoli, 490
Ham-N-Cheddar Broccoli Quiche, 212
Lasagna Roll-Ups, 477
Mighty Vegetable Casserole, 511
Slow Cooker Broccoli Soup, 299
Veggie Burgers, 332–333

BROWNIES
Apple Brownies, 86–87
Bake Shop Brownies, 91

Brown Sugar Brownies, 87
Just Plain Great Brownies, 90
Kahlúa Brownies, 88
Oatmeal Brownies, 89
Surprise Brownies, 86
Toffee-Topped Brownie Trifle Delight, 130
Turtle Brownies, 89

BRUSSELS SPROUTS
Brussels Sprout Salad, 271
Brussels Sprouts Gratinée, 490
Zesty Brussels Sprouts, 177

BUTTERS
Banana Butter, 247
Herb Butter, 522

CABBAGE
Caraway Cabbage Toss, 293
Cranberry-Walnut Cabbage Slaw, 294
Picnic German Coleslaw, 294
Scalloped Cabbage, 489
Stuffed Cabbage Rolls, 396
"Unstuffed" Cabbage Roll Casserole, 441

CAKES. See also Cheesecakes
All-American Chocolate Cake, 38–39
Almond Joy Cake, 28
Almond Lovers' Cake, 48–49
Applesauce Cake, 250–251
Apricot Nectar Cake, 11
Banana-Nut Cake, aka Grammy Cake, 16–17
Black Forest Cake, 40
Black Russian Cake, 48
Black Walnut Cake, 46
Blueberry Cake, 13
Blue Ribbon Banana Coconut Cake, 12–13

CAKES (*continued*)
Butter Cake, 5
Chewy Carrot Date Cake, 11
Chocolate Chip Kahlúa Cake, 47
Chocolate Chip Rum Cake, 40
Chocolate-Chocolate Cake to Die For, 35
Chocolate Mayonnaise Cake, 38
Chocolate Pudding Cake, 129
Chocolate Upside-Down Cake, 33
Chocolate Zucchini Cake, 58
Cool Coconut Do-Ahead Cake, 15
Crazy Cake, 43
Delicious Spice Cake, 15
Dreamsicle Cake, 24–25
Earthquake Cake, 43
Fresh Apple Cake, 9
Graham Cracker Cake with Mocha Frosting, 41
The Great Pumpkin Cake, 18
Holiday Pecan Cake, 22–23
It's-a-Sin Cake, 24
Japanese Fruitcake, 20
Jewish Apple Cake, 9
Kentucky Jam Cake, 51
Lamingtons, 126
Last-Minute Chocolate Cake, 39
Lemon Cake, 26–27
Lemon Jell-O Cake, 29
Lemon Lime Cake, 28–29
Lemon Meringue Cake, 30
Lemon Nut Crunch, 29
Milky Way Cake, 52–53
Mississippi Mud Cake, 36–37
Molten Chocolate Cakes with Vanilla Ice Cream, 36
Nova Scotia Blueberry Cream Cake, 25
Oatmeal Chocolate Chip Cake, 49
Old-Fashioned Devil's Food Cake, 39
Old-Fashioned Raisin Cake, 14–15
Past-Perfect Fruit Cake, 19

Peanut Butter Sheet Cake, 54
Peanut Butter Squares, 56
Pineapple Angel Food Cake, 32
Pineapple Coconut Cake, 32
Pink Champagne Cake, 54
Pink Lady Cake, 23
Pistachio Cake, 46–47
Pistachio Marble Cake, 47
Popcorn Candy Cake, 45
Poppy Seed Bundt Cake, 53
pound cakes
    Apricot Cream Cheese Pound Cake, 4
    Blueberry Pound Cake, 5
    Chocolate Pound Cake, 6–7
    Coconut Lovers Pound Cake, 8–9
    Cream Cheese Pound Cake, 6
    Hurry-Up Pound Cake, 6
    Lavender Pound Cake, 7
    Pecan Pound Cake, 251
Pumpkin Cake Roll, 14
Pumpkin Pie Cake, 17
Red Hat Cranberry Pudding Cake with Butter Sauce, 137
Red Hatters Red Cake, 37
Red Hot Momma's Party Cake, 30–31
Rollicking Red Beet Cake, 10
Royal Carrot Cake, 12
Ruby Slipper Cake, 23
Rum Cake, 42–43
Shoofly Cake, 49
Solid Walnut Cake, 46
Stack Cake, 10
Strawberry Shortcut Cake, 24
Strawberry YaYa Cake, 55
Sunshine Cake, 27
Swedish Pineapple Cake, 31
Tangerine Cake, 27
Texas Hot Cocoa Cake, 40–41
Texas White Sheet Cake, 4–5
Tres Leches Cake, 57

Triple Chocolate Mess Cake, 35
Triple Fudge Cake, 34
Upside-Down Rhubarb Cake, 51
Watermelon Cake, 32–33
White Wine Cake, 56–57

CANDY
Almond Butter Crunch, 158
Buckeyes, 162–163
Butter Mints, 157
Butterscotch Haystacks, 158
Creamy Pralines, 164
Crunchy Candy, 160
Crunchy Peanut Bark, 163
English Toffee, 160–161
Macadamia Nut Truffles, 161
Micro Fudge, 158–159
Microwave Peanut Brittle, 163
Orange-Coconut Balls, 162
Peanut Butter Snowballs, 162
Pecan Caramel Candies, 161
Quick Foolproof Fudge, 159
Sherry Pralines, 164
Stained Glass Windows, 160
Toffee Bar Squares, 164
Velveeta Fudge, 157

CANTALOUPE
Cantaloupe Chiffon Pie, 65
Cantaloupe Surprise, 273
Fluffy Lime Cantaloupe, 143
Fresh Fruit Salad Pita, 206
Mint Melon Soup, 310

CARAMELS
Blueberry Bread Pudding with Caramel Sauce, 123
Caramel Ice Bream, 139
Caramel Syrup, 150
German Chocolate Luscious Bars, 87

Pecan Caramel Candies, 161
Strawberry and Caramel-Banana
   Trifle, 150
Turtle Brownies, 89

CARROTS
Apricot Carrot Mélange, 491
Carrot and Leek Soup, 303
Carrot-Date-Nut Bread, 229
Carrot Marmalade, 519
Carrot Soufflé, 490–491
Carrot Soup with Ginger, 303
Chewy Carrot Date Cake, 11
Copper Pennies, 492
Herb-Baked Veggies, 509
Mighty Vegetable Casserole, 511
Royal Carrot Cake, 12
Turnip & Carrot Casserole, 506
Veggie Burgers, 332–333

CASHEWS
Cashew Nut Chicken, 403
Wheat Germ-Cashew Granola, 205

CASSEROLES. *See also* Bread
   puddings and stratas
Baked Noodle Cups, 480–481
Broccoli Bake, 453
California Casserole, 482
Cheesy Chicken Vegetable
   Casserole, 446
Chicken Tetrazzini, 467
Corn Casserole, 455
Creamy Chicken and Stuffing
   Casserole, 445
Creamy Potato Bake, 456
Crunchy Chicken Bake, 446
Easy Chicken Enchilada
   Casserole, 449
Eggplant Casserole, 455
Five-Bean Casserole, 453
Green and Gold Casserole, 484–485

GREEN BEAN & GROUND BEEF
   CASSEROLE, 536
Green Bean & Swiss Cheese
   Casserole, 497
GREEN BEAN CASSEROLE, 548
Haddock Casserole, 450
Hot Chicken Salad, 446–447
Impossibly Easy Cheeseburger Pie, 394
Italian Eggplant and Ground Chuck
   Casserole, 391
King Ranch Chicken, 448
Layered Reuben Bake, 442
Mac and Texas Cheeses with Roasted
   Chiles, 460
Macaroni and Cheese Scallop, 464
Mexican Beef and Bean Casserole,
   440–441
Microwave Spanish Rice, 441
Mighty Vegetable Casserole, 511
Never-Fail Macaroni and Cheese, 464
One, Two Sausage and Rice Bake, 444
One-Dish Chicken and Rice Bake, 410
Pepperoni Zucchini Casserole, 450
Poppy Seed Chicken, 451
Potluck Spaghetti, 458
Ravioli Lasagna, 475
Red Pepper Lasagna, 478
Salmon Noodle Casserole, 451
Seafood Lasagna, 478–479
Shepherd's Pie, 440
Shrimp and Wild Rice Casserole,
   450–451
Slow Cooker Pizza Casserole, 443
Sour Cream Noodle Bake, 440
Southwest Hominy Casserole, 447
Spicy Corn Bread Casserole, 442
Spinach Lasagna, 477
Spinach Ziti, 476
Squash, Corn Bread, and Green Chile
   Bake, 456
Squash or Eggplant Casserole, 455
String Pie, 459

Sweet-and-Sour Green Bean
   Casserole, 495
Taco Casserole, 449
Texas Hash, 442–443
Three-Cheese Macaroni and Cheese,
   462–463
Turkey Crunch Casserole, 452–453
Turnip & Carrot Casserole, 506
"Unstuffed" Cabbage Roll
   Casserole, 441
Vegetarian Chili Corn Bread
   Casserole, 484
Wild Rice Casserole, 513
Wild Rice Chicken Casserole, 448
Zucchini Pie, 458
Zucchini Stuffing Bake, 457

CAULIFLOWER
Cauliflower Salad, 272
Corn Bread Salad, 275
Creamy Roasted Cauliflower Soup,
   300–301
Mighty Vegetable Casserole, 511
Swedish Cauliflower, 491

CHAMPAGNE
Pink Champagne Cake, 54
Strawberry Champagne Fancy
   Schmancy Drink, 196

CHEESE. *See also* Blue cheese; Cream
   cheese; Parmesan Cheese; Ricotta
   cheese
ALMOND-CRUSTED CHICKEN WITH
   CARAMELIZED PEAR AND BRIE
   CREAM SAUCE, 539
Baked Cheese, 213
Beef and Chile Cheese Rolls, 330–331
Cake-Pan Cheese Soufflé, 482
Cheddar-Apple Breakfast Lasagna,
   222–223
Cheese Biscuits, 239
Cheese Bombay, 169

CHEESE (*continued*)
Cheese Soufflé, 481
Cheesy Artichoke Hearts Appetizer, 180–181
Cheesy Baked Apples, 507
Cheesy Meatloaf, 393
Cheesy New Potatoes, 501
Chili Cheese Chicken, 398
Chili Cheese Dip, 170
Colby Bean Dip, 168
A Cup, A Cup, A Cup Dip, 173
Dutch Tart, 481
Feta Cheese Orzo, 463
Feta-Spinach Pie, 485
Gougères, 181
Green Bean & Swiss Cheese Casserole, 497
Ham-N-Cheddar Broccoli Quiche, 212
HAM 'N' CHEESE MASHED POTATOES, 538–539
Hot Corn Cheese Dip, 170
Impossibly Easy Cheeseburger Pie, 394
Layered Nacho Dip, 172
Mac and Texas Cheeses with Roasted Chiles, 460
Macaroni and Cheese Salad, 277
Macaroni and Cheese Scallop, 464
Magnolia Special, 344
Meal in a Bun, 330
Melt-In-Your-Mouth Cheese Tarts, 262–263
Mississippi Sin Dip, 174–175
Nearly Instantaneous Swiss Onion Soup, 312
Never-Fail Macaroni and Cheese, 464
Pasta and Brie, 466
Port Wine Cheese Spread, 247
Potato Crust Ham and Cheese Quiche, 216–217
Salmon Cheese Chowder, 324
Slap-It-Together Beer Cheese Soup, 305
Slow-Cooker Macaroni and Cheese, 466
Spinach Florentine Antipasto, 186–187
Swiss & Cream Cheese Chicken Enchiladas, 413
SWISS CHEESE SOUFFLÉ, 548
Three-Cheese Macaroni and Cheese, 462–463
Tomato and Gorgonzola Pizza, 354
Velveeta Fudge, 157
Zesty Texan Chicken Alfredo, 467
Zucchini Cheese Puff, 507

CHEESECAKES
Cassis & White Chocolate Cheesecake, 132
Cheesecake Cake, 18–19
Classic Cheesecake, 134–135
Cottage Cheese Cake, 19
Fudge Rum Cheesecake, 134
Italian Cheesecake, 131
No-Need-to-Share Individual Cheesecakes, 133
Peanut Butter Cheesecake, 132–133
Roasted Red Pepper Cheesecake, 179
Spiced Eggnog Cheesecake, 22

CHERRIES
Banana Cream Salad, 276
Black Forest Cake, 40
Cherries in the Snow, 127
Cherry Bread, 229
Cherry Coconut Tea Dainties, 252
Choco-Cherry Bars, 90
Overnight Pancakes with Fruit Sauce, 202–203
Pink Stuff, 276

CHICKEN
ALMOND-CRUSTED CHICKEN WITH CARAMELIZED PEAR AND BRIE CREAM SAUCE, 539
Artichoke Chicken Pasta Salad, 268
Bacon & Tomato Chicken, 399
Baked Yogurt Chicken, 415
Berry Easy Red Chicken, 401
BOB HOPE'S FAVORITE CHICKEN HASH, 544
Cajun Skillet Jambalaya, 412
Cashew Nut Chicken, 403
casseroles
    Cheesy Chicken Vegetable Casserole, 446
    Chicken Tetrazzini, 467
    Creamy Chicken and Stuffing Casserole, 445
    Crunchy Chicken Bake, 446
    Easy Chicken Enchilada Casserole, 449
    Hot Chicken Salad, 446–447
    King Ranch Chicken, 448
    One-Dish Chicken and Rice Bake, 410
    Poppy Seed Chicken, 451
    Wild Rice Chicken Casserole, 448
Celebration Chicken, 399
Chicken Asiago, 398
CHICKEN BASILICO, 543
Chicken Chipotle Pasta, 468–469
Chicken Fajita Pizza, 354–355
Chicken Marsala, 410
Chicken Paprikash, 422–423
Chicken Piccata, 408
Chicken Reuben, 410–411
Chicken Salad Delight, 262
Chicken Sicilian, 409
CHICKEN-STUFFED ACORN SQUASH, 544
Chicken-Stuffed Manicotti, 466–467

Chicken Supreme, 545
Chicken Thighs with Wine, 418–419
Chicken Vermouth, 415
Chicken with Tarragon Cream
    Sauce, 412
Chili Cheese Chicken, 398
Crunchy Chicken, 404
Crunchy Oven-Fried Chicken, 404
Cuban Chicken and Rice (Arroz Con
    Pollo), 419
Easy Chicken Dijon, 405
Garlic Fried Chicken Sesame Soy
    Glaze, 402
Great Grilled Chicken, 398–399
Grilled Chicken with White BBQ
    Sauce, 362
Herbed Chicken in Wine Sauce, 406
Honeymoon Special Chicken, 406
Honey Mustard Chicken, 542
Honey-Pecan Chicken Salad, 337
Italian Baked Chicken, 416
Jalapeño-Lime Chicken for Fajitas,
    406–407
Korean-Style Chicken in a
    Lettuce Leaf, 542–543
Lazy Chicken Cordon Bleu, 416
Lemon Chicken, 407
Lemon Chicken Pilaf, 541
Malaysian Pizza, 355
Mediterranean Chicken, 418
Mexican Citrus-Marinated Chicken, 403
Mexican Meat Loaf, 389
Mother's Potato Chip Chicken, 408
Pineapple-Soy Sauce Chicken,
    402–403
Presto Change-O Chicken and Rice
    Salad, 286–287
Prosciutto-Stuffed Chicken, 417
Purple Chicken with Plum Sauce,
    408–409
sandwiches
    Apple-Almond Chicken
        Sandwiches, 259

Baked Chicken Sandwiches, 337
Bonnet Tea Chicken Cranberry
    Sandwiches, 261
Hot Brown Sandwich, 342–343
Simple Asian-Style Chicken or
    Chop, 542
Simple Cordon Blue, 540
Slow Cooker Chicken and Corn
    Bread Dressing, 405
Slow Cooker Chicken and Dressing, 445
soups
    Chicken Barley Soup, 306
    Chicken-Cheese Tortellini Soup
        with Spinach, 306
    Fast and Easy Chicken
        Chili, 308
    Mulligatawny Soup, 309
    Wild Rice Soup, 322–323
Sour Cream Chicken, 414
Spinach-Stuffed Chicken Cutlets, 417
Swiss & Cream Cheese Chicken
    Enchiladas, 413
Taste of Hawaii Chicken Salad, 274
Tequila-Lime Chicken, 414–415
Teriyaki Chicken, 414
Teriyaki Grilled Chicken, 413
Two-Step Parmesan-Garlic
    Chicken, 407
Warm Chicken Dip, 170
White Meatloaf, 420
Zesty Texan Chicken Alfredo, 467

CHICK PEAS. See Garbanzo beans

CHILI
Fast and Easy Chicken Chili, 308
The Ol' Ball Game Hot Dog Chili,
    333
Rowdy Red Chili, 306–307
Vegetarian Chili Corn Bread
    Casserole, 484
White Chili, 307

CHOCOLATE
brownies
    Bake Shop Brownies, 91
    Just Plain Great Brownies, 90
    Kahlúa Brownies, 88
    Surprise Brownies, 86
    Toffee-Topped Brownie Trifle
        Delight, 130
    Turtle Brownies, 89
cakes
    All-American Chocolate Cake,
        38–39
    Almond Joy Cake, 28
    Black Forest Cake, 40
    Chocolate Chip Kahlúa Cake, 47
    Chocolate Chip Rum Cake, 40
    Chocolate-Chocolate Cake to
        Die For, 35
    Chocolate Mayonnaise Cake, 38
    Chocolate Pound Cake, 6–7
    Chocolate Pudding Cake, 129
    Chocolate Upside-Down Cake, 33
    Chocolate Zucchini Cake, 58
    Crazy Cake, 43
    Graham Cracker Cake with
        Mocha Frosting, 41
    Last-Minute Chocolate Cake, 39
    Milky Way Cake, 52–53
    Mississippi Mud Cake, 36–37
    Molten Chocolate Cakes with
        Vanilla Ice Cream, 36
    Oatmeal Chocolate Chip Cake, 49
    Old-Fashioned Devil's Food
        Cake, 39
    Red Hatters Red Cake, 37
    Rollicking Red Beet Cake, 10
    Texas Hot Cocoa Cake, 40–41
    Triple Chocolate Mess Cake, 35
    Triple Fudge Cake, 34
candy
    Almond Butter Crunch, 158
    Buckeyes, 162–163

CHOCOLATE (*continued*)

    Crunchy Candy, 160

    English Toffee, 160–161

    Micro Fudge, 158–159

    Peanut Butter Snowballs, 162

    Quick Foolproof Fudge, 159

    Velveeta Fudge, 157

cheesecakes

    Cassis & White Chocolate
      Cheesecake, 132

    Fudge Rum Cheesecake, 134

Chocolate Chip Cheese Ball, 169

Chocolate Glaze, 136–137

Chocolate Ice Cream, 139

Chocolate Zucchini Bread, 253

cookies

    Chewy Double Chocolate
      Cookies, 95

    Choco-Cherry Bars, 90

    Chocolate Chip Crisps, 101

    Chocolate Turtles, 96

    Coconut Kiss Cookies, 98–99

    Coconut Mounds Bars, 98

    Forget-Me-Nots, 94

    German Chocolate Luscious
      Bars, 87

    Peanut Butter Kisses, 109

    Peanut Butter Squares, 56

    Pumpkin & Chocolate Chip
      Cookies, 110–111

    Sour Cream Chocolate Drops, 96

desserts

    Chocolate Cream Torte Delight,
      127

    Chocolate Hazelnut Torte, 244

frostings

    Chocolate Frosting, 36–37

    Chocolate Ganache, 56

    Mocha Frosting, 41

Hot Fudge Sauce, 156

Microwave Hot Fudge Sauce, 155

pies

    Chocolate Angel Pie, 62–63

    Chocolate Chess Pie, 64

    Fresh Strawberry Tart, 82

    Microwave Choc Pie, 66

    Raspberry White Chocolate
      Pie, 81

Snowman Soup, 192

CHOWDERS

Clam Chowder, 301

Crawfish and Corn Chowder, 304

Fish Chowder, 532

Fresh Shrimp Chowder, 323

Manhattan Fish Chowder, 324

Salmon Cheese Chowder, 324

CLAMS

Clam Chowder, 301

Shrimp or Clam Marinara Pasta, 475

COCONUT

Aloha Loaf, 231

cakes

    Almond Joy Cake, 28

    Blue Ribbon Banana Coconut
      Cake, 12–13

    Coconut Lovers Pound Cake, 8–9

    Cool Coconut Do-Ahead Cake, 15

    Earthquake Cake, 43

    Pineapple Coconut Cake, 32

Cherry Coconut Tea Dainties, 252

cookies

    Coconut Kiss Cookies, 98–99

    Coconut Macaroons with Red
      Tops, 99

    Coconut Mounds Bars, 98

    Josephines, 102–103

    Piña Colada Squares, 111

    Swedish Courtyard Coconut
      Cookies, 98

    World's Greatest Corn Flake
      Cookie, 102

Dream Bars, 246

Great Granola, 205

Orange-Coconut Balls, 162

pies

    Coconut Buttermilk Pies, 68

    Crustless Coconut Pies, 65

    Hospitality Pies, 66

    Macaroon Pie, 68

Refrigerator Fruit Cake, 117

Taste of Hawaii Chicken Salad, 274

Wheat Germ-Cashew Granola, 205

COFFEE

Baby Back Ribs with Java Sauce,
    372–373

Coffee Punch, 190

Java Sauce, 372–373

Tender-to-the-Bone Spareribs in
    Quick Joe Sauce, 374

COFFEECAKES AND PASTRIES

Banana Cream Coffeecake, 223

The Best Darn Coffeecake Ever, 225

Cherry Coconut Tea Dainties, 252

Cranberry Coffeecake, 224

Crunchy-Top Coffee Cake, 527

Danish Kringle, 201

Danish Puff, 200–201

Pecan-Cinnamon Tea Ring, 249

Red Raspberry Cheese Danish, 202

Sour Cream Coffeecake, 226

COOKIES. *See also* Bars and squares

Amaretto Apricot Chews, 253

Amaretto Cookies, 92–93

Apricot Fold-Ups, 93

Bourbon Balls, 157

Chewy Double Chocolate Cookies, 95

Chocolate Chip Crisps, 101

Chocolate Turtles, 96
Christmas Cake Cookies, 106
Coconut Kiss Cookies, 98–99
Coconut Macaroons with Red Tops, 99
Cookie Dough Cream Cheese Cups, 96–97
Cornflake Macaroons, 248
Corn Flake No-Bakes, 100
Cranberry-Pistachio Biscotti, 101
Date Swirl Cookies, 100
Dunking Platter Cookies, 103
Fancy Rich Butter Cookies, 248–249
Forget-Me-Nots, 94
Frosted Cranberry-Orange Cookies, 104–105
Fruitcake Cookies, 105
Ginger-Lavender Sugar Cookies, 108
Homemade Crème Sandwiches, 95
Josephines, 102–103
Macadamia Snowballs, 106
Melt-In-Your-Mouth Butter Cookies, 94
Nut Balls, 103
Peanut Butter Cups, 159
Peanut Butter Kisses, 109
Peanut Butter Miracles, 111
Potato Chip Cookies, 109
Pumpkin & Chocolate Chip Cookies, 110–111
Raspberry Meringue Kisses, 112
Real Scottish Shortbread, 254
Ricotta Cookies, 110
Root Beer Cookies, 112–113
Snappy Gingersnaps, 106–107
Snicker Cookies, 114
Sour Cream Chocolate Drops, 96
Spice Cookies, 113
Spiced Oatmeal Cookies, 107
Swedish Courtyard Coconut Cookies, 98
Viennese Apricot Jam Macaroons, 91

World's Greatest Corn Flake Cookie, 102
Zucchini Cookies, 114

CORN
Confetti Corn Scallop, 496
Corn & Zucchini Gratin, 495
Corn Bread Bake, 513
Corn Casserole, 455
Corn Fritters, 493
Corn Soufflé, 492–493
Crawfish and Corn Chowder, 304
Creamy Slow Cooker Corn, 493
Fresh Fried Corn, 493
Green and Gold Casserole, 484–485
Hot Corn Cheese Dip, 170
Mexicorn Dip, 171
Micro-Scalloped Corn, 492
Shoe Peg Salsa, 175
Spicy Corn Bread Casserole, 442
Summer Corn Gazpacho, 300

CORNED BEEF
Corned Beef Extra, 383
Corned Beef Pâté, 168
Layered Reuben Bake, 442
Queen's Cream of Reuben Soup, 316
Reuben Spread, 174

CORN FLAKES
Chocolate Chip Crisps, 101
Cornflake Macaroons, 248
Corn Flake No-Bakes, 100
Dunking Platter Cookies, 103
World's Greatest Corn Flake Cookie, 102

CRABMEAT
Baked Crab Rolls, 338–339
Chesapeake Bay Crab Cakes, 430–431

Crabby Tilapia, 425
Crab Quiche Deluxe, 210
Crab Salad Rounds, 338
Crab Soufflé, 211
Deluxe Crab Soup, 302
Easy Crab Imperial, 432
Hampton Crab Cakes, 431
Hot Crab Dip, 171
Hot Crab Sandwiches, 339
In-a-Snap Crab Bisque, 301
Joyce Moore's Crab Crunch, 171
Maryland Crab Cake Sandwich, 338
Seafood Lasagna, 478–479
Seafood Rangoon, 345
Seafood Soup, 318
Texas Crab Grass, 172

CRANBERRIES
Berry Easy Red Chicken, 401
Bonnet Tea Chicken Cranberry Sandwiches, 261
Cranberry Apple Crisp, 138
Cranberry Coffeecake, 224
Cranberry Marmalade, 517
Cranberry-Pear Sauce, 368
Cranberry-Pistachio Biscotti, 101
Cranberry Swirl Salad, 512
Cranberry-Walnut Cabbage Slaw, 294
Cranberry Walnut Pie, 64–65
Crown Pork Roast with Cranberry Pear Sauce, 368
Czarina's Cranberry Borscht Salad with Horseradish Dressing, 278
Double Berry Multi-Grain Pancakes, 208
Frosted Cranberry-Orange Cookies, 104–105
Overnight Pancakes with Fruit Sauce, 202–203
Peach & Cranberry Pie, 73
Red Hat Cranberry Pudding Cake with Butter Sauce, 137

CRANBERRIES (continued)
Red Jewel Bread, 230
Ruby Sweet Pork Chops, 370
Spiced Cranberry-Orange Sauce, 518–519

CRAWFISH
Crawfish and Corn Chowder, 304
Crawfish Jambalaya in a Rice Cooker, 433
Seafood Soup, 318

CREAM CHEESE
Apricot Cream Cheese Pound Cake, 4
Baked Cheese Bundles, 182
Blender Cheese Pie, 64
Blueberries and Cream Dessert, 124
Cheese and Pesto Spread, 178
Cherries in the Snow, 127
Chocolate Chip Cheese Ball, 169
Chocolate Cream Torte Delight, 127
Cookie Dough Cream Cheese Cups, 96–97
Cream Cheese Filling, 86
Cream Cheese Pound Cake, 6
Crescent Cream Squares, 151
Dessert Cheese Ball, 135
Grapes and Cream, 144
Pineapple Cheese Ball, 173
Red Raspberry Cheese Danish, 202
Swiss & Cream Cheese Chicken Enchiladas, 413

CUCUMBERS
Big Batch Tea Sandwich, 260–261
Cool Cucumber Soup, 308
Cucumber Cream Salad, 273
Cucumber Tea Sandwiches, 261
Freezer Pickles, 520
Seven-Day Sweet Pickles, 520
Summer Sandwich, 345

DATES
Carrot-Date-Nut Bread, 229
Chewy Carrot Date Cake, 11
Christmas Cake Cookies, 106
Date-Nut Bread, 232–233
Date Swirl Cookies, 100
Dunking Platter Cookies, 103
Figgy Date Bars, 251

DESSERTS. See also Bars and squares; Bread puddings and stratas; Brownies; Cakes; Cheesecakes; Cookies; Pies and tarts; Puddings
APPLE CRUNCH, 524
Apple Dumplings, 121
Apple Slices, 245
Baked Custard with Caramel Sauce, 138
Baked Peaches, 145
BAKED PEARS, 525
Banana Cream Salad, 276
Banana Split Dessert, 122
Blueberries and Cream Dessert, 124
Blueberry Nut Crunch, 124
Cherries in the Snow, 127
CHILLED STRAWBERRY CREAM, 526
Christmas Plum Duff, 146
Cranberry Apple Crisp, 138
Creamy Cream Puffs, 136–137
Dessert Cheese Ball, 135
Dirt Dessert, 128
Dream Bars, 246
Easy Amaretto Flan, 120–121
eating first, 1
Eggnog Flan, 125
Fluffy Lime Cantaloupe, 143
French Cream, 136
frozen desserts
    Creamy Strawberry Freeze, 149
    Foundation Ice Cream, 139
    Frosty Fruit Pops, 142
    Frozen Fruit Cups, 219

Heavenly Ice Cream Dessert, 139
Homemade Crème Sandwiches, 95
Hospitality Pies, 66
Lemonade Stand Pie, 69
Margarita Pie, 71
Toffee Bar Crunch Pie, 82
Fruit Pizza, 143
Funnel Cakes, 130
Grapes and Cream, 144
Kiwi-Banana Kuchen, 140
Lazy Peach Party Dessert, 146
Lemon Lush, 140–141
Mini Hamburger Dessert, 145
Nut Baklava, 144–145
Pineapple Upside-Down Biscuits, 147
Pink Stuff, 276
Pumpkin Crunch, 148
Quick Lemon Mousse, 142–143
Rhubarb Dessert, 148–149
Simplified Fruit Cobbler, 123
Tiramisu, 152
Toasted Almond Dessert, 121
tortes
    Blitz Torten, 152–153
    Chocolate Cream Torte Delight, 127
    Chocolate Hazelnut Torte, 244
    Ice Cream Crunch Torte, 140
    Pistachio Delight Torte, 148
    Praline Pumpkin Torte, 146–147
trifles
    Charlotte Royale Mousse Trifle, 129
    Red Hat Gelatin Trifle, 128
    Simple Strawberry Trifle, 151
    Strawberry and Caramel-Banana Trifle, 150
    Toffee-Topped Brownie Trifle Delight, 130
Twinkie Casserole, 153

Vanilla Pecan Delight, 154
Vanilla Snowbank, 153
Zeppole, 154

DIPS
Beefy Picadillo Dip, 169
BLT Dip, 168
Chili Cheese Dip, 170
Colby Bean Dip, 168
A Cup, A Cup, A Cup Dip, 173
Fresh Vegetable Dip, 174
High Society Dip, 172
Hot Corn Cheese Dip, 170
Hot Crab Dip, 171
Hot Onion Dip, 173
Layered Nacho Dip, 172
Marshmallow Fruit Dip, 246
Mexicorn Dip, 171
Mississippi Sin Dip, 174–175
Orange Sour Cream Fruit Dip, 246
Peppernut Sandwich Spread or Dip, 264
Taco Dip, 174
Warm Chicken Dip, 170

DRESSINGS. See Salad dressings;
    Stuffings and dressings

DUCK
Kentucky Duck, 420

EGGNOG
Eggnog, 190–191
Eggnog Flan, 125
Orange Eggnog, 191
Spiced Eggnog Cheesecake, 22

EGGPLANTS
Eggplant Casserole, 455
Eggplant Timbale, 494–495
Feta Cheese Orzo, 463

Italian Eggplant and Ground Chuck
    Casserole, 391
Ratatouille (Summer Veggie Medley),
    511
Roasted Vegetables, 508–509
Squash or Eggplant Casserole, 455

EGGS. See also Bread puddings and
    stratas; Quiche
Baked Custard with Caramel Sauce,
    138
Baked Eggs Dijon, 214
Breakfast Burrito Bar, 214–215
Dill Egg Spread, 265
Egg Spread, 340
MIGAS FOR ONE, 527
Omelet Biscuit Cups, 224
Omelets in a Bag, 222
Red Head's Irish Cream, 194–195

ENCHILADAS
Easy Chicken Enchilada Casserole, 449
Microwave Green Chile Enchiladas, 350
Real Green Chile Enchiladas, 350
Swiss & Cream Cheese Chicken
    Enchiladas, 413

ESCAROLE AND BEAN SOUP, 309

FIGS
Figgy Date Bars, 251

FISH. See also Salmon; Tuna
BAKED ORANGE ROUGHY WITH
    VEGGIES, 546
Company Halibut, 426
Crabby Tilapia, 425
FISH CHOWDER, 532
Fish Tacos, 349
Foil Dinner, 424–425
Grilled Perch and Pine Nuts, 426

Haddock Casserole, 450
Halibut Parmesan, 425
Manhattan Fish Chowder, 324
Marinated Tilapia, 426–427
Panamanian Seviche, 427
Pan-Seared Tilapia, 427
Sole Meuniere with Baby Bella
    Mushrooms, 424
Southwestern Flounder, 423
SUN-DRENCHED COD, 544–545

FROSTINGS AND FILLINGS. See
    also Glazes
Chocolate Frosting, 36–37
Chocolate Ganache, 56
Cream Cheese Filling, 86
Creamy Nut Filling, 13
Decorator Buttercream Icing, 44–45
French Cream Frosting, 55
Mocha Frosting, 41
Quick Caramel Frosting, 11

FRUIT
Autumn Treasure Green Salad, 293
Banana Cream Salad, 276
Charlotte Royale Mousse Trifle, 129
Fresh Fruit Salad Pita, 206
Frosty Fruit Pie, 72
Frosty Fruit Pops, 142
Frozen Fruit Cups, 219
Fruit and Cream Cooler, 135
Fruit Ice Cream, 139
Fruit Pizza, 143
Glazed Fruit Tarts, 70–71
Hot Fruit Casserole, 219
Hot Sherried Fruit, 512
Japanese Fruitcake, 20
Mint Melon Soup, 310
Overnight Pancakes with Fruit Sauce,
    202–203

FRUIT (continued)
Pineapple Boat Salad, 282–283
Red Hat Summer Salad, 290
Simplified Fruit Cobbler, 123

FRUIT, DRIED
Christmas Cake Cookies, 106
Fruitcake Cookies, 105
Past-Perfect Fruit Cake, 19
Refrigerator Fruit Cake, 117
Stovetop Raisin Cakes, 265

FRUIT DIPS
Marshmallow Fruit Dip, 246
Orange Sour Cream Fruit Dip, 246

GARBANZO BEANS
Chick Pea Soup, 297
Five-Bean Casserole, 453

GLAZES
Banana Glaze, 15
Chocolate Glaze, 136–137

GRANOLA
Great Granola, 205
Wheat Germ-Cashew Granola, 205

GRAPES
Fresh Fruit Salad Pita, 206
Frozen Fruit Cups, 219
Grapes and Cream, 144
Red Hat Summer Salad, 290

GRAVY
Country-Style Sausage Gravy,
    220–221
Hot Turkey and Gravy for
    Sandwiches, 343
Italian Gravy a la Rutigliano, 461

GREEN BEANS
Barbecued Green Beans, 496
Farmer's Green Beans, 496
Fresh Green Bean and Squash
    Salad, 271
GREEN BEAN & GROUND BEEF
    CASSEROLE, 536
Green Bean & Swiss Cheese
    Casserole, 497
Green Bean Bundles, 499
GREEN BEAN CASSEROLE, 548
Sweet-and-Sour Green Bean
    Casserole, 495

GREEN CHILES
Beef and Chile Cheese Rolls, 330–331
California Casserole, 482
Chili Cheese Chicken, 398
Green Chili Stew, 314
Microwave Green Chile Enchiladas, 350
Real Green Chile Enchiladas, 350
Squash, Corn Bread, and Green Chile
    Bake, 456

GRITS
Grits Soufflé, 218–219
Kentucky Derby Grits, 514–515
Shrimp and Grits, 437

HAM
Big Bunch Barbecued Chopped
    Ham, 339
BROCCOLI HAM MUFFINS, 528–529
Easy Ham Tortillas, 346
"Golf Balls" with Sauce, 376
Ham and Egg Strata, 216
Ham in a Blanket, 364
Ham Loaf, 377
Ham-N-Cheddar Broccoli Quiche, 212
HAM 'N' CHEESE MASHED
    POTATOES, 538–539

Lazy Chicken Cordon Bleu, 416
Little Swedish Meatballs, 377
Meal in a Bun, 330
Mississippi Sin Dip, 174–175
Monte Cristo Sandwiches, 346
Muffulettas, 340–341
Omelet Biscuit Cups, 224
Pajama Party Breakfast Bake, 209
Peach and Ham Stir-Fry, 366
Pear Tea Sandwiches, 263
Potato Crust Ham and Cheese
    Quiche, 216–217
SIMPLE CORDON BLUE, 540
Stromboli, 358

HAZELNUTS
Chocolate Hazelnut Torte, 244

HEARTS OF PALM
Big-Hearted Salad, 280

HOMINY
Southwest Hominy Casserole, 447

HOT DOGS
Drunken Hot Dogs, 183
The Ol' Ball Game Hot Dog Chili, 333

JALAPEÑO PEPPERS
Hot Hot Jalapeño Corn Bread, 238
Jalapeño-Lime Chicken for Fajitas,
    406–407
Jalapeño-Stuffed Bacon-Wrapped
    Grilled Shrimp, 435

JAMS AND MARMALADES
Carrot Marmalade, 519
Cranberry Marmalade, 517
Green Tomato Jam, 521
Kentucky Jam Cake, 51
Pineapple-Kiwi Microwave Jam, 521

Rich Nut and Jam Squares, 254
Viennese Apricot Jam Macaroons, 91

KAHLÚA
Black Russian Cake, 48
Chocolate Chip Kahlúa Cake, 47
Homemade Kahlúa, 194
Kahlúa Baked Beans, 488
Kahlúa Brownies, 88
Toasted Almond Dessert, 121

KIELBASA
Oh-So-Easy Sweet Kielbasa, 182
Slow-Cooker Kielbasa and Kraut, 377

KIWIFRUIT
Kiwi-Banana Kuchen, 140
Pineapple-Kiwi Microwave Jam, 521

LAMB
PAN-FRIED LIVER WITH THYME, 537
Roast Leg of Lamb, 397

LAVENDER
Ginger-Lavender Sugar Cookies, 108
Lavender Pound Cake, 7

LEEKS
Carrot and Leek Soup, 303
Ice Cold Vichyssoise, 316–317

LEMONS
Citrus Meringue Pie, 73
Coronation Citrus Tea Punch, 244
Lemonade Stand Pie, 69
Lemon Asparagus Soup, 295
Lemon Cake, 26–27
Lemon Cake Pie, 68–69
Lemon-Caper Sauce, 396–397
Lemon Chicken, 407
LEMON CHICKEN PILAF, 541

Lemon Fluff Sauce, 155
Lemon Jell-O Cake, 29
Lemon Lime Cake, 28–29
Lemon Lush, 140–141
Lemon Meringue Cake, 30
Lemon Nut Crunch, 29
LITTLE LEMON MERINGUE PIES, 524–525
Low-Fat Lemon Icebox Pie, 83
Microwave Lemon Curd, 247
Pink Hatter Lemonade, 192–193
Pink Lemonade Pie, 71
Quick Lemon Mousse, 142–143
Self-Frosting Lemon Pie, 69
Veal with Lemon-Caper Sauce, 396–397

LIMA BEANS
Candied Lima Beans, 498

LIMES
Fluffy Lime Cantaloupe, 143
Jalapeño-Lime Chicken for Fajitas, 406–407
Lemon Lime Cake, 28–29
Lime Vinaigrette, 384
Mexican Citrus-Marinated Chicken, 403
Tequila-Lime Chicken, 414–415

LOBSTER
Curried Lobster Bake, 438

MACADAMIA NUTS
Macadamia Nut Truffles, 161
Macadamia Snowballs, 106
Taste of Hawaii Chicken Salad, 274

MARINADES
Best Steak Marinade Ever, 396
Fresh Albacore with Onion Marinade, 428–429

GRILLED TUNA WITH HONEY-MUSTARD MARINADE, 545

MARMALADES. *See* Jams and marmalades

MUFFINS
Baking Mix Muffins, 229
BROCCOLI HAM MUFFINS, 528–529
Flowerpot Apple Muffins, 245
Gridiron Blueberry Muffins, 230
Nutty Rhubarb Muffins, 231
Pound Cake Muffins, 233
Sour Cream Muffins, 244
SOUR CREAM MUFFINS, 530

MUSHROOMS
Fresh Mushroom Soup, 321
Garlic Mushrooms Morgan Hill, 184
LINGUINE WITH SHRIMP AND MUSHROOMS, 550
Marinated Fresh Mushrooms, 278
MUSHROOM RISOTTO, 548–549
Portobello Pizza, 355
Roasted Vegetables, 508–509
Sole Meuniere with Baby Bella Mushrooms, 424
Stuffed Mushrooms, 184
Vegetable Kabobs, 486, 508

NOODLES
Baked Noodle Cups, 480–481
Beef Stroganoff, 390–391
Hamburger Noodle Soup, 302
Microwave Beef Stroganoff, 388
Noodle Kugel, 514
Pennsylvania Dutch Beef and Noodles, 384–385
Salmon Noodle Casserole, 451
Sour Cream Noodle Bake, 440

NUTS. *See also* Almonds; Cashews; Macadamia nuts; Pecans; Walnuts
Banana-Nut Cake, aka Grammy Cake, 16–17
Carrot-Date-Nut Bread, 229
Christmas Cake Cookies, 106
Date-Nut Bread, 232–233
Lemon Nut Crunch, 29
Nut Tea Sandwiches, 263
Nutty Rhubarb Muffins, 231

OATMEAL
Amaretto Cookies, 92–93
Dunking Platter Cookies, 103
Great Granola, 205
Oat Cakes, 266
Oatmeal Bread, 235
Oatmeal Brownies, 89
Oatmeal Chocolate Chip Cake, 49
Spiced Oatmeal Cookies, 107
Wheat Germ-Cashew Granola, 205

OLIVES
Muffulettas, 340–341
Potatoes Smashed with Olives, 500
Slumguneon, 264–265
Smashed Green Olives, 187

ONIONS
Balsamic Onions with Honey, 499
The Best French Onion Soup Ever, 312
A Cup, A Cup, A Cup Dip, 173
French Onion Meatloaf, 389
Fresh Albacore with Onion Marinade, 428–429
Holiday Scalloped Onions, 498–499
Hot Onion Dip, 173
Nearly Instantaneous Swiss Onion Soup, 312
Onion and Wine Soup, 310–311
Onion Bread, 241

Onion Tart, 497
ORANGE & BERMUDA ONION SALAD, 532
Tomato-Onion Phyllo Pizza, 357
Vidalia Onion Salad, 280–281

ORANGES
Balsamic Orange Dressing, 280
Banana Cream Salad, 276
Citrus Meringue Pie, 73
Coronation Citrus Tea Punch, 244
Fresh Fruit Salad Pita, 206
Frosted Cranberry-Orange Cookies, 104–105
Frozen Fruit Cups, 219
Fruit Pizza, 143
Ginger-Orange Scones, 256
Mexican Citrus-Marinated Chicken, 403
ORANGE & BERMUDA ONION SALAD, 532
Orange-Coconut Balls, 162
Orange Cream Scones, 254–255
Orange Eggnog, 191
Orange Sour Cream Fruit Dip, 246
Pineapple Boat Salad, 282–283
Pink Stuff, 276
Soy Orange Ginger Dressing, 281
Spiced Cranberry-Orange Sauce, 518–519
SUN-DRENCHED COD, 544–545
Sunshine Cake, 27

OYSTERS
Oyster Stew, 311
Scalloped Oysters, 432

PANCAKES
APPLE OVEN PANCAKE, 526
Double Berry Multi-Grain Pancakes, 208

Oven Puff Pancake, 528
Overnight Pancakes with Fruit Sauce, 202–203
Sourdough Pancakes, 208

PARMESAN CHEESE
ASPARAGUS WITH FRESH CHEESE, 550
Halibut Parmesan, 425
Two-Step Parmesan-Garlic Chicken, 407

PASTA. *See also* Noodles
Cheese Ravioli with Pumpkin-Sage Sauce, 464–465
Chicken-Cheese Tortellini Soup with Spinach, 306
Chicken Chipotle Pasta, 468–469
Chicken-Stuffed Manicotti, 466–467
Chicken Tetrazzini, 467
Depression Spaghetti, 457
Feta Cheese Orzo, 463
Garlic Parsley Spaghetti, 469
Italian Gravy a la Rutigliano, 461
Italian Pasta Fazool, 296
lasagna
    Ravioli Lasagna, 475
    Red Pepper Lasagna, 478
    Seafood Lasagna, 478–479
    Spinach Lasagna, 477
Lasagna Roll-Ups, 477
Linguine with Roasted Peppers, 471
LINGUINE WITH SHRIMP AND MUSHROOMS, 550
macaroni and cheese
    Mac and Texas Cheeses with Roasted Chiles, 460
    Macaroni and Cheese Salad, 277
    Macaroni and Cheese Scallop, 464
    Never-Fail Macaroni and Cheese, 464

Slow-Cooker Macaroni and Cheese, 466

Three-Cheese Macaroni and Cheese, 462–463

Mama Mia Manicotti, 465

Pasta and Brie, 466

Pasta and Peas, 470

PASTA FAGIOLI, 547

Pasta with Garlic and Oil, 469

Pasta with Marinated Tomatoes, 474

Pasta with Pizzazz, 472

Pasta with Sun-Dried Tomato Cream, 468

Pierogies, 479

Potluck Spaghetti, 458

salads

Artichoke Chicken Pasta Salad, 268

Festive Layered Salad, 292

Green Pearls Salad, 282

Italian Macaroni Salad, 277

Layered Spinach Salad, 272

Macaroni and Cheese Salad, 277

Orzo & Pine Nut Salad, 281

Sun-Dried Tomato Pasta Salad, 280

Sunflower Pasta Salad, 288

Sausage and Peppers over Pasta, 472–473

Seafood Pasta, 473

Shrimp and Fresh Tomato Pasta, 474–475

Shrimp and Sausage Penne, 472

Shrimp Fettuccine, 471

Shrimp or Clam Marinara Pasta, 475

Slow Cooker Pizza Casserole, 443

SPAGHETTI AND MEATBALLS FOR ONE, 535

Spaghetti Sauce, 459

Spaghetti with Tuna Sauce, 476

Spinach Ziti, 476

String Pie, 459

Tuscan-Style Shrimp and Linguine, 474

Yugoslavian Spaghetti Sauce, 460–461

Zesty Texan Chicken Alfredo, 467

PASTRIES. See Coffeecakes and pastries

PEACHES

Baked Peaches, 145

Bloomer Droppers, 196

Fresh Peach Custard Pie, 74

Fresh Peach Pie with No-Roll Crust, 74

Hot Fruit Casserole, 219

Hot Sherried Fruit, 512

Lazy Peach Party Dessert, 146

Peach & Cranberry Pie, 73

Peach and Ham Stir-Fry, 366

Peaches-and-Cream Pie, 72

Peach Iced Tea, 192

PeachRazNana Smoothie, 529

PEANUT BUTTER

Buckeyes, 162–163

Corn Flake No-Bakes, 100

Peanut Butter Cheesecake, 132–133

Peanut Butter Cups, 159

Peanut Butter Kisses, 109

Peanut Butter Miracles, 111

Peanut Butter Sheet Cake, 54

Peanut Butter Snowballs, 162

Peanut Butter Squares, 56

PEANUTS

Crunchy Peanut Bark, 163

Hot Peanuts, 187

Microwave Peanut Brittle, 163

Peanut Brittle Ice Cream, 139

Peas and Peanuts Salad, 282

PEARS

ALMOND-CRUSTED CHICKEN WITH CARAMELIZED PEAR AND BRIE CREAM SAUCE, 539

Autumn Treasure Green Salad, 293

BAKED PEARS, 525

Cranberry-Pear Sauce, 368

Crown Pork Roast with Cranberry Pear Sauce, 368

Hot Fruit Casserole, 219

Hot Sherried Fruit, 512

Pear Custard Pie, 74–75

Pear Tea Sandwiches, 263

PEAS

Green Pearls Salad, 282

Pasta and Peas, 470

Peas and Peanuts Salad, 282

Scrumptious Green Pea Soup, 313

PECANS

Apple-Stuffed French Toast with Praline Topping, 208–209

Baby Blue Salad, 274–275

Blueberry Nut Crunch, 124

Bourbon Pecan Pie, 75

Creamy Pralines, 164

Earthquake Cake, 43

Fresh Strawberry Pie with Pecan Crust, 81

Fruitcake Cookies, 105

Holiday Pecan Cake, 22–23

Honey-Pecan Chicken Salad, 337

Hospitality Pies, 66

Nut Ice Cream, 139

Past-Perfect Fruit Cake, 19

Pecan Caramel Candies, 161

Pecan-Cinnamon Tea Ring, 249

Pecan Pound Cake, 251

Pecan Tarts, 76–77

Pecan-Topped Pumpkin Pie Squares, 78

PECANS (continued)

Pecan-Tuna Crunch Spread, 264
Praline Pumpkin Torte, 146–147
Praline-Top Sweet Potatoes, 504
Sally's Apple and Nut Bread
    Pudding, 122
Sherry Pralines, 164
Spiced Pecan Halves, 188
Vanilla Pecan Delight, 154

PEPPERONI

Grilled Pizza Margherita, 357
Pepperoni Loaf, 183
Pepperoni Zucchini Casserole, 450
Pizza Burgers, 331
Portobello Pizza, 355
Slow Cooker Pizza Casserole, 443
Stromboli, 358

PEPPERS

Linguine with Roasted Peppers, 471
Mac and Texas Cheeses with Roasted
    Chiles, 460
Peppernut Sandwich Spread or
    Dip, 264
Red Pepper Lasagna, 478
Red Pepper Sauce, 478
Roasted Red Pepper Cheesecake, 179
Sausage and Peppers over Pasta,
    472–473
Sausage-Stuffed Pepper Boats, 376
STUFFED PEPPERS, 536
Terry's Veal and Peppers, 395

PESTO

Cheese and Pesto Spread, 178
Fresh Tomato Pizza with Pesto, 356

PHYLLO PASTRY

Nut Baklava, 144–145
Tomato-Onion Phyllo Pizza, 357

PICKLES

Dill Pickle Meat Loaf, 388
Dill Pickle Soup, 311
Freezer Pickles, 520
Seven-Day Sweet Pickles, 520

PIES AND TARTS

Blender Cheese Pie, 64
Bourbon Pecan Pie, 75
Brown Bag Apple Pie, 60
Butterscotch Pie, 62
Cantaloupe Chiffon Pie, 65
Chocolate Angel Pie, 62–63
Chocolate Chess Pie, 64
Citrus Meringue Pie, 73
Coconut Buttermilk Pies, 68
Cranberry Walnut Pie, 64–65
Crustless Coconut Pies, 65
Fresh Peach Custard Pie, 74
Fresh Peach Pie with No-Roll Crust, 74
Fresh Strawberry Pie with Pecan
    Crust, 81
Fresh Strawberry Tart, 82
Frosty Fruit Pie, 72
Glazed Fruit Tarts, 70–71
Grandma's Apple Pot Pie, 60–61
Hospitality Pies, 66
Lemonade Stand Pie, 69
Lemon Cake Pie, 68–69
LITTLE LEMON MERINGUE PIES,
    524–525
Low-Fat Lemon Icebox Pie, 83
Macaroon Pie, 68
Margarita Pie, 71
Microwave Choc Pie, 66
Peach & Cranberry Pie, 73
Peaches-and-Cream Pie, 72
Pear Custard Pie, 74–75
Pecan Tarts, 76–77
Pecan-Topped Pumpkin Pie Squares, 78

Pink Lemonade Pie, 71
Raspberry White Chocolate Pie, 81
Red and Purple Berry Pie, 79
Red Hat Berry Cream Pie, 79
Rhubarb Cream Pie, 77
savory dishes
    Dutch Tart, 481
    Feta-Spinach Pie, 485
    Fresh Tomato Tart, 180,
        482–483
    Melt-In-Your-Mouth Cheese
        Tarts, 262–263
    Onion Tart, 497
    Squash Pie, 510
Self-Frosting Lemon Pie, 69
Sugar-Free Pineapple Pie, 77
Three Sisters Pie, 61
Toffee Bar Crunch Pie, 82
Unbaked Fresh Blueberry Pie, 62

PINEAPPLE

Aloha Loaf, 231
Banana Cream Salad, 276
Escalloped Pineapple, 512
Frosty Fruit Pie, 72
Frozen Fruit Cups, 219
Fruit Pizza, 143
Hot Fruit Casserole, 219
Hot Sherried Fruit, 512
Piña Colada Squares, 111
Pineapple & Black Bean Salsa, 519
Pineapple Angel Food Cake, 32
Pineapple Boat Salad, 282–283
Pineapple Cheese Ball, 173
Pineapple Coconut Cake, 32
Pineapple-Kiwi Microwave Jam, 521
Pineapple Pork Loin Roast with
    Horseradish Sauce, 366–367
Pineapple-Soy Sauce Chicken,
    402–403
Pineapple Upside-Down Biscuits, 147

Pink Stuff, 276
Sugar-Free Pineapple Pie, 77
Swedish Pineapple Cake, 31
Taste of Hawaii Chicken Salad, 274

PINE NUTS
Feta Cheese Orzo, 463
Grilled Perch and Pine Nuts, 426
Orzo & Pine Nut Salad, 281

PISTACHIOS
Cranberry-Pistachio Biscotti, 101
Pistachio Cake, 46–47
Pistachio Delight Torte, 148
Pistachio Marble Cake, 47

PIZZA
Almond Spinach Pizza, 351
Chicken Fajita Pizza, 354–355
Chilled Vegetable Pizza, 346–347
Cocktail Pizza, 358
Crazy Crust Pizza, 354
Deep-Dish Broccoli Pizza, 353
Four Favorites Pizza, 356
Fresh Tomato Pizza with Pesto, 356
Grilled Pizza Margherita, 357
Malaysian Pizza, 355
Pizza Burgers, 331
PIZZA FOR ONE, 549
Pizza-wiches, 336
Portobello Pizza, 355
Quick Bubble Pizza, 352
Rice Pizza, 360
Stir-and-Roll Pizza Dough, 359
Stromboli, 358
Tomato and Gorgonzola Pizza, 354
Tomato-Onion Phyllo Pizza, 357
Upside-Down Pizza, 351
White Pizza, 359

PLUMS
Plum Luscious Roast, 378
Plum Sauce, 368–369
Roast Pork with Plum Sauce, 368–369

POPCORN
Popcorn Candy Cake, 45
Popcorn Salad, 284

PORK
Apple Pie Pork Dinner, 369
Asian-Style Lettuce Wraps, 347
Barbecued Pork Loin, 365
Big Pig Gig, 362–363
chops
    BAKED PORK CHOPS WITH
        APPLES, 538
    Beer Garden Pork Chops, 371
    Ruby Sweet Pork Chops, 370
    SIMPLE ASIAN-STYLE CHICKEN
        OR CHOP, 542
    TROPICAL PORK CHOPS, 540
    Whiskey-Glazed Pork Chops,
        370–371
Crown Pork Roast with Cranberry
    Pear Sauce, 368
Cuban Roast Pork Loin, 366
Gorgeous Grilled Pork Loin, 364–365
Green Chili Stew, 314
Half-Time Pulled Pork, 367
Ham Loaf, 377
Little Swedish Meatballs, 377
Meat Puffs, 392–393
Pineapple Pork Loin Roast with
    Horseradish Sauce, 366–367
ribs
    Baby Back Ribs with Java Sauce,
        372–373
    Kamahamaha Pork Spareribs, 374
    Maple-Glazed Ribs, 373

Sweet and Sour
    StovetopSpareribs, 372
Tender-to-the-Bone Spareribs in
    Quick Joe Sauce, 374
Roast Pork Tenderloin, 365
Roast Pork with Plum Sauce, 368–369
Stuffed Cabbage Rolls, 396

POTATOES
Baked Potato Soup, 314–315
Cheesy New Potatoes, 501
Crazy Potatoes, 503
Creamy Potato Bake, 456
CUBE STEAK AND POTATOES FOR
    TWO, 535
Dilly Mashed Idaho Potatoes, 501
HAM 'N' CHEESE MASHED
    POTATOES, 538–539
Herb-Baked Veggies, 509
Hidden Valley Potatoes, 500–501
Ice Cold Vichyssoise, 316–317
Italian Potatoes, 502
Little Baby Reds, 501
Make-Ahead Mashed Potatoes, 500
Morning Potatoes, 222
ONE POTATO, 551
Potato and Sausage Soup, 313
Potato Crust Ham and Cheese
    Quiche, 216–217
Potatoes Smashed with Olives, 500
salads
    Never-Fail Secret Potato
        Salad, 284
    Old-Fashioned German-Style
        Potato Salad, 285
    Something-In-Red Potato
        Salad, 286
    Southwest-Style Potato
        Salad, 288
Shepherd's Pie, 440
Timber Lodge Hash Browns, 504
Vegetable Kabobs, 486, 508

PROSCIUTTO
Four Favorites Pizza, 356
Prosciutto-Stuffed Chicken, 417

PUDDINGS
Banana Cream Salad, 276
Caramel Apple Salad, 268
Dirt Dessert, 128
Fruit and Cream Cooler, 135
Paradise Pudding, 120
Rice Pudding, 149

PUMPKIN
Cheese Ravioli with Pumpkin-Sage
    Sauce, 464–465
The Great Pumpkin Cake, 18
Pecan-Topped Pumpkin Pie Squares, 78
Praline Pumpkin Torte, 146–147
Pumpkin & Chocolate Chip Cookies,
    110–111
Pumpkin Cake Roll, 14
Pumpkin Crunch, 148
Pumpkin Pie Cake, 17
Pumpkin Spice Bread, 234
Pumpkin Tea Bread, 258

QUICHE
Crab Quiche Deluxe, 210
Ham-N-Cheddar Broccoli Quiche, 212
Potato Crust Ham and Cheese
    Quiche, 216–217
Sausage Quiche, 217

RAISINS
Cinnamon-Raisin French Toast
    Soufflé, 206
Old-Fashioned Raisin Cake, 14–15
Raisin Scones, 256
Refrigerator Fruit Cake, 117
Stovetop Raisin Cakes, 265

RASPBERRIES
Asparagus Raspberry Salad, 269
Cantaloupe Surprise, 273
PEACHRAZNANA SMOOTHIE, 529
Raspberry Meringue Kisses, 112
Raspberry White Chocolate Pie, 81
Red and Purple Berry Pie, 79
Red Raspberry Cheese Danish, 202
Three Sisters Pie, 61

RED HAT SOCIETY
Are We There Yet?, 320
Birth of, 50, 243
Foreseeing the Future, 204
Gathering Together, 421
Pink Hatters, 197
Playing Dress-Up, 80
Red Hat Magic, 279
Reduation, 197
Ruby Redhat, 375
Stone Soup analogy, 267
Website, 115

RHUBARB
Nutty Rhubarb Muffins, 231
Red and Purple Berry Pie, 79
Rhubarb Cream Pie, 77
Rhubarb Dessert, 148–149
Rhubarb Slush, 192
Upside-Down Rhubarb Cake, 51

RICE
Baked Rice, 513
"Brown" Rice, 516
Brown Rice Pilaf, 515
Cajun Skillet Jambalaya, 412
California Casserole, 482
Chilled Rice Salad, 285
Crawfish Jambalaya in a Rice
    Cooker, 433

Cuban Chicken and Rice (Arroz Con
    Pollo), 419
Fragrant Curried Rice, 514
German Rice Salad, 287
LEMON CHICKEN PILAF, 541
Microwave Spanish Rice, 441
MUSHROOM RISOTTO, 548–549
One, Two Sausage and Rice Bake, 444
One-Dish Chicken and Rice Bake, 410
Presto Change-O Chicken and Rice
    Salad, 286–287
Rice Croquettes, 220
Rice Pilaf, 515
Rice Pizza, 360
Rice Pudding, 149
Sausage-Rice Brunch Casserole,
    212–213
Shrimp Over Rice, 436
Texas Hash, 442–443

RICOTTA CHEESE
Italian Cheesecake, 131
Mama Mia Manicotti, 465
Ricotta Cookies, 110
Roasted Red Pepper Cheesecake, 179
White Pizza, 359

RUM
Chocolate Chip Rum Cake, 40
Doughnut Bread Pudding with Butter
    Rum Sauce, 126
Fresh Strawberry Daiquiri, 198
Fudge Rum Cheesecake, 134
Red Head's Irish Cream, 194–195
Rum Cake, 42–43

SALAD DRESSINGS.
    See also Vinaigrettes
Balsamic Orange Dressing, 280
Real Italian Salad Dressing, 286
Roquefort Dressing, 288–289

RUBY RED DRESSING, 532
Soy Orange Ginger Dressing, 281

SALADS
Artichoke Chicken Pasta Salad, 268
Asparagus Raspberry Salad, 269
Autumn Treasure Green Salad, 293
Avocado Cocktail, 269
Baby Blue Salad, 274–275
Banana Cream Salad, 276
Big-Hearted Salad, 280
Black-Eyed-Pea Salad, 270
Broccoli Bacon Salad, 270
Brussels Sprout Salad, 271
Caramel Apple Salad, 268
Caraway Cabbage Toss, 293
Cauliflower Salad, 272
Chicken Salad Delight, 262
Chilled Rice Salad, 285
Corn Bread Salad, 275
Cranberry Swirl Salad, 512
Cranberry-Walnut Cabbage Slaw, 294
Cucumber Cream Salad, 273
Curried Beet Salad, 272–273
Czarina's Cranberry Borscht Salad
    with Horseradish Dressing, 278
Festive Layered Salad, 292
Fresh Green Bean and Squash
    Salad, 271
German Rice Salad, 287
Gracious Goodness Tossed Green
    Salad, 292
Grapefruit Salad, 276–277
Green Pearls Salad, 282
Honey-Pecan Chicken Salad, 337
Italian Macaroni Salad, 277
Layered Spinach Salad, 272
Macaroni and Cheese Salad, 277
Marinated Asparagus Salad, 268–269
Marinated Fresh Mushrooms, 278
Never-Fail Secret Potato Salad, 284

Old-Fashioned German-Style Potato
    Salad, 285
ORANGE & BERMUDA ONION
    SALAD, 532
Orzo & Pine Nut Salad, 281
Peas and Peanuts Salad, 282
Picnic German Coleslaw, 294
Pineapple Boat Salad, 282–283
Pink Stuff, 276
Pomegranate Salad, 284–285
Popcorn Salad, 284
Presto Change-O Chicken and Rice
    Salad, 286–287
Redelicious Red Hat Salad, 291
Red Hat Summer Salad, 290
Scarlet Sparkle Spinach Salad, 289
Something-In-Red Potato Salad, 286
Southwest-Style Potato Salad, 288
Summer Tomato and Basil Salad, 291
Sun-Dried Tomato Pasta Salad, 280
Sunflower Pasta Salad, 288
Tancook Island Sauerkraut Salad, 289
Taste of Hawaii Chicken Salad, 274
Tofu Ginger Salad, 290–291
Vidalia Onion Salad, 280–281
Wilted Spinach Salad, 290

SALMON
Dilled Red Salmon, 429
Gingered Grilled Salmon, 430
Honey Salmon, 428
Salmon Cheese Chowder, 324
Salmon Noodle Casserole, 451
Slow-Roasted Salmon with Wilted
    Spinach, 430
Whiskey-Soused Salmon, 428

SALSAS
Annie's Sassy Salsa, 175
Avocado Salsa, 348–349
Gawdy Girls Party Salsa, 176–177

Mango Salsa, 177
Pineapple & Black Bean Salsa, 519
Shoe Peg Salsa, 175
Shrimp Salsa, 188

SANDWICHES AND WRAPS
Asian-Style Lettuce Wraps, 347
Asparagus Lovelies, 258–259
BAJA TURKEY WRAP, 530
Baked Chicken Sandwiches, 337
Baked Crab Rolls, 338–339
Beef and Bean Wraps, 348
Beef and Chile Cheese Rolls, 330–331
Beef Barbecue for a Bunch, 336
Beef-Stuffed French Loaf, 332
A Big Sandwich, Red-Hat Style, 335
Big Bunch Barbecued Chopped
    Ham, 339
Black Bean Pitas with Avocado Salsa,
    348–349
Bologna Sandwich Spread, 336
burgers
    Gourmet Gingerburgers, 328
    Memories of Philly Burgers, 330
    Pizza Burgers, 331
    Shrimp Burger, 328–329
    Tunaburgers, 331
    Veggie Burgers, 332–333
Chicken Reuben, 410–411
Crab Salad Rounds, 338
Dynamites, 329
Easy Ham Tortillas, 346
Egg Spread, 340
Honey-Pecan Chicken Salad, 337
Hot Brown Sandwich, 342–343
Hot Crab Sandwiches, 339
Hot Turkey and Gravy for
    Sandwiches, 343
Italian Hero Sandwich, 344
Magnolia Special, 344
Maryland Crab Cake Sandwich, 338

SANDWICHES AND WRAPS
(continued)

Meal in a Bun, 330
Monte Cristo Sandwiches, 346
Muffulettas, 340–341
The Ol' Ball Game Hot Dog Chili, 333
Pizza-wiches, 336
Quicker Beef Pastries, 394
Red Hot Topper, 333
Shrimp Pocket Sandwich, 342
Sirloin French Dip, 334
Slow Cooker Italian Sandwich
    Beef, 335
Sourdough Turkey Sandwich, 342
Summer Sandwich, 345
tea sandwiches
    Apple-Almond Chicken
        Sandwiches, 259
    Big Batch Tea Sandwich,
        260–261
    Bonnet Tea Chicken Cranberry
        Sandwiches, 261
    Chicken Salad Delight, 262
    Cucumber Tea Sandwiches, 261
    Dill Egg Spread, 265
    Nut Tea Sandwiches, 263
    Pear Tea Sandwiches, 263
    Pecan-Tuna Crunch Spread, 264
    Peppernut Sandwich Spread or
        Dip, 264
    Slumguneon, 264–265
    Strawberry Tea Sandwiches, 262
Tuna Cheese Broil, 332

SAUCES AND SYRUPS

Banana Butter, 247
Bruschetta Sauce, 328
Burgundy Sauce, 387
Butter Rum Sauce, 126
Butter Sauce, 137
Caramel Sauce, 123

Caramel Syrup, 150
Cranberry-Pear Sauce, 368
Cream Sauce, 450–451
Devonshire Cream, 248
Fruit Sauce, 203
Herb Butter, 522
Hot Fudge Sauce, 156
Italian Gravy a la Rutigliano, 461
Java Sauce, 372–373
Lemon-Caper Sauce, 396–397
Lemon Fluff Sauce, 155
Microwave Hot Fudge Sauce, 155
Microwave Lemon Curd, 247
Nutmeg Sauce, 478
Plum Sauce, 368–369
Red Pepper Sauce, 478
Spaghetti Sauce, 459
Spanish Sauce, 218
Spiced Cranberry-Orange Sauce,
    518–519
White Sauce, 497
Yugoslavian Spaghetti Sauce, 460–461

SAUERKRAUT

Chicken Reuben, 410–411
Layered Reuben Bake, 442
Queen's Cream of Reuben Soup, 316
Reuben Meat Loaf, 392
Reuben Spread, 174
Sauerkraut Soup, 322
Slow-Cooker Kielbasa and Kraut, 377
Tancook Island Sauerkraut Salad, 289

SAUSAGE

Breakfast Burrito Bar, 214–215
Cajun Skillet Jambalaya, 412
Cocktail Pizza, 358
Country-Style Sausage Gravy, 220–221
Creamy Sausage Brunch Soufflè, 214
Deep-Dish Broccoli Pizza, 353

Down-East Low Country Shrimp
    Boil, 432
English Toad in the Hole, 213
Five-Bean Casserole, 453
Four Favorites Pizza, 356
German Rice Salad, 287
High Society Dip, 172
Hot Sweet Little Sausages, 186
Mexican Kitchen Black Bean and
    Sausage Posole, 296–297
One, Two Sausage and Rice Bake, 444
Oysterless Turkey Dressing, 516–517
Pasta with Pizzazz, 472
Potato and Sausage Soup, 313
Potluck Spaghetti, 458
Sausage and Peppers over Pasta,
    472–473
Sausage and Rye Brunch Bake, 218
Sausage Balls, 182
Sausage Fondue, 216
Sausage Quiche, 217
Sausage-Rice Brunch Casserole,
    212–213
Sausage Soup, 317
Sausage Stars, 212
Sausage-Stuffed Pepper Boats, 376
Savory Heartland Poultry Stuffing, 516
Shrimp and Sausage Penne, 472
Special Red Bean Recipe, 299
Stuffed Mushrooms, 184
Upside-Down Pizza, 351
White Meatloaf, 420
White Pizza, 359

SCALLOPS

Coquilles St. Jacques, 433
Seafood Pasta, 473

SCONES

Ginger-Orange Scones, 256
Orange Cream Scones, 254–255

Raisin Scones, 256
Swedish Scones, 257

SEAFOOD DISHES
Seafood Lasagna, 478–479
Seafood Pasta, 473
Seafood Rangoon, 345
Seafood Soup, 318

SHRIMP
Down-East Low Country Shrimp Boil, 432
Easy Scampi, 435
Fresh Shrimp Chowder, 323
Green Pearls Salad, 282
Jalapeño-Stuffed Bacon-Wrapped Grilled Shrimp, 435
LINGUINE WITH SHRIMP AND MUSHROOMS, 550
Pickled Shrimp, 185
Seafood Lasagna, 478–479
Seafood Pasta, 473
Seafood Rangoon, 345
Seafood Soup, 318
Shrimp and Fresh Tomato Pasta, 474–475
Shrimp and Grits, 437
Shrimp and Sausage Penne, 472
Shrimp and Wild Rice Casserole, 450–451
SHRIMP BISQUE, 531
Shrimp Burger, 328–329
Shrimp Creole, 434
Shrimp Curry, 437
Shrimp Etouffé, 436
Shrimp Fettuccine, 471
Shrimp for Tapas, 434
Shrimp or Clam Marinara Pasta, 475
Shrimp Over Rice, 436
Shrimp Pocket Sandwich, 342
Shrimp Puff Oriental, 185

Shrimp Salsa, 188
Tuscan-Style Shrimp and Linguine, 474

SLOW-COOKER DISHES
Apple Pie Pork Dinner, 369
Baked Beef Stew, 382
Chick Pea Soup, 297
Creamy Slow Cooker Corn, 493
Fast and Easy Chicken Chili, 308
Green Chili Stew, 314
Hidden Valley Potatoes, 500–501
Hot Mulled Apple Cider, 189
Hot Turkey and Gravy for Sandwiches, 343
Oh-So-Easy Sweet Kielbasa, 182
Pumpkin Tea Bread, 258
Red Hot Taco Soup, 310
Salpicon, 384
Slow Cooker Broccoli Soup, 299
Slow Cooker Chicken and Corn Bread Dressing, 405
Slow Cooker Chicken and Dressing, 445
Slow Cooker Italian Sandwich Beef, 335
Slow-Cooker Kielbasa and Kraut, 377
Slow-Cooker Macaroni and Cheese, 466
Slow Cooker Pizza Casserole, 443
SLOW-COOKER STEW FOR TWO, 533
Triple Chocolate Mess Cake, 35
Warm Chicken Dip, 170

SNAP PEAS
Sesame Snap Peas, 498

SOUFFLÉS
Cake-Pan Cheese Soufflé, 482
Carrot Soufflé, 490–491
Corn Soufflé, 492–493
SPINACH SOUFFLÉ, 547
SWISS CHEESE SOUFFLÉ, 548

SOUPS AND STEWS. See also Chili; Chowders
Acorn Squash Soup, 295
Baked Beef Stew, 382
Baked Potato Soup, 314–315
The Best French Onion Soup Ever, 312
Carrot and Leek Soup, 303
Carrot Soup with Ginger, 303
Chicken Barley Soup, 306
Chicken-Cheese Tortellini Soup with Spinach, 306
Chick Pea Soup, 297
Cool Cucumber Soup, 308
Cream of Fresh Broccoli Soup, 297
Creamy Roasted Cauliflower Soup, 300–301
Deluxe Crab Soup, 302
Dill Pickle Soup, 311
Escarole and Bean Soup, 309
Fresh Mushroom Soup, 321
Greek Beef Stew, 386
Green Chili Stew, 314
Hamburger Noodle Soup, 302
Ice Cold Vichyssoise, 316–317
In-a-Snap Crab Bisque, 301
Italian Pasta Fazool, 296
ITALIAN TOMATO SOUP FOR TWO, 533
Lemon Asparagus Soup, 295
Lentil Spinach Soup, 325
Meatball Soup, 304
Mexican Kitchen Black Bean and Sausage Posole, 296–297
Microwave Cream of Zucchini Soup, 325
Mint Melon Soup, 310
Mulligatawny Soup, 309
Nearly Instantaneous Swiss Onion Soup, 312
One Tomato, Two Tomato Soup, 321
Onion and Wine Soup, 310–311

SOUPS AND STEWS (continued)
Oyster Stew, 311
Pantry Soup, 298
Potato and Sausage Soup, 313
Queen's Cream of Reuben Soup, 316
Quick Creamy Tomato-Basil Soup, 319
Red Hot Taco Soup, 310
Sauerkraut Soup, 322
Sausage Soup, 317
Scrumptious Green Pea Soup, 313
Seafood Soup, 318
Slap-It-Together Beer Cheese Soup, 305
Slow Cooker Broccoli Soup, 299
SLOW-COOKER STEW FOR TWO, 533
Steak Lovers' Soup, 298–299
Strawberry Soup, 314
Summer Corn Gazpacho, 300
SWEET POTATO SOUP FOR TWO,
    530–531
Turkey Soup (My Way), 318–319
Turkey Tortilla Soup, 322
Tuscan Soup, 319
Wild Rice Soup, 322–323

SOUR CREAM
BLT Dip, 168
Cucumber Cream Salad, 273
Nova Scotia Blueberry Cream Cake, 25
Orange Sour Cream Fruit Dip, 246
Sour Cream Chicken, 414
Sour Cream Chocolate Drops, 96
Sour Cream Coffeecake, 226
Sour Cream Muffins, 244
SOUR CREAM MUFFINS, 530
Sour Cream Noodle Bake, 440

SPINACH
Almond Spinach Pizza, 351
Chicken-Cheese Tortellini Soup with
    Spinach, 306
Feta-Spinach Pie, 485

Layered Spinach Salad, 272
Lentil Spinach Soup, 325
Scarlet Sparkle Spinach Salad, 289
Slow-Roasted Salmon with Wilted
    Spinach, 430
Spinach Florentine Antipasto,
    186–187
Spinach Lasagna, 477
SPINACH SOUFFLÉ, 547
Spinach-Stuffed Chicken Cutlets, 417
Spinach Things, 190
Spinach Ziti, 476
Texas Crab Grass, 172
Tuscan Soup, 319
Wilted Spinach Salad, 290

SQUASH. See also Acorn squash
Butternut Squash Bake with Snap-
    Crackle-Pop Topping, 505
Fresh Green Bean and Squash
    Salad, 271
Herb-Baked Veggies, 509
Quick Squash Stir-Fry, 503
Ratatouille (Summer Veggie
    Medley), 511
Roasted Vegetables, 508–509
Squash, Corn Bread, and Green Chile
    Bake, 456
Squash or Eggplant Casserole, 455
Squash Pie, 510
Two-Squash Bake, 504–505

STORIES
A+ for Ingenuity, 67
The Accountant Chef, 315
All Puffed Up, 221
An Apple Pie to Remember, 76
Apple Sauce, 510
The Baked Ham, 379
Baptist Punch, 189
Bay Leaves or Bailey's, 194

Beef Barley Soup, 305
Big Pig Gig, 363
Breakfast of Champions, 334
Celebration Dinner in Red and
    Purple, 283
The Cheesecake Dog, 131
Coal Camp Survivor Cooking, 250
College Appetite, 411
Cookie Decorating, 104
Cookie Surprise, 112
Dirty Potatoes, 502
Doggone Surprise, 26
Duck for Thanksgiving Dinner, 422
The Eggnog Debacle, 156
Electric Mixer Trauma, 8
A Fish Story, 429
Flammable Corn, Do Not Eat!, 494
Go, Dough, Go!, 232
"Grandpa, What's for Breakfast?", 239
Greaseless Potatoes, 341
The Great Meatloaf Debacle, 390
Iced Tee, 480
Little Baker, 52
Little Hat on the Prairie, 176
Madame, S'il Vous Plaît, Guillotine
    the Turkey!, 452
Making a Treasure, 260
Maybe the Boys Should Learn to
    Cook, 21
The Melting Turkey, 400–401
Mom!, 215
Monday Night Baking, 92
One Lump or Two, 370
Oops!, 352
Peanut Brittle Block, 97
Pie in the Sky, 70
Polka-Dot Cake, 42
Rise of the Yeast Monster, 207
Scary Cake, 16
Special Homemade Pie, 63
The Substitution Shuffle, 470

Sugar Storm, 44–45
Then vs. Now, 462
What Goes Quack and Sits on a
    Plate?, 444
The Whole Egg, 34

STRATA. *See* Bread puddings and
    stratas

STRAWBERRIES
Chilled Strawberry Cream, 526
Creamy Strawberry Freeze, 149
Fresh Fruit Salad Pita, 206
Fresh Strawberry Daiquiri, 198
Fresh Strawberry Pie with Pecan
    Crust, 81
Fresh Strawberry Tart, 82
Frozen Fruit Cups, 219
Fruit Pizza, 143
It's-a-Sin Cake, 24
Pineapple Boat Salad, 282–283
Red Hat Berry Cream Pie, 79
Red Hat Gelatin Trifle, 128
Simple Strawberry Trifle, 151
Strawberry and Caramel-Banana
    Trifle, 150
Strawberry and Cream Cooler, 196
Strawberry Bread, 258
Strawberry Champagne Fancy
    Schmancy Drink, 196
Strawberry Shortcut Cake, 24
Strawberry Soup, 314
Strawberry Tea Sandwiches, 262
Strawberry YaYa Cake, 55
Three Sisters Pie, 61

STUFFINGS AND DRESSINGS
Oysterless Turkey Dressing, 516–517
Raise-a-Toast Turkey Dressing, 518
Savory Heartland Poultry Stuffing, 516

SWEET POTATOES
Praline-Top Sweet Potatoes, 504
Shrimp Bisque, 531
Spirited Sweet Potato Bake, 503
Sweet Potato Soup for Two,
    530–531

SYRUPS. *See* Sauces and syrups

TACOS
Fish Tacos, 349
Minnesota "Uff da" Tacos, 347
Taco Casserole, 449

TARTS. *See* Pies and tarts

TOMATOES
Bacon & Tomato Chicken, 399
Baked Dijon Tomatoes, 505
BLT Bites, 183
BLT Dip, 168
Bonna's Tipsy Tomatoes, 188
Fresh Tomato Pizza with Pesto, 356
Fresh Tomato Tart, 180, 482–483
Fried Green Tomatoes, 506
Green Tomato Bread, 240
Green Tomato Jam, 521
Italian Tomato Soup for Two, 533
Magnolia Special, 344
Mighty Vegetable Casserole, 511
One Tomato, Two Tomato Soup, 321
Pantry Soup, 298
Pasta with Marinated Tomatoes, 474
Pasta with Sun-Dried Tomato
    Cream, 468
Quick Creamy Tomato-Basil Soup,
    319
Redelicious Red Hat Salad, 291
Roasted Vegetables, 508–509
Salpicon, 384

salsas
    Annie's Sassy Salsa, 175
    Gawdy Girls Party Salsa,
        176–177
    Mango Salsa, 177
    Shoe Peg Salsa, 175
Shrimp and Fresh Tomato Pasta,
    474–475
Spanish Sauce, 218
Stuffed Tomatoes, 506
Summer Corn Gazpacho, 300
Summer Sandwich, 345
Summer Tomato and Basil Salad, 291
Sun-Dried Tomato Pasta Salad, 280
Tomato and Gorgonzola Pizza, 354
Tomato-Onion Phyllo Pizza, 357
Vegetable Kabobs, 486, 508

TORTILLAS
Beef and Bean Wraps, 348
Breakfast Burrito Bar, 214–215
Easy Ham Tortillas, 346
Fish Tacos, 349
Flat and Uglies, 178–179
Jalapeño-Lime Chicken for Fajitas,
    406–407
Microwave Green Chile
    Enchiladas, 350
Migas for One, 527
Pizza for One, 549
Real Green Chile Enchiladas, 350
Salpicon, 384
Swiss & Cream Cheese Chicken
    Enchiladas, 413
Tortilla Rollups, 186

TUNA
Blackened Ahi Tuna with
    Horseradish Vinaigrette, 546
Fresh Albacore with Onion Marinade,
    428–429

TUNA (*continued*)
GRILLED TUNA WITH HONEY-
    MUSTARD MARINADE, 545
Pecan-Tuna Crunch Spread, 264
Spaghetti with Tuna Sauce, 476
Tunaburgers, 331
Tuna Cheese Broil, 332
Tuna Spread, 179

TURKEY
BAJA TURKEY WRAP, 530
Hot Brown Sandwich, 342–343
Hot Turkey and Gravy for
    Sandwiches, 343
Mexican Meat Loaf, 389
Monte Cristo Sandwiches, 346
Oysterless Turkey Dressing, 516–517
Sourdough Turkey Sandwich, 342
Turkey Crunch Casserole, 452–453
TURKEY PICCATA FOR TWO, 541
Turkey Soup (My Way), 318–319
Turkey Tortilla Soup, 322
White Chili, 307
White Meatloaf, 420

VEAL
Asian-Style Lettuce Wraps, 347
Mexican Meat Loaf, 389
Terry's Veal and Peppers, 395
Veal Paprikash, 397
Veal with Lemon-Caper Sauce,
    396–397

VEGETABLES
BAKED ORANGE ROUGHY WITH
    VEGGIES, 546
Cheesy Chicken Vegetable
    Casserole, 446
Chilled Vegetable Pizza, 346–347
"Cooks By Itself" Brisket and
    Vegetables, 380

Fresh Vegetable Dip, 174
Herb-Baked Veggies, 509
Mighty Vegetable Casserole, 511
Ratatouille (Summer Veggie
    Medley), 511
Roasted Vegetables, 508–509
Vegetable Kabobs, 486, 508
Vegetable Strata, 483
Vegetarian Chili Corn Bread
    Casserole, 484
Veggie Burgers, 332–333

VINAIGRETTES
Balsamic Vinaigrette, 281
Curry Vinaigrette, 272–273
HORSERADISH VINAIGRETTE, 546
Lime Vinaigrette, 384

WALNUTS
Black Walnut Cake, 46
caramelized walnuts, 465
Cranberry-Walnut Cabbage Slaw, 294
Cranberry Walnut Pie, 64–65
Honey-Sweet Banana-Nut Bread, 228
Nut Baklava, 144–145
Nut Balls, 103
Rich Nut and Jam Squares, 254
Solid Walnut Cake, 46
Viennese Apricot Jam Macaroons, 91

WHISKEY. *See* Bourbon

WILD RICE
Shrimp and Wild Rice Casserole,
    450–451
Wild Rice Casserole, 513
Wild Rice Chicken Casserole, 448
Wild Rice Soup, 322–323

WINE
Burgundy Beef Loaf with Burgundy
    Sauce, 386–387
Chicken Marsala, 410
Chicken Thighs with Wine, 418–419
Chicken Vermouth, 415
Flank Steak in Wine Sauce, 380
Herbed Chicken in Wine Sauce, 406
Holiday Wine Coolers, 198
Hot Sherried Fruit, 512
Onion and Wine Soup, 310–311
Port Wine Cheese Spread, 247
Sherry Pralines, 164
White Wine Cake, 56–57

ZUCCHINI
Chocolate Zucchini Bread, 253
Chocolate Zucchini Cake, 58
Corn & Zucchini Gratin, 495
Green and Gold Casserole, 484–485
Herb-Baked Veggies, 509
Microwave Cream of Zucchini
    Soup, 325
Pepperoni Zucchini Casserole, 450
Quick Squash Stir-Fry, 503
Ratatouille (Summer Veggie
    Medley), 511
Roasted Vegetables, 508–509
STUFFED ZUCCHINI, 537
Two-Squash Bake, 504–505
Veggie Burgers, 332–333
Zucchini (Crab) Cakes, 508
Zucchini Cheese Puff, 507
Zucchini Cookies, 114
Zucchini Pie, 458
Zucchini Stuffing Bake, 457